HUMAN DEVELOPMENT 98/99

Twenty-Sixth Edition

Editor

Karen L. Freiberg

University of Maryland, Baltimore County

Dr. Karen Freiberg has an interdisciplinary educational and employment background in nursing, education, and developmental psychology. She received her B.S. from the State University of New York at Plattsburgh, her M.S. from Cornell University, and her Ph.D. from Syracuse University. Freiberg has worked as a school nurse, a pediatric nurse, a public health nurse for the Navajo Indians, an associate project director for a child development clinic, a researcher in several areas of child development, and a university professor. She is the author of an award-winning textbook, *Human Development: A Life-Span Approach*, which is now in its fourth edition. Dr. Freiberg is currently on the faculty at the University of Maryland, Baltimore County.

A Library of Information from the Public Press

Dushkin/McGraw·Hill

Sluice Dock, Guilford, Connecticut 06437

Visit us on the Internet—http://www.dushkin.com/

The Annual Editions Series

ANNUAL EDITIONS, including GLOBAL STUDIES, consist of over 70 volumes designed to provide the reader with convenient, low-cost access to a wide range of current, carefully selected articles from some of the most important magazines, newspapers, and journals published today. ANNUAL EDITIONS are updated on an annual basis through a continuous monitoring of over 300 periodical sources. All ANNUAL EDITIONS have a number of features that are designed to make them particularly useful, including topic guides, annotated tables of contents, unit overviews, and indexes. For the teacher using ANNUAL EDITIONS in the classroom, an Instructor's Resource Guide with test questions is available for each volume. GLOBAL STUDIES titles provide comprehensive background information and selected world press articles on the regions and countries of the world.

VOLUMES AVAILABLE

ANNUAL EDITIONS
Abnormal Psychology
Accounting
Adolescent Psychology
Aging
American Foreign Policy
American Government
American History, Pre-Civil War
American History, Post-Civil War
American Public Policy
Anthropology
Archaeology
Astronomy
Biopsychology
Business Ethics
Child Growth and Development
Comparative Politics
Computers in Education
Computers in Society
Criminal Justice
Criminology
Developing World
Deviant Behavior
Drugs, Society, and Behavior
Dying, Death, and Bereavement
Early Childhood Education

Economics
Educating Exceptional Children
Education
Educational Psychology
Environment
Geography
Geology
Global Issues
Health
Human Development
Human Resources
Human Sexuality
International Business
Macroeconomics
Management
Marketing
Marriage and Family
Mass Media
Microeconomics
Multicultural Education
Nutrition
Personal Growth and Behavior
Physical Anthropology
Psychology
Public Administration
Race and Ethnic Relations

Social Problems
Social Psychology
Sociology
State and Local Government
Teaching English as a Second
   Language
Urban Society
Violence and Terrorism
Western Civilization,
   Pre-Reformation
Western Civilization,
   Post-Reformation
Women's Health
World History, Pre-Modern
World History, Modern
World Politics

GLOBAL STUDIES
Africa
China
India and South Asia
Japan and the Pacific Rim
Latin America
Middle East
Russia, the Eurasian Republics,
   and Central/Eastern Europe
Western Europe

Cataloging in Publication Data
Main entry under title: Annual Editions: Human development. 1998/99.
    1. Child study—Periodicals. 2. Socialization—Periodicals. 3. Old age—
Periodicals. I. Freiberg, Karen L., *comp.* II. Title: Human development.
   ISBN 0-697-39185-X   155'.05   72-91973   HQ768.A44   ISSN 0278-4661

Twenty-Sixth Edition

Cover image © 1998 PhotoDisc, Inc.

Printed in the United States of America

Printed on Recycled Paper

Editors/Advisory Board

Members of the Advisory Board are instrumental in the final selection of articles for each edition of ANNUAL EDITIONS. Their review of articles for content, level, currentness, and appropriateness provides critical direction to the editor and staff. We think that you will find their careful consideration well reflected in this volume.

EDITOR

Karen L. Freiberg
University of Maryland, Baltimore County

ADVISORY BOARD

Staff

To the Reader

In publishing ANNUAL EDITIONS we recognize the enormous role played by the magazines, newspapers, and journals of the *public press* in providing current, first-rate educational information in a broad spectrum of interest areas. Many of these articles are appropriate for students, researchers, and professionals seeking accurate, current material to help bridge the gap between principles and theories and the real world. These articles, however, become more useful for study when those of lasting value are carefully *collected, organized, indexed,* and *reproduced* in a *low-cost format,* which provides easy and permanent access when the material is needed. That is the role played by ANNUAL EDITIONS. Under the direction of each volume's *academic editor,* who is an expert in the subject area, and with the guidance of an *Advisory Board,* each year we seek to provide in each ANNUAL EDITION a current, well-balanced, carefully selected collection of the best of the public press for your study and enjoyment. We think that you will find this volume useful, and we hope that you will take a moment to let us know what you think.

The public press, voice media, and the Internet are chock-full of the pop psychology of the 1990s. Is scientology scientific? Human development is considered on a daily basis with a legion of explanations for what might be normal or abnormal, correct or incorrect, healthy or unhealthy. Selecting a few representative articles of good quality is difficult due to the magnitude of the product. I am grateful to all the members of my advisory board for helping me cull through the collection and select some of the best articles available for 1998/99.

Annual Editions: Human Development 98/99 is organized according to the *absolute* time concept of chronos, chronological time, from conception through death. However, the reader should be aware of other *relative* time concepts: kairos (God's time); preterition (retrospective time), and futurity (prospective time); transientness (short duration) and diuturnity (long duration); and recurrent time. Human development is more akin to a continuous circle of life than to a line with a distinct beginning and end. Like stars whose light reaches us thousands of years after they expire, our ancestors influence our behaviors long after their deaths. Our hopes for our own futures and for our children's futures also predestine our developmental milestones: education, initiations, employment, births, weddings, retirements. With an eye to the circle of life, articles have been selected which bridge the gap left by clocked time and discrete ages and stages. Thus, prenatal articles may discuss adult development and late adulthood articles may focus on grandchildren.

As you explore this anthology, you will discover that many articles ask questions that have no answers. As a student, I felt frustrated by such writing. I wanted answers, right answers, right away. Part of the lessons in tolerance that are necessary to achieve maturity are lessons in accepting relativity and in acknowledging extenuating circumstances. Life frequently has no right or wrong answers, but rather various alternatives with multiple consequences. Instead of right versus wrong, a more helpful consideration is "What will bring about the greater good for the greater number?" Controversies promote healthy mental exercise. Different viewpoints should be weighed against societal standards. Different cultural communities should be celebrated for what they offer in creativity and adaptability to changing circumstances. Many selections in this anthology reflect the cultural diversity and the cultural assimilation with which we live today.

The selections for *Annual Editions: Human Development 98/99* have attempted to reflect an ecological view of growth and change. Some articles deal with microsystems such as family, school, and employment. Some deal with exosystems such as television and community. Some writers discuss macrosystems such as economics and government. Most of the articles deal with mesosystems, those which link systems such as economics, health and nutrition, schools and culture, or heredity and environment. The unique individual's contribution to every system and every system linkage is always paramount.

We hope you will be energized and enriched by the readings in this compendium. Please complete and return the postage-paid article rating form on the last page to express your opinions. We value your input and will heed it in future revisions of *Human Development.*

Karen Freiberg

Karen Freiberg, Ph.D.
Editor

Contents

UNIT 1

Genetic and Prenatal Influences on Development

Six selections discuss genetic influences on development, reproductive technology, and the effects of substance abuse on prenatal development.

The concepts in bold italics are developed in the article. For further expansion please refer to the Topic Guide and the Index.

UNIT 2

Development during Infancy and Early Childhood

Seven selections profile the impressive abilities of infants and young children, examine the ways in which children learn, and look at sex differences.

UNIT 3

Development during Childhood: Cognition and Schooling

Seven selections examine human development during childhood, paying specific attention to social and emotional development, cognitive and language development, and development problems.

The concepts in bold italics are developed in the article. For further expansion please refer to the Topic Guide and the Index.

UNIT 4

Development during Childhood: Family and Culture

Nine selections discuss the impact of home and culture on childrearing and child development. The topics include parenting styles, family structure, and cultural influences.

The concepts in bold italics are developed in the article. For further expansion please refer to the Topic Guide and the Index.

UNIT 5

Development during Adolescence and Young Adulthood

Nine selections explore a wide range of issues and topics concerning adolescence and early adulthood.

The concepts in bold italics are developed in the article. For further expansion please refer to the Topic Guide and the Index.

UNIT 6

Development during Middle and Late Adulthood

Seven selections review a variety of biological and psychological aspects of aging, questioning the concept of set life stages.

The concepts in bold italics are developed in the article. For further expansion please refer to the Topic Guide and the Index.

x

The concepts in bold italics are developed in the article. For further expansion please refer to the Topic Guide and the Index.

Topic Guide

This topic guide suggests how the selections in this book relate to topics of traditional concern to students and professionals involved with the study of human development. It is useful for locating articles that relate to each other for reading and research. The guide is arranged alphabetically according to topic. Articles may, of course, treat topics that do not appear in the topic guide. In turn, entries in the topic guide do not necessarily constitute a comprehensive listing of all the contents of each selection. **In addition, relevant Web sites, which are annotated on the next two pages, are noted in bold italics under the topic articles.**

TOPIC AREA	TREATED IN	TOPIC AREA	TREATED IN
Adolescence	30. Growing Up Goes On and On 31. Adolescence: Whose Hell Is It? 32. Working with the Emotionally Sensitive Adolescent 33. What Is a Bad Kid? 34. HIV Infected Youth Speaks *(22, 23, 24, 25, 26, 31)*	Depression	13. Parents Speak 28. Biology of Soul Murder 30. Growing Up Goes On and On 31. Adolescence: Whose Hell Is It? 32. Working with the Emotionally Sensitive Adolescent 38. Why They Stay: A Saga of Spouse Abuse *(18, 23, 24, 37)*
Aggression	20. Dealing with Misbehavior 21. Fathers' Time 27. TV Violence: Myth and Reality 29. Children at Risk 31. Adolescence: Whose Hell Is It? 33. What Is a Bad Kid? *(9, 10, 12, 22, 23, 24, 25, 29, 30)*	Divorce	36. Who Stole Fertility? 38. Why They Stay: A Saga of Spouse Abuse *(31)*
		Drug Abuse	4. Role of Lifestyle 5. Prenatal Drug Exposure 6. Sperm under Siege 29. Children at Risk 31. Adolescence: Whose Hell Is It? 32. Working with the Emotionally Sensitive Adolescent 33. What Is a Bad Kid? 34. HIV Infected Youth Speaks 37. Addicted *(11, 22, 23, 24, 29, 31)*
AIDS	34. HIV Infected Youth Speaks 35. Psychotrends		
Child Abuse	25. Lasting Effects of Child Maltreatment 26. WAAAH!! Why Kids Have a Lot to Cry About 28. Biology of Soul Murder 29. Children at Risk 34. HIV Infected Youth Speaks *(23, 24, 29)*		
		Early Childhood	5. Prenatal Drug Exposure 11. Your Child's Brain 12. Changing Demographics 13. Parents Speak *(10, 11, 12, 13, 14)*
Cognitive Development	5. Prenatal Drug Exposure 8. Fertile Minds 10. Studies Show Talking with Infants Shapes Basis of Ability to Think 11. Your Child's Brain 14. It's Magical! It's Malleable! It's . . . Memory 15. Basic Teaching on Piaget's Constructivism 16. Reconceputalization of the Effects of Undernutrition 17. Life in Overdrive 21. Fathers' Time 31. Adolescence: Whose Hell Is It? 39. Man's World, Woman's World? 43. Studies Suggest Older Minds are Stronger than Expected *(2, 5, 6, 7, 8, 9, 18, 25, 26, 37)*	Education/School	12. Changing Demographics 18. Bell, Book, and Scandal 19. EQ Factor 20. Dealing with Misbehavior 25. Lasting Effects of Child Maltreatment 42. Age Boom 44. Grandparent Development and Influence *(15, 16, 17, 18, 19, 20, 21)*
		Emotional Development/ Personality	8. Fertile Minds 9. Realistic View of Biology and Behavior 11. Your Child's Brain 13. Parents Speak 16. Reconceptualization of the Effects of Undernutrition 17. Life in Overdrive 19. EQ Factor 21. Fathers' Time 22. Invincible Kids 24. Children Who Witness Domestic Violence 25. Lasting Effects of Child Maltreatment 30. Growing Up Goes On and On 32. Working with the Emotionally Sensitive Adolescent 39. Man's World, Woman's World? *(2, 3, 4, 7, 10, 12, 26, 38)*
Creativity	14. It's Magical! It's Malleable! It's . . . Memory 17. Life in Overdrive 32. Working with the Emotionally Sensitive Adolescent *(6, 8, 9, 18, 21, 24, 26)*		
Culture	18. Bell, Book, and Scandal 26. WAAAH!! Why Kids Have a Lot to Cry About 27. TV Violence: Myth and Reality 28. Biology of Soul Murder 29. Children at Risk 31. Adolescence: Whose Hell Is It? 33. What Is a Bad Kid? 35. Psychotrends 41. Getting Over Getting Older 42. Age Boom 44. Grandparent Development and Influence 45. Solace of Patterns *(1, 3, 10, 25, 26, 27, 30, 34, 37)*	Ethics/Morality	1. Unraveling the Mystery of Life 2. World after Cloning 9. Realistic View of Biology and Behavior 38. Why They Stay: A Saga of Spouse Abuse *(1, 8, 9, 10)*

TOPIC AREA	TREATED IN	TOPIC AREA	TREATED IN
Family/Parenting	12. Changing Demographics 13. Parents Speak 21. Fathers' Time 22. Invincible Kids 23. Right to a Family Environment 24. Children Who Witness Domestic Violence 25. Lasting Effects of Child Maltreatment 26. WAAAH!! Why Kids Have a Lot to Cry About 29. Children at Risk 31. Adolescence: Whose Hell Is It? 32. Working with the Emotionally Sensitive Adolescent 42. Age Boom *(7, 10, 11, 12, 14, 15, 23, 24, 28, 29, 30, 31)*	Occupation/Work	25. Lasting Effects of Child Maltreatment 40. Sleep Pays Attention 41. Getting Over Getting Older 42. Age Boom *(28, 29, 30, 31, 33, 34, 37)*
Fertility	3. Nature's Clones 36. Who Stole Fertility? *(1, 8)*	Peers	26. WAAAH!! Why Kids Have a Lot to Cry About 29. Children at Risk 31. Adolescence: Whose Hell Is It? 33. What Is a Bad Kid? *(2, 3, 23, 25, 27, 29, 30, 31)*
Genetics	1. Unraveling the Mystery of Life 2. World after Cloning 3. Nature's Clones 9. Realistic View of Biology and Behavior 37. Addicted *(1, 8)*	Physical Development	7. How Breast Milk Protects Newborns 8. Fertile Minds 11. Your Child's Brain 16. Reconceptualization of the Effects of Undernutrition 18. Bell, Book, and Scandal 30. Growing Up Goes On and On 31. Adolescence: Whose Hell Is It? 37. Addicted *(4, 5, 9, 11, 12, 13, 14, 22, 23, 24, 25)*
Health	4. Role of Lifestyle 7. How Breast Milk Protects Newborns 13. Parents Speak 16. Reconceputalization of the Effects of Undernutrition 26. WAAAH!! Why Kids Have a Lot to Cry About 28. Biology of Soul Murder 31. Adolescence: Whose Hell Is It? 34. HIV Infected Youth Speaks 37. Addicted 40. Sleep Pays Attention 41. Getting Over Getting Older *(4, 11, 15, 22, 24, 37)*	Prenatal Development	3. Nature's Clones 4. Role of Lifestyle 5. Prenatal Drug Exposure 6. Sperm Under Siege 8. Fertile Minds *(4, 5, 6, 7, 8, 9)*
Infant Development	7. How Breast Milk Protects Newborns 8. Fertile Minds 9. Realistic View of Biology and Behavior 10. Studies Show How Talking with Infants Shapes Basis of Ability to Think 13. Parents Speak *(4, 7, 10, 11, 12, 13, 14)*	Self-Esteem	29. Children at Risk 30. Growing Up Goes On and On 36. Who Stole Fertility? 37. Addicted 38. Why They Stay: A Saga of Spouse Abuse 44. Grandparent Development and Influence *(2, 21, 26, 34, 37, 38)*
Language/ Communication	5. Prenatal Drug Exposure 10. Studies Show How Talking with Infants Shapes Basis of Ability to Think 11. Your Child's Brain 21. Fathers' Time 39. Man's World, Woman's World? *(3, 12, 14, 17, 18, 30, 31, 34)*	Sex Differences	21. Fathers' Time 35. Psychotrends 39. Man's World, Woman's World? *(30, 31, 34)*
Late Adulthood	42. Age Boom 43. Studies Suggest Older Minds Are Stronger than Expected 44. Grandparent Development and Influence 45. Solace of Patterns *(32, 33, 34, 35, 36, 37, 38)*	Stress	14. It's Magical! It's Malleable! It's . . . Memory 26. WAAAH!! Why Kids Have a Lot to Cry About 28. Biology of Soul Murder 36. Who Stole Fertility? *(10, 22, 23, 24, 30, 31)*
Marriage	35. Psychotrends 36. Who Stole Fertility? 38. Why They Stay: A Saga of Spouse Abuse 44. Grandparent Development and Influence *(27, 28, 29, 30, 31, 34)*	Television	26. WAAAH!! Why Kids Have a Lot to Cry About 27. TV Violence: Myth and Reality
Middle Adulthood	39. Man's World, Woman's World? 40. Sleep Pays Attention 41. Getting Over Getting Older *(34, 35, 38)*	Teratogens	4. Role of Lifestyle 5. Prenatal Drug Exposure 6. Sperm under Siege
Nutrition	4. Role of Lifestyle 7. How Breast Milk Protects Newborns 16. Reconceptualization of the Effects of Undernutrition *(7, 11, 12, 22)*	Violence/Rape	24. Children Who Witness Domestic Violence 25. Lasting Effects of Child Maltreatment 26. WAAAH! Why Kids Have a Lot to Cry About 27. TV Violence: Myth and Reality 28. Biology of Soul Murder 29. Children at Risk 32. Working with the Emotionally Sensitive Adolescent 34. HIV Infected Youth Speaks 37. Addicted 38. Why They Stay: A Saga of Spouse Abuse *(22, 23, 24, 25, 27, 28, 29, 30, 31)*
		Young Adulthood	35. Psychotrends 36. Who Stole Fertility? 37. Addicted 38. Why They Stay: A Saga of Spouse Abuse *(22, 23, 24, 25, 26)*

Selected World Wide Web Sites for
Annual Editions: Human Development

All of these Web sites are hot-linked through the *Annual Editions* home page: *http://www.dushkin.com/annualeditions* (just click on a book). In addition, these sites are referenced by number and appear where relevant in the Topic Guide on the previous two pages.

Some Web sites are continually changing their structure and content, so the information listed may not always be available.

General Human Development Issues

1. Association for Moral Education—*http:;//www.usask.ca/education/ coruswrk/ame/ame.html*—The Association for Moral Education is dedicated to fostering comunication, cooperation, training, curriculum development, and research that links moral theory with educational practices. From this site it is possible to connect to several areas on moral development.

2. Behavior Analysis Resources—*http://www.coedu.usf.edu/behavior/ bares.htm*—This site is dedicated to promoting the experimental, theoretical, and applied analysis of behavior. It encompasses contemporary scientific and social issues, theoretical advances, and the dissemination of professional and public information.

3. Social Influence—*http://www.public.asu.edu/~kelton/*—The Social Influence Web site focuses on persuasion, compliance, and propaganda. Lots of practical examples and applications can be found here.

Genetic and Prenatal Influences on Development

4. American Academy of Pediatrics—*http://www.aap.org/*—This organization provides data for optimal physical, mental, and social health for all children. The site provides links to publications, professional educational sources, and current research.

5. Basic Neural Processes—*http://psych.hanover.edu/Krantz/neurotut. html*—This site is highly interactive, and provides an extensive tutorial on brain structures.

6. Evolutionary Psychology: A Primer—*http://www.psych.ucsb.edu/ research/cep/primer.htm*—The goal of research in evolutionary psychology is to discover and understand the design of the human mind. This site provides a complete paper describing evolutionary psychology and a great deal of background information is included.

7. Family Internet—*http://www.familyinternet.com/babycare/babycare. htm*—The Baby Care Corner at this site presents a collection of information related to the care of babies and children. It contains special topics including health risks and immunizations.

8. Human Genetics and Human Genome Project—*http:/kumchttp. mc.ukans.edu/instruction/medicine/genetics/homepage.html*—The University of Kansas Medical Center provides information on human genetics and the human genome project on this site. A number of links to research areas are available.

9. Variability in Brain Function and Behavior—*http://serendip. brynmawr.edu/serendip/*—Organized into five subject areas (brain and behavior, complex systems, genes and behavior, science and culture, and science education), this site contains interactive exhibits, articles, links to other resources, and a forum.

Development during Infancy and Early Childhood

10. Aggression and Cooperation: Helping Young Children Develop Constructive Strategies—*http:ericps.crc.uiuc.edu/eece/pubs/ digests/1992/jewett92.html*—Jan Jewett wrote this ERIC Digest report on how to help children deal effectively with aggression. Helping children develop prosocial attitudes and behaviors is its goal.

11. Children's Nutrition Research Center (CNRC)—*http:www.bcm.tmc. edu/cnrc/*—CNRC, one of six USDA/ARS (Agricultural Research Service) facilities, is dedicated to defining the nutrient needs of healthy children, from conception through adolescence, and pregnant and nursing mothers.

12. Early Childhood Care and Development—*http://www.ecdgroup. com/*—Dedicate to the improvement of conditions of young children at risk, the Consultative Group provides an Early Childhood Care and Development International Resources site. Child development theory, programming data, parenting data, and research can be found on this site.

13. Society of Pediatric Psychology (SPP)—*http://macserv.psy.miami. edu/SPP/*—The homepage for the Society of Pediatric Psychology, which provides a forum for scientists and professionals who are interested in the health care of children, adolescents, and their families, presents a connection to publications and other sites of interest.

14. Zero to Three: National Center for Infants, Toddlers, and Families—*http://www.zerotothree.org*—This national organization is dedicated solely to infants, toddlers, and their families. It is headed by recognized experts in the field and provides technical assistance to communities, states, and the federal government.

Development during Childhood: Cognition and Schooling

15. Children Now—*http:www.childrennow.org/*—Children Now focuses on improving conditions for children who are poor or at risk. Articles include information on education, health, and security.

16. Educational Resources Information Center (ERIC)—*http://www.ed. gov.pubs/pubdb.html*—This Web site is sponsored by the United States Department of Education and will lead to numerous documents related to elementary and early childhood education.

17. Council for Exceptional Children—*http://www.cec.sped.org/*— This is the home page for the Council for Exceptional Children, which is dedicated to improving education for children with exceptionalities, students with disabilities, and the gifted child.

18. Federation of Behavioral, Psychological, and Cognitive Science—*http://www.am.org/federation/*—The Federation's mission is fulfilled through legislative and regulatory advocacy, education, and information dissemination to the scientific community. Hotlink to the National Institutes of Health's medical database, government network, and the Project on the Decade of the Brain.

19. The National Association for the Education of Young Children (NAEYC)—*http:www.america-tomorrow.com/naeyc/*—The NAEYC is the nation's largest organization of early childhood professionals

devoted to improving the quality of early childhood education programs for children from birth through the age of eight.

20. National Institute on Out-of-School Time—*http://www.wellesley.edu/WCE/CRW/SAC/*—Directed by the Wellesley College Center for Research on Women, this project conducts policy-oriented research on issues that affect the lives of women, children, families and society. The Center reaches a wide range of audiences, including educational agencies, corporations, and individuals.

21. What is Project Zero?—*http://pzweb.harvard.edu/*—Harvard Project Zero has investigated the development of learning processes in children and adults for 30 years. Today, Project Zero is building on this research to help create communities of reflective, independent learners; to enhance deep understanding within disciplines; and to promote critical and creative thinking.

Development during Adolescence and Young Adulthood

22. AMA—Adolescent Health On Line—*http://www.ama-assn.org/adolhlth/adolhlth.htm*—This major AMA adolescent health initiative is a proliferation of comprehensive clinical preventive services that primary care physicians and other health professionals can provide to young people.

23. American Academy of Child and Adolescent Psychology—*http://www.psyuch.med.umich.edu/web/aacap/brochure.htm*—This site provides up-to-date data on topics that include childhood depression, teen suicide, helping children after a disaster, discipline, learning disabilities, and child sexual abuse.

24. Ask NOAH About: Mental Health—*http://www.noah.cuny.edu/illness/mentalhealth/mental.html*—This enormous resource contains information about child and adolescent family problems, mental conditions and disorders, suicide prevention, and much more.

25. Biological Changes in Adolescence—*http://www.personal.psu.edu/faculty/n/x/nxd/biologic2.htm*—This site offers a discussion of puberty, sexuality, biological changes, cross-cultural differences, and nutrition for adolescents, including obesity.

26. The Opportunity of Adolescence—*http://www.winternet.com/*—This paper calls adolescence the turning point, after which the future is redirected and confirmed, and goes on to discuss the opportunities and problems of this period to the individual and society, using quotations from Erik Erikson, Jean Piaget, and others.

Development during Childhood: Family and Culture

27. Cross-cultural Psychology Journals—*http://pilot.msu.edu/user/lyubansk/journals.htm*—This site offers a number of links that are related to cross-cultural psychology and development.

28. Families and Work Institute—*http://www.familiesandworkinst.org*—The Families and Work Institute conducts policy research on issues related to the changing workforce and operates a national clearinghouse on work and family life.

29. National Committee to Prevent Child Abuse (NCPCA)—*http://www.childabuse.org/*—This site, dedicated to the NCPCA's abuse prevention efforts, provides statistics and parenting tips.

30. The National Parent Information Network (NPIN)—*http://ericps.ed.uiuc.edu/npin*—This site contains resources related to many of the controversial issues faced by parents raising children in contemporary society. Discussion groups are also available.

31. The Single Parent Resource—*http://www.parentsplace.com/readroom/spn/articles.html*—This site focuses on issues concerning single parents and their children. Although the articles range from parenting children from infancy through adolescence, most of the materials deal with middle childhood.

Development during Middle and Late Adulthood

32. The Alzheimer Page—*http://www.biostat.wustl.edu/ALZHEIMER*—This site is sponsored by the Washington University in St. Louis Alzheimer's Disease Research Center, and links to a wide range of other sites devoted to Alzheimer's disease and dementia.

33. American Psychological Association's Division 20, Adult Development and Aging—*http://wwwiog.wayne.edu/APADIV20/lowdiv20.htm*—Dedicated to studying the psychology of adult development and aging, this division provides links to research guides, laboratories, instructional resources, and other related areas.

34. Communication and Gender—*http://cyberschool3j.lane.edu/people/faculty/giesen/commg/Lessons/Lessons.htm*—This site provides a number of lessons from a course on communication and gender. It contains information on gender roles and identity.

35. Grief Net—*http://revendell.org/*—Produced by a nonprofit group, Rivendell Resources, this site provides many links to the Web on the bereavement process, resources for grievers, and support groups.

36. Huffington Center on Aging—*http://www.bcm.tmc.edu/hcoa/*—The Huffington Center on Aging home page offers links to sites on aging and Alzheimer's disease.

37. The Institute of Gerontology, Gero Web—*http://www.iog.wayne.edu/GeroWebd/GeroWeb.html*—This virtual library on aging contains information on gerontology, geriatrics, and the process of aging.

38. The Personality Project—*http://fas.psych.nwu.edu/personality.html*—The Personality Project is meant to guide those interested in personality theory and research on current personality research information.

We highly recommend that you review our Web site for expanded information and our other product lines. We are continually updating and adding links to our Web site in order to offer you the most usable and useful information that will support and expand the value of your Annual Editions. You can reach us at: *http://www.dushkin.com/annualeditions/*.

Genetic and Prenatal Influences on Development

Genetic Influences (Articles 1–3)
Prenatal Influences (Articles 4–6)

In February 1997 the world was shocked to learn that a Scottish research team had cloned a sheep. By August of 1997, a Wisconsin research team reported its success in cloning a cow. Suddenly, possibilities for genetic engineering of human beings loomed large. Genetic makeup will be more easily altered because of the technology that produced Dolly (the cloned sheep) and Gene (the cloned cow). A clone is an organism that is genetically identical to another. Will it be desirable to clone humans? Cloning might be used to prevent disease, or cure disease, or be used to replace diseased body parts. Science fiction notwithstanding, would you like to clone yourself? Would you support cloning for medical purposes?

The field of genetic knowledge is burgeoning. The human genome (23 pairs of chromosomes with their associated genes) is being mapped with great speed. As the arrangement of gene sites on chromosomes is uncovered, so too are genetic markers (DNA sequences associated with particular traits). This is of vast significance to students of human development. No longer are genes just thought of as important because some carry certain diseases. Genes can be compared to an incredibly complicated computer program. They dictate every aspect of human development: physical structure and cognitive, social, and emotional traits.

Human embryology (the study of the first through seventh weeks after conception) and human fetology (the study of the eighth week of pregnancy through birth) have given verification to the idea that behavior precedes birth. The developing embryo/fetus reacts to the internal and external environments provided by the mother and to substances that diffuse through the placental barrier from the mother's body. The embryo reacts to toxins (viruses, antigens) that pass through the umbilical cord. The fetus reacts to an enormous number of other stimuli, such as the sounds from the mother's body (digestive rumblings, heartbeat) and the mother's movements, moods, and medicines. How the embryo/fetus reacts (e.g., weakly to strongly; positively to negatively) depends, in large part, on his or her genetic preprogramming. Genes and

environment are so inextricably intertwined that the effect of each cannot be studied separately. Prenatal development always has strong genetic influences and vice versa.

The first article included in the genetic section of this unit gives an articulate overview of the history and current research efforts in the science of human genetics. It provides the lay reader with a short dictionary of terms helpful in understanding the descriptions of genome research. It highlights the research being carried out in the Boston, Massachusetts, area but also describes other important studies worldwide. It probes the question "Should we use gene markers to proactively diagnose disease, when the disease is, as yet, incurable?" It also explains why a "Genetic Privacy Act" has been proposed for future legislative action. Prospective parents frequently wonder about genetic screening and what uncovering of deleterious genes will mean to their lives and to the lives of their future offspring.

The second article presents the most frequently asked questions about cloning today, such as "Could a human being be cloned?" and "Would a cloned person have its own soul?" Scientists, philosophers, and theologians, who are considered experts in these areas, have given perspicacious answers to each intriguing question. Their opinions may not please everyone, but they open up mind-boggling implications for future developments in cloning. The exercise of reading the questions and answers will expand every reader's range of knowledge and most probably will stimulate many new questions.

The third genetic selection contemplates the phenomenon of twinning. Are identical twins nature's handmade clones? What behaviors, if any, of monozygotic twins are predetermined by their identical genes? Research studies are reviewed that both support and refute the twin evidence of biological behavior propensities. The role of environmental limitations to biological propensities is also judiciously considered. The play of nature-nurture in twins is telling and spirit-stirring.

The study of teratology (malformations of the embryo/fetus) and the study of normal prenatal develop-

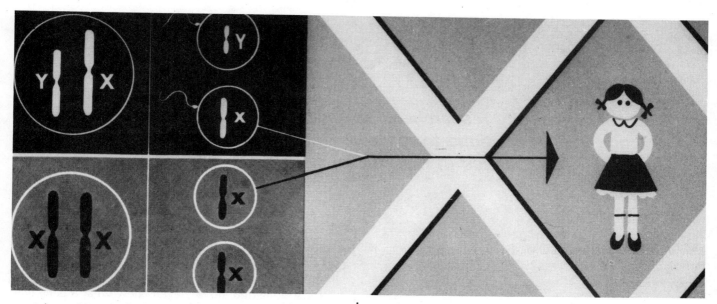

ment have historically focused on environmental factors. Until recently, genetic influences on how the embryo/fetus would react to teratogens or nutrients was ignored. Today we know that the same environmental factors may influence uniquely developing babies in different ways. Likewise, the age of the developing embryo/fetus makes a difference in the effect of an environmental factor. Keeping individual differences in mind, certain teratogens are dangerous to all unborn babies, and certain nutrients are necessary for all unborn babies.

The first article in the prenatal-influence section of this unit explores the role of the mother's lifestyle in protecting her baby from, or subjecting her baby to, an "at-risk" birth status. At-risk infants are born with low birth weights and immature organ systems that put them in danger of dying or of experiencing delayed or disabled development. The authors discuss not only lifestyle choices but also demographic risks and stress risks, assessment of risk factors, barriers to change, and directions for prevention and intervention. It is an important paper that highlights the need for healthy mothers in order to have healthy babies.

The second prenatal-influence selection is an excellent discussion of prenatal drug exposure and its behavioral effects on infants and young children. The compounding issues of the number of drugs to which a baby has been exposed, how much exposure, and length of exposure are explained. Regardless of the uniqueness of each drug-exposed baby, certain complications are common in childhood. These anomalies are presented in both narrative and tabular form. Suggestions are given for improving the lives of children who have prenatal drug-effect characteristics.

The third article in the prenatal section has been retained once again, despite its age, because of rave reviews from readers. A father provides one half the chromosomes with one half of the genetic materials needed to produce a new human being. A mother provides the other half. She also provides the gestational setting for pregnancy and prenatal development in her uterus. The contributions of fathers to prenatal growth and change have long been overlooked. Not only do fathers provide one half of the genetic influences on development, but they also indirectly influence the environment that the gestational mother provides. This article discusses the ways in which teratogens can affect developing sperm and shows how important it is for prospective fathers to practice health maintenance and to protect themselves from toxins (chemicals, alcohol, tobacco, drugs) for their sperm's sake. It is an eye-opening article for both males and females.

Looking Ahead: Challenge Questions

How much do we know about the human genome? What dilemmas will we face as a human society when the genome is completely mapped?

What controversies are emerging from cloning technology? How do you feel about the moral/ethical questions?

Do studies of identical twins give answers to the age-old nature-nurture questions?

What strategies can reduce the numbers of babies born with low birth weight and at risk of developmental disabilities?

What behavioral effects are seen in infants and young children who have been exposed to illicit drugs prenatally?

How do sperm contribute to prenatal development?

Unraveling the Mystery of Life

Boston University researchers, in collaboration with other medical science teams, continue to make significant contributions with their discoveries in the field of genetic knowledge.

Mariette DiChristina

Mariette DiChristina (COM '86) *is a senior editor at Popular Science.*

EACH OF THESE SAMPLES HOLDS A PIECE OF genetic code," says Chris Amemiya, Ph.D., his scarlet and navy paisley tie and khakis poking out from a long white lab coat. In tiny breakers resting atop a black ice bucket like shrimp cocktail, these crucial codes look surprisingly inconsequential—rather like simple tap water.

Yet codes like these have awesome power over human destiny. They determine whether you are tall or short, have blue eyes or brown, curly hair or straight. And more important, they may tell whether you will get sick someday, and from what. There are perhaps 3,000 to 4,000 ailments caused by genetic defects.

In this tidy, well-lit lab, Amemiya, an assistant professor at the Center for Human Genetics at the Boston University School of Medicine, and others are working to help figure out, or characterize, sequences of these genetic codes. Their efforts are just one small part of the impressive ongoing genetic research at the University.

Individually as well as in collaboration with other medical science teams, BU scientists have contributed to many nationally recognized achievements in the complex arena of genetic research. Their work covers the spectrum of discovery—from persevering with pipettes in the lab to number-crunching reams of data with computers to dealing with the human consequences of the search for greater genetic knowledge.

On the world stage, genome research has seen some remarkable advances. So far, some two dozen genes have been linked to human diseases. The past year alone has seen the discovery of a gene commonly implicated in many varieties of cancer, as well as ones for breast cancer,

obesity, a form of youth-onset Alzheimer's, even the general site of a gene linked with persistent bed-wetting in children.

Not so long ago, no one even knew what a gene was. Since Gregor Mendel's famous work with peas, scientists have known the importance of heritage. But it wasn't until 1952 that scientists discovered the DNA is the basic stuff of heredity. Short for deoxyribonucleic acid, DNA is a long thread-like molecule that is part of a gene (see "A Genetic Dictionary"). Today we know that DNA acts like a biological computer program some three billion bits long. This program spells out the key instructions for making proteins, the basic building blocks of life. If you could print it out, the entire human genome—the blueprint that makes each of us a unique individual—would fill a thousand 1,000-page telephone books.

The genome is so large and the work to decipher it so painstaking that fewer than 5 percent of these genetic codes have been sequenced. To explain why this is so, many researchers cite the example of the landmark 1989 discovery of the gene for cystic fibrosis. The many independent groups that worked simultaneously on the project often duplicated one another's efforts, and the total cost probably exceeded $120 million.

5,000 Genes a Year

Enter the Human Genome Project. Launched in 1990, the massive, multibillion-dollar project seeks to identify an estimated 50,000 to 100,000 human genes by the year 2005. An international effort involving hundreds of scientists at dozens of universities and medical institutions, the project is supported in the

United States by the National Institutes of Health and the Department of Energy.

A pioneer was Charles DeLisi, Ph.D., who initiated the project in the 1980s as a director of the Department of Energy's health and environment research programs. An internationally recognized researcher in molecular structure and function, DeLisi is now professor of biomedical engineering and dean of BU's College of Engineering.

Among those continuing in the wake of DeLisi's efforts are scientists at the BU Center for Advanced Biotechnology, on the Charles River Campus. Charles Cantor, Ph.D., the center's director and a member of the National Academy of Sciences, says a key goal of the researchers is to reduce the tremendous cost and time involved in genetic research.

Shortcuts

To ease the arduous task of sifting through forty-six human chromosomes of marvelous complexity, many scientists seek to create some basic road maps. Cassandra L. Smith, Ph.D., deputy director of the Center for Advanced Biotechnology, is one researcher who focuses on new methods of faster DNA mapping and sequencing.

"The technical problem is that the genome is very large and you can't look at the whole genome at one time with current technology," says Smith. "So we've developed methods of looking at subsets of the genome that are likely to have changes that might cause diseases. When a gene falls into such a region, you already might have a lot of the resources to help pinpoint it."

To explain the point, Smith offers an analogy. Imagine you're looking for a certain house in a city. You could start at any random street and then search block by block. Or you could look at an overall map of the city and get a general idea of where to begin. Having the genetic markers, she says, "is like having a map of the city."

One marking technique is to use restriction enzymes, which chemically clip DNA at places where the enzymes recognize specific base sequences. Eventually gene mappers would like to create a regularly spaced set of markers at close intervals. Using these markers as signposts for genetic "neighborhoods" on the imaginary city map, scientists can then find the important "streets" and "houses." When there are differences around these markers in family members who have a genetic disease—but not in disease-free members—scientists can locate the genetic cause.

This method of gene hunting has produced some notable successes at BU: location of the genes for Waardenburg's syndrome as well as for Huntington's disease.

In 1992 a team led by Clinton T. Baldwin, Ph.D., an associate professor of pediatrics and the director of molecular genetics research at the Center for Human Genetics, found the genetic cause of a form of deafness called Waardenburg's syndrome. Waardenburg's, which is accompanied by pigment disorders of the skin, eyes, and hair, causes about 3 percent of all cases of congenital deafness.

"We determined the [key part of a] DNA sequence of an individual with the disease, compared it to a person without the disease, and found a single base change that resulted in a single amino acid change," explains Baldwin. "This was sufficient to destroy the ability of the protein to function." Using earlier research done on the genetics of mice and fruit flies—which have some genes similar to human genes—also helped the researchers understand the genes involved.

The gene for Huntington's was also located with this search technique. Huntington's is a deadly neurodegenerative disease whose best known victim was folksinger Woodie Guthrie. Unlike Waardenburg's, Huntington's is not a single error. Rather, explains Richard Myers, Ph.D., of the BU Medical Center, it is a "stutter" flaw. There are too many repeats of one tiny bit of code, as if the genetic photocopier went haywire. Myers, who was part of the team that made the 1993 discovery of the Huntington's gene after a decade-long search, says the more copies of this gene a Huntington's patient has, the more severe the symptoms and the earlier the onset of the disease. Continuing in his research, Myers is exploring some puzzling

A GENETIC DICTIONARY

DNA—Two yards of DNA are packed into each one of the 100 trillion cells in your body. A strand of DNA, or deoxyribonucleic acid, is more than 37,000 times thinner than a human hair. The DNA is on twenty-three pairs of chromosomes; you get one set of twenty-three chromosomes from each of your parents.

CHROMOSOME—Each of the forty-six human chromosomes contains the DNA for thousands of individual genes, the chemical units of heredity.

GENE—A gene is a snippet, or sequence, of DNA that holds the recipe for making a specific molecule, usually a protein. These recipes are spelled out in four chemical bases: adenine (A), thymine (T), guanine (G), and cytosine (C). The bases form interlocking pairs. A always pairs with T and G pairs with C. In some cases, genetic defects are caused by the substitution of just one base pair for another.

PROTEIN—Amino acids make up proteins, which are key components of all human organs and chemical activities in your body. Their function depends on their shape, which is determined by the 50,000 to 100,000 genes in the cell nucleus.—MD differences in the complexity of nerve cells of Huntington's patients and those without the disease.

Another place scientists look for gene clues is in people whose relationship is even closer than most family members: identical twins. Because identical twins develop from the same fertilized egg, they have the same genetic material.

Studies of gay men and their twin brothers by psychiatrists Richard Pillard of the BU School of Medicine and J. Michael Bailey of Northeastern University indicate that there is a heredity factor in homosexuality. When one brother is gay, they discovered, there is a far greater likelihood that the identical twin is gay too.

If one twin has a trait that the other doesn't have, this gives scientists a hint about where to look for the specific gene that causes that trait. For example, Cassandra Smith is conducting studies with twins in the search for genes responsible for schizophrenia. "I take identical twins who are discordants—that is, one has and one doesn't have schizophrenia—and compare the DNA to find the differences," she says. By doing so she seeks the triggers for this chronic disease.

A third way to shorten the search for genes is to differentiate between the 3 percent of DNA that creates coding and the 97 percent that is noncoding. Noncoding DNA is called *junk* because no one knows its purpose. "What could this 97 percent be doing?" asks H. Eugene Stanley, Ph.D., professor of physics and director of the

Center for Polymer Studies at BU. "One idea is that it's just accumulated during evolution the way junk accumulates in my office," he says with a sweep of his arm taking in stacks of books and piles of paper.

Work by Stanley and colleagues at Boston University and Harvard indicates that the junk may be a language. One language feature in junk—a discovery led by team member S. Martina Ossadnik—is that it has correlations. That is, certain bits of information generally follow certain others—the way u follows q in English. Taking that a step further, Rosario Mantegna, then a BU graduate student and now a research associate in the physics department, computer-analyzed the junk, applying tests used by linguists. He found "word" repetitions, another common language feature. "Language is a structured thing," adds Stanley. "There is a lot of redundancy: I could leave out a word and you would understand me. A code is the opposite. It is very strict; you cannot make a mistake." Genetic codes do not share these language features.

So what does the junk say? No one is certain. "We can't prove it's a language," stresses Stanley, "but it passes the tests for language."

Once you find a gene for a disease, you can work to develop predictive tests. Richard Myers founded and heads Huntington's testing and counseling at the University. Boston University and Johns Hopkins University, which set up programs simultaneously in 1986, were the first institutions to offer such testing. Today more people

TESTING WITHOUT CURES

Genetic research will undoubtedly bring unmatched abilities to improve the human condition. But rapidly advancing lab work is leaving society to face some difficult issues. While scientists have found the genetic causes of several diseases and developed predictive tests, treatments remain elusive.

The result, says George Annas, J.D., M.P.H., a professor of health law at the Boston University School of Public Health who has been widely quoted on genome ethics, is that "it gives you scary information that is not terribly useful in your daily life."

Perhaps few have come to know these punishing issues as well as Richard Myers at the BU Medical Center. Myers, whose twenty-year experience with the deadly, incurable Huntington's disease began with his dissertation, participated in the gene's discovery (see main article). At the University, he founded one of the first U.S. testing and counseling programs for Huntington's.

Considering the brutal, relentless progress of Huntington's, Myers

speaks of its victims in measured tones tinged with sympathy. "There are plenty of diseases that are pretty nasty. A lot of times you might be better off not knowing how bad it can get," he says. "But for a person to get Huntington's disease, a parent would have had it. They [the children] would have had to watch." Many who come in for couseling choose not to be tested.

Worse, there are fears about twenty-first-century discrimination based on an individual's genetic heritage. For instance, Myers knows of one New England woman in her twenties who was fired from her pharmacy job after her boss discovered that the woman's mother had Huntington's and thus she was vulnerable to developing the disease. Anticipating such cases, the U.S. Equal Opportunity Commission this year concluded that the Americans with Disabilities Act protects healthy people carrying abnormal genes from discrimination.

Annas and two School of Public Health colleagues—Leonard Glantz,

J.D., health law professor, and Patricia Roche, J.D., instructor—aim to take that a step further: this spring they proposed legislation to prevent the collection, analysis, and storage of DNA, and disclosure of information derived from such analysis, without the individual's written authorization. The proposed legislation, called the Genetic Privacy Act, was developed over two years under a grant awarded from that portion of the Human Genome Project's budget that goes to ethics research. The act has been introduced in a half-dozen state legislatures, says Annas, who also expects it to be considered as a federal statute.

"Everyone has some bad genes," says Annas. "The problem is these genes are being discovered long before there is any hope for treating these conditions. Nonetheless, there are many opportunities for employers, insurance companies, and others to discriminate on the basis of someone's genetic makeup."—MD have undergone testing for Huntington's than for any other disease that appears in adulthood (see sidebar, "Testing Without Cures").

While locating a gene doesn't guarantee a cure, it may point the way. Researchers hope to design drugs that can target the cause of an ailment rather than the symptoms. In collaboration with colleagues from other universities and biotechnology companies, Charles Cantor of the Biotechnology Center is working to take advantage of the natural lock-and-key mechanism of a type of protein—a string of amino acids—called streptavidin. One example of a natural lock and key is how antibodies fight infection in your body; the antibody chemically matches the infecting virus and adheres to it—rendering the virus harmless. Streptavidin's lock-and-key binding, however, is a million times stronger than that of antibodies. "You could use this natural mechanism to bring radiation right to the site of a cancerous tumor in a precise way," says Cantor.

Another possible way to treat genetic disease is to correct or replace the altered gene through gene therapy. This involves inserting corrective DNA into human cells to replace flawed genes or to produce proteins that

stimulate the body's natural immune system. Such experimental gene therapy to treat Parkinson's disease is just one example of the more than 100 gene-therapy procedures now undergoing testing.

In some cases, too, finding out you are predisposed to a genetic ailment could help you take preventive actions or enable you to get treatment earlier, when it is more likely to be effective. Clinical research will also provide a piece of the genetic puzzle.

A leader in this area is Aubrey Milunsky, M.D., a professor of human genetics, pediatrics, pathology, and obstetrics at BU's School of Medicine and director of the Center for Human Genetics. As head of the human genetics program, Milunsky's landmark work has supported the development of national guidelines for folic acid supplementation to prevent neural tube defects and has focused on prenatal diagnosis and early pregnancy screening for birth defects.

"The power of genetics is that if you have the time and money, you are almost guaranteed to find the gene," says Cassandra Smith. Speaking for many researchers, she adds, "It's just a matter of perseverance."

The world after cloning

A reader's guide to what Dolly hath wrought

By WRAY HERBERT, JEFFERY L. SHELER, AND TRACI WATSON

At first it was just plain startling. Word from Scotland last week that a scientist named Ian Wilmut had succeeded in cloning an adult mammal—a feat long thought impossible—caught the imagination of even the most jaded technophobe. The laboratory process that produced Dolly, an unremarkable-looking sheep, theoretically would work for humans as well. A world of clones and drones, of *The Boys From Brazil* and *Multiplicity,* was suddenly within reach. It was science fiction come to life. And scary science fiction at that.

In the wake of Wilmut's shocker, governments scurried to formulate guidelines for the unknown, a future filled with mind-boggling possibilities. The Vatican called for a worldwide ban on human cloning. President Clinton ordered a national commission to study the legal and ethical implications. Leaders in Europe, where most nations already prohibit human cloning, began examining the moral ramifications of cloning other species.

Like the splitting of the atom, the first space flight, and the discovery of "life" on Mars, Dolly's debut has generated a long list of difficult puzzles for scientists and politicians, philosophers and theologians. And at dinner tables and office coolers, in bars and on street corners, the development of wild scenarios spun from the birth of a simple sheep has only just begun. *U.S. News* sought answers from experts to the most intriguing and frequently asked questions.

Why would anyone want to clone a human being in the first place?

The human cloning scenarios that ethicists ponder most frequently fall into two broad categories: 1) parents who want to clone a child, either to provide transplants for a dying child or to replace that child, and 2) adults who for a variety of reasons might want to clone themselves.

Many ethicists, however, believe that after the initial period of uproar, there won't be much interest in cloning humans. Making copies, they say, pales next to the wonder of creating a unique human being the old-fashioned way.

Could a human being be cloned today? What about other animals?

It would take years of trial and error before cloning could be applied successfully to other mammals. For example, scientists will need to find out if the donor egg is best used when it is resting quietly or when it is growing.

Will it be possible to clone the dead?

Perhaps, if the body is fresh, says Randall Prather, a cloning expert at the University of Missouri-Columbia. The cloning method used by Wilmut's lab requires fusing an egg cell with the cell containing the donor's DNA. And that means the donor cell must have an intact membrane around its DNA. The membrane starts to fall apart after death, as does DNA. But, yes, in theory at least it might be possible.

Can I set up my own cloning lab?

Yes, but maybe you'd better think twice. All the necessary chemicals and equipment are easily available and relatively low-tech. But out-of-pocket costs would run $100,000 or more, and that doesn't cover the pay for a skilled developmental biologist. The lowest-priced of these scientists, straight out of graduate school, makes about $40,000 a year. If you tried to grow the cloned embryos to maturity, you'd encounter other difficulties. The Scottish team implanted 29 very young clones in 13 ewes, but only one grew into a live lamb. So if you plan to clone Fluffy, buy enough cat food for a host of surrogate mothers.

Would a cloned human be identical to the original?

Identical genes don't produce identical people, as anyone acquainted with identical twins can tell you. In fact, twins are more alike than clones would be, since they have at least shared the uterine environment, are usually raised in the same family, and so forth. Parents could clone a second child who eerily resembled their first in appearance, but all the evidence suggests the two would have very different personalities. Twins separated at birth do sometimes share quirks of personality, but such quirks in a cloned son or daughter would be haunting reminders of the child who was lost—and the failure to re-create that child.

Even biologically, a clone would not be identical to the "master copy." The clone's cells, for example, would have energy-processing machinery (mitochondria) that came from the egg donor, not from the nucleus donor. But most of the physical differences between originals and copies wouldn't be detectable without a molecular-biology lab. The one possible exception is fertility. Wilmut and his coworkers are not sure that Dolly will be able to have lambs. They will try to find out once she's old enough to breed.

Will a cloned animal die sooner or have other problems because its DNA is older?

Scientists don't know. For complex biological reasons, creating a clone from an older animal differs from breeding an older animal in the usual way. So clones of adults probably wouldn't risk the same birth defects as the offspring of older women, for example. But the age of the DNA used for the clone still might

 From *U.S. News & World Report,* March 10, 1997, pp. 59-63. © 1997 by U.S. News & World Report. Reprinted by permission.

What if parents decided to clone a child in order to harvest organs?

Most experts agree that it would be psychologically harmful if a child sensed he had been brought into the world simply as a commodity. But some parents already conceive second children with nonfatal bone marrow transplants in mind, and many ethicists do not oppose this. Cloning would increase the chances for a biological match from 25 percent to nearly 100 percent.

If cloned animals could be used as organ donors, we wouldn't have to worry about cloning twins for transplants. Pigs, for example, have organs similar in size to humans'. But the human immune system attacks and destroys tissue from other species. To get around that, the Connecticut biotech company Alexion Pharmaceuticals Inc. is trying to alter the pig's genetic codes to prevent rejection. If Alexion succeeds, it may be more efficient to massproduce porcine organ donors by cloning than by current methods, in which researchers inject pig embryos with human genes and hope the genes get incorporated into the embryo's DNA.

Wouldn't it be strange for a cloned twin to be several years younger than his or her sibling?

When the National Advisory Board on Ethics in Reproduction studied a different kind of cloning a few years ago, its members split on the issue of cloned twins separated in time. Some thought the children's individuality might be threatened, while others argued that identical twins manage to keep their individuality intact.

John Robertson of the University of Texas raises several other issues worth pondering: What about the cloned child's sense of free will and parental expectations? Since the parents chose to duplicate their first child, will the clone feel obliged to follow in the older sibling's footsteps? Will the older child feel he has been duplicated because he was inadequate or because he is special? Will the two have a unique form of sibling rivalry, or a special bond? These are, of course, just special versions of questions that come up whenever a new child is introduced into a family.

Could a megalomaniac decide to achieve immortality by cloning an "heir"?

Sure, and there are other situations where adults might be tempted to clone themselves. For example, a couple in which the man is infertile might opt to clone one of them rather than introduce an outsider's sperm. Or a single woman might choose to clone herself rather than involve a man in any way. In both cases, however, you would have adults raising children who are also their twins—a situation ethically indistinguishable from the megalomaniac cloning himself. On adult cloning, ethicists are more united in their discomfort. In fact, the same commission that was divided on the issue of twins was unanimous in its conclusion that cloning an adult's twin is "bizarre . . . narcissistic and ethically impoverished." What's more, the commission argued that the phenomenon would jeopardize our very sense of who's who in the world, especially in the family.

How would a human clone refer to the donor of its DNA?

"Mom" is not right, because the woman or women who supplied the egg and the womb would more appropriately be called Mother. "Dad" isn't right, either. A traditional father supplies only half the DNA in an offspring. Judith Martin, etiquette's "Miss Manners," suggests, "Most honored sir or madame." Why? "One should always respect one's ancestors," she says, "regardless of what they did to bring one into the world."

That still leaves some linguistic confusion. Michael Agnes, editorial director of *Webster's New World Dictionary,* says that "clonee" may sound like a good term, but it's too ambiguous. Instead, he prefers "original" and "copy." And above all else, advises Agnes, "Don't use 'Xerox.' "

A scientist joked last week that cloning could make men superfluous. Is it true?

Yes, theoretically. A woman who wanted to clone herself would not need a man. Besides her DNA, all she would require are an egg and a womb—her own or another woman's. A man who wanted to clone himself, on the other hand, would need to buy the egg and rent the womb—or find a very generous woman.

What are the other implications of cloning for society?

The gravest concern about the misuse of genetics isn't related to cloning directly, but to genetic engineering—the deliberate manipulation of genes to enhance human talents and create human beings according to certain specifications. But some ethicists also are concerned about the creation of a new (and stigmatized) social class: "the clones." Albert Jonsen of the University of Washington believes the confrontation could be comparable to what occurred in the 16th century, when Europeans where perplexed by the unfamiliar inhabitants of the New World and endlessly debated their status as humans.

Whose pockets will cloning enrich in the near future?

Not Ian Wilmut's. He's a government employee and owns no stock in PPL Therapeutics, the British company that holds the rights to the cloning technology. On the other hand, PPL stands to make a lot of money. Also likely to cash in are pharmaceutical and agricultural companies and maybe even farmers. The biotech company Genzyme has already bred goats that are genetically engineered to give milk laced with valuable drugs. Wilmut and other scientists say it would be much easier to produce such animals with cloning than with today's methods. Stock breeders could clone champion dairy cows or the meatiest pigs.

Could cloning be criminally misused?

If the technology to clone humans existed today, it would be almost impossible to prevent someone from cloning you without your knowledge or permission, says Philip Bereano, professor of technology and public policy at the University of Washington. Everyone gives off cells all the time—whenever we give a blood sample, for example, or visit the dentist—and those cells all contain one's full complement of DNA. What would be the goal of such "drive-by" cloning? Well, what if a woman were obsessed with having the child of an apathetic man? Or think of the commercial value of a dynasty-building athletic pedigree or a heavenly singing voice. Even though experience almost certainly shapes these talents as much as genetic gifts, the unscrupulous would be unlikely to be deterred.

Is organized religion opposed to cloning?

Many of the ethical issues being raised about cloning are based in theology. Concern for preserving human dignity and individual freedom, for example, is deeply rooted in religious and biblical principles. But until last week there had been surprisingly little theological discourse of the implications of cloning per se. The response so far from the religious community, while overwhelmingly negative, has been far from monolithic.

Roman Catholic, Protestant, and Jewish theologians all caution against applying the new technology to humans, but for varying reasons. Catholic opposition stems largely from the church's belief that "natural moral law" prohibits most kinds of tampering with human reproduction. A 1987 Vatican document, *Donum Vitae,* condemned cloning because it violates "the dignity both of human procreation and of the conjugal union."

Protestant theology, on the other hand, emphasizes the view that nature is "fallen" and subject to improvement. "Just because something occurs naturally doesn't mean it's automatically good," explains Max Stackhouse of Princeton Theological Seminary. But while they tend to support using technology to fix flaws in nature, Protestant theologians say cloning of humans crosses the line. It places too much power in the hands of sinful humans, who, says philosophy Prof. David Fletcher of Wheaton College in Wheaton, Ill., are subject to committing "horrific abuses."

Judaism also tends to favor using technology to improve on nature's shortcomings, says Rabbi Richard Address of the Union of American Hebrew Congregations. But cloning humans, he says, "is an area where we cannot go. It violates the mystery of what it means to be human."

Doesn't cloning encroach on the Judeo-Christian view of God as the creator of life? Would a clone be considered a creature of God or of science?

Many theologians worry about this. Cloning, at first glance, seems to be a usurpation of God's role as creator of humans "in his own image." The scientist, rather than God or chance, determines the outcome. "Like Adam and Eve, we want to be like God, to be in control," says philosophy Prof. Kevin Wildes of Georgetown University. "The question is, what are the limits?"

But some theologians argue that cloning is not the same as creating life from scratch. The ingredients used are alive or contain the elements of life, says Fletcher of Wheaton College. It is still only God, he says, who creates life.

Would a cloned person have its own soul?

Most theologians agree with scientists that a human clone and its DNA donor would be separate and distinct persons. That means each would have his or her own body, mind, and soul.

Would cloning upset religious views about death, immortality, and even resurrection?

Not really. Cloned or not, we all die. The clone that outlives its "parent"—or that is generated from the DNA of a dead person, if that were possible—would be a different person. It would not be a reincarnation or a resurrected version of the deceased. Cloning could be said to provide immortality, theologians say, only in the sense that, as in normal reproduction, one might be said to "live on" in the genetic traits passed to one's progeny.

Nature's Clones

Can genes explain our passions and prejudices, the mates we choose, that mystery we call the self? New research on twins upsets some of our most cherished notions about how we become who we are—and gives nature and nurture a whole new meaning. By JILL NEIMARK

Last April I went down to West 27th Street in Manhattan to sit in the audience of the *Maury Povich* show, and meet four sets of identical twins who had been separated at birth and adopted into different families. I wanted to see if the same soul stared out of those matched pairs of eyes, to contemplate the near miracle of DNA—double helix twisting around itself like twin umbilical cords—ticking out a perfect code for two copies of a human. One pair, a Polish nun and a Michigan housewife, had been filmed at the airport by CNN the week before, reunited for the first time in 51 years and weeping in each other's arms, marveling at their instinctive rapport. Yet how alike were they really, if one spent her days on rescue missions to places like Rwanda, while the other cleaned houses to supplement her husband's income?

Twins are nature's handmade clones, doppelgangers moving in synchrony through circumstances that are often eerily similar, as if they were unwitting dancers choreographed by genes or fate or God, thinking each other's thoughts, wearing each other's clothes, exhibiting the same quirks and odd habits. They leave us to wonder about our own uniqueness and loneliness, and whether it's possible to inhabit another person's being. Twins provoke questions about the moment our passions first ignite—for they have been seen on sonogram in the womb, kissing, punching, stroking each other. They are living fault lines in the ever shifting geography of the nature/nurture debate, and their peculiar puzzle ultimately impacts politics, crime and its punishment, education, and social policy. It isn't such a short leap from studies of behavioral genetics to books like the infamous *The Bell Curve* (by Richard Herrnstein and Charles Murray) and a kind of sotto-voce eugenics. And so everything from homosexuality to IQ, religious affiliation, alcoholism, temperament, mania, depression, height, weight, mortality, and schizophrenia has been studied in identical and fraternal twins and their relatives.

Yet the answers—which these days seem to confirm biology's power—raise unsettling questions. Twin research is flawed, provocative, and fascinating, and it topples some of our most cherished notions—the legacies of Freud and Skinner included—such as our beliefs that parenting style makes an irrevocable difference, that we can mold our children, that we are free agents piecing together our destinies.

Today, we've gone twin-mad. Ninety thousand people gather yearly at the International Twins Day Festival in Twinsburg, Ohio. We're facing a near epidemic of twins. One in 50 babies born this year will have a fraternal or identical double; the number of such births rose 33 percent in 1994 alone, peaking at over 97,000—largely due to women delaying childbirth (which skewers the odds in favor of twins) and to the fertility industry, which relies on drugs that superovulate would-be mothers. Recently, a stunning scientific feat enabled an ordinary sheep to give up a few cells and produce a delayed identical twin—a clone named Dolly, who was born with her donor's 6-year-old nucleus in every cell of her body. The international furor this Scottish lamb engendered has at its heart some of the same wonder and fear that every twin birth evokes. Twins are a break, a rift in the customary order, and they call into question our own sense of self. Just how special and unique are we?

The history of twins is rich with stories that seem to reveal them as two halves of the same self—twins adopted into different families falling down stairs at the same age, marrying and miscarrying in the same year, identical twins inventing secret languages, "telepathic" twins seemingly connected across thousands of miles, "evil" twins committing arson or murder together, conjoined twins sharing a single body, so that when one coughs the other reflexively raises a hand to cover the first one's mouth. And yet the lives of twins are full of just as many instances of discordance, differences, disaffection. Consider the 22-year-old Korean twins, Sunny and Jeen Young Han of San Diego County; Jeen hired two teenagers to murder her sister, hoping to assume her identity.

So what is truly *other*, what is *self*? As the living embodiment of that question, twins are not just the mirrors of each other, they are a mirror for us all.

Reprinted with permission from *Psychology Today*, July/August 1997, pp. 36–44, 64, 66–69. © 1997 by Sussex Publishers, Inc.

MY TWIN MARRIAGE

A few years ago, I was playing the messages back on my answering machine just as my husband, Jeff, was coming into the apartment. He heard a familiar voice and ran for the answering machine.

"It's Phil!" he yelled, shrugging out of his coat. "Pick up the phone. Phil's calling."

Only it wasn't Phil. It was Phil's identical twin brother, Jeff.

"Oh, it's me," my husband said sheepishly. Sheepish in the sense of Dolly, the cloned sheep.

When I was first dating Jeff, the prospect of marrying an identical twin seemed magical. Jeff spoke of his brother as if he were talking about himself, almost as if he could bi-locate and live two contrasting yet mutually enriching lives. Jeff worked at a literary agency in Manhattan and loved boy fiction, thrillers, and horror novels, while Phil was overtly spiritual, editing a journal dedicated to the study of myth and tradition. When they were together they seemed to merge into one complex yet cohesive personality. They talked like hyper-bright little boys, each of them bringing equal heat and erudition to Stephen King and esoteric teachings, baseball, and the possibility of spiritual transformation. They argued—and still argue—like Trotsky and Lenin, desperate to define themselves as individuals, yet they define themselves against each other. Jeff and Phil love their wives and children, but they obey the orders they get from the mothership of their identical DNA.

My husband and his twin brother live by E. M. Forster's admonition, "Only connect." The pair e-mail each other at their respective offices two, four, even more times a day. A few weeks ago, Phil wrote Jeff that he was trying to decide his favorite 10 films of all time. He listed *Journey to the Center of the Earth, Star Wars,* seven other boy classics, and asked for Jeff's help thinking up a 10th.

"Phil and I decided that *Jurassic Park* is our favorite movie of all time," announced Jeff the other evening at dinner. In the course of dozens of soothing little dispatches Phil's movie list and Jeff's movie list had become one.

My marriage to Jeff has locked me into a triangle. The bond between these twins amazes and amuses me, yet it fills me with an unappeasable longing. After all, unlike Phil's wife, Carol, who is an only child, I was conditioned even before I was born to be with a twin. I am a fraternal twin, a girl born 10 minutes after a boy.

"What do you get out of being a twin?" I asked my husband the first day we had lunch. "What insight does it give you that's harder for single people to understand?"

"Trust," said my husband. "That pure physical trust that comes when you know someone loves and accepts you completely because they are just like you are."

I knew the primordial closeness he was talking about. As tiny premature babies, my brother Steve and I used to cuddle in the same crib holding hands. My earliest memory is of being lifted up high and feeling incredible joy as I gazed into my mother's vast, radiant face. I was put back down on a big bed. I remember sensing another baby lying next to me, my twin. His presence felt deeply familiar, and I know I had sensed him before we were born. For me, in the beginning there was the light but there was also the son. In addition to the vertical relationship I had with Mommy, I also had a lateral relationship, a constant pre-verbal reassurance that I had a peer. I was in it with somebody else. This feeling of extending in two directions, horizontal and vertical, made up the cross of my emotional life.

Separated at Birth But Joined at the Hip

The woman seated alone onstage at the opening of the *Maury Povich* show was already famous in the twin literature: Barbara Herbert, a plump 58-year-old with a broad, pretty face and short, silver hair, found her lost twin, Daphne Goodship, 18 years ago. Both had been adopted as babies into separate British families after their Finnish single mother killed herself.

The concordances in their lives send a shiver up the spine: both women grew up in towns outside of London, left school at 14, fell down stairs at 15 and weakened their ankles, went to work in local government, met their future husbands at age 16 at the Town Hall dance, miscarried in the same month, then gave birth to two boys and a girl. Both tinted their hair auburn when young, were squeamish about blood and heights, and drank their coffee cold. When they met, both were wearing cream-colored dresses and brown velvet jackets. Both had the same crooked little fingers, a habit of pushing up their nose with the palm of their hand—which both had nicknamed "squidging"—and a way of bursting into laughter that soon had people referring to them as the Giggle Twins. The two have been studied for years now at the University of Minnesota's Center for Twin and Adoption Research, founded by Thomas J. Bouchard, Ph.D. It is the largest, ongoing study of separated twins in the world, with nearly 100 pairs registered, and they are poked, probed, and prodded by psychologists, psychiatrists, cardiologists, dentists, ophthalmologists, pathologists, and geneticists, testing everything from blood pressure to dental caries.

At the center, it was discovered that the two women had the same heart murmurs, thyroid problems, and allergies, as well as IQ's a point apart. The two showed remarkably similar personalities on psychological tests. So do the other sets of twins in the study—in fact, the genetic influence is pervasive across most domains tested. Another set of twins had been reunited in a hotel room when they were young adults, and as they unpacked found that they used the same brand of shaving lotion (Canoe), hair tonic (Vitalis), and toothpaste (Vademecum). They both smoked Lucky Strikes, and after they met they returned to their separate cities and mailed each other identical birthday presents. Other pairs have discovered they like to read magazines from back to front, store rubber bands on their wrists, or enter the ocean backwards and only up to their knees. Candid photos of every pair of twins in the study show virtually all the identicals posed the same way; while fraternal twins positioned hands and arms differently.

Bouchard—a big, balding, dynamic Midwesterner who can't help but convey his irrepressible passion about this research—recalls the time he reunited a pair of twins in their mid-30s at the Minneapolis airport. "I was following them down the ramp to baggage claim and they started talking to each other. One would stop and a nanosecond later the other would start, and when she stopped a nanosecond later the other would start. They never once interrupted each other. I said to myself, 'This is incredible, I can't carry on a conversation like that with my wife and we've been married for 36 years. No psychologist would believe this is happening.' When we finally got to baggage claim they turned around and said, 'It's like we've known each other all our lives.' "

Just Puppets Dancing To Music of the Genes?

I asked Bouchard if the results of his research puncture our myth that we consciously shape who we are.

"You're not a believer in free will, are you?" he laughed, a little too heartily. "What's free will, some magical process in the brain?"

Yet I am a believer (a mystical bent and fierce independence actually run in my family, as if my genes have remote controlled a beguiling but misbegotten sense of freedom and transcendence). I was mesmerized and disturbed by the specificity of the twins' concordances. David Teplica, M.D., a Chicago plastic surgeon who for the last 10 years has been photographing more than 100 pairs of twins, has found the same number of crow's feet at the corners of twins' eyes, the same skin cancer developing behind twins' ears in the same year. Says Teplica, "It's almost beyond comprehension that one egg and one sperm could predict that."

I could imagine, I told Bouchard, that since genes regulate hormones and neurochemicals, and thus impact sexual attraction and behavior, DNA might influence the shaving lotion twins liked or the hue they tinted their hair. But the same esoteric brand of toothpaste? Walking into the sea backwards? This implies an influence so far-reaching it's unnerving.

"Nobody has the vaguest idea how that happens," he admitted, unfazed. "We're studying a set of triplets now, two identical females and a brother, and all three have Tourette's syndrome. How can the genes get so specific? I was talking yesterday in Houston to a bunch of neuroscientists and I said, 'This is the kind of thing you guys have to figure out.' There is tons of stuff to work on here, it's all open territory."

He paused to marvel over the tremendous shift in our understanding of human behavior. "When we began studying twins at the university in 1979, there was great debate on the power of genetics. I remember arguing in one graduate school class that the major psychoses were largely genetic in origin. Everyone in the classroom just clobbered me. It was the era of the domination of behaviorism, and although there's nothing wrong with Skinner's work, it had been generalized to explain everything under the sun. Nothing explains everything. Even genetics influences us, on the average, about 50 percent."

Yet that 50 percent seems omnipresent. It impacts everything from extroversion to IQ to religious and so-

At the age of 3, I remember standing in the grass on a hot, bright day in El Paso, Texas, aware as never before that my brother was different from me, not just because he was smaller then and a boy, but because he was different inside. I loved him and felt protective towards him, as I would throughout my childhood, but I also felt the first stirrings of rebellion, of wanting to go vertical in my identity, to make it clear to my parents and everybody else that I was not the same as Steve.

I began to relish the idea of not being completely knowable. I developed a serious underground life. At 8, I twinned myself with an invisible black panther I called Striker. At 10, I became a spy. I made cryptic notes in a notebook. I had sinister passport photos taken. I had a plastic revolver I carried in a plastic attaché case. You may call me one of the twins, I thought to myself, but I come from a foreign country that has malevolent designs on your own.

No one ever calls me and Steve "the twins" anymore, except as an artifact of childhood. I tend to think of my birth twin, who is now a Porsche mechanic and a big, outdoorsy guy who lives with his wife and two kids in a small town outside of Boston, as the brother who was with me when I was born, who shared space with me in the womb. I feel close to him not because we are exactly the same, but because I still have bedrock sensation and empathy for his life.

Jeff claimed that his knowledge of trust from being an identical let him know that I was the person he wanted to marry. He felt twinship towards me right from the start he said, and I wasn't surprised. Accustomed to being twins, my husband and I fell right into acting like twins. We co-authored a book and both edit at Publisher's Weekly, yet we sometimes argue over who gets to use the little study in our apartment as if our identities were at stake. Lately, I've noticed that when I feel dominated by Jeff I tend to yearn for a "real" twin, a twin who mirrors me so lovingly and acceptingly that I can let go and be myself without fear or explanation. A single person might escape by daydreaming about a perfect lover, but my fantasies of romantic enmeshment have always incorporated the twin.

Years ago in Manhattan I was invited to attend a ceremony for the Santeria religion's god of thunder, Shango, because Shango loves twins. On the way, a revered old Cuban santera told me that twins were sacred in Santeria and in the African mother religion of Yoruba because they reflect the intersection of spirit and matter. Girl and boy twins were especially fascinating, according to the santera. Most girls were killed by the boy energy, they believed. A girl had to be very strong to survive.

The moment I heard that I realized that being a twin has heightened the drama of my life. Human beings are born double, pulled between the desire to merge with another yet emerge as an authentic self. Twins fascinate, I believe, because we are an externalized representation of an internal struggle everybody lives with all their lives. We cast the illusion of solving the unsolvable, though we're no closer than anyone else.—*Tracy Cochran*

cial attitudes—and drops only in the influence on homosexuality and death. Though some researchers have criticized Minnesota's twin sample for being too small and perhaps self-selected (how many separated twins out there don't participate or don't even know they're twins?), it generally confirms the results of larger studies

BEYOND NATURE AND NURTURE: TWINS AND QUANTUM PHYSICS

I've been interested in identical twins ever since I was old enough to realize I am one. When my brother and I were young we were close but nonetheless epitomized the struggle of twins to achieve individual identities. Now in our 50s, we have both noticed a real convergence of our intellectual, spiritual and philosophical views.

Are the strikingly similar thoughts and behaviors of twins, even those reared apart, due to nature or nurture—or to a third factor? What if what I call the "nonlocal" nature of the mind is involved?

Nonlocal mind is a term I introduced in 1989 to account for some of the ways consciousness manifests, ways suggesting that it is not completely confined or localized to specific points in space or time. Nobel physicist Erwin Schrödinger believed that mind by its very nature is singular and one, that consciousness is not confined to separate, individual brains, that it is ultimately a unified field. David Chalmers, a mathematician and cognitive scientist from the University of California at Santa Cruz, has suggested that consciousness is fundamental in the universe, perhaps on a par with matter and energy, and that it is not derived from, nor reducible to, anything else. Nobel physicist Brian Josephson, of Cambridge University's Cavendish Laboratory, has proposed that nonlocal events at the subatomic level for example, the fact that there are correlations between the spin of subatomic particles, even after they are separated—can be amplified and may emerge in our everyday experience.

In other words, the macrocosm reflects the microcosm. Systems theorist Erwin Laszlo has suggested that nonlocal mind may mediate events such as intercessory prayer, telepathy, precognition, and clairvoyance.

If consciousness is unbounded and unitary, strikingly similar thoughts and behaviors of identical twins, even separated twins, would not be surprising. Genes do determine how individual brains function, how we each process information, and nonlocal mind could be easier to access if two brains were almost identical in their functioning. Indeed, some people see analogies between the behavior of separated, identical twins and separated, identical subatomic particles.

According to the late Irish physicist John S. Bell, if two subatomic particles once in contact are separated to some arbitrary distance, a change in one is correlated with a change in the other—instantly and to the same degree. There is no travel time for any known form of energy to flow between them. Yet experiments have shown these changes do occur, instantaneously. Neither can these nonlocal effects be blocked or shielded—one of the hallmarks of nonlocality. Perhaps distant twins are mysteriously linked, like distant particles—or, to quote Ecclesiastes, "All things go in pairs, one the counterpart of the other."
—*Larry Dossey, M.D.*

of twins reared together—studies that have taken place around the world.

Twin studies allow us to double blind our nature/nurture research in a unique way. Identical twins share 100 percent of their genes, while fraternals share 50 percent. But usually they grow up together, sharing a similar environment in the womb and the world. When separated, they give us a clue about the strength of genetic influence in the face of sometimes radically different environments. Soon Bouchard and his colleagues will study siblings in families that have adopted a twin, thus testing environmental influences when no genes are shared. Like a prism yielding different bands of light, twin studies are rich and multifaceted. Here are some of the major findings on nature and nurture thus far:

• **Political and social attitudes,** ranging from divorce to the death penalty, were found to have a strong genetic influence in one Australian study. A Swedish study found genes significantly influenced two of the so-called "big five" personality traits—"openness to experience" and "conscientiousness"—while environment had little impact. In contrast, environment influenced "agreeableness" more than genes did. (The two other traits are "neuroticism" and "extroversion.") Another study, at the University of Texas at Austin, found that personality in identicals correlated 50 percent, in fraternals about 25 percent.

• **Body fat is under genetic influence.** Identical twins reared together will have the same amount of body fat 75 percent of the time; for those reared apart it's 61 percent, showing a heavy genetic and mild environmental influence, according to a 1991 study.

• **Both optimism and pessimism** are heavily influenced by genes, but shared environment influences only optimism, not pessimism, according to a study of 522 pairs of middle-aged identical and fraternal twins. Thus family life and genes can be equal contributors to an optimistic outlook, which influences both mental and physical health. But pessimism seems largely controlled by genes.

• **Religiosity is influenced by genes.** Identical and fraternal twins, raised together and apart, demonstrate that 50 percent of religiosity (demonstrated by religious conviction and church attendance) can be attributed to genes.

• **Sexual orientation** is under genetic influence, though not solely, according to studies by Michael Bailey, Ph.D., associate professor of psychology at Northwestern University. In one study he found that if one identical twin is gay, the other is also gay 50 percent of the time. However, when Bailey analyzed a sample of 5,000 twins from the Australian twin registry, the genetic impact was less. In identical male twins, if one was gay the likelihood of his twin being gay was 20 percent; in fraternal twins the likelihood was almost zero. In women, there was little evidence of heritability for homosexuality.

• **When substance abuse** was studied in 295 identical and fraternal twin pairs, year of birth was the most powerful predictor of drug use. Younger twins were most likely to have abused drugs, reflecting widespread drug use in the culture at large. Alcoholism, however, has a significant genetic component, according to Andrew Heath, Ph.D., at the Virginia Institute for Psychiatric and

Behavioral Genetics at Virginia Commonwealth University School of Medicine.

• **Attention deficit disorder** may be influenced by genes 70 percent of the time, according to Lindon Eaves, M.D., director of the Virginia Institute for Psychiatric and Behavioral Genetics. Eaves and colleagues studied 1,400 families of twins and found genetic influence on "all the juvenile behavior disorders," usually in the range of 30 to 50 percent.

• **Twins tend to start dating,** to marry, and to start having children at about the same time. David Lykken, Ph.D., and Matthew McGue, Ph.D., at the University of Minnesota, found that if an identical twin had divorced, there was a 45 percent chance the other had also. For fraternals, the chance was 30 percent. The researchers think this is due to inherited personality traits.

• **Schizophrenia** occurs more often in identical twins, and if one twin suffers from the disorder, the children of the healthy identical sibling are also at greater risk, according to psychiatrist Irving Gottesman, M.D., of the University of Virginia. The risk is about twice as high for the children of a twin whose identical counterpart is ill, as it is for the children of a twin whose fraternal counterpart is ill.

Hidden Differences Between Twins

A few fascinating kinks in the biology of twin research have recently turned up, weaving an even more complex pattern for us to study and learn from. It turns out that not all identical twins are truly identical, or share all their genetic traits. In one tragic instance, one twin was healthy and a gymnast, while the other suffered from severe muscular dystrophy, a genetic disorder, and was dead by age 16. Yet the twins were identical.

One way twins can differ is in the sex chromosomes that turn them into a male or female, and which contain other genes as well, such as those that code for muscular dystrophy or color blindness. All girls inherit two X chromosomes, one from each parent, while boys inherit an X and a Y. Girls automatically shut off one X in every cell—sometimes some of the mother's and some of the father's, in other cases all the mother's or all the father's. A girl may not shut off her extra set of X chromosomes in the same pattern as her identical twin does.

Identical twins may not be exposed to the same world in the womb, either. It depends on the time their mother's fertilized egg splits—and that timing may explain why some identical twins seem more eerily alike than others. At Lutheran University, researchers have looked at the placentas of some 10,000 twin births. They've found that an egg that separates in the first four days of pregnancy develops not only into separate twins, but results in separate placentas, chorionic casings, and amniotic sacs. These twins are like two singletons in the womb and have the best chance of survival. Twins who

separate between the fifth and eighth days share a single placenta and chorion, but still have the benefit of two amniotic sacs. Here, one twin can have a distinct advantage over the other. The umbilical cord may be positioned centrally on one sac, while the other is on the margin, receiving fewer nutrients. Studies of these twins show that with a nurturing environment, the weaker twin will catch up in the first few years of life. However, it's possible that viruses may penetrate separate sacs at

> Some twins are bonded by a lifelong passion for each other that the rest of us experience only in the almost unbearably intense first flush of romantic love. England's notorious Gibbons twins were one such pair.

different rates or in different ways—perhaps increasing the risk for schizophrenia or other illnesses later in life.

Twins who split between the eighth and 12th days share their amniotic sac, and often their cords get entangled. One cord may be squeezed until no blood flows through it, and that twin dies. Finally, twins who split after the 12th day become conjoined—and even though they share organs and limbs, anecdotal evidence suggests that they often have distinctly different temperaments, habits, and food cravings.

In one hotly debated hypothesis, pediatrician and geneticist Judith Hall, of the University of British Columbia in Vancouver, speculates that twinning occurs because of genetic differences within in an embryo. Perhaps mutations occur at a very early stage in some cells, which then are sensed as different, and expelled from the embryo. Those cells may survive and grow into a twin. Hall suggests this could account for the higher incidence of birth defects among twins.

While identical twins can be more distinct than we imagine, fraternal twins might come from the same egg, according to behavioral geneticist Charles Boklage, M.D., of the East Carolina University School of Medicine. Boklage proposes that occasionally an older egg may actually split before it is fertilized by two of the father's sperm. With advances in gene mapping and blood testing, he says, we may find that one-egg fraternal twins occur as often as do two-egg fraternals. We may be mistaking some same sex fraternal twins for identical twins.

Twins Who Vanish, Twins Who Merge

Whatever the cause of twinning, once it beings, mysterious and unsettling events can occur. Some twins disappear or even merge together into one person. Ultrasound equipment has revealed twin pregnancies that later turn into singletons. One of the twins is absorbed into the body, absorbed by the other twin, or shed and noticed by the mother only as some extra vaginal bleeding.

"Only one in 80 twin conceptions makes it to term as two living people," notes Boklage. "For every one that results in a twin birth, about 12 make it to term as a sole survivor. And those people never know they were twins." Because twins tend to be left-handed more often than singletons, Boklage speculates that many left-handers could be the survivors of a twin pregnancy. And a few of those twin pregnancies may lead to what Boklage terms a "chimera," based on the Greek monster with a tail of a serpent, body of a goat, and head of lion—a mosaic of separate beings. "We find people entirely by accident who have two different blood types or several different versions of a single gene. Those people look perfectly normal, but I believe they come from two different cell lines."

It's as if fantastical, primitive acts of love, death, merging, and emerging occur from the very moment life ignites, even as the first strands of DNA knit themselves into the human beings we will later become—carrying on those same acts in the world at large, acts that define us, and that we still are not certain we can call our own.

When Twins Die, Kill, Hate, and Burn

Though it doesn't happen often, occasionally in history a set of mythic twins seem to burst into our awareness, more wedded and bonded than any couple, even darkly so. Some twins live with a passion the rest of us experience only in the almost unbearably intense first flush of romantic love. England's Gibbons twins are one such pair.

Jennifer and June Gibbons were born 35 years ago, the youngest children of Aubrey Gibbons, a West Indian technician for the British Royal Air Force. The girls communicated with each other in a self-made dialect and were elective mutes with the rest of the world. By the time they were 11, they refused to sit in the same room with their parents or siblings. Their mother delivered their meals on a tray and slipped mail under the door. They taught themselves to read, and eventually locked themselves in their bedroom, writing literally millions of words in diaries.

Later they lost their virginity to the same boy within a week of each other, triggering jealous rage. Jennifer tried to strangle June with a cord, and June tried to drown Jennifer in a river. When publishers rejected their work, they went on a spree of arson and theft, and were committed to Broadmoor, England's most notorious institution for the criminally insane.

"Nobody suffers the way I do," June wrote in her diary. "This sister of mine, a dark shadow robbing me of sunlight, is my one and only torment." In another passage, Jennifer described June lying in the bunk bed above her: "Her perception was sharper than steel, it sliced through to my own perception . . . I read her mind, I knew all about her mood . . . My perception. Her perception . . . clashing, knowing, cunning, sly."

After more than a decade of confinement, they were set free. That same afternoon, Jennifer was rushed to the hospital with viral myocarditis, an inflammation of the heart, and that night she died. The pathologist who saw her heart seemed to be speaking poetically of their lethal passion when he described Jennifer's illness as "a fulminating, roaring inflammation with the heart muscle completely destroyed." June, the survivor, has said that she was "born in captivity, trapped in twinship." Eventually, June claims, they began to accept that one must die so the other could be free. Today, June lives in Wales.

Another set of twins, 22-year-old Jeen Young Han (nicknamed Gina) and her sister Sunny, have been dubbed the "evil" and "good" twins by the media, after one tried to murder the other. Although the twins were both valedictorians at their small country high school in San Diego County and got along well, after they graduated they began to battle one another. Both sisters were involved in petty crime, but when Gina stole Sunny's BMW and credit cards, Sunny had her jailed. She escaped, but in November 1996 Sunny and her roommate were attacked and Gina was arrested for conspiracy to commit murder. She'd planned to have Sunny killed at her Irvine condominium, and then assume her identity.

For twin researcher and obstetrician Louis Keith, M.D., of Northwestern University Medical School, the idea of killing a twin is practically unthinkable. "I'm an identical twin, and yesterday I attended the funeral of another identical twin. I kept trying to imagine what my life would be like without my twin. My brother and I have had telepathic experiences. I was in East Germany, being driven on a secluded highway with evening snow falling, and suddenly felt intense heat over the entire front of my body and knew it could only mean one thing, that my brother was sending intense signals to me to call him. When one of the Communist telephone operators agreed to put the call through, I found out that my aunt had died and my twin wanted me to come to the funeral. The twin bond is greater than the spousal bond, absolutely."

Raymond Brandt, publisher of *Twins World* magazine, agrees. "I'm 67, and my identical twin died when we were 20. I love my wife and sons in a very special way, but my twin was one half of me, he was my first love. Living without my twin for 47 years has been a hell of an existence."

These remarkable stories seem to indicate an extra dimension to the twin bond, as if they truly shared a common, noncorporeal soul. What little study has been done on paranormal phenomena and twins, however, indicates that—once again—genes may be responsible. A study by British parapsychologist Susan Blackmore found that when twins were separated in different rooms and asked to draw whatever came into their minds, they often drew the same things. When one was asked to draw an object and transmit that to the other twin, who then was asked to draw what she telepathically received, the results were disappointing. Blackmore concluded that when twins seem to be clairvoyant, it's simply because their thought patterns are so similar.

Is There No Nurture?

Over a century ago, in 1875, British anthropologist Francis Galton first compared a small group of identical and fraternal twins and concluded that "nature prevails enormously over nurture." Time and research seem to have proved him right. "It's no accident that we are what we are," contends Nancy Segal, Ph.D., professor of developmental psychology at California State University at Fullerton and director of the Twin Studies Center there. "We are born with biological propensies that steer us in one direction or another."

Yet critics of twin studies scoff. Richard Rose, Ph.D., professor of psychology and medical genetics at Indiana University in Bloomington, has studied personality in more than 7,000 pairs of identical twins and concluded that environment, both shared and unshared, has nearly twice the influence of genes.

However, both the nature and nurture camps may be looking at the same data and interpreting it differently. According to Lindon Eaves, unshared environment may actually be "chosen" by the genes, selected because of biological preferences. Scientists dub this the "nature of nurture." Genetically influenced personality traits in a child may cause parents to respond in specific ways. So how can we ever tease out the truth? Nature and nurture interact in a never-ending Mobius strip that can't be traced back to a single starting point.

Yet if genes are a powerful and a-priori given, they nonetheless have a range of activity that is calibrated in the womb by nutrition and later in life by the world. "Remember," says Eaves, "only 50 percent of who you are is influenced by genes. The other 50 percent includes the slings and arrows of outrageous fortune, accidents of development, sheer chaos, small and cumulative changes both within and without."

Environment, it turns out, may be most powerful when it limits—through trauma, deprivation, malnutrition. Studies by Sandra Scarr, Ph.D., professor of psychology at the University of Virginia, show that IQ scores for white twins at the bottom of the socioeconomic ladder, and for all black twins, are heavily influenced by environment. Social and economic deprivation keep scores artificially lower than twins' genetic potential.

Otherwise, Scarr postulates, genes bias you in a certain direction, causing you to select what you are already genetically programmed to enjoy. Children may be tiny gene powerhouses, shaping their parents' behavior as much as parents shape their children.

"Where does this leave us?" concludes Bouchard. "Your job as a parent is really to maximize the environment so that you and your children can manifest your full genetic potential." Under the best of environmental circumstances, our genes might be free to play the entire symphony of self.

And yet what of Irina, the Michigan housewife, and her twin, Yanina, the Polish nun? I sat with them over lunch, newly united twins who couldn't stop smiling at each other, clasping each other's hands. Their luminous hazel eyes were virtual replicas, but the two women couldn't have appeared more different otherwise: Irina bejeweled and blonde, Yanina in a combat-green nun's habit, a few tufts of brown hair peeping out, skin weathered. She described rescuing bloodied children from the arms of mothers who'd been shot to death and rising at dawn in the convent to pray silently for hours; her American counterpart portrayed a life filled with errands, cleaning homes, and caring for family.

"Rushing, rushing, rushing to get everything done" was Irina's summary of her life. "Teaching love, the kind of love that will make you happy," was her sister's. Listening to them speak, one in slow, gentle Midwestern cadences, the other in the rolled drumbeat of a Slavic tongue enriched by laughter and hand gestures, it was hard to believe they carried the same genetic imprint.

To me, their differences are so striking they seem to defy the last 20 years of twin research. "Right now we understand a little bit about human behavior and its biological and cultural roots," says Eaves. "But our lived understanding is far richer than any of that. People are yielding the ground too easily to genetics."

As I mused over the intricate turnings of twin research, I could only conclude the findings were as complex as the self we hope to illuminate with these studies. Fascinating, tantalizing, yes, but twin research, like any great scientific endeavor, ultimately points us toward the ineffable, inexplicable.

As Charles Boklage notes: "The development of the self is chaotic, nonlinear, and dynamic. Very small variations in conditions can lead to huge changes. Different twin studies give different answers. And whenever the mind tries to understand something, it has to be bigger than the subject it compasses. You cannot bite your own teeth."

"In the end," says Eaves, "I don't give a damn whether you call it God or natural selection, we're trying to find words that instill reverence for the mysterious stuff from which we are made."

God, fate, genes, luck, a random event like a move to America or Poland, or perhaps something stubbornly individual and free about us all, something that can never be quantified but can only be lived . . . The play of self goes on, and whatever hand or eye has orchestrated us, who in the end, twin or not, can know the dancer from the dance?

The Role of Lifestyle in Preventing Low Birth Weight

Virginia Rall Chomitz
Lilian W. Y. Cheung
Ellice Lieberman

Abstract

Lifestyle behaviors such as cigarette smoking, weight gain during pregnancy, and use of other drugs play an important role in determining fetal growth. The relationship between lifestyle risk factors and low birth weight is complex and is affected by psychosocial, economic, and biological factors. Cigarette smoking is the largest known risk factor for low birth weight. Approximately 20% of all low birth weight could be avoided if women did not smoke during pregnancy. Reducing heavy use of alcohol and other drugs during pregnancy could also reduce the rate of low birth weight births. Pregnancy and the prospect of pregnancy provide an important window of opportunity to improve women's health and the health of children. The adoption before or during pregnancy of more healthful lifestyle behaviors, such as ceasing to smoke, eating an adequate diet and gaining enough weight during pregnancy, and ceasing heavy drug use, can positively affect the long-term health of women and the health of their infants. Detrimental lifestyles can be modified, but successful modification will require large-scale societal changes. In the United States, these societal changes should include a focus on preventive health, family-centered workplace policies, and changes in social norms.

Virginia Rall Chomitz, Ph.D., is project manager of the Eat Well and Keep Moving Project, Department of Nutrition, Harvard School of Public Health.

Lilian W. Y. Cheung, D.Sc., R.D., is a lecturer in the Department of Nutrition and director of the Harvard Nutrition and Fitness Project, Harvard School of Public Health, Department of Nutrition and Center for Health Communication.

Ellice Lieberman, M.D., Dr.PH., is assistant professor in the Department of Obstetrics, Gynecology, and Reproductive Biology, Harvard Medical School and in the Department of Maternal and Child Health, Harvard School of Public Health.

Many of the known risk factors associated with low birth weight, such as socioeconomic status, ethnicity, genetic makeup, and obstetric history, are not within a woman's immediate control. However, there are things that a woman can do to improve her chances of having a normal, healthy child. Lifestyle behaviors, such as cigarette smoking, use of other drugs, and nutrition, play an important role in determining fetal growth. Detrimental habits can be modified, but successful modification requires more than just a dose of individual "self control." Stopping lifelong addictive behaviors is very difficult, and a woman who suffers from them requires support and assistance not only from family members and individuals close to her, but also from the health care system and society.

The relationship between lifestyle risk factors and low birth weight is very complex and is affected by psychosocial, socioeconomic, and biological factors. While it is important to describe the independent effects of different behavioral and socioeconomic risk factors, we must bear in mind that these factors are not isolated events in women's lives, but are a part of many interrelated complex behaviors and environmental risks. Factors associated with the perinatal health of women and children include demographic factors, medical risks, and maternal behaviors. These risk factors may influence maternal and infant health directly (in terms of physiology) or indirectly (in terms of health behavior). In this article we focus primarily on lifestyle behavioral risk factors that are amenable to change and that, if modified before or during pregnancy, can improve the likelihood of the delivery of a full-term healthy infant of appropriate size.

> *There are things that a woman can do to improve her chances of having a normal, healthy child.*

This paper is based on Healthy Mothers—Healthy Beginnings, *a paper written with a grant from the CIGNA Foundation and CIGNA Corporation, 1992.*

Demographic Factors

Socioeconomic status and race/ethnicity are indicators of complex linkages among environmental events, psychological states, and physiologic factors which may lead to low birth weight or preterm delivery. While we do not fully understand the specific biological pathways responsible, we do know that a woman's social and economic status will influence her general health and access to resources. (See the article by Hughes and Simpson in this journal issue for a detailed analysis of the effects of social factors on low birth weight.) In this section, we review the effects of some demographic indicators.

Socioeconomic Status

Low birth weight and infant mortality are closely related to socioeconomic disadvantage. Socioeconomic status, however, is difficult to measure accurately. Educational attainment, marital status, maternal age, and income are interrelated factors and are often used to approximate socioeconomic status, but no single factor truly measures its underlying influence.

Maternal education, maternal age, and marital status are all reflective of socioeconomic status and predictive of low birth weight. Twenty-four percent of the births in 1989 were to women with less than a high school education.[1] Low educational attainment is associated with higher rates of low birth weight.[2] For example, relative to college graduates, white women with less than a high school education were 50% more likely to have babies with very low birth weight (less than 1,500 grams, or 3 pounds, 5 ounces) and more than twice as likely to have babies with moderately low birth weight (between 1,500 grams and 2,500 grams, or 3 pounds, 5 ounces and 5 pounds, 8 ounces) than were women who graduated from college.[2] Teenage mothers are at greater risk of having a low birth weight baby than are mothers aged 25 to 34.[1] However, it is not clear if the risk of teenage childbearing is due to young maternal age or to the low socioeconomic status that often accompanies teenage pregnancy.

The marital status of the mother also appears to be independently associated with the rate of low birth weight,[2,3] although the relationship appears to vary by maternal age and race. The association of unmarried status with low birth weight is probably strongest for white women over 20 years of age.[2,4] Marital status may also serve as a marker for the "wantedness" of the child, the economic status of the mother, and the social support that the mother has—all of which are factors that may influence the health of the mother and infant.

It has been hypothesized that economic disadvantage may be a risk factor for low birth weight partly because of the high levels of stress and negative life events that are associated with being poor. Both physical stress and fatigue—particularly related to work during pregnancy—and psychological distress have been implicated.[5] In addition, stress and negative life events are associated with health behaviors such as smoking.[6] Social support may act as a moderator or as a buffer from the untoward effects of stressful life experiences and emotional dysfunction.[7]

Race/Ethnicity

The prevalence of low birth weight among white infants is less than half of that for African-American infants (6% and 13%, respectively). This difference reflects a twofold increase of preterm and low birth weight births among African-American mothers.[1] African-American mothers are more likely to have less education, not to be married, and to be younger than white mothers.[1] However, at almost all educational levels and age categories, African-American women have about double the rates of low birth weight as white women.[8] This fact indicates that these demographic differences in education, marital status, and age do not account for the large disparity between African Americans and whites in the incidence of low birth weight.

Among infants of Hispanic origin, who represented approximately 15% of live births in 1989, the rate of low birth weight was relatively low (6.1% overall), particularly given that Hispanic women (except Cuban women) had limited educational attainment and were not as likely as non-Hispanic white women to receive prenatal care early in pregnancy.[1]

However, Hispanics are a very diverse group, and the low birth weight rates vary considerably by national origin. Low birth weight rates range from 9.4% among Puerto Rican mothers to 5.6% among Cuban mothers. Among Asian infants in 1989, the incidence of low birth weight ranged from 5.1% for Chinese births to 7.3% for Filipino births.[1]

It is not known why infants of African-American mothers are twice as likely as all other infants to be born with low birth weights. The etiology of racial disparities in infant mortality and low birth weight is probably multifactorial in nature and is not completely explained by differences in demographics, use of tobacco and other drugs, or medical illnesses.[9] During the primary childbearing years (ages 15 to 29), the general mortality of African-American women exceeds that of white women for virtually every cause of death.

African-American women have higher rates of hypertension, anemia, and low-level lead exposure than other groups,[10] suggesting that the general health status of African-American women may be suboptimal. Infants of African-American foreign-born mothers have lower risks of neonatal mortality than infants of African-American U.S.-born mothers, a relationship that is not seen between foreign- and U.S.-born white women.[11] In addition, racial or ethnic differences in familial structure and social networks may affect morbidity and mortality.[12] More research will be needed to clarify the reasons for these disparities.

Nutrition and Weight Gain

Concerns about nutrition during pregnancy fall into two basic areas, maternal weight gain and nutrient intake, both of which can potentially affect the health of the mother and infant. As with other lifestyle factors, a woman's nutrition and weight gain are closely linked to her socioeconomic status, cigarette smoking, and other health-related behaviors.

Maternal Weight Gain

Maternal weight gain during pregnancy results from a variety of factors, including maternal dietary intake, prepregnancy weight and height, length of gestation, and size of the fetus. The mother's prepregnancy weight and height are, in turn, a consequence of her genetic makeup, past nutritional status, and environmental factors. The relationship between a woman's caloric intake during pregnancy and her infant's birth weight is complex and is moderated through maternal weight gain and other mechanisms during pregnancy.[13,14]

Epidemiologic evidence has demonstrated a nearly linear association between maternal weight gain during pregnancy and birth weight,[15,16] and an inverse relationship to the rate of low birth weight.[16] It comes as no surprise that maternal weight gain during pregnancy is highly correlated with the birth weight of the infant because a large propor-

It is not known why infants of African-American mothers are twice as likely as all other infants to be born with low birth weights.

tion of the weight gain is due to the growth of the fetus itself. Women with total weight gains of 22 pounds (10 kilograms) or less were two to three times more likely to have growth-retarded full-term babies than were women with a gain of more than 22 pounds. Once corrected for the duration of pregnancy, the relationship between weight gain and preterm delivery is uncertain.[17,18]

On average, women gain about 30 pounds during pregnancy. Teenage mothers, older mothers, unmarried mothers, and mothers with less than a high school education are most likely to have low or inadequate weight gain during pregnancy. Even after accounting for gestational age and socioeconomic status, African-American mothers gain less weight than white mothers (28 versus 31 pounds).[19] It has been estimated that from 15% to 33% of women gain an inadequate amount of weight (less than 22 pounds) during pregnancy.[13,19] Low weight gain may in part be the result of outdated medical advice and personal beliefs. In one study, one-quarter of the pregnant women believed that they should not gain more than 20 pounds during pregnancy.[20] In addition, belief that a smaller baby is easier to deliver and thus that weight gain and fetal birth weight should be limited influences the amount of weight gained by some women.[21]

tionship between specific vitamins and minerals and low birth weight is unclear, and controversy exists over the association between maternal hematocrit levels (which is a marker for anemia) and preterm birth.[23–26]

A pregnant woman's current nutritional status is determined by her prepregnant nutritional status, her current intake of nutrients, and her individual physiological nutrient requirements. Members of the National Academy of Sciences recently reviewed the available literature on dietary intake of nutrients and minerals among pregnant women. They found that the energy intake (calories) for U.S. women was consistently below recommended levels and that the amount of important vitamins and minerals in their diet was also substantially lower than the recommended daily allowance. On average, intakes of protein, riboflavin, vitamin B-12, niacin, and vitamin C exceeded the recommended daily allowance.[27]

Women at particular risk of nutritional inadequacy during pregnancy may require nutritional counseling. Groups at risk include women voluntarily restricting caloric intake or dieting; pregnant adolescents; women with low income or limited food budgets; women with eating patterns or practices that require balancing food choices, such as strict

Approximately 20% to 25% of American women smoke cigarettes during pregnancy.[31,32] White, young, unmarried, and unemployed women, as well as women with fewer than 12 years of education and low socioeconomic status, are more likely to smoke during pregnancy, compared with nonwhite, older, married women with more than 12 years of education and higher socioeconomic status.[27,30,33,34] For example, 35% of mothers with less than a high school education smoke compared with 5% of college graduates.[35]

Smoking retards fetal growth. Birth weight is reduced by 150 to 320 grams (5.3 to 11.4 ounces) in infants born to smokers compared with those born to nonsmokers.[36] It has been consistently reported that, even after controlling other factors, women who smoke are about twice as likely to deliver a low birth weight baby as are women who do not smoke.[37] A dose-response relationship exists between the amount smoked and birth weight: the percent of low birth weight births increases with increasing number of cigarettes smoked during pregnancy. In addition, exposure to environmental cigarette smoke has also been associated with low birth weight.[38] Preterm birth is associated with smoking, but the association is weak compared with the association between low birth weight and smoking.[9,37] Cigarette smoking during pregnancy may account for up to 14% of preterm deliveries.[37]

Studies of women who quit cigarette smoking at almost any point during pregnancy show lower rates of low birth weight. Most fetal growth takes place in the last trimester, so that quitting early in pregnancy can decrease the negative effect of smoking on birth weight.[33] Quitting even as late as the seventh or eighth month has a positive impact on birth weight.[39]

Overall, about one-quarter of women who smoke prior to pregnancy quit upon learning of their pregnancies, and an additional one-third reduce the number of cigarettes they smoke.[33,40] Older women and more educated women are more likely to quit smoking during pregnancy.[41] Light smokers are more likely to quit smoking than heavier smokers. Heavier smokers are likely to reduce the amount they smoke, but are unlikely to quit.[42] Social support appears to be a critical factor in changing smoking behavior.[40]

Even among women who do quit smoking during pregnancy, about a third will relapse before childbirth.[43] In addition, nearly 80% of women who stop smoking during pregnancy relapse within one year after the delivery.[40] These high relapse rates reflect the physiological addictive nature of nicotine. While 57% of the pregnant smokers in one study were able to decrease their intake, 40% "tried and failed" to reduce.[44] Of women who both drank and smoked before pregnancy, fewer women were able to decrease

---

Smoking during pregnancy has been linked to 20% to 30% of low birth weight births.

While higher maternal weight gain is linked with healthier fetal weight gains, women and clinicians are concerned that women may retain weight after delivery and be at greater risk for obesity. Recent studies have shown that weight retention following delivery increased as weight gain increased, and African-American women retained more weight than white women with comparable weight gains during pregnancy (7.2 versus 1.6 pounds).[22] Thus, weight management programs would be appropriate for some women after delivery, but not during pregnancy.

Diet and Nutrient Intake

During pregnancy, the need for calories and nutrients, such as protein, iron, folate, and the other B vitamins, is increased to meet the demands of the fetus as well as the expansion of maternal tissues that support the fetus. As noted by Nathanielsz in this journal issue, the nutritional needs of the fetus are second only to the needs of the mother's brain. Thus, it is important for a pregnant woman to have a well-balanced, nutritious diet to meet the changing needs of her body and her fetus. Unfortunately, the direct rela-

vegetarians; women with emotional illness; smokers; women with poor knowledge of nutrition due to lack of education of illiteracy; and women with special difficulties in food resource management because of limited physical abilities and poor cooking or budgeting skills.[28]

Lifestyle Choices: Cigarette Smoking, Alcohol, Caffeine, and Illicit Drugs

Cigarette Smoking

Since the 1970s, the Surgeon General has reported that cigarette smoking during pregnancy is linked to fetal growth retardation and to infant mortality.[29] Smoking during pregnancy has been linked to 20% to 30% of low birth weight births and 10% of fetal and infant deaths.[30] Cigarette smoking is unequivocally the largest and most important known modifiable risk factor for low birth weight and infant death.

or quit smoking than drinking, despite feelings of social pressure to quit and feelings of guilt at continuing to smoke.[44] The high recidivism rate after childbirth also reflects diminished maternal contact with the health care system as health care provision shifts from obstetrics to pediatrics.[45]

The bulk of evidence shows a clear and consistent association between low birth weight (primarily due to growth retardation, not preterm birth) and infant mortality and smoking during pregnancy. Smoking also impacts on other aspects of the health status of women and infants. Smoking has been linked to long-term effects in infants such as physical, mental, and cognitive impairments.[46,47] The linkages between smoking and illnesses, such as cancer and cardiovascular and respiratory disease, are well known.[48] In addition, research on the effects of passive smoke indicates an increased frequency of respiratory and ear infections among infants and children exposed to this smoke.[33,49]

Alcohol Use

Alcohol use during pregnancy has long been associated with both short- and long-term negative health effects for infants. Alcohol abuse during pregnancy is clearly related to

Heavy alcohol consumption has been cited as the leading preventable cause of mental retardation worldwide.

a series of congenital malformations described as fetal alcohol syndrome. However, the effects of moderate drinking on the fetus are not well established. Alcohol use among women of childbearing age and, specifically, among pregnant women has apparently declined significantly in the past decades.[44] This decreasing trend has generally been confined to more educated and older women. However, there has been little or no change in drinking during pregnancy among smokers, younger women, and women with less than a high school education.[50]

Heavy Drinking During Pregnancy

Numerous studies report an association between chronic alcohol abuse and a series of fetal malformations. Fetal alcohol syndrome is characterized by a pattern of severe birth defects related to alcohol use during pregnancy which include prenatal and postnatal growth retardation, central nervous system

disorders, and distinct abnormal craniofacial features.[51] Heavy alcohol consumption has been cited as the leading preventable cause of mental retardation worldwide.[52] It has been estimated that the prevalence of fetal alcohol syndrome is 1 to 3 per 1,000 live births with a significantly increased rate among alcoholics of 59 per 1,000 live births. Prenatally alcohol-exposed babies with birth defects who do not meet all required criteria for the syndrome are categorized as having fetal alcohol effects. The prevalence of fetal alcohol effects may be threefold that of fetal alcohol syndrome.[52]

The children of women who continued to drink an average of greater than one drink daily throughout their pregnancies are significantly smaller, shorter, and have smaller head circumferences than infants of control mothers who stop drinking.[53] The risk of low birth weight to women drinking three to five drinks per day was increased twofold over nondrinking mothers and almost threefold for those drinking six or more drinks daily when compared with women who did not drink.[54] A study of French women showed that those who consumed 35 drinks or more a week gave birth to infants that weighed 202 grams (about 7 ounces) less than the infants of women who consumed six or fewer drinks per week.[55]

Moderate Drinking During Pregnancy

While the effects of heavy daily drinking are well documented, the impact of moderate drinking is not as well established. Approximately 40% to 60% of pregnant women consume one drink or less a day. Alcohol use exceeding one drink daily ranges from 3% to 13%. Abstinence levels in pregnant women have been reported to range from 16% to 53%.[50,54,56] Women who consumed less than one alcoholic drink per day had only an 11% increased chance of delivering a growth-retarded infant.[54] Decrements in birth weight from 32 to 225 grams (1.1 to 8 ounces) have been reported for children born to women who drank one to three drinks daily.[55,57] Some studies with long-term follow-up have reported deleterious short-term effects and long-term effects, such as growth, mental, and motor delays, for infants of mothers who drink alcohol during pregnancy.[58,59] However, a number of studies demonstrate insignificant or no effects of "low to moderate" intake on growth at birth[60] and at four and five years of age.[58,61] The role of binge drinking is unknown.

Profile of the Pregnant Drinker

The profile of the pregnant drinker varies by the type of drinking. Any alcohol use during pregnancy is associated with older, white, professional, college-educated women with few previous children. Drinkers are also more likely to be unmarried and to smoke than are nondrinkers.[50] However, heavier alcohol use, in excess of two drinks daily, has been associated with African-American and Hispanic race/ethnicity, less than a high school education, and multiparity. Conversely, women who abstained during pregnancy were more likely to be younger, African-American, and/or of moderate income.[62]

During pregnancy, many women reduce their drinking[63] with decreases occurring in all types of drinkers.[64] In addition, as pregnancy advances, the proportion of women drinking decreases. In one study, 55% of women drank in the week prior to conception, 50% drank after 32 weeks, and only 20% drank in the last week of their pregnancies.[65]

Many of the studies investigating the relationship of maternal alcohol use to fetal effects suffer from methodologic problems common to substance use research. Most of the studies rely on self-reporting which, because of the stigma attached to alcohol use during pregnancy, may be inaccurate. Studies of drug use also often fail to consider other important factors, such as maternal nutrition, general health, or marijuana use. In addition, the usual dose, frequency of intake, and timing of drinking during pregnancy may result in different consequences, but this information is often lacking.

Caffeine Consumption

Caffeine is one of the most commonly used drugs. At least 52% of people in the United States drink coffee, 29% drink tea, and 58% consume soft drinks.[66] Caffeine is most commonly consumed in beverages such as coffee, tea, and soft drinks; eaten in the form of chocolate; and also taken as part of various prescription and nonprescription drugs. No consistent associations between caffeine and low birth weight or preterm birth have been observed.[67] Most studies have found no association between caffeine use and low birth weight, but some studies report positive yet inconsistent associations.[67] Several studies have found an interaction between caffeine and cigarette smoking, where the adverse effects of caffeine were observed only among smokers. The existence of such an interaction may help to explain the conflicting results.

Illicit Drug Use

In recent years, the rise in use of illegal drugs, particularly prenatal drug and cocaine, or "crack," use has received extensive coverage in the popular press and sparked many investigations. Prenatal cocaine and heroin abuse are clearly associated with adverse birth outcomes. Other factors in a drug addict's lifestyle, including malnutrition, sexually transmitted diseases, and polysubstance abuse, may contribute to an increased risk of adverse pregnancy outcome and often complicate the ability to examine the effects of individual drugs. The effect of marijuana use on the health of women and their infants is not as clear, nor are the effects of the occasional use of cocaine and other drugs.

Several methodologic problems hinder the interpretation and generalizability of much of the research on both the prevalence and effects of prenatal drug exposure. Studies are often based on small, nonrepresentative samples of mothers, and the bulk of the literature regarding illicit drug use relies on self-reporting. It is difficult to elicit valid information about illegal drug use, and a significant amount of underreporting probably takes place.[68] It is also unclear whether some of the effects of drug use are due to fetal drug exposure or to the generally poorer health and limited prenatal care of many addicted women. Finally, most research has been conducted with low-income urban women who are often in poorer health and under greater stress than their middle-class counterparts. The timing of drug use during the course of pregnancy and the dosage undoubtedly influences the consequences of the actions. However, most studies have been

Prenatal cocaine and heroin abuse are clearly associated with adverse birth outcomes.

unable to characterize accurately the use of drugs in pregnancy. In addition, interactive effects of illicit drugs with alcohol, tobacco, or other drugs have not as yet been adequately examined.

Despite the limitations of the research, a number of studies have shown significant effects of individual illicit substances on women and infants. Elevated rates of fetal growth retardation, perinatal death, and pregnancy and delivery complications—such as abruptio placentae, high blood pressure, and preeclampsia—have been observed among drug-abusing women and their infants.[69-73]

Cocaine Use

Maternal cocaine use has been associated with low birth weight, preterm labor, abruptio placentae, and fetal distress.[68,74,75] Brain damage and genitourinary malformations of the neonate have been reported, as well as fetal hyperthermia, thyroid abnormalities, stroke, and acute cardiac events.[76] Neurobehavioral effects found in neonates born to cocaine-abusing mothers have also been reported. These effects include decreased interactive behavior and poor organizational response to environmental stimuli.[72,74]

Marijuana Use

The effects of prenatal marijuana use on pregnancy and infant outcomes are inconclusive. Children exposed to marijuana *in utero* may be smaller than nonexposed infants.[68] Other reports suggest that pregnant women who smoke marijuana are at higher risk of preterm labor, miscarriage, and stillbirth.[76] However, other studies find no difference between users of marijuana and nonusers in terms of rate of miscarriage, type of presentation at birth, Apgar status, and frequency of complications or major physical anomalies at birth.[77]

Very little is known about the number of women who use drugs while pregnant, their pattern of drug usage during pregnancy, or the intensity of use. The prevalence of illicit drug use among pregnant women has been estimated using state level and hospital-based studies. Based on anonymous urine toxicology analysis combined with self-reporting, the prevalence of drug use among pregnant women has been estimated at 7.5% to 15%.[78,79]

Cocaine use among pregnant women has been estimated at 2.3% to 3.4%.[79,80] Regional and hospital-based data report marijuana use during pregnancy in the range of 3% to 12% and opiate (heroin) use in the range of 2% to 4%.[78,79] Regional data, such as New York City birth certificate data,[81] documented the dramatic increase in cocaine use relative to other drugs during the 1980s.

Figure 1 presents a profile of substance use among one sample of pregnant women.[62] Extrapolation of the data suggests that about half of all pregnant women may completely abstain from cigarette, alcohol, or drug use. However, approximately 14% of pregnant women engage in two or more high-risk behaviors during pregnancy, with about 2.5% of pregnant women, possibly about 100,000 nationwide, combining smoking, drinking, and recreational drug use.

Recent evidence suggests that, for pregnant women who receive treatment for drug abuse before their third trimester, the risks of low birth weight and preterm birth due to cocaine use may be minimized.[82] Little is known about which women quit or reduce drug use and why. In one study, college-educated, employed women were more likely to quit recreational drug use during pregnancy

Stress is widely cited in the popular literature as a serious risk to mothers and infants, but current research has not characterized its effects.

than were teenagers. The cessation rates were similar by racial/ethnic background and household income.[62] In another study, 14% of white women who used marijuana stopped using it upon starting prenatal care, as compared with 6% of African-American women.[83]

Stress, Physical Activity, Employment, Social Support, Violence, and Sexually Transmitted Diseases

As discussed in the previous section on demographic risk factors, physical and psychosocial stress may be associated with low birth weight. Stress is widely cited in the popular literature as a serious risk to mothers and infants, but current research has not characterized its effects. The scientific literature linking stress and anxiety to obstetric outcome has been equivocal, but there is some basis for the notion that maternal emotional distress may be linked to poor reproductive outcome.[84]

Stress

Stress is believed to influence maternal and infant health via changes in neuroendocrine functioning, immune system responses, and health behaviors. Thus, stress may influence pregnancy outcome directly (in terms of physiology) or indirectly (in terms of health behavior). Physiologically, stress has been associated with anxiety and depression.[85] It has been suggested that anxiety may increase metabolic expenditure and may lead to a lower gestational weight gain or to an anxiety-mediated change in catecholamine or hormonal balance which could provoke preterm labor.[37] Maternal psychological stress or emotional distress may interfere with the utilization of prenatal care of co-occur with particular health behaviors such as smoking and alcohol consumption.

However, the many methodological problems in much of the literature on stress and social support limit the extent to which studies can inform and guide policy and research. The studies are often based on small and ungeneralizable samples, and suffer from possible recall biases, poor reliability, and validity of study instruments and confounding. These difficulties arise from the

multifactorial nature of stress and social support and from the problems inherent in trying to characterize these poorly understood elements of people's lives.

Physical Activity

Concerns about weight gain and health have resulted in a high level of consciousness about weight control. More than one-third of American women participate in some form of regular physical activity.[86] Moderate aerobic exercise during pregnancy appears to have little adverse effect on pregnancy outcomes, and the potential benefits of exercise appear to be considerable.[87] Moderate exercise may be particularly beneficial for women at risk of developing diabetes during pregnancy. Lower levels of blood sugar were observed among diabetic women who were randomly assigned to moderate exercise regimens.[88] Decreases in the discomforts of pregnancy, improved self-esteem, and reduced tensions were reported among women who had participated in moderate physical conditioning programs during pregnancy.[89]

Employment

The majority of American women are employed during pregnancy.[90] Women are employed in a wide range of occupations, which have varying degrees of physical and emotional demands, and varying levels of exposure to employment-related chemicals, radiation, or other toxic substances. Thus, defining a particular "exposure" that characterizes the potential risks of employment has been difficult. In addition, the interrelationship between employment and socioeconomic status is unavoidable. Employed mothers also may accrue positive effects of employment through increased socioeconomic status, better access to medical care, and improved overall lifestyle.[91]

In general, the results of studies evaluating the relationship between employment and low birth weight have been inconclusive.[92] Studies conducted outside the United States have found increased rates of low birth weight and preterm birth among employed women whose jobs required heavy physical labor. However, results of studies conducted in the United States are more mixed and have even demonstrated positive effects of employment. Further advances in this area will be hampered until we are able to better understand the complex relationship among socioeconomic status, employment, stress, and lifestyle.

Domestic Violence

Depending on the population surveyed and the questions asked, the prevalence of battering of pregnant women has been estimated to be 8% to 17%.[93,94] There is some evidence of low birth weight among women

Figure 1

Profile of Substance Use Among Pregnant Women

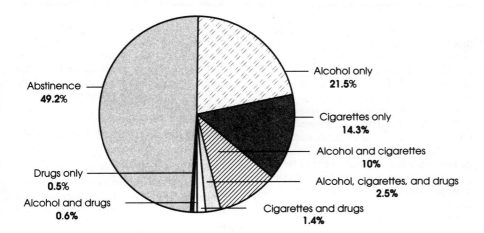

Abstinence
49.2%

Drugs only
0.5%

Alcohol and drugs
0.6%

Alcohol and drugs
0.6%

Alcohol only
21.5%

Cigarettes only
14.3%

Alcohol and cigarettes
10%

Alcohol, cigarettes, and drugs
2.5%

Cigarettes and drugs
1.4%

Source: Adapted from Johnson, S. F., McCarter, R. J., and Ferencz, C. Changes in alcohol, cigarette, and recreational drug use during pregnancy: Implications for intervention. *American Journal of Epidemiology* (1987) 126,4:701. Reprinted with permission of the *American Journal of Epidemiology.*

who have been abused during pregnancy,[95] possibly due to a physical trauma that initiates abruption, infections, or uterine contractions leading to early onset of labor. In addition, victimization of women may lead to a neglect of chronic medical conditions or to later initiation of prenatal care.[94]

Sexually Transmitted Diseases

Whether or not a woman gets infected with a sexually transmitted disease is highly associated with her sexual behavior and the sexual behavior of her partners. The chance of being infected increases with the number of sexual partners. There is increasing evidence to indicate that various genital infections are associated with low birth weight and preterm delivery.[96] However, the large number of implicated organisms combined with the numerous genital tract sites that they might infect has made the investigation of sexually transmitted diseases and low birth weight very challenging. Aside from the devastating effects on the fetus of untreated syphilis or gonorrhea, few specific organisms or defined genital tract infections have conclusively been shown to be highly correlated with preterm birth or low birth weight.[96] Most of the evidence linking genital organisms or infections to birth outcomes has been inconsistent and has shown only a low to moderate association. Clinical trials of antibiotics aimed at removing the organisms or infections have not consistently improved pregnancy outcomes.[96]

Other maternal infections during pregnancy, such as cytomegalovirus, genitourinary infections, pyelonephritis, and HIV, as well as food- or environmentally-borne infections such as toxoplasmosis and listeriosis, may endanger the health of the mother and fetus.[5,97–99]

Assessing the Impact of Lifestyle Risk Factors on Maternal and Infant Health

In this section, we try to estimate the number of excess low birth weight or small-for-gestational-age babies born due to maternal lifestyle risk factors. As noted earlier, the risk factors for low birth weight described above do not occur as isolated events; rather, they are part of a complex web of social, environmental, and individual factors. To understand the importance of these individual risk factors, we must try to fit them into a framework that represents a realistic picture of what is occurring in women's lives. This task is made more difficult because of our limited knowledge of the many common risk factors and the many potential interactions between factors which would result in a compounding of adverse effects—such as alcohol abuse and heavy cigarette smoking—as well as the role of protective factors.

Figure 2

Prevalence of Low Weight Gain and Substance Use Among Pregnant Women

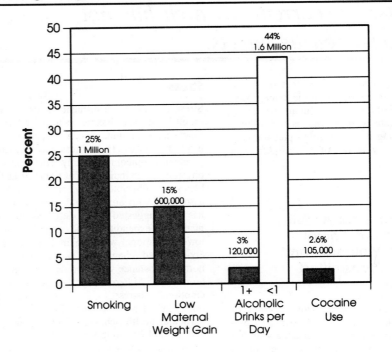

Source: Chomitz, V. R., Cheung, L., and Lieberman, E. *Healthy mothers—Healthy beginnings*. A white paper prepared by the Center for Health Communication, Harvard School of Public Health, Boston: President and Fellows of Harvard College, 1992.

The prevalence of battering of pregnant women has been estimated to be 8% to 17%.

We started by selecting the risk factors that have a consistent relationship with low birth weight and have been shown to be modifiable. These risk factors are cigarette smoking, alcohol abuse, cocaine abuse, and inadequate weight gain during pregnancy. The data on the prevalence of these factors and the risk incurred were derived from a variety of national and regional studies, and thus the estimates presented reflect the demographic and regional profile of the sample used. The estimates are not the result of a meta-analysis, but are based on published analyses that represent conservative and plausible risk.

We estimated the extra adverse birth outcomes attributed to high-risk lifestyle factors by applying the rate of low birth weight deliveries among cigarette smokers, women with inadequate weight gain, alcohol drinkers, and cocaine users, minus a baseline rate

of low birth weight among low-risk women. The effects of reducing stress and exposure to infectious agents cannot be quantified at this time. The numbers we derived are very rough estimates and should be regarded only as order of magnitude estimates.

Prevalence of Lifestyle Risk Factors

From the literature, we extrapolated estimates of the prevalence of high-risk behaviors among pregnant women to the number of live births in the United States in 1989. Some 20% to 25% of pregnant women, or approximately one million, smoked during pregnancy.[32,33] (see Figure 2.) Approximately 15%, or about 600,000 nonobese women, may have an inadequate total weight gain of less than 22 pounds during their pregnancy. More than 40% of women may not completely abstain from alcohol but consume less than one drink per day during pregnancy; about 3%, or 120,000 women, may have one or more drinks per day.[54] Approximately 105,000, or 2.6% of women, may use cocaine around the time of delivery.[79]

Excess Adverse Birth Outcomes

In 1990, there were 4,158,212 births in the United States, and 6.97% (approximately 290,000) of these infants were born low birth weight.[100] It comes as no surprise that reducing cigarette smoking has the largest potential to reduce the incidence of low birth weight. Approximately 48,000 low birth weight births could have been prevented if women had not smoked during pregnancy.

Women who failed to gain adequate weight (less than 22 pounds) by term gave birth to approximately 22,000 extra low birth weight babies who were born at full term. Approximately 14,000 infants a year may be born small for their gestational age due to

maternal alcohol consumption, and 10,000 excess low birth weight births could be attributed to prenatal cocaine abuse.

The low birth weight births that are potentially preventable due to smoking, inadequate weight gain, and alcohol use would generally reduce the number of infants who were born too small due to growth retardation but would have little effect on the number of infants born preterm. The lack of a relationship between these risk factors and preterm birth indicates that little improvement in preterm birth rates could be expected with the elimination of these risk factors.

Our estimates of the number of low birth weight births are very rough and may be inaccurate, as these numbers are only as good as our current knowledge of the true relationships between these risk factors and birth outcomes. The number of low birth weight births estimated to be due to each of these factors cannot simply be added together to

derive the total number of births that might be prevented by lifestyle changes because these estimates do not take into consideration the interrelationships among the risk factors. For example, a woman who is a heavy smoker and drinker would be counted twice in these calculations.

Directions for Future Research: Identifying Barriers to Change

Women face systemic, psychosocial, biological, or knowledge and attitudinal barriers to lifestyle changes. Further research must identify successful strategies for influencing behaviors. Figure 3 illustrates the complexity and interrelationship of common barriers to improving prenatal care and nutritional status, and for modifying smoking, drinking, and drug use.

Figure 3

Barriers to Behavioral Change

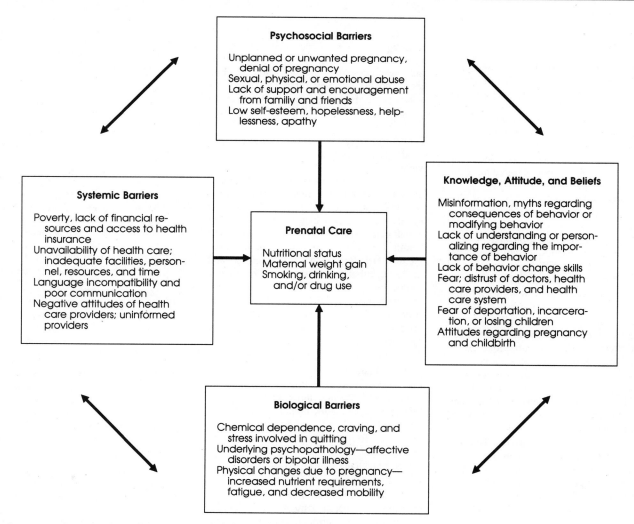

Source: Center for Health Communication, Harvard School of Public Health.

Although some individuals within an economically depressed or stressful situation may be involved in adverse lifestyle behaviors, most women are not. It is therefore important not only to conduct research with those individuals who have less healthy lifestyles, but also to profile and learn from those who, given similar environmental pressures, do not engage in high-risk behaviors or who have been able to change; that is, we

must overcome. Expecting women simply to change or modify their behavior without support and attention from the health care system, society, and influential people in their lives is unrealistic and may help to foster the belief that women are solely to blame for undesirable behaviors.

Barriers to successful intervention will not be overcome in the short term and will require both system-level reform and indi-

Strategies that can reduce the burden of low birth weight do exist. The public and private sectors must work together to define, develop, and implement these strategies.

Pregnancy and the prospect of pregnancy provide a window of opportunity to improve a woman's health before pregnancy, during pregnancy, and after the birth of her child.

must discover the protective strategies or resilience among individuals who are not engaged in adverse lifestyle behaviors, and apply the lessons learned to intervention programs.

Directions for Prevention/Intervention

Pregnancy and the prospect of pregnancy provide a window of opportunity to improve a woman's health before pregnancy, during pregnancy, and after the birth of her child. Pregnancy provides an opportunity for increased contact with the health care system and is associated with a heightened concern regarding health. Moreover, healthier mothers are more likely to provide more healthful beginnings for their children.

The adoption of healthful lifestyle behaviors before or during pregnancy, such as ceasing to smoke cigarettes, eating foods that supply adequate nutrition and produce an appropriate pregnancy weight gain, ceasing or reducing alcohol consumption, and ceasing illicit drug use, can also positively affect the long-term health of women, future pregnancy outcomes, and the health of children.

The health of the family, in general, may also be improved through household dietary changes and the reduction of environmental risks such as secondhand smoke. However, it must be reiterated that behaviors should not be isolated from the environment (society, community, and family) that fosters and supports them, and thus a change in the elements within the environment will facilitate an individual's ability to change his or her behavior. Despite the importance of maternal behavior modification to the health of mothers, infants, and families, it is important to recognize that there are systemic, biological, psychosocial, and belief and attitudinal barriers to behavioral change which women also

vidual efforts. Many women who smoke, engage in high-risk behaviors, eat poorly, or lack access to health care also live surrounded by poverty and violence, and go without adequate housing or employment. Under such circumstances, living a healthful lifestyle may not be a priority compared with day-to-day survival.

Overcoming these social circumstances will require increased access and availability to quality health care, as well as other affiliated resources and facilities such as child care, social services, law enforcement services, affordable and quality food, transportation, and maternity provisions during employment.

Finding ways to improve maternal and infant health and decrease the low birth weight rate is difficult, at least in part because the known causes of low birth weight are multifactorial, and much of the etiology remains unknown. The independent effects of economic disadvantage and inadequate health care coverage on maternal and infant health are difficult to isolate. In addition, medical risk factors that are identified and managed either before or during pregnancy can positively influence the health of women and their infants. Thus, linking women to continuous health care early in pregnancy or, ideally, before conception is a high priority for intervention.

Health promotion efforts aimed at improving infant health must do so by improving women's health. Improving women's health before, during, and after pregnancy is the key to reducing the human and economic costs associated with infant mortality and morbidity. To improve both women's and infants' health, efforts must target long-term, societal elements that involve policy or legislative changes.

These efforts should include an emphasis on preventive health care services, family-oriented work site options, changes in social norms, and individual behavior modification.

Notes

1. National Center for Health Statistics. *Advance report of final natality statistics, 1991.* Monthly Vital Statistics Report, Vol. 42, No. 3, Suppl. Hyattsville, MD: Public Health Service, September 9, 1993.
2. Kleinman, J., and Kessel, S. Racial differences in low birthweight: Trends and risk factors. *New England Journal of Medicine* (1987) 317,12:749–53.
3. Ahmed, F. Unmarried mothers as a high-risk group for adverse pregnancy outcomes. *Journal of Community Health* (1990) 15,1:35–44.
4. Bennett, T. Marital status and infant health outcomes. *Social Science Medicine* (1992) 35,9:1179–87.
5. Institute of Medicine, Committee to Study the Prevention of Low Birthweight. *Preventing low birthweight.* Washington, DC: National Academy Press, 1985.
6. McCormick, M. C., Brooks-Gunn, J., Shorter, T., et al. Factors associated with smoking in low income pregnant women: Relationship to birthweight, stressful life events, social support, health behaviors, and mental distress. *Journal of Clinical Epidemiology* (1990) 43:441–48.
7. Brooks-Gunn, J. Support and stress during pregnancy: What do they tell us about low birthweight? In *Advances in the prevention of low birthweight: An international symposium.* H. Berendes, S. Kessel, and S. Yaffe, eds. Washington, DC: National Center for Education in Maternal and Child Health, 1991, pp. 39–60.
8. Collins, Jr., J. W., and David, R. J. The differential effect of traditional risk factors on infant birthweight among blacks and whites in Chicago. *American Journal of Public Health* (1990) 80,6:679.
9. Shiono, P., Klebanoff, M., and Rhoads, G. Smoking and drinking during pregnancy. *Journal of the American Medical Association* (1986) 255:82–84.
10. Geronimus, A. T., and Bound, J. Black/white differences in women's reproductive-related health status: Evidence from vital statistics. *Demography* (1990) 27,3:457–66.
11. Kleinman, J., Fingerhut, L. A., and Prager K. Differences in infant mortality by race, nativity status, and other maternal characteristics. *American Journal of Diseases of Children* (1991) 145:194–99.
12. Moss, N. Demographic and behavioral sciences five year research plan. Draft. Bethesda, MD: National Institute of Child Health and Human Development, 1991.
13. Scholl, T., Hediger, J., Khoo, C., et al. Maternal weight gain, diet and infant birth weight: Correlations during adolescent pregnancy. *Journal of Clinical Epidemiology* (1991) 44:423–18.
14. Susser, M. Maternal weight gain, infant birth weight, and diet: Causal sequences. *American Journal of Clinical Nutrition* (1991) 53,6:1384–96.
15. Kleinman, J. *Maternal weight gain during pregnancy: Determinants and consequences.*

Working Paper No. 33. Hyattsville, MD: National Center for Health Statistics, 1990.

16. Luke, B., Dickinson, C., and Petrie, R. H. Intrauterine growth: Correlations and maternal nutritional status and rate of gestational weight gain. *European Journal of Obstetrics, Gynecology, and Reproductive Biology* (1981) 12:113–21.

17. Kramer, M. S., McLean, F. H., Eason, E. L., and Usher, R. H. Maternal nutrition and spontaneous preterm birth. *American Journal of Epidemiology* (1992) 136:574–83.

18. Kramer, M. S., Coates, A. L., Michoud, M., and Hamilton, E. F. Maternal nutrition and idiopathic preterm labor. *Pediatric Research* (1994) 35,4:277A.

19. National Center for Health Statistics. *Advance report of maternal and infant health data from the birth certificate, 1990.* Monthly Vital Statistics Report, Vol. 42, No. 2, Suppl. Hyattsville, MD: Public Health Service, July 8, 1993.

20. Carruth, B. R., and Skinner, J. D. Practitioners beware: Regional differences in beliefs about nutrition during pregnancy. *Journal of American Dietetic Association* (1991) 91,4:435–40.

21. Chez, R. Weight gain during pregnancy. *American Journal of Public Health* (1986) 76:1390–91.

22. Keppel, K. G., and Taffel, S. M. Pregnancy-related weight gain and retention: Implications of the 1990 Institute of Medicine Guidelines. *American Journal of Public Health* (1993) 83:1100–1103.

23. Klein, L. Premature birth and maternal prenatal anemia. *American Journal of Obstetrics and Gynecology* (1962) 83,5:588–90.

24. Klebanoff, M. A., Shiono, P. H., Selby, J. V., et al. Anemia and spontaneous preterm birth. *American Journal of Obstetrics and Gynecology* (1991) 164:59–63.

25. Lieberman, E., Ryan, K., Monson, R. R., and Schoenbaum, S. C. Association of maternal hematocrit with premature labor. *American Journal of Obstetrics and Gynecology* (1988) 159:107–14.

26. Klebanoff, J., and Shiono, P. H. Facts and artifacts about anemia and preterm birth. *Journal of the American Medical Association* (1989) 262:511–15.

27. Institute of Medicine, Subcommittee on Nutritional Status and Weight Gain During Pregnancy. *Nutrition during pregnancy.* Washington, DC: National Academy Press, 1990.

28. Dwyer, J. Impact of maternal nutrition on infant health. *Medical Times* (1983) 111:30–38.

29. U.S. Department of Health, Education, and Welfare. *The health consequences of smoking.* DHEW/HSM 73–8704. Washington, DC: DHEW, 1973.

30. Kleinman, J., and Madans, J. H. The effects of maternal smoking, physical stature, and educational attainment on the incidence of low birth weight. *American Journal of Epidemiology* (1985) 121:832–55.

31. National Center for Health Statistics. *Advance report of new data from the 1989 birth certificate, 1989: Final data from the National Center for Health Statistics.* Monthly Vital Statistics Report, Vol. 40, No. 12. Hyattsville, MD: Public Health Service, April 15, 1992.

32. National Center for Health Statistics. *Advance report of final mortality statistics, 1989: Final data from the National Center for Health Statistics.* Monthly Vital Statistics Report, Vol. 40, No. 8, Suppl. 2. Hyattsville, MD: Public Health Service, January 7, 1992.

33. U.S. Department of Health and Human Services. *The health benefits of smoking cessation: A report of the Surgeon General.* DHHS/CDC 90–8416. Washington, DC: DHHS, 1990.

34. Cardoza, L. D., Gibb, D. M. F., Studd, J. W. W., and Cooper, D. J. Social and obstetric features associated with smoking in pregnancy. *British Journal of Obstetrics and Gynecology* (1982) 89:622–27.

35. See note no. 32, National Center for Health Statistics, for mortality statistics in 1989.

36. Butler, N., Goldstein, H., and Ross, E. Cigarette smoking in pregnancy: Its influence on birth weight and perinatal mortality. *British Medical Journal* (1972) 2:127–30.

37. Kramer, M. S. Determinants of low birth weight: Methodological assessment and meta-analysis. *Bulletin of the World Health Organization* (1987) 65:663–737.

38. Martin, T., and Bracken, M. Association of low birth weight with passive smoke exposure in pregnancy. *American Journal of Epidemiology* (1986) 124:633–42.

39. Rush, D., and Cassano, P. Relationship of cigarette smoking and social class to birth weight and perinatal mortality among all births in Britain, 5–11 April 1970. *Journal of Epidemiology and Community Health* (1983) 37:249–55.

40. Wilner, S., Secker-Walker, R. H., Flynn, B. S., et al. How to help the pregnant woman stop smoking. In *Smoking and reproductive health.* M. J. Rosenberg, ed. Littleton, MA: PSG Publishing, 1987, pp. 215–22.

41. Fingerhut, L. A., Kleinman, J. C., and Kendrick, J. S. Smoking before, during, and after pregnancy. *American Journal of Public Health* (1990) 80:541–44.

42. Waterson, E. J., and Murray-Lyon, I. M. Drinking and smoking patterns amongst women attending an antenatal clinic—II. During pregnancy. *Alcohol and Alcoholism* (1989) 24,2:163–73.

43. Windsor, R. *The handbook to plan, implement and evaluate smoking cessation programs for pregnant women.* White Plains, NY: March of Dimes Birth Defects Foundation, 1990.

44. Condon, J. T., and Hilton, C. A. A comparison of smoking and drinking behaviors in pregnant women: Who abstains and why. *Medical Journal of Australia* (1988) 148:381–85.

45. Burns, D., and Pierce, J. P. *Tobacco use in California 1990–1991.* Sacramento: California Department of Health Services, 1992.

46. Brandt. E. N. Smoking and reproductive health. In *Smoking and reproductive health.* M. J. Rosenberg, ed. Littleton, MA: PSG Publishing, 1987, pp 1–3.

47. Weitzman, M., Gortmaker, S., Walker, D. K., and Sobol, A. Maternal smoking and childhood asthma. *Pediatrics* (1990) 85:505–11.

48. U.S. Department of Health and Human Services. *Reducing the health consequences of smoking: A report of the Surgeon General.* DHHS/CDC 89–8411. Rockville, MD: DHHS, 1989.

49. Samet, J. M., Lewit, E. M., and Warner, K. E. Involuntary smoking and children's health. *The Future of Children.* (Winter 1994) 4,3:94–114.

50. Serdula, M., Williamson, D., Kendrick, J., et al. Trends in alcohol consumption by pregnant women. *Journal of the American Medical Association* (1991) 265:876–79.

51. Ouellette, E. M., Rosett, H. L., Rosman, N. P., and Weiner, L. Adverse effects on offspring of maternal alcohol abuse during pregnancy. *New England Journal of Medicine* (1977) 297,10:528–30.

52. Abel, E. L., and Sokol, R. J. Incidence of fetal alcohol syndrome and economic impact of FAS-related anomalies. *Drug and Alcohol Dependence* (1987) 19:51–70.

53. Day, N. L., Jasperse, D., Richardson, G., et al. Prenatal exposure to alcohol: Effect on infant growth and morphologic characteristics. *Pediatrics* (1989) 84,3:536–41.

54. Mills, J. L., Graubard, B. I., Harley, E. E., et al. Maternal alcohol consumption and birth weight: How much drinking during pregnancy is safe? *Journal of the American Medical Association* (1984) 252,14:1875–79.

55. Larroque, B., Kaminski, M., Lelong, N., et al. Effects on birth weight of alcohol and caffeine consumption during pregnancy. *American Journal of Epidemiology* (1993) 137:941–50.

56. Halmesmaki, E., Raivio, K., and Ylikorkala, O. Patterns of alcohol consumption during pregnancy. *Obstetrics and Gynecology* (1987) 69:594–97.

57. Little, R., Asker, R. L., Sampson, P. D., and Renwick, J. H. Fetal growth and moderate drinking in early pregnancy. *American Journal of Epidemiology* (1986) 123,2:270–78.

58. Streissguth, A. P., Bookstein, F. L., Sampson, P. D., and Barr, H. M. Neurobehavioral effects of prenatal alcohol: Part III. PLS analyses of neuropsychologic tests. *Neurotoxicology and Teratology* (1989) 11,5:493–507.

59. Streissguth, A. P., Barr, H. M., and Sampson, P. D. Moderate prenatal alcohol exposure: Effects on child IQ and learning problems at age 7½ years. *Alcoholism, Clinical and Experimental Research* (1990) 14,5:662–69.

60. Walpole, I., Zubrick, S., and Pontre, J. Is there a fetal effect with low to moderate alcohol use before or during pregnancy? *Journal of Epidemiology and Community Health* (1990) 44,4:297–301.

61. Ernhart, C. B., Sokol. R. J., Ager, J. W., et al. Alcohol-related birth defects: Assessing the risk. *Annals of the New York Academy of Sciences* (1989) 562:159–72.

62. Johnson, S. F., McCarter, R. J., and Ferencz, C. Changes in alcohol, cigarette, and recreational drug use during pregnancy: Implications for intervention. *American Journal of Epidemiology* (1987) 126,4:695–702.

63. Little, R. Schultz, F., and Mandell, W. Alcohol consumption during pregnancy. *Journal of Studies on Alcohol* (1976) 37:375–79.

64. Russell, M. Drinking and pregnancy: A review of current research. *New York State Journal of Medicine* (1983) 8:1218–21.

65. See note no. 56, Halmesmaki, Raivio, and Ylikorkala, for more information about alcohol consumption patterns during pregnancy.

66. Lecos, C. Caffeine jitters: Some safety questions remain. *FDA Consumer* (December 1987/January 1988) 21:22.

67. Shiono, P. H., and Klebanoff, M. A. Invited commentary: Caffeine and birth outcomes. *American Journal of Epidemiology* (1993) 137:951–54.

68. Zuckerman, B., Frank, D. A., Hingson, R., et al. Effects of maternal marijuana and cocaine use on fetal growth. *New England Journal of Medicine* (1989) 320:762–68.

69. Zelson, C., Rubio, E., and Wasserman, E. Neonatal narcotic addiction: 10 year observation. *Pediatrics* (1971) 48,2:178–89.

70. Fricker, H., and Segal, S. Narcotic addiction, pregnancy, and the newborn. *American Journal of Diseases of Children* (1978) 132:360–66.

71. Lifschitz, M., Wilson, G., Smith, E., et al. Fetal and postnatal growth of children born to narcotic-dependent women. *Journal of Pediatrics* (1983) 102:686–91.

72. Robins, L. N., and Mills, J. L., Krulewitch, C., and Herman, A. A. Effects of in utero exposure to street drugs. *American Journal of Public Health* (December 1993) 83,12:S9.

73. Oleske, J. Experiences with 118 infants born to narcotic-using mothers. *Clinical Pediatrics* (1977) 16:418–23.

74. Dattel, B. J. Substance abuse in pregnancy. *Seminars in Perinatology* (1990) 14,2:179–87.

75. Bateman, D. A., Ng, S. K. C., Hansen, C. A., and Heagarty, M. C. The effects of intrauterine cocaine exposure in newborns. *American Journal of Public Health* (1993) 83,2:190–93.

76. Office for Substance Abuse Prevention. *Alcohol and other drugs can harm an unborn baby: Fact sheet and resource list.* Rockville, MD: National Clearinghouse for Alcohol and Drug Information, 1989, pp 1–19.

77. Fried, P. A., and Makin, J. E. Neonatal behavioral correlates of prenatal exposure to marjuana, cigarettes and alcohol in a low risk population. *Neurotoxicology and Teratology* (1986) 9:1–7.

78. Chasnoff, I. J., Landress, H. J., and Barrett, M. E. The prevalence of illicit-drug or alcohol use during pregnancy and discrepancies in mandatory reporting in Pinellas County, Florida. *New England Journal of Medicine* (1990) 322:1202–6.

79. Centers for Disease Control and Prevention. Statewide prevalence of illicit drug use by pregnant women—Rhode Island. *Morbidity and Mortality Weekly Report* (1990) 39,14:225–27.

80. Handler, A., Kistin, N., Davis, F., and Ferré, C. Cocaine use during pregnancy: Perinatal outcomes. *American Journal of Epidemiology* (1991) 133:818–25.

81. Zeitel, L., Bauer, T. A., and Brooks, P. *Infants at risk: Solutions within our reach.* New York: Greater New York March of Dimes/United Hospital Fund of New York, 1991.

82. U.S. General Accounting Office. *Drug abuse: The crack cocaine epidemic: Health consequences and treatment.* HRD-91–55FS. Washington, DC: GAO, 1991.

83. McCaul, M. E., Svikis, D. S., and Feng, T. Pregnancy and addition: Outcomes and interventions. *Maryland Medical Journal* (1991) 40:995–1001.

84. Newberger, E. H., Barkan, S. E., Leiberman, E. S., et al. Abuse of pregnant women and adverse birth outcome: Current knowledge and implications for practice. *Journal of the American Medical Association* (1992) 267,17:2370–72.

85. McAnarney, E. R., and Stevens-Simon, C. Maternal psychological stress/depression and low birth weight. *American Journal of Diseases of Children* (1990) 144:789–92.

86. Katch, F. I., and McArdle, W. E. *Introduction to nutrition, exercise and health.* 4th ed. Philadelphia: Lea and Febiger, 1993.

87. Dewey, K. G., and McCrory, M. A. Effects of dieting and physical activity on pregnancy and lactation. *American Journal of Clinical Nutrition* (1994) 59:446S–53S.

88. Jovanovic-Peterson, L., Durak, E. P., and Peterson, C. M. Randomized trial of diet versus diet plus cardiovascular conditioning on glucose levels in gestational diabetes. *American Journal of Obstetrics and Gynecology* (1989) 161:415–19.

89. Hall, D. C., and Kaufmann, D. A. Effects of aerobic and strength conditioning on pregnancy outcomes. *American Journal of Obstetrics and Gynecology* (1987) 157:1199–1203.

90. U.S. Bureau of the Census. *Work and family patterns of American women.* Current Population Reports, Series P-23, No. 165. Washington, DC: U.S. Government Printing Office, 1990.

91. Poerksen, A., and Petitti, D. B. Employment and low birth weight in black women. *Social Science and Medicine* (1991) 33:1281–96.

92. Simpson, J. L., Are physical activity and employment related to preterm birth and low birth weight? *American Journal of Obstetrics and Cynecology* (1993) 168:1231–38.

93. Helton, A. S., McFarlane, J., and Anderson, E. T. Battered and pregnant: A prevalence study. *American Journal of Public Health* (1987) 77,10:1337–39.

94. Mcfarlane, J., Parker, B., Soeken, K., and Bullock, L. Assessing for abuse during pregnancy: Severity and frequency of injuries and associated entry into prenatal care. *Journal of the American Medical Association* (1992) 267,23:3176–78.

95. Bullock, L. F., and Mcfarlane, J. The birthweight/battering connection. *American Journal of Nursing* (September 1989):1153–55.

96. Gibbs, R. S., Romero, R., Hillier, S. L., et al. A review of premature birth and subclinical infection. *American Journal of Obstetrics and Gynecology* (1992) 166:1515–28.

97. Carroll, J. C. Chalmaydia trachomatis during pregnancy: To screen or not to screen? *Canadian Family Physician* (1993) 39:97–102.

98. Kramer, M. S. The etiology and prevention of low birthweight: Current knowledge and priorities for future research. In *Advances in the prevention of low birthweight: An international symposium.* H. Berendes, S. Kessel, and S. Yaffe, eds. Washington, DC: National Center for Education in Maternal and Child Health, 1991, pp. 25–39.

99. Zygmunt, D. J. Toxoplasma gondii. *Infection Control and Hospital Epidemiology* (1990) 11,4:207–11.

100. Wegman, M. E. Annual summary of vital statistics—1992. *Pediatrics* (1993) 92,6:743–54.

Prenatal Drug Exposure

Meeting the Challenge

Linda C. Sluder, Lloyd R.
Kinnison and Dennis Cates

*Linda C. Sluder is Associate Professor, Early Childhood and
Lloyd R. Kinnisonis Professor, Special Education, Texas Woman's University, Denton.
Dennis Cates is Associate Professor, Special Education, Cameron University, Lawton, Oklahoma.*

Educators and child care providers today face a challenging new community of children identified as one of the fastest growing at-risk populations in America (Poulsen, 1992). These children have been labeled as "crack babies," "prenatal drug exposed," "peri-natal cocaine addicted" or "substance exposed infants and children" (Kinnison, Sluder & Cates, 1995, p. 35).

The mainstream media first identified such children in the early 1990s, focusing on demographic projections and associated statistical implications. The pressing issue now, however, is that these children have reached school age. As these children enter early childhood programs, educators must be prepared to nurture and encourage them.

Children with prenatal drug exposure exhibit a complex range of cognitive abilities and behaviors (Chasnoff, 1992; Howard, Beckwith, Rodning & Kropenske, 1989). Wright (1994) emphasizes that identifying specific traits is difficult, however, because prenatal exposure has diverse effects.

THE CASE OF TWO CHILDREN

Treavor

To the casual observer, Treavor appears to be a typical 5-year-old. He lives with his grandparents, who provide him with a caring and nurturing environment. His size is average for his age. Although his gross motor development appears to be age appropriate, he has some difficulty with fine motor tasks. In general, his physical responses are spasmodic, limiting his ability to independently accomplish directed activities, such as placing wooden pegs into specific holes.

Psychoeducational test evaluations (e.g., measures of cognitive ability and adaptive behavior) indicate that Treavor functions in the severe-profound range of mental retardation. He becomes excited and distracted when individuals enter the learning environment, often soiling his diaper or outer clothing.

Treavor's receptive language is adequate to deal with simple tasks. He is able to follow basic verbal directions and participate, to some extent, in classroom activities. Treavor usually responds during group language activities with gestures and grunts or by showing recognition through directed eye movements. He is able to identify size ("big"

and "little"), pictures of his immediate family, and his teacher and classmates when their names are given as prompts. Over the past year, the teacher noticed that Treavor improved in receptive language, attempts at expressive language, motor skills and attention span. Treavor attends a half-day early childhood program for disabled children.

Melissa

Melissa, a 2nd-grader, participates in a special education resource room one hour each day. She is small for her age, but otherwise displays no physical indications of prenatal drug exposure. While pregnant, Melissa's birth mother ingested alcohol, marijuana and various other drugs, including, possibly, cocaine. Melissa lives with adoptive parents in what appears to be a positive environment.

Melissa suffered from seizures at an early age, for which anticonvulsive medications were prescribed. Additionally, she takes Ritalin daily to help control her attention deficit disorder with hyperactivity and possible obsessive conduct disorder. A psychoeducational assessment indicates that Melissa's cognitive ability is above average. Her reading skills range from one to two standard

deviations above the mean. Melissa's math achievement is on grade level and her written language skills are one standard deviation above the mean. Assessments indicate that she has average oral language development. In contrast to the assessment scores, Melissa's classroom teacher reports extreme variations in her daily academic performance.

Melissa's teachers maintain daily logs that illustrate her erratic behavior. Her teachers say that Melissa "tries hard, [is] inattentive, lacks small muscle control, [is] slow, in constant motion and has extremes in emotions." She appears to work best in a relatively small space and in one-on-one teaching situations.

In the regular classroom, she is compulsive—always giving an answer. She can also be mentally inflexible, needs constant redirection and has limited attention. Her regular education teacher is frustrated and has threatened to resign if Melissa is not removed from her classroom.

Melissa's medication has been invaluable. Without prescriptive intervention, her behavior is unpredictable. Consequently, she does not seem to have control of her actions. Records document that prior to taking her medication, Melissa had, among other

---

Table 1

BEHAVIORAL INDICATORS OF PRENATAL DRUG EXPOSURE IN YOUNG CHILDREN

Motor Development

■ Awkward eye and hand coordination
■ Trembling arms and legs when reaching for objects
■ Excessive fidgeting and/or hyperactivity
■ Clumsy or immature use of tools such as spoons, crayons or small toys

Language Development

■ Limited early vocalizations
■ Prolonged articulation errors
■ Difficulty in picture identification
■ Problems following directions
■ Limited vocabulary

Play Development

■ Reluctance to initiate play activities
■ Aimless wandering through the play area
■ Inability to stack blocks
■ Apparent confusion in some play situations
■ Awkward understanding of and response to social cues
■ Occasional aggressive behavior in group situations

Affective Development

■ Avoidance of eye contact
■ Low tolerance for change of environment or caregiver
■ Difficulty in dealing with changes in routines
■ Low ability to self-regulate own behavior
■ Frequent limit testing
■ Decreased response to verbal praise as a reinforcer
■ Poor interactions with caregivers
■ Increased frequency of temper tantrums
■ Fearfulness of strangers

Cognitive Development

■ Decreased imitative play
■ Less pretend play or exploration of the environment
■ Difficulty concentrating
■ Disorganization
■ Inability to structure work or play activities
■ Diminished ability to stay on task
■ Less goal-directed behavior
■ Increasingly disruptive behavior
■ Greater need for a more controlled learning environment

Adapted from: Kinnison, L., Sluder, L., & Cates, D. (1995). Prenatal drug exposure: Implications for teachers of young children. *Day Care & Early Education, 22*(3), 35–37.

things, threatened to beat her adoptive mother. After receiving treatment, Melissa was remorseful and expressed sorrow for such behavior.

COMPOUNDING ISSUES

Approximately 375,000 children are prenatally exposed to illicit drugs each year (Behrman, 1990; Feig 1990). A rapidly growing proportion of these children are exposed to crack cocaine. Feig (1990) estimates that 30,000 to 50,000 "crack babies" are born each year.

A survey by the National Institute on Drug Abuse (1989) revealed that approximately 9 percent of all women of child-bearing age admitted to using illicit drugs. The number of women in this age group testing positive for drug use increased from 25 percent in 1972 to 40 percent in 1988. Other data indicate that prenatal drug use has remained at a consistent level ("Children of Cocaine: Facing New Issues," 1990). Women who use drugs while pregnant come from all socioeconomic and ethnic backgrounds (Feig, 1990; Weston, Ivins, Zuckerman, Jones & Lopez, 1989).

The severity of cognitive, social, behavioral and motor deficiencies are compounded by the multiple ingestion of tobacco, alcohol and combined drugs. Table 1 offers some behavioral characteristics that may be associated with prenatal drug exposure.

COMPLICATIONS

Motor Development

Although a small number of drug-exposed children exhibit gross motor difficulties, the influences on fine motor development are far more apparent. Researchers report that cocaine-exposed infants and toddlers often avoid eye contact and negatively respond to multiple stimuli (Zuckerman, Jones, La Rue & Lopez, 1990). Other studies suggest that these infants appear to have underdeveloped muscle tone and poor reflexes, and that their arms and hands may tremble when they reach for objects (Daberczak, Shaner, Senie & Kendal, 1988; Feig, 1990). Behrman (1990) suggests that such visual-perceptual and fine motor problems persist as these children mature. Van Dyke and Fox (1990) suggest that fetal exposure to various types of illicit drugs (e.g., cocaine or cocaine used with other drugs) may cause other developmental problems. These complications' characteristics may be similar to those of hyperactivity.

Cognitive Development

Many factors related to prenatal drug exposure directly and indirectly influence cognitive development. Drugs such as cocaine

may force blood vessels in an expectant woman to constrict, reducing the blood flow and decreasing the amount of oxygen delivered to the fetus's brain (Woods & Plessinger, 1990). Bellisimo (1990) emphasizes that the "high" brought on by drug use may cause the fetus to suffer small strokes or seizures. These findings suggest that central nervous system damage and subsequent learning problems are possible.

Children prenatally exposed to drugs tend to perform more poorly on tests designed to measure concentration, group interaction and the ability to cope within an instructional environment, according to Viadero (1990). Further studies suggest that these children are often disorganized, unstructured, irritable, less goal-directed and have problems processing information.

Language Development

Drug exposed infants and children are less likely to spontaneously vocalize or use gestures to communicate. In preschool, these children experience prolonged difficulty in articulating, identifying pictures and using expressive language (Chapman & Worthington, 1994).

Some children may have better success with receptive language (what is understood), as in Treavor's case. In this instance, receptive language may be superior to expressive language development. Treavor's behavior suggests he understands oral language, but cannot verbally communicate.

Affective-Behavioral Development

Children prenatally exposed to harmful substances may undergo a variety of emotional and behavioral swings, sometimes shifting rapidly from apathy to aggression. "A giggle becomes a scream, or a response to a question becomes an outburst" (Bellisimo, 1990, p. 25). Changes in environmental stimuli, such as visitors or minor disruptions in routines, may prompt the child to suddenly act uncontrollably. Melissa's behavior is characteristic of these extremes. It appears that prenatally drug exposed children commonly insist on addressing tasks in their own terms and persistently refuse to comply with requests.

These children interact poorly with others. Cocaine-exposed infants may become easily frustrated and throw temper tantrums when adults provide inconsistent directional cues (Bellisimo, 1990; Howard et al., 1989). Often, the children resist attachments to new adults or children. Some children actually avoid adult interactions.

Play Development

Howard, Beckwith, Rodning and Kropenske (1989) observed less representational play among drug exposed children. Instead, their play was characterized by randomly scattering toys, and then indiscriminately picking up and discarding them. These behaviors are

in sharp contrast to children's typical play behavior.

Substance exposed infants and children often have difficulty initiating independent play activities. Consequently, they aimlessly wander through the learning environment. Many of these youngsters do not seem to have the necessary skills to spontaneously stack blocks or engage in representational play. They appear confused and unable to select a particular material for play or focus.

ACCEPTING THE CHILD

Children with suspected prenatal drug exposure need assurances from the adults in their lives. Educators who work with this population must understand the child's social, legal and educational needs. Unfortunately, accurate information about the extent of prenatal drug exposure is limited. Admitting that their child has been prenatally exposed to drugs places the mother or parents at risk for legal action. Moreover, as many states consider prenatal drug exposure to be child abuse, admission of such activity will be rare.

Other issues also prevent parents from fully disclosing their drug use. Increased public awareness of the effects of prenatal drug exposure places the parent in a precarious situation. Many fear the reactions of their families, friends, the community and their children. Fetal alcohol children interviewed in Michael Dorris's *The Broken Cord* (1989) expressed difficulty understanding their disability and their parents' reasons for engaging in drug use.

Often, these children come from chaotic and dangerous home environments where the potential for continued drug abuse is high. Their mothers may be estranged from the family because of their drug use, which perpetuates a lack of support systems for both mother and child. Careful consideration and effort must be given to ensure that extensive time and opportunity are provided for these children to develop bonds with the family or other caregivers.

IMPLICATIONS AND SUGGESTIONS

Children who are exposed prenatally to illicit drugs present myriad challenges for early childhood professionals. The cognitive and behavior extremes associated with prenatal exposure precludes drawing up an explicit list of "best practices" or pedagogical approaches.

Compounding the problem is researchers' inability to systematically identify children who have been exposed to illicit drugs. Many research studies have samples that are too small with poorly defined subjects or no control groups (Chapman & Worthington, 1994). Other studies have been narrowly defined and use highly selective strategies, offering limited general application.

The following suggestions for early childhood professionals are based on the most current review of research and experience. Educators should pay special attention to the learning environment, ensuring that programs are predictable and restricting the number of nonessential people who enter and leave the environment. Howard et al. (1989) reported that a small room or learning area is superior to large, open areas.

Education professionals must carefully consider these children's unique learning styles when determining the classroom environment and teacher-to-student ratios. Daily routines must allow the children to engage in self-directed exploration. The educator or care provider, however, must always be aware that these children do not tend to engage in spontaneous activities. Adult intervention may be necessary to direct the child toward cooperative play and work opportunities.

Many potentially volatile situations can be diffused by alerting children to transitions and providing time to adjust to new activities. When a child is cognitively and emotionally involved with a special activity, adults can reduce children's frustration by providing notice that the activity is about to end. A statement such as "We have five more minutes left in math before lunch" will alert the child that the activity is closing.

CONCLUSION

Educators and care providers must be aware that children may exhibit multiple disabilities—including physical, medical, emotional, social and/or educational. A team of professionals should work together to focus on individual children's needs. Community-based, family-centered solutions should be emphasized, as should confidentiality.

Early childhood education and care providers need to establish close working relationships with local and state agencies. Joint efforts should promote specific caregiver training, substance abuse counseling, activities to raise mothers' self-esteem and training in basic parenting skills. These efforts may be university-based or associated with community and state agencies. Only through such collaborative efforts can substantial help be given to children with prenatal drug exposure.

References

Behrman, J. (1990). Care for and educating the children of drug-using mothers: A challenge for society and schools in the 1990s. *Counterpoint, 11*(2), 15–16.

Bellisimo, V. (1990, January). Crack babies: The school's new high at risk student. *Thrust,* 23–26.

Chapman, J., & Worthington, L. (1994, April). *Illicit drug-exposed children: Four critical needs areas.* Paper presented at the annual convention of the Council for Exceptional Children, Denver, CO.

Chasnoff, I. (1992, October). *NAPARE today: People and programs. Update.* Chicago, IL: National Association for Perinatal Addiction Research and Education.

Children of cocaine: Facing new issues. (1990). (ERIC Document Reproduction Service No. ED 320 358)

Daberczak, T., Shanzer, S., Senie, T., & Kendal, S. (1988). Neonatal neurologic and electroencephalograms effects of intrauterine cocaine exposure. *Journal of Pediatrics, 113,* 354–358.

Dorris, M. (1989). *The broken cord.* New York: Harper.

Feig, L. (1990). *Drug-exposed infants and children: Service needs and policy questions.* Washington, DC: U.S. Department of Health and Human Services, Office of Human Services Policy, Division of Children and Youth.

Howard, J., Beckwith, L., Rodning, C., & Kropenske, Y. (1989). The development of young children of substance-abusing parents: Insights from seven years of intervention and research. *Zero to Three, 9*(5), 1–7.

Kinnison, L., Sluder, L., & Cates, D. (1995). Prenatal drug exposure: Implications for teachers of young children. *Day Care & Early Education, 22*(3), 35–37.

National Institute on Drug Abuse, Department of Health and Human Services. (1989). *National Institute on Drug Abuse: Household Survey on Drug Abuse 1988, Population Estimates.* Rockville, MD: Author. (DHHS Publication No. ADM 89-1636).

Poulsen, M. (1992). *Schools meet the challenge: Educational needs of children at risk due to prenatal substance exposure.* (ERIC Document Reproduction Service No. ED 348 800)

Van Dyke, D., & Fox, A. (1990). Fetal drug exposure and implications for learning in the preschool and school-age populations. *Journal of Learning Disabilities, 28*(3), 160–162.

Viadero, D. (1990). Drug exposed children pose special problems. *Education Week, 9*(8), 1–10.

Weston, D., Ivins, B., Zuckerman, B., Jones, C., & Lopez, R. (1989). Drug-exposed babies: Research and clinical issues. *Zero to Three, 9*(5), 1–7.

Woods, J., & Plessinger, M. (1990). Pregnancy increases cardiovascular toxicity to cocaine. *American Journal of Obstetrics-Gynecology, 162*(2), 529–535.

Wright, R. (1994). Drugged out. *Texas Monthly, 20*(11), 136, 150–154.

Zuckerman, B., Jones, C., LaRue, C., & Lopez, R. (1990). Effects of maternal marijuana and cocaine use on fetal growth. In J. R. Meratz & J. E. Thompson (Eds.), *Perspectives on prenatal care.* New York: Elsevier.

SPERM UNDER SIEGE

MORE THAN WE EVER GUESSED, HAVING A HEALTHY BABY MAY DEPEND ON DAD

Anne Merewood

IT DIDN'T MAKE SENSE. Kate Malone's* first pregnancy had gone so smoothly. Yet when she and her husband Paul* tried to have a second child, their efforts were plagued by disaster. For two years, Kate couldn't become pregnant. Then she suffered an ectopic pregnancy, in which the embryo began to grow in one of her fallopian tubes and had to be surgically removed. Her next pregnancy heralded more heartache—it ended in miscarriage at four months and tests revealed that the fetus was genetically abnormal. Within months, she became pregnant and miscarried yet again. By this point, some four years after their troubles began, the couple had adopted a son; baffled and demoralized by the string of apparent bad luck, they gave up trying to have another child. "We had been to the top doctors in the country and no one could find a reason for the infertility or the miscarriages," says Kate.

Soon, however, thanks to a newspaper article she read, Kate uncovered what she now considers the likely cause of the couple's reproductive woes. When it all started, Paul had just been hired by a manufacturing company that used a chemical called paradichlorobenzene, which derives from benzene, a known carcinogen. The article discussed the potential effects of exposure to chemicals, including benzene, on a man's sperm. Kate remembered hearing that two other men in Paul's small office were also suffering from inexplicable infertility. Both of their wives had gone through three miscarriages as well. Kate had always considered their similar misfortunes to be a tragic coincidence. Now she became convinced that the chemical (which has not yet

been studied for its effects on reproduction) had blighted the three men's sperm.

Paul had found a new job in a chemical-free workplace, so the couple decided to try once more to have a baby. Kate conceived immediately—and last August gave birth to a healthy boy. The Malones are now arranging for the National Institute for Occupational Safety and Health (NIOSH), the federal agency that assesses work-related health hazards for the public, to inspect Paul's former job site. "Our aim isn't to sue the company, but to help people who are still there," says Kate.

The Malones' suspicions about sperm damage echo the concerns of an increasing number of researchers. These scientists are challenging the double standard that leads women to overhaul their lives before a pregnancy—avoiding stress, cigarettes and champagne—while men are left confident that their lifestyle has little bearing on their fertility or their future child's health. Growing evidence suggests that sperm is both more fragile and potentially more dangerous than previously thought. "There seems to have been both a scientific resistance, and a resistance based on cultural preconceptions, to accepting these new ideas," says Gladys Friedler, Ph.D., an associate professor of psychiatry and pharmacology at Boston University School of Medicine.

But as more and more research is completed, sperm may finally be stripped of its macho image. For example, in one startling review of data on nearly 15,000 newborns, scientists at the University of North Carolina in Chapel Hill concluded that a father's drinking and smoking habits, and even his age, can increase his child's risk of birth defects—ranging from cleft palates to *hydrocephalus*, an abnormal accumulation of spinal fluid in the brain. Other new and equally worrisome

---

*These names have been changed.

From *Health*, April 1991, pp. 53–57, 76–77. © 1991 by Anne Merewood. Reprinted by permission.

studies have linked higher-than-normal rates of stillbirth, premature delivery and low birthweight (which predisposes a baby to medical and developmental problems) to fathers who faced on-the-job exposure to certain chemicals. In fact, one study found that a baby was more likely to be harmed if the father rather than the mother worked in an unsafe environment in the months before conception.

The surprising news of sperm's delicate nature may shift the balance of responsibility for a newborn's well-being. The research may also have social and economic implications far beyond the concerns of couples planning a family. In recent years a growing number of companies have sought to ban women of childbearing age from jobs that entail exposure to hazardous substances. The idea is to protect the women's future children from defects—and the companies themselves from lawsuits. Already, the "fetal protection policy" of one Milwaukee-based company has prompted female employees to file a sex discrimination suit that is now before the U.S. Supreme Court. Conversely, if the new research on sperm is borne out, men whose future plans include fatherhood may go to court to *insist* on protection from hazards. Faced with potential lawsuits from so many individuals, companies may be forced to ensure that workplaces are safe for *all* employees.

SPERM UND DRANG

At the center of all this controversy are the microscopic products of the male reproductive system. Sperm (officially, spermatozoa) are manufactured by *spermatagonia*, special cells in the testes that are constantly stimulated by the male hormone testosterone. Once formed, a sperm continues to mature as it travels for some 80 days through the *epididymis* (a microscopic network of tubes behind the testicle) to the "waiting area" around the prostate gland, where it is expelled in the next ejaculation.

A normal sperm contains 23 chromosomes—the threadlike strands that house DNA, the molecular foundation of genetic material. While a woman is born with all the eggs she will ever produce, a man creates millions of sperm every day from puberty onwards. This awesome productivity is also what makes sperm so fragile. If a single sperm's DNA is damaged, the result may be a mutation that distorts the genetic information it carries. "Because of the constant turnover of sperm, mutations caused by the environment can arise more frequently in men than in women," says David A. Savitz, Ph.D., an associate professor of epidemiology and chief researcher of the North Carolina review.

If a damaged sperm fertilizes the egg, the consequences can be devastating. "Such sperm can lead to spontaneous abortions, malformations, and functional or behavioral abnormalities," says Marvin Legator, Ph.D., director of environmental toxicology at the department of preventative medicine at the University of Texas in Galveston. And in some cases, sperm may be too badly harmed even to penetrate an egg, leading to mysterious infertility.

Though the findings on sperm's vulnerability are certainly dramatic, researchers emphasize that they are also preliminary. "We have only a very vague notion of how exposure might affect fetal development, and the whole area of research is at a very early stage of investigation," says Savitz. Indeed, questions still far outnumber answers. For starters, there is no hard evidence that a chemical damages an infant by adversely affecting the father's sperm. A man who comes in contact with dangerous substances might harm the baby by exposing his partner indirectly—for example, through contaminated clothing. Another theory holds that the harmful pollutants may be carried in the seminal fluid that buoys sperm. But more researchers are becoming convinced that chemicals can inflict their silent damage directly on the sperm itself.

THE CHEMICAL CONNECTION

The most well-known—and most controversial—evidence that chemicals can harm sperm comes from research on U.S. veterans of the Vietnam war who were exposed to the herbicide Agent Orange (dioxin), used by the U.S. military to destroy foliage that hid enemy forces. A number of veterans believe the chemical is responsible for birth defects in their children. The latest study on the issue, published last year by the Harvard School of Public Health, found that Vietnam vets had almost twice the risk of other men of fathering infants with one or more major malformations. But a number of previous studies found conflicting results, and because so little is known about how paternal exposure could translate into birth defects, the veterans have been unsuccessful in their lawsuits against the government.

Scientific uncertainty also dogs investigations into other potentially hazardous chemicals and contaminants. "There seem to be windows of vulnerability for sperm: Certain chemicals may be harmful only at a certain period during sperm production," explains Donald Mattison, M.D., dean of the School of Public Health at the University of Pittsburgh. There isn't enough specific data to make definitive lists of "danger chemicals." Still, a quick scan of the research shows that particular substances often crop up as likely troublemakers. Chief among them: lead, benzene, paint solvents, vinyl chloride, carbon disulphide, the pesticide DBCP, anesthetic gases and radiation. Not surprisingly, occupations that involve contact with these substances also figure heavily in studies of sperm damage. For example, men employed in the paper, wood, chemical, drug and paint industries may have a greater chance of siring stillborn children. And increased leukemia rates have been detected among children whose fathers are medical workers, aircraft or auto mechanics, or who are exposed regularly to paint or radiation. In fact, a study of workers at Britain's Sellafield nuclear power plant in West Cambria found a sixfold leukemia risk among children whose fathers were exposed to the plant's highest radiation levels (about 9 percent of all employees).

Workers in "high-risk" industries should not panic, says Savitz. "The credibility of the studies is limited because we have no firm evidence that certain exposures cause certain birth defects." Yet it makes sense to be watchful for warning signs. For example, if pollution levels are high enough to cause skin irritations, thyroid trouble, or breathing problems, the reproductive system might also be at risk. Another danger signal is a clustered outbreak of male infertility or of a particular disease: It was local concern about high levels of childhood leukemia, for instance, that sparked the investigation at the Sellafield nuclear plant.

The rise in industrial "fetal protection policies" is adding even more controversy to the issue of occupational hazards to sperm. In 1984, employees brought a class-action suit against Milwaukee-based Johnson Controls, the nation's largest manufacturer of car batteries, after the company restricted women "capable of bearing children" from holding jobs in factory areas where lead exceeded a specific level. The suit—which the Supreme Court is scheduled to rule on this spring—

focuses on the obstacles the policy creates for women's career advancement. Johnson Controls defends its regulation by pointing to "overwhelming" evidence that a mother's exposure to lead can harm the fetus.

In effect, the company's rule may be a case of reverse discrimination against men. Males continue to work in areas banned to women despite growing evidence that lead may not be safe for sperm either. In several studies over the past 10 years, paternal exposure to lead (and radiation) has been connected to Wilms' tumor, a type of kidney cancer in children. In another recent study, University of Maryland toxicologist Ellen Silbergeld, Ph.D., exposed male rats to lead amounts equivalent to levels below the current occupational safety standards for humans. The rats were then mated with females who had not been exposed at all. Results: The offspring showed clear defects in brain development.

Johnson Controls claims that evidence linking fetal problems to a father's contact with lead is insufficient. But further research into chemicals' effects on sperm may eventually force companies to reduce pollution levels, since *both* sexes can hardly be banned from the factory floor. Says Mattison: "The workplace should be safe for everyone who wants to work there, men and women alike!"

FATHER TIME

Whatever his occupation, man's age may play an unexpected role in his reproductive health. When researchers at the University of Calgary and the Alberta Children's Hospital in Canada examined sperm samples taken from 30 healthy men aged 20 to 52, they found that the older men had a higher percentage of sperm with structurally abnormal chromosomes. Specifically, only 2 to 3 percent of the sperm from men between ages 20 and 34 were genetically abnormal, while the figure jumped to 7 percent in men 35 to 44 and to almost 14 percent in those 45 and over. "The findings are logical," says Renée Martin, Ph.D., the professor of pediatrics who led the study. "The cells that create sperm are constantly dividing from puberty onwards, and every time they divide they are subject to error."

Such mistakes are more likely to result in miscarriages than in unhealthy babies. "When part of a chromosome is missing or broken, the embryo is more likely to abort as a miscarriage [than to carry to term]," Martin says.

Yet her findings may help explain why Savitz's North Carolina study noted a doubled rate of birth defects like cleft palate and hydrocephalus in children whose fathers were over 35 at the time of conception, no matter what the mothers' age.

Currently, there are no tests available to pre-identify sperm likely to cause genetic defects. "Unfortunately there's nothing offered, because [the research] is all so new," says Martin. But tests such as amniocentesis, alpha fetoprotein (AFP) and chorionic villi sampling (CVS) can ferret out some fetal genetic defects that are linked to Mom *or* Dad. Amniocentesis, for example, is routinely recommended for all pregnant women over 35 because with age a woman increases her risk of producing a Down's syndrome baby, characterized by mental retardation and physical abnormalities.

With respect to Down's syndrome, Martin's study provided some good news for older men: It confirmed previous findings that a man's risk of fathering a child afflicted with the syndrome actually drops with age. Some popular textbooks still warn that men over 55 have a high chance of fathering Down's syndrome babies. "That information is outdated," Martin insists. "We now know that for certain."

THE SINS OF THE FATHERS?

For all the hidden dangers facing a man's reproductive system, the most common hazards may be the ones most under his control.

Smoking. Tobacco addicts take note: Smoke gets in your sperm. Cigarettes can reduce fertility by lowering sperm count—the number of individual sperm released in a single ejaculation. "Most than half a pack a day can cause sperm density to drop by 20 percent," says Machelle Seibel, M.D., director of the Faulkner Centre for Reproductive Medicine in Boston. One Danish study found that for each pack of cigarettes a father tended to smoke daily (assuming the mother didn't smoke at all), his infant's birthweight fell 4.2 ounces below average. Savitz has found that male smokers double their chances of fathering infants with abnormalities like hydrocephalus, *Bell's palsy* (paralysis of the facial nerve), and mouth cysts. In Savitz's most recent study, children whose fathers smoked around the time of conception were 20 percent more likely to develop brain cancer, lymphoma and leukemia than were children whose fathers did not

smoke (the results still held regardless of whether the mother had a tobacco habit).

This is scary news—and not particularly helpful: Savitz's studies didn't record how frequently the fathers lit up, and no research at all suggests why the links appeared. Researchers can't even say for sure that defective sperm was to blame. The babies may instead have been victims of passive smoking—affected by Dad's tobacco while in the womb or shortly after birth.

Drinking. Mothers-to-be are routinely cautioned against sipping any alcohol while pregnant. Now studies suggest that the father's drinking habits just before conception may also pose a danger. So far, research hasn't discovered why alcohol has an adverse effect on sperm, but it does suggest that further investigation is needed. For starters, one study of laboratory rats linked heavy alcohol use with infertility because the liquor lowered testosterone levels. Another study, from the University of Washington in Seattle, discovered that newborn babies whose fathers drank at least two glasses of wine or two bottles of beer per day weighed an average of 3 ounces less than babies whose fathers were only occasional sippers—even when all other factors were considered.

Illicit Drugs. Many experts believe that a man's frequent use of substances such as marijuana and cocaine may also result in an unhealthy fetus, but studies that could document such findings have yet to be conducted. However, preliminary research has linked marijuana to infertility. And recent tests at the Yale Infertility Clinic found that long-term cocaine use led to both very low sperm counts and a greater number of sperm with motion problems.

WHAT A DAD CAN DO

The best news about sperm troubles is that many of the risk factors can be easily prevented. Because the body overhauls sperm supplies every 90 days, it only takes a season to get a fresh start on creating a healthy baby. Most experts advise that men wait for three months after quitting smoking, cutting out drug use or abstaining from alcohol before trying to sire a child.

Men who fear they are exposed to work chemicals that may compromise the health of future children can contact NIOSH. (Write the Division of Standards Development and Technology Transfer, Technical Information

Branch, 4676 Columbia Parkway, Mailstop C-19, Cincinnati, OH 45226. Or call [800] 356–4674.) NIOSH keeps files on hazardous chemicals and their effects, and can arrange for a local inspection of the workplace. Because it is primarily a research institution, NIOSH is most useful for investigating chemicals that haven't been studied previously for sperm effects (which is why the Malones approached NIOSH with their concerns about paradichlorobenzene). For better-known pollutants, it's best to ask the federal Occupational Safety and Health Administration (OSHA) to inspect the job site (OSHA has regional offices in most U.S. cities).

There is also advice for men who are concerned over exposure to radiation during medical treatment. Direct radiation to the area around the testes can spur infertility by halting sperm production for more than three years. According to a recent study, it can also triple the number of abnormal sperm the testes produce. Men who know they will be exposed to testicular radiation for medical reasons should consider "banking" sperm before the treatment, for later use in artificial in-semination. Most hospitals use lead shields during radiation therapy, but for routine X-rays, even dental X-rays, protection might not be offered automatically. If it's not offered, patients should be sure to request it. "The risks are really, really low, but to be absolutely safe, patients—male or female—should *always* ask for a lead apron to protect their reproductive organs," stresses Martin.

Though the study of sperm health is still in its infancy, it is already clear that a man's reproductive system needs to be treated with respect and caution. Women do not carry the full responsibility for bearing a healthy infant. "The focus should be on both parents—not on 'blaming' either the mother or the father, but on accepting that each play a role," says Friedler.

Mattison agrees: "Until recently, when a woman had a miscarriage, she would be told it was because she had a 'blighted ovum' [egg]. We never heard anything about a 'blighted sperm.' This new data suggests that both may be responsible. That is not unreasonable," he concludes, "given that it takes both an egg and a sperm to create a baby!"

Development during Infancy and Early Childhood

Infancy (Articles 7–10)
Early Childhood (Articles 11–13)

Newborns are quite well developed in some areas, and incredibly deficient in others. Babies' brains, for example, already have their full complement of neurons (worker cells). The neuroglia (supportive cells) are almost completely developed and will reach their final numbers by age one. In contrast, babies' legs and feet are tiny, weak, and barely functional. Looking at newborns from another perspective, however, makes their brains seem somewhat less superior. The neurons and neuroglia present at birth must last a lifetime. Neurons cannot replace themselves by mitosis after birth. If they die, the brain's number of neurons remains forever diminished. By contrast, the cells of the baby's legs and feet (skin, fat, muscles, bones, blood vessels) are able to replace themselves by mitosis indefinitely. Their numbers will continue to grow through early adulthood; then their quantity and quality can be retained through old age.

In order to protect the brain and nervous system of the newborn, as well as encourage growth and development of other vital systems, the eating, sleeping, and elimination functions are critical. All three functions are enhanced by human breast milk. The first article included in this unit of *Human Development* gives scientific explanations of why human milk is so much better for babies than milk derived from soy, or taken from cows, goats, or sheep. Human milk aids digestion, stimulates the gut, prevents infection, selectively kills harmful bacteria while leaving good bacteria alone, strengthens the baby's immune response, stimulates growth and development and, by extension, allows for sounder sleep. The author, a Canadian pediatrician who has worked in Central and South America as well as New Zealand and Africa, brings cross-cultural knowledge to his invocation of the benefits of breast milk.

The developing brain in infancy is a truly fascinating organ. At birth it is poorly organized. The lower (primitive) brain parts (brain stem, pons, medulla, cerebellum) are well enough developed to allow the infant to live. The lower brain directs vital organ systems (heart, lungs, kidneys, etc.). The higher (advanced) brain parts (cerebral hemispheres) have all their neurons, but the nerve cells and cell processes (axon, dendrites) are small, underde-veloped, and unorganized. During infancy, these higher (cerebral) nerve cells (that allow the baby to think, reason, and remember) grow at astronomical rates. They migrate to permanent locations in the hemispheres, develop myelin sheathing (insulation), and conduct messages. Piaget, the father of cognitive psychology, wrote that all brain activity in the newborn was reflexive, based on instincts for survival. Now researchers are discovering that fetuses can learn, and newborns can think as well as learn.

The second article in this unit addresses some of the new discoveries about brain development that have poured out of neuroscience labs recently. The role played by electrical activity of neurons in actively shaping the physical structure of the brain is particularly breathtaking. The neurons are produced prenatally. After birth, the flood of sensory inputs from the environment (sights, sounds, smells, tastes, touch, and kinesthetic sensations) drives the neurons to form circuits and become wired to each other. Trillions of connections are established in a baby's brain. During childhood the connections that are seldom or never used are eliminated, or pruned. Madeleine Nash suggests that the first 3 years are critical for establishing these connections. Environments that provide lots of sensory stimulation really do produce richer, more connected brains. Specific suggestions are presented about wiring vision, feelings, language, and movement as well as wiring the total brain.

The third article in this unit invokes more attention to the development of social and emotional behaviors in infancy, rather than to physical and cognitive development. Author Jerome Kagan is a Harvard professor with a worldwide reputation as an expert in socioemotional aspects of development. In this article, he contends that neither environmental explanations of human behavior (popular in the 1960s and 1970s) nor biological explanations of traits (popular today) are sufficient to explain temperament. He sees a danger in excusing antisocial behaviors and unrestrained emotions because they are due to inheritance. He stresses the need for socialization practices that focus on moral obligations to be civil and responsible.

The last selection on infancy deals with language development as it is affected by infant experiences. Sandra

Blakeslee supports the evidence provided in the article, "Fertile Minds." The richer the language stimulation of babies, the richer will be the language area of the brain. The article reviews research that suggests a generalized trend toward less talking to babies by poorly educated parents and more talking to babies by professionally educated parents. It includes suggestions for what types of language stimulation work best in the first month, in months 1 to 3, 3 to 5, etc., throughout the first 18 months. Cautionary statements are made about extreme beliefs from "Love is enough" to "The more activities the better."

The selections about toddlers and preschoolers that are included in this anthology continue the trend of looking at development physically, cognitively, and socioemotionally. Each of the articles, while focusing on one topic, views the whole child across all three domains considering both hereditary and environmental factors.

"Your Child's Brain" continues the discussion of the rapid myelinization of neurons and their migration to permanent locations in the brain during early childhood. The author contends that extra experience in the pursuit of an area of knowledge (e.g., math, language, music) can trigger more neurons to be sent to the area of the cerebral

hemisphere involved in acquiring, storing, and retrieving that kind of information. This accommodation is a clear-cut example of nature-nurture interaction.

The next article, on changing demographics, focuses on cognitive development as it relates to early childhood education programs. Donald Hernandez asserts that we are experiencing a child-care revolution. Single parenting and two-wage-earner families have made the need for excellence in early childhood education critical. The possibility of public funding to ensure quality control is discussed.

The concluding article in this unit addresses parental knowledge about raising young children in the 1990s. Although parents recognize the importance of early childhood, they do not see its full significance. Parents may not recognize their power to affect their child's intellectual potential or to affect his or her social development. Many parents feel that a child will "catch-up" socially and that lack of social interaction from birth to age 3 is irrelevant. Time constraints, child-care arrangements, and lack of "how-to" information are seen as barriers to more effective parenting. The author gives suggestions about helpful and welcome ways to support parents who are raising young children.

Looking Ahead: Challenge Questions

How can a human mother's milk actively enhance her newborn's growth and development?

What are the intellectual potentials of babies?

Is infant reactivity and temperamental style a factor in the development of personal and social skills?

Can talking to infants shape their ability to think? What kinds of talking work better at different months of age?

How can environmental exposure and exercise help form the brain's circuitry for areas such as music and math?

In what ways might young children's cognitive development be stimulated by early childhood education programs?

What are parents' views of early childhood development? Where do parents need more information and support?

How Breast Milk Protects Newborns

*Some of the molecules and cells
in human milk actively help
infants stave off infection*

Jack Newman

Doctors have long known that infants who are breast-fed contract fewer infections than do those who are given formula. Until fairly recently, most physicians presumed that breast-fed children fared better simply because milk supplied directly from the breast is free of bacteria. Formula, which must often be mixed with water and placed in bottles, can become contaminated easily. Yet even infants who receive sterilized formula suffer from more meningitis and infection of the gut, ear, respiratory tract and urinary tract than do breast-fed youngsters.

The reason, it turns out, is that mother's milk actively helps newborns avoid disease in a variety of ways. Such assistance is particularly beneficial during the first few months of life, when an infant often cannot mount an effective immune response against foreign organisms. And although it is not the norm in most industrial cultures, UNICEF and the World Health Organization both advise breast-feeding to "two years and beyond." Indeed, a child's immune response does not reach its full strength until age five or so.

All human babies receive some coverage in advance of birth. During

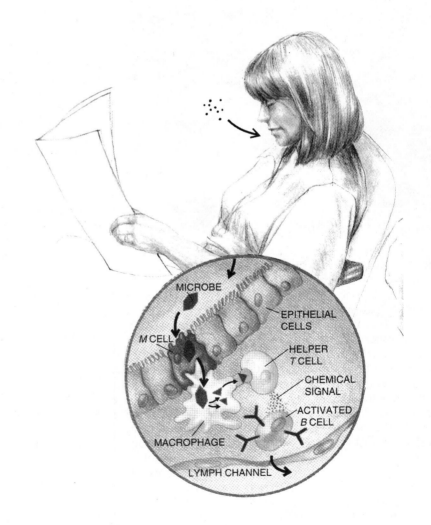

AFTER INGESTING A MICROBE (*left*), a new mother manufactures antibody molecules termed secretory IgA that enter breast milk (*center*) and help to protect the breast-fed baby from pathogens in its environment (*right*). More specifically, a microbe is taken up by the mother's M cells (*inset at left*)—specialized cells in the epithelial lining of the digestive tract—and passed to immune cells known as macrophages. The macro-

MICROBE
EPITHELIAL CELLS
M CELL
HELPER *T* CELL
CHEMICAL SIGNAL
ACTIVATED *B* CELL
MACROPHAGE
LYMPH CHANNEL

pregnancy, the mother passes antibodies to her fetus through the placenta. These proteins circulate in the infant's blood for weeks to months after birth, neutralizing microbes or marking them for destruction by phagocytes—immune cells that consume and break down bacteria, viruses and cellular debris. But breast-fed infants gain extra protection from antibodies, other proteins and immune cells in human milk.

Once ingested, these molecules and cells help to prevent microorganisms from penetrating the body's tissues. Some of the molecules bind to microbes in the hollow space (lumen) of the gastrointestinal tract. In this way, they block microbes from attaching to and crossing through the mucosa—the layer of cells, also known as the epithelium, that lines the digestive tract and other body cavities. Other molecules lessen the supply of particular minerals and vitamins that harmful bacteria need to survive in the digestive tract. Certain immune cells in human milk are

phagocytes that attack microbes directly. Another set produces chemicals that invigorate the infant's own immune response.

Breast Milk Antibodies

Antibodies, which are also called immunoglobulins, take five basic forms, denoted as IgG, IgA, IgM, IgD and IgE. All have been found in human milk, but by

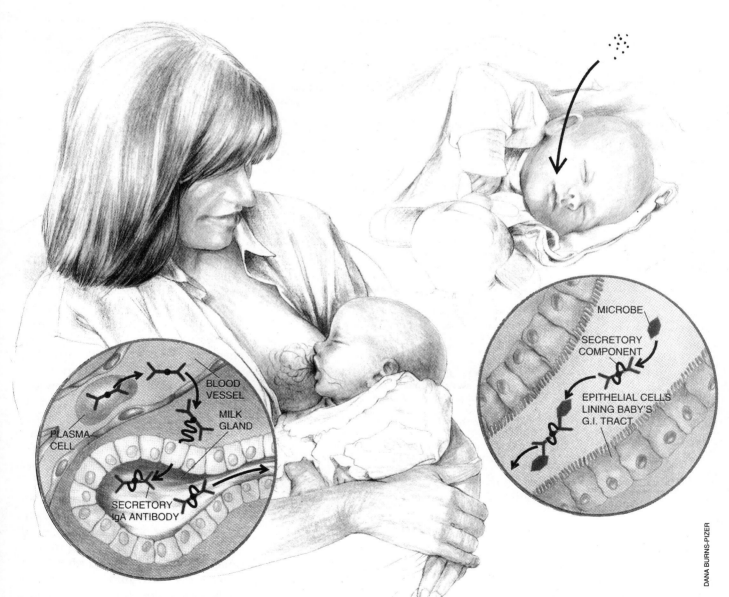

BLOOD VESSEL

MILK GLAND

PLASMA CELL

SECRETORY IgA ANTIBODY

MICROBE

SECRETORY COMPONENT

EPITHELIAL CELLS LINING BABY'S G.I. TRACT

DANA BURNS-PIZER

phages break down the pathogen and display fragments of its (antigens) to other immune cells called helper *T* lymphocytes, which secrete chemicals that activate still other immune cells, *B* lymphocytes. The *B* cells, in turn, mature into so-called plasma cells that travel to epithelial tissues in the breast and release antibodies (*inset at center*). Some of these molecules enter the milk and are swallowed by the baby. In the infant's digestive tract (*inset at right*), the antibodies, which are protected from breakdown by a so-called secretory component, prevent microorganisms from penetrating the baby's gut.

Immune Benefits of Breast Milk at a Glance

Component	Action
White Blood Cells	
B lymphocytes	Give rise to antibodies targeted against specific microbes.
Macrophages	Kill microbes outright in the baby's gut, produce lysozyme and activate other components of the immune system.
Neutrophils	May act as phagocytes, ingesting bacteria in baby's digestive system.
T lymphocytes	Kill infected cells directly or send out chemical messages to mobilize other defenses. They proliferate in the presence of organisms that cause serious illness in infants. They also manufacture compounds that can strengthen a child's own immune response.
Molecules	
Antibodies of secretory IgA class	Bind to microbes in baby's digestive tract and thereby prevent them from passing through walls of the gut into body's tissues.
B_{12} binding protein	Reduces amount of vitamin B_{12}, which bacteria need in order to grow.
Bifidus factor	Promotes growth of *Lactobacillus bifidus,*, a harmless bacterium, in baby's gut. Growth of such nonpathogenic bacteria helps to crowd out dangerous varieties.
Fatty acids	Disrupt membranes surrounding certain viruses and destroy them.
Fibronectin	Increases antimicrobial activity of macrophages; helps to repair tissues that have been damaged by immune reactions in baby's gut.
Gamma-interferon	Enhances antimicrobial activity of immune cells.
Hormones and growth factors	Stimulate baby's digestive tract to mature more quickly. Once the initially "leaky" membranes lining the gut mature, infants become less vulnerable to microorganisms.
Lactoferrin	Binds to iron, a mineral many bacteria need to survive. By reducing the available amount of iron, lactoferrin thwarts growth of pathogenic bacteria.
Lysozyme	Kills bacteria by disrupting their cell walls.
Mucins	Adhere to bacteria and viruses, thus keeping such microorganisms from attaching to mucosal surfaces.
Oligosaccharides	Bind to microorganisms and bar them from attaching to mucosal surfaces.

far the most abundant type is IgA, specifically the form known as secretory IgA, which is found in great amounts throughout the gut and respiratory system of adults. These antibodies consist of two joined IgA molecules and a so-called secretory component that seems to shield the antibody molecules from being degraded by the gastric acid and digestive enzymes in the stomach and intestines. Infants who are bottle-fed have few means for battling ingested pathogens until they begin making secretory IgA on their own, often several weeks or even months after birth.

The secretory IgA molecules passed to the suckling child are helpful in ways that go beyond their ability to bind to microorganisms and keep them away from the body's tissues. First, the collection of antibodies transmitted to an infant is highly targeted against pathogens in that child's immediate surroundings. The mother synthesizes antibodies when she ingests, inhales or otherwise comes in contact with a disease-causing agent. Each antibody she makes is specific to that agent; that is, it binds to a single protein, or antigen, on the agent and will not waste time attacking irrelevant substances. Because the mother makes antibodies only to pathogens in her environment, the baby receives the protection it most needs— against the infectious agents it is most likely to encounter in the first weeks of life.

Second, the antibodies delivered to the infant ignore useful bacteria normally found in the gut. This flora serves to crowd out the growth of harmful organisms, thus providing another measure of resistance. Researchers do not yet know how the mother's immune system knows to make antibodies against only pathogenic and not normal bacteria, but whatever the process may be, it favors the establishment of "good bacteria" in a baby's gut.

Secretory IgA molecules further keep an infant from harm in that, unlike most other antibodies, they ward off disease without causing inflammation—a process in which various chemicals destroy microbes but potentially hurt healthy tissue. In an infant's developing gut, the mucosal membrane is extremely delicate, and an excess of these chemicals can do considerable damage.

Interestingly, secretory IgA can probably protect mucosal surfaces other than those in the gut. In many countries, particularly in the Middle East, western South America and northern Africa, women put milk in their infants' eyes to treat infections there. I do not know if this remedy has ever been tested scientifically, but there are theoretical reasons to believe it would work. It probably does work at least some of the time, or the practice would have died out.

An Abundance of Helpful Molecules

Several molecules in human milk besides secretory IgA prevent microbes from attaching to mucosal surfaces. Oligosaccharides, which are simple chains of sugars, often contain domains that resemble the binding sites through which bacteria gain entry into the cells lining the intestinal tract. Thus, these sugars can intercept bacteria, forming harmless complexes that the baby excretes. In addition, human milk contains large molecules called mucins that include a great deal of protein and carbohydrate. They, too, are capable of adhering to bacteria and viruses and eliminating them from the body.

The molecules in milk have other valuable functions as well. Each molecule of a protein called lactoferrin, for example, can bind to two atoms of iron. Because many pathogenic bacteria thrive on iron, lactoferrin halts their spread by making iron unavailable. It is especially effective at stalling the proliferation of organisms that often cause serious illness in infants, including *Staphylococcus aureus*. Lactoferrin also disrupts the process by which bacteria digest carbohydrates, further limiting their growth. Similarly, B_{12} binding protein, as its name suggests, deprives microorganisms of vitamin B_{12}.

Bifidus factor, one of the oldest known disease-resistance factors in human milk, promotes the growth of a beneficial organism named *Lactobacillus bifidus*. Free fatty acids present

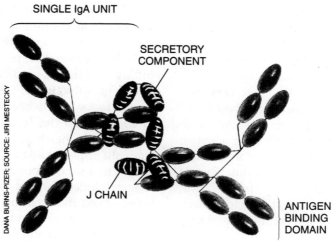

SINGLE IgA UNIT

SECRETORY COMPONENT

J CHAIN

ANTIGEN BINDING DOMAIN

DANA BURNS-PIZER; SOURCE: JIRI MESTECKY

SECRETORY IgA ANTIBODY, depicted schematically, consists of two IgA molecules "glued" together by a protein fragment known as the J chain. The secretory element (*stripes*) wraps around the joined molecules. The ellipses represent functional domains. Each of the four arms in such antibodies contains an antigen binding domain.

in milk can damage the membranes of enveloped viruses, such as the children pox virus, which are packets of genetic material encased in protein shells. Interferon, found particularly in colostrum—the scant, sometimes yellowish milk a mother produces during the first few days after birth—also has strong antiviral activity. And fibronectin, present in large quantities in colostrum, can make certain phagocytes more aggressive so that they will ingest microbes even when the microbes have not been tagged by an antibody. Like secretory IgA, fibronectin minimizes inflammation; it also seems to aid in repairing tissue damaged by inflammation.

Cellular Defenses

As is true of defensive molecules, immune cells are abundant in human milk. They consist of white blood cells, or leukocytes, that fight infection themselves and activate other defense mechanisms. The most impressive amount is found in colostrum. Most of the cells are neutrophils, a type of phagocyte that normally circulates in the bloodstream. Some evidence suggests that neutrophils continue

to act as phagocytes in the infant's gut. Yet they are less aggressive than blood neutrophils and virtually disappear from breast milk six weeks after birth. So perhaps they serve some other function, such as protecting the breast from infection.

The next most common milk leukocyte is the macrophage, which is phagocytic like neutrophils and performs a number of other protective functions. Macrophages make up some 40 percent of all the leukocytes in colostrum. They are far more active than milk neutrophils, and recent experiments suggest that they are more motile than are their counterparts in blood. Aside from being phagocytic, the macrophages in breast milk manufacture lysozyme, increasing its amount in the infant's gastrointestinal tract. Lysozyme is an enzyme that destroys bacteria by disrupting their cell walls.

In addition, macrophages in the digestive tract can rally lymphocytes into action against invaders. Lymphocytes constitute the remaining 10 percent of white cells in the milk. About 20 percent of these cells are *B* lymphocytes, which give rise to antibodies; the rest are *T* lymphocytes, which kill infected cells directly or send out chemical messages that mobilize still other components of the immune system. Milk lymphocytes seem to behave differently from blood lymphocytes. Those in milk, for example, proliferate in the presence of *Escherichia coli*, a bacterium that can cause life-threatening illness in babies, but they are far less responsive than blood lymphocytes to agents posing less threat to infants. Milk lymphocytes also manufacture several chemicals—including gamma-interferon, migration inhibition factor and monocyte chemotactic factor—that can strengthen an infant's own immune response.

Added Benefits

Several studies indicate that some factors in human milk may induce an infant's immune system to mature more quickly than it would were the child fed artificially. For example, breast-fed babies produce higher levels of antibodies in response to immunizations. Also, certain hormones in milk (such as cortisol) and smaller proteins (including epidermal growth factor, nerve growth factor, insulin-like growth factor and somatomedin C) act to close up the leaky mucosal lining of the newborn, making it relatively impermeable to unwanted pathogens and other potentially harmful agents. Indeed, animal studies have demonstrated that postnatal development of the intestine occurs faster in animals fed their mother's milk. And animals that also receive colostrum, containing the highest concentrations of epidermal growth factor, mature even more rapidly.

Other unknown compounds in human milk must stimulate a baby's own production of secretory IgA, lactoferrin and lysozyme. All three molecules are found in larger amounts in the urine of breast-fed babies than in that of bottle-fed babies. Yet breast-fed babies cannot absorb these molecules from human milk into their gut. It would appear that the molecules must be produced in the mucosa of the youngsters' urinary tract. In other words, it seems that breast-feeding induces local immunity in the urinary tract.

In support of this notion, recent clinical studies have demonstrated that the breast-fed infant has a lower risk of acquiring urinary tract infections. Finally, some evidence also suggests that an unknown factor in human milk may cause breast-fed infants to produce more fibronectin on their own than do bottle-fed babies.

All things considered, breast milk is truly a fascinating fluid that supplies infants with far more than nutrition. It protects them against infection until they can protect themselves.

The Author

JACK NEWMAN founded the breast-feeding clinic at the Hospital for Sick Children in Toronto in 1984 and serves as its director. He has more recently established similar clinics at Doctors Hospital and St. Michael's Hospital, both in Toronto. Newman received his medical degree in 1970 from the University of Toronto, where he is now an assistant professor. He completed his postgraduate training in New Zealand and Canada. As a consultant for UNICEF, he has worked with pediatricians in Africa. He has also practiced in New Zealand and in Central and South America.

Further Reading

MUCOSAL IMMUNITY: THE IMMUNOLOGY OF BREAST MILK. H. B. Slade and S. A. Schwartz in *Journal of Allergy and Clinical Immunology*, Vol. 80, No. 3, pages 348–356; September 1987.
IMMUNOLOGY OF MILK AND THE NEONATE. Edited by J. Mestecky et al. Plenum Press, 1991.
BREASTFEEDING AND HEALTH IN THE 1980's: A GLOBAL EPIDEMIOLOGIC REVIEW. Allan S. Cunningham in *Journal of Pediatrics*, Vol. 118, No. 5, pages 659–666; May 1991.
THE IMMUNE SYSTEM OF HUMAN MILK: ANTIMICROBIAL, ANTIINFLAMMATORY AND IMMUNOMODULATING PROPERTIES. A. S. Goldman in *Pediatric Infectious Disease Journal*, Vol. 12, No. 8, pages 664–671; August 1993.
HOST-RESISTANCE FACTORS AND IMMUNOLOGIC SIGNIFICANCE OF HUMAN MILK. In *Breastfeeding: A Guide for the Medical Profession*, by Ruth A. Lawrence. Mosby Year Book, 1994.

FERTILE MINDS

From birth, a baby's brain cells proliferate wildly,
making connections that may shape a lifetime of experience.
The first three years are critical

By J. MADELEINE NASH

RAT-A-TAT-TAT. RAT-A-TAT-TAT. RAT-A-tat-tat. If scientists could eavesdrop on the brain of a human embryo 10, maybe 12 weeks after conception, they would hear an astonishing racket. Inside the womb, long before light first strikes the retina of the eye or the earliest dreamy images flicker through the cortex, nerve cells in the developing brain crackle with purposeful activity. Like teenagers with telephones, cells in one neighborhood of the brain are calling friends in another, and these cells are calling their friends, and they keep calling one another over and over again, "almost," says neurobiologist Carla Shatz of the University of California, Berkeley, "as if they were autodialing."

But these neurons—as the long, wiry cells that carry electrical messages through the nervous system and the brain are called—are not transmitting signals in scattershot fashion. That would produce a featureless static, the sort of noise picked up by a radio tuned between stations. On the contrary, evidence is growing that the staccato bursts of electricity that form those distinctive rat-a-tat-tats arise from coordinated waves of neural activity, and that those pulsing waves, like currents shifting sand on the ocean floor, actually change the shape of the brain, carving mental circuits into patterns that over time will enable the newborn infant to perceive a father's voice, a mother's touch, a shiny mobile twirling over the crib.

Of all the discoveries that have poured out of neuroscience labs in recent years, the finding that the electrical activity of brain cells changes the physical structure of the brain is perhaps the most breathtaking. For the rhythmic firing of neurons is no longer assumed to be a by-product of building the brain but essential to the process, and it begins, scientists have established, well before birth. A brain is not a computer. Nature does not cobble it together, then turn it on. No, the brain begins working long before it is finished. And the same processes that wire the brain before birth, neuroscientists are finding, also drive the explosion of learning that occurs immediately afterward.

At birth a baby's brain contains 100 billion neurons, roughly as many nerve cells as there are stars in the Milky Way. Also in place are a trillion glial cells, named after the Greek word for glue, which form a kind of honeycomb that protects and nourishes the neurons. But while the brain contains virtually all the nerve cells it will ever have, the pattern of wiring between them has yet to stabilize. Up to this point, says Shatz, "what the brain has done is lay out circuits that are its best guess about what's required for vision, for language, for whatever." And now it is up to neural activity—no longer spontaneous, but driven by a flood of sensory experiences—to take this rough blueprint and progressively refine it.

During the first years of life, the brain undergoes a series of extraordinary changes. Starting shortly after birth, a baby's brain, in a display of biological exuberance, produces trillions more connections between neurons than it can possibly use. Then, through a process that resembles Darwinian competition, the brain eliminates connections, or synapses, that are seldom or never used. The excess synapses in a child's brain undergo a draconian pruning, starting around the age of 10 or earlier, leaving behind a mind whose patterns of emotion and thought are, for better or worse, unique.

Deprived of a stimulating environment, a child's brain suffers. Researchers at Baylor College of Medicine, for example, have found that children who don't play much or are rarely touched develop brains 20% to 30% smaller than normal for their age. Laboratory animals provide another provocative parallel. Not only do young rats reared in toy-strewn cages exhibit more complex behavior than rats confined to sterile, uninteresting boxes, researchers at the University of Illinois at Urbana-Champaign have found, but the brains of these rats contain as many as 25% more synapses per neuron. Rich experiences, in other words, really do produce rich brains.

The new insights into brain development are more than just interesting science. They have profound implications for parents and policymakers. In an age when mothers and fathers are increasingly pressed for time—and may already be feeling guilty about how many hours they spend away from their children—the results coming out of the labs are likely to increase concerns about leaving very young children in the care of others. For the data underscore the importance of

From *Time*, February 3, 1997, pp. 48-56. © 1997 by Time Inc. Magazine Company. Reprinted by permission.

hands-on parenting, of finding the time to cuddle a baby, talk with a toddler and provide infants with stimulating experiences.

The new insights have begun to infuse new passion into the political debate over early education and day care. There is an urgent need, say child-development experts, for preschool programs designed to boost the brain power of youngsters born into impoverished rural and inner-city households. Without such programs, they warn, the current drive to curtail welfare costs by pushing mothers with infants and toddlers into the work force may well backfire. "There is a time scale to brain development, and the most important year is the first," notes Frank Newman, president of the Education Commission of the States. By the age of three, a child who is neglected or abused bears marks that, if not indelible, are exceedingly difficult to erase.

But the new research offers hope as well. Scientists have found that the brain during the first years of life is so malleable that very young children who suffer strokes or injuries that wipe out an entire hemisphere can still mature into highly functional adults. Moreover, it is becoming increasingly clear that well-designed preschool programs can help many children overcome glaring deficits in their home environment. With appropriate therapy, say researchers, even serious disorders like dyslexia may be treatable. While inherited problems may place certain children at greater risk than others, says Dr. Harry Chugani, a pediatric neurologist at Wayne State University in Detroit, that is no excuse for ignoring the environment's power to remodel the brain. "We may not do much to change what happens before birth, but we can change what happens after a baby is born," he observes.

Strong evidence that activity changes the brain began accumulating in the 1970s. But only recently have researchers had tools powerful enough to reveal the precise mechanisms by which those changes are brought about. Neural activity triggers a biochemical cascade that reaches all the way to the nucleus of cells and the coils of DNA that encode specific genes. In fact, two of the genes affected by neural activity in embryonic fruit flies, neurobiologist Corey Goodman and his colleagues at Berkeley reported late last year, are identical to those that other studies have linked to learning and memory. How thrilling, exclaims Goodman, how intellectually satisfying that the snippets of DNA that embryos use to build their brains are the very same ones that will later allow adult organisms to process and store new information.

As researchers explore the once hidden links between brain activity and brain structure, they are beginning to construct a sturdy bridge over the chasm that previously separated genes from the environment. Experts now agree that a baby does not come into

Wiring Vision

WHAT'S GOING ON Babies can see at birth, but not in fine-grained detail. They have not yet acquired the knack of focusing both eyes on a single object or developed more sophisticated visual skills like depth perception. They also lack hand-eye coordination.

WHAT PARENTS CAN DO There is no need to buy high-contrast black-and-white toys to stimulate vision. But regular eye exams, starting as early as two weeks of age, can detect problems that, if left uncorrected, can cause a weak or unused eye to lose its functional connections to the brain.

WINDOW OF LEARNING Unless it is exercised early on, the visual system will not develop.

AGE (in years)	Birth	1	2	3	4	5	6	7	8	9	10
Visual acuity											
Binocular vision											

the world as a genetically preprogrammed automaton or a blank slate at the mercy of the environment, but arrives as something much more interesting. For this reason the debate that engaged countless generations of philosophers—whether nature or nurture calls the shots—no longer interests most scientists. They are much too busy chronicling the myriad ways in which genes and the environment interact. "It's not a competition," says Dr. Stanley Greenspan, a psychiatrist at George Washington University. "It's a dance."

THE IMPORTANCE OF GENES

THAT DANCE BEGINS AT AROUND THE THIRD week of gestation, when a thin layer of cells in the developing embryo performs an origami-like trick, folding inward to give rise to a fluid-filled cylinder known as the neural tube. As cells in the neural tube proliferate at the astonishing rate of 250,000 a minute, the brain and spinal cord assemble themselves in a series of tightly choreographed steps. Nature is the dominant partner during this phase of development, but nurture plays a vital supportive role. Changes in the environment of the womb—whether caused by maternal malnutrition, drug abuse or a viral infection—can wreck the clockwork precision of the neural assembly line. Some forms of epilepsy, mental retardation, autism and schizophrenia appear to be the results of developmental processes gone awry.

But what awes scientists who study the brain, what still stuns them, is not that things occasionally go wrong in the devel-

oping brain but that so much of the time they go right. This is all the more remarkable, says Berkeley's Shatz, as the central nervous system of an embryo is not a miniature of the adult system but more like a tadpole that gives rise to a frog. Among other things, the cells produced in the neural tube must migrate to distant locations and accurately lay down the connections that link one part of the brain to another. In addition, the embryonic brain must construct a variety of temporary structures, including the neural tube, that will, like a tadpole's tail, eventually disappear.

What biochemical magic underlies this incredible metamorphosis? The instructions programmed into the genes, of course. Scientists have recently discovered, for instance, that a gene nicknamed "sonic hedgehog" (after the popular video game Sonic the Hedgehog) determines the fate of neurons in the spinal cord and the brain. Like a strong scent carried by the wind, the protein encoded by the hedgehog gene (so called because in its absence, fruit-fly embryos sprout a coat of prickles) diffuses outward from the cells that produce it, becoming fainter and fainter. Columbia University neurobiologist Thomas Jessell has found that it takes middling concentrations of this potent morphing factor to produce a motor neuron and lower concentrations to make an interneuron (a cell that relays signals to other neurons, instead of to muscle fibers, as motor neurons do).

Scientists are also beginning to identify some of the genes that guide neurons in their long migrations. Consider the problem faced by neurons destined to become part of the cerebral cortex. Because they arise relatively late in the development of the mammalian brain, billions of these cells must push and shove their way through dense colonies established by earlier migrants. "It's as if the entire population of the East Coast decided to move en masse to the West Coast," marvels Yale University neuroscientist Dr. Pasko Rakic, "and marched through Cleveland, Chicago and Denver to get there."

But of all the problems the growing nervous system must solve, the most daunting is posed by the wiring itself. After birth, when the number of connections explodes, each of the brain's billions of neurons will forge links to thousands of others. First they must spin out a web of wirelike fibers known as axons (which transmit signals) and dendrites (which receive them). The objective is to form a synapse, the gap-like structure over which the axon of one neuron beams a signal to the dendrites of another. Before this can happen, axons and dendrites must almost touch. And while the short, bushy dendrites don't have to travel very far, axons—the heavy-duty cables of the nervous system—must traverse distances that are the microscopic equivalent of miles.

What guides an axon on its incredible voyage is a "growth cone," a creepy, crawly sprout that looks something like an amoeba. Scientists have known about growth cones since the turn of the century. What they didn't know until recently was that growth cones come equipped with the molecular equivalent of sonar and radar. Just as instruments in a submarine or airplane scan the environment for signals, so molecules arrayed on the surface of growth cones search their surroundings for the presence of certain proteins. Some of these proteins, it turns out, are attractants that pull the growth cones toward them, while others are repellents that push them away.

THE FIRST STIRRINGS

UP TO THIS POINT, GENES HAVE CONTROLLED the unfolding of the brain. As soon as axons make their first connections, however, the nerves begin to fire, and what they do starts to matter more and more. In essence, say scientists, the developing nervous system has strung the equivalent of telephone trunk lines between the right neighborhoods in the right cities. Now it has to sort out which wires belong to which house, a problem that cannot be solved by genes alone for reasons that boil down to simple arithmetic. Eventually, Berkeley's Goodman estimates, a human brain must forge quadrillions of connections. But there are only 100,000 genes in human DNA. Even though half these genes—some 50,000—appear to be dedicated to constructing and maintaining the nervous system, he observes, that's not enough to specify more than a tiny fraction of the connections required by a fully functioning brain.

In adult mammals, for example, the axons that connect the brain's visual system arrange themselves in striking layers and columns that reflect the division between the left eye and the right. But these axons start out as scrambled as a bowl of spaghetti, according to Michael Stryker, chairman of the physiology department at the University of California at San Francisco. What sorts out the mess, scientists have established, is neural activity. In a series of experiments viewed as classics by scientists in the field, Berkeley's Shatz chemically blocked neural activity in embryonic cats. The result? The axons that connect neurons in the retina of the eye to the brain never formed the left eye–right eye geometry needed to support vision.

But no recent finding has intrigued researchers more than the results reported in October by Corey Goodman and his Berkeley colleagues. In studying a deceptively simple problem—how axons from motor neurons in the fly's central nerve cord establish connections with muscle cells in its limbs—the Berkeley researchers made an

Wiring Feelings

WHAT'S GOING ON Among the first circuits the brain constructs are those that govern the emotions. Beginning around two months of age, the distress and contentment experienced by newborns start to evolve into more complex feelings: joy and sadness, envy and empathy, pride and shame.
WHAT PARENTS CAN DO Loving care provides a baby's brain with the right kind of emotional stimulation. Neglecting a baby can produce brainwave patterns that dampen happy feelings. Abuse can produce heightened anxiety and abnormal stress responses.
WINDOW OF LEARNING Emotions develop in layers, each more complex than the last.

AGE (in years)	Birth	1	2	3	4	5	6	7	8	9	10
Stress Response											
Empathy, Envy											

unexpected discovery. They knew there was a gene that keeps bundles of axons together as they race toward their muscle-cell targets. What they discovered was that the electrical activity produced by neurons inhibited this gene, dramatically increasing the number of connections the axons made. Even more intriguing, the signals amplified the activity of a second gene—a gene called CREB.

The discovery of the CREB amplifier, more than any other, links the developmental processes that occur before birth to those that continue long after. For the twin processes of memory and learning in adult animals, Columbia University neurophysiologist Eric Kandel has shown, rely on the CREB molecule. When Kandel blocked the activity of CREB in giant snails, their brains changed in ways that suggested that they could still learn but could remember what they learned for only a short period of time. Without CREB, it seems, snails—and by extension, more developed animals like humans—can form no long-term memories. And without long-term memories, it is hard to imagine that infant brains could ever master more than rudimentary skills. "Nurture is important," says Kandel. "But nurture works through nature."

EXPERIENCE KICKS IN

WHEN A BABY IS BORN, IT CAN SEE and hear and smell and respond to touch, but only dimly. The brain stem, a primitive region that controls vital functions like heartbeat and breathing, has completed its wiring. Elsewhere the connections between neurons are wispy and weak. But over the first few

months of life, the brain's higher centers explode with new synapses. And as dendrites and axons swell with buds and branches like trees in spring, metabolism soars. By the age of two, a child's brain contains twice as many synapses and consumes twice as much energy as the brain of a normal adult.

University of Chicago pediatric neurologist Dr. Peter Huttenlocher has chronicled this extraordinary epoch in brain development by autopsying the brains of infants and young children who have died unexpectedly. The number of synapses in one layer of the visual cortex, Huttenlocher reports, rises from around 2,500 per neuron at birth to as many as 18,000 about six months later. Other regions of the cortex score similarly spectacular increases but on slightly different schedules. And while these microscopic connections between nerve fibers continue to form throughout life, they reach their highest average densities (15,000 synapses per neuron) at around the age of two and remain at that level until the age of 10 or 11.

This profusion of connections lends the growing brain exceptional flexibility and resilience. Consider the case of 13-year-old Brandi Binder, who developed such severe epilepsy that surgeons at UCLA had to remove the entire right side of her cortex when she was six. Binder lost virtually all the control she had established over muscles on the left side of her body, the side controlled by the right side of the brain. Yet today, after years of therapy ranging from leg lifts to math and music drills, Binder is an A student at the Holmes Middle School in Colorado Springs, Colorado. She loves music, math and art—skills usually associated with the right half of the brain. And while Binder's recuperation is not 100%—for example, she has never regained the use of her left arm—it comes close. Says UCLA pediatric neurologist Dr. Donald Shields: "If there's a way to compensate, the developing brain will find it."

What wires a child's brain, say neuroscientists—or rewires it after physical trauma—is repeated experience. Each time a baby tries to touch a tantalizing object or gazes intently at a face or listens to a lullaby, tiny bursts of electricity shoot through the brain, knitting neurons into circuits as well defined as those etched onto silicon chips. The results are those behavioral mileposts that never cease to delight and awe parents. Around the age of two months, for example, the motor-control centers of the brain develop to the point that infants can suddenly reach out and grab a nearby object. Around the age of four months, the cortex begins to refine the connections needed for depth perception and binocular vision. And around the age of 12 months, the speech centers of the brain are poised to produce what is perhaps the most magical moment of childhood: the first word that marks the flowering of language.

When the brain does not receive the right information—or shuts it out—the result can be devastating. Some children who display early signs of autism, for example, retreat from the world because they are hypersensitive to sensory stimulation, others because their senses are underactive and provide them with too little information. To be effective, then, says George Washington University's Greenspan, treatment must target the underlying condition, protecting some children from disorienting noises and lights, providing others with attention-grabbing stimulation. But when parents and therapists collaborate in an intensive effort to reach these abnormal brains, writes Greenspan in a new book, *The Growth of the Mind* (Addison-Wesley, 1997), three-year-olds who begin the descent into the autistic's limited universe can sometimes be snatched back.

Indeed, parents are the brain's first and most important teachers. Among other things, they appear to help babies learn by adopting the rhythmic, high-pitched speaking style known as Parentese. When speaking to babies, Stanford University psychologist Anne Fernald has found, mothers and fathers from many cultures change their speech patterns in the same peculiar ways. "They put their faces very close to the child," she reports. "They use shorter utterances, and they speak in an unusually melodious fashion." The heart rate of infants increases while listening to Parentese, even Parentese delivered in a foreign language. Moreover, Fernald says, Parentese appears to hasten the process of connecting words to the objects they denote. Twelve-month-olds, directed to "look at the ball" in Parentese, direct their eyes to the correct picture more frequently than when the instruction is delivered in normal English.

In some ways the exaggerated, vowel-rich sounds of Parentese appear to resemble the choice morsels fed to hatchlings by adult birds. The University of Washington's Patricia Kuhl and her colleagues have conditioned dozens of newborns to turn their heads when they detect the *ee* sound emitted by American parents, vs. the *eu* favored by doting Swedes. Very young babies, says Kuhl, invariably perceive slight variations in pronunciation as totally different sounds. But by the age of six months, American babies no longer react when they hear variants of *ee,* and Swedish babies have become impervious to differences in *eu.* "It's as though their brains have formed little magnets," says Kuhl, "and all the sounds in the vicinity are swept in."

TUNED TO DANGER

EVEN MORE FUNDAMENTAL, SAYS Dr. Bruce Perry of Baylor College of Medicine in Houston, is the role parents play in setting

Wiring Language

WHAT'S GOING ON Even before birth, an infant is tuning into the melody of its mother's voice. Over the next six years, its brain will set up the circuitry needed to decipher—and reproduce—the lyrics. A six-month-old can recognize the vowel sounds that are the basic building blocks of speech.

WHAT PARENTS CAN DO Talking to a baby a lot, researchers have found, significantly speeds up the process of learning new words. The high-pitched, singsong speech style known as Parentese helps babies connect objects with words.

WINDOW OF LEARNING Language skills are sharpest early on but grow throughout life.

AGE (in years)	Birth 1 2 3 4 5 6 7 8 9 10
Recognition of speech	
Vocabulary	

up the neural circuitry that helps children regulate their responses to stress. Children who are physically abused early in life, he observes, develop brains that are exquisitely tuned to danger. At the slightest threat, their hearts race, their stress hormones surge and their brains anxiously track the nonverbal cues that might signal the next attack. Because the brain develops in sequence, with more primitive structures stabilizing their connections first, early abuse is particularly damaging. Says Perry: "Experience is the chief architect of the brain." And because these early experiences of stress form a kind of template around which later brain development is organized, the changes they create are all the more pervasive.

Emotional deprivation early in life has a similar effect. For six years University of Washington psychologist Geraldine Dawson and her colleagues have monitored the brainwave patterns of children born to mothers who were diagnosed as suffering from depression. As infants, these children showed markedly reduced activity in the left frontal lobe, an area of the brain that serves as a center for joy and other lighthearted emotions. Even more telling, the patterns of brain activity displayed by these children closely tracked the ups and downs of their mother's depression. At the age of three, children whose mothers were more severely depressed or whose depression lasted longer continued to show abnormally low readings.

Strikingly, not all the children born to depressed mothers develop these aberrant brain-wave patterns, Dawson has found. What accounts for the difference appears to be the emotional tone of the exchanges be-

tween mother and child. By scrutinizing hours of videotape that show depressed mothers interacting with their babies, Dawson has attempted to identify the links between maternal behavior and children's brains. She found that mothers who were disengaged, irritable or impatient had babies with sad brains. But depressed mothers who managed to rise above their melancholy, lavishing their babies with attention and indulging in playful games, had children with brain activity of a considerably more cheerful cast.

When is it too late to repair the damage wrought by physical and emotional abuse or neglect? For a time, at least, a child's brain is extremely forgiving. If a mother snaps out of her depression before her child is a year old, Dawson has found, brain activity in the left frontal lobe quickly picks up. However, the ability to rebound declines markedly as a child grows older. Many scientists believe that in the first few years of childhood there are a number of critical or sensitive periods, or "windows," when the brain demands certain types of input in order to create or stabilize certain long-lasting structures.

For example, children who are born with a cataract will become permanently blind in that eye if the clouded lens is not promptly removed. Why? The brain's visual centers require sensory stimulus—in this case the stimulus provided by light hitting the retina of the eye—to maintain their still tentative connections. More controversially, many linguists believe that language skills unfold according to a strict, biologically defined timetable. Children, in their view, resemble certain species of birds that cannot master their song unless they hear it sung at an early age. In zebra finches the window for acquiring the appropriate song opens 25 to 30 days after hatching and shuts some 50 days later.

WINDOWS OF OPPORTUNITY

WITH A FEW EXCEPTIONS, THE WINDOWS OF opportunity in the human brain do not close quite so abruptly. There appears to be a series of windows for developing language. The window for acquiring syntax may close as early as five or six years of age, while the window for adding new words may never close. The ability to learn a second language is highest between birth and the age of six, then undergoes a steady and inexorable decline. Many adults still manage to learn new languages, but usually only after great struggle.

The brain's greatest growth spurt, neuroscientists have now confirmed, draws to a close around the age of 10, when the balance between synapse creation and atrophy abruptly shifts. Over the next several years, the brain will ruthlessly destroy its weakest synapses, preserving only those that have been magically transformed by experience. This magic, once again, seems to be encoded in the genes. The ephemeral bursts of electricity that travel through the brain, creating everything from visual images and pleasurable sensations to dark dreams and wild thoughts, ensure the survival of synapses by stimulating genes that promote the release of powerful growth factors and suppressing genes that encode for synapse-destroying enzymes.

By the end of adolescence, around the age of 18, the brain has declined in plasticity but increased in power. Talents and latent tendencies that have been nurtured are ready to blossom. The experiences that drive neural activity, says Yale's Rakic, are like a sculptor's chisel or a dressmaker's shears, conjuring up form from a lump of stone or a length of cloth. The presence of extra material expands the range of possibilities, but cutting away the extraneous is what makes art. "It is the overproduction of synaptic connections followed by their loss that leads to patterns in the brain," says neuroscientist William Greenough of the University of Illinois at Urbana-Champaign. Potential for greatness may be encoded in the genes, but whether that potential is realized as a gift for mathematics, say, or a brilliant criminal mind depends on patterns etched by experience in those critical early years.

Wiring Movement

WHAT'S GOING ON At birth babies can move their limbs, but in a jerky, uncontrolled fashion. Over the next four years, the brain progressively refines the circuits for reaching, grabbing, sitting, crawling, walking and running.
WHAT PARENTS CAN DO Give babies as much freedom to explore as safety permits. Just reaching for an object helps the brain develop hand-eye coordination. As soon as children are ready for them, activities like drawing and playing a violin or piano encourage the development of fine motor skills.
WINDOW OF LEARNING Motor-skill development moves from gross to increasingly fine.

AGE (in years)	Birth	1	2	3	4	5	6	7	8	9	10
Basic motor skills											
Fine motor ability											
Musical fingering											

Psychiatrists and educators have long recognized the value of early experience. But their observations have until now been largely anecdotal. What's so exciting, says Matthew Melmed, executive director of Zero to Three, a nonprofit organization devoted to highlighting the importance of the first three years of life, is that modern neuroscience is providing the hard, quantifiable evidence that was missing earlier. "Because you can see the results under a microscope or in a PET scan," he observes, "it's become that much more convincing."

What lessons can be drawn from the new findings? Among other things, it is clear that foreign languages should be taught in elementary school, if not before. That remedial education may be more effective at the age of three or four than at nine or 10. That good, affordable day care is not a luxury or a fringe benefit for welfare mothers and working parents but essential brain food for the next generation. For while new synapses continue to form throughout life, and even adults continually refurbish their minds through reading and learning, never again will the brain be able to master new skills so readily or rebound from setbacks so easily.

Rat-a-tat-tat. Rat-a-tat-tat. Rat-a-tat-tat. Just last week, in the U.S. alone, some 77,000 newborns began the miraculous process of wiring their brains for a lifetime of learning. If parents and policymakers don't pay attention to the conditions under which this delicate process takes place, we will all suffer the consequences—starting around the year 2010.

The Realistic View of Biology and Behavior

Jerome Kagan

Jerome Kagan is professor of psychology at Harvard University. He is the author of Galen's Prophecy: Temperament in Human Nature *(BasicBooks, 1994).*

Although families with more than one child know that each infant brings into the world a distinctive mood and manner, during most of this century Americans have resisted the idea that biology might form at least part of the foundation of some personality traits. The strength of American skepticism is odd, because generations of previous commentators on human nature, beginning with the ancient Greeks, acknowledged that each person's physiology made a small contribution to his or her energy, emotional adaptability, and style of interaction with others.

The source of American resistance, though, is the laudable, egalitarian hope that benevolent home and school experiences can overcome individual biological variations and create a society of relative equals. Because that hope sustains liberal legislation, many people—including scholars—believe that it is dangerous to challenge it, no matter how mildly.

However, the evidence for physiology's influence on some behavior is sufficient to overcome any hesitation to discuss openly the nature of biologically based predispositions. Research in many laboratories, including my own, reveals that many people inherit a physiology that can affect, for example, a proneness to be melancholic or sanguine. At the same time, we must not become so enamored of such discoveries that we forget biology's real limits.

The campaign to suppress discussion of biology grew strong during the opening decades of this century. Politically liberal scholars, joined by journalists of like mind, wished to mute the arguments of conservatives who argued for halting immigration from Eastern Europe on the ground that the immigrants had genetic flaws. The liberals were helped by Ivan Pavlov's discovery of conditioning, in the early 1900's, in a St. Petersburg laboratory. If a dog could be taught to salivate at a sound, surely a child could be taught anything, was the message John Watson, America's first behaviorist, brought to American parents after World War I. That bold claim was congruent with Sigmund Freud's creative hypothesis that family experiences in the early years could create or prevent a future neurosis.

By the late 1920's, the broad acceptance of inherited temperamental traits, which had lasted for two millennia, had been banished, its demise speeded by our society's need to believe in the power of social experience.

As the discipline of psychology—born in Europe during the last quarter of the 19th century—became recognized at American colleges and universities, many faculty members began to emphasize the influence of social experience on behavior. This approach became easier to defend after Hitler proposed the repugnant philosophy that Aryans were superior to other people.

After World War II, social science in America also became more positivistic, demanding objective evidence for all theoretical statements. Neuroscience was still young in the late 1940's and was unable to supply evidence that could explain, for example, how a particular physiological profile might be the foundation of an anxious or an angry mood.

By the 1970's, however, the historical context had again changed. Hundreds of studies of the way families influence growing children had not

> "Hundreds of studies of the way families influence growing children had not produced the powerful generalizations that had been anticipated a half century earlier."

produced the powerful generalizations that had been anticipated a half century earlier. Equally important, engineers and scientists had invented ingenious ways to study the brain. Suddenly it became possible to speculate about how a particular neurochemistry could produce excessive anxiety, sadness, or anger. Scientists who put forward such explanations were not treated as intellectual terrorists for suggesting, for example, that a woman with panic attacks might have inherited a neurochemistry that rendered her especially vulnerable to a sudden, inexplicable sharp rise in heart rate, a feeling of suffocation, and a surge of fear.

But I believe that some psychiatrists and neuroscientists are moving too quickly toward a biological determinism that is as extreme as the earlier loyalty of some psychologists to an environmental explanation of behavior. Fortunately, a majority of scientists recognize that no human psychological profile is a product of genes alone. To rephrase a graceful sentence by the philosopher W. V. O. Quine, every behavior can be likened to a pale gray fabric composed of black threads, for biology, and white threads, for experience, but it is not possible to detect any purely black threads nor any white ones.

Support for this more complex, but realistic, view of the relation between brain and behavior is found in the fact that if one member of a pair of identical twins develops schizophrenia, the odds are less than 50 per cent that the other twin will come down with the same psychosis. Because inherited biological propensities do not affect all psychological outcomes equally, the proper strategy is to ask which psychological characteristics are most, and which least, vulnerable to biological forces. Serious depression belongs to the former category, while preference for a seaside holiday belongs to the latter.

At the moment, two psychological categories, which can be observed clearly in children, appear to be heavily influenced by biology. Between 15 per cent and 20 per cent of a large group of healthy infants we studied, who were born into secure homes, were found to have inherited a tendency to be unusually aroused and distressed by new, unexpected events. When they were observed in our laboratory at four months of age, they thrashed their limbs and cried when they saw colorful, moving mobiles or heard tape recordings of human speech. About two-thirds of these easily aroused infants, whom we call "high reactive," became extremely shy, fearful, subdued toddlers. Based on other data, we estimate that about one-half of this group of toddlers will become quiet, introverted adolescents. Not all of the high-reactive infants will become introverted, however, because their life experiences lead them to develop differently.

A second, larger group of infants—about 35 per cent of the children we studied—are the opposite of the high-reactive, shy children. These infants are relaxed and rarely cry when they experience new events. Two-thirds of this group become sociable, relatively fearless young children. Stressful events, however, can produce a fearful or shy manner in such children, even though they began life with a minimally excitable temperament.

Support for a biological contribution to the development of these two types of children comes from the fact that the two groups differ in many aspects of their physiological functioning, as well as in their body build. The fearful children show larger increases in heart rate and blood pressure when they are challenged—signs of a more reactive sympathetic nervous system. They have a higher prevalence of the allergies that produce hay fever and hives (and, surprisingly, possess narrower faces). Studies of identical and fraternal twins support the belief that each of these temperamental types is influenced, in part, by heredity.

Hippocrates and Galen of Pergamon would not have been surprised by these discoveries. Many Americans, however, will be troubled, because they will misinterpret the evidence as implying an exaggerated biological influence on behavior. Some social scientists will also resist acknowledging the contribution of brain chemistry and physiology to behavior because they will worry that, if they let the camel's nose under the tent, the animal will soon be inside, forcing all the residents to leave.

All the more reason that we who study the relationship of biology to behavior must make clear that psychological phenomena, like a fearful or a fearless style of behavior, cannot be reduced completely to a person's biology: The child's life history influences the adult's psychological profile. Because the course of that life history is unknown when children are very young, we cannot at that time select the very small proportion of the 5 per cent to 10 per cent of children whose temperaments dispose them to be fearless, impulsive, and aggressive who will go on to develop an asocial or criminal personality. It would be unethical, for example, to tell parents that their 3-year-old son is at serious risk for delinquent behavior.

Similar arguments can be made about predicting which children will develop panic attacks, depression, or schizophrenia. A small group of children are at risk for each of these disorders because of the physiology they inherit, but we are unable at the present time to say which of the children will eventually develop a particular disorder—because we do not know what vicissitudes life will hold for them.

Perhaps future discoveries will supply the information that will make such predictions accurate enough to warrant benevolent intervention early in the child's life. We will have to wait and see whether that promise can be fulfilled.

A more subtle implication of the research on temperament involves people's willingness to take responsibility for their own actions. I trust that most Americans still believe in the notion of free will—that we can decide what action we will take or not take—and that each of us has a moral obligation to be civil and responsible, even when we wake up feeling blue, angry, or anxious. Our culture still insists that we should pull up our socks and act responsibly, even if that posture comes at some emotional price.

The danger in the new romance with biology is that many people will begin to award temperament too strong a voice, deciding, for example, to be permissive and accepting of friends who lose their tempers too easily. Each of us does inherit a temperamental bias for one or more characteristics, but we also inherit the human capacity for restraint. Most of the time, humans are able to control the behavior that their temperament presses upon them, if they choose to do so. The new research on temperament and biology should not be used to excuse asocial behavior. Rather, the purpose of the inquiry is to help us understand the bases for the extraordinary variation in human motivation, mood, and social behavior.

We would do well to remember that although the poet-philosopher Lucretius believed in temperamental variation he was also convinced that the "lingering traces of inborn temperament that cannot be eliminated by philosophy are so slight that there is nothing to prevent men from leading a life worthy of the gods."

Studies Show Talking With Infants Shapes Basis of Ability to Think

By SANDRA BLAKESLEE

When a White House conference on early child development convenes today, one of the findings Hillary Rodham Clinton will hear from scientists is that the neurological foundations for rational thinking, problem solving and general reasoning appear to be largely established by age 1—long before babies show any signs of knowing an abstraction from a pacifier.

Furthermore, new studies are showing that spoken language has an astonishing impact on an infant's brain development. In fact, some researchers say the number of words an infant hears each day is the single most important predictor of later intelligence, school success and social competence. There is one catch—the words have to come from an attentive, engaged human being. As far as anyone has been able to determine, radio and television do not work.

"We now know that neural connections are formed very early in life and that the infant's brain is literally waiting for experiences to determine how connections are made," said Dr. Patricia Kuhl, a neuroscientist at the University of Washington in Seattle

and a key speaker at today's conference. "We didn't realize until very recently how early this process begins," she said in a telephone interview. "For example, infants have learned the sounds of their native language by the age of six months."

This relatively new view of infant brain development, supported by many scientists, has obvious political and social implications. It suggests that infants and babies develop most rapidly with caretakers who are not only loving, but also talkative and articulate, and that a more verbal family will increase an infant's chances for success. It challenges some deeply held beliefs—that infants will thrive intellectually if they are simply given lots of love and that purposeful efforts to influence babies' cognitive development are harmful.

If the period from birth to 3 is crucial, parents may assume a more crucial role in a child's intellectual development than teachers, an idea sure to provoke new debates about parental responsibility, said Dr. Irving Lazar, a professor of special education and resident scholar at the Center for Research in Human Development at Vanderbilt University

in Nashville. And it offers yet another reason to provide stimulating, high quality day care for infants whose primary caretakers work, which is unavoidably expensive.

Environmental factors seem to take over for genetic influence.

The idea that early experience shapes human potential is not new, said Dr. Harry Chugani, a pediatric neurologist at Wayne State University in Detroit and one of the scientists whose research has shed light on critical periods in child brain development. What is new is the extent of the research in the field known as cognitive neuroscience and the resulting synthesis of findings on the influence of both nature and nurture. Before birth, it appears that genes predominantly direct how the brain establishes basic wir-

TIMETABLE

The Growing Brain: What Might Help Your Infant

Dr. William Staso, an expert in neurological development, suggests that different kinds of stimulation should be emphasized at different ages. At all stages, parental interaction and a conversational dialogue with the child are important. Here are some examples:

FIRST MONTH: A low level of stimulation reduces stress and increases the infant's wakefulness and alertness. The brain essentially shuts down the system when there is overstimulation from competing sources. When talking to an infant, for example, filter out distracting noises, like a radio.

MONTHS 1 TO 3 Light/dark contours, like high-contrast pictures or objects, foster development in neural networks that encode vision. The brain also starts to discriminate among acoustic patterns of language, like intonation, lilt and pitch. Speaking to the infant, especially in an animated voice, aids this process.

MONTHS 3 TO 5 The infant relies primarily on vision to acquire information about the world. Make available increasingly complex designs that correspond to real objects in the baby's environment; motion also attracts attention. A large-scale picture of a fork, moved across the field of vision, would offer more stimulation than just an actual fork.

MONTHS 6 TO 7 The infant becomes alert to relationships like cause and effect, the location of objects and the functions of objects. Demonstrate and talk about situations like how the turning of a doorknob leads to the opening of a door.

MONTHS 7 TO 8 The brain is oriented to make associations between sounds and some meaningful activity or object. For example, parents can deliberately emphasize in conversation that the sound of water running in the bathroom signals an impending bath, or that a doorbell means a visitor.

MONTHS 9 TO 12 Learning adds up to a new level of awareness of the environment and increased interest in exploration; sensory and motor skills coordinate in a more mature fashion. This is the time to let the child turn on a faucet or a light switch, under supervision.

MONTHS 13 TO 18 The brain establishes accelerated and more complex associations, especially if the toddler experiments directly with objects. A rich environment will help the toddler make such associations, understand sequences, differentiate between objects and reason about them.

---

ing patterns. Neurons grow and travel into distinct neighborhoods, awaiting further instructions.

After birth, it seems that environmental factors predominate. A recent study found that mice exposed to an enriched environment have more brain cells than mice raised in less intellectually stimulating conditions. In humans, the inflowing stream of sights, sounds, noises, smells, touches—and most importantly, language and eye contact—literally makes the brain take shape. It is a radical and shocking concept.

Experience in the first year of life lays the basis for networks of neurons that enable us to be smart, creative and adaptable in all the years that follow, said Dr. Esther Thelen, a neurobiologist at Indiana University in Bloomington.

The brain is a self-organizing system, Dr. Thelen said, whose many parts co-operate to produce coherent behavior. There is no master program pulling it together but rather the parts self-organize. "What we know about these systems is that they are very sensitive to initial conditions," Dr. Thelen said. "Where you are now depends on where you've been."

The implication for infant development is clear. Given the explosive growth and self-organizing capacity of the brain in the first year of life, the experiences an infant has during this period are the conditions that set the stage for everything that follows.

In later life, what makes us smart and creative and adaptable are networks of neurons which support our ability to use abstractions from one memory to help form new ideas and solve problems, said Dr. Charles Stevens, a neurobiologist at the Salk Institute in San Diego. Smarter people may have a greater number of neural networks that are more intri-

cately woven together, a process that starts in the first year.

The complexity of the synaptic web laid down early may very well be the physical basis of what we call general intelligence, said Dr. Lazar at Vanderbilt. The more complex that set of interconnections, the brighter the child is likely to be since there are more ways to sort, file and access experiences.

Of course, brain development "happens" in stimulating and dull environments. Virtually all babies learn to sit up, crawl, walk, talk, eat independently and make transactions with others, said Dr. Steven Petersen, a neurologist at Washington University School of Medicine in St. Louis. Such skills are not at risk except in rare circumstances of sensory and social deprivation, like being locked in a closet for the first few years of life. Subject to tremendous variability within the normal range of environments are the abilities to perceive, conceptualize, understand, reason, associate and judge. The ability to function in a technologically complex society like ours does not simply "happen."

One implication of the new knowledge about infant brain development is that intervention programs like Head Start may be too little, too late, Dr. Lazar said. If educators hope to make a big difference, he said, they will need to develop programs for children from birth to 3.

Dr. Bettye Caldwell, a professor of pediatrics and an expert in child development at the University of Arkansas in Little Rock, who supports the importance of early stimulation, said that in early childhood education there is a strong bias against planned intellectual stimulation. Teachers of very young children are taught to follow "developmentally appropriate practices," she said, which means that the child chooses what he or she wants to do. The teacher is a responder and not a stimulator.

Asked about the bias Dr. Caldwell described, Matthew Melmed, executive director of Zero to Three, a research and training organization for early childhood development in Washington, D.C., said that knowing how much stimulation is too much or too little, especially for infants, is "a really tricky question. It's a dilemma parents and educators face every day," he said.

In a poll released today, Zero to Three found that 87 percent of parents think that the more stimulation a baby receives the better off the baby is, Mr. Melmed said. "Many parents have the concept that a baby is something you fill up with information and that's not good," he said.

"We are concerned that many parents are going to take this new information about brain research and rush to do more things with their babies, more activities, forgetting that it's not the activities that are impor-

tant. The most important thing is connecting with the baby and creating an emotional bond," Mr. Melmed said.

There is some danger of overstimulating an infant, said Dr. William Staso, a school psychologist from Orcutt, Calif., who has written a book called "What Stimulation Your Baby Needs to Become Smart." Some people think that any interaction with very young children that involves their intelligence must also involve pushing them to excel, he said. But the "curriculum" that most benefits young babies is simply common sense, Dr. Staso said. It does not involve teaching several languages or numerical concepts but rather carrying out an ongoing dialogue with adult speech. Vocabulary words are a magnet for a child's thinking and reasoning skills.

This constant patter may be the single most important factor in early brain development, said Dr. Betty Hart, a professor emeritus of human development at the University of Kansas in Lawrence. With her colleague, Dr. Todd Ridley of the University of Alaska, Dr. Hart recently co-authored a book—"Meaningful Differences in the Everyday Experience of Young American Children."

Challenging the deep belief that lots of love is enough.

The researchers studied 42 children born to professional, working class or welfare parents. During the first two and a half years of the children's lives, the scientists spent an hour a month recording every spoken word and every parent-child interaction in every home. For all the families, the data include 1,300

hours of everyday interactions, Dr. Hart said, involving millions of ordinary utterances.

At age 3, the children were given standard tests. The children of professional parents scored highest. Spoken language was the key variable, Dr. Hart said.

A child with professional parents heard, on average, 2,100 words an hour. Children of working-class parents heard 1,200 words and those with parents on welfare heard only 600 words an hour. Professional parents talked three times as much to their infants, Dr. Hart said. Moreover, children with professional parents got positive feedback 30 times an hour—twice as often as working-class parents and five times as often as welfare parents.

The tone of voice made a difference, Dr. Hart said. Affirmative feedback is very important. A child who hears, "What did we do yesterday? What did we see?" will listen more to a parent than will a child who always hears "Stop that," or "Come here!"

By age 2, all parents started talking more to their children, Dr. Hart said. But by age two, the differences among children were so great that those left behind could never catch up. The differences in academic achievement remained in each group through primary school.

Every child learned to use language and could say complex sentences but the deprived children did not deal with words in a conceptual manner, she said.

A recent study of day care found the same thing. Children who were talked to at very young ages were better at problem solving later on.

For an infant, Dr. Hart said, all words are novel and worth learning. The key to brain development seems to be the rate of early learning—not so much what is wired but how much of the brain gets interconnected in those first months and years.

A baby's brain is a work in progress, trillions of neurons waiting to be wired into a mind. The experiences of childhood, pioneering research shows, help form the brain's circuits—for music and math, language and emotion.

Your Child's Brain

Sharon Begley

YOU HOLD YOUR NEWBORN SO his sky-blue eyes are just inches from the brightly patterned wallpaper. *ZZZt:* a neuron from his retina makes an electrical connection with one in his brain's visual cortex. You gently touch his palm with a clothespin; he grasps it, drops it, and you return it to him with soft words and a smile. *Crackle:* neurons from his hand strengthen their connection to those in his sensory-motor cortex. He cries in the night; you feed him, holding his gaze because nature has seen to it that the distance from a parent's crooked elbow to his eyes exactly matches the distance at which a baby focuses. *Zap:* neurons in the brain's amygdala send pulses of electricity through the circuits that control emotion. You hold him on your lap and talk . . . and neurons from his ears start hard-wiring connections to the auditory cortex.

And you thought you were just playing with your kid.

When a baby comes into the world her brain is a jumble of neurons, all waiting to be woven into the intricate tapestry of the mind. Some of the neurons have already been hard-wired, by the genes in the fertilized egg, into circuits that command breathing or control heartbeat, regulate body temperature or produce reflexes. But trillions upon trillions more are like the Pentium chips in a computer before the factory preloads the software. They are pure and of almost infinite potential, unprogrammed circuits that might one day compose rap songs and do calculus, erupt in fury and melt in ecstasy. If the neurons are used they become integrated into the circuitry of the brain by connecting to other neurons; if they are not used, they may die. It is the experiences of childhood, determining which neurons are used, that wire the circuits of the brain as surely as a programmer at a key-

board reconfigures the circuits in a computer. Which keys are typed—which experiences a child has—determines whether the child grows up to be intelligent or dull, fearful or self-assured, articulate or tongue-tied. Early experiences are so powerful, says pediatric neurobiologist Harry Chungani of Wayne State University, that "they can completely change the way a person turns out."

By adulthood the brain is crisscrossed with more than 100 billion neurons, each reaching out to thousands of others so that, all told, the brain has more than 100 trillion connections. It is those connections—more than the number of galaxies in the known universe—that give the brain its unrivaled powers. The traditional view was that the wiring diagram is predetermined, like one for a new house, by the genes in the fertilized egg. Unfortunately, even though half the genes—50,000—are involved in the central nervous system in some way, there are not enough of them to specify the brain's incomparably complex wiring. That leaves another possibility: genes might determine only the

brain's main circuits, with something else shaping the trillions of finer connections. That something else is the environment, the myriad messages that the brain receives from the outside world. According to the emerging paradigm, "there are two broad stages of brain wiring," says developmental neurobiologist Carla Shatz of the University of California, Berkeley: "an early period, when experience is not required, and a later one, when it is."

Yet, once wired, there are limits to the brain's ability to create itself. Time limits. Called "critical periods," they are windows of opportunity that nature flings open, starting before birth, and then slams shut, one by one, with every additional candle on the child's birthday cake. In the experiments that gave birth to this paradigm in the 1970s, Torsten Wiesel and David Hubel found that sewing shut one eye of a newborn kitten rewired its brain: so few neurons connected from the shut eye to the visual cortex that the animal was blind even after its eye was reopened. Such rewiring did not occur in adult cats

The Logical Brain

SKILL: Math and logic
LEARNING WINDOW: Birth to 4 years
WHAT WE KNOW: Circuits for math reside in the brain's cortex, near those for music. Toddlers taught simple concepts, like one and many, do better in math. Music lessons may help develop spatial skills.

WHAT WE CAN DO ABOUT IT: Play counting games with a toddler. Have him set the table to learn one-to-one relationships—one plate, one fork per person. And, to hedge your bets, turn on a Mozart CD.

The Language Brain

SKILL: Language
LEARNING WINDOW: Birth to 10 years
WHAT WE KNOW: Circuits in the auditory cortex, representing the sounds that form words, are wired by the age of 1. The more words a child hears by 2, the larger her vocabulary will grow. Hearing problems can impair the ability to match sounds to letters.

WHAT WE CAN DO ABOUT IT: Talk to your child—a lot. If you want her to master a second language, introduce it by the age of 10. Protect hearing by treating ear infections promptly.

whose eyes were shut. Conclusion: there is a short, early period when circuits connect the retina to the visual cortex. When brain regions mature dictates how long they stay malleable. Sensory areas mature in early childhood; the emotional limbic system is wired by puberty; the frontal lobes—seat of understanding—develop at least through the age of 16.

The implications of this new understanding are at once promising and disturbing. They suggest that, with the right input at the right time, almost anything is possible. But they imply, too, that if you miss the window you're playing with a handicap. They offer an explanation of why the gains a toddler makes in Head Start are so often evanescent: this intensive instruction begins too late to fundamentally rewire the brain. And they make clear the mistake of postponing instruction in a second language. As Chugani asks, "What idiot decreed that foreign-language instruction not begin until high school?"

Neurobiologists are still at the dawn of understanding exactly which kinds of experiences, or sensory input, wire the brain in which ways. They know a great deal about the circuit for vision. It has a neuron-growth spurt at the age of 2 to 4 months, which corresponds to when babies start to really notice the world, and peaks at 8 months, when each neuron is connected to an astonishing 15,000 other neurons. A baby whose eyes are clouded by cataracts from birth will, despite cataract-removal surgery at the age of 2, be forever blind. For other systems, researchers know what happens, but not—at the level of neurons and molecules—how. They nevertheless remain confident that cognitive abilities work much like sensory ones, for the brain is parsimonious in how it conducts its affairs: a mechanism that works fine for wiring vision is not likely to be abandoned when it comes to circuits for music. "Connections are not forming willy-nilly," says Dale Purves of Duke University, "but are promoted by activity."

Language: Before there are words, in the world of a newborn, there are sounds. In English they are phonemes such as sharp ba's and da's, drawn-out ee's and ll's and sibilant sss's. In Japanese they are different—barked *hi's,* merged rr/ll's. When a child hears a phoneme over and over, neurons from his ear stimulate the formation of dedicated connections in his brain's auditory cortex. This "perceptual map," explains Patricia Kuhl of the University of Washington, reflects the apparent distance—and thus the similarity—between sounds. So in English-speakers, neurons in the auditory cortex that respond to "ra" lie far from those that respond to "la." But for Japanese, where the sounds are nearly identical, neurons that respond to "ra" are practically intertwined, like L.A. freeway spaghetti, with those for "la." As a result, a Japanese-speaker will have trouble distinguishing the two sounds.

Researchers find evidence of these tendencies across many languages. By 6 months of age, Kuhl reports, infants in English-speaking homes already have different auditory maps (as shown by electrical measurements that identify which neurons respond to different sounds) from those in Swedish-speaking homes. Children are functionally deaf to sounds absent from their native tongue. The map is completed by the first birthday. "By 12 months," says Kuhl, "infants have lost the ability to discriminate sounds that are not significant in their language. And their babbling has acquired the sound of their language."

Kuhl's findings help explain why learning a second language after, rather than with, the first is so difficult. "The perceptual map of the first language constrains the learning of a second," she says. In other words, the circuits are already wired for Spanish, and the remaining undedicated neurons have lost their ability to form basic new connections for, say, Greek. A child taught a second language after the age of 10 or so is unlikely ever to speak it like a native. Kuhl's work also suggests why related languages such as Spanish and French are easier to learn than unrelated ones: more of the existing circuits can do double duty.

With this basic circuitry established, a baby is primed to turn sounds into words. The more words a child hears, the faster she learns language, according to psychiatrist Janellen Huttenlocher of the University of Chicago. Infants whose mothers spoke to them a lot knew 131 more words at 20 months than did babies of more taciturn, or less involved, mothers; at 24 months, the gap had widened to 295 words. (Presumably the findings would also apply to a father if he were the primary caregiver.) It didn't matter which words the mother used—monosyllables seemed to work. The sound of words, it seems, builds up neural circuitry that can then absorb more words, much as creating a computer file allows the user to fill it with prose. "There is a huge vocabulary to be acquired," says Huttenlocher, "and it can only be acquired through repeated exposure to words."

Music: Last October researchers at the University of Konstanz in Germany reported that exposure to music rewires neural circuits. In the brains of nine string players examined with magnetic resonance imaging, the amount of somatosensory cortex dedicated to the thumb and fifth finger of the left hand—the fingering digits—was significantly larger than in nonplayers. How long the players practiced each day did not affect the cortical map. But the age at which they had been introduced to their muse did: the younger the child when she took up an instrument, the more cortex she devoted to playing it.

Like other circuits formed early in life, the ones for music endure. Wayne State's Chugani played the guitar as a child, then gave it up. A few years ago he started taking

The Musical Brain

SKILL: Music
LEARNING WINDOW: 3 to 10 years
WHAT WE KNOW: String players have a larger area of their sensory cortex dedicated to the fingering digits on their left hand. Few concert-level performers begin playing later than the age of 10. It is much harder to learn an instrument as an adult.

WHAT WE CAN DO ABOUT IT: Sing songs with children. Play structured, melodic music. If a child shows any musical aptitude or interest, get an instrument into her hand early.

piano lessons with his young daughter. She learned easily, but he couldn't get his fingers to follow his wishes. Yet when Chugani recently picked up a guitar, he found to his delight that "the songs are still there," much like the muscle memory for riding a bicycle.

Math and logic: At UC Irvine, Gordon Shaw suspected that all higher-order thinking is characterized by similar patterns of neuron firing. "If you're working with little kids," says Shaw, "you're not going to teach them higher mathematics or chess. But they are interested in and can process music." So Shaw and Frances Rauscher gave 19 preschoolers piano or singing lessons. After eight months, the researchers found, the children "dramatically improved in spatial reasoning," compared with children given no music lessons, as shown in their ability to work mazes, draw geometric figures and copy patterns of two-color blocks. The mechanism behind the "Mozart effect" remains murky, but Shaw suspects that when children exercise cortical neurons by listening to classical music, they are also strengthening circuits used for mathematics. Music, says the UC team, "excites the inherent brain patterns and enhances their use in complex reasoning tasks."

Emotions: The trunk lines for the circuits controlling emotion are laid down before birth. Then parents take over. Perhaps the strongest influence is what psychiatrist Daniel Stern calls attunement—whether caregivers "play back a child's inner feelings." If a baby's squeal of delight at a puppy is met with a smile and hug, if her excitement at seeing a plane overhead is mirrored, circuits for these emotions are reinforced. Apparently, the brain uses the same pathways to generate an emotion as to respond to one. So if an emotion is reciprocated, the electrical and chemical signals that produced it are reinforced. But if emotions are repeatedly met with indifference or a clashing response—Baby is proud of building a skyscraper out of Mom's best pots, and Mom is terminally annoyed—those circuits become confused and fail to strengthen. The key here is "repeatedly": one dismissive harrumph will not scar a child for life. It's the pattern that counts, and it can be very powerful: in one of Stern's studies, a baby whose mother never matched her level of excitement became extremely passive, unable to feel excitement or joy.

Experience can also wire the brain's "calm down" circuit, as Daniel Goleman describes in his best-selling "Emotional Intelligence." One father gently soothes his crying infant, another drops him into his crib; one mother hugs the toddler who just skinned her knee, another screams "It's your own stupid fault!" The first responses are attuned to the child's distress; the others are wildly out of emotional sync. Between 10 and 18 months, a cluster of cells in the rational prefrontal cortex is busy hooking up to the emotion regions. The circuit seems to grow into a control switch, able to calm agitation by infusing reason into emotion. Perhaps parental soothing trains this circuit, strengthening the neural connections that form it, so that the child learns how to calm herself down. This all happens so early that the effects of nurture can be misperceived as innate nature.

Stress and constant threats also rewire emotion circuits. These circuits are centered on the amygdala, a little almond-shaped structure deep in the brain whose job is to scan incoming sights and sounds for emotional content. According to a wiring diagram worked out by Joseph LeDoux of New York University, impulses from eye and ear reach the amygdala before they get to the rational, thoughtful neocortex. If a sight, sound or experience has proved painful before—Dad's drunken arrival home was followed by a beating—then the amygdala floods the circuits with neurochemicals before the higher brain knows what's happening. The more often this pathway is used, the easier it is to trigger: the mere memory of Dad may induce fear. Since the circuits can stay excited for days, the brain remains on high alert. In this state, says neuroscientist Bruce Perry of Baylor College of Medicine, more circuits attend to nonverbal cues—facial expressions, angry noises—that warn of impending danger. As a result, the cortex falls behind in development and has trouble assimilating complex information such as language.

Movement: Fetal movements begin at 7 weeks and peak between the 15th and 17th weeks. That is when regions of the brain controlling movement start to wire up. The critical period lasts a while: it takes up to two years for cells in the cerebellum, which controls posture and movement, to form functional circuits. "A lot of organization takes place using information gleaned from when the child moves about in the world," says William Greenough of the University of Illinois. "If you restrict activity you inhibit the formation of synaptic connections in the cerebellum." The child's initially spastic movements send a signal to the brain's motor cortex; the more the arm, for instance, moves, the stronger the circuit, and the better the brain will become at moving the arm intentionally and fluidly. The window lasts only a few years: a child immobilized in a body cast until the age of 4 will learn to walk eventually, but never smoothly.

THERE ARE MANY MORE CIRcuits to discover, and many more environmental influences to pin down. Still, neuro labs are filled with an unmistakable air of optimism these days. It stems from a growing understanding of how, at the level of nerve cells and molecules, the brain's circuits form. In the beginning, the brain-to-be consists of only a few advance scouts breaking trail: within a week of conception they march out of the embryo's "neural tube," a cylinder of cells extending from head to tail. Multiplying as they go (the brain adds an astonishing 250,000 neurons per minute during gestation), the neurons clump into the brain stem which commands heartbeat and breathing, build the little cerebellum at the back of the head which controls posture and movement, and form the grooved and rumpled cortex wherein thought and perception originate. The neural cells are so small, and the distance so great, that a neuron striking out for what will be the prefrontal cortex migrates a distance equivalent to a human's walking from New York to California, says developmental neurobiologist Mary Beth Hatten of Rockefeller University.

Only when they reach their destinations do these cells become true neurons. They grow a fiber called an axon that carries electrical signals. The axon might reach only to a neuron next door, or it might wend its way clear across to the other side of the brain. It is the axonal connections that form the brain's circuits. Genes determine the main highways along which axons travel to make their connection. But to reach particular target cells, axons follow chemical cues strewn along their path. Some of these chemicals attract: this way to the motor cortex! Some repel: no, *that* way to the olfactory cortex. By the fifth month of gestation most axons have reached their general destination. But like the prettiest girl in the bar, target cells attract way more suitors—axons—than they can accommodate.

How does the wiring get sorted out? The baby neurons fire electrical pulses once a minute, in a fit of what Berkeley's Shatz calls auto-dialing. If cells fire together, the target cells "ring" together. The target cells then release a flood of chemicals, called trophic factors, that strengthen the incipient connections. Active neurons respond better to trophic factors than inactive ones, Barbara Barres of Stanford University reported in October. So neurons that are quiet when others throb lose their grip on the target cell. "Cells that fire together wire together," says Shatz.

The same basic process continues after birth. Now, it is not an auto-dialer that sends signals, but stimuli from the senses. In experiments with rats, Illinois's Greenough found that animals raised with playmates and toys and other stimuli grow 25 percent more synapses than rats deprived of such stimuli.

Rats are not children, but all evidence suggests that the same rules of brain development hold. For decades Head Start has fallen short of the high hopes invested in it: the children's IQ gains fade after about three years. Craig Ramey of the University of Alabama suspected the culprit was timing: Head Start enrolls 2-, 3-, and 4-year-olds. So in 1972 he launched the Abecedarian Project.

Children from 20 poor families were assigned to one of four groups: intensive early education in a day-care center from about 4 months to age 8, from 4 months to 5 years, from 5 to 8 years, or none at all. What does it mean to "educate" a 4-month-old? Nothing fancy: blocks, beads, talking to him, playing games such as peek-a-boo. As outlined in the book "Learningames,"* each of the 200-odd activities was designed to enhance cognitive, language, social or motor development. In a recent paper, Ramey and Frances Campbell of the University of North Carolina report that children enrolled in Abecedarian as preschoolers still scored higher in math and reading at the age of 15 than untreated children. The children still retained an average IQ edge of 4.6 points. The earlier the children were enrolled, the more enduring the gain. And intervention after age 5 conferred no IQ or academic benefit.

All of which raises a troubling question. If the windows of the mind close, for the most part, before we're out of elementary school, is all hope lost for children whose parents did not have them count beads to stimulate their math circuits, or babble to them to build their language loops? At one level, no: the brain retains the ability to learn throughout life, as witness anyone who was befuddled by Greek in college only to master

it during retirement. But on a deeper level the news is sobering. Children whose neural circuits are not stimulated before kindergarten are never going to be what they could have been. "You want to say that it is never too late," says Joseph Sparling, who designed the Abecedarian curriculum. "But there seems to be something very special about the early years."

And yet . . . there is new evidence that certain kinds of intervention can reach even the older brain and, like a microscopic screwdriver, rewire broken circuits. In January, scientists led by Paula Tallal of Rutgers University and Michael Merzenich of UC San Francisco described a study of children who have "language-based learning disabilities"—reading problems. LLD affects 7 million children in the United States. Tallal has long argued that LLD arises from a child's inability to distinguish short, staccato sounds—such as "d" and "b." Normally, it takes neurons in the auditory cortex something like .015 second to respond to a signal from the ear, calm down and get ready to respond to the next sound; in LLD children, it takes five to 10 times as long. (Merzenich speculates that the defect might be the result of chronic middle-ear infections in infancy: the brain never "hears" sounds clearly and so fails to draw a sharp auditory map.) Short sounds such as "b" and "d" go by too

fast—.04 second—to process. Unable to associate sounds with letters, the children develop reading problems.

The scientists drilled the 5- to 10-year-olds three hours a day with computer-produced sound that draws out short consonants, like an LP played too slow. The result: LLD children who were one to three years behind in language ability improved by a full two years after only four weeks. The improvement has lasted. The training, Merzenich suspect, redrew the wiring diagram in the children's auditory cortex to process first sounds. Their reading problems vanished like the sounds of the letters that, before, they never heard.

Such neural rehab may be the ultimate payoff of the discovery that the experiences of life are etched in the bumps and squiggles of the brain. For now, it is enough to know that we are born with a world of potential—potential that will be realized only if it is tapped. And that is challenge enough.

With MARY HAGER

*Joseph Sparling and Isabelle Lewis
(226 pages. Walker. $8.95).

Changing Demographics: Past and Future Demands for Early Childhood Programs

Donald J. Hernandez

Donald J. Hernandez, Ph.D., is chief of the Marriage and Family Statistics Branch of the U.S. Bureau of the Census.

Abstract

This article provides a historical analysis of how demographic changes in the organization of American family life from the mid-1800s to the present have shaped the demand for programs to complement the efforts of families to educate and care for their children. The author asserts that the United States is in the midst of a second child care revolution. The first occurred in the late 1800s, when families left farming to enable fathers to take jobs in urban areas and when compulsory free public schooling was established for children age six and above. The second has developed over the past 55 years as the proportion of children under six living in families with two wage earners or a single working parent has escalated and propelled more and more young children into the early childhood care and education programs discussed throughout this journal issue.

Looking to the future, the author sees indications that the demand for early childhood care and education programs will continue to grow while the needs of the children to be served will become increasingly diverse. To meet these dual pressures, the author argues that public funding for early childhood programs—like funding for public schools—is justified by the value such programs have for the broader society.

Today's children are the adults—the parents, workers, and citizen's—of tomorrow. Yet while they learn and develop the abilities they will need later in life, children depend almost entirely upon adults to meet their needs and to make decisions on their behalf. Key among those are decisions about the roles parents and children will take on both inside and outside the home. This article takes a historical look at how changing patterns of employment among parents have been linked to changes in children's attendance at school and out-of-home child care programs like those discussed throughout this issue.

During the past 150 years, the family economy was revolutionized twice, as fathers and then mothers left the home to spend much of the day away at jobs as family breadwinners. With these changes, with instability in fathers' work, and with increasing divorce and out-of-wedlock childbearing, never during the past half century were a majority of children born into "Ozzie and Harriet" families in which the father worked full time year round, the mother was a full-time homemaker, and all of the children were born after the parents' only marriage. Corresponding revolutions in child care occurred, as children age six and over, and then younger children, began to spend increasing amounts of time in school or in the care of someone other than their parents.

This article reviews each of these revolutions to clarify the factors that lie behind the growing demand for out-of-home programs to serve preschool-age children, drawing on census and survey data charting a wide array of family and economic changes from the mid-1800s to the present.[1] It addresses the following questions:

1. To what extent have young children experienced a decline in parental time potentially available for their care?

2. How have increasing employment among mothers and the rise in one-parent families contributed to the decline in parental availability to care for children at home?

3. What major demographic and family trends are responsible for increasing employment of mothers and for one-parent family living?

From *The Future of Children*, Winter 1995, pp. 145-160. © 1995 by the Center for the Future of Children of the David and Lucile Packard Foundation. Reprinted by permission. *The Future of Children* journals and executive summaries are available free of charge by faxing mailing information to: Circulation Department (650) 948-6498.

4. How may demographic trends influence the demand for child care during the coming decades?

5. What lessons from the first child care revolution—compulsory public schooling—can guide child care policy today?

The focus on historical changes as experienced by children provides a unique vantage point for understanding the child care revolution young children are now experiencing and for speculating about what the future may hold.

The Decline in Parental Availability for Child Care

The daily experiences young children have at home, in school, or in child care depend in important ways on the composition of their families. In the middle of the twentieth century, most children under the age of six lived in breadwinner-homemaker families, that is, in two-parent families where the father worked outside the home to support the family, and the mother could care for the children at home because she was not in the paid labor force. In 1940, 87% of young children (throughout this article, the term "young children" refers to children under the age of six) had a nonemployed parent who

could provide full-time care. By 1989, however, the same could be said of only 48% of children under six.

This dramatic decline resulted from the growing prevalence of dual-earner families and one-parent families with an employed head. As Figure 1 shows, between 1940 and 1989, the percentage of young children living in dual-earner families (that is, two-parent families with both parents in the labor force) increased sevenfold, from 5% to 38%. During the same period, the proportion of children living with a lone parent who worked increased fivefold, from 2% to 13%. In about half the families, the parents worked full time; in the others, one or both parents worked part time. Together, the trends toward dual-earner households and one-parent families increased by 43 percentage points the proportion of young children who did not have a parent at home who could provide full-time care. From 1940 to 1989, the percentage of children under six who needed alternative child care arrangements rose from 8% to 51%.

About three-fourths of the increased demand for child care was accounted for by dual-earner families, and the remaining one-fourth stemmed from one-parent families with working parents. Because the growing demand for child care for preschool-age children is rooted in the new prevalence of

dual-earner families and one-parent employed families, an understanding of what the future may hold must rest upon an examination of the earlier historical changes that led to these transformations in the family lives of children.

The Revolutionary Increase in Mothers' Employment

The proportion of young children with employed mothers jumped from about 7% in 1940 to 43% in 1980. Since then it increased again to 51% in 1990, but no further change had occurred as of 1993.[2] The explanation for much of this increase in mothers' employment after 1940 can be found in earlier historic changes that occurred in fathers' work and family residence, in family size, and in children's school attendance and educational attainment. Each of those factors paved the way for the growing participation of mothers in the paid labor force.

Fathers' Increasing Nonfarm Work

For hundreds of years, agriculture and the two-parent farm family were the primary forms of economic production and family organization in Western countries. On the family farm, economic production, parenting, and child care were combined as parents and children worked together to support themselves. This life pattern changed with the Industrial Revolution, however. Families moved to urban areas, and childhood was transformed in unprecedented ways. Fathers in urban families spent much of the day away from home working at jobs to earn the income required to support their families, while mothers remained at home to care for their children and to perform other household chores.

The shift away from farming, when it occurred, was very rapid. Figure 2 provides a historical view of the likelihood that children would live in each of four basic family types between 1790 and the present. Between 1830 and 1930, the proportion of children living in two-parent farm families dropped from about 70% to only 30%, while the proportion living in nonfarm families with breadwinner fathers and homemaker mothers jumped from 15% to 55%. The shift from farming to urban occupations enabled many families to improve their relative economic status because comparatively favorable economic opportunities existed in urban areas. Urban jobs generated incomes higher than many people could earn through farming, and, given the precarious economic situations faced by many rural families, even poorly paid or dangerous jobs in urban areas were attractive.

Falling Family Size

The massive migration to urban areas was accompanied by a dramatic decline in family size. Figure 3 depicts the number of siblings

Figure 1

Children Ages 0 to 5 Years in Dual-Earner Families and One-Parent Families with an Employed Parent, 1940–1989

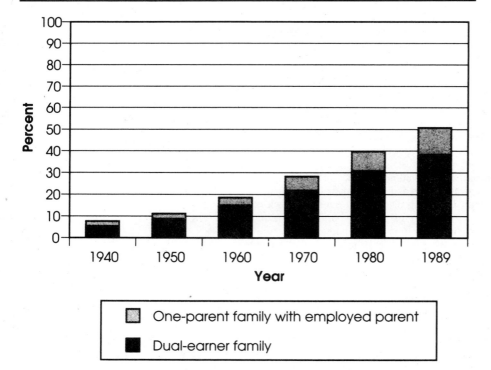

Source: Hernandez, D. J. *America's Children: Resources from family, government, and the economy.* New York: Russell Sage Foundation, 1993, Table 5.2. Reprinted by permission of the Russell Sage Foundation.

Figure 2

Children Ages 0 to 17 Years in Farm Families, Father-as-Breadwinner Families, and Dual-Earner Families, 1790–1989

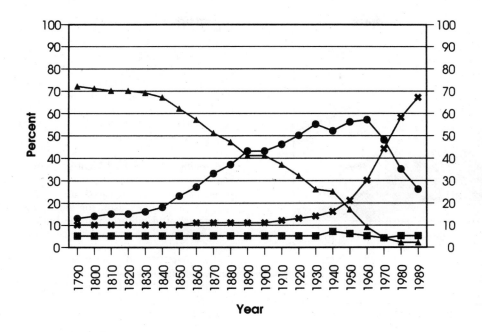

Year

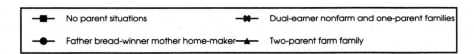

- ■ No parent situations
- ● Father bread-winner mother home-maker
- ✕ Dual-earner nonfarm and one-parent families
- ▲ Two-parent farm family

Estimates are for 10-year intervals to 1980, and for 1989.

Source: Hernandez, D. J. *America's Children: Resources from family, government, and the economy*. New York: Russell Sage Foundation, 1993, p. 103. Reprinted by permission of the Russell Sage Foundation.

in typical families from 1865 to the present. Among children born in 1865, 82% lived in families with five or more children, but only 30% of those born in 1930 had such large families. The median number of siblings in a typical family dropped from more than seven siblings to only two or three.

Parents may have restricted themselves to a small number of children for reasons of household economics. Moving from the farm to urban areas meant that housing, food, clothing, and other necessities had to be paid for with cash, so the costs of supporting additional children became increasingly apparent. Also, as economic growth led to increases in the quality and quantity of available consumer products and services, expected consumption standards rose. Individuals had to spend more money simply to maintain the standard of living they considered normal, and their rising expectations also increased the costs of supporting each additional child at a "normal" level.

Meanwhile, the economic contribution that children could make to their parents and families was sharply reduced by the passage of laws restricting child labor. More and more parents limited their families to a comparatively small number of children, ensuring that available family income could be spread less thinly and that the family's expected standard of living could be maintained.

Increasing Schooling and Educational Attainments

A third revolutionary change in children's lives resulted from the enormous increase in school enrollment and educational attainments that took place between 1870 and 1940. As farming was overshadowed by an industrial economy in which fathers worked for pay at jobs located away from home, the economic role of children also changed with the enactment of compulsory school attendance and child labor laws. School enrollment rates jumped sharply. In 1870, about 50% of children 5 through 19 years old were enrolled in school. By 1940, 95% of children 7 through 13 years old were enrolled, as were 79% of children 14 through 17. The

length of the school year also increased over that period. The number of days that enrolled students spent in school doubled from 21% to 42% of the total days in the year, or 59% of the nonweekend days. This represented a dramatic change in how children who were six or over spent much of their waking time.

Why did parents send their children to school in greater numbers and for longer periods? There are several plausible explanations. School enrollments increased during the period when laws limiting child labor were passed. Labor unions sought these laws to ensure that jobs would be available for adults (mainly fathers), while the child welfare movement sought them to protect children from unsafe and unfair working conditions. Compulsory education laws supported by the same movements led to universal schooling that was mandated and paid for by local governments.

In addition, as time passed, higher educational attainments were needed to obtain jobs with higher incomes and greater prestige. Hence, parents encouraged their children's educational attainments as a path to achieving economic success in adulthood. Because the children of today are the parents of tomorrow, this enormous increase in schooling led to significant later increases in the education levels of parents. For example, as Figure 4 shows, only 15% of children born in 1920 had fathers who had completed four years of high school, compared with 39% of those born in 1940. Levels of education among mothers increased as well. By 1940, fully 44% of young children had mothers with four years of high school education. Today, more than 80% of adolescents have parents who completed at least four years of high school.

Explaining the Increasing Employment of Mothers

How did the historic shifts toward nonfarm work, urban residence, smaller families, and increased educational attainments that took place between the Industrial Revolution and about 1940 lead to increased employment by mothers? One explanation focuses on efforts parents made to maintain, improve, or regain their economic standing relative to other families.

Until about 1940, three major avenues were open to parents who wanted to improve their economic standing. First, they could move off the farm to allow the husband to work in a better-paid job in the growing urban-industrial economy. Second, they could limit themselves to a smaller number of children so that available family income could be spread less thinly. Third, they could increase their educational attainments so as to be qualified to enter well-paid occupations. By 1940, however, most families had already taken these steps. Only 23% of Americans still lived on farms; 70% of parents had only

Figure 3

Actual and Expected Sibsizes for Children Born from 1865 through 1994

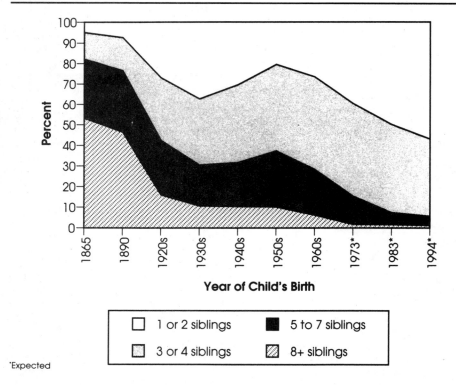

Year of Child's Birth

- ☐ 1 or 2 siblings
- ▨ 3 or 4 siblings
- ■ 5 to 7 siblings
- ▧ 8+ siblings

*Expected

Source: Hernandez, D. J. *America's Children: Resources from family, government, and the economy.* New York: Russell Sage Foundation, 1993, p. 34. Reprinted by permission of the Russell Sage Foundation.

one or two dependent children in the home; and adults beyond age 25 often found it difficult or impractical to pursue additional schooling. Consequently, for many parents, these historical avenues for improving their economic standing had run their course.

A fourth major avenue to increasing family income emerged between 1940 and 1960, namely, paid work by wives and mothers. The traditional supply of female nonfarm labor—unmarried women—was limited, while the war effort and the economic boom created an escalating demand for additional female workers.[3] Meanwhile, mothers also were becoming more available and qualified for work outside the home. By 1940, the enrollment of children over six in school had released mothers with school-age children from child care responsibilities for about two-thirds of a full-time workday, and for about two-thirds of a full-time work year. In addition, many women were highly educated because compulsory, free schooling applied to girls as well as boys and the educational attainments of women had increased along with those of men. By 1940, young women were more likely than young men to graduate from high school, and they were about two-thirds as likely to graduate from college.

Paid work for mothers was becoming increasingly attractive both as an economic advantage in a competitive, consumption-oriented society and as a hedge against possible economic disaster. Families with two earners could jump ahead economically of many families with only a single earner.[4] Moreover, a woman of 24 could look forward to about 40 years during which she could work for pay to help support her family. Additional motivations that drew many wives and mothers into the labor force included the personal nonfinancial rewards of working, the opportunity to be productively involved with other adults, and career satisfactions for those who entered a high-prestige occupation. In addition, the historic rise in divorce (discussed below) made paid work attractive to mothers who feared they might lose most or all of their husband's income through divorce.

Economic insecurity among families in which the fathers faced low wages or joblessness made mothers' work virtually essential. Many families experienced economic insecurity and need when widespread unemployment prevailed during the Great Depression. In 1940, 40% of children lived with fathers who did not work full time year round. While this proportion declined after the Great Depression, it has continued at high levels. Throughout the past 50 years, at least one-fifth of children have lived with fathers who, during any given year, experienced part-time work or joblessness. This has been a powerful incentive for many mothers to work for pay.

The Rising Number of Mother-Only Families

In addition to increasing employment among mothers, a second reason for the decline in parental availability to provide full-time child care lies in the new prevalence of one-parent, working-parent families that became evident after 1960, 20 years after the rise in dual-earner families began. Most one-parent families are mother-child families, created through separation, divorce, or out-of-wedlock childbearing. By 1993, about 24% of young children lived in mother-child families (another 4% lived with their fathers only). In about half those families, the parent worked: 12% of young children lived with a lone working mother, and an added 3% lived with a lone working father. A number of earlier changes in family life help explain these revolutionary changes in family structure.

High Rates of Divorce

As Figure 5 shows, a remarkably steady rise in rates of divorce is evident between the 1860s and the 1960s, resulting in an eightfold increase during the century. (See also the Spring 1994 issue of *The Future of Children,* which focused on Children and Divorce).[5] One way of explaining this long-term increase focuses on the role the family plays as an economic unit. On preindustrial farms, fathers and mothers had to work together to sustain the family, but with a nonfarm job, the father could depend on his own work alone for his income. He could leave his family but keep his income. And, at the same time as urban employment weakened the economic interdependence of husbands and wives, by moving to urban areas families also left behind the rural small-town social controls that once censured divorce.

By 1993, about 24% of young children lived in mother-child families; in about half those families, the parent worked.

Figure 4

Proportion of Children Born Between the 1920s and the 1980s Where Parents Have Specified Education Attainment

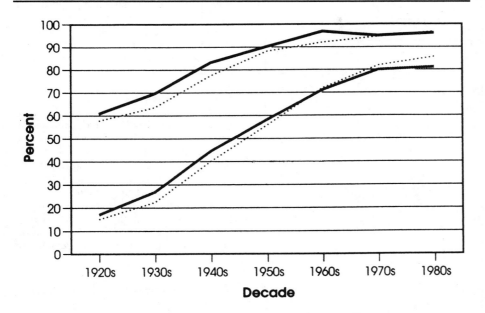

Legend:
— Mother eight or more years of schooling   ▬ Mother four years of high school or more

··· Father eight or more years of schooling   ··· Father four years of high school or more

Source: Hernandez, D. J. *America's Children: Resources from family, government, and the economy.* New York: Russell Sage Foundation, 1993, p. 197. Reprinted by permission of the Russell Sage Foundation.

In addition, recent research suggests that the economic insecurity and need that result from erratic or limited employment prospects for men can also increase hostility between husbands and wives, decrease marital quality, and increase the risk of divorce.[6–8] In fact, during each of the three economic recessions that occurred between 1970 and 1982, the proportion of mother-only families increased substantially more than during the preceding nonrecessionary period. Those recessions can account for about 30% of the overall increase in mother-child families between 1968 and 1988 or for about 50% of the increase in families headed by separated or divorced mothers.[1]

Stresses on Black Families

Between 1940 and 1960, black children experienced much larger increases than white children in the proportion who lived in a mother-child family with a divorced or separated mother. The factors that led to increased separation and divorce were similar among whites and among blacks—movement off the farm and exposure to economic insecurity. Those forces affected black families with special intensity, however. The proportion of blacks living on farms dropped precipitously during the 20-year period between 1940 and 1960. In 1940, 44% of black children lived on farms, while by 1960, this figure had plummeted to only 11%. This startling drop and the extraordinary economic pressures and hardships faced by black families may account for the fact that a much higher proportion of black children than white children came to live in mother-child families.[1]

In addition, especially since 1970, black children have experienced extremely large increases in the proportion who live with a never-married mother. One explanation for this difference is offered by William Julius Wilson, who points out that unemployment among young males makes marriage less likely and so contributes to the rate of births that occur out of wedlock.[9] Calculations using survey data show that in 1955 there was little difference in rates of joblessness for young black and young white men. However, by 1976–1989, white men 16 to 24 years old were 15 to 25 percentage points more likely to be employed than were black men of the same ages.[1] The large and rapid drop in the ability of black men in the main family-building ages to secure employment and provide significant support to a family appears to have depressed marriage rates. Many young black women may be reluctant to initiate a marriage that would likely be temporary and unrewarding, instead choosing to bear children out of wedlock.

Summary

In short, the growing reliance of American families on nonparental child care is rooted in several historical changes. First was the revolutionary increase in mothers' labor force participation that occurred during the past half-century. By 1940, many mothers were potentially available for work, and mothers' work had become the only major avenue available to most couples over age 25 who sought to improve their relative social and economic status. Parents had earlier limited themselves to smaller families and moved off the farm so that fathers could work at better-paid jobs in urban areas. Increasing rates of school attendance by children six years old and over freed many mothers from the need to stay home, and, over time, public schooling increased the educational attainments of young women and made them better qualified as employees. After 1940, not only was there an increasing economic demand for married women to enter the labor force, they also faced the need to work and experienced the attractions of work.

In addition, the proportion of young children living in one-parent, working-parent families has increased substantially since 1960. Underlying this increase are sharply rising rates of divorce and out-of-wedlock childbearing. The incomes of working women helped to weaken the economic interdependence between husbands and wives, setting the stage for a historic rise in rates of separation and divorce. The experience of economic insecurity associated with fathers' part-time work, joblessness, or difficulties finding employment also made marriage less at-

By 1989 about 40% of preschoolers spent considerable time in the care of someone other than their parents while the parents worked.

Figure 5

Divorces per 1,000 Married Women 15 Years Old and Over, 1860–1990

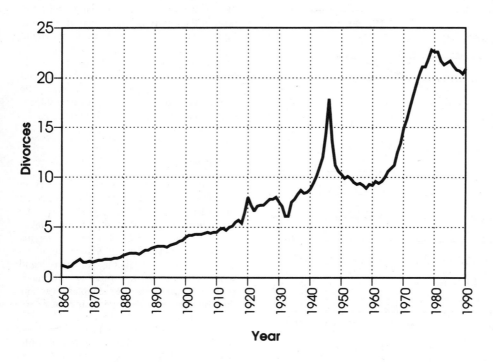

Source: Jacobson, P. H. *American Marriage and Divorce.* New York: Rinehart, 1950; U.S. National Center for Health Statistics. *Advance report of final divorce statistics,* 1988, vol. 39, no. 12, supplement 2. Washington, DC: USNCHS, 1991.

tractive and less sustainable for many families.

The consequence of all these trends is the fact that today most children live either in dual-earner families in which both parents work at jobs away from home or in one-parent families. As a result, a growing proportion of children under six need care by people other than their parents for a significant portion of the day.

Demographic Trends: Implications for Child Care

The family and economic circumstances in which children live have important implications for the development of early childhood programs. By 1989, although about 12% of children lived in dual-earner families in which the parents worked different hours or days and could personally care for their children, about 40% of preschoolers spent considerable time in the care of someone other than their parents while the parents worked. If mothers' labor force participation continues to rise, the demand for non-parental child care will rise with it.

Continued Growth in the Demand for Child Care

The revolutionary increase in mothers' labor force participation during the past half-century led to enormous increases in nonparental care of young children. Looking to the future, between 1992 and 2005, the labor force participation rate for women between the ages of 25 and 54 is projected to increase from 75% to 83%.[10] Continued increases in rates of employment among women are likely to lead to a further decline in the availability of mothers who can be home to provide full-time care for their children.

The rising prevalence of one-parent families also is likely to continue. The divorce rate reached a peak in 1979 and declined

slightly thereafter, but the graph in Figure 5 shows that the divorce rate remains extremely high by historical standards. Meanwhile, the proportion of births occurring out of wedlock continues to increase at a steady pace. If this trend persists, the proportion of children in one-parent families with working parents will rise even further.

Some families headed by single mothers with limited labor force participation have been able to rely financially on public assistance through the Aid to Families with Dependent Children (AFDC) program. Most current welfare reform proposals, however, aim to increase labor force participation among AFDC recipients. If such reforms are enacted and if they successfully increase employment rates, there will be a corresponding increase in the need for non-parental child care for children of these mothers.[11]

As a result of all these demographic and policy changes, the need for nonparental child care for children in one-parent, working-parent families is likely to continue to rise.

Characteristics of the Children Who Will Need Child Care

This article has focused thus far on how family and economic change is increasing the demand for nonparental child care. But the changing family life of children can also influence the nature and content of the care that children will need. Ongoing demographic trends suggest that, in the coming decades, early childhood programs will be serving a population of children which is increasingly diverse in economic resources, racial and ethnic background, and family structure.

Increasing Economic Inequality
Economic well-being can be viewed in terms of absolute levels of family income or in terms of relative economic standing compared with other families. Economists from Adam Smith to John Kenneth Galbraith have argued that poverty must be defined in terms of contemporary standards of living.[12] In Galbraith's words, " . . . people are poverty-stricken when their income, even if adequate for survival, falls markedly behind that of the community."

In an absolute sense, real income levels and living standards rose dramatically between 1940 and 1973, as median family in-

The proportion of children under age 18 who are white is projected to decline steadily and rapidly, from 69% in 1990 to only 50% in 2030.

Figure 6

Distribution of Children Ages 0 to 5 Years by Relative Income Levels, 1939–1988

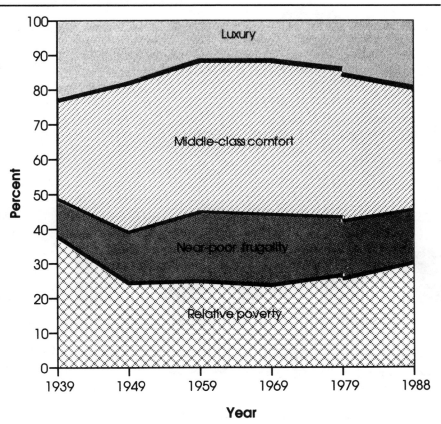

Lines separating areas appear broken at 1979 to account for the change from using Decennial Census poverty data to current Population Survey poverty data.

Source: Hernandez, D. J. *America's Children: Resources from family, government, and the economy.* New York: Russell Sage Foundation, 1993, p. 260. Reprinted by permission of the Russell Sage Foundation.

come more than doubled, although it has changed comparatively little since then. Since 1959, however, economic expansion has done little to reduce the uneven distribution of income across families, and since 1969, economic inequality had increased. To examine the income distribution, families can be classified as living in relative poverty; near-poor fugality, middle-class comfort, or luxury, based on income thresholds set at 50%, 75%, and 150% of median family income in specific years and adjusted for family size.[1]

Figure 6 is a graph showing the distribution of children into these income categories from 1939 to 1988. This measure shows that the proportion of young children from birth to five years living in relative poverty dropped from a high of 38% after the Great Depression to remain at less than 25% from 1949 through 1979, before it jumped to 30% in 1988 and 33% in 1993. Another 15% of children in 1988 and 1993 lived in near-poor frugality. At the opposite extreme, the pro-

portion of young children in families with luxury level incomes declined from 23% in 1939 to about 12% in the 1950s, before increasing to 20% in 1988 and to 23% in 1993. The years from 1969 to 1993 saw a significant decline in middle class comfort, as more and more children lived at the extremes of luxury and poverty.

In other words, the past 25 years—when the demand for nonparental child care was growing fastest—also brought a substantial expansion in economic inequality among families. As a result, the quantitative increases in the total need for nonparental care during the past quarter-century have been accompanied by increased qualitative differences in the educational needs of the children who enter child care.

In families with higher incomes, parents can usually afford to provide resources and educational experiences that foster the development of their children, while children from poor homes rely more on child care and preschool programs to provide those ex-

periences.[13] As a result, children from families at different income levels may enter child care situations with different needs. In recognition of the unmet developmental needs of many children who live in poverty, for example, the Head Start program adds to its preschool educational activities a comprehensive set of nutritional, health, and social services that are not typically offered to children from more advantaged families.[14] Research, policies, and programs that explicitly address these differences are sorely needed.

Growing Racial and Ethnic Diversity

Race and ethnic origin define another dimension along which it seems likely that educational needs of young children may differ.[15] American children were already quite racially and ethnically diverse as of 1990, when 69% of children under age 18 were white (and not of Hispanic origin), 15% were black, 12% were Hispanic, and 4% were from another racial or ethnic group.

Immigration and differential birthrates across ethnic groups will likely increase that diversity in the coming years. Looking to the future, Figure 7 shows that the proportion of children under age 18 who are white is projected to decline steadily and rapidly, from 69% in 1990 to only 50% in 2030. Conversely, the proportion of all children who are Hispanic or who are black or of another nonwhite race is expected to climb from 31% to 50%.

Poverty, language barriers, and cultural isolation are important factors that influence many nonwhite or Hispanic children, who may have educational needs (and related social needs) that differ from those of white children. As a result, these projections highlight an increasing need to understand these differences through research and to plan new child care policies and programs appropriate to a diverse population of children.[16]

Diverse Family Living Arrangements

Children also vary greatly in their family living arrangements, and this is true separately for children within specific racial and ethnic groups. Even among children under age one, historical data show that, in 1940, 7% of white infants and 25% of black infants lived in a one-parent family or were separated from their parents. By 1980, these rates had doubled to 13% for whites and 54% for blacks. In 1993, the proportion of children under age six with one parent in the home was 21% for whites, 66% for blacks, and 34% for Hispanics.

Recent evidence indicates that, compared with children in two-parent families, children in one-parent families have higher risks of dropping out of high school, bearing children as teenagers, and not being employed by their early twenties. The low incomes and sudden declines in income experienced by children in these families are the most important reason for their disadvantaged out-

Figure 7

Percentage of Children Who Are Non-Hispanic White, Black, and Hispanic, 1980, 1990, and Projected Through 2050

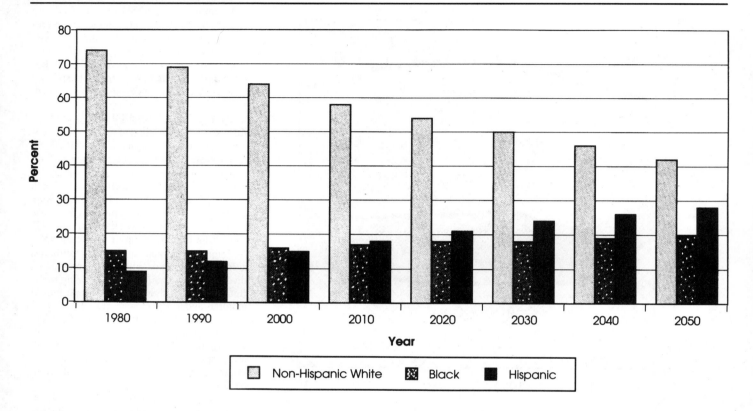

Percentages do not sum to 100 within each year because no bar is included to represent children from other racial or ethnic groups.

Source: U.S. Bureau of the Census. *U.S. Population Estimates by Age, Sex, and Hispanic Origin: 1980–1991.* Current Population Reports, Series P-25, No. 1095. Washington, DC: U.S. Government Printing Office, 1993; U.S. Bureau of the Census. *Population Projections of the United States, by Age, Sex, Race, and Hispanic Origin: 1993–2050.* Current Population Reports, Series P-25, No. 1104. Washington, DC: U.S. Government Printing Office, 1993.

comes, although research suggests that other differences in family life also play a significant role.[17] Children in one-parent families are therefore likely to have educational needs that differ from children in two-parent families and that should be understood and addressed.

Summary

In short, the United States is in the midst of a child care revolution, as more and more young children under the age of six are cared for by someone other than their parents. Broad demographic trends as well as efforts to reform the welfare system are likely to increase rates of labor force participation by mothers with young children, further expanding the demand for nonparental child care. At the same time, the diversity in the characteristics and needs of the nation's children has also increased, particularly in terms of their economic circumstances, their racial and ethnic backgrounds, and their family living arrangements. Child care policies and

programs must be designed to respond to the differing needs of the many children who use them.

Lessons to Guide Child Care Policy

The first child care revolution began more than 100 years ago, and it affected children over age five. Through compulsory education laws, government both mandated and paid for universal schooling for all children age six and over. As time passed, the upper age limit for compulsory schooling was raised, and public funding for schooling increased. This led to enormous improvements in the skills and knowledge of the labor force, thereby contributing to economic development and rising real incomes.

Today, as global economic competition becomes an increasing concern, the United States is in the midst of a second child care revolution, one affecting children under age

six whose parent or parents work. From this perspective, one can see child care as valuable or essential to society at large. It facilitates the work of mothers and their contribution both to their family income and to the economy. The quality of child care may also influence the future international competitiveness of the U.S. economy by fostering the development of productive workers who will support the baby boom generation as it reaches retirement.

When high-quality child care, like the preschool programs that are the subject of this journal issue, leads to improved educational and developmental outcomes for children, it has value not only for the child and the parents, but also for the broader society. Child care is expensive, however. Overall, families with a preschool child who pay for child care devote about 10% of their incomes to child care, but this figure ranges from only 6% for families with annual incomes of $50,000 or more to 23% for families with annual incomes under $15,000.[18] The relative cost of child care as an expense associated with having a job is quite high for low-income families. The question then arises: Should the cost of that care be borne mainly or solely by parents?

The first child care revolution was mandated and paid for by government as a social good in the public interest. Today, evolving economic conditions effectively require that an increasing proportion of mothers work, and proposed welfare reforms will mandate that other mothers of young children find employment to support their families. In this context, it is important that new research inform the public policy debate about the kinds, the costs, and the quality of child care available to the youngest members of American society. Research about the value of child care to children, parents, and society at large may also help inform policy debate about the appropriate role of government in fostering and funding quality care for American children.

The author is indebted to Arthur J. Norton for institutional leadership, scholarly counsel, and personal enthusiasm and encouragement which created an indispensable and nurturing home in the U.S. Bureau of the Census for writing the book which provides the foundation for this article. Thanks are due also to Edith Reeves and Catherine O'Brien for statistical support, and to Stephanie Kennedy for secretarial support. The author bears sole responsibility for the results and opinions presented here.

Notes

1. This article draws especially on research reported in the author's recent book which used census and survey data for 1940, 1950, 1960, 1970, 1980, and 1989 to develop the first-ever statistics using children as the unit of analysis. These data chart a wide array of family and economic changes that affected children from the Great Depression through the 1980s. Additional analyses of previously published data extend the investigation back an additional 150 years. Hernandez, D. J. *America's children: Resources from government, family, and the economy.* New York: Russell Sage Foundation, 1993. This research was also reported in Hernandez, D. J. Children's changing access to resources: A historical perspective. *Social Policy Report* (1993) 8,1:1–23.

2. The precise estimate, of 6% to 8% is obtained from note no. 1, Hernandez, *America's children*, Table 5.2. The estimates for 1980, 1990, and 1993 were provided by the U.S. Bureau of Labor Statistics, Howard Hayghe.

3. Oppenheimer, V. K. *The female labor force in the United States.* Population Monograph Series, No. 5. Berkeley, CA: Institute of international Studies, University of California Press, 1970.

4. Oppenheimer, V. K. *Work and family.* New York: Academic Press, 1982.

5. *The Future of Children* (Spring 1994) 5,1.

6. Conger, R. D., Elder, G. H., Jr., Lorenz, F. O., et al. Linking economic hardship to marital quality and instability. *Journal of Marriage and the Family* (1990) 52:643–56.

7. Conger, R. D., Elder, G. H., Jr., with Lorenz, F. O., Simons, R. L., and Whitbeck, L. B. *Families in troubled times: Adapting to change in rural America.* New York: Aldine de Gruyter, 1994.

8. Liker, J. K., and Elder, G. H., Jr. Economic hardship and marital relations in the 1930s. *American Sociological Review* (1983) 48:343–59.

9. Wilson, W. J. *The truly disadvantaged: The inner city, the underclass, and public policy.* Chicago: University of Chicago Press, 1987.

10. U.S. Department of Labor, Bureau of Labor Statistics. Bulletin 2452. Washington, DC: U.S. Government Printing Office, April 1994, Table A-1.

11. Another important goal of many welfare reform proposals is to reduce out-of-wedlock childbearing, but available evidence suggests that the effect of welfare on out-of-wedlock childbearing is small. For a discussion of the extent to which welfare programs have contributed to the increase in mother-only families, see note no. 1, Hernandez, *America's children,* pp. 291–300.

12. Adam Smith was cited in U.S. Congress. *Alternative measures of poverty.* Staff study prepared for the Joint Economic Committee. Washington, DC, October 18, 1994, p. 10. The quote from Galbraith can be found in Galbraith, J. K. *The affluent society.* Boston: Houghton, Mifflin, 1958, pp. 323–24.

13. For recent studies on the effects for children of poverty and economic inequality, see papers from the Consequences of Growing Up Poor conference, held February 2–3, 1995, at the National Academy of Sciences, organized by the National Institute of Child Health and Development (NICHD) Family and Child Well-Being Network, the Russell Sage Foundation, and the National Academy of Sciences Board on Children and Families.

14. U.S. General Accounting Office. *Early childhood centers: Services to prepare children for school often limited.* GAO/HEHS-95-21. Washington, DC: U.S. GAO, March 1995.

15. For additional discussions of child indicators pertaining to race, ethnicity, and educational needs, see Lewit, E. M. and Baker, L. G. Race and ethnicity—changes for children. *The Future of Children* (Winter 1994) 4,3:134–44.

16. Phillips, D., and Crowell, N. A., eds. *Cultural diversity and early education.* Washington, DC: National Academy Press, 1994.

17. McLanahan, S., and Sandefur, G. *Growing up with a single parent: What hurts, what helps.* Cambridge, MA: Harvard University Press, 1994.

18. Hofferth, S. L., Brayfield, A., Deich, S., and Holcomb, P. *National Child Care Survey.* 1990. Washington, DC: Urban Institute Press, 1991.

Parents Speak:

Zero to Three's Findings from Research on Parents' Views of Early Childhood Development

Matthew Melmed

How much do parents of babies and toddlers know about their children's intellectual, social, and emotional development at the earliest ages? What are parents doing to encourage healthy development of their babies in these interrelated domains? Zero to Three commissioned a study that included focus groups and a national poll to determine what parents know and believe about early childhood development, where they go for information and support, and how receptive they are to new information.

Both the focus groups and the poll revealed that parents have much less knowledge and information about their children's emotional, intellectual, and social development than they do about their physical development. Parents thirst for more information on how to promote their young children's healthy development.

As new findings in brain research emerge (see *Young Children*, May 1997, pp. 4–9), they should provide a major impetus for parents to understand their own ability to im-

Matthew Melmed is executive director of ZERO TO THREE: National Center for Infants, Toddlers and Families (formerly the National Center for Clinical Infant Programs), a national organization dedicated to advancing the healthy development of babies and young children that is based in Washington, D.C.

prove their children's lives and indeed to show all of us—parents, grandparents, other relatives, educators, child care providers, employers, policy-makers, and others—how we can positively impact children's development. Crafting such messages effectively requires knowledge of what parents know and value about early childhood development. Following are the major conclusions of our research, designed to address these questions.

1. Although parents recognize the importance of early childhood, they do not see its full significance.

There is much progress to be made to convince parents of babies that the period from birth to age three is *particularly* significant and provides a unique opportunity for growth and learning. In our study, parents said they felt that all of childhood is important, but they saw birth to three as important years of child development only in general terms and within limits. These parents lack much of the new information that can help them as their child's first teacher. The focus group parents understood that babies need more than love—including stimulation, consistency, and sense of security—but they were mostly unaware of the depth of their influences on their babies' long-term development.

2. Parents feel most able to impact babies' emotional development.

Our inquiry looked at attitudes and knowledge in three developmental domains: intellectual, emotional, and social. Of the three, *emotional development may be the area in which parents believe they can have the most impact.* The parents in our research groups stressed the importance of making babies feel secure and loved from the very beginning. They said babies' feelings can be hurt and that babies read and interpret their parents' and other people's emotional cues.

The national poll found that 39% of parents felt they had the greatest influence over their child's emotional development as compared to the child's intellectual (19%) or social (16%) development. However, one out of every four parents report having the least information on how a child develops emotionally.

3. Laying down a foundation for social growth in the early years is not seen as critical.

When it comes to social development, the attitudes expressed by the parents in this study were quite different. Parents were often unsure that what happens to a child from birth to age three has long-term impact on social development. They see *social development as an area where a child can "catch up,"* and they feel that this area is less crucial than the other domains.

4. Parents may not recognize their power to shape their child's intellectual development.

The parents in this study said their young children are always learning. Yet the parents felt *less able to impact intellectual development than any other area of childhood development.* The parents described intellectual development as a process of absorption rather than as a process of *creation* of more capacity or development of cognitive abilities, as suggested by emerging brain research. Some said that an unstimulating environment does not deny a child intellectual development, because much of the intellectual self is "nature" not "nurture."

The poll revealed that only 44% of the parents felt totally sure that they could tell if their infant or toddler's intellectual development was on track. Parents (53%) were more certain about signs to watch for to see if their child's physical develop-

ment was on track; 37% felt this way about milestones of social development and 38% about emotional development.

5. Caregiver continuity and consistency is a hot-button issue for many parents.

According to research, the individuals with whom an infant or toddler spends the most time play a critical role in that child's emotional, social, and intellectual development, and limiting the number of caregivers is important for creating strong relationships that form the basis of learning. Yet the focus groups found limiting the number of caregivers is a hot-button issue with parents. The suggestion that either the consistency or a limited number of caregivers really matters made some parents—particularly those with multiple child care arrangements—feel uncomfortable, guilty, or nervous. These feelings unfortunately may lead to some of these parents rejecting the notion that caregivers have important relationships with babies. Some parents believe that if a child has a stable home life, whatever happens during child care may not be as important.

The poll found that caregivers other than these mothers or fathers played a major role in the lives of their young children. Only one in five babies or toddlers were cared for since birth exclusively by a parent; 60% of babies and toddlers are currently cared for on a regular basis by someone other than their parents. Half of all parents surveyed thought that the more caregivers a child has before age three, the better that child will be at adapting and coping with change.

6. Get parents the good news early on about the opportunity of children's first three years.

The parents in the focus groups made it clear that they learned about child development *on the job* as parents. It is important to raise the consciousness of parents *before* they have children or when their babies are very young. Reaching parents early may avoid having to battle guilt feelings of parents who feel they have failed if they took few steps to enhance their child's development before the age of two or three.

Parental guilt and denial could thwart efforts to increase parents' involvement in their children's early development. Learning that the period from birth to age three is extremely important in child development and that parents can actively influence it is not good news for those parents who feel they have missed the boat. It is motivating, on the other hand, to new and expectant parents.

7. Parents want specific information on what they can do with their child.

These results suggest that many parents of young children may need guidance if they are to maximize experiences in the early years. What

---

Sources of Data and Further Information

Zero to Three used two different research methodologies—focus groups and in-depth telephone surveys—to collect information from parents of very young children.

Focus groups— The public opinion research firm Belden and Russonello conducted eight focus groups with parents of children younger than age three and expectant parents, exploring their knowledge and perceptions of child development. Held between October 1996 and February 1997, the groups convened parents of varying levels of education and income, segmented by gender and race.

In-depth telephone survey— Between March 21 and April 1, 1997, Peter D. Hart Research Associates conducted an in-depth telephone survey among a representative sample of 1,022 mothers and fathers and legal guardians of children aged 36 months and younger.

More detailed information about the results of both studies is available at the ZERO TO THREE Website: **http://www.zerotothree.org**; see the "newsroom."

Parents' Perspectives on Their Children's Development: Selected Comments of Focus Group Participants

"If they get the emotional—the proper attachments, the love, the support that they need—they will feel confident to go out in the social situations . . . explore things and learn intellectually."— *a mother, Richmond*

"No matter what you do . . . not everything is programmable. . . . Whether a child's going to be intelligent or not is more or less something they're born with, the level of intelligence they can achieve. That is kind of hardwired."—*a father, Boston*

"Really [it] is your innate abilities which affect how you do in school, more so than your experiences. But the more experience you have, that's going to give you more curiosity and interest. But your performance is really based on your native intelligence."—*a mother, New York*

"I hope [having a limited number of caregivers is] not that important, because my child's on her third [caregiver]. Just don't tell me that I'm wrong."—*a mother, Boston*

"I feel that I'm getting better—that when she was born I was just so new at everything—and I'm hoping I get better and better day by day, month by month, and year by year. It scares me to death thinking [that in] a year—that's it—my time is up."—*a mother, Richmond*

"[The statement about child development before age three] makes me paranoid. . . . Even though I'm trying, I do the best I can, like if I do one thing wrong . . . I'm an idiot. . . . So, I think you always question yourself, even though you do the best that you can for them."—*a mother, New York*

"It is like you communicate with someone who speaks a foreign language—basically that's what you're doing."—*a mother, Richmond*

"[Babies] don't have instructions."—*a mother, Boston*

they lack is not just information on the importance of the earliest years but also specific steps, ideas, activities, and concepts for making the most of this time. For example, the parents in the focus group research said they believe babies communicate and are interpretable almost from birth; however, parents have difficulty understanding what their babies are communicating and what their behaviors mean. Many said it is hard to read a baby's cues and would appreciate help in learning how to do so.

The poll indicated that 60% of the parents of babies and toddlers were extremely or very interested in information about early brain development and how children learn, and an additional 21% said that they were somewhat interested. According to the poll, parents relied most on their informal networks—their parents or friends and neighbors—for information or advice. Only 2% mentioned their child's caregiver as someone to whom they usually turned for help.

8. Many parents do not recognize that they can create capacity by stimulating a child's brain in ways that match the child's level and interest.

According to the focus group research, many parents see their role largely as keeping their children from harm. The participating parents often stressed the negative impact of a poor emotional or social environment, situations they seek to avoid. Making a creative difference in the lives of children, through *improving the quality of their experiences and their relationships with the important people in their lives*, is a different way of thinking for many parents than what they have traditionally held to be their obligations to their children.

Nearly all the parents (95% of those polled) recognized that children learn from the moment they are born. Most parents (87%) assumed that the more stimulation a baby receives, the better. But, in fact,

parents and caregivers need to carefully match the amount and kind of stimulation to a child's development, interests, temperament, and mood at the moment.

9. Many parents see time as a major barrier to better parenting.

In the poll, more than one-third of parents (37%) indicated that one of the chief reasons they may need to improve as parents is because they don't spend as much quality time with their child as they would like. Half of all parents said that they ended most days feeling that they had spent less time with their young child than they wanted to—either a lot less time (20%) or a little less (27%).

What these results mean to early childhood professionals

In this study, parents seemed well aware of the general importance of the love and time they give their infants and toddlers, but they wanted more information about exactly *how* to influence their children's emotional and intellectual development in positive ways. These moms and dads feel good about many aspects of being parents to young children. Yet they recognize their ability to improve, and they display a genuine interest in doing so.

Indeed, the data reveal these parents' desire to play the most positive role they can in their children's development. They want to understand how to prepare in advance for parenthood; where to turn for day-to-day information, especially when their children are young; how to provide the best care for their children, even when they cannot provide it exclusively themselves; how to recognize signals and cues that inform them about their children's development; how they can affect most positively a young and growing brain; and what specific strategies and techniques they can use to help practice better parenting and give their young children the best possible start in life.

Early childhood professionals, especially those working in programs that serve infants and toddlers, are in an excellent position to respond to parents' desire for more information and support. New and creative ways of providing this type of assistance may be needed, however, as most of the parents surveyed do not automatically turn to their child's caregiver as an information source.

Finally, early childhood professionals should recognize what parents think would help them become better parents: (1) information to help them understand their child's feelings or needs and ways to handle difficult situations, and (2) more quality time with their child. Actions and strategies that especially support parents in these ways are likely to be the most helpful and the most welcome.

Development during Childhood: Cognition and Schooling

Cognition (Articles 14–17)
Schooling (Articles 18–20)

Cognition is the mental process of knowing. It includes aspects such as awareness, perception, reasoning, and judgment. Intelligence is the capacity to acquire and apply knowledge. It is usually assumed that intelligence can be measured. The ratio of tested mental age to chronological age is expressed as an intelligence quotient (IQ). For years, schoolchildren have been classified and tracked educationally by IQ scores. This practice has been both obsequiously praised and venomously opposed. The links between IQ scores and school achievement are positive, but no significant correlations exist between IQ scores and life success. Many kinds of achievement that require superb cognitive processes (awareness, perception, reasoning, judgment) cannot be measured with intelligence tests or with achievement tests. Consider, for example, the motor coordination and kinesthetic abilities of a baseball player such as Cal Ripken Jr. A Harvard psychologist, Howard Gardner, has suggested that there are at least seven different kinds of intelligences. These include the body movement skills of athletes and dancers and musical linguistic, logical-mathematical, spatial, self-understanding, and social understanding types. The 1990s have been host to a spate of research about the last two types of intelligences: self-understanding and social understanding. Some psychologists have suggested that measuring one's emotional quotient (EQ) might make more sense than measuring one's intelligence quotient (IQ). The typical tests of intelligence only measure achievement and abilities in the logical-mathematical, spatial, and linguistic areas of intelligence.

Jean Piaget, the Swiss founder of cognitive psychology, was involved in the creation of the world's first intelligence test, the Binet-Simon Scale. He became disillusioned with trying to quantify how much children knew at different chronological ages. He was much more intrigued with what they did not know, what they knew incorrectly, and how they came to know the world in the ways in which they knew it. He started a Centre for Genetic Epistemology in Geneva, Switzerland, and began to study the nature, extent, and validity of children's knowledge. He discovered qualitative, rather than quantitative,

differences in cognitive processes over the life span. Infants know the world through their senses and their motor responses. After language develops, toddlers and preschoolers know the world through their language/symbolic perspectives. Piaget likened early childhood cognitive processes to bad thought, or thought akin to daydreams. By school age, children know things in concrete terms, which allows them to number, seriate, classify, conserve, think backwards and forwards, and to think about themselves thinking (metacognition). They are able to use reason. However, Piaget believed that children do not acquire the cognitive processes necessary to think abstractly and to use clear, consistent, logical patterns of thought until early adolescence.

Contemporary cognitive researchers are refining Piaget's theories. They are discovering that children acquire many abilities earlier than Piaget postulated. In the first article in this unit, Jill Neimark discusses the extraordinary intricacy of a child's cognitive processes. An event may be processed at several levels and in several areas of the brain. For example, a part of an event may be stored unconsciously, a part of it may be stored in a content area, and another part of it may be stored in an emotional area. Piaget's belief that early childhood cognitive processes are akin to daydreams may be due to a young child's inability to consolidate memory traces from multiple areas. However, new research on cognition suggests that older children and adults may consolidate false memory traces along with those that are true. Jill Neimark's exposition on memory attempts to explain malleable, lost, and recovered memories as well as the physiology that is known about information coding, storage, and retrieval.

The second article in this unit explains Piaget's theory that learning originates from inside the child. Constance Kamii and Janice Ewing believe that school teaching should be based on Piaget's view of cognitive constructivism. Piaget makes a distinction between three kinds of knowledge: physical knowledge, social (conventional) knowledge, and logico-mathematical knowledge. These cognitions are constructed very differently inside the child. The sources of each and their modes of being structured are very important

UNIT 3

building blocks for education. Teaching based on scientific theories of how children construct knowledge is more potent than teaching based on fads, pendulum swings, or superficial impressions of what works.

The third article on cognition summarizes what is known about the effects of undernutrition on cognitive development. Lack of essential nutrients will alter the brain structurally and biochemically and reduce learning abilities. In addition, structural and biochemical brain changes affect personality, emotionality, and behavior in children. This contributes to a cycle of factors that further disrupt the learning process. The main research findings that support the above statement are reviewed in the article.

The fourth article presents some aspects of a genetic/biological predetermined brain functioning that may influence the capacity to acquire and apply knowledge. Children (and adults) with attention deficit hyperactive disorder (ADHD) may have frontal-lobe circuitry different from non-ADHD affected persons. This may give them certain advantages: creativity, spontaneity, effervescence. However, their short attention spans and impulsivity, brought on by frontal-lobe differences, may inhibit some reasoning and judgment. If children with ADHD are labeled less intelligent, they may have little incentive to learn and perform to their maximum genetic potentialities.

The first two articles in the schooling subsection of this unit address the issues of defining and testing intelligence for purposes of school placement and educational programming. Politicians play with the rhetoric about what our children should and should not learn in school. "Bell, Book and Scandal" gives an historic overview of IQ testing and the use of IQ tests to differentiate children by achievement in the logical-mathematical type of intelligence. To what extent is this placement practice discriminating against other children who demonstrate high motivation and potential to achieve but different types of intelligences? How important is self-understanding and social understanding? Should schools teach empathy? Is emotional control the true yardstick of human intellectual potential?

The final article of this unit outlines the diagnostic approach to prevention and/or management of misbehavior that interferes with school learning. The author suggests that teachers must learn as much as possible about pupils: from IQ tests, EQ assessments, previous teachers, significant people in the students' lives, and from the pupils themselves. With adequate information, teachers can determine the causes of most behavior problems and take steps to eliminate them or modify them so they do not interfere with scholarship.

Looking Ahead: Challenge Questions

How are memories encoded, stored, and retrieved?

Why should Piaget's cognitive constructivism be used to shape lesson plans for students?

What are the effects of undernutrition on cognitive development and the learning process?

Is attention deficit a different cognitive style rather than a "disorder"? Explain.

Why is *The Bell Curve* so controversial? Is it a scandalous idea?

Can gathering as much information as possible about students help a teacher deal more effectively with classroom misbehavior that interferes with the learning process?

It's Magical! It's Malleable! It's . . . Memory

So complex and evanescent is memory, our best metaphors fall short, bogged down in materialism. Yet through the creative blending and reblending of experience and emotion, memory builds that about us which often seems most solid—our sense of self. We remember, therefore we are.

Jill Neimark

We never know exactly why certain subjects—like certain people—claim us, and do not let us go. Elizabeth Loftus is a research psychologist who has devoted her life to the study of memory, its mystery and malleability. Of late, she has gained ingenious experiments, which have shown repeatedly that about 25 percent of individuals can be easily induced to remember events that never happened to them—false memories that feel absolutely real.

So it was something of a shock when, at a family gathering, an uncle informed the then 44-year-old Loftus that 30 years earlier, when her mother had drowned, she had been the one to discover the body in the pool. Loftus believed she had never seen her mother's dead body; in fact, she remembered little about the death itself.

Almost immediately after her uncle's revelation, "the memories began to drift back," she recalls in her recent book, *The Myth of Repressed Memory* (St. Martin), "like the crisp, piney smoke from evening camp fires. My mother, dressed in her nightgown, was floating face down. . . . I started screaming. I remembered the police cars, their lights flashing. For three days my memory expanded and swelled.

"Then, early one morning, my brother called to tell me that my uncle had made a mistake. Now he remembered (and other relatives confirmed) that Aunt Pearl found my mother's body." Suddenly Loftus understood firsthand what she had been studying for decades. "My own experiment had inadvertently been performed on me! I was left with a sense of wonder at the inherent credulity of even my skeptical mind."

Memory has become a lightning rod of late. This has been a time of fascinating, grisly stories—of recovered memories of satanic cults, butchered babies, and incest that have spawned church scandals, lawsuits, suicides, splintered families, murders, and endless fodder for talk shows. Three major books on the fallibility of memory were reviewed on the front page of the *New York Times Book Review* last spring, and three more were published this fall. The essential nature of memory, which ought by rights to be a scientific debate, has so galvanized the culture that laws have actually been revoked and repealed over it; in Illinois, for example, a law that bars people over 30 from filing lawsuits based on remembered abuse was repealed in 1992, and is now being reinstated.

Memory is the likelihood that, among a vast tangle of neurons, the pathway of connections an experience forges in the brain can be reactivated again. It is the ability to repeat a performance— albeit with mistakes.

Memory's ambiguities and paradoxes seem to have suddenly claimed us as they have claimed researchers for decades. This fascination cannot be explained away by the human need to memorialize the past—a need that expresses itself beautifully and indelibly in monuments like the Vietnam memorial or the AIDS quilt, and in projects like Steven Spielberg's ongoing documentary of holocaust survivors.

It's as if we've awakened, at the turn of the millennium, and realized that memory is the bedrock of the self—and that it may be perpetually shifting and terrifically malleable. That image of memory, whose river runs into tabloids and traumas, seems both terrifying and baptismal. If we can repress life-shaping events (such as sexual or physical abuse), or actually invent memories of events that never happened (from UFO abductions to rapes and murders), memory carries a power that promises to utterly reshape the self.

And so it's exciting news that in the past few years, scientists have begun to piece together a picture of memory that is stunning in its specifics:

• Sophisticated PET (positron emission tomography) scans can record the actual firing of the neurons that hold the pictures of our lives, and observe memory move like a current across the brain while it sleeps or wakes.

• How and where the brain lays down and consolidates memory—that is, makes it permanent—is yielding to understanding. As one researcher states, we are seeing "an explosion of knowledge about what parts of the brain are doing what."

• Hormones that help engrave the narrative of our lives into our cells have now been identified.

• Certain drugs block or enhance memory, and they may hold the key to preventing disorders as wide-ranging as Alzheimer's disease and posttraumatic stress disorder (PTSD).

• The well-known "fight-or-flight" response to stress can sear "indelible" memories into the brain.

• Memory is not a single entity residing in a single place. It is the likelihood that the pathway of neurons and connections an experience forges in the brain can be reactivated again. It involves multiple systems in the brain. The emotion associated with a memory, for example, is stored in a different place than the content of the memory itself.

• Some memories occur in a primitive part of the brain, unknown to conscious perception. That part functions "below" the senses, as it were. That is why individuals with brain damage can sometimes learn and remember—without knowing they do so.

• There is a growing understanding that an infant's early experience of emotional attachment can direct the nature and durability of childhood memories and the way they are stored in the brain.

Memory, it turns out, is both far more complex and more primitive than we knew. Ancient parts of the brain can record memory before it even reaches our senses—our sight and hearing, for instance. At the same time, "there are between 200 and 400 billion neurons in the brain and each neuron has about 10,000 connections," notes psychiatrist Daniel Siegel, M.D. "The parallel processing involved in memory is so complex we can't even begin to think how it works."

The one thing that we can say for certain is this: If memory is the bedrock of the self, then even though that self may seem coherent and unchanging, it is built on shifting sands.

13 WAYS OF LOOKING AT THE BRAIN

Moments after being removed from the skull, the brain begins to collapse into a jellylike mass. And yet this wet aspic of tissue contains a fantastic archeology of glands, organs, and lobes, all of which have their own specialized jobs. . . . Much of this archeology is devoted to the complex tasks of memory.

But just what is memory? According to Nobel Prize-winning neuroscientist Gerald Edelman, Ph.D., author of *Bright Air, Brilliant Fire* (Basic Books), memory is the ability to repeat a performance—with mistakes. Without memory, life itself would never have evolved. The genetic code must be able to repeat itself in DNA and RNA; an immune cell must be able to remember an antigen and repeat a highly specific defense next time they meet; a neuron in the brain must be able to send the same signal each time you encounter (for example) a lion escaped from the local zoo. Every living system must be able to remember; but what is most dangerous and wonderful about memory is that it must occasionally make errors. It must be wrong. Mere repetition might explain the way a crystal grows but not the way a brain works. Memory classifies and adapts to our environment. That adaptation requires flexibility. The very ability to make mistakes is precious.

Now you can bravely step into the hall of mirrors that is memory. And though our words to describe this evanescent process are still crude and oversimplistic, here are a few tools to travel with:

Memory can be implicit or explicit. Implicit memory is involved in learning habits—such as riding a bicycle or driving a car. It does not require "conscious" awareness, which is why you can sometimes be lost in thought as you drive and find you've driven home without realizing it. Explicit memory is conscious, and is sometimes called declarative. One form of declarative memory is autobiographical memory—our ability to tell the story of our life in the context of time.

We often talk of memory storage and retrieval, as if memory were filed in a honeycomb of compartments, but these words are really only metaphors. If memory is the reactivation of a weblike network of neurons that were first activated when an event occurred, each time that network is stimulated the memory is strengthened, or consolidated. Storage, retrieval, consolidation—how comforting and solid they sound; but in fact they consist of electrical charges leaping among a vast tangle of neurons.

In truth, even the simplest memory stimulates complex neural networks at several different sites in the brain. The content (what happened) and meaning (how it felt) of an event are laid down in separate parts of the brain. In fact, research at Yale University by Patricia Goldman-Rakic, Ph.D., has shown that neurons themselves are specialized for different types of memories—features, patterns, location, direction. "The coding is so specific that it can be mapped to different areas . . . in the prefrontal region."

What is activating these myriad connections? We still don't know. Gerald Edelman calls this mystery "the homunculus crisis." Who is thinking? Is memory remembering us? "The intricacy and numerosity of brain connections are extraordinary," writes Edelman. "The layers and loops between them are dynamic, they continually change."

Yet the center holds. The master regulator of memory, the hub at the center of the wheel, is a little seahorse-shaped organ called the hippocampus. Like the rest of the brain, it is lateralized; it exists in both the right and left hemispheres. Without it, we learn and remember nothing—in fact, we are lost to ourselves.

THE SEAHORSE AND THE SELF

"He's 33 years old, and he never remembers that his father is dead. Every time he rediscovers this fact he goes through the whole grieving process again," Mark Gluck, Ph.D., a professor at the Center for Molecular and Behavioral Neuroscience at Rutgers University, says of M.P., a young man who lost his memory after a stroke six years ago. Gluck has been studying M.P. for several years. After his stroke, M.P. forgot that on that very morning he had proposed marriage to his girlfriend. "He can store no new information in his long-term memory. If you tell him a phone number and ask him to repeat it, he will; but if you change the subject and then ask him the number, he can't remember. M.P. is going to be living in the present for the rest of his life. He has lost the essential ability of the self to evolve."

M.P. is uncannily similar to one of the most remarkable and intensively studied patients of all time, a man called H.M., who lost his memory after undergoing brain surgery to treat epilepsy. This type of memory loss, called anterograde amnesia, stops time. It usually results from damage to the hippocampus, which normally processes, discards, or dispatches information by sending signals to other parts of the brain.

"The hippocampus is critical for learning," says Gluck, "and it's also one of the most volatile, unstable parts of the brain—one of the first parts damaged if oxygen is cut off. Think of it as a highly maneuverable kayak; it has to immediately capture a whole range of information about an event and needs the ability to go rapidly through many changes. We think the hippocampus serves as a filter, learning new associations and deciding what is important and what to ignore or compress. That's why it's critical for learning." The hippocampus is, in a sense, a collating machine, sorting and then sending various packets of information to other parts of the brain.

One of the most exciting advances in neuroscience may lie ahead as researchers begin to actually model the living brain on the computer—creating a new era of artificial intelligence called neural networks. Gluck and researchers at New York University have begun to model the hippocampus, creating "lesions" and watching what happens—in the hope that they can develop specialized tests that will identify Alzheimer's in its early stages, as well as develop machinery that can learn the way a brain does. Thus far their predictions about its role have been borne out—in fact, Gluck is developing applications for the military so that hippocampal-like computers can learn the early signals of engine malfunctions and sound the alarm long before a breakdown.

The hippocampus does not store memories permanently. It is a way station, though a supremely important one. Like a football player in the heat of the game, it passes the ball to other parts of the brain. This takes minutes, or maybe even hours, according to James McGaugh, Ph.D., of the University of California at Irvine. At that point, memories can still be lost. They need to be consolidated; the network of neurons responsible for a memory needs to be strengthened through repeated stimuli, until the memory exists independent of the hippocampus, a process known as long-term potentiation (LTP).

Once again, a word picture of this process is extremely crude. In actuality, Edelman points out, "the circuits of the brain look like no others we have seen before. The neurons have treelike arbors that overlap in myriad ways. Their signaling is like the vast aggregate of interactive events in a jungle."

No one is certain how long it takes to fully consolidate a memory. Days? Weeks? Perhaps it takes even years until the linkages of networks are so deeply engraved that the memory becomes almost crystallized—easy to recall, detailed and clear. Individuals like M.P. seem to lose several years of memory just prior to hippocampal damage; so do Alzheimer's patients, who usually suffer hippocampal damage as their brains begin to malfunction, and who recall their childhood days with fine-etched clarity but find the present blurred.

A MAGIC RHYTHM OF MEMORY?

Just how and when do memories become permanent? Scientists now have direct evidence of what they have long suspected—that consolidation of memories, or LTP, takes place during sleep or during deeply relaxed states. It is then that brain waves slow to a rhythm known as "theta," and perhaps, according to McGaugh, the brain releases chemicals that enhance storage.

In an ingenious experiment reported in the journal *Science* last July, researchers planted electrodes in different cells in rats' hippocampi, and watched each cell fire as the animals explored different parts of a box. After returning to their cages, the rats slept. And during sleep the very same cells fired.

There seems to be a specific brain rhythm dedicated to LTP. "It's the magic rhythm of theta! The theta rhythm is the natural, indigenous rhythm of the hippocampus," exclaims neuroscientist Gary Lynch, Ph.D., of the University of California at Irvine. Lynch is known for his inspiring, if slightly mad, brilliance. His laboratory found that LTP is strongest when stimulation is delivered to the hippocampus in a frequency that corresponds to the slow rhythms of theta, of deep relaxation. Research by James McGaugh seems to confirm this: the more theta waves that appear in an animal's EEG (electroencephalogram), the more it remembers.

No wonder, then, that recent experiments show sleep improves memory in humans—and specifically, the sleep associated with dreaming, REM (rapid eye movement) sleep. In Canada, students who slept after cramming for an exam retained more information than those who pulled an all-nighter. In Israel, researchers Avi Karni and Dov Sagi at the Weizmann Institute found that interrupting REM sleep 60 times in a night completely blocked learning; interrupting non-REM sleep just as often did not. These findings give scientific punch to "superlearning" methods like that of Bulgarian psychiatrist Georgi Lozanov, which utilizes deep relaxation through diaphragmatic breathing and music, combined with rhythmic bursts of information.

THE HAUNTED BRAIN

What happens when memory goes awry? It seems that some memories are so deeply engraved in the brain that they haunt an individual as if he were a character in an Edgar Allen Poe story. How, asks Roger Pittman, M.D., coordinator of research and development at the Manchester (New Hampshire) Veterans Administration Medical Center and associate professor at Harvard Medical School, does the traumatic event "carve its canyons and basins of memory into the living brain?"

'We believe that the brain takes advantage of hormones and chemicals, released during stress and powerful emotions, to regulate the strength of memory.' We owe our very lives to this; a dangerous event needs to be recalled.

In any kind of emotionally arousing experience, the brain takes advantage of the fight-or-flight reaction, which floods cells with two powerful stress hormones, adrenaline and noradrenaline. "We believe that the brain takes advantage of the chemicals released during stress and powerful emotions," says James McGaugh, "to regulate the strength of storage of the memory." These stress hormones stimulate the heart to pump faster and the muscles to tense; they also act on neurons in the brain. A memory associated with emotionally charged information gets seared into the brain. We owe our very lives to this: a dangerous, threatening, or exciting event needs to be recalled well so that we may take precautions when meeting similar danger again.

Scientists are now beginning to understand just how emotional memory works and why it is so powerful. According to Joseph Ledoux, Ph.D., of the Center for Neural Science at New York University, the hormones associated with strong emotion stimulate the amygdala, an almond-shaped organ in the brain's cortex.

It's long been known that when rats are subjected to the sound of a tone and a shock, they soon learn to respond fearfully to the tone alone. The shocker is that when the auditory cortex—the part of the brain that receives sound—is completely destroyed, the rats are still able to learn the exact same fear response. How can a rat learn to be afraid of a sound it cannot hear?

The tone, it appears, is carried directly back to the amygdala, as well as to the auditory cortex. Destroy the amygdala, and even a rat with perfect hearing will never learn to be afraid of the sound. As neurologist Richard Restak, M.D., notes, this "implies that much of our brain's emotional processing occurs unconsciously. The amygdala may process many of our unconscious fear responses." This explains in part why phobias are so difficult to treat by psychotherapy. The brain's memory for emotional experiences is an enduring one.

But the ability of the brain to utilize stress hormones can go badly awry—and a memory can become not simply permanent but intrusive and relentless. "Suppose somebody shoots you and years later you're still waking up in a cold sweat with nightmares," says McGaugh. "The hormonal regulation of memory, when pushed to an extreme in a traumatic situation, may make memories virtually indelible."

Such memories seem so powerful that even an innocuous stimulus can arouse them. Roger Pittman compares the inescapable memories of PTSD, where flashbacks to a nightmarish trauma intrude relentlessly on daily life, to a black hole, "a place in space-time that has such high gravity that even light cannot pass by without being drawn into it."

So with ordinary associations and memories in PTSD: "As all roads lead to Rome, all the patient's thoughts lead to the trauma. A war veteran can't look at his wife's nude body without recalling with revulsion the naked bodies he saw in a burial pit in Vietnam, can't stand the sight of children's dolls because their eyes remind him of the staring eyes of the war dead."

The tragic twist is that, Pittman believes, each time a memory floods in again, the same stress hormones are released, running the same neural paths of that particular memory and binding the victim ever tighter in the noose of the past. Yet in response to the stress of recalling trauma, the body releases a flood of calming opiates. These neurochemicals, which help us meet the immediate demands of stress and trauma, might create a kind of unfortunate biochemical reward for the traumatic memory. "This whole question of an appetitive component to trauma is really fascinating and as yet unexplored," notes Pittman. "It may explain the intrusive, repeating nature of these memories. Maybe, however horrible the trauma, there's something rewarding in the brain chemicals released."

A solution, then, to treating the kind of PTSD we see in war veterans and victims of rape and child abuse, might lie in blocking the action of some of these stress hormones. And perhaps a key to enhancing ordinary learning is to create a judicious amount of stress—excitement, surprise, even a healthy dose of fear (like the kind one may feel before cramming for a demanding final exam).

A landmark study recently reported by James McGaugh and Larry Cahill, in *Nature*, indicates that any emotion, even ordinary emotion, is linked to learning. They gave two groups of college students a drug that blocks the effects of adrenaline and noradrenaline, then showed the students a series of 12 slides that depicted scenes such as a boy crossing the street with his mother or visiting a man at a hospital. A control group was told an ordinary story (son and mother visit the boy's surgeon father) that corresponded to some of the slides. The experimental group heard a story of disaster (boy is hit by car; a surgeon attempts to reattach his severed feet).

Two weeks later, the volunteers were given a surprise memory test. Students who heard the ordinary story recalled all 12 slides poorly. The second group, however, recalled significantly better the slides associated with the story of disaster.

Then, in an ingenious twist, McGaugh and Cahill repeated the experiment with new volunteers. Just before the slide show, the experimental group was given a beta blocker—a drug that acts on nerve cells to block the effect of stress hormones. Two weeks later they could not be distinguished from the control group. They similarly remembered all 12 slides poorly.

The implications of this elegant experiment are far reaching. "Let's suppose," postulates McGaugh, "that a plane crashes near Pittsburgh and you're hired to pick out the body parts. If we give you a beta blocker, we impair your 'emotional' memory, the memory for the trauma, without impairing your normal memory."

Pittman looks forward in the next decade to drugs that not only block PTSD but help ameliorate it. "There seems to be a window of opportunity, up to six hours or so in rats in any case, before memories are consolidated." During that time effective drugs, such as beta blockers, might be administered.

MEMORY LOST AND REGAINED

The stories are legendary. Elizabeth Loftus has found ordinary memory to be so malleable that she can prompt volunteers to "remember nonexistent broken glass and tape recorders; to think of a clean-shaven man as having a mustache, of straight hair as curly, of hammers as screwdrivers, to place a barn in a bucolic scene that contained no buildings at all, to believe in characters who never existed and events that never happened."

Sometimes the memories become so seemingly fantastical that they lead to court cases and ruined lives. "I testified in a case recently in a small town in the state of Washington," Loftus recalls, "where the memories went from, 'Daddy made me play with his penis in the shower' to 'Daddy made me stick my fist up the anus of a horse,' and they were bringing in a veterinarian to talk about just what a horse would do in that circumstance. The father is ill and will be spending close to $100,000 to defend himself."

Nobody is quite sure how memories might be lost to us and then later retrieved—so-called repression. Whatever it is, it is a different process than traumatic amnesia, a well-known phenomenon where a particular horrendous event is forgotten because it was never consolidated in long-term memory in the first place. Such is the amnesia of an accident victim who loses consciousness after injury. Repressed memory, on the other hand, is alleged to involve repeated traumas.

According to UCLA's Daniel Siegel, both amnesia and repression may be due to a malfunction of the hippocampus. In order to recall an explicit memory, and to be able to depict it in words and pictures, the hippocampus must process it first. Perhaps, postulates Siegel, the work of the hippocampus is disrupted during trauma—while other components of memory carry on. We know, for example, that primitive responses like fear or excitement stimulate the amygdala directly; learning can occur without our "knowing" it.

If explicit memory is impaired—you forget what happened to you—but implicit memory is intact, you may still be profoundly influenced by an experience. Siegel thinks that some individuals remove conscious attention during repeated trauma, say from an unbearable event like repeated rapes. In the parlance of the mind trade, they "dissociate."

While his theory may explain repressed memory plausibly, it doesn't suggest how the memory emerges decades later, explicit and intrusive. And it doesn't answer the contention of many researchers that such repression is probably rare, and that the wave of repressed memories we are hearing about today may be due to invention.

It turns out that it's relatively easy to confuse imagery with perception. The work of Stephen Kossyln, Ph.D., a psychologist at Harvard University and author of *Image and Brain* (MIT press), has shown that the exact same centers in the brain are activated by both imagination and perception. "PET studies have shown that, when subjects close their eyes and form visual images, the same areas are activated as if they were actually seeing." The strength of the imagined "signal" (or image) is about half that of a real one. Other research shows that the source of a memory—the time, place, or way the memory began—is the first part to fade. After all, the source of a memory is fragile.

If we concentrate on generating images that then get recorded in the web of neurons as if they were real, we might actually convince ourselves that confabulations are true. (This might also explain how some individuals who lie about an event eventually convince themselves, through repeated lying, that the lie is true.)

The fragility of source memory explains why, in a famous experiment by psychologist John Neisser, John Dean's testimony about Richard Nixon was shown to be both incredibly

---

'It's easy to confuse memory with experience. The exact same brain centers are activated by imagination and perception.'

---

accurate and hugely inaccurate. "His initial testimony was so impressive that people called him a human tape recorder," recalls psychologist Charles Thompson, Ph.D. "Neisser then compared the actual tapes to his testimony, and found that if you really looked at the specifics, who said what and when, Dean was wrong all over the place. But if you just looked at his general sense of what was going on in the meetings he was right on target. His confusion was about the source." In general, supposes Thompson, this is how memory works. We have an accurate sense of the core truth of an event, but we can easily get the details wrong.

"Memory is more reconstructive than reproductive. As time passes, details are lost. We did a study where we asked people to keep a daily diary for up to a year and a half, and later asked them questions about recorded events. The memory of the core event and its content stayed at a high level of about 70 percent, while the peripheral details dropped quickly."

CAN MEMORY CREATE THE SELF?

From Freud on down, it was believed that memories from infancy or early childhood were repressed and somehow inaccessible—but that their clues, like the bits of bread dropped by Hansel and Gretel in the forest, could be found in dreams or in the pathology of waking life. Now we know better. It's that the brain systems that support declarative memory develop late—two or three years into life.

If we don't actually lay down any memories of our first few years, how can they shape our later life? An intriguing answer can be pieced together from findings by far-flung researchers.

Daniel Siegel plows the field of childhood memory and attachment theory. He finds that memory is profoundly affected in children whose mothers had rejected or avoided them. "We don't know why this happens, but at 10 years old, these children have a unique paucity in the content of their spontaneous autobiographical narratives." As adults, they do not recall childhood family experiences.

It may be that memory storage is impaired in the case of childhood trauma. Or it may be, Siegel suggests, that avoidant parents don't "talk to children about their experiences and memories. Those children don't have much practice in autobiographical narrative. Not only are their memories weak or nonexistent, the sense of self is not as rich. As a psychotherapist, I try to teach people to tell stories about their lives. It helps them develop a richer sense of self."

As far as the biology of the brain goes, this may be no different than training an 18-year-old boy to distinguish between whales and submarines; if the hippocampus is continually fed a stimulus, it will allocate more of the brain's capacities to recording and recognizing that stimulus. In the case of autobiographical narrative, however, what emerges is magical and necessary: the self.

That is almost like saying memory creates the self, and in a sense it does. But memory is also created and recreated by the self. The synergy between the two is like two sticks rubbed together in a forest, creating fire. "We now have a new paradigm of memory," notes Loftus, "where memories are understood as creative blendings of fact and fiction, where images are alchemized by experience and emotion into memories."

"I think it's safe to say we make meaning out of life, and the meaning-making process is shaped by who we are as self," says Siegel. Yet that self is shaped by the nature of memory. "It's this endless feedback loop which maintains itself and allows us to come alive."

When we think of our lives, we become storytellers—heroes of our own narrative, a tale that illumines that precious and mysterious "self" at the center. That "I am" cannot be quantified or conveyed precisely and yet it feels absolute. As Christopher Isherwood wrote long ago in *The Berlin Stories,* "I am a camera." Yet, as the science is showing us, there is no single camera—or if there is, it is more like the impressionist, constantly shifting camera of *Last Year at Marienbad.* Memory is malleable—and so are we.

Basing Teaching on Piaget's Constructivism

Constance Kamii and Janice K. Ewing

Constance Kamii is Professor, Department of Curriculum and Instruction, University of Alabama at Birmingham. Janice K. Ewing is Assistant Professor, Department of Social Sciences and Education, Colby-Sawyer College, New London, New Hampshire.

Constructivism, the view that much of learning originates from *inside* the child, has become increasingly popular in recent years. Many educators, however, use the term "construct" loosely without knowing, for example, that children construct a system of writing very differently from how they construct mathematical understanding. And some people think that Piaget had nothing to do with constructivism, crediting him only with discovering the stages of children's development.

The purpose of this article is to explain three main reasons for basing teaching on Piaget's constructivism: 1) it is a scientific theory that explains the nature of human knowledge, 2) it is the only theory in existence that explains children's construction of knowledge from birth to adolescence and 3) it informs educators of how Piaget's distinction among the three kinds of knowledge changes the way we should teach many subjects.

From *Childhood Education*, Annual Theme Issue, 1996, pp. 260-264. © 1996 by the Association for Childhood Education International, 17904 Georgia Avenue, Suite 215, Olney, MD. Reprinted by permission.

A Scientific Explanation of Human Knowledge

Philosophers have debated for centuries about how human beings attain truth, or knowledge. The two main views—the empiricist and rationalist views—developed in answer to this question differ, especially in the way philosophers thought about the role of experience.

Empiricists (such as Locke, Berkeley and Hume) argued, in essence, that knowledge has its source outside the individual, and that it is acquired by internalization through the senses. Empiricists further argued that the individual at birth is like a clean slate on which experiences are "written" as he or she grows up. As Locke wrote in 1690, "The senses at first let in particular ideas, and furnish the yet empty cabinet, and the mind by degrees growing familiar with some of them, they are lodged in the memory . . ." (1690/1947, p. 22).

Although rationalists such as Descartes, Spinoza and Kant did not deny the necessity of experience, they argued that reason is more important than sensory experience because reason enables us to know with certainty many truths that observation can never ascertain. We know, for example, that every event has a cause, in spite of the fact that we cannot examine every event in the entire past and future of the universe. Rationalists also pointed out that since our senses often deceive us through perceptual illusions, the senses cannot be trusted to provide reliable knowledge. The rigor, precision and certainty of mathematics, a purely deductive system, was the rationalists' prime example supporting the power of reason. When asked to explain the origin of reason, many proclaimed it was innate in human beings.

As a biologist trained in scientific methods, Piaget decided that the way to resolve the debate between empiricism and rationalism was to study knowledge scientifically, rather than continuing to argue on the basis of speculation. Piaget also believed that to understand the nature of knowledge, we must study its formation rather than examining only the end product. This is why he wanted to study the evolution of science from its prehistoric beginning, to examine the roles of sensory information and reason. Prehistoric evidence did not exist anymore, however, and the closest data available to him were babies' and children's knowledge. For Piaget, the study of children was thus a means of explaining the nature of human knowledge (Bringuier, 1977/1980).

The outcome of more than 50 years of research was Piaget's sharp disagreement with empiricism. Although he did not agree completely with rationalism, he did align himself with rationalism when required to place himself in a broad sense in one tradition or the other. With regard to the empiri-

cist belief that we know objects through our senses, he argued that we never know objects as they are "out there" in external reality. Objects can be known only by assimilation into the schemes that we bring to each situation.

The famous conservation-of-liquid task offers an example of Piaget's opposition to empiricism. Until children construct a certain level of logic from the inside, they are nonconservers because they can base their judgment only on what they can *see*. Their *reason* later enables them to *interpret* the empirical data and deduce that the amount

of liquid is the same even if one glass appears to have more than the other.

The Construction of Knowledge from Birth to Adolescence

To teach 3-year-olds, 7-year-olds or any other age group, educators must understand how children have acquired the knowledge they already have, and how this knowledge is related to that of adolescents and adults. The only theory in existence that shows this development from birth to adolescence is Piaget's. In his books about babies (Piaget, 1936/1952, 1937/1954, 1945/1962), especially *The Construction of Reality in the*

Child, we can read in meticulous detail about infants' construction of objects and of object permanence and the roots of logico-mathematical knowledge.

Although gaps are still being filled in Piaget's theory, we can clearly see children's subsequent construction of logic at ages 4–16 in *The Growth of Logical Thinking from Childhood to Adolescence* (Inhelder & Piaget, 1955/1958) and *The Early Growth of Logic in the Child* (Inhelder & Piaget, 1959/1964). An example related to the conservation-of-liquid task is given below to il-

lustrate older children's construction of knowledge (Piaget & Inhelder, 1968/1973).

Children between 4 and 15 years of age were shown two U-shaped glass tubes (Figure 1a) mounted on a board and containing colored water. The subjects were asked to take a good look at the objects because they would later be asked to describe and draw them from memory.

Figure 1b shows examples of the children's drawings. At level 1, they drew only the containers (tubes) or the substance contained therein (liquid). At level 2, they made the water level the same everywhere. At level 3, while the water level became unequal, both tubes looked the same. The drawings be-

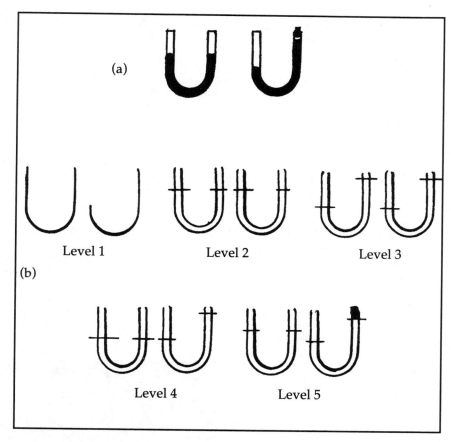

Figure 1

came more accurate at level 4, but the children did not notice that the water level in the second tube went up on one side as much as it went down on the other side. At level 5, however, they inferred the initial equality of quantity in the two tubes, conserved this equality and noticed the significance of the stopper. As can be seen in Table 1, only the oldest children were frequently at levels 4 and 5.

Table 1

Relationship Between Ages and Levels in a Memory Task

Ages	Levels					Total number
	1	2	3	4	5	
4–5	12(54%)	6(27%)	2(9%)	2(9%)	0(0%)	22
6–7	4(22%)	4(22%)	1(5%)	8(44%)	1(5%)	18
8–15	0(0%)	1(5%)	1(5%)	9(45%)	9(45%)	20

This task is one of the countless examples that enable us to trace the roots of adolescents' knowledge all the way back to infancy. It again supports Piaget's view that we do not know objects as they are "out there" in external reality. Six-year-olds cannot even *see* the inequality of the water level in one of the tubes. When they can make more precise spatial relationships, they become able to notice what is obvious to older children.

Hundreds of other tasks can be found in Piaget's books that reveal the surprising process of children's construction of knowledge. In this process, children go from one level of being "wrong" to another, rather than simply accumulating more and more knowledge quantitatively. Nonconservation may be "wrong," but basing one's judgment on water level is an enormous achievement compared to what babies do, without even understanding the word "more."

The roles of sensory information and reason discussed earlier can be understood only in light of the distinction Piaget made among three kinds of knowledge. We, therefore, now turn to a discussion of the three kinds of knowledge and the difference this distinction can make to teaching.

Three Kinds of Knowledge

The three kinds of knowledge are physical, social (conventional) and logico-mathematical knowledge. Piaget's distinction among the three is based on their ultimate sources and modes of structuring.

Physical knowledge is knowledge of objects in external reality. The color and weight of a block are examples of physical properties that are in objects in external reality and can be known empirically by observation.

Examples of *social knowledge* are holidays, written and spoken languages, and the rule of saying "Good morning" under certain circumstances. The ultimate source of physical knowledge is partly in objects, and the ultimate source of social knowledge is partly in man-made conventions. The reason for saying "partly" is clarified shortly.

Logico-mathematical knowledge consists of relationships created by each individual and is the hardest kind to understand. When we are presented with a red block and a blue block and think that they are *similar,* for instance, the similarity is an example of logico-mathematical knowledge. Almost everybody thinks that the similarity between the blocks is observable, but this is not true.

The blocks themselves are observable, but the similarity between them is not. The similarity exists neither *in* the red block nor *in* the blue one. If a person did not put the objects into this relationship, the similarity would not exist for him or her. The source of logico-mathematical knowledge, therefore, is *in* each child's mind. Other relationships the individual can create between the same blocks are *different, the same in weight* and *two.* Mathematical knowledge such as 2 + 2 = 4 and 3 × 4 = 12 is constructed by each child by making new relationships out of previously created relationships.

It was stated earlier that the source of physical knowledge is only *partly* in objects. Piaget's reason for saying "partly" was that a logico-mathematical framework, or a classificatory framework, is necessary even to recognize a block as a block or to recognize water as a liquid. Classification is also necessary to think about the color of an object and to recognize the color as blue. Without classification, it would be impossible to construct physical knowledge. Likewise, it would be impossible to construct social (conventional) knowledge without a logico-mathematical framework. To recognize a certain word as a "bad one," for example, the child has to categorize words into "good ones" and "bad ones."

The conservation of amount of liquid mentioned earlier is an example of the child's logico-mathematization of physical knowledge. The conservation of quantity of liquid involves spatio-temporal and other relationships, which belong to logico-mathematical knowledge. This is why we say that conservation is a logical deduction and not empirical knowledge.

The memory task described earlier also illustrates children's logico-mathematization of physical knowledge. We do not see facts only with our eyes. To the extent that we can make higher-level relationships and have more physical knowledge about contents such as air pressure, we obtain higher-level knowledge from the objects we see. In other

---

Armed with Piaget's theory about the nature of logico-mathematical knowledge, Kamii set out to test the hypothesis that children can invent their own procedures for the four arithmetical operations . . .

The Hindu Scratch Method for Solving 278 + 356 by Proceeding from Left to Right

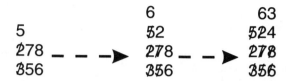

The rules followed:

1. Add 200 and 300, write the result (5 in the hundreds place), and cross out the 200 and 300.

2. Add 70 and 50, write the result (120), and cross out the 70 and 50. Because there was already a 5 in the hundreds place, this 5 was crossed out and changed to 6.

3. Add 8 and 6, write the result (14), and cross out the 8 and the 6. Because there was already a 2 in the tens place, this 2 was crossed out and changed to 3.

Figure 2

words, we observe the stopper in the task only if we bring a certain level of knowledge to it.

Physics and all the other branches of science involve the logico-mathematization of objects that are observable. Educators who understand the nature of science focus science education on children's reasoning about observable phenomena, rather than on transmission of scientific facts and terminology (social knowledge). An example of this emphasis on reasoning in physics can be found in Kamii and DeVries (1978/1993).

The teaching of mathematics also changes drastically when we understand the nature of logico-mathematical knowledge. Since 1980, Kamii (1985, 1989, 1994) has been developing an approach to primary mathematics based on Piaget's constructivism. This approach is described below as an example of how Piaget's theory can change the way we teach.

Elementary Mathematics Education

Traditional mathematics educators are usually not aware of Piaget's distinction among the three kinds of knowledge. Much of traditional elementary mathematics is therefore taught according to associationist-behavioristic principles, as if mathematics were social (conventional) knowledge. Teaching rules such as "carrying" and "borrowing" is an example of this social-knowledge approach.

Armed with Piaget's theory about the nature of logico-mathematical knowledge, Kamii set out to test the hypothesis that children can invent their own procedures for the four arithmetical operations, without any teaching of conventional rules. While this hypothesis was amply confirmed, an unexpected finding surfaced. The rules that are now taught in almost all the elementary schools throughout the United States are harmful to children's development of numerical reasoning.

Two reasons can be given to explain the harm. First, children have to give up their own thinking to use the rules of "carrying," "borrowing" and so forth. These rules make children proceed from right to left; that is, from the column of ones to those of tens, hundreds and so on. When children are free to do their own thinking, however, they invariably proceed in the opposite direction, from left to right. To add 38 + 16, for example, they typically do 30 + 10 = 40, 8 + 6 = 14, and 40 + 14 = 54. To subtract 18 from 32, they often say, "30 – 10 = 20. I can take only 2 from 2; so I have to take 6 more away from 20; so the answer is 14." In multiplication, likewise, children's typical way of doing 5 × 234, for example, is: 5 × 200 = 1,000, 5 × 30 = 150, 5 × 4 = 20, and 1,000 + 150 + 20 = 1170. Because a compromise is not possible between going from left to right and going from right to left, children have to give up their own thinking to obey their teachers.

The second reason for saying that algorithms are harmful is that these rules "unteach" place value and prevent children from developing number sense. While solving the preceding multiplication problem, for example, children who are taught algorithms say, "Five times four is twenty, put down the zero, and carry the two. Five times three is fifteen, plus two is seventeen, put down the seven, and carry the one. Five times two is ten," and so on. Treating every digit as ones is efficient for adults, who already know that the 2 in 234 is 200. For primary-age children, who have a tendency to think that the 2 in 234 means *two,* however, algorithms reinforce their "errors."

The history of computation is full of methods that are similar to the way today's children think. The Hindu Scratch Method shown in Figure 2 is an example of a method our ancestors used. It illustrates the constructive process through which the human species created knowledge (see Kamii, 1994, for other examples). Educators who impose algorithms on primary-age children think that mathematics is a cultural heritage that they must *transmit* to children. While their intentions are good, they impose on children in ready-made form the results of centuries of construction by adult mathematicians. An example of the outcome of this teaching is that the great majority of 4th-graders who had been taught algorithms gave outlandish answers such as 848, 783, 194 and 134 when asked to do 6·+ 53 + 185 without paper and pencil (Kamii, 1994).

Conclusion

Education entered a scientific era when it embraced associationism and behaviorism. While both these theories are scientific, Piaget's constructivism has gone beyond them. Many educators cannot accept constructivism, however, because associationism and behaviorism seem too valid to reject.

It is not necessary to reject associationism and behaviorism completely to embrace constructivism. The reason is that Piaget's constructivism surpassed associationism and behaviorism in a way similar to the way Copernicus's theory went beyond the geocentric theory. Copernicus proved the geocentric theory wrong not by eliminating it, but by encompassing it. This is why even today we speak of sunrise and sunset, knowing perfectly well that the sun does not revolve around the earth. From the limited perspective of earth, it is still true that the sun rises and sets.

In a similar way, associationism and behaviorism still remain true from the limited perspective of surface behavior and specific bits of knowledge. In certain situations, therefore, associationism and behaviorism can still be used by educators. Science, too, advances by going through one level after another of being "wrong." Older, "wrong" knowledge is not eliminated completely. It is *modified* when we construct more adequate theories.

Although education has entered a scientific era, much of it remains at a stage of folk art based on opinions and trial-and-error. Because education is based mainly on opinions, it remains vulnerable to fads and the swinging of the pendulum. Progressive Education went out of fashion by the 1950s, for example, and came back in part in the 1960s as Open Education. But Open Education was quickly defeated by the forces of "back to basics."

Constructivist teaching has the potential of becoming another resurrection of Progressive Education. It is true that education cannot be based on scientific knowledge alone. But if education is to keep advancing and free itself from bandwagons and the swinging of the pendulum,

we must study human knowledge with scientific rigor. Teaching will always remain an art, just as medicine is an art. But teaching must become an art based on scientific knowledge because science advances only in one direction and does not return to obsolete theories.

References

Bringuier, J.-C. (1980). *Conversations with Jean Piaget.* Chicago: University of Chicago Press. (Original work published 1977)

Inhelder, B., & Piaget, J. (1958). *The growth of logical thinking from childhood to adolescence.* New York: Basic Books. (Original work published 1955)

Inhelder, B., & Piaget, J. (1964). *The early growth of logic in the child.* New York: Harper & Row. (Original work published 1959)

Kamii, C. (1985). *Young children reinvent arithmetic.* New York: Teachers College Press.

Kamii, C. (1989). *Young children continue to reinvent arithmetic, 2nd grade.* New York: Teachers College Press.

Kamii, C. (1994). *Young children continue to reinvent arithmetic, 3rd grade.* New York: Teachers College Press.

Kamii, C., & DeVries, R. (1993). *Physical knowledge in preschool education.* New York: Teachers College Press. (Original work published 1978)

Locke, J. (1947). *Essay concerning human understanding.* Oxford, England: Oxford University Press. (Original work published 1690)

Piaget, J. (1952). *The origins of intelligence in children.* New York: Basic Books. (Original work published 1936)

Piaget, J. (1954). *The construction of reality in the child.* New York: Basic Books. (Original work published 1937)

Piaget, J. (1962). *Play, dreams, and imitation in childhood.* New York: Norton. (Original work published 1945)

Piaget, J., & Inhelder, B. (1973). *Memory and intelligence.* New York: Basic Books. (Original work published 1968)

A Reconceptualization of the Effects of Undernutrition on Children's Biological, Psychosocial, and Behavioral Development

Ernesto Pollitt, chair
Mari Golub, Kathleen Gorman, Sally Grantham-McGregor, David Levitsky, Beat Schürch, Barbara Strupp, Theodore Wachs

Task Force on Nutrition and Behavioral Development of the International Dietary Energy Consultative Group

Introduction

About 40%—approximately 190 million—of the world's children below 5 years of age are underweight (that is, weight-for-age two standard deviations below the medians of the National Center for Health Statistics of the United States [NCHS/World Health Organization [WHO])[1] and may, according to international organizations such as WHO, be assumed to be suffering from or to have suffered from varying degrees of undernutrition (International Conference on Nutrition, 1992). The numbers are particularly high in southern Asia and are increasing in Africa, especially sub-Saharan Africa. Severe clinical undernutrition, much less common than mild-to-moderate undernutrition, affects up to 10% of preschool children, depending on the country surveyed.

In many of these societies, chronic undernutrition during infancy and early childhood has significant adverse effects on subsequent cognitive development and school performance. Ultimately, a high prevalence of undernutrition stands to interfere with the formation of human capital, the cornerstone of social and economic development and welfare within a society.

In 1973 a subcommittee on Nutrition, Brain Development and Behavior of the Committee on International Nutrition Programs of the Food and Nutrition Board of the National Academy of Sciences (NAS) of the United States published a position paper on the relationship of nutrition to brain and cognitive development (NAS, 1973). This paper reported that although the fundamental mechanisms by which nutritional and environmental factors may affect the central nervous system were not known, three putative pathways for causal action were recognized:

1. Structural and biochemical changes in the brain may alter brain function and reduce learning abilities.
2. These factors may decrease exposure and responsiveness to environmental stimuli and thereby limit development.
3. Changes in personality, emotionality, and behavior of the child may disrupt the learning process.

The authors added, however, that there was no evidence to claim that undernutrition "per se contributes more or less to the depressed cognitive development of previously malnourished children than do unfortunate social and environmental conditions" (1973, p. 4). Evidence did suggest, nevertheless, that severe undernutrition does impair intellectual development, above and beyond the effects of social influences. Since then, a number of reviews have been published by independent investigators who considered available evidence in the context of the mechanisms postulated by the NAS position paper (Barrett & Frank, 1987; Buzina et al., 1989; Levitsky, 1979; Lozoff, 1988; Pollitt, 1987, 1988; Pollitt & Thomson, 1977; Simeon & Grantham-McGregor, 1990). Overall these reviewers concurred that severe malnutrition in early life impairs cognitive function, but they considered the evidence on mild-to-moderate malnutrition insufficient for definitive conclusions.

New information on undernutrition has recently led to a reconceptualization of its effects on human development. Combined with results of new experiments using animal models (Almeida, Oliveira, & Graeff, 1991; Austin et al., 1992; Bedi, 1992; Diaz-Cintra, Cintra, Ortega, Kemper, & Morgane, 1990; Keller, Cuadra, Molina, & Orsingher, 1990; Medvedev & Babichenko, 1988), new evidence is emerging from a variety of studies in human populations:

1. Clinical trials of dietary (Husaini et al., 1991) and iron (Lozoff, 1990) supplementation;
2. Follow-up assessments of previously severely malnourished (Grantham-McGregor, Powell, Walker, Chang, & Fletcher, 1994) and supplemented (Pollitt, Gorman, Engle, Martorell, & Rivera, 1993) children;
3. Studies of specific nutrients and contextual risk factors as predictors of functional competence at different ages (McCullough et al., 1990; Sigman, Neumann, Baksh, Bwibo, & McDonald, 1989; Wachs et al., 1995).

Whereas researchers previously focused on protein energy malnutrition (PEM) as a central causal agent, they have become increasingly aware that such an approach is limited because PEM is not a distinct clinical entity but a syndrome having multiple causes (Schürch, 1995). PEM coexists with micronutrient deficiencies and imbalances that can affect central nervous system (CNS) function and divert development from a normal trajectory (Golub, Keen, Gershwin, & Hendrickx, 1995; Pollitt, 1995). But the social environmental context also plays a key role. Investigators have thus shifted away from measuring the contribution of undernutrition to cognitive deficits, per se, toward identifying and measuring the interactions and transactions among undernutrition and contextual factors that determine the final outcome of the undernourished child. Mild-to-moderate malnutrition is now recognized as indeed a developmental risk factor. Conjointly, stunted brain growth is considered too simple an explanation in light of recent evidence, so that other biological mediators, such as alterations in neuroreceptor sensitivity, are now being considered (Levitsky & Strupp, 1995; Strupp & Levitsky, 1995).

These new scientific developments led the International Dietary Energy Consultative Group (IDECG) to convene a task force to assess current knowledge of the relationship between undernutrition and behavioral development in children and to interpret this information in the context of current theories of nutrition and developmental psychobiology. The Task Force, consisting of nutritionists, physiologists, physicians, and psychologists, presents in this report a review and interpretation of the main findings currently available on the effects of several types of undernutrition. Also included are new perspectives on undernutrition which point to a theoretical reconceptualization of the issues.

Reconceptualizing the Relationship of Nutrition and Development

The following section describes how the strategy for investigating the relationship between undernutrition and cognitive development has changed and is continuing to evolve. Also discussed are some of the problems in defining the nutritional and outcome variables of interest and how biological and environmental factors can modify the effects of undernutrition.

Assessing Nutrition

Protein and energy. In the 1960s, when researchers and policymakers were becoming increasingly concerned that early PEM could result in permanent impairment of intellectual development, it was widely accepted that protein was the limiting nutrient in the diet of populations at risk. During the next decade, however, dietary energy was held to be the more critical factor (McLaren, 1974). It was understood that to provide undernourished children with protein without also providing sufficient energy was futile, because the dietary protein would be used to supply energy rather than essential amino acids.

Iron, iodine, and zinc. Accompanying the new focus on energy was a recognition that, in most circumstances, energy deficiency may be closely linked to political and socioeconomic problems not easily addressed by simple nutritional intervention. Such political complexity and the fact that dietary energy is inextricably confounded with a mix of nutrients were two of numerous reasons that led subsequent research and policy interest to shift from the study of PEM effects to the effects of specific nutrients, especially Vitamin A, iron, iodine, and zinc. Whereas iron deficiency was known to be a cause of anemia, zinc deficiency a cause of growth retardation, and iodine deficiency a cause of goiter and cretinism, studies established further that deficiencies in these nutrients have broader systemic effects that lead to multiple threats to child health and development (United Nations ACC/SCN, 1993).

Complexities of deficiencies. Mild-to-moderate protein-energy malnutrition is difficult to diagnose, because it does not produce a specific set of symptoms and signs. It also coexists with other nutrient deficiencies. The same foods, particularly those from animal origin (from meat, fish, and poultry), are often sources of energy, protein, and distinct micronutrients (e.g., iron and zinc). Children that do not have access to these foods are at risk of multiple nutritional deficiencies. Further, some constituents of a habitual diet can limit the absorption of some important nutrients. This is the case, for example, with phytates, tea, and coffee which inhibit the absorption of non-heminic iron. Dietary quality[2] is critically important, requiring diversity and, to the extent possible for a family, the inclusion of foods of animal origin.

Where food is scarce and dietary quality is poor, diets consist primarily of staples such as cereals and legumes. Such diets typically contain few animal products, fresh fruits, or vegetables, and are therefore associated with low intakes of certain vitamins and minerals, high intakes of phytates and fiber, and poor bioavailability[3] (Allen, 1993). Moreover, bioavailability is reduced when the supply of nutrients that enhance absorption is low. Finally, when food availability and quality are inadequate, the incidence of morbidity is usually high, with several nutrients simultaneously depleted through anorexia, malabsorption, and/or diarrhea with its associated inflammatory responses (Chen, 1983; Martorell & Yarbrough, 1983; Sahni & Chandra, 1983).

Thus, with both the nature of nutritional deficiency and the relationship among nutrients unclear, it remains a challenge not only to understand effects but to utilize findings in designing intervention strategies. In populations where general undernutrition is common, supplementation with a single nutrient, with the exception perhaps of iodine, will often be ineffective because as one deficiency is ameliorated, others may become limiting.

Measuring Outcome

Investigations of both the nature and range of effects of undernutrition on intellectual development have been limited by the restricted nature of the psychological tests commonly used to assess children's cognitive development. Availability and convenience of the test seem to have been the dominant criteria for test selection, rather than considered theory and well-defined hypotheses that would test the psychological processes most likely to be affected. Consequently, it is possible that deficits in specific cognitive functions, e.g., attention, have not been adequately assessed by IQ or achievement tests, and may have been underestimated or missed entirely (Diamond et al., 1992). This concern is borne out by suggestive evidence of impaired attentiveness in previously undernourished children (Galler, Ramsey, Solimano, & Lowell, 1983).

Effects of undernutrition on social and emotional development have been generally disregarded. The few researchers who have investigated such effects have observed that social and emotional development is sensitive to undernutrition (Barrett, 1984; Espinosa, Sigman, Neumann, Bwibo, & McDonald, 1992) and can moderate effects on other processes. Detriments in these domains, observed repeatedly in animal studies (Levitsky & Strupp, 1995), may well have significant effects on the child's ability to adapt to the educational and social environment.

The traditional approach of focusing exclusively on cognitive development, independent of other psychological processes and systems, contradicts both current understanding of psychological development and the results of experimental studies based on animal models. Such a restricted approach also gives the mistaken impression that the effects of undernutrition on cognition are direct. Current data indicate strong reciprocal interactions between cognitive and emotional development so that changes in one may contribute to changes in the other (Rothbart, Derryberry, & Posner, 1994; Steinmetz, 1994).

Incorporating the Context

Adopting a contextual approach acknowledges that we can not interpret the contributions of specific biological or psychosocial factors to development independent of the individual's specific environment. Within this framework, the study of nutritional influences on development must account for not just the biological but also the psychosocial stressors that accompany undernutrition (Horowitz, 1989; Pollitt, 1987; Ricciuti, 1981, 1993). Available evidence clearly demonstrates that undernourished individuals have a higher probability of simultaneous exposure to other risk factors (Golden, 1991; Grantham-McGregor, 1984; Pollitt, 1987), including

1. *biological factors* (e.g., morbidity, parasitic infection, lead exposure);
2. *psychosocial factors* (e.g., child neglect, poor-quality schools);
3. *socioeconomic factors* (e.g., parental underemployment, lack of access to medical care).

Conversely, the detrimental impact of an adversity may be attenuated (though not necessarily eliminated) by *protective factors*, such as maternal education (Rutter, 1983; Zimmerman & Arunkumar, 1994). For example, in one study among impoverished rural communities in Guatemala, maternal education ensured that the children benefited from a nutrition program. Independent of the distance between home and the center where the foods were distributed, the mothers with higher levels of education took the children to the center to eat the food distributed without charge. This was not the case among children of mothers with low levels of education: these children were likely to be taken to the center only if they lived nearby (Carmichael, Pollitt, Gorman, & Martorell, 1994).

Traditionally, environmental influences have been regarded as complicating nuisances, to be controlled for by elements of the research design or statistical procedures. But this view has tended to oversimplify or obscure inherent complexities of causation that can only be captured if the most relevant biological, psychosocial, and socioeconomic factors (the covariates) are an integral part of the research plan (Lozoff, 1990).

Main Research Findings

The following is not intended to be a comprehensive review of the literature. Rather, it is restricted to what members of the Task Force held to be the main and strongest findings. More extensive reviews are provided in papers prepared by Task Force members and published in the *Journal of Nutrition Supplement*, "The Relationship between Undernutrition and Behavioral Development in Children," (volume 125, number 8S). This present review focuses first on data from observational and intervention studies of intrauterine growth retardation and PEM and then describes findings from intervention studies of micronutrient deficiencies.

Intrauterine Growth Retardation

Three strategies have been used to test the effects of mild-to-moderate prenatal undernutrition on behavioral and cognitive development:

1. Assess the development of growth-retarded newborns.
2. Follow children born into periods of famine.
3. Track the effects of supplementing the diet of nutritionally at-risk mothers on the development of the offspring.

Development of growth-retarded newborns. This is a very heterogeneous group. Although social class is the strongest predictor of intrauterine growth retardation, other factors, including genetics, infection, placental damage, and maternal malnutrition, may also cause growth retardation (Kramer, 1987). This report focuses exclusively on those relatively few studies that investigate nutritional factors. In Guatemala, for example, one study found that birth weight below the 10th percentile of the reference weight distribution for gestational age was associated with cognitive delays at 36 and 48 months (Gorman & Pollitt, 1992; Villar, Smeriglio, Martorell, Brown, & Klein, 1984), but birth weight was unrelated to cognitive test performance at 60 months and in adolescence (Pollitt, Gorman, & Metallinos-Katsaras, 1992).

Studies in more affluent countries suggest that the timing of malnutrition can moderate the outcome (Wachs, 1995). Comparatively poor postnatal performance deficits were more likely when prenatal stunting occurred before 24 weeks of gestation (Harvey, Princie, Burton, Parkison, & Campbell, 1982). But other social, educational, and biological factors can also moderate the effects of prenatal undernutrition. As noted by Wachs (1995), postnatal developmental risk is decreased among infants from socially and economically advantaged families (Vohr, Garcia-Coll, & Oh, 1989); they tend to have fewer postnatal biomedical complications (Eckerman, Sturm, & Gross, 1985) and are more likely to be exposed to programs of early cognitive stimulation (Padin-Rojas et al., 1991).

Children of famine. Children born to Dutch women whose second half of pregnancy coincided with the famine in the winter of 1944–45 had an average birth weight 327 grams below the norm. In early adulthood, however, they showed no deficits in intelligence (Stein, Susser, Saenger, & Marolla, 1975).

In Kenya, a period of drought and food shortage compromised further the energy intake of families among a nutritionally at-risk population. Besides showing weight loss, school children became less attentive in the classroom and reduced their motor activity in the playground. Toddlers were protected through family adjustments: Neither their energy intake nor their body weight was reduced; play and language behavior also remained stable (McDonald, Sigman, Espinosa, & Neumann, 1994).

Nutritional supplementation of mothers. Supplementation trials of pregnant women have yielded mixed findings. One study in Harlem, New York, found no effects of protein supplementation during pregnancy on the performance of offspring on developmental tests administered at 12 months of age, but the subjects did show beneficial effects on measures of habituation and play behavior (Rush, Stein, & Susser, 1980). A second study in Sui Lin Township, Taiwan, found sparse effects: infants at 8 months of age whose mothers had received a protein and energy supplement during pregnancy and lactation showed no effects on mental development and modest beneficial effects on motor development (Joos, Pollitt, Mueller, & Albright, 1983). At 5 years of age the children's performance on an IQ test showed no effects of the supplement (Hsueh & Meyer, 1981).

In summary, empirical evidence favoring the assumption that intrauterine growth retardation causes cognitive delays is weak. The number of relevant studies is small, and the data are not supportive, particularly in studies of middle childhood and adolescence. Further, a recent review of studies of children 7 years old and older, conducted in the United States and Europe, found little to support that intrauterine growth retardation is a risk factor for later development (Hack, 1996).

Concurrent and Later Effects of Undernutrition

Two sets of data are cited in this section: The first includes observational studies that tested the relationship between anthropometry (human body measurement) and dietary intake, on the one hand, and performance on mental and motor tests, on the other. In some of the studies the nutritional and outcome measures were concurrent; in others the anthropometric and dietary measures preceded the outcome measures. The second set of data comes from studies in which subjects' daily dietary intake was controlled, amounting to a nutritional supplement.

Body size, diet, and development. Measurements of linear growth (i.e., recumbent length and height), body weight, and other anthropometric measurements (e.g., skin-fold thickness) are widely used in clinical work and nutrition epidemiology to classify the nutritional status of children from infancy to adolescence. Children whose growth is slow or arrested in populations where malnutrition is endemic are assumed to be or to have been undernourished. In this light it would seem reasonable to postulate that an association between poor physical growth (e.g., stunting) and slow mental development was explained primarily by nutritional factors. That is, if undernutrition explained children's physical growth retardation, and retardation was associated with slow mental development, then undernutrition must also explain delays in mental development. This interpretation is speculative, however: both physical growth in early and late childhood and cognitive development are influenced by many other factors besides nutrition.

Independent of prenatal nutritional history, chronic mild-to-moderate PEM during the first 2 years of life has frequently, but not always, been found related to concurrent delays of mental and motor development (Wachs, 1995). In one study of young children in Jamaica, stunting was associated with reduced motor activity and exploratory behavior (Simeon & Grantham-McGregor, 1990). Later, again in Jamaica, better-nourished children exhibited increases in exploratory behavior and social interaction (Meeks Gardner et al., 1993). A study in West Java, Indonesia, found an association between body length and delays in the acquisition of gross motor milestones leading to bipedal locomotion (Pollitt et al., 1994). Self-locomotion is presently considered a critical experience for normal cognitive development (Bertenthal & Campos, 1990).

While undernutrition of infants is a concern, undernutrition among preschoolers and school-age children is also a serious public health problem. Undernourished preschool children accustomed to diets that do not meet their physiological requirements are at risk for lower levels of attention, learning impairment, and poor school attendance and achievement (Simeon & Grantham-McGregor, 1990; Wachs, 1995). A study in Kenya, for example, found that, after taking demographic factors into account, energy and animal protein intakes during the preschool years were associated with play and cognitive performance at 5 years of age (Sigman, McDonald, Neumann, & Bwibo, 1991). Other evidence from school-age children indicated that body size, particularly height-for-age, was related to performance on cognitive and achievement tests (Wachs, 1995).

Anthropometric indicators of undernutrition during the first 3 years of life also predict cognitive test performance in later childhood and adolescence. In the same study in Kenya, body size in infancy predicted performance on cognitive tests administered at 5 years of age (Sigman, Neumann, Janson, & Bwibo, 1989). Rural Guatemalan subjects also showed an association between height at 3 years of age and performance on a battery of psychoeducational tests administered 15 years later (Martorell, Rivera, Kaplowitz, & Pollitt, 1992).

Regarding diet, studies in Egypt (Wachs et al., 1995) and Kenya (Sigman, Neumann, Baksh, et al., 1989) showed that among toddlers intake of energy and total protein were positively associated with level of symbolic play and mental competence. In the Kenyan study, animal protein intake, compared to total protein, assessed at 18 and 30 months of age, was the better predictor of cognitive test performance at 5 years of age (Sigman et al., 1991).

Cognitive test performance among school children was also related to the quantity and quality of the diet. For example, the total energy and protein intakes of school-age children in Kenya were positively related to cognitive development (Sigman, Neumann, Janson, et al., 1989). However, in Kenya, as in Egypt, the intake of a better-quality protein (from animal sources) was a better predictor of performance in this age group (Wachs et al., 1995).

Protein and energy malnutrition. Laboratory animals which are severely undernourished early in life show a wide range of changes in responsiveness to environmental contingencies (Strupp & Levitsky, 1995). The most pervasive and permanent changes appear to be in emotionality, motivation, and anxiety level, which in turn affect all aspects of behavior, including those indicative of cognitive status. Affective changes that seem to be associated with changes in neural receptor functions and lowered cognitive flexibility persist after rehabilitation (Strupp & Levitsky, 1995).

Severely undernourished children are apathetic, not very responsive to their environment and inclined to stay close to their mother (Grantham-McGregor, 1995). Some of these behavioral characteristics persist into early childhood. For example, in a study in Barbados school-age children who were severely undernourished as infants were characterized as quiet, withdrawn, and passive (Galler et al., 1983). Severe undernutrition in early childhood was also associated with later cognitive deficits and poor school achievement in a study of children in Jamaica (Grantham-McGregor, 1995), particularly for children who continue to live under conditions that are not supportive of their growth and development. The early placement of such children in environments where they receive good nutrition, psychosocial support, and education can substantially reduce or even eliminate cognitive deficits (Colombo, de la Parra, & Lopez, 1992; Grantham-McGregor, Powell, Walker, & Himes, 1991; Winick, Meyer, & Harris, 1975).

Supplementary feeding. A meta-analysis of experimental and quasi-experimental studies showed that supplementary feeding during pregnancy and the child's first months of postnatal life enhanced motor development among infants (8 to 12 months) and toddlers (12 to 24 months) and also mental development among toddlers (Pollitt & Oh, 1994). In a study in Mexico early supplementary feeding influenced the quality of the mother's caregiving behavior (Chavez & Martinez, 1984). A relationship between the child's diet and maternal behavior was also observed in a study in Egypt, even after statistically controlling for the adequacy of the mother's own dietary intake (Wachs et al., 1992). These findings illustrate the influence that nutrition has on the reciprocal relationship between parent and child—the parent's caregiving practices influencing infant development and the infant's behaviors influencing parent's caregiving practices.

Supplementary feeding during the first 2 years of life has also been found to have long-term effects on cognitive development. In rural Guatemala, nutritional supplementation of pregnant and lactating women and their offspring for at least the first 2 years of postnatal life improved the later performance, in adolescence, on tests of reading, vocabulary, arithmetic, and general knowledge. Effects were strongest among children whose families were at the low end of the social and economic distribution within their rural communities (Pollitt et al., 1993).

Evidence suggests further that supplementary feeding beyond the period of peak growth of the central nervous system has long-term effects on cognitive development. In the Guatemalan study, supplementary feeding *after* the first 2 years of life also led to improved performance, in adolescence, on tests of arithmetic, general knowledge, and reading (Pollitt et al., 1993). In one intervention in Cali, Colombia, which began at 42 months of age or later and combined nutritional supplementation (protein, energy, and vitamins A and B plus iron) with health support and educational stimulation, undernourished preschool children showed improved cognitive test performance. At the beginning of primary school, however, when the intervention was discontinued, the amount of benefit children showed varied, depending on the timing and duration of support: the earlier the intervention was begun and the longer it lasted, the greater the benefit (McKay, Sinisterra, McKay, Gomez, & Lloreda, 1978).

Theoretically, school nutrition should enhance children's achievement by improving attendance, preventing hunger, and correcting nutritional deficiencies. Evaluations of school nutritional programs have yielded equivocal results overall; however, in those with stronger research designs (i.e., in Jamaica, Peru, and the United States) the expected effects were observed (Jacoby, Cueto, & Pollitt, 1996; Meyers, Sampson, Weitzman, Rogers, & Kayne, 1989; Pollitt, Jacoby, & Cueto, 1996; Powell, Grantham-McGregor, & Elaston, 1983).

Contextual Factors

Assuring the best prediction of an undernourished child's later development requires that we account for not only the nutritional risk but also the context in which malnourishment occurred (Wachs, 1995). Undernutrition, with few exceptions, is closely associated with economic impoverishment, limited educational opportunity, limited access to health

care, poor hygiene and sanitation, and continuous exposure to vectors of infection (Mata, 1978). But even where such conditions prevail, those families that are socially and economically better off are less likely to house an undernourished child (Espinosa et al., 1992; Grantham-McGregor, 1984; Kirksey et al., 1991; Wachs et al., 1995). Contextual conditions also explain, by themselves or through their interaction with malnutrition, part of the retarded physical growth and the delays in motor, mental, and socio-emotional development of undernourished infants and children. Further, in more affluent countries, young children who are undernourished owing to medical reasons are generally free of any cognitive deficits (Pollitt, 1987).

An interaction between socioeconomic background and early supplementary feeding was observed in Guatemala. As noted earlier, the effectiveness of an early energy and protein supplement on later performance in adolescence was greatest for those children who were at the lowest end of the social and economic distribution (Pollitt et al., 1993). The supplement appeared to compensate for low status.

In summary, nutritional indicators (e.g., anthropometry and dietary intake) among infants and preschool children are positively related to performance on tests of mental and motor development. Anthropometry (particularly height-for-age) also relates to school-age children's performance on cognitive and psycho-educational tests. Supplementary feeding during pregnancy and during the first 2 years of postnatal life enhances the development of nutritionally at-risk children and improves cognitive competence as measured 10 years later. Some of these benefits result even if the intervention started after the peak period of central nervous system growth. Nutritional factors, however, do not fully explain delays in development or the comparatively poor test performance of undernourished children. Contextual factors, rooted in poverty, must be invoked. Assessing the combination of these factors and nutritional risk yields the best prediction of the development of these children.

Micronutrient Deficiencies

As noted earlier, some micronutrient deficiencies that coexist with protein and energy deficiency have adverse effects on behavior in laboratory animals, on mental and motor development of infants and toddlers, and on the cognitive functioning of older children. It is important that we not overlook the role of micronutrient deficiencies in studies of the effects of undernourishment on child development. In some investigations such deficiencies are a confound; in others they can be conceptualized as an effect modifier. In the first instance, the dietary intake of children in populations previously considered at risk of PEM were likely to have been deficient in vitamins and minerals, *not* in energy and protein, thus confounding results (Allen, 1993; Beaton, Calloway, & Murphy, 1992). In the second, nutritional factors that cause PEM could also be causing micronutrient deficiencies (e.g., in iron and zinc) that are known to affect, in turn, mental and motor development in children (Golub et al., 1995; Pollitt, 1995); thus, the outcomes may vary, depending on the presence or absence and severity of deficiencies.

Iron. Infants and toddlers who are iron-deficient anemic consistently perform less well on tests of mental and motor development than their peers whose body iron stores are replete (Lozoff, 1990; Walter, 1989). Yet supplementary iron has not generally reversed the developmental delay in this age group, except in a randomized trial in West Java, Indonesia (Idjradinata & Pollitt, 1993). In other studies, the developmental reversal was restricted to those cases where the iron supplementation resulted in normalizing the child's hemoglobin level. A preventative trial with the same age group yielded equivocal findings. The motor, but not mental, development of infants fed iron-fortified formulas was accelerated, compared to controls, up to 12 months of age; but this advantage was lost at 15 months (Moffatt, Longstaffe, Besant, & Dureski, 1994).

Evidence on the effects of iron deficiency on preschoolers and older school-age children is clearer. Compared to controls, children with iron deficiency scored lower on cognitive tests and performed less well on school tests (Pollitt, Hathirat, Kotchabharkdi, Missell, & Valyasevi, 1989; Seshadri & Gopaldas, 1989). Iron supplementation led to significantly improved performance on measures of overall intelligence and on tests of specific cognitive processes among iron-deficient children (Seshadri & Gopaldas, 1989; Soemantri, Pollitt, & Kim, 1985; Soewondo, Husaini, & Pollitt, 1989).

Research has yet to determine the role of iron in the brain in the cognitive and emotional detriments observed in iron-deficient children. It has been proposed that such effects are mediated by a deficiency in the functional activity of dopamine receptors (Yehuda & Youdim, 1989), but this hypothesis has yet to be fully tested in humans (Dallman, 1990). Alternatively, the impact of iron on cognitive performance may be mediated by changes in motivation or emotion that interfere with attentional processes which, in turn, interfere with cognitive performance. This question—how changes in iron status translate into changes in cognitive and noncognitive performance—remains an important area for future research.

Iodine. Maternal iodine deficiency in early pregnancy and associated thyroxine deficiency impair the development of the fetal central nervous system and can result in frank, irreversible cretinism in the child. Studies in Ecuador (Fierro-Benitez et al., 1989; Trowbridge, 1972) showed that correction of the maternal iodine deficiency before conception or in early pregnancy can improve the mental performance of offspring. Comparisons of primary school children in China, in areas with iodine deficiency versus areas with normal iodine intake (Ma, Wang, Wang, Chen, & Chi, 1989) and of goitrous vs. non-goitrous children in Chile (Muzzo, Levia, & Carrasco, 1987) showed better mental and psychomotor performance in the latter groups.

Two double-blind[4] intervention studies of primary school children yielded contradictory results. An intervention with goitrous Bolivian primary school children reduced the goiter rate but had no effect on physical or mental performance (Bautista, Barker, Dunn, Sanchez, & Kaiser, 1982), whereas iodized oil given to iodine-deficient children of similar age in Malawi did have a positive effect on mental and certain psychomotor test performance (Shrestha, 1994).

Zinc. Severe developmental zinc deficiency in laboratory rats disrupted brain growth and morphology and led to long-term behavioral changes that were qualitatively similar in many respects to those produced by general undernutrition (Golub et al., 1995). However, since severe induced zinc deficiency produces anorexia, it is difficult to discriminate between the effects of low zinc intake and an overall decrease in nutrient intake. Studies of marginal and moderate zinc deficiency in young monkeys have demonstrated effects on activity level, exploration, and performance on some cognitive tasks (Golub, Gershwin, Hurley, & Saito, 1985). In stunted school-age children, however, no differences were found between groups varying in zinc status, or within groups in response to zinc supplements, in scores on standardized tests of attention (Gibson et al., 1989).

At present, no experimental studies have discriminated among the effects of deficiencies of zinc, iron, protein, and energy. Thus, how different deficiencies may interact is unknown.

Future Directions

New understanding of the role of nutrition in child development points to suggestions for future research.

Biological and Behavioral Mechanisms

Research efforts are gradually revealing a finer-grained picture of the processes linking nutrition and observable behavior. Various mechanisms involving both biological and behavioral aspects of development are implicated and bear investigating.

Biological. Earlier research linking PEM and behavior suggested that undernutrition interfered with the development of the central nervous system. Undernutrition reduced brain weight and the number of brain cells, which in turn were seen as the cause of irreversible detriments in cognitive and motor performance (NAS, 1973). This emphasis on brain growth focused attention almost exclusively on the period of maximal brain growth, seen as the period of greatest vulnerability.

New findings indicate, however, that periods before and after that of maximal brain growth may be equally important. It is now understood that critical aspects of central nervous system development—for example, gliogenesis, macroneurogenesis, and early glial and neuronal migrations—precede the period of maximal brain growth. Other later processes, such as synaptogenesis and myelinization, may also be sensitive to insult and remediation (Levitsky & Strupp, 1995; Strupp & Levitsky, 1995).

Research during the last decade has shown that the effects of undernutrition late in gestation are similar to those occurring early. In the case of previously undernourished animals, for instance, the period of brain growth can be extended, and remarkable recovery has been observed. Such evidence is leading researchers to consider a broader range of possible biological mediators, including brain differentiation and changes in neuroreceptor sensitivity. For example, perturbations at the sub-cellular level, as suggested by alterations in sensitivity to pharmacological challenges, persist after periods of early undernutrition and nutritional rehabilitation (Levitsky & Strupp, 1995).

Behavioral. In the mid 1970s the concept of *functional isolation*, referring to restricted interaction with the environment, was proposed to explain the long-term behavioral effects of early undernutrition (Levitsky, 1979; Levitsky & Barnes, 1972). It was hypothesized that it is the differential experience of the organism rather than disrupted brain growth that mediates the effects of early undernutrition over time. The child who is undernourished attempts to maintain energy balance by reducing energy expenditure and withdrawing from environment stimulation. Such withdrawal limits the child's capacity to take in environmental information and thereby acquire the skills and knowledge necessary for normal behavioral development (Levitsky & Strupp, 1984). This concept arose from evidence suggesting that the behaviors affected by early undernutrition were similar to those produced by early environmental isolation.

Although the functional isolation hypothesis was initially developed as an alternative to a purely biological explanation of nutrition-mediated behavioral deficits, the two explanations may in fact be compatible rather than conflicting. Functional isolation may actually influence both central nervous system and behavioral development. While not all aspects of the CNS may be sensitive to environmental influences, and the extent of effects may be relatively small (Bedi & Bhide, 1988), evidence from behavioral neuroscience studies illustrates how restricting experience may adversely influence development (Diamond, 1988; Greenough & Black, 1992) and efficiency (Stone, 1987) of specific brain structures and processes. In addition to the influence of functional isolation on both brain and behavior, subsequent neural changes may further accentuate the effects of functional isolation on ultimate development.

Recently, the functional isolation proposition has been elaborated to explain in greater detail some of the mechanisms that may contribute to long-term adverse effects of undernutrition on cognitive development (Pollitt et al., 1993). This revised proposal hinges on the well-documented effects of undernutrition on body size, neuromotor development, and physical activity. If the child is small and physically underdeveloped and inactive, he or she may

1. induce behaviors and social responses from caretakers that would generally be reserved for younger children;
2. undertake less exploration of the environment; and
3. consequently lag in acquiring the motor skills, cognitive abilities, and social behaviors that typify normal development.

These patterns can operate independently and interactively, with cumulative effects, such that the child ultimately falls behind in competencies attained by well-nourished children. Investigating how nutrition promotes individual differences in children's motor skills, exploration, and play behavior would provide a welcome test of this hypothesis.

Assessing Nutrition

Focusing on individual nutrient deficiencies is particularly problematic within populations in which undernutrition is a major public health concern. With the possible exception of populations where this is not a problem, studies of single nutrients are no longer adequate (Golub et al., 1995; Pollitt, 1995)—as indicated by the coexistence of multiple nutrient deficiencies (Schürch, 1995), complex interactions in the absorption and utilization of nutrients, and the demonstrated effects of different nutrients on CNS function. Moreover, failure to account for the relationship between PEM and micronutrient deficiencies has led to inconclusive findings regarding the causal role of distinct nutrients on cognitive outcomes (Pollitt et al., 1993).

Too often studies are marred by a lack of information on the overall nutritional status of the population in question. For example, studies testing the functional consequences of particular nutritional deficits (e.g., energy) have floundered, because the prevalence of the deficit in the populations under study was negligible (Allen, 1993). It is important, therefore, to obtain survey data on nutritional indicators before implementing field studies. Further, if limits in knowledge and technology preclude the use of laboratory measures to determine nutrient status (as in the case of zinc), then alternative procedures (e.g., response to treatment) should be used to establish baseline values. While this approach could be costly, the yield to science would be rewarding.

Measuring Outcome

Just as the field is moving beyond an emphasis on single nutrients, so the focus on cognitive development to the exclusion of biological and psychosocial development no longer suffices in the investigation of undernutrition effects. Research is expanding to encompass the broader context and the multiple risks that interact with nutrition in determining outcomes for the undernourished child.

Assessments of affective characteristics, e.g., temperament, reactivity to stress, self-regulation, and emotional regulation, stand to shed light on the effects of undernutrition on the behavioral adjustment and psychological functioning of undernourished children. Although such attributes are typically treated as innate, increasing knowledge of the CNS processes that underlie individual differences in temperament and link temperament and cognitive processes makes research in this domain promising. One issue is whether the nutritional environment could modify the genotype of temperament.

Likewise, studying the effects of undernutrition on the simultaneous or sequential relationships between developmental systems is also critical. The link, for example, between neuromotor and cognitive delays in the undernourished infant merits attention in light of new information showing that self-locomotion is an antecedent to perceptual development (Bertenthal & Campos, 1990; Lockman & Thelen, 1993).

We must understand more about the neural mechanisms through which undernutrition and related factors translate into individual differences in behavior and development. Recent advances in biomedical methodology promise a more direct assessment of critical nutrition-sensitive CNS processes. For example, nuclear magnetic resonance spectroscopy allows noninvasive assessment of changes in CNS energy metabolism (Holtzman, McFarland, Jacobs, Offut, & Neuringer, 1991) and has been used with some success to distinguish the CNS metabolic concentrations of at-risk and normal infants (Cady et al., 1983).

Finally, the possible effects of undernutrition across generations must be identified. At issue is how biological and behavioral mechanisms may contribute to the transfer of a burden of undernutrition from one generation to the next (Susser & Stein, 1994). Several longitudinal studies of severe and mild-to-moderate undernutrition in early life, launched in the past, offer unique opportunities for the follow-up of new generations.

Accounting for Factors That Modify Effects

Studies are needed of the effects of undernutrition over the lifespan, from the earliest stages, including the prenatal, to old age. But, while age may be related to the outcome, we must identify what factors related to increasing age act to modify outcomes. Obviously, effects are not necessarily mediated only by changes in the CNS occurring during the specific period of maximal brain growth (Levitsky & Strupp, 1995). How for instance, is the educational achievement and progress of children hampered by undernutrition (Soemantri et al., 1985)? Or how does formal education limit the adverse effects of early undernutrition?

Future studies should also attend to the role of intra-individual and environmental factors that protect against or accentuate the risks of undernutrition. Research designs that would, for example, track the chain of relationships—of effects of undernutrition on the child's behavior, the child's behavior on caregiver behavior and vice versa, and possible buffering or deleterious factors on these relationships—would go a long way toward clarifying how undernutrition affects behavioral outcomes and development.

Finally, what is needed are studies that capture the broader context, the "human condition." Undernutrition among children in economically impoverished populations is likely compounded by multiple risk factors—by conditions besides undernutrition. With few exceptions (Chavez & Martinez, 1984), the recognition that such interactions do exist has failed to lead to studies that attempt to disentangle them or that seek to identify the factors that either increase or decrease the risks. It is, for example, important to understand why, in one study, poor, undernourished children experienced significant developmental delays, while middle-class children who suffered from severe undernutrition secondary to medical problems showed no such effects (Pollitt, 1987).

Conclusion

In summary, there is convincing evidence that general undernutrition and iodine and iron deficiency can impair behavioral and cognitive development. Iodine deficiency has its maximal effect in utero, while that of iron deficiency and general undernutrition is greatest in the early postnatal period. These effects, however, are no longer believed to be limited to the phase of maximal brain growth or to be mediated exclusively through neuroanatomical structural changes. Studies intended to show or reverse the effects of PEM do not allow a clear causal attribution to protein or energy as determining factors, and confounding with iron remains a possibility. Other single nutrients could have effects on behavioral development, but this has not yet been convincingly demonstrated in humans. The incidence and magnitude of nutritional effects on behavior can be greatly exacerbated by other risk factors and insults; they can also be reduced or eliminated by buffering factors. Such effect modifiers should be considered in all research and policy discussions.

While we encourage further research on the effects of undernutrition on human development, there is, finally, a great need to study the societal impact of undernutrition in populations in which most members are affected. Of great concern are populations which have been exposed to natural and man-made famine conditions. Such research would involve calculating the social and economic cost of limiting the potential of human capital within a society and estimating the benefits that would accrue through the prevention of malnutrition.

Notes

1. Anthropometric (human body) measurements are generally used around the world to classify children as well-nourished or nutritionally at risk (i.e., stunted or wasted). The World Health Organization (WHO) has a set of reference standards for weight and height used to compare trends among different countries and to estimate the prevalence of undernutrition. The 50th percentile, that is, the median of the normal distribution of a particular anthropometric measurement (e.g., weight) at a given age, is generally used as the criterion for comparisons. The WHO references are based on the respective anthropometric measurements obtained by the United States National Center for Health Statistics (NCHS). Although weight-for-age is a criterion often used to classify children at-risk, it is recognized that this measure is not a fully satisfactory criterion because the weights of some children, which may be low for their chronological age according to the WHO reference, may be in line with their short stature.

2. Dietary quality refers to a diverse diet that includes protein and micronutrients (e.g., iron) of animal origin.

3. In this context, bioavailability indicates that absorption of nutrients varies depending on their source. For the human infant, for example, the iron contained in human milk has a higher bioavailability than that in

cow's milk. This difference explains in part why the prevalence of iron-deficiency anemia is much lower among infants who are breast fed, compared to those fed cow's milk.

4. In a double-blind experiment, neither the subject nor the person who implements the treatment nor the person who analyzes the data knows which subjects make up the experimental group and which the comparison group.

References

Allen, L. H. (1993). The nutrition CRSP: What is marginal undernutrition, and does it affect human function? *Nutrition Reviews, 9*, 255–267.

Almeida, S. S., de Oliveira, L. M., & Graeff, F. G. (1991). Early life protein malnutrition changes exploration of the elevated plus-maze and reactivity to anxyolytics. *Psychopharmacology, 103*, 513–518.

Austin, K. B., Beiswanger, C., Bronzino, J. D., Austin-Lafrance, R. J., Galler, J. R., & Morgane, P. J. (1992). Prenatal protein malnutrition alters behavioral state modulation of inhibition and facilitation in the dentate gyms. *Brain Research Bulletin, 28*, 245–255.

Barrett, D. (1984). Malnutrition and child behavior: Conceptualization, assessment, and an empirical study of social-emotional functioning. In B. Schürch & J. Brozek (Eds.), *Malnutrition and behavior: A critical assessment of key issues* (pp. 280–306). Lausanne, Switzerland: Nestlé Foundation for the Study of Nutrition Problems in the World.

Barrett, D., & Frank, D. (1987). *The effects of undernutrition on children's behavior.* New York: Gordon and Breach.

Bautista, A., Barker, P. A., Dunn, J. T., Sanchez, M., & Kaiser, D. L. (1982). The effects of oral iodized oil on intelligence, thyroid status, and somatic growth in school-age children from an area of endemic goiter. *American Journal of Clinical Nutrition, 35*, 127–134.

Beaton, G. H., Calloway, D. H., & Murphy, S. P. (1992). Estimated protein intakes of toddlers: Predicted prevalence of inadequate intakes in village populations in Egypt, Kenya, and Mexico. *American Journal of Clinical Nutrition, 55*, 902–911.

Bedi, K. (1992). Malnutrition, environment, brain and behavior. *Proceedings of the Australasian Society for Human Biology, 5*, 125–142.

Bedi, K., & Bhide, P. (1988). Effects of environmental diversity on brain morphology. *Early Human Development, 17*, 107–143.

Bertenthal, B., & Campos, J. (1990). A system approach to the organizing effects of self-produced locomotion during infancy. In C. Rovee-Collier & L. P. Lipsitt (Eds.), *Advances in infancy research* (Vol. 6, pp. 2–60). Norwood, NJ: Ablex Publishing.

Buzina, R., Bates, C. J., Beek, v.d.J., Brubacher, G., Chandra, R. K., Hallberg, L., Heseker, J., Mertz, W., Pietrzik, K., Pollitt, E., Pradilla, A., Suboticanec, K., Sandstead, H. H., Schalch, W., Spurr, G. B., & Westenhofer, J. (1989). Workshop on functional significance of mild to moderate malnutrition. *American Journal of Clinical Nutrition, 50*, 172–176.

Cady, E. B., Costello, A. M., Dawson, M. J., Delpy, D. T., Hope, P. L., Reynolds, E. O., Tofts, P. S., & Wilkie, D. R. (1983). Non-invasive investigation of cerebral metabolism in newborn infants by phosphorus nuclear magnetic resonance spectroscopy. *Lancet, 14*, 1059–1062.

Carmichael, S. L., Pollitt, E., Gorman, K. S., & Martorell, R. (1994). Determinants of participation in a nutritional supplementation project in rural Guatemala. *Nutrition Research, 14*(2), 163–176.

Chavez, A., & Martinez, C. (1984). Behavioral measurements of activity in children and their relation to food intake in a poor community. In E. Pollitt & P. Amante

(Eds.), *Energy intake and activity* (pp. 303–321). New York: Liss.

Chen, L. (1983). Diarrhea and malnutrition. In L. Chen & N. Scrimshaw (Eds.), *Energy intake and activity* (pp. 3–19). New York: Plenum Publishing Corp.

Colombo, M., de la Parra, A., & Lopez, I. (1992). Intellectual and physical outcome of children undernourished in early life is influenced by later environmental conditions. *Developmental Medicine and Child Neurology, 34*, 611–622.

Dallman, P (1990). Commentary. In J. Dobbing (Ed.), *Brain, behavior and iron in the infant diet* (pp. 101–103). London: Springer-Verlag.

Diamond, M. (1988). *Enriching heredity: The impact of the environment on the anatomy of the brain.* New York: Free Press.

Diamond, A., Ciaramitaro, V., Donner, E., Hurwitz, W., Lee, E., Grover, W., & Minarcik, C. (1992). Prefrontal cortex cognitive deficits in early-treated PKU: Results of a longitudinal study in children and of an animal model. *Society of Neuroscience Abstracts, 18*, 1063 (abs.).

Diaz-Cintra, S., Cintra, L., Ortega, A., Kemper, T., & Morgane, P. J. (1990). Effects of protein deprivation on pyramidal cells of the visual cortex in rats of three age groups. *Journal of Comparative Neurology, 292*, 117–126.

Eckerman, C., Sturm, L., & Gross, S. (1985). Different developmental courses for very-low-birthweight infants differing in early growth. *Developmental Psychology, 21*, 813–827.

Espinosa, M. P., Sigman, M. D., Neumann, C. G., Bwibo, N. O., & McDonald, M. A. (1992). Playground behaviors of school-age children in relation to nutrition, schooling and family characteristics. *Developmental Psychology, 28*, 1188–1195.

Fierro-Benitez, R., Sandoval-Valencia, H., Sevilla-Munoz, B., Rodriguez, E., Gualotuna, E., Fierro-Carrion, G., Pacheco-Bastides, V., Andrade, J., Wang, P. H., & Stanbury, J. B. (1989). Influence of nutritional state on the disposal of orally and intramuscularly administered iodized oil to iodine repleted older children and adult women. *Journal of Endocrinological Investigation, 12*, 405–407.

Galler, J. R., Ramsey, F., Solimano, G., & Lowell, W. E. (1983). The influence of early malnutrition on subsequent behavioral development. II. Classroom behavior. *Journal of the American Academy of Child Psychiatry, 22*, 16–22.

Gibson, R. S., Smit Vanderkooy, P. D., MacDonald, A. C., Goldman, A., Ryan B. A., & Berry, M. (1989). A growth limiting, mild zinc deficiency syndrome in some Southern Ontario boys with low height percentiles. *American Journal of Clinical Nutrition, 49*, 1266–1273.

Golden, M. (1991). The nature of nutritional deficiency in relation to growth failure and poverty. *Acta Paediatrica Scandinavia Supplement, 374*, 95–110.

Golub, M. S., Gershwin, M. E., Hurley, L. S., Hendrickx, A. G., & Saito, W Y. (1985). Studies of marginal zinc deprivation in rhesus monkeys: Infant behavior. *American Journal of Clinical Nutrition, 42*, 1229–1239.

Golub, M., Keen, C. L., Gershwin, E., & Hendrickx, A. G. (1995). Developmental zinc deficiency and behavior. *Journal of Nutrition Supplement, 125*, 2263S–2271S.

Gorman, K., & Pollitt, E. (1992). Relationship between weight and body proportionality at birth, growth during the first year of life, and cognitive development at 36, 48, and 60 months. *Infant Behavior and Development, 15*, 279–296.

Grantham-McGregor, S. M. (1984). The social background of childhood malnutrition. In J. Brozek & B. Schürch (Eds.), *Malnutrition and behaviour: Critical assessment of key issues* (pp. 358–374). Lausanne, Switzerland: Nestlé Foundation.

Grantham-McGregor, S. (1995). A review of studies of the effect of severe malnutrition on mental development. *Journal of Nutrition Supplement, 125*, 2233S–2238S.

Grantham-McGregor, S., Powell, C., Walker, S., Chang, S., & Fletcher, P. (1994). The long-term follow-up of severely malnourished children who participated in an intervention program. *Child Development, 65,* 428–439.

Grantham-McGregor, S., Powell, C., Walker, S., & Himes, J. (1991). Nutritional supplementation, psychosocial stimulation, and mental development of stunted children: The Jamaican study. *Lancet, 338,* 1–5.

Greenough, W., & Black, J. (1992). Induction of brain structure by experience: Substrates for cognitive development. In M. Gunnar & C. Nelson (Eds.), *Developmental behavior neuroscience: The Minnesota symposia on child psychology* (Vol. 24, pp. 155–200). Hillsdale, NJ: Erlbaum Assoc., Inc.

Hack, M. (1996, November). *Effects of intrauterine growth retardation on mental performance and behavior: Outcomes during adolescence and adulthood.* Paper presented at the workshop on Intrauterine Growth Retardation organized by the International Dietary Consultative Group, Baton Rouge, Louisiana.

Harvey, D., Princie, J., Burton, J., Parkison, L., & Campbell, S. (1982). Ability of children who were small-for-gestational-age babies. *Pediatrics, 69,* 296–300.

Holtzman, D., McFarland, E., Jacobs, D., Offut, M., & Neuringer, L. (1991). Maturational increase in mouse brain creatine kinase reaction rates shown by phosphorus magnetic resonance. *Developmental Brain Research, 58,* 181–188.

Horowitz, F. (1989). Using developmental theory to guide the search for the effects of biological risk factors on the development of children. *American Journal of Clinical Nutrition Supplement, 50,* 589–595.

Hsueh, A. M., & Meyer, B. (1981). Maternal dietary supplementation and 5-year-old Stanford Binet test on the offspring in Taiwan. *Federation Proceedings, 40,* 897 (Abs.). [FASEB Journal–Abstracts (Federation of American Societies for Experimental Biology)].

Husaini, M. A., Karyadi, L., Husaini, Y. K., Sandjaja, Karyadi, D., & Pollitt, E. Developmental effects of short-term supplementary feeding in nutritionally at-risk Indonesian infants. *American Journal of Clinical Nutrition, 54,* 799–804.

Idjradinata, P., & Pollitt, E. (1993). Reversal of developmental delays in iron-deficient anaemic infants treated with iron. *Lancet, 341,* 1–4.

International Conference on Nutrition, FAO/Rome & WHO/Geneva. (1992). *Nutrition and development: A global assessment.* Author.

Jacoby, E., Cueto, S., & Pollitt, E. (1996). Benefits of a school breakfast program among Andean children in Huaraz, Peru. *Food and Nutrition Bulletin, 17*(1), 54–64.

Joos, S. K., Pollitt, E., Mueller, W. H., & Albright, D. (1983). The Bacon Chow Study: Maternal supplementation and infant behavioral development. *Child Development, 54,* 669–676.

Keller, E. A., Cuadra, G. R., Molina, V. A., & Orsingher, O. A. (1990). Perinatal undernutrition affects brain modulatory capacity of beta-adrenergic receptors in adult rats. *Journal of Nutrition, 120,* 305–338.

Kirksey, A., Rahmanifar, A., Wachs, T. D., McCabe, G. P., Bassily, N. S., Bishry, Z., Galal, O. M., Harrison, G. G., & Jerome, N. W. (1991). Determinants of pregnancy outcome and newborn behavior of a semirural Egyptian population. *American Journal of Clinical Nutrition, 54,* 657–667.

Kramer, M. S. (1987). Determinants of low birth weight: Methodological assessment and meta-analysis. *Bulletin of the World Health Organization, 65,* 663–737.

Levitsky, D. A. (1979). Malnutrition and the hunger to learn. In D. A. Levitsky (Ed.), *Malnutrition, environment, and behavior* (pp. 161–179). Ithaca, NY: Cornell University Press.

Levitsky, D. A., & Barnes, R. H. (1972). Nutritional and environmental interactions in behavioral development of the rat: Long-term effects. *Science, 176,* 68–72.

Levitsky, D. A., & Strupp, B. J. (1984). Functional isolation in rats. In J. Brozek & B. Schürch (Eds.), *Malnutrition and behavior: Critical assessment of key issues* (Vol. 4, pp. 411–420). Lausanne, Switzerland: Nestlé Foundation Publication Series.

Levitsky, D. A., & Strupp, B. J. (1995). Malnutrition and the brain: Changing concepts, changing concerns. *Journal of Nutrition Supplement, 125,* 2212S–2220S.

Lockman, J., & Thelen, E. (1993). Developmental biodynamics—brain, body, behavior connections—introduction. *Child Development, 64,* 953–959.

Lozoff, B. (1988). Behavioral alterations in iron deficiency. *Advances in Pediatrics, 35,* 331–359.

Lozoff, B. (1990). Has iron deficiency been shown to cause altered behavior in infants? In J. Dobbing (Ed.), *Brain, behavior, and iron in the infant diet* (pp. 107–31). London: Springer-Verlag.

Ma, T., Wang, Y. Y., Wang, D., Chen, Z. P., & Chi, S. P. (1989). Neuropsychological studies in iodine deficiency areas in China. In G. R. DeLong, J. Robbins, & G. Condiffe (Eds.), *Iodine and the brain* (pp. 259–268). New York: Plenum Press.

Martorell, R., Rivera, J., Kaplowitz, H., & Pollitt, E. (1992). Long term consequences of growth retardation during early childhood. In M. Hernandez & J. Argente (Eds.), *Human growth: Basic and clinical aspects* (pp. 143–149). Amsterdam, The Netherlands: Elsevier.

Martorell, R., & Yarbrough, C. (1983). The energy cost of diarrheal diseases and other common illnesses in children. In L. Chen & N. Scrimshaw (Eds.), *Diarrhea and malnutrition* (pp. 125–141). New York: Plenum Publishing Corp.

Mata, L. (1978). *The children of Santa Maria Cauque: A prospective field study of health and growth* (International Nutrition Policy Series). Cambridge, MA: MIT Press.

McCullough, A. L., Kirksey, A., Wachs, T. D., McCabe, G. P, Bassily, N. S., Bishry, Z., Galal, O. M., Harrison, G. G., & Jerome, N. W. (1990). Vitamin B-6 status of Egyptian mothers: Relation to infant behavior and maternal-infant interactions. *American Journal of Clinical Nutrition, 51,* 1067–1074.

McDonald, M. A., Sigman, M., Espinosa, M. P., & Neumann, C. G. (1994). Impact of a temporary food shortage on children and their mothers. *Child Development, 65,* 404–415.

McKay, H., Sinisterra, L., McKay, A., Gomez, H., & Lloreda, P. (1978). Improving cognitive ability in chronically deprived children. *Science, 200,* 270–278.

McLaren, D. S. (1974). The great protein fiasco. *Lancet, 2,* 93–96.

Medvedev, D. I., & Babichenko, I. I. (1988). Characteristics of the effect of protein-calorie insufficiency on synaptic contacts in the neocortex. *Biulleten Eksperimentalnoi. Biologii i Meditsiny* (USSR), *105,* 393–397.

Meeks Gardner, J., Grantham-McGregor, S. M., & Chang, S. (1993). Behavior of stunted children and the relationship to development. *Proceedings, Nutrition Society, 52,* 36A (abs.).

Meyers, A., Sampson, A., Weitzman, M., Rogers, B., & Kayne, H. (1989). School breakfast program and school performance. *American Journal of Diseases of Children, 142,* 1234–1239.

Moffatt, M. E. K., Longstaffe, S., Besant, J., & Dureski, C. (1994). Prevention of iron deficiency and psychomotor decline in high-risk infants through use of iron-fortified infant formula: A randomized clinical trial. *Journal of Pediatrics, 125,* 527–534.

Muzzo, S., Levia, L., & Carrasco, D. (1987). Influence of a moderate iodine deficiency upon intellectual coefficient of school-age children. In G. Medeiros-Neto, R. M. B. Maciel, & A. Halpern (Eds.), *Iodine deficiency disorders and congenital hypothyroidism* (pp. 40–45). São Paulo, Brazil: ACHE.

National Academy of Sciences. (1973). *National Research Council of the National Academy of Sciences Position Paper.* Washington, DC: Author.

Padin-Rojas, Y. Y., Garcia Coll, C. T., Gomez, G., Bonet, L., Escobar, M., & Varcarcel, M. (1991). Early intervention in infants with intrauterine growth retardation: Its effects on neuropsychological development. *Boletin Asociacion Medica de Puerto Rico, 83,* 378–382.

Pollitt, E. (1987). A critical review of three decades of research on the effects of chronic energy malnutrition on behavioral development. In B. Schürch & N. S. Scrimshaw (Eds.), *Chronic energy deficiency: Consequences and related issues* (pp. 77–93). Lausanne, Switzerland: International Dietary Energy Consultative Group.

Pollitt, E. (1988). Developmental impact of nutrition on pregnancy, infancy and childhood: Public health issues in the United States. In N. W. Bray (Ed.), *International review of research in mental retardation* (Vol. 15, pp. 33–80). San Diego, CA: Academic Press.

Pollitt, E. (1995). Functional significance of the covariance between protein energy malnutrition and iron deficiency anemia. *Journal of Nutrition Supplement, 125,* 2272S–2277S.

Pollitt, E., Gorman, K. S., Engle, P., Martorell, R., & Rivera, J. (1993). Early supplementary feeding and cognition: Effects over two decades. *Monographs of the Society for Research in Child Development, 58*(7, Serial No. 238).

Pollitt, E., Gorman, K., & Metallinos-Katsaras, E. (1992). Long-term developmental consequences of intrauterine and postnatal growth retardation in rural Guatemala. In G. J. Suci & S. Robertson (Eds.), *Future directions in infant development research* (pp. 43–70). New York: Springer-Verlag.

Pollitt, E., Hathirat, P., Kotchabharkdi, N., Missell, L., & Valyasevi, A. (1989). Iron deficiency and educational achievement in Thailand. *American Journal of Clinical Nutrition Supplement, 50,* 687–696.

Pollitt, E., Husaini, M. A., Harahap, H., Halati, S., Nugraheni, A., & Sherlock, A. (1994). Stunting and delayed motor development in rural West Java. *American Journal of Human Biology, 6,* 627–635.

Pollitt, E., Jacoby, E., & Cueto, S. (1996). *Desayuno escolar y rendimiento.* Lima, Peru: Editorial Apoyo.

Pollitt, E., & Oh, S.-Y. (1994). Early supplementary feeding, child development and health policy. *Food and Nutrition Bulletin, 15,* 208–214.

Pollitt, E., & Thomson, C. (1977). Protein-calorie malnutrition and behavior: A view from psychology. In R. Wurtman & J. Wurtman (Eds.), *Nutrition and the brain* (Vol. 2, pp. 261–306). New York: Raven Press.

Powell, C., Grantham-McGregor, S., & Elston, M. (1983). An evaluation of giving the Jamaican government school meal to a class of children. *Human Nutrition. Clinical Nutrition, 37C,* 381–388.

Riciutti, H. (1981). Developmental consequences of malnutrition in early childhood. In M. Lewis & L. Rosenblum (Eds.), *The uncommon child: Genesis of behavior* (Vol. 3, pp. 151–172). New York: Plenum Press.

Ricciuti, H. N. (1993). Nutrition and mental development. *Current Directions in Psychological Science, 2,* 43–46.

Rothbart, M., Derryberry, D., & Posner, M. (1994). A psychobiological approach to the development of temperament. In J. Bates & T. D. Wachs (Eds.), *Temperament: Individual differences at the interface of biology and behavior* (pp. 83–116). Washington, DC: American Psychological Association, Science Volumes.

Rush, D., Stein, Z., & Susser, M. (1980). *Diet in pregnancy: A randomized controlled trial of nutritional supplements.* New York: Alan R. Liss, Inc.

Rutter, M. (1983). Statistical and personal interactions: Facets and perspectives. In D. Magnusson & V. Allen (Eds.), *Human development: An interactional perspective* (pp. 295–319). New York: Academic Press.

Sahni, S., & Chandra, R. K. (1983). Malnutrition and susceptibility to diarrhea, with special reference to the antiinfective properties of breast milk. In L. Chen & N. Scrimshaw (Eds.), *Diarrhea and Malnutrition* (pp. 99–109). New York: Plenum Press.

Schurch, B. (1995). Malnutrition and behavioral development: The nutrition variable. *Journal of Nutrition Supplement, 125,* 2255S–2262S.

Seshadri, S., & Gopaldas, T. (1989). Impact of iron supplementation on cognitive functions in preschool and school-aged children: The Indian experience. *American Journal of Clinical Nutrition Supplement, 50,* 675–686.

Shrestha, R. M. (1994). *Effect of iodine and iron supplementation on physical, psychomotor and mental development in primary school children in Malawi.* The Hague: CIP-Data Koninklijke Bibliotheek.

Sigman, M., McDonald, M. A., Neumann, C., & Bwibo, N. (1991). Prediction of cognitive competence in Kenyan children from toddler nutrition, family characteristics and abilities. *Journal of Child Psychology and Psychiatry, 32,* 307–320.

Sigman, M., Neumann, C., Baksh, M., Bwibo, N., & McDonald, M. A. (1989). Relationship between nutrition and development in Kenyan toddlers. *Journal of Pediatrics, 115,* 357–364.

Sigman, M., Neumann, C., Jansen, A. A. J., & Bwibo, N. (1989). Cognitive abilities of Kenyan children in relation to nutrition, family characteristics, and education. *Child Development, 60,* 1462–1474.

Simeon, D. T., & Grantham-McGregor, S. (1990). Nutritional deficiencies and children's behavior and mental development. *Nutrition Research Reviews, 3,* 1–24.

Soemantri, A. G., Pollitt, E., & Kim, I. (1985). Iron deficiency anemia and educational achievement. *American Journal of Clinical Nutrition Supplement, 42,* 1221–1228.

Soewondo, S., Husaini, M., & Pollitt, E. (1989). Effects of iron deficiency on attention and learning processes in preschool children: Bandung, Indonesia. *American Journal of Clinical Nutrition Supplement, 50,* 667–674.

Stein, Z., Susser, M., Saenger, G., & Marolla, F. (1975). *Famine and human development: The Dutch hunger winter of 1944/45.* New York: Oxford University Press.

Steinmetz, J. (1994). Brain substrates of emotion and temperament. In J. Bates & T. D. Wachs (Eds.), *Temperament: individual differences at the interface of biology and behavior* (pp. 17–46). Washington, DC: American Psychological Association, Science Volumes.

Stone, E. A. (1987). Central cyclic-AMP-linked noradrenergic receptors: New findings on properties as related to the actions of stress. *Neuroscience and Biobehavior Review 11,* 391–398.

Strupp, B. J., & Levitsky, D. A. (1995). Enduring cognitive effects of early malnutrition: A theoretical reappraisal. *Journal of Nutrition Supplement, 125,* 2221S–2232S.

Susser, M., & Stein, Z. (1994). Timing in prenatal nutrition: A reprise of the Dutch famine study. *Nutrition Reviews, 52,* 84–94.

Trowbridge, F. L. (1972). Intellectual assessment in primitive societies, with a preliminary report of a study of the effects of early iodine supplementation on intelligence. In *Human development and the thyroid gland: Relation to endemic cretinism, Advances in Experimental Medicine and Biology* (Vol. 30, pp. 137–150). Proceedings of Symposium on Endemic Cretinism held at The Kroc Foundation, Santa Ynez Valley, CA. New York: Plenum Press.

United Nations Administrative Committee on Coordination, Subcommittee on Nutrition (ACC/SCN). (1993). *SCN News, no. 9.*

Villar, J., Smeriglio, J., Martorell, R., Brown, C. H., & Klein, R. (1984). Heterogeneous growth and mental development of intrauterine growth retarded infants during the first 3 years of life. *Pediatrics, 74,* 783–791.

Vohr, B., Garcia Coll, C., & Oh, W. (1989). Language and neurodevelopmental outcome of low-birth-weight infants at three years. *Developmental Medicine and Child Neurology, 31,* 582–590.

Wachs, T. D. (1995). Relation of mild-to-moderate malnutrition to human development: correlational studies. *Journal of Nutrition Supplement, 125,* 2245S–2254S.

Wachs, T. D., Bishry, Z., Moussa, W., Yunis, F., McCabe, G., Harrison, G., Swefi, I., Kirksey, A., Galal, O., Jerome, N., & Shaheen, E. (1995). Nutritional intake and context as predictors of cognition and adaptive behavior of Egyptian school-age children. *International Journal of Behavioral Development, 18,* 425–450.

Wachs, T. D., Sigman, M., Bishry, Z., Moussa, W., Jerome, N., Neumann, C., Bwibo, N., & McDonald, M. A. (1992). Caregiver-child interaction patterns in two cultures in relation to nutritional intake. *International Journal of Behavioral Development, 15,* 1–18.

Walter, T. (1989). Infancy: Mental and motor development. *American Journal of Clinical Nutrition, 50,* 655–664.

Winick, M., Meyer, K. K., & Harris, R. C. (1975). Malnutrition and environmental enrichment by early adoption. *Science, 190,* 1173–1175.

Yehuda, S., & Youdim, M. B. H. (1989). Brain iron: A lesson from animal models. *American Journal of Clinical Nutrition, 50,* 618–629.

Zimmerman, M. A., & Arunkumar, R. (1994). Resiliency research: Implications for schools and policy. *Social Policy Report, 8*(4), 1–18.

About the Authors

The authors are members of the Task Force on Nutrition and Behavioral Development of the International Dietary Energy Consultative Group (IDECG):

Ernesto Pollitt, Ph.D., chair, University of California, Davis

Mari Golub, Ph.D., University of California, Davis

Kathleen Gorman, Ph.D., University of Vermont

Sally Grantham-McGregor, M.D., University of the West Indies

David Levitsky, Ph.D., Cornell University

Beat Schürch, M.D., Ph.D., Nestlé Foundation, Lausanne, Switzerland

Barbara Strupp, Ph.D., Cornell University

Theodore Wachs, Ph.D., Purdue University

IDECG was established in 1986 to study dietary energy intake in relation to the health and welfare of individuals and societies. The IDECG is sponsored by the United Nations University, with the endorsement of the Administrative Committee on Coordination of the United Nations/Subcommittee on Nutrition and the International Union of Nutritional Sciences. One of the objectives of the IDECG is the compilation and interpretation of relevant research data on functional and other consequences of deficiency, change, or excess of dietary energy intake.

Acknowledgements

The work of the Task Force was done under the auspices of the International Union of Nutritional Sciences, the United Nations University, the Nestlé Foundation, and Kraft Foods.

LIFE IN OVERDRIVE

Doctors say huge numbers of kids and adults have attention deficit disorder. Is it for real?

CLAUDIA WALLIS

DUSTY NASH, AN ANGELIC-looking blond child of seven, awoke at 5 one recent morning in his Chicago home and proceeded to throw a fit. He wailed. He kicked. Every muscle in his 50-lb. body flew in furious motion. Finally, after about 30 minutes, Dusty pulled himself together sufficiently to head downstairs for breakfast. While his mother bustled about the kitchen, the hyperkinetic child pulled a box of Kix cereal from the cupboard and sat on a chair.

But sitting still was not in the cards this morning. After grabbing some cereal with his hands, he began kicking the box, scattering little round corn puffs across the room. Next he turned his attention to the TV set, or rather, the table supporting it. The table was covered with a checkerboard Con-Tact paper, and Dusty began peeling it off. Then he became intrigued with the spilled cereal and started stomping it to bits. At this point his mother interceded. In a firm but calm voice she told her son to get the stand-up dust pan and broom and clean up the mess. Dusty got out the dust pan but forgot the rest of the order. Within seconds he was dismantling the plastic dust pan, piece by piece. His next project: grabbing three rolls of toilet paper from the bathroom and unraveling them around the house.

It was only 7:30, and his mother Kyle Nash, who teaches a medical-school course on death and dying, was already feeling half dead from exhaustion. Dusty was to see his doctors that day at 4, and they had asked her not to give the boy the drug he usually takes to control his hyperactivity and attention problems, a condition known as attention deficit hyperactivity disorder (ADHD). It was going to be a very long day without help from Ritalin.

Karenne Bloomgarden remembers such days all too well. The peppy, 43-year-old entrepreneur and gym teacher was a disaster as a child growing up in New Jersey. "I did very poorly in school," she recalls. Her teachers and parents were constantly on her case for rowdy behavior. "They just felt I was being bad—too loud, too physical, too everything." A rebellious tomboy with few friends, she saw a psychologist at age 10, "but nobody came up with a diagnosis." As a teenager she began prescribing her own medication: marijuana, Valium and, later, cocaine.

The athletic Bloomgarden managed to get into college, but she admits that she cheated her way to a diploma. "I would study and study, and I wouldn't remember a thing. I really felt it was my fault." After graduating, she did fine in physically active jobs but was flustered with administrative work. Then, four years ago, a doctor put a label on her troubles: ADHD. "It's been such a weight off my shoulders," says Bloomgarden, who takes both the stimulant Ritalin and the antidepressant Zoloft to improve her concentration. "I had 38 years of thinking I was a bad person. Now I'm rewriting the tapes of who I thought I was to who I really am."

Fifteen years ago, no one had ever heard of attention deficit hyperactivity disorder. Today it is the most common behavioral disorder in American children, the subject of thousands of studies and symposiums and no small degree of controversy. Experts on ADHD say it afflicts as many as 3½ million American youngsters, or up to 5% of those under 18. It is two to three times as likely to be diagnosed in boys as in girls. The disorder has replaced what used to be popularly called "hyperactivity," and it includes a broader collection of symptoms. ADHD has three main hallmarks: extreme distractibility,

an almost reckless impulsiveness and, in some but not all cases, a knee-jiggling, toe-tapping hyperactivity that makes sitting still all but impossible. (Without hyperactivity, the disorder is called attention deficit disorder, or ADD.)

For children with ADHD, a ticking clock or sounds and sights caught through a window can drown out a teacher's voice, although an intriguing project can absorb them for hours. Such children act before thinking; they blurt out answers in class. They enrage peers with an inability to wait their turn or play by the rules. These are the kids no one wants at a birthday party.

Ten years ago, doctors believed that the symptoms of ADHD faded with maturity. Now it is one of the fastest-growing diagnostic categories for adults. One-third to two-thirds of ADHD kids continue to have symptoms as adults, says psychiatrist Paul Wender, director of the adult ADHD clinic at the University of Utah School of Medicine. Many adults respond to the diagnosis with relief—a sense that "at last my problem has a name and it's not my fault." As more people are diagnosed, the use of Ritalin (or its generic equivalent, methylphenidate), the drug of choice for ADHD, has surged: prescriptions are up more than 390% in just four years.

As the numbers have grown, ADHD awareness has become an industry, a passion, an almost messianic movement. An advocacy and support group called CHADD (Children and Adults with Attention Deficit Disorders) has exploded from its founding in 1987 to 28,000 members in 48 states. Information bulletin boards and support groups for adults have sprung up on CompuServe, Prodigy and America Online. Numerous popular books have been published on the subject. There are summer camps designed to help ADHD kids, videos and children's books with titles like *Jumpin' Johnny Get Back to Work!* and, of course, therapists, tutors and workshops offering their services to the increasingly self-aware ADHD community.

I T IS A COMMUNITY THAT VIEWS ITSELF with some pride. Popular books and lectures about ADHD often point out positive aspects of the condition. Adults see themselves as creative; their impulsiveness can be viewed as spontaneity; hyperactivity gives them enormous energy and drive; even their distractibility has the virtue of making them alert to changes in the environment. "Kids with ADHD are wild, funny, effervescent. They have a love of life. The rest of us sometimes envy them," says psychologist Russell Barkley of the University of Massachusetts Medical Center. "ADHD adults," he notes, "can be incredibly successful. Sometimes being impulsive means being decisive." Many ADHD adults gravitate into creative fields or work that provides an outlet for emotions, says Barkley. "In our clinic we saw an adult poet who couldn't write poetry when she was on Ritalin. ADHD people make good salespeople. They're lousy at desk jobs."

In an attempt to promote the positive side of ADHD, some CHADD chapters circulate lists of illustrious figures who, they contend, probably suffered from the disorder: the messy and disorganized Ben Franklin, the wildly impulsive and distractible Winston Churchill. For reasons that are less clear, these lists also include folks like Socrates, Isaac Newton, Leonardo da Vinci—almost any genius of note. (At least two doctors interviewed for this story suggested that the sometimes scattered Bill Clinton belongs on the list.)

However creative they may be, people with ADHD don't function particularly well in standard schools and typical office jobs. Increasingly, parents and lobby groups are demanding that accommodations be made. About half the kids diagnosed with ADHD receive help from special-education teachers in their schools, in some cases because they also have other learning disabilities. Where schools have failed to provide services, parents have sometimes sued. In one notable case that went to the U.S. Supreme Court last year, parents argued—successfully—that since the public school denied their child special education, the district must pay for her to attend private school. Another accommodation requested with increasing frequency: permission to take college-entrance exams without a time limit. Part of what motivates parents to fight for special services is frightening research showing that without proper care, kids with ADHD have an extremely high risk not only of failing at school but also of becoming drug abusers, alcoholics and lawbreakers.

Adults with ADHD are beginning to seek special treatment. Under the 1990 Americans with Disabilities Act, they can insist upon help in the workplace. Usually the interventions are quite modest: an office door or white-noise machine to reduce distractions, or longer deadlines on assignments. Another legal trend that concerns even ADHD advocates: the disorder is being raised as a defense in criminal cases. Psychologist Barkley says he knows of 55 such instances in the U.S., all in the past 10 years. ADHD was cited as a mitigating factor by the attorney for Michael Fay, the 19-year-old American who was charged with vandalism and caned in Singapore.

Many of those who treat ADHD see the recognition of the problem as a humane breakthrough: finally we will stop blaming kids for behavior they cannot control. But some are worried that the disorder is being embraced with too much gusto. "A lot of people are jumping on the bandwagon," complains psychologist Mark Stein, director of a special ADHD clinic at the University of Chicago. "Parents are putting pressure on health professionals to make the diagnosis." The allure of ADHD is that it is "a label of forgiveness," says Robert Reid, an assistant professor in the department of special education at the University of Nebraska in Lincoln. "The kid's problems are not his parents' fault, not the teacher's fault, not the kid's fault. It's better to say this kid has ADHD than to say this kid drives everybody up the wall." For adults, the diagnosis may provide an excuse for personal or professional failures, observes Richard Bromfield, a psychologist at Harvard Medical School. "Some people like to say, 'The biological devil made me do it.'"

A DISORDER WITH A PAST Other than the name itself, there is nothing new about this suddenly ubiquitous disorder. The world has always had its share of obstreperous kids, and it has generally treated them as behavior problems rather than patients. Most of the world still does so: European nations like France and England report one-tenth the U.S. rate of ADHD. In Japan the disorder has barely been studied.

The medical record on ADHD is said to have begun in 1902, when British pediatrician George Still published an account of 20 children in his practice who were "passionate," defiant, spiteful and lacking "inhibitory volition." Still made the then radical suggestion that bad parenting was not to blame; instead he suspected a subtle brain injury. This theory gained greater credence in the years following the 1917–18 epidemic of viral encephalitis, when doctors observed that the infection left some children with impaired attention, memory and control over their impulses. In the 1940s and '50s, the same constellation of symptoms was called minimal brain damage and, later, minimal brain dysfunction. In 1937 a Rhode Island pediatrician reported that giving stimulants called amphetamines to children with these symptoms had the unexpected effect of calming them down. By the mid-1970s, Ritalin had become the most prescribed drug for what was eventually termed, in 1987, attention deficit hyperactivity disorder.

Nobody fully understands how Ritalin and other stimulants work, nor do doctors have a very precise picture of the physiology of ADHD. Researchers generally suspect a defect in the frontal lobes of the brain, which regulate behavior. This region is rich in the neurotransmitters dopamine and norepinephrine, which are influenced by drugs like Ritalin. But the lack of a more specific explanation has led some psychologists to question whether ADHD is truly a disorder at all or merely a set of characteristics that tend to cluster together. Just because something responds to a drug doesn't mean it is a sickness.

ADHD researchers counter the skeptics by pointing to a growing body of biological clues. For instance, several studies have found that people with ADHD have decreased blood flow and lower levels of electrical activity in the frontal lobes than normal adults and children. In 1990 Dr. Alan Zametkin at the National Institute of Mental Health found that in PET scans, adults with ADD showed slightly lower rates of metabolism in areas of the brain's cortex known to be involved in the control of attention, impulses and motor activity.

Zametkin's study was hailed as the long-awaited proof of the biological basis of ADD, though Zametkin himself is quite cautious. A new study used another tool—magnetic resonance imaging—to compare the brains of 18 ADHD boys with those of other children and found several "very subtle" but "striking" anatomical differences, says co-author Judith Rapoport, chief of the child psychiatry branch at NIMH. Says Zametkin: "I'm absolutely convinced that this disorder has a biological basis, but just what it is we cannot yet say."

W HAT RESEARCHERS DO say with great certainty is that the condition is inherited. External factors such as birth injuries and maternal alcohol or tobacco consumption may play a role in less than 10% of cases. Suspicions that a diet high in sugar might cause hyperactivity have been discounted. But the influence of genes is unmistakable. Barkley estimates that 40% of ADHD kids have a parent who has the trait and 35% have a sibling with the problem; if the sibling is an identical twin, the chances rise to between 80% and 92%.

Interest in the genetics of ADHD is enormous. In Australia a vast trial involving

3,400 pairs of twins between the ages of 4 and 12 is examining the incidence of ADHD and other behavioral difficulties. At NIMH, Zametkin's group is recruiting 200 families who have at least two members with ADHD. The hope: to identify genes for the disorder. It is worth noting, though, that even if such genes are found, this may not settle the debate about ADHD. After all, it is just as likely that researchers will someday discover a gene for a hot temper, which also runs in families. But that doesn't mean that having a short fuse is a disease requiring medical intervention.

TRICKY DIAGNOSIS In the absence of any biological test, diagnosing ADHD is a rather inexact proposition. In most cases, it is a teacher who initiates the process by informing parents that their child is daydreaming in class, failing to complete assignments or driving everyone crazy with thoughtless behavior. "The problem is that the parent then goes to the family doctor, who writes a prescription for Ritalin and doesn't stop to think of the other possibilities," says child psychiatrist Larry Silver of Georgetown University Medical Center. To make a careful diagnosis, Silver argues, one must eliminate other explanations for the symptoms.

The most common cause, he points out, is anxiety. A child who is worried about a problem at home or some other matter "can look hyperactive and distractible." Depression can also cause ADHD-like behavior. "A third cause is another form of neurological dysfunction, like a learning disorder," says Silver. "The child starts doodling because he didn't understand the teacher's instructions." All this is made more complicated by the fact that some kids—and adults—with ADHD also suffer from depression and other problems. To distinguish these symptoms from ADHD, doctors usually rely on interviews with parents and teachers, behavior-ratings scales and psychological tests, which can cost from $500 to $3,000, depending on the thoroughness of the testing. Insurance coverage is spotty.

Among the most important clues doctors look for is whether the child's problems can be linked to some specific experience or time or whether they have been present almost from birth. "You don't suddenly get ADD," says Wade Horn, a child psychologist and former executive director of CHADD. Taking a careful history is therefore vital.

For kids who are hyperactive, the pattern is unmistakable, says Dr. Bruce Roseman, a pediatric neurologist with several offices in the New York City area, who has ADHD himself. "You say to the mother, 'What kind of personality did the chid have as a baby? Was he active, alert? Was he colicky?' She'll say, 'He wouldn't stop—waaah, waaah, waaah!' You ask, 'When did he start to walk?' One mother said to me, 'Walk? My son didn't walk. He got his pilot's license at one year

of age. His feet haven't touched the ground since.' You ask, 'Mrs. Smith, how about the terrible twos?' She'll start to cry, 'You mean the terrible twos, threes, fours, the awful fives, the horrendous sixes, the God-awful eights, the divorced nines, the I-want-to-die tens!' "

Diagnosing those with ADD without hyperactivity can be trickier. Such kids are often described as daydreamers, space cases. They are not disruptive or antsy. But, says Roseman, "they sit in front of a book and for 45 minutes, nothing happens." Many girls with ADD fit this model; they are often misunderstood or overlooked.

Christy Rade, who will be entering the ninth grade in West Des Moines, Iowa, is fairly typical. Before she was diagnosed with ADD in the third grade, Christy's teacher described her to her parents as a "dizzy blond and a space cadet." "Teachers used to get fed up with me," recalls Christy, who now takes Ritalin and gets some extra support from her teachers. "Everyone thought I was purposely not paying attention." According to her mother Julie Doy, people at Christy's school were familiar with hyperactivity but not ADD. "She didn't have behavior problems. She was the kind of kid who could fall through the cracks, and did."

Most experts say ADHD is a lifelong condition but by late adolescence many people can compensate for their impulsiveness and disorganization. They may channel hyperactivity into sports. In other cases, the symptoms still wreak havoc, says UCLA psychiatrist Walid Shekim. "Patients cannot settle on a career. They cannot keep a job. They procrastinate a lot. They are the kind of people who would tell their boss to take this job and shove it before they've found another job."

Doctors diagnose adults with methods similar to those used with children. Patients are sometimes asked to dig up old report cards for clues to their childhood behavior—an essential indicator. Many adults seek help only after one of their children is diagnosed. Such was the case with Chuck Pearson of Birmingham, Michigan, who was diagnosed three years ago, at 54. Pearson had struggled for decades in what might be the worst possible career for someone with ADD: accounting. In the first 12 years of his marriage, he was fired from 15 jobs. "I was frightened," says Zoe, his wife of 35 years. "We had two small children, a mortgage. Bill collectors were calling perpetually. We almost lost the house." Chuck admits he had trouble focusing on details, completing tasks and judging how long an assignment would take. He was so distracted behind the wheel that he lost his license for a year after getting 14 traffic tickets. Unwittingly, Pearson began medicating himself: "In my mid-30s, I would drink 30 to 40 cups of coffee a day. The caffeine helped." After he was diagnosed, the Pearsons founded the Adult Attention Deficit Foundation, a clearinghouse for information

about ADD; he hopes to spare others some of his own regret: "I had a deep and abiding sadness over the life I could have given my family if I had been treated effectively."

PERSONALITY OR PATHOLOGY? While Chuck Pearson's problems were extreme, many if not all adults have trouble at times sticking with boring tasks, setting priorities and keeping their minds on what they are doing. The furious pace of society, the strain on families, the lack of community support can make anyone feel beset by ADD. "I personally think we are living in a society that is so out of control that we say, 'Give me a stimulant so I can cope.' " says Charlotte Tomaino, a clinical neuropsychologist in White Plains, New York. As word of ADHD spreads, swarms of adults are seeking the diagnosis as an explanation for their troubles. "So many really have symptoms that began in adulthood and reflected depression or other problems," says psychiatrist Silver. In their best-selling new book, *Driven to Distraction,* Edward Hallowell and John Ratey suggest that American life is "ADD-ogenic": "American society tends to create ADD-like symptoms in us all. The fast pace. The sound bite. The quick cuts. The TV remote-control clicker. It is important to keep this in mind, or you may start thinking that everybody you know has ADD."

And that is the conundrum. How do you draw the line between a spontaneous, high-energy person who is feeling overwhelmed by the details of life and someone afflicted with a neurological disorder? Where is the boundary between personality and pathology? Even an expert in the field like the University of Chicago's Mark Stein admits, "We need to find more precise ways of diagnosing it than just saying you have these symptoms." Barkley also concedes the vagueness. The traits that constitute ADHD "are personality characteristics," he agrees. But it becomes pathology, he says, when the traits are so extreme that they interfere with people's lives.

THE RISKS There is no question that ADHD can disrupt lives. Kids with the disorder frequently have few friends. Their parents may be ostracized by neighbors and relatives, who blame them for failing to control the child. "I've got criticism of my parenting skills from strangers," says the mother of a hyperactive boy in New Jersey. "When you're out in public, you're always on guard. Whenever I'd hear a child cry, I'd turn to see if it was because of Jeremy."

School can be a shattering experience for such kids. Frequently reprimanded and tuned out, they lose any sense of self-worth and fall ever further behind in their work. More than a quarter are held back a grade; about a third fail to graduate from high school. ADHD kids are also prone to accidents, says neurologist Roseman. "These are the kids I'm going to see in the emergency room this summer. They rode their bicycle right into the street and didn't look. They jumped off the deck and forgot it was high."

But the psychological injuries are often greater. By ages five to seven, says Barkley, half to two-thirds are hostile and defiant. By ages 10 to 12, they run the risk of developing what psychologists call "conduct disorder"—lying, stealing, running away from home and ultimately getting into trouble with the law. As adults, says Barkley, 25% to 30% will experience substance-abuse problems, mostly with depressants like marijuana and alcohol. One study of hyperactive boys found that 40% had been arrested at least once by age 18—and these were kids who had been treated with stimulant medication; among those who had been treated with the drug plus other measures, the rate was 20%—still very high.

It is an article of faith among ADHD researchers that the right interventions can prevent such dreadful outcomes. "If you can have an impact with these kids, you can change whether they go to jail or to Harvard Law School," says psychologist James Swanson at the University of California at Irvine, who co-authored the study of arrest histories. And yet, despite decades of research, no one is certain exactly what the optimal intervention should be.

TREATMENT The best-known therapy for ADHD remains stimulant drugs. Though Ritalin is the most popular choice, some patients do better with Dexedrine or Cylert or even certain antidepressants. About 70% of kids respond to stimulants. In the correct dosage, these uppers surprisingly "make people slow down," says Swanson. "They make you focus your attention and apply more effort to whatever you're supposed to do." Ritalin kicks in within 30 minutes to an hour after being taken, but its effects last only about three hours. Most kids take a dose at breakfast and another at lunchtime to get them through a school day.

When drug therapy works, says Utah's Wender, "it is one of the most dramatic effects in psychiatry." Roseman tells how one first-grader came into his office after trying Ritalin and announced, "I know how it works." "You do?" asked the doctor. "Yes," the child replied. "It cleaned out my ears. Now I can hear the teacher." A third-grader told Roseman that Ritalin had enabled him to play basketball. "Now when I get the ball, I turn around, I go down to the end of the room, and if I look up, there's a net there. I never used to see the net, because there was too much screaming."

For adults, the results can be just as striking. "Helen," a 43-year-old mother of three in northern Virginia, began taking the drug after being diagnosed with ADD in 1983. "The very first day, I noticed a difference," she marvels. For the first time ever, "I was able to sit down and listen to what my husband had done at work. Shortly after, I was able to sit in bed and read while my husband watched TV."

Given such outcomes, doctors can be tempted to throw a little Ritalin at any problem. Some even use it as a diagnostic tool, believing—wrongly—that if the child's concentration improves with Ritalin, then he or she must have ADD. In fact, you don't have to have an attention problem to get a boost from Ritalin. By the late 1980s, over-prescription became a big issue, raised in large measure by the Church of Scientology, which opposes psychiatry in general and launched a vigorous campaign against Ritalin. After a brief decline fostered by the scare, the drug is now hot once again. Swanson has heard of some classrooms where 20% to 30% of the boys are on Ritalin. "That's just ridiculous!" he says.

Ritalin use varies from state to state, town to town, depending largely on the attitude of the doctors and local schools. Idaho is the No. 1 consumer of the drug. A study of Ritalin consumption in Michigan, which ranks just behind Idaho, found that use ranged from less than 1% of boys in one county to as high as 10% in another, with no correlation to affluence.

Patients who are taking Ritalin must be closely monitored, since the drug can cause loss of appetite, insomnia and occasionally tics. Doctors often recommend "drug holidays" during school vacations. Medication is frequently combined with other treatments, including psychotherapy, special education and cognitive training, although the benefits of such expensive measures are unclear. "We really haven't known which treatment to use for which child and how to combine treatments," says Dr. Peter Jensen, chief of NIMH's Child and Adolescent Disorders Research Branch. His group has embarked on a study involving 600 children in six cities. By 1998 they hope to have learned how medication alone compares to medication with psychological intervention and other approaches.

BEYOND DRUGS A rough consensus has emerged among ADHD specialists that whether or not drugs are used, it is best to teach kids—often through behavior modification—how to gain more control over their impulses and restless energy. Also recommended is training in the fine art of being organized: establishing a predictable schedule of activities, learning to use a date book, assigning a location for possessions at school and at home. This takes considerable effort on the part of teachers and parents as well as the kids themselves. Praise, most agree, is vitally important.

Within the classroom "some simple, practical things work well," says Reid. Let hyperactive kids move around. Give them stand-up desks, for instance. "I've seen kids who from the chest up were very diligently working on a math problem, but from the chest down, they're dancing like Fred Astaire." To minimize distractions, ADHD kids should sit very close to the teacher and be permitted to take important tests in a quiet area. "Unfortunately," Reid observes, "not many teachers are trained in behavior management. It is a historic shortfall in American education."

In Irvine, California, James Swanson has tried to create the ideal setting for teaching kids with ADHD. The Child Development Center, an elementary school that serves 45 kids with the disorder, is a kind of experiment in progress. The emphasis is on behavior modification: throughout the day students earn points—and are relentlessly cheered on—for good behavior. High scorers are rewarded with special privileges at the end of the day, but each morning kids start afresh with another shot at the rewards. Special classes also drill in social skills: sharing, being a good sport, ignoring annoyances rather than striking out in anger. Only 35% of the kids at the center are on stimulant drugs, less than half the national rate for ADHD kids.

Elsewhere around the country, enterprising parents have struggled to find their own answers to attention deficit. Bonnie and Neil Fell of Skokie, Illinois, have three sons, all of whom have been diagnosed with ADD. They have "required more structure and consistency than other kids," says Bonnie. "We had to break down activities into clear time slots." To help their sons, who take Ritalin, the Fells have employed tutors, psychotherapists and a speech and language specialist. None of this comes cheap: they estimate their current annual ADD-related expenses at $15,000. "Our goal is to get them through school with their self-esteem intact," says Bonnie.

The efforts seem to be paying off. Dan, the eldest at 15, has become an outgoing A student, a wrestling star and a writer for the school paper. "ADD gives you energy and creativity," he says. "I've learned to cope. I've become strong." On the other hand, he is acutely aware of his disability. "What people don't realize is that I have to work harder than everyone else. I start studying for finals a month before other people do."

COPING Adults can also train themselves to compensate for ADHD. Therapists working with them typically emphasize organizational skills, time management, stress reduction and ways to monitor their own distractibility and stay focused.

IN HER OFFICE IN WHITE PLAINS, Tomaino has a miniature Zen garden, a meditative sculpture and all sorts of other items to help tense patients relax. Since many people with ADHD also have learning disabilities, she tests each patient and then often uses computer programs to strengthen weak areas. But most important is helping people define their goals and take orderly steps to reach them. Whether working with a stockbroker or a homemaker, she says, "I teach adults basic rewards and goals. For instance, you can't go out to lunch until you've cleaned the kitchen."

Tomaino tells of one very hyperactive and articulate young man who got all the way through college without incident, thanks in good measure to a large and tolerant extended family. Then he flunked out of law school three times. Diagnosed with ADHD, the patient took stock of his goals and decided to enter the family restaurant business, where, Tomaino says, he is a raging success. "ADHD was a deficit if he wanted to be a lawyer, but it's an advantage in the restaurant business. He gets to go around to meet and greet."

For neurologist Roseman, the same thing is true. With 11 offices in four states, he is perpetually on the go. "I'm at rest in motion," says the doctor. "I surround myself with partners who provide the structure. My practice allows me to be creative." Roseman has accountants to do the bookkeeping. He starts his day at 6:30 with a hike and doesn't slow down until midnight. "Thank God for my ADD," he says. But, he admits, "had I listened to all the negative things that people said when I was growing up, I'd probably be digging ditches in Idaho."

LESSONS Whether ADHD is a brain disorder or simply a personality type, the degree to which it is a handicap depends not only on the severity of the traits but also on one's environment. The right school, job or home situation can make all the difference. The lessons of ADHD are truisms. All kids do not learn in the same way. Nor are all adults suitable for the same line of work.

Unfortunately, American society seems to have evolved into a one-size-fits-all system. Schools can resemble factories: put the kids on the assembly line, plug in the right components and send 'em out the door. Everyone is supposed to go to college; there is virtually no other route to success. In other times and in other places, there have been alternatives: apprenticeships, settling a new land, starting a business out of the garage, going to sea. In a conformist society, it becomes necessary to medicate some people to make them fit in.

This is not to deny that some people genuinely need Ritalin, just as others need tranquilizers or insulin. But surely an epidemic of attention deficit disorder is a warning to us all. Children need individual supervision. Many of them need more structure than the average helter-skelter household provides. They need a more consistent approach to discipline and schools that tailor teaching to their individual learning styles. Adults too could use a society that's more flexible in its expectations, more accommodating to differences. Most of all, we all need to slow down. And pay attention. *—With reporting by Hannah Bloch/New York, Wendy Cole/Chicago and James Willwerth/Irvine*

Bell, book and scandal

For more than a century intelligence testing has been a field rich in disputed evidence and questionable conclusions. "The Bell Curve", by Charles Murray and Richard Herrnstein, has ensured it will remain so

THERE is plenty of room for debate about which was the most amusing book of 1994, or which the best written. But nobody can seriously quibble about which was the most controversial. "The Bell Curve: Intelligence and Class Structure in American Life", an 845-page tome by Charles Murray and Richard Herrnstein*, has reignited a debate that is likely to rage on for years yet, consuming reputations and research grants as it goes.

"The Bell Curve" is an ambitious attempt to resuscitate IQ ("intelligence quotient") testing, one of the most controversial ideas in recent intellectual

history; and to use that idea to explain some of the more unpalatable features of modern America. Mr Murray, a sociologist, and Herrnstein, a psychologist who died shortly before the book's publication, argue that individuals differ substantially in their "cognitive abilities"; that these differences are inherited as much as acquired; and that intelligence is distributed in the population along a normal distribution curve—the bell curve of the book's title—with a few geniuses at the top, a mass of ordinary Joes in the middle and a minority of dullards at the bottom (see chart).

Then, into this relatively innocuous cocktail, Messrs Murray and Herrnstein mix two explosive arguments.

The first is that different races do not perform equally in the IQ stakes—that, in America, Asians score, on average, slightly above the norm, and blacks, on average, substantially below it. The second is that America is calcifying into impermeable castes. The bright are inter-marrying, spawning bright offspring and bagging well-paid jobs; and the dull are doomed to teenage pregnancy, welfare dependency, drugs and crime.

For the past three months it has been almost impossible to pick up an American newspaper or tune into an American television station without learning more about Mr Murray's views. Dozens of academics are hard at work rebutting (they would say refuting) his arguments.

*The Free Press. New York, 1994

Thanks to the controversy, "The Bell Curve" has sold more than a quarter of a million copies.

Undoubtedly, Mr Murray has been lucky in his timing. Left-wingers point out that Americans have seldom been so disillusioned with welfare policy: the voters are turning not just to Republicans, but to Republicans who are arguing seriously about the merits of state orphanages and of compulsory adoption. Mr Murray's arguments answer to a feeling that social policies may have failed not because they were incompetently designed or inadequately funded, but because they are incompatible with certain "facts" of human nature.

Right-wingers retort that it is liberals' addiction to "affirmative action" that has supplied Mr Murray with much of his material. Affirmative action has institutionalised the idea that different ethnic groups have different cognitive abilities: "race norming", now *de rigueur* in academia, means that a black can perform significantly less well than, say, an Asian, and still beat him into a university. It has also resulted in America's having a compilation of statistics about race unequalled outside South Africa.

Differently weird

The regularity with which discussion of IQ testing turns into an argument that ethnic groups differ in their innate abilities, with blacks at the bottom of the cognitive pile, has done more than anything else to make theorists and practitioners of IQ testing into figures of academic notoriety reviled everywhere from Haight-Ashbury to Holland Park. The early 1970s saw a furious argument about "Jensenism", named after Arthur Jensen, a psychologist at the University of California, Berkeley, who published an article arguing, among other things, that the average black had a lower IQ than the average white. William Shockley, also known as a co-inventor of the transistor, drew the anti-Jensenists' fire by saying that blacks' and whites' brains were "differently wired".

But, even if it could be extricated from arguments about ethnic differences, IQ testing would remain controversial. One reason is that few people like the idea that inequality might be inevitable, the result of natural laws rather than particular circumstances (and the more so, perhaps, when economic inequalities seem likely to widen as labour markets put an ever-higher premium on intelligence). The implication is that egalitarian policies are self-defeating: the more inherited prejudices are broken down, the more society resolves into intellectual castes.

A second reason for controversy is that IQ testers are all too prone to the fatal conceit of thinking that their discipline equips them to know what is best for their fellow men. To most parents the idea that a man with a book of tests and a clipboard can divine what is best for their children is an intolerable presumption (who can know a child as well as its parents?) and an insupportable invasion of lib-

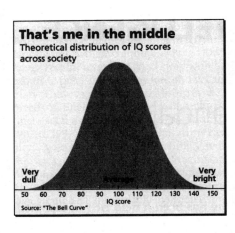

That's me in the middle
Theoretical distribution of IQ scores across society

Very dull   Average   Very bright

50 60 70 80 90 100 110 120 130 140 150
IQ score
Source: "The Bell Curve"

erty (surely people should be free to choose the best school for their children?). Nor has the IQ testers' image been helped by their having often been asked—as in England in the days of the 11-plus school entry examination—to help make already contentious decisions.

A third reason IQ testers excite concern is that they seem to make a fetish of intelligence. Many people feel instinctively that intelligence is only one of the qualities that make for success in life—that looks, luck and charm also play their part; they also like to feel that intelligence is less important than what they call "character", which can turn even a dull person into a useful citizen.

But the thing which, in the end, really frightens people about IQ testing is its message of genetic Calvinism: that IQ both determines one's destiny, and is dictated by one's genes. This flies in the face of the liberal notion that we are each responsible for fashioning our own fate. It also upsets two beliefs held particularly firmly in America: that anybody can win out, provided they have "the right stuff"; and that everybody

should be given as many educational chances as possible, rather than sorted out and classified at the earliest possible opportunity. (Thus "Forrest Gump", a film that appeared shortly before publication of "The Bell Curve", enjoyed great popularity and critical acclaim for its portrayal of a well-meaning simpleton who won all America's glittering prizes.)

Hunting down Sir Humphrey

How, then, did so widely distrusted a discipline originate? To answer that question means a trip to a rather unexpected place, the Whitehall of the mid-19th century. Traditionally, jobs in the British civil service had been handed out on the basis of family connections, in a sort of affirmative-action programme for upper-class twits. But as Britain developed a world-beating economy and a world-spanning empire, reformers argued that preferment should go to the most intelligent candidates, their identity to be discovered by competitive examinations.

This innovation proved so successful that policy-makers applied the same principle to the universities and schools. Their aim was to construct an educational system capable of discovering real ability wherever it occurred, and of matching that ability with the appropriate opportunities.

Ironically, it was children at the other end of the ability scale who inspired the first IQ tests as such. The introduction of compulsory schooling for the masses confronted teachers with the full variety of human abilities, and obliged them to distinguish between the lazy and the congenitally dull. Most investigators contented themselves with measuring children's heads. But in 1905 Alfred Binet, a French psychologist, came up with the idea of assigning an age level to a variety of simple intellectual operations, determined by the earliest age at which the average child could perform them, and ranking children both against their peers and against a normal development curve. Binet's idea was refined soon afterwards by introducing the arithmetical device of dividing mental age by chronological age and multiplying by 100.

Two English psychologists turned intelligence testing into a sort of scientific movement. The first was Francis Galton, a rich and well connected man (Charles Darwin was a cousin) who devoted his life to the nascent sciences of statistics and genetics. His motto was "wherever you can, count", and he measured everything from the distended buttocks of Hottentot women (with a theodolite) to the distribution of "pulchritude" in the British Isles. He compiled family trees of everybody from Cambridge wranglers to West Country wrestlers to prove his belief that "characteristics cling to families" and "ability goes by descent."

Combining his two passions, Galton speculated that abilities in the British population were distributed along a "bell curve", with the upper classes at the top and an underclass at the bottom. He was so worried that those at the bottom of the curve were outbreeding those at the top that he spent most of his fortune bankrolling another "science", eugenics.

Galton's mission was completed by a retired soldier, Charles Spearman. Deciding that the results of certain tests correlated with each other to a remarkable degree, Spearman concluded, in a seminal article published in 1904, that all mental abilities were manifestations of a single general ability, which he called "g": all individuals inherited a fixed quantity of mental energy, which infused every intellectual act they performed and determined what they were capable of in life. The right tests could capture how much "g" each individual possessed and express it as a single number.

Intelligence testing went on to enjoy decades of growing popularity. The American army used it on recruits in the first world war, employing more than 300 psychologists, and other armies followed. Schools used tests to help in streaming or selecting their pupils. Bureaucrats and businessmen used them to identify talented recruits. Tests were thought indispensable for discovering and diagnosing learning problems.

Only in the 1960s did opinion turn sharply against the IQ testers. Educationalists accused them of allowing an obsession with classification to blind them to the full range of human abilities. Sociologists (and sociologically minded psychologists) argued that intellectual differences owed more to social circumstances than to genes. In Britain, disillusionment with IQ tests hastened the introduction of comprehensive schools. In the United States, schools abandoned the use of IQ tests to classify children. In 1978 a district court in San Francisco even ruled unconstitutional the use of IQ tests to place children in classes for the backward if the use of such tests meant that the classes contained a "grossly disproportionate" number of black children.

Dropping clangers

"The Bell Curve" thus represents an attempt to rehabilitate an idea that had fallen into two or three decades of disfavour. But have Messrs Murray and Herrnstein got their science right?

So far, the debate on "The Bell Curve" has been billed as if it were psychometrists (mind-measurers) versus the rest. In fact, IQ testers divide among themselves on all sorts of key issues, from the structure of the mind to the reliability of tests; moreover, Messrs Murray and Herrnstein occupy a rather eccentric position among psychometrists. They are unabashed supporters of Charles Spearman, believing that intelligence is a unitary quality expressible in a single number, such that people who are good at one thing will also be good at others. Yet this is one of the most hotly disputed topics within psychometry. A British pioneer, Godfrey Thomson, argued that the correlations which so excited Spearman might be explained by the laws of chance. He concluded that the mind had no fixed structure and that intelligence tests gave little more than a hint of a person's mental powers.

Among other psychologists, L.L. Thurstone argued for the existence of dozens of different types of mental abilities, such as mathematical, verbal and visio-spatial abilities. Liam Hudson has found IQ tests to reward a particular type of "convergent" thinker. Howard Gardner thinks there are many sorts of "intelligence".

Synaptitude

IQ testers have clashed and go on clashing over less arcane issues too. They endorse widely different estimates of the heritability of IQ, ranging from 40% to 80%. They squabble about the accuracy of IQ tests: some argue that such tests are nothing more than estimates that need to be repeated frequently and to be supplemented by personal interviews (and indeed, observably, children can learn, or be taught, to raise their IQ scores). Some of the most illustrious psychometrists are even starting to argue that IQ tests should be replaced by physical tests to measure the speed of reactions, the production of glucose in the brain, the speed of neural transmission and even the size of the brain.

Psychometrists disagree, too, about the validity of generalising about groups in the way that Murray and Herrnstein do. It is widely accepted that differences within groups may reflect hereditary factors; but differences between groups are susceptible to other explanations (just as people in one place may be taller on average than people in another place, for example, but for reasons of nutrition, not genetics).

Oddly, Messrs Murray and Herrnstein have chosen to dispute (or ignore) one of the few arguments on which other psychometrists agree: that children do not necessarily have the same IQ as their parents. "The Bell Curve" argues that society is fixing itself into impermeable castes. But psychometry is a theory of social mobility, not social stasis. It tries to explain why bright people often have dull children and dull people often have bright children. Sex ensures that genes are resorted in each generation.

In fact, it is hereditarianism's sworn enemy, environmentalism, which is really a theory of social stasis: if the rich and educated can pass on their advantages to their children undisturbed by the dance of the chromosomes, then social mobility will always be something of a freak. Messrs Murray and Herrnstein are, perhaps, environmentalists in hereditarian clothing.

Politically, "The Bell Curve" has reinforced the impression that IQ testers are anti-welfare conservatives. Some are. But IQ tests have been invoked in defence of a wide variety of political positions, respectable and otherwise. American psychologists have popped up to support abominations such as compulsory sterilisation and ethnically sensitive immigration laws. Others have been socialists, keen on upward mobility, child-centred education and generous provision for the backward. In Britain between the wars Labour Party intellectuals such as R.H. Tawney argued for IQ testing as a way to ensure educational opportunities were allocated on the basis of innate ability rather than family connections; psychologists such as Cyril Burt have been passionate supporters of nursery-school education and better treatment of backward children. (The fusty T.S. Eliot, on the other hand, thought IQ tests were a plot to promote social mobility and debase education. A particularly crusty Cambridge don, Edward Welbourne, denounced them as "devices invented by Jews for the advancement of Jews.")

Too clever by half

What makes the IQ debate particularly frustrating is that both sides have long been addicted to exaggeration. The earliest IQ testers were guilty of hubris when they argued that they had invented an infallible technique for measuring mental abilities and distributing educational and occupational opportunities. As if that was not bad enough, they exacerbated their error by claiming that their method contributed to economic efficiency (by making the best use of human resources) and personal happiness (by ensuring that people were given jobs suited to their abilities).

The enemies of IQ testing were also guilty of terrible exaggeration when they accused testers of shoring up capitalism, perpetuating inequality, and justifying sexism, racism, even fascism. In fact, the IQ testers were never anywhere near as influential as they, or their opponents, imagined.

IQ theory played no part in persuading the American Congress to pass the Immigration Restriction Act of 1924; British grammar schools used IQ tests only to supplement other, more traditional selection procedures, such as scholastic examinations and interviews; Hitler and Mussolini had no time for IQ tests that were liable to contradict their own racial prejudices.

What the IQ debate needs now is a dash of cold water. Opponents of testing should forget their over-heated rhetoric about legitimising capitalism and racism. Supporters should fold up their more grandiose blueprints for building the meritocracy, and limit themselves to helping with practical problems. They should point out that IQ tests are useful ways of identifying and diagnosing mental deficiency, just so long as they are administered along with other diagnostic tools by a trained psychologist. They should add that IQ tests can also be useful in helping to allocate places in oversubscribed schools; that, indeed, they are less class-biased than scholastic tests (which favour the well-taught) or personal interviews (which favour the well-brought up). It is a pity that Charles Murray and Richard Herrnstein have chosen to douse the debate not with cold water but with petrol.

The EQ Factor

New brain research suggests that emotions, not IQ, may be the true measure of human intelligence

NANCY GIBBS

IT TURNS OUT THAT A SCIENTIST CAN SEE THE future by watching four-year-olds interact with a marshmallow. The researcher invites the children, one by one, into a plain room and begins the gentle torment. You can have this marshmallow right now, he says. But if you wait while I run an errand, you can have two marshmallows when I get back. And then he leaves.

Some children grab for the treat the minute he's out the door. Some last a few minutes before they give in. But others are determined to wait. They cover their eyes; they put their heads down; they sing to themselves; they try to play games or even fall asleep. When the researcher returns he gives the children their hard-earned marshmallows. And then, science waits for them to grow up.

By the time the children reach high school, something remarkable has happened. A survey of the children's parents and teachers found that those who as four-year-olds had the fortitude to hold out for the second marshmallow generally grew up to be better adjusted, more popular, adventurous, confident and dependable teenagers. The children who gave in to temptation early on were more likely to be lonely, easily frustrated and stubborn. They buckled under stress and shied away from challenges. And when some of the students in the two groups took the Scholastic Aptitude Test, the kids who held out longer scored an average of 210 points higher.

When we think of brilliance we see Einstein, deep-eyed, woolly haired, a thinking machine with skin and mismatched socks. High achievers, we imagine, were wired for greatness from birth. But then you have to wonder why, over time, natural talent seems to ignite in some people and dim in others. This is where the marshmallows come in. It seems that the ability to delay gratification is a master skill, a triumph of the reasoning brain over the impulsive one. It is a sign, in short, of emotional intelligence. And it doesn't show up on an IQ test.

For most of this century, scientists have worshiped the hardware of the brain and the software of the mind; the messy powers of the heart were left to the poets. But cognitive theory could simply not explain the questions we wonder about most: why some people just seem to have a gift for living well; why the smartest kid in the class will probably not end up the richest; why we like some people virtually on sight and distrust others; why some people remain buoyant in the face of troubles that would sink a less resilient soul. What qualities of the mind or spirit, in short, determine who succeeds?

The phrase "emotional intelligence" was coined by Yale psychologist Peter Salovey and the University of New Hampshire's John Mayer five years ago to describe qualities like understanding one's own feelings, empathy for the feelings of others and "the regulation of emotion in a way that enhances living." Their notion is about to bound into the national conversation, handily shortened to EQ, thanks to a new book, *Emotional Intelligence* (Bantam; $23.95) by Daniel Goleman. Goleman, a Harvard psychology Ph.D. and a *New York Times* science writer with a gift for making even the chewiest scientific theories digestible to lay readers, has brought together a decade's worth of behavioral research into how the mind processes feelings. His goal, he announces on the cover, is to redefine what it means to be smart. His thesis: when it comes to predict-ing people's success, brainpower as measured by IQ and standardized achievement tests may actually matter less than the qualities of mind once thought of as "character" before the word began to sound quaint.

At first glance, there would seem to be little that's new here to any close reader of fortune cookies. There may be no less original idea than the notion that our hearts hold dominion over our heads. "I was so angry," we say, "I couldn't think straight." Neither is it surprising that "people skills" are useful, which amounts to saying, it's good to be nice. "It's so true it's trivial," says Dr. Paul McHugh, director of psychiatry at Johns Hopkins University School of Medicine. But if it were that simple, the book would not be quite so interesting or its implications so controversial.

This is no abstract investigation. Goleman is looking for antidotes to restore "civility to our streets and caring to our communal life." He sees practical applications everywhere for how companies should decide whom to hire, how couples can increase the odds that their marriages will last, how parents should raise their children and how schools should teach them. When street gangs substitute for families and schoolyard insults end in stabbings, when more than half of marriages end in divorce, when the majority of the children murdered in this country are killed by parents and stepparents, many of whom say they were trying to discipline the child for behavior like blocking the TV or crying too much, it suggests a demand for remedial emotional education. While children are still young, Goleman argues, there is a "neurological window of opportunity" since the brain's prefrontal circuitry, which regulates how we act on what we feel, probably does not mature until mid-adolescence.

And it is here the arguments will break out. Goleman's highly popularized conclusions, says McHugh, "will chill any veteran scholar of psychotherapy and any neuroscientist who worries about how his research may come to be applied." While many researchers in this relatively new field are glad to see emotional issues finally taken seriously, they fear that a notion as handy as EQ invites misuse. Goleman admits the danger of suggesting that you can assign a numerical yardstick to a person's character as well as his intellect; Goleman never even uses the phrase EQ in his book. But he (begrudgingly) approved an "unscientific" EQ test in *USA Today* with choices like "I am aware of even subtle feelings as I have them," and "I can sense the pulse of a group or relationship and state unspoken feelings."

"You don't want to take an average of your emotional skill," argues Harvard psychology professor Jerome Kagan, a pioneer in child-development research. "That's what's wrong with the concept of intelligence for mental skills too. Some people handle anger well but can't handle fear. Some people can't take joy. So each emotion has to be viewed differently."

EQ is not the opposite of IQ. Some people are blessed with a lot of both, some with little of either. What researchers have been trying to understand is how they complement each other; how one's ability to handle stress, for instance, affects the ability to concentrate and put intelligence to use. Among the ingredients for success, researchers now generally agree that IQ counts for about 20%; the rest depends on everything from class to luck to the neural pathways that have developed in the brain over millions of years of human evolution.

It is actually the neuroscientists and evolutionists who do the best job of explaining the reasons behind the most unreasonable behavior. In the past decade or so, scientists have learned enough about the brain to make judgments about where emotion comes from and why we need it. Primitive emotional responses held the keys to survival: fear drives the blood into the large muscles, making it easier to run; surprise triggers the eyebrows to rise, allowing the eyes to widen their view and gather more information about an unexpected event. Disgust wrinkles up the face and closes the nostrils to keep out foul smells.

Emotional life grows out of an area of the brain called the limbic system, specifically the amygdala, whence come delight and disgust and fear and anger. Millions of years ago, the neocortex was added on, enabling humans to plan, learn and remember. Lust grows from the limbic system; love, from the neocortex. Animals like reptiles that have no neocortex cannot experience anything like maternal love; this is why baby snakes have to hide to avoid being eaten by their parents. Humans, with their capacity for love, will protect their offspring, allowing the brains of the young time to develop. The more connections between limbic system and the neocortex, the more emotional responses are possible.

It was scientists like Joseph LeDoux of New York University who uncovered these cerebral pathways. LeDoux's parents owned a meat market. As a boy in Louisiana, he first learned about his future specialty by cutting up cows' brains for sweetbreads. "I found them the most interesting part of the cow's anatomy," he recalls. "They were visually pleasing—lots of folds, convolutions and patterns. The cerebellum was more interesting to look at than steak." The butchers' son became a neuroscientist, and it was he who discovered the short circuit in the brain that lets emotions drive action before the intellect gets a chance to intervene.

A hiker on a mountain path, for example, sees a long, curved shape in the grass out of the corner of his eye. He leaps out of the way before he realizes it is only a stick that looks like a snake. Then he calms down; his cortex gets the message a few milliseconds after his amygdala and "regulates" its primitive response.

Without these emotional reflexes, rarely conscious but often terribly powerful, we would scarcely be able to function. "Most decisions we make have a vast number of possible outcomes, and any attempt to analyze all of them would never end," says University of Iowa neurologist Antonio Damasio, author of *Descartes' Error: Emotion, Reason and the Human Brain*. "I'd ask you to lunch tomorrow, and when the appointed time arrived, you'd still be thinking about whether you should come." What tips the balance, Damasio contends, is our unconscious assigning of emotional values to some of those choices. Whether we experience a somatic response—a gut feeling of dread or a giddy sense of elation—emotions are helping to limit the field in any choice we have to make. If the prospect of lunch with a neurologist is unnerving or distasteful, Damasio suggests, the invitee will conveniently remember a previous engagement.

When Damasio worked with patients in whom the connection between emotional brain and neocortex had been severed because of damage to the brain, he discovered how central that hidden pathway is to how we live our lives. People who had lost that linkage were just as smart and quick to reason, but their lives often fell apart nonetheless. They could not make decisions because they didn't know how they felt about their choices. They couldn't react to warnings or anger in other people. If they made a mistake, like a bad investment, they felt no regret or shame and so were bound to repeat it.

If there is a cornerstone to emotional intelligence on which most other emotional skills depend, it is a sense of self-awareness, of being smart about what we feel. A person whose day starts badly at home may be grouchy all day at work without quite knowing why. Once an emotional response comes into awareness—or, physiologically, is processed through the neocortex—the chances of handling it appropriately improve. Scientists refer to "metamood," the ability to pull back and recognize that "what I'm feeling is anger," or sorrow, or shame.

Metamood is a difficult skill because emotions so often appear in disguise. A person in mourning may know he is sad, but he may not recognize that he is also angry at the person for dying—because this seems somehow inappropriate. A parent who yells at the child who ran into the street is expressing anger at disobedience, but the degree of anger may owe more to the fear the parent feels at what could have happened.

In Goleman's analysis, self-awareness is perhaps the most crucial ability because it allows us to exercise some self-control. The idea is not to repress feeling (the reaction that has made psychoanalysts rich) but rather to do what Aristotle considered the hard work of the will. "Anyone can become angry—that is easy," he wrote in the *Nicomachean Ethics*. "But to be angry with the right person, to the right degree, at the right time, for the right purpose, and in the right way—that is not easy."

Some impulses seem to be easier to control than others. Anger, not surprisingly, is one of the hardest, perhaps because of its evolutionary value in priming people to action. Researchers believe anger usually arises out of a sense of being trespassed against—the belief that one is being robbed of what is rightfully his. The body's first response is a surge of energy, the release of a cascade of neurotransmitters called catecholamines. If a person is already aroused or under stress, the threshold for release is lower, which helps explain why people's tempers shorten during a hard day.

Scientists are not only discovering where anger comes from; they are also exposing myths about how best to handle it. Popular wisdom argues for "letting it all hang out" and having a good cathartic rant. But Goleman cites studies showing that dwelling on anger actually increases its power; the body needs a chance to process the adrenaline through exercise, relaxation techniques, a well-timed intervention or even the old admonition to count to 10.

Anxiety serves a similar useful purpose, so long as it doesn't spin out of control. Worrying is a rehearsal for danger; the act of fretting focuses the mind on a problem so it can search efficiently for solutions. The danger comes when worrying blocks thinking, becoming an end in itself or a path to resignation instead of perseverance. Over-worrying about failing increases the likelihood of failure; a salesman so concerned about his falling sales that he can't bring himself to pick up the phone guarantees that his sales will fall even further.

But why are some people better able to "snap out of it" and get on with the task at hand? Again, given sufficient self-awareness, people develop coping mechanisms. Sadness and discouragement, for instance, are "low arousal" states, and the dispirited salesman who goes out for a run is triggering a high arousal state that is incompatible with staying blue. Relaxation works better for high energy moods like anger or anxiety. Either way, the idea is to shift to a state of arousal that breaks the destructive cycle of the dominant mood.

The idea of being able to predict which salesmen are most likely to prosper was not an abstraction for Metropolitan Life, which in the mid-'80s was hiring 5,000 salespeople a year and training them at a cost of more than $30,000 each. Half quit the first year, and four out of five within four years. The reason: selling life insurance involves having the door slammed in your face over and over again. Was it possible to identify which people would be better at handling frustration and take each refusal as a challenge rather than a setback?

The head of the company approached psychologist Martin Seligman at the University of Pennsylvania and invited him to test some of his theories about the importance of optimism in people's success. When optimists fail, he has found, they attribute the failure to something they can change, not some innate weakness that they are helpless to overcome. And that confidence in their power to effect change is self-reinforcing. Seligman tracked 15,000 new workers who had taken two tests. One was the company's regular screening exam, the other Seligman's test measuring their levels of optimism. Among the new hires was a group who flunked the screening test but scored as "superoptimists" on Seligman's exam. And sure enough, they did the best of all; they outsold the pessimists in the regular group by 21% in the first year and 57% in the second. For years after that, passing Seligman's test was one way to get hired as a MetLife salesperson.

Perhaps the most visible emotional skills, the ones we recognize most readily, are the "people skills" like empathy, graciousness, the ability to read a social situation. Researchers believe that about 90% of emotional communication is nonverbal. Harvard psychologist Robert Rosenthal developed the PONS test (Profile of Nonverbal Sensitivity) to measure people's ability to read emotional

One Way to Test Your EQ

UNLIKE IQ, WHICH IS GAUGED BY THE FAMOUS STANFORD-Binet tests, EQ does not lend itself to any single numerical measure. Nor should it, say experts. Emotional intelligence is by definition a complex, multifaceted quality representing such intangibles as self-awareness, empathy, persistence and social deftness.

Some aspects of emotional intelligence, however, can be quantified. Optimism, for example, is a handy measure of a person's self-worth. According to Martin Seligman, a University of Pennsylvania psychologist, how people respond to setbacks—optimistically or pessimistically—is a fairly accurate indicator of how well they will succeed in school, in sports and in certain kinds of work. To test his theory, Seligman devised a questionnaire to screen insurance salesmen at MetLife.

In Seligman's test, job applicants were asked to imagine a hypothetical event and then choose the response (A or B) that most closely resembled their own. Some samples from his questionnaire:

You forget your spouse's (boyfriend's/girlfriend's) birthday.
A. I'm not good at remembering birthdays.
B. I was preoccupied with other things.

You owe the library $10 for an overdue book.
A. When I am really involved in what I am reading, I often forget when its due.
B. I was so involved in writing the report, I forgot to return the book.

You lose your temper with a friend.
A. He or she is always nagging me.
B. He or she was in a hostile mood.

You are penalized for returning your income-tax forms late.
A. I always put off doing my taxes.
B. I was lazy about getting my taxes done this year.

You've been feeling run-down.
A. I never get a chance to relax.
B. I was exceptionally busy this week.

A friend says something that hurts your feelings.
A. She always blurts things out without thinking of others.
B. My friend was in a bad mood and took it out on me.

You fall down a great deal while skiing.
A. Skiing is difficult.
B. The trails were icy.

You gain weight over the holidays, and you can't lose it.
A. Diets don't work in the long run.
B. The diet I tried didn't work.

Seligman found that those insurance salesman who answered with more B's than A's were better able to overcome bad sales days, recovered more easily from rejection and were less likely to quit. People with an optimistic view of life tend to treat obstacles and setbacks as temporary (and therefore surmountable). Pessimists take them personally; what others see as fleeting, localized impediments, they view as pervasive and permanent.

The most dramatic proof of his theory, says Seligman, came at the 1988 Olympic Games in Seoul, South Korea, after U.S. swimmer Matt Biondi turned in two disappointing performances in this first two races. Before the Games, Biondi had been favored to win seven golds—as Mark Spitz had done 16 years earlier. After those first two races, most commentators thought Biondi would be unable to recover from his setback. Not Seligman. He had given some members of the U.S. swim team a version of his optimism test before the races; it showed that Biondi possessed an extraordinarily upbeat attitude. Rather than losing heart after turning in a bad time, as others might, Biondi tended to respond by swimming even faster. Sure enough, Biondi bounced right back, winning five gold medals in the next five races. —*By Alice Park* cues. He shows subjects a film of a young woman expressing feelings—anger, love, jealousy, gratitude, seduction—edited so that one or another nonverbal cue is blanked out. In some instances the face is visible but not the body, or the woman's eyes are hidden, so that viewers have to judge the feeling by subtle cues. Once again, people with higher PONS scores tend to be more successful in their work and relationships; children who score well are more popular and successful in school, even [though] their IQs are quite average.

Like other emotional skills, empathy is an innate quality that can be shaped by experience. Infants as young as three months old exhibit empathy when they get upset at the sound of another baby crying. Even very young children learn by imitation; by watching how others act when they see someone in distress, these children acquire a repertoire of sensitive responses. If, on the other hand, the feelings they begin to express are not recognized and reinforced by the adults around them, they not only cease to express those feelings but they also become less able to recognize them in themselves or others.

Empathy too can be seen as a survival skill. Bert Cohler, a University of Chicago psychologist, and Fran Stott, dean of the Erikson Institute for Advanced Study in Child Development in Chicago, have found that children from psychically damaged families frequently become hypervigilant, developing an intense attunement to their parents' moods. One child they studied, Nicholas, had a horrible habit of approaching other kids in his nursery-school class as if he were going to kiss them, then would bite them instead. The scientists went back to study videos of Nicholas at 20 months interacting with his psychotic mother and found that she had responded to his every expression of anger or independence with compulsive kisses. The researchers dubbed them "kisses of death," and their true significance was obvious to Nicholas, who arched his back in horror at her approaching lips—and passed his own rage on to his classmates years later.

Empathy also acts as a buffer to cruelty, and it is a quality conspicuously lacking in child molesters and psychopaths. Goleman cites some chilling research into brutality by Robert Hare, a psychologist at the University of British Columbia. Hare found that psychopaths, when hooked up to electrodes and told they are going to receive a shock, show none of the visceral responses that fear of pain typically triggers: rapid heartbeat, sweating and so on. How could the threat of punishment deter such people from committing crimes?

It is easy to draw the obvious lesson from these test results. How much happier would we be, how much more successful as individuals and civil as a society, if we were more alert to the importance of emotional

Square Pegs in the Oval Office?

I F A HIGH DEGREE OF EMOTIONAL INTELLIGENCE IS A PREREQUISITE FOR OUTSTANDING achievement, there ought to be no better place to find it than in the White House. It turns out, however, that not every man who reached the pinnacle of American leadership was a gleaming example of self-awareness, empathy, impulse control and all the other qualities that mark an elevated EQ.

Oliver Wendall Holmes, who knew intelligence when he saw it, judged Franklin Roosevelt "a second-class intellect, but a first-class temperament." Born and educated as an aristocrat, F.D.R. had polio and needed a wheelchair for most of his adult life. Yet, far from becoming a self-pitying wretch, he developed an unbridled optimism that served him and the country well during the Depression and World War II—this despite, or because of, what Princeton professor Fred Greenstein calls Roosevelt's "tendency toward deviousness and duplicity."

Even a first-class temperament, however, is not a sure predictor of a successful presidency. According to Duke University political scientist James David Barber, the most perfect blend of intellect and warmth of personality in a Chief Executive was the brilliant Thomas Jefferson, who "knew the importance of communication and empathy. He never lost the common touch." Richard Ellis, a professor of politics at Oregon's Willamette University who is skeptical of the whole EQ theory, cites two 19th century Presidents who did not fit the mold. "Martin Van Buren was well adjusted, balanced, empathetic and persuasive, but he was not very successful," says Ellis. "Andrew Jackson was less well adjusted, less balanced, less empathetic and was terrible at controlling his own impulses, but he transformed the presidency."

Lyndon Johnson as Senate majority leader was a brilliant practitioner of the art of political persuasion, yet failed utterly to transfer that gift to the White House. In fact, says Princeton's Greenstein, L.B.J. and Richard Nixon would be labeled "worst cases" on any EQ scale of Presidents. Each was touched with political genius, yet each met with disaster. "To some extent," says Greenstein, "this is a function of the extreme aspects of their psyches; they are the political versions of Van Gogh, who does unbelievable paintings and then cuts off his ear."

History professor William Leuchtenburg of the University of North Carolina at Chapel Hill suggests that the 20th century Presidents with perhaps the highest IQs—Wilson, Hoover and Carter—also had the most trouble connecting with their constituents. Woodrow Wilson, he says, "was very high strung [and] arrogant; he was not willing to strike any middle ground. Herbert Hoover was so locked into certain ideas that you could never convince him otherwise. Jimmy Carter is probably the most puzzling of the three. He didn't have a deficiency of temperament; in fact, he was too temperate. There was an excessive rationalization about Carter's approach."

That was never a problem for John Kennedy and Ronald Reagan. Nobody ever accused them of intellectual genius, yet both radiated qualities of leadership with an infectious confidence and openheartedness that endeared them to the nation. Whether President Clinton will be so endeared remains a puzzle. That he is a Rhodes scholar makes him certifiably brainy, but his emotional intelligence is shaky. He obviously has the knack for establishing rapport with people, but he often appears to eager to please that he looks weak. "As for controlling his impulses," says Willamette's Ellis, "Clinton is terrible." **—By Jesse Birnbaum. Reported by James Carney/Washington and Lisa H. Towle/Raleigh**

intelligence and more adept at teaching it? From kindergartens to business schools to corporations across the country, people are taking seriously the idea that a little more time spent on the "touchy-feely" skills so often derided may in fact pay rich dividends.

In the corporate world, according to personnel executives, IQ gets you hired, but EQ gets you promoted. Goleman likes

to tell of a manager at AT&T's Bell Labs, a think tank for brilliant engineers in New Jersey, who was asked to rank his top performers. They weren't the ones with the highest IQs; they were the ones whose E-mail got answered. Those workers who were good collaborators and networkers and popular with colleagues were more likely to get the cooperation they needed to reach their goals than the socially awkward, lone-wolf geniuses.

When David Campbell and others at the Center for Creative Leadership studied "derailed executives," the rising stars who flamed out, the researchers found that these executives failed most often because of "an interpersonal flaw" rather than a technical inability. Interviews with top executives in the U.S. and Europe turned up nine so-called fatal flaws, many of them classic emotional failings, such as "poor working relations," being "authoritarian" or "too ambitious" and having "conflict with upper management."

At the center's executive-leadership seminars across the country, managers come to get emotionally retooled. "This isn't sensitivity training or Sunday-supplement stuff," says Campbell. "One thing they know when they get through is what other people think of them." And the executives have an incentive to listen. Says Karen Boylston, director of the center's team-leadership group: "Customers are telling businesses, 'I don't care if every member of your staff graduated with honors from Harvard, Stanford and Wharton. I will take my business and go where I am understood and treated with respect.' "

Nowhere is the discussion of emotional intelligence more pressing than in schools, where both the stakes and the opportunities seem greatest. Instead of constant crisis intervention, or declarations of war on drug abuse or teen pregnancy or violence, it is time, Goleman argues, for preventive medicine. "Five years ago, teachers didn't want to think about this," says principal Roberta Kirshbaum of P.S. 75 in New York City. "But when kids are getting killed in high school, we have to deal with it." Five years ago, Kirshbaum's school adopted an emotional literacy program, designed to help children learn to manage anger, frustration, loneliness. Since then, fights at lunchtime have decreased from two or three a day to almost none.

Educators can point to all sorts of data to support this new direction. Students who are depressed or angry literally cannot learn. Children who have trouble being accepted by their classmates are 2 to 8 times as likely to drop out. An inability to distinguish distressing feelings or handle frustration has been linked to eating disorders in girls.

Many school administrators are completely rethinking the weight they have been giving to traditional lessons and standardized tests. Peter Relic, president of the National Association of Independent Schools, would like to junk the SAT completely. "Yes, it may cost a heck of a lot more money to assess someone's EQ rather than using a machine-scored test to measure IQ," he says. "But if we don't, then we're saying that a test score is more important to us than who a child is as a human being. That means an immense loss in terms of human potential because we've defined success too narrowly."

This warm embrace by educators has left some scientists in a bind. On one hand, says Yale psychologist Salovey, "I love the idea that we want to teach people a richer understanding of their emotional life, to help them achieve their goals." But, he adds, "what I would oppose is training conformity to social expectations." The danger is that any campaign to hone emotional skills in children will end up teaching that there is a "right" emotional response for any given situation—laugh at parades, cry at funerals, sit still at church. "You can teach self-control," says Dr. Alvin Poussaint, professor of psychiatry at Harvard Medical School. "You can teach that it's better to talk out your anger and not use violence. But is it good emotional intelligence not to challenge authority?"

SOME PSYCHOLOGISTS GO further and challenge the very idea that emotional skills can or should be taught in any kind of formal, classroom way. Goleman's premise that children can be trained to analyze their feelings strikes Johns Hopkins' McHugh as an effort to reinvent the encounter group: "I consider that an abominable idea, an idea we have seen with adults. That failed, and now he wants to try it with children? Good grief!" He cites the description in Goleman's book of an experimental program at the Nueva Learning Center in San Francisco. In one scene, two fifth-grade boys start to argue over the rules of an exercise, and the teacher breaks in to ask them to talk about what they're feeling. "I appreciate the way you're being assertive in talking with Tucker," she says to one student. "You're not attacking." This strikes McHugh as pure folly. "The author is presuming that someone has the key to the right emotions to be taught to children. We don't even know the right emotions to be taught to adults. Do you really think a child of eight or nine really understands the difference between aggressiveness and assertiveness?"

The problem may be that there is an ingredient missing. Emotional skills, like intellectual ones, are morally neutral. Just as a genius could use his intellect either to cure cancer or engineer a deadly virus, someone with great empathic insight could use it to inspire colleagues or exploit them. Without a moral compass to guide people in how to employ their gifts, emotional intelligence can be used for good or evil. Columbia University psychologist Walter Mischel, who invented the marshmallow test and others like it, observes that the knack for delaying gratification that makes a child one marshmallow richer can help him become a better citizen or—just as easily—an even more brilliant criminal.

Given the passionate arguments that are raging over the state of moral instruction in this country, it is no wonder Goleman chose to focus more on neutral emotional skills than on the values that should govern their use. That's another book—and another debate. **—Reported by Sharon E. Epperson and Lawrence Mondi/New York, James L. Graff/Chicago and Lisa H. Towle/Raleigh**

Dealing with Misbehavior: Two Approaches

J. Michael Palardy

Two approaches that have proven effective in teachers' dealings with student misbehavior, namely, the behaviorist and the diagnostic, are described and discussed. Of the two, the diagnostic approach is preferred, principally for the reasons that the behaviorist approach fails to treat the causes of misbehavior, does not emphasize prevention, has little transfer value, and results at best in "managed conduct."

Two major approaches to dealing with classroom discipline seem to be promulgated today by most authorities. Respectively, these are the behaviorist and the diagnostic approaches. Is each of these a legitimate approach, particularly in reference to teaching at-risk youngsters? Yes, in my opinion, but not equally legitimate. A review of the basic characteristics and strategies of each seems warranted, particularly in light of the fact that discipline remains atop the list of teachers' major concerns (Palardy, 1992).

The Behaviorist Approach

The psychology of behaviorism has been a key force in American education for at least 50 years. Its offshoot, *behavior modification*, is a relative newcomer in education, having gained widespread popularity only within the past couple of decades through highly publicized techniques such as "assertive discipline" (Canter, 1988). The purpose of behavior modification is to reshape behavior, i.e., to change pupils' undesirable classroom behavior to desirable—and is effected through four "simple" steps.

The first step is identification of the behavior problem itself. Teachers must identify the behavior they find undesirable. The key is to be specific. It is insufficient, for example, for teachers to say that Marcus misbehaves. Rather, they must pinpoint the specific way(s) he misbehaves. Does he keep getting out of his seat; does he throw spitwads; does he bully Harry; does he come to class late; does he talk out of turn; does he sleep in class? The more specifically the behavior is identified, the better.

The second step is identification of the appropriate behavior. Teachers must identify the specific way(s) they want the pupil to act. In almost every case, such identification is the

J. Michael Palardy, College of Education, University of Alabama.

Correspondence concerning this article should be addressed to J. Michael Palardy, College of Education, the University of Alabama, P.O. Box 870130, Tuscaloosa, Alabama 35487-0130.

From *Journal of Instructional Psychology*, June 1995, pp. 135-140. © 1995 by the Journal of Instructional Psychology. Reprinted by permission.

reverse of step one. For example, Marcus remains seated; he refrains from throwing spitwads; he acts kindly toward Harry; he raises his hand before answering; he is prompt and on-task. This step may seem to be an unnecessary duplication of effort, but for behavior modifiers it is critical.

The third step is the use of reward. When the pupil behaves in the way that was spelled out in the second step, teachers must reward him/her. To return to our example, not even Marcus is out of his seat every minute of every reading class. When Marcus is seated, it is important for teachers to reward him. Actually, for behavior modifiers, this is the most important of the steps. The quickest and surest way of eliminating misbehavior is rewarding its opposite.

Furthermore, teachers must keep in mind that good behavior is not necessarily its own reward. When teachers object to students' misbehavior, they typically tell them "not to do it again." Then, when the students do what they have been told not to, teachers usually react, often by punishing. But when the students are doing what they are supposed to do, too frequently teachers do nothing. Perhaps thinking that good behavior is its own reward, teachers fail to commend students for their *good* conduct. According to the behaviorist approach, these omissions are deadly.

The fourth and final step is the use of extinction procedures to help *eliminate* the inappropriate behavior identified in the first step. The key words are to help eliminate. Let's return to Marcus. He has two choices in reading group: to sit or not to sit. Even if teachers consistently reward Marcus when he chooses to sit, there will be occasions, particularly at first, when he will choose not to. When Marcus opts to leave his seat, teachers can do one of two things. They can either ignore his behavior or react to it. Each of these responses is what behaviorists refer to as an extinction procedure.

Critics often ask why teachers should ever ignore inappropriate behavior. As one example, suppose that Marcus gets out of his seat during reading class to attract attention. When teachers react to his behavior by saying, "Marcus, please sit down!" what have they done? They have given him exactly what he wants—attention. In essence, they have rewarded Marcus for behaving inappropriately. Even worse, they have reinforced his knowledge that, whenever he wants attention, all he has to do to get it is to get out of his seat.

There are times, then, when reacting to misbehavior has an effect entirely different from the one wanted.

Other types of misbehavior, of course, demand that teachers react. They cannot simply stand by and watch a pupil deface school property or bully another youngster. They have to intervene immediately. But it is important to note that intervening or reacting is not synonymous with punishing. Reminding Marcus that he is supposed to be seated during reading class is reacting. Keeping him in at recess because he needed reminding is punishing. To repeat, teachers can react to misbehavior without punishing.

As stated earlier, the key to behavior modification is not the use of punishment, but the use of reward. Pupils can be conditioned to act in desirable ways if teachers will reward them for acting in these ways. Then, as pupils begin to be conditioned, their need for reward lessens. At first, Marcus needs immediate and frequent payoffs for staying seated. Later, as he gradually becomes conditioned to remaining seated, the payoffs can and should become less frequent. Finally, it is hoped, the conditioning process will work so well that payoffs will not longer be necessary.

Is this a legitimate hope? Does behavior modification work? Yes, it does, but in my opinion not to the degree or with the frequency behaviorists predict. Elsewhere (Palardy, 1992) I have written that the approach has at least four limitations. These are: it fails to treat the causes of misbehavior; there is little emphasis on prevention; there is little transfer value; it results in "managed conduct," but not self discipline.

The Diagnostic Approach

The most comprehensive and legitimate approach to discipline is called the diagnostic approach. Contrary to behavior modification, this approach assumes that there can be lasting effects on certain behavior problems *only after* their causes are ferreted out and treated.

According to the diagnostic approach, what can teachers do to prevent behavior problems? What are some strategies of prevention? Below I have listed nine strategies that, in my opinion, are essential. But I need to emphasize that others are possible. I also must emphasize that preventive strategies are not fail proof. Even if all the preventive strategies described here are used, behavior problems may still emerge. But from the diagnostic point of view and my own, if the strategies described here are used, the number of these problems will be significantly reduced.

Prevention

Here are nine strategies to prevent discipline problems.

1. Teachers must feel comfortable with themselves, their students, and their subject matter. One of the major reasons that student teachers and first-year teachers often have difficulties with discipline is their uneasiness—uneasiness with themselves because being on the other side of that desk, particularly at first, is no easy task; uneasiness with their students because they may be "so different" or "so little"; uneasiness with their subject matter because, in terms of the real world, content courses taken in high school and college often leave much to be desired. But regardless of the cause, and regardless of their years of experience, teachers who are uneasy are going to communicate that uneasiness to their students. And when this happens, the door to restlessness among students is wide open.

2. Teachers must believe in their pupils' capacity and propensity for appropriate classroom conduct. For according to sociologists, teachers' beliefs serve as "self-fulfilling prophecies." If teachers believe that pupils can and will act in socially acceptable ways, pupils will tend to do so. But if teachers believe, for any number of reasons, including race of socioeconomic background, that pupils neither can nor will behave appropriately, they will tend, in fact, to misbehave. The principle of the self-fulfilling prophecy is profoundly, and often painfully, clear: the tendency of pupils, as of every other social group, is to live and act as others expect them to live and act.

3. Teachers must ensure that their instructional activities are interesting and relevant. The words *interesting* and *relevant* may be overworked in educational literature, but there can be no mistaking their importance. Nor can there be any mistaking the fact that dreary classrooms, monotonous routines, ir-

relevant, antiquated content, and tedious methods of presentation are more characteristic of more educational settings than many care to admit. There is little doubt that these characteristics are major causes of misbehavior. Some pupils, to be sure, become acculturated to drabness in school life, learn to play the game, and become "model" citizens in school. But just as certainly, and perhaps even more expectedly, other pupils become indifferent, rebel, and become troublemakers.

4. Teachers must match their instructional activities and requirements with their pupils' capabilities. Behavior problems are often the result of the teacher's failure to adapt their instruction to their pupils' abilities. When pupils are handed materials that are too difficult, when they're required to complete assignments for which they lack readiness, when they're given directions they can't possibly understand, is it any wonder that some become frustrated and cause problems? I think not. When other pupils are assigned tasks that insult their intelligence, is it any wonder that some lose interest and cause trouble? Again, I think not. Teachers must see to it that all pupils are challenged appropriately, not over- or underwhelmed. Failing this, teachers should at least lay the blame for misbehavior where the blame belongs.

5. Teachers must involve their pupils in setting up "the rules." There are two major reasons for following this practice, one long range and one short term. From the long-range perspective, a democracy requires that citizens have the skills to participate actively and intelligently in group decision-making. Schools, in my opinion, are potentially the single best medium through which youngsters can practice and master these skills in a gradual, nonthreatening way. From the short-term perspective, when groups of individuals help make the decisions that affect their lives, they are more likely to live within the framework of these decisions. Groups of pupils are no exception. Pupils who help establish the rules and regulations of the classroom better understand the necessity of having the rules and are more committed to following them than pupils who have had no voice in classroom regulations.

6. Teachers must make certain that their pupils know and understand "the routine." No two teachers hold the exact same set of expectations for pupils. No two teachers have the same classroom routine. Given differing ex-

pectations and differing routines, the problem confronting pupils is real. In this day of earlier and earlier departmentaliztion, even very young pupils daily come into contact with several teachers. Pupils must remember what routine to follow as well as whose routine. This is no easy task, but one that teachers often take for granted. Too frequently, teachers make the mistake of assuming that their standards for proper behavior are the only standards for proper behavior. In fact, though, a good amount of behavior is relative, and its appropriateness can only be determined in context. Given differing routines or contexts, what one teacher perceives as proper behavior another teacher may perceive as misbehavior. And pupils are caught in the middle!

7. Teachers must identify their problem times. When do pupils tend to act up? When they first get to class? Or toward the end of the period? On the playground? In the lunchroom? In the halls? On Monday, or Wednesday, or Friday? The day before or after a big dance, test, or ball game? Knowing when the problem times are is an important first step in being able to make plans to prevent them.

8. Teachers must remember that pupils are not adults. Rather, they're five- or six-year-olds to teenagers. These youngsters cannot and should not be expected to display the same control over their behavior as adults. Yet, in too many instances, they're expected to display more. There is no doubt that teachers would save their pupils much frustration, and themselves many headaches, if they simply refrained from insisting on proper adult conduct from nonadults.

9. Teachers must give evidence that they genuinely respect their pupils. Teachers do not give such evidence when they complain about pupils in the halls and lounges; when they criticize and laugh at pupils behind their backs; when they tell pupils in hundreds of different ways that their culture is deficient, that their homes are inadequate; when they do not take the time to make a home visit or prepare an extra lesson. The list could go on, but the point is unmistakable. Teachers do not give evidence that they respect pupils by voicing platitudes. Teachers give evidence mainly through their actions, or lack thereof, and only through such will they succeed in earning pupils' respect. To earn it is probably the most important preventive strategy of all.

These nine strategies are measures teachers can and must take to prevent behavior prob-

lems. But even with these measures, some behavior problems will still emerge. When they do, what guidelines does the diagnostic approach give teachers? What can teachers do when behavior problems occur?

Intervention

According to the diagnostic approach, there is no one method of dealing with behavior problems, just as there is no one method of preventing them. There is no single strategy of intervention that works every time. Rather, there are many intervention strategies, and only teachers themselves can assess which ones work best in various situations. There are, however, seven strategies that I believe should be in every teacher's repertory. Again, these seven strategies in no way constitute a comprehensive list, but they do provide teachers with as sound a point of departure as I think there is.

1. The use of nonverbal techniques, particularly at the beginning stages of misbehavior, can be an effective way of letting pupils know that one or all of them had better settle down. Eye contact, body posture, facial expressions, and silence are probably the most noteworthy of these techniques. Verbal techniques can also be effective. But they are so overused that their long-term impact seems questionable. Witness the number of teachers who intersperse every other sentence with "sh."

2. When a pupil is misbehaving, merely walking up to and standing beside him/her can frequently bring about the desired result. When proximity control is used, few pupils fail to get the message, and even fewer are brazen enough to disregard it.

3. Removing the source of a disturbance can bring about the desired result. One form of removal is the "take-it-away" type. The teacher may take away rubber bands, water pistols, food, and contraband reading materials. Most teachers are familiar with this form of removal. Another form is the "let-it-run-its course" type. Teachers may be less familiar with this type. Almost daily, in the classroom and outside, there are phenomena that pupils are naturally interested in, that they naturally give their attention to. Hailstorms, ambulance sirens, Johnny's new shoes, Sarah's coiffure, and Ms. Smith's new student teacher are but a few examples. When such attractions cap-

ture pupils' attention, the surest way of recapturing it is simply to let pupils have a few minutes of exploration.

4. Pointing out to pupils the consequences of their misbehavior can be an effective method of intervention. The key is to find the right consequence. To tell Marcus that he will have a terrible time with long division if he does not stop horsing around in second-grade addition is probably not a very meaningful consequence to him. But to tell him that he will not be able to sit next to Billy might be. Matching the pupil with the right consequence is no easy task. But making false matches yields no benefits whatsoever.

5. The use of behavior modification techniques can be an effective method of intervention. These techniques, as well as some of their limitations, were described earlier.

6. Asking a pupil to leave the room or sending him to a time-out corner can be an important intervention strategy. This technique has one overarching purpose: to give the pupil a chance to cool off. Trying to deal with a pupil who is on the verge of losing self-control is almost inevitably a lost cause. In such situations teachers often become angry and end up losing their own self control.

7. Punishing pupils can be a necessary and an effective strategy. But when punishment is being considered, five principles should be kept in mind.

First, punishment should be used sparingly. The more often punishment is used, the less effective it becomes. Teachers who frequently resort to punishment find that they have to punish more often and more severely just to maintain the status quo.

Second, punishment should never constitute retaliation. It is beneath the dignity of professionals to punish pupils "to get back at them." Teachers who do so do not belong in education.

Third, subject matter should not be used as punishment. In most cases, requiring pupils to do another page of mathematics or to write an extra book report reduces the chance that they will develop favorable attitudes in these areas. In the long run, much more is lost than gained.

Fourth, mass punishment should not be used. Teachers should never punish the entire class for the transgressions of a few members. Many teachers fall into this trap; few escape without some loss of respect.

Fifth, corporal punishment should not be used. I know that there are strong differences of opinion about whether corporal punishment is effective. I happen to believe it generally is not. But this is not the key point. The key is that corporal punishment, by those who support its use, is intended to be a last-ditch effort to change behavior. The implication is that if corporal punishment fails, nothing else can be done. This implication, from the diagnostic point of view and my own, is anathema.

According to the diagnostic approach, then, if the strategies of prevention and intervention are used, most common forms of misbehavior can either be eliminated or be dealt with effectively. But some behavior problems cannot be. These are the problems that are symptoms of underlying causes and, consequently, continue to recur until the causes are diagnosed and treated.

Diagnosis

There is no quick, easy or fail-proof formula for diagnosing the causes of pupils' behavior problems. But there is one absolutely essential step: to learn as much as possible about the pupils. To do so, teachers must draw on all possible sources of information. These include achievement and intelligence tests, social and psychological inventories, attendance records, cumulative folders, previous teachers, clergymen, parents, relatives, siblings, peers, social workers, visiting teachers, medical personal, employers, coaches, and, most important of all, the pupils themselves.

After the information from these sources has been gathered and analyzed, it is my contention that teachers can make a reasonably reliable determination of the causes of most behavior problems. Certainly, teachers are not psychiatrists and psychologists. But discovering most behavior problems of youngsters does not require that sort of expertise. It is also my contention that teachers can take steps to eliminate many of these causes and the resulting behavioral symptoms. But, as I said earlier, neither of these contentions is universally supported.

Most critics of this approach argue that the whole effort of diagnosis is a waste of time because nothing *can be done anyway*. These critics are quick to assert that teachers cannot force parents to love their children or feed them adequately, that teachers cannot mend broken homes, that they cannot keep Joe's father off the bottle or Karen's mother off the streets or needle.

But I disagree with this argument. First, because it assumes that the causes of students' behavior problems are not school related or school induced. Like it or not, many are.

Second, even if the diagnosis shows that the causes are not school related, much can still be done. Pupils' ego needs can be met in school, their self-respect enhanced, their enjoyment of life increased. In school, pupils can be given love and can learn to give it in return. Schools can provide food and clothing. They can make medical, dental, and psychological referrals. They can contact community action programs, welfare departments, civic organizations, churches, and even law enforcement agencies. Schools can provide for adult education, drug and sex education, and early education. I disagree that diagnosis is a waste of time because nothing can be done. This logic has long been refuted by schools and teachers who have done all these things and more.

I said earlier that there are no easy answers to discipline problems. But I know that the judicious and consistent use of diagnostic approaches will place students and teachers alike in the best possible classroom environment.

References

Canter, L. (1988). More than names on the board and marbles in a jar. *Phi Delta Kappan, 75,* 103–108.

Palardy, J.M. (1992). Behavior modification: It does work, but. . . . *Journal of Instructional Psychology, 22.* 127–132.

Development during Childhood: Family and Culture

Family (Articles 21–25)
Culture (Articles 26–29)

Is there a set of family values that is superior to another set of family values? Is there a culture that has more correct answers than another culture? It is often assumed by the layperson that children's behaviors and personalities have a direct correlation with the behaviors and personalities of the person or persons who provided their socialization during infancy and childhood. Are you a mirror image of the person or persons who raised you? Why or why not? How many of their behaviors do you reflect?

During childhood, a person's family values get compared to, and tested against, the values of school, community, and culture. Peers, schoolmates, teachers, neighbors, extracurricular activity leaders, religious leaders, even shopkeepers, play increasingly important roles. Culture influences the developing child not only through the people with whom the child has one-on-one interaction, but also through holidays, styles of dress, music, television, movies, slang, games played, parents' jobs, transportation, and exposure to sex, drugs, and violence. The ecological theorist, Urie Bronfenbrenner, calls these exosystem and macrosystem influences. The developing personality of a child has multiple interwoven influences: from genetic potentialities through family values and socialization practices to community and cultural pressures for behaviors.

The first article in this unit appeals to partnerships in parenting: fathers plus mothers. Fathers have been relegated to "second banana" position, often viewed as breadwinners and disciplinarians. School-age children need parents who are both responsive and demanding. Discipline is crucial to a healthy personality. However, mothers as well as fathers need to be disciplinarians, and fathers as well as mothers need to provide tender, loving, and responsive caregiving. The authors are both fathers who have important things to say about their roles in their children's lives.

The second article reviews several important parenting factors that can help children develop resiliency and healthy self-esteem. Bad environments (e.g., poverty, use of drugs, violence, psychotic behaviors) do not always signal calamity for children. Good parenting can help children overcome, and even grow stronger, in times of ad-

versity. Joseph Shapiro and his coauthors review research on resiliency-building factors, which are assets for children. They give vignettes of strengths in the lives of several people, including Bill Clinton (and his mother).

The third article affirms the rights of all children, including those with disabilities, to live in a family environment. Separating a child from his or her parents may deprive that child of the resiliency-building factors mentioned in the previous article. Resiliency is an asset all children need. Children with disabilities have the right to all the same supports as every other child. Society should afford them nothing less. Separating them from their parents for education or for therapy deprives them of their right to have their safety, love, and belongingness needs met in family environments by the people to whom they are emotionally attached.

The fourth and fifth articles in the family section present the opposite dimensions of loving responsiveness and caring discipline. The first presents some of the long-term consequences upon school-age children of witnessing physical abuse between their parents. The second, retained from previous editions because of reader accolades, speaks to the long-term consequences to children of being themselves physically abused. Violence begets violence. Children who witness violence, or have it perpetrated against themselves, are at risk of many types of dysfunctional behavior later in life. They can benefit from counseling intervention.

The first article in the culture section is a classic description of childhood culture by the prolific writer and cognitive psychologist, David Elkind. This essay has been retained because of its importance and its continued usefulness to readers.

The second article in this section deals with the question of television as a pervasive influence on the psyche of the school-age child. The reality is that the average child spends more time in front of a television set than in a school classroom. Despite early psychological studies that suggested that the effect of television might be cathartic (a relief of tension and anxiety by bringing repressed feelings and fears to consciousness), current research explicitly demon-

peers, and religious leaders. Is a loved adult's opinion more important than the majority opinion? What is the opinion of the greater society in a rapidly changing culture? What beliefs continue to exert pressure? What social climate should be maintained? The third article in this section suggests that the presence of a loving adult can be a powerful antidote for some stress-ridden children. Nevertheless, the article also points out that too much culture shock and stressful living can cause brain changes that may or may not be reversible.

The fourth article in this section on culture addresses the problem of children whose brain chemistry or architecture has already been affected by biology, stressful environments, or both. Diagnoses such as attention-deficit hyperactive disorder, learning disorder, anxiety disorder, conduct disorder, or emotional/behavioral disorder often leave children at increased risk for drug abuse, teen pregnancy, and psychiatric problems later in life. Robert Brooks reviews domains of resilience and self-esteem. His article offers intervention strategies to foster the hope and courage needed to survive in our contemporary culture.

Looking Ahead: Challenge Questions

How important are fathers in the lives of their children?

What can parents do to turn a foundering child into a thriving survivor?

Why should parents be encouraged to keep a child with disabilities at home?

What happens to children who witness domestic violence?

What happens to children who experience child abuse?

What is there in today's culture that causes insecurity and stress?

What are the myths and what is the reality about viewing televised violence?

What is "The Biology of Soul Murder"? Does stress have a devastating effect on biological processes in childhood?

How can interventions give stressed children resiliency and hope for their futures?

strates that children learn violent behaviors from television and practice them in their real worlds.

School-age children base right and wrong on criteria such as the approval of others, relationship maintenance, social order maintenance, and respect for authority. When adult role models condone an environment that includes violence, drugs, and sexual promiscuity, children come to think of these behaviors as socially and morally acceptable. Some children experience a great deal of stress in trying to figure out why what they hear and see all around them is labeled wrong by some parents, teachers,

Fathers' Time

Their style is vastly different, but dads can no longer be looked on as second bananas in the parenting biz. New studies show fathers are crucial for the emotional and intellectual growth of their kids, influencing how they ultimately turn out. Writer/father PAUL ROBERTS reports on the importance of being a papa. Actor/father BILL MOSELEY's dispatches reveal what it's like on the front lines.

Paul Roberts

PAUL ROBERTS is a Seattle-based freelance writer. Actor BILL MOSELEY interviewed Timothy Leary for *PT* in 1995.

This was supposed to be the Golden Era of Paternity. After decades of domestic aloofness, men came charging into parenthood with an almost religious enthusiasm. We attended Lamaze classes and crowded into birthing rooms. We mastered diapering, spent more time at home with the kids, and wallowed in the flood of "papa" literature unleashed by Bill Cosby's 1986 best-seller Fatherhood.

Yet for all our fervor, the paternal revolution has had a slightly hollow ring. It's not simply the relentless accounts of fatherhood's dark side—the abuse, the neglect, the abandonment—that make us so self-conscious. Rather, it's the fact that for all our earnest sensitivity, we can't escape questions of our psychological necessity: What is it, precisely, that fathers do? What critical difference do we make in the lives of our children?

Think about it. The modern mother, no matter how many nontraditional duties she assumes, is still seen as the family's primary nurturer and emotional guardian. It's in her genes. It's in her soul. But mainstream Western society accords no corresponding position to the modern father. Aside from chromosomes and feeling somewhat responsible for household income, there's no similarly celebrated deep link between father and child, no

widely recognized "paternal instinct." Margaret Mead's quip that fathers are "a biological necessity but a social accident" may be a little harsh. But is does capture the second-banana status that many fathers have when it comes to taking their measure as parents.

Happily, a new wave of research is likely to substantially boost that standing. Over the

Diary of a Dad

I love this time. Jane Moseley puts her hunter mare through its paces. Time slows to a trot, works up to a canter, drops to a lazy walk.

She announces she won't wear her riding hat. I insist she must. She refuses, would rather not ride. I can't believe she'd give up The Most Important Thing in her life over this. Fine, don't ride. This triggers an outpouring of vitriol. I pay attention, but don't take it personally. Thirty minutes later she's holding my hand as we walk down Melrose.

last decade, researchers like Jay Belsky, Ph.D., at Pennsylvania State University, and Ross Parke, Ph.D., of the University of California/Riverside Center for Family Studies, have been mapping out the psychology of the father-child bond, detailing how it functions and how it differs—sometimes substantially—from the bond between mother and child. What emerges from their work is the beginning of a truly modern concept of paternity, one in which old assumptions are overturned or, at the very least, cast in a radically different light. Far from Mead's "social accident," fatherhood turns out to be a complex and unique phenomenon with huge consequences for the emotional and intellectual growth of children.

Key to this new idea of fatherhood is a premise so mundane that most of us take it for granted: Fathers parent differently than mothers do. They play with their children more. Their interactions tend to be more physical and less intimate, with more of a reliance on humor and excitement. While such distinctions may hardly seem revelatory, they can mean a world of difference to kids. A father's more playful interactive style, for example, turns out to be critical in teaching a child emotional self-control. Likewise, father-child interactions appear to be central to the development of a child's ability to maintain strong, fulfilling social relationships later in life.

But it's not simply a matter of paternal behavior differing from maternal methods. The fabric of the father-child bond is also different. Studies show that fathers with low self-esteem have a greater negative impact on their children than do mothers who don't like themselves. In addition, the father-child bond seems to be more fragile—and therefore more easily severed—during periods of strife between parents.

Amid this welter of findings two things are clear. First, given our rapidly evolving conceptions of "father" and "family," fatherhood in the 1990s is probably tougher, psychologically, than at any other time in recent history. Plainly put, there are precious few positive role models to guide today's papas. Yet at the same time, the absence of any guidance holds hidden promise. Given the new information on fatherhood, the potential for a rich and deeply rewarding paternal experience is significantly greater today than even a generation ago. "The possibilities for fathering have never been better," Belsky says. "Culturally

After Jane and I had a walk, she wanted to box. So we waltzed around for 20 minutes, floating like a butterfly (me), stinging like a bee (Jane). I've taught her the rudiments of pugilism: how to make a fist (don't wrap your fingers around your thumb); how she should always stand sideways to her opponent, watching the hands not the eyes, etc. After a few fun-filled injury-free rounds, I came to my senses and ended our play.

Jane is an only child, so I figure it's my job to play with her as a brother or provide her with a sibling—playing with her is easier!

speaking, there is so much more that fathers are 'allowed' to do."

OUR FOREFATHERS

The surge of interest in fatherhood has a distinctly modern feel, as if after thousands of years of unquestioned maternal preeminence, men are just now discovering and asserting their parental prerogatives. But in fact, this unquestioned maternal dominance is itself a relatively recent development. Up until the mid-1700s, when most fathers worked in or near the home and took a much greater hand in child rearing, Western culture regarded them and not mothers as the more competent parent—and ultimately held them more responsible for how their children turned out. Not only were books and manuals on parenting written chiefly for men, according to R. L. Griswold, author of *Fatherhood in America*, men were routinely awarded custody of their kids in cases of divorce.

With the Industrial Revolution, however, more fathers began working outside their homes and thus were effectively removed from domestic life. As Vicky Phares, Ph.D., assistant professor of psychology at the University of South Florida, wrote in *Fathers and Developmental Psychopathology*, industrialization ushered in the "feminization of the domestic sphere and the marginalization of fathers' involvement with their children." By the mid-1800s, Phares notes, "child-rearing manuals were geared toward mothers, and this trend continued for the most part until the mid 1970s."

The implication here—that parental roles have largely been defined by economics—is still a subject of cultural debate. Less arguable, however, is the fact that by the turn of the twentieth century, both science and society saw the psychology of parenting largely as the psychology of motherhood. Not only were mothers somehow more "naturally" inclined to parent, they were also genetically better prepared for the task. Indeed, in 1916, Phares notes, one prominent investigator went so far as to "prove" the existence of the maternal instinct—and the lack of paternal equivalent—largely based on the notion that "few fathers were naturally skilled at taking care of infants."

Granted, bogus scientific claims were plentiful in those times. But even Freud, who believed fathers figured heavily in children's development of conscience and sexual identity, dismissed the idea that they had any impact until well past a child's third year. And even then, many psychologists argued, these paternal contributions consisted primarily of providing income, discipline, and a masculine role model, along with periodic injections of what might be called "real world" experience—that is, things that took place outside the home. "The classical psychological view held that a father's 'job' was to expand his children's horizon beyond the bosom of the family and the mother-child relationship," Belsky observes. "Mothers preserved and protected children from discomfort. But fathers imposed a realistic, the-world-is-tough perspective."

By the 1920s, the classic "mother-centric" view was showing its cracks. Not only did subsequent empirical studies find little hard evidence of any unique maternal instinct but, as Phares points out, the phenomenon of "mother-blaming"—that is, blaming mothers for all the emotional and behavioral problems of their children—prodded some researchers (and, no doubt, a good many mothers) to ask whether fathers might share some of the responsibility.

I crave adult company, but I don't have a baby-sitter for tonight. So I'm trying to lug Jane all the way to Santa Monica to see Wing Chung, a kung-fu movie she says she doesn't want to see. Oh, no you don't, kid, it's my time now, and we're going to Santa Monica. Of course, Jane winds up loving the movie. Later that night we watch a video of Captains Courageous. I am reminded of all the songs that the two of us have made up over the past several years: "Feed Lot," "Ain't No Bridge," "Don't Drink the Water," "When the Vulture Swoops," etc. (Lyrics upon request).

By the 1950s, science began to recognize that there was some paternal impact on early childhood—even if it was only in the negative context of divorce or the extended absence of a father. Psychologist Michael Lamb, Ph.D., research director at the National Institute for Child Health and Human Development in Bethesda, Maryland, explains: "The assumption was that by comparing the behavior and personalities of children raised with and without fathers, one could—essentially by a process of subtraction—estimate what sort of influence fathers typically had."

What Dads Do

It wasn't until the feminist movement of the 1970s that researchers thought to ask whether dads could be as nurturing as moms. To everyone's astonishment, the answer was yes.

Actually, that was half the answer. Subsequent inquiries showed that while fathers could be as nurturing as mothers, they tended to leave such duties to moms. Hardly news to millions of overworked women, this finding was crucial. For the first time, researchers began systematically studying how and why male and female parenting strategies diverged, and more to the point, what those differences meant for children.

Although the total fatherhood experience runs from conception on, research has focused most keenly on the first few years of the parent-child relationship. It's here that children are most open to parental influence; they function primarily as receivers, consuming not only huge quantities of nourishment and comfort but stimuli as well. For decades, investigators have understood that infants not only enjoy taking in such rudimentary knowledge but absolutely require it for intellectual, physical, and especially emotional growth.

Without such constant interaction, argues W. Andrew Collins, Ph.D., of the University of Minnesota's Institute for Child Development, infants might never fully develop a sense of comfort and security. As important, they might not develop a sense of being connected to—and thus having some degree of control over—the world around them. "The key ingredient is a 'contingent responsiveness,'" says Collins, "where infants learn their actions will elicit certain reliable responses from others."

It's also during this crucial period that one of the most fundamental differences between

male and female parenting styles takes place. Work by several psychiatrists, including San Diego's Martin Greenberg, M.D., and Kyle Pruett, M.D., a professor of psychiatry at the Yale Child Study Center, suggests that while new mothers are inclined to relate to their infants in a more soothing, loving, and serious way, new fathers "hold their children differ-

Made Jane cry—down on her for not helping me put away the groceries, make dinner. She wanted to play Super Mario Bros. (So did I.) She called me an idiot. I yelled at her about not pulling her oar—sounded just like my dad—and sent her to her room. I kept her in there for a few minutes, felt bad, knocked on the door, and sat on her bed and apologized for losing my temper. "You hurt my feelings," she sniffed.

CREATING A NEW PATRIARCHY

Even the most dedicated dads quickly discover that the road to modern fatherhood is strewn with obstacles. Positive role models are in short supply and personal experiences are usually no help. Jerrold Lee Shapiro, Ph.D., professor of psychology at Santa Clara University, says understanding your relationship with your own father is the first step. If not, you're bound to automatically and unconciously replicate things from your childhood.

Here are several strategies both parents can use to strengthen the father-child bond.

◆ Start early. While involvement doesn't always equal intimacy, fathers who immerse themselves in all aspects of parenting from birth on are more likely to be closer to their children. Take part in as many prenatal activities as possible and schedule at least a week away from work after the baby is born to practice parenting skills and overcome anxieties about handling the baby.

◆ Create "fathering space": Schedule times and activities in

which you take care of your newborn entirely on your own. The traditional practice of deferring to mothers as "experts" gives new fathers few chances to hone their parenting skills, bolster their confidence, and build solid bonds with baby.

Sue Dickinson, M.S.W., a marriage and family therapist in Cle Elum, Washington, suggests persuading mom to go out of the house so you can have the experience of being the parent. Martin Greenberg, M.D., recommends bundling your baby in a chest pack and going for walks. The feeling of a baby's body—together with his or her warmth and smell—is captivating.

◆ Articulate feelings. Although fatherhood is routinely described as "the most wonderful experience" a man can have, new fathers may feel anxious, fearful, and frustrated. They may also be jealous of the time their wives spend with the baby and of their wives' "natural" parenting skills. These feelings may only make it harder for you to wholeheartedly participate in parenting and create distance

between you and your child. New fathers need to identify such feelings and discuss them with their wives.

◆ Mind the details. Tune in to your children and avoid relying on mom to "read" what your baby wants.

◆ Respect diversity. Accept your partner's parenting style without criticizing. Mothers often regard fathers' more boisterous style as too harsh or insensitive. But such criticism can derail a dad's desire for involvement. "Just because he's doing something you wouldn't do doesn't make it wrong," says Jay Belsky, Ph.D. Mothers have to temper their need to protect and remember dads offer things moms don't.

◆ Be realistic. Fathers who want to adopt a more hands-on approach than they themselves experienced are often frustrated when kids don't immediately respond. But children accustomed to having mom as the primary caregiver simply cannot adapt to "sudden" paternal involvement overnight. Above all, parenting requires patience.

ently and have a different kind of patience and frustration cycle than mothers," Pruett observes.

Why it is fathers behave this way isn't entirely clear. (And when fathers are primary caregivers, they are likely to display many of the so-called maternal traits.) Some studies suggest these gender differences are part of a larger male preference for stimulating, novel activities that arises from neurobiological differences in the way stimuli and pleasure are linked in male and female brains, and likely a result of genetics. Individuals high in the sensation-seeking trait are far more likely to engage in new and exciting pastimes. Though not all guys qualify as sensation seekers, the trait is far more common in men—particularly young ones—than it is in women, and might help explain why [m]any young fathers start off having a parenting style that's stimulating for them as well as their child.

THE DADDY DYNAMIC

Whatever its origins, this more playful, jocular approach carries major consequences for developing children. Where the "average" mother cushions her baby against irritating stimulation, the "average" father heaps it on, consistently producing a broader range of arousal. The resulting ups and downs force children to "stretch," emotionally and physically.

This emotion-stretching dynamic becomes more pronounced as father-child relationships enter into their second and third years. When playing, fathers tend to be more physical with their toddlers—wrestling, playing tag, and so on—while mothers emphasize verbal exchanges and interacting with objects, like toys. In nearly all instances, says Lamb, fathers are much more likely "to get children worked up, negatively or positively, with fear as well as delight, forcing them to learn to regulate their feelings."

In a sense, then, fathers push children to cope with the world outside the mother-child bond, as classical theory argued. But more than this, fathering behavior also seems to make children develop a more complex set of interactive skills, what Parke calls "emotional communication" skills.

First, children learn how to "read" their father's emotions via his facial expressions, tone of voice, and other nonverbal cues, and respond accordingly. Is Daddy really going to chase me down and gobble me up, or is he joking? Did I really hurt Daddy by poking him in the eye? Is Daddy in the mood to play, or is he tired?

Second, children learn how to clearly communicate their own emotions to others. One common example is the child who by crying lets her daddy know that he's playing too roughly or is scaring her. Kids also learn to indicate when interactions aren't stimulating enough; they'll show they've lost interest by not responding or wandering off.

Finally, children learn how to "listen" to their own emotional state. For instance, a child soon learns that if he becomes too "worked up" and begins to cry, he may in effect drive his play partner away.

The consequences of such emotional mastery are far-reaching. By successfully coping with stimulating, emotionally stretching interactions, children learn that they can indeed effect change both on internal matters (their feelings) and in the outside world (their father's actions). In that regard, links have been found between the quality of father-child interactions and a child's later development of certain life skills, including an ability to manage frustration, a willingness to explore new things and activities, and persistence in problem solving.

Anna's sleeping over. Earlier in the evening, Jane was on the floor of her bedroom looking up my shorts, laughing, saying she saw my penis. Later, I spy Jane and Anna holding up our cat Jackson. Must be a penis hunt, little-girl style. It's already in full swing and they're seven and eight!

In addition to being cook, chauffeur, maid, and spiritual protector, I am also Sex Authority! Two years ago, I explained, in a general way, the birds and the bees to Jane, correcting the misinformation she'd been given by her good friend Olivia.

As important as learning to regulate the emotional intensity of their interactions is children's ability to master the larger interactive process, the give and take that makes up social communication. "Kids who learn how to decode and encode emotions early on will be better off later when it comes to any social encounter," Parke says.

Such benefits have been intensely studied in the area of sibling relationships. Work by Belsky and Brenda Volling, Ph.D., an assistant professor of psychology at the University of Michigan, suggests that the emotion-management "lessons" learned by children from their fathers during play are applied later in interactions with siblings—and ultimately with people outside the family—and lead to more cooperation and less fighting. The press release announcing Belsky and Volling's research quipped, "If Adam had been a better father, things might have turned out differently for Cain and Abel."

Such findings come with plenty of caveats. A mother's more comforting manner is just as crucial to her children, helping them foster, among other things, a critical sense of security and self-confidence. Indeed, a mere preference for stimulating activities does not a good father make; obviously, the quality of father-child interactions is important. Successful fathers both monitor and modulate their play, maintaining a level of stimulation that keeps children engaged without making them feel like they've been pushed too far. This requires complete engagement—something many of today's busy fathers find difficult to manage. "What often happens is fathers don't pay attention to the cues their kids are sending," Belsky says. "A kid is crying 'uncle' and his father doesn't hear it."

Of course, fathers aren't the only parent who can teach these coping skills. Mothers physically play with their kids and, depending on the dynamics and history of the family, may also be the ones providing more of a "paternal" influence—teaching coping skills through play. Yet this "stretching" role typically falls to fathers because men gravitate toward less intimate, more physical interactions. And, as Reed Larson, Ph.D., a psychologist at the University of Illinois-Champaign, observes, "when dads stop having fun interacting with their kids, they're more likely than mothers to exit."

Whether these differences are genetic, cultural, or, more likely, a combination of the two, is still hotly debated. But the fact remains

Jane's legs hurt tonight; she calls them growing pains. I got mad, then simmered down (when my fear subsided), gave her Tylenol after she brushed her teeth. Read her a chapter from Great Expectations.

When Jane's sick, her mother takes such good care of her with medicines, doctors. I was raised Christian Scientist, taught that sickness and injury are illusions that should be healed with prayer and proper thinking. I'm just getting over my anger, my fear of disease, doctors, medicine.

that in terms of time spent with children, fathers typically spend more of it playing with their kids than mothers do—a difference that from very early on, children pick up on. Studies show that during stressful situations, one-year-old and 18-month-old babies more often turn to their primary caretaker—in most families, mom—for help. By contrast, when researchers measured so-called affiliative behaviors like smelling and vocalizing, during their first two years, babies showed a preference for their fathers. Just as dramatic, almost as soon as a child can crawl or walk, he or she will typically seek out dad for play and mom for comfort and other needs.

DOWNSIDE OF THE DADDY TRACK

On the face of it, fathers would seem to enjoy considerable advantages over mothers during their children's first years. Not only do they do less of the dirty work, but it's almost as if they've been anointed to handle the fun art of parenting. Yet as time goes on this situation changes dramatically. While a mother's more intimate, need-related approach to parenting generally continues to cement her bond with her children, a father's more playful and stimulating style steadily loses its appeal. By the age of eight or nine, a child may already be angry at his father's teasing, or bored or annoyed by his I'm-gonna-gitcha style.

This discrepancy often becomes quite pronounced as children reach adolescence. Research suggests that preteens and teens of both sexes continue to rely on their mothers for intimacy and needs, and increasingly view her as the favored parent for topics requiring sensitivity and trust. By contrast, Parke says, the joking, playful style that serves fathers so well during children's first years may begin to alienate teens, giving them the impression that their father doesn't take their thoughts and needs seriously.

Adding to this tension is the father's traditional role as the dispenser of discipline and firmness. It's hypothesized that fathers' less intimate interactive style may make it easier—although not more pleasant—for them to play the "heavy." In any case, adolescents come to see their fathers as the harsher, more distant parent. This feeling may increase teenagers' tendency to interact more often and intimately with their mothers, which in turn only heightens the sense of estrangement and tension between fathers and their kids.

As to whether fathers' possibly not being at home as much as mothers makes it easier or more difficult for them to be the disciplinarian, Parke says there are too many other factors involved to make such a determination. He does note, however, that many mothers faced with unruly kids still employ the threat, "Wait 'til your father gets home."

Clearly, the distance between fathers and adolescent children is not solely a result of fathers' playfulness earlier on. A central function of adolescence is a child's gradual movement toward emotional and physical autonomy from both parents. But studies suggest this movement is more directly and forcefully spurred by fathers' less intimate ways.

Does a father's parenting style during adolescence produce more closeness between father and child? The answer is probably no, says Parke. But if the question is, does a father's style serve a launching, independence-gaining function, the answer is probably yes. "Mothers' continued nurturance maintains a child's connectedness to the family, while fathers encourage differentiation," Parke says. In fact, according to a recent survey of adolescents by Israeli researchers Shmuel Shulman, Ph.D., and Moshe Klein, Ph.D., most perceived their fathers as being the primary source of support for their teenage autonomy.

Such notions will undoubtedly strike some as disturbingly regressive, as if researchers have simply found new, complex ways to justify outdated stereotypes of paternal behavior. For as any sensitive observer knows, the totality of fatherhood goes well beyond a tendency toward stimulating interactions and away from intimacy. Nonetheless, this does appear to be a central component of fathering behavior and may help explain why some seemingly antiquated modes of fathering persist. Despite evolution in gender roles, Belsky says, fathers are still more likely to provide less sensitivity, require kids to adjust to 'tough' realities, and perhaps be less understanding and empathetic.

Yet if the father-child bond truly serves as a mechanism for preparing children for the external world, the bond itself seems remarkably sensitive, even vulnerable, to that world. External variables, such as a father's relationships beyond his family—and in particular his experience in the workplace—appear to be linked to both the kind of fathering behavior he exhibits and the success he achieves with it. Some of these links are obvious. Few would be surprised to learn that fathers with high-stress jobs are apt to be more distant from their kids or use harsher, physical discipline when dealing with youthful infractions.

Other links between a man's external world and the way he fathers are more subtle. According to Parke, there are significant and intriguing fathering differences between men whose jobs involve a great degree of independence and those who are heavily managed. Fathers with workplace autonomy tend to expect and encourage more independence in their children. Moreover, they generally place grater emphasis on a child's intent when assessing misbehavior, and aren't inclined toward physical discipline. By contrast, men in highly supervised jobs with little autonomy are more likely to value and expect conformity from their kids. They're also more likely to consider the consequences of their children's misbehavior when meting out punishment, and discipline them physically.

This so-called spillover effect is hardly mysterious. We would expect parents whose jobs reward them for creativity, independence, and intent to value those qualities, and to emphasize them in their interactions with their children. Not that men have a monopoly on job spillover. A mother whose job is stressful probably isn't able to parent at one hundred percent either.

Lately, I've felt a little more thin-skinned with Jane. I think it dates back to around the time of her Christmas break. Jane's not as cuddly, pliable, obedient as she was before. Rather, she's more headstrong, defiant, sometimes openly mocking of me, my authority.

I guess she's becoming independent, setting her own boundaries. Yipes! Thankfully, Lucinda explained this. I figured Jane was going through a bad patch, or maybe her friends or mother were encouraging her to resist my fine parenting! Instead, it's my parenting that's helped foster her confidence.

Bill Moseley

Dads Who Disconnect

Other factors may also have a greater impact on the father-child bond than on the bond between mother and child. "If things aren't going well in a marriage," says Lamb, "it's more likely to have a negative impact on a father's relationship with his child." This is surely due in part to a child's history of intimacy with his or her mother. But Lamb also speculates that fathers simply find it easier to "disconnect" from their kids during times of conflict.

Speculations like these raise the specter of some genetic explanation. If fathers are inclined to relate to their children in a less intimate way, they may naturally be less capable of building and maintaining strong parent-child bonds. Yet while Lamb and Parke acknowledge some degree of innate, gender-related parenting differences, they place far more emphasis on cultural or learned factors.

Of these, the most important may be the parenting models today's men and women have from their own childhoods—models that very likely ran along traditional lines, and most significantly indicated mothering was mandatory and fathering far more discretionary. A mother may be angry and depressed, Lamb says, "but parenting has to be done and the buck stops with her, whereas dads have traditionally been given leeway."

It's changing, of course. New legal sanctions, such as those against deadbeat dads, coupled with a rising sense—not just among conservatives—of fathers' familial obligations, are making it tougher for men to simply walk away physically or emotionally. Today men getting divorced are likely to fight for primary or joint custody of their kids. We may even reach a point where one parent isn't deemed mandatory and the other "allowed" to drop back.

Bringing the Revolution Home

Researchers say the more compelling changes in fathering are, or ought to be, taking place not just on a social level but on a personal one. One of the simplest steps is refiguring the division of parental duties: mom takes on some of the play master role, while dad does more of the need-based parenting—everything from changing diapers to ferrying the kids to dance lessons. By doing more of the "mandatory" parenting, Parke says, fathers will encourage their kids to see them not simply as a playmate, but as a comfort provider too.

No one's advocating a complete role reversal, or suggesting a complete shift is possible. Parke says men have difficulty "giving up their robust interactive styles, even when they are the parent staying at home." Instead, families should take advantage of the difference between men's and women's parenting approaches. Since fathers' boisterous antics seem to help prepare children for life outside the family, mothers shouldn't cancel this out by intervening or being overly protective.

At the same time, a more androgynous approach has its advantages. Children will be less inclined to mark one parent for fun and the other for comfort. For fathers this might mean more opportunities to deal with emotional ups and downs and develop the empathy and emotional depth.

Of course, fathers will experience difficulties making this shift. Yet the potential rewards are huge. Not only will we give our children more progressive examples of parenting—examples that will be crucial when they raise their own children—but we'll greatly enhance our own parenting experiences.

Fatherhood may be more confusing and open-ended than ever before, but the possibilities—for those willing to take the risks—are endless. "In the theater of modern family life," says Belsky, "there are just many more parts that fathers can play."

CULTURE & IDEAS

INVINCIBLE KIDS

Why do some children survive
traumatic childhoods unscathed?
The answers can help every child

Child psychologist Emmy Werner went looking for trouble in paradise. In Hawaii nearly 40 years ago, the researchers began studying the offspring of chronically poor, alcoholic, abusive and even psychotic parents to understand how failure was passed from one generation to the next. But to her surprise, one third of the kids she studied looked nothing like children headed for disaster. Werner switched her focus to these "resilient kids," who somehow beat the odds, growing into emotionally healthy, competent adults. They even appeared to defy the laws of nature: When Hurricane Iniki flattened Kauai in 1992, leaving nearly 1 in 6 residents homeless, the storm's 160-mph gusts seemed to spare the houses of Werner's success stories.

Werner's "resilient kids," in their late 30s when Iniki hit, helped create their own luck. They heeded storm warnings and boarded up their properties. And even if the squall blew away their roofs or tore down their walls, they were more likely to have the financial savings and insurance to avoid foreclosure—the fate of many of Iniki's victims. "There's not a thing you can do personally about being in the middle of a hurricane," says the University of California–Davis's Werner, "but [resilient kids] are planners and problem solvers and picker-uppers."

For many of America's children, these are difficult times. One in five lives in poverty. More than half will spend some of their childhood living apart from one parent—the result of divorce, death or out-of-wedlock birth.

Child abuse, teen drug use and teen crime are surging. Living in an affluent suburb is no protection: Suburban kids are almost as likely as those in violent neighborhoods to report what sociologists call "parental absence"—the lack of a mother and father who are approachable and attentive, and who set rules and enforce consequences.

In the face of these trends, many social scientists now are suggesting a new way of looking at kids and their problems: Focus on survivors, not casualties. Don't abandon kids who fail, but learn from those who succeed.

Such children, researchers find, are not simply born that way. Though genes play a role, the presence of a variety of positive influences in a child's environment is even more crucial; indeed, it can make the difference between a child who founders and one who thrives.

The implications of such research are profound. The findings mean that parents, schools, volunteers, government and others can create a pathway to resiliency, rather than leaving success to fate or to hard-wired character traits. Perhaps most important, the research indicates that the lessons learned from these nearly invincible kids can teach us how to help *all* kids—regardless of their circumstances—handle the inevitable risks and turning points of life. The Search Institute, a Minneapolis-based children's research group, identified 30 resiliency-building factors. The more of these "assets" present in a child's environment, the more likely the child was to avoid school problems, alco-

hol use, early sexual experimentation, depression and violent behavior.

Like the factors that contribute to lifelong physical health, those that create resilience may seem common-sensical, but they have tremendous impact. Locate a resilient kid and you will also find a caring adult—or several—who has guided him. Watchful parents, welcoming schools, good peers and extracurricular activities matter, too, as does teaching kids to care for others and to help out in their communities.

From thug to Scout. The psychologists who pioneered resiliency theory focused on inborn character traits that fostered success. An average or higher IQ was a good predictor. So was innate temperament—a sunny disposition may attract advocates who can lift a child from risk. But the idea that resiliency can be molded is relatively re-

ROBERT DOLE. He came of age during the tough years of the Great Depression. Later, he overcame a nearly fatal war injury.

"Why me, I demanded? ... Maybe it was all part of a plan, a test of endurance and strength and, above all, of faith."

From *U.S. News & World Report*, November 11, 1996, pp. 60-71. © 1996 by U.S. News & World Report. Reprinted by permission.

cent. It means that an attentive adult can turn a mean and sullen teenage thug—a kid who would smash in someone's face on a whim—into an upstanding Boy Scout.

That's the story of Eagle Scout Rudy Gonzalez. Growing up in Houston's East End barrio, Gonzalez seemed on a fast track to prison. By the time he was 13, he'd already had encounters with the city's juvenile justice system—once for banging a classmate's head on the pavement until blood flowed, once for slugging a teacher. He slept through classes and fought more often than he studied. With his drug-using crew, he broke into warehouses and looted a grocery store. His brushes with the law only hardened his bad-boy swagger. "I thought I was macho," says Gonzalez. "With people I didn't like, [it was], 'Don't look at me or I'll beat you up.'"

Many of Gonzalez's friends later joined real gangs. Several met grisly deaths; others landed in prison for drug dealing and murder. More than a few became fathers and dropped out of school. Gonzalez joined urban scouting, a new, small program established by Boy Scouts of America to provide role models for "at risk" youth. At first glance, Gonzalez's path could hardly seem more different than that of his peers. But both gangs and Boy Scouts offer similar attractions: community and a sense of purpose, a hierarchical system of discipline and a chance to prove loyalty to a group. Gonzalez chose merit badges and service over gang colors and drive-by shootings.

Now 20, Gonzalez wears crisply pressed khakis and button-down shirts and, in his sophomore year at Texas A&M, seems well on his way to his goal of working for a major accounting firm. Why did he succeed when his friends stuck to crime? Gonzalez's own answer is that his new life is "a miracle." "Probably, God chose me to do this," he says.

There were identifiable turning points. Scoutmaster John Trevino, a city policeman, filled Gonzalez's need for a caring adult who believed in him and could show him a different way to be a man. Gonzalez's own father was shot and killed in a barroom fight when Rudy was just 6. Fate played a role, too. At 14, using survival skills he'd learned in scouting, Gonzalez saved the life of a younger boy stuck up to his chin in mud in a nearby bayou. The neighborhood hero was lauded in the newspaper and got to meet President Bush at the White House. Slowly, he began to feel the importance of serving his community—another building block of resiliency. For a Scout project he cleaned up a barrio cemetery.

Something special. Once his life started to turn around, Gonzalez felt comfortable enough to reveal his winning personality and transcendent smile—qualities that contributed further to his success. "When I met him, I wanted to adopt him," says his high school counselor, Betty Porter. "There's something about him." She remembers Gonzalez as a likable and prodigious networker who made daily visits to her office to tell her about college scholarships—some she didn't even know about.

BILL CLINTON. He lost his father in an auto wreck before he was born. Later, he coped with an alcoholic, occasionally violent stepfather.

"My mother taught me about sacrifice. She held steady through tragedy after tragedy and, always, she taught me to fight."

A little bit of help—whether an urban scouting program or some other chance to excel—can go a long way in creating resiliency. And it goes furthest in the most stressed neighborhoods, says the University of Colorado's Richard Jessor, who directs a multimillion-dollar resiliency project for the John D. and Catherine T. MacArthur Foundation. Looking back, Gonzalez agrees. "We were just guys in the barrio without anything better to do," he says. "We didn't have the YMCA or Little League, so we hung out, played sports, broke into warehouses and the school." Adds Harvard University's Katherine Newman: "The good news is that kids are motivated. They want to make it. The bad news is that there are too few opportunities."

Resiliency theory brightens the outlook for kids. Mental health experts traditionally have put the spotlight on children who emerge from bad childhoods damaged and scarred. But statistics show that many—if not most—children born into unpromising circumstances thrive, or at least hold their own. Most children of teen mothers, for example, avoid becoming teen parents themselves. And though the majority of child abusers were themselves abused as children, most abused children do not become abusers. Similarly, children of schizophrenics and children who grew up in refugee camps also tend to defy the odds. And many Iowa youths whose families lost their farms during the 1980s farm crisis became high achievers in school.

Living well. A person who has faced childhood adversity and bounced back may even fare *better* later in life than someone whose childhood was relatively easy—or so Werner's recently completed follow-up of the Kauai kids at age 40 suggests. Resilient children in her study reported stronger marriages and better health than those who enjoyed less stressful origins. Further, none had been on welfare, and none had been in trouble with the law. Many children of traumatic, abusive or neglectful childhoods suffer severe consequences, including shifts in behavior, thinking and physiology that dog them into adulthood. But though Werner's resilient kids turned adults tended to marry later, there was little sign of emotional turmoil. At midlife, these resilient subjects were more likely to say they were happy and only one third as likely to report mental health problems.

Can any child become resilient? That remains a matter of debate. Some kids, researchers say, simply may face too many risks. And the research can be twisted to suggest that there are easy answers. "Resiliency theory assumes that it's all or nothing, that you have it or you don't," complains Geoffrey Canada, who runs neighborhood centers for New York's poorest youth. "But for some people it takes 10,000 gallons of water, and for some kids it's just a couple of little drops."

In fact, as Canada notes, most resilient kids do not follow a straight line to success. An example is Raymond Marte, whom Canada mentored, teaching the youth karate at one of his Rheedlen Centers for Children and Families. Today, Marte, 21, is a freshman at New York's Bard College. But only a few years ago, he was just another high school dropout and teenage father, hanging out with gang friends and roaming the streets with a handgun in his pocket. "This is choice time," Canada told

DR. RUTH WESTHEIMER. The sex therapist fled the Nazis at 10; her parents died in the Holocaust, and she grew up in a Swiss orphanage.

"The values my family [instilled] left me with the sense I must make something out of my life to justify my survival."

Marte after five of the boy's friends were killed in three months. Marte re-enrolled in school, became an Ameri-Corps volunteer and won a college scholarship. Today, when he walks the streets of his family's gritty Manhattan neighborhood, he is greeted as a hero, accepting high-fives from friends congratulating the guy who made it out.

Good parenting can trump bad neighborhoods. That parents are the first line in creating resilient children is no surprise. But University of Pennsylvania sociologist Frank Furstenberg *was* surprised to find that adolescents in the city's most violence prone, drug-ridden housing projects showed the same resilience as middle-class adolescents. The expectation was that the worst neighborhoods would overwhelm families. Inner-city housing projects do present more risk and fewer opportunities. But good parenting existed in roughly equal proportions in every neighborhood.

Sherenia Gibbs is the type of dynamo parent who almost single-handedly can instill resiliency in her children. The single mother moved her three children from a small town in Illinois to Minneapolis in search of better education and recreation. Still, the new neighborhood was dangerous, so Gibbs volunteered at the park where her youngest son, T. J. Williams, played. Today, six years later, Gibbs runs a city park, where she has started several innovative mentoring programs. At home, Gibbs sets aside time to spend with T. J., now 14, requires him to call her at work when he gets home from school or goes out with friends and follows his schoolwork closely. Indeed, how often teens have dinner with their family and whether they have a curfew are two of the best predictors of teen drug use, according to

the National Center on Addiction and Substance Abuse at Columbia University. How often a family attends church—where kids are exposed to both values and adult mentors—also makes a difference. Says Gibbs: "The streets will grab your kids and eat them up."

Some resiliency programs study the success of moms like Gibbs and try to teach such "authoritative parenting" skills to others. When a kid has an early brush with the law, the Oregon Social Learning Center brings the youth's whole family together to teach parenting skills. Not only is the training effective with the offending youth, but younger brothers and sisters are less likely to get in trouble as well.

Despite the crucial role of parents, few—rich or poor—are as involved in their children's lives as Gibbs. And a shocking number of parents—25 percent—ignore or pay little attention to how their children fare in school, according to Temple University psychology professor Laurence Steinberg. Nearly one third of students across economic classes say their parents have no idea how they are doing in school. Further, half the parents Steinberg surveyed did not know their children's friends, what their kids did after school or where they went at night. Some schools are testing strategies for what educator Margaret Wang, also at Temple, calls "educational resilience."

One solution: teaching teams, which follow a student for a few years so the child always has a teacher who knows him well. In Philadelphia, some inner-city schools have set up "parents' lounges," with free coffee, to encourage moms and dads to be regular school visitors.

Given the importance of good parenting, kids are at heightened risk when parents themselves are troubled. But it is a trait of resilient kids that in such circumstances, they seek out substitute adults. And sometimes they become substitute adults themselves, playing a parental role for younger siblings. That was true of Tyrone Weeks. He spent about half his life without his mother as she went in and out of drug rehabilitation. Sober now for three years, Delores Weeks maintains a close relationship with her son. But Tyrone was often on his own, living with his grandmother and, when she died, with his basketball coach, Tennis Young. Young and Dave Hagan, a neighborhood priest in north

Philadelphia, kept Weeks fed and clothed. But Weeks also became a substitute parent for his younger brother, Robert, while encouraging his mother in her struggle with cocaine. Says Weeks, "There were times when I was lost and didn't want to live anymore."

Like many resilient kids, Weeks possessed another protective factor: a talent. Basketball, he says, gave him a self-confidence that carried him through the lost days. Today, Weeks rebounds and blocks shots for the University of Massachusetts. Obviously, not all kids have Weeks's exceptional ability. But what seems key is not the level of talent but finding an activity from which they derive pride and sense of purpose.

Mon Ye credits an outdoor leadership program with "keeping me out of gang life." Born in a Cambodian refugee camp, Ye has lived with an older brother in a crime-ridden Tacoma, Wash., housing project since his mother's death a few years ago. Outdoor adventure never interested him. But then parks worker LeAnna Waite invited him to join a program at a nearby recreation center (whose heavy doors are dented with bullet marks from gang fights). Last year, Ye led a youth climb up Mount Rainier and now plans to go to college to become a recreation and park supervisor.

It helps to help. Giving kids significant personal responsibility is another way to build resiliency, whether it's Weeks pulling his family together or Ye supervising preteens. Some of the best youth programs value both service to others and the ability to plan and make choices, according to Stanford University's Shirley Brice Heath. The Food Project—in which kids raise 40,000 pounds of vegetables for Boston food kitchens—is directed by the young par-

KWEISI MFUME. The NAACP chief's stepdad was abusive. After his mom died, he ran with gangs and had five sons out of wedlock.

"We're all inbred with a certain amount of resiliency. It's not until it's tested . . . that we recognize inner strength."

ticipants, giving them the chance to both learn and then pass on their knowledge. Older teens often find such responsibility through military service.

Any program that multiplies contacts between kids and adults who can offer advice and support is valuable. A recent study of Big Brothers and Big Sisters found that the nationwide youth-mentoring program cuts drug use and school absenteeism by half. Most youth interventions are set up to target a specific problem like violence or teen sex—and often have little impact. Big Brothers and Big Sisters instead succeeds with classic resiliency promotion: It first creates supportive adult attention for kids, then expects risky behavior to drop as a consequence.

The 42,490 residents of St. Louis Park, Minn., know all about such holistic approaches to creating resiliency. They've made it a citywide cause in the ethnically diverse suburb of Minneapolis. Children First is the city's call for residents to think about the ways, big and small, they can help all kids succeed, from those living in the city's Meadowbrook housing project to residents of parkside ranch houses. The suburb's largest employer, HealthSystem Minnesota, runs a free kids' health clinic. (Doctors and staff donate their time.) And one of the smallest businesses, Steve McCulloch's flower shop,

DIANNE FEINSTEIN. The California senator was raised in privilege, but her mother was mentally ill and at times violent.

"I've never believed adversity is a harbinger of failure. On the contrary, [it] can provide a wellspring of strength."

gives away carnations to kids in the nearby housing project on Mother's Day. Kids even help each other. Two high school girls started a Tuesday night baby-sitting service at the Reformation Lutheran Church. Parents can drop off their kids for three hours. The cost: $1.

The goal is to make sure kids know that they are valued and that several adults outside their own family know and care about them. Those adults might include a police officer-volunteering to serve lunch in the school cafeteria line. Or Jill Terry, one of scores of volunteers who stand at school bus stops on frigid mornings. Terry breaks up fights, provides forgotten lunch money or reassures a sad-faced boy about his parents' fighting. The adopt-a-bus-stop program

was started by members of a senior citizens' group concerned about an attempted abduction of a child on her way to school.

Another volunteer, Kyla Dreier, works in a downtown law firm and mentors Angie Larson. The 14-year-old has long, open talks with her mother but sometimes feels more comfortable discussing things with another adult, like Dreier.

Spreading out. St. Louis Park is the biggest success story of over 100 communities nationwide where the Search Institute is trying to develop support for childhood resiliency. In a small surburb, it was relatively easy to rally community leaders. Now Search is trying to take such asset building to larger cities like Minneapolis and Albuquerque, N.M.

In St. Louis Park, resiliency is built on a shoestring budget. About $60,000 a year—all raised from donations—covers the part-time staff director and office expenses. But that's the point, says Children First Coordinator Karen Atkinson. Fostering resiliency is neither complicated nor costly. It's basic common sense—even if practiced too rarely in America. And it pays dividends for all kids.

BY JOSEPH P. SHAPIRO WITH DORIAN FRIEDMAN IN NEW YORK, MICHELE MEYER IN HOUSTON AND MARGARET LOFTUS

The Right to a Family Environment for Children With Disabilities

Victoria Weisz and Alan J. Tomkins

University of Nebraska–Lincoln

To access services for children with disabilities, the children often have been required to leave their families of origin. However, social science evidence indicates that there are substantial psychological benefits for children to remain with their families whenever possible. The U.N. Convention on the Rights of the Child (U.N. General Assembly, 1989) supports policies and programs that enable children with disabilities to receive services without leaving their family environment. This article briefly reviews the social science literature and the U.N. Convention, and it documents trends in U.S. law consistent with the implications of the scientific evidence and international consensus. The authors conclude that it is important for the federal government to maintain these progressive programs and policies even as responsibilities for social programs shift to the states.

W hat is a right to a family environment? What would be the result if such a right were taken seriously in policy planning for children? The recognition of a right to a family environment would provide guidance for planning even for children who do not have families who can care for them (e.g., a policy preference for foster families rather than institutions for children of abusive families). For children who do have families, the recognition of such a right would be still more powerful. Policies that separate children from their families would necessarily be replaced by those that maintain children within their families. Although the recognition of individual rights in the United States does not require government spending to enable the exercise of rights (*Rust v. Sullivan*, 1991), the establishment of the right to a family environment for children would mean that policies would need to reflect the priority of keeping children with their families.

This article focuses on a particular group of children, children with disabilities. Children with disabilities are a useful example to explore the policy implications of advancing a child's right to a family environment. We point out that for many years, when children with disabilities received services for their disabilities, they often were separated from their families. We note that recently there has been a shift toward serving these children in their homes and communities. We show that this shift is consistent with social science evidence suggesting that there are substantial psychological benefits for children to receive services in their homes and communities. The social science data and the trend toward home-based services are consistent with direction advocated in the U.N. Convention on the Rights of the Child (U.N. General Assembly, 1989). We then turn our attention to U.S. laws and policies and find that they too have been evolving in a direction consistent with the social science evidence and the international consensus. We conclude with

Victoria Weisz, Center on Children, Families and the Law, University of Nebraska–Lincoln; Alan J. Tomkins, Law/Psychology Program, University of Nebraska–Lincoln.

A version of this article was presented at the Second International Interdisciplinary Study Group on Ideologies of Children's Rights, May 14–18, 1994, Charleston, SC. Victoria Weisz was supported, in part, by National Institute of Mental Health Postdoctoral Fellowship MH 5T32-16156 during the preparation of this article.

Special acknowledgment is extended to Gary B. Melton, whose support and encouragement have been greatly valued.

Correspondence concerning this article should be addressed to Victoria Weisz, Center on Children, Families and the Law, University of Nebraska, 121 South 13th Street, Suite 302, Lincoln, NE 68588-0227. Electronic mail may be sent via Internet to vweisz@unlinfo.unl.edu.

a plea for ratification by the United States of the U.N. Convention on the Rights of the Child, because it would help to ensure that there will be no backtracking on the progress that has been made in the past 25 years in serving children with disabilities.

The Change in Vision Regarding Services for Children With Disabilities

Children with disabilities have represented a class of individuals for whom governmental policies have typically interfered with the child's place within his or her family (e.g., Agosta & Melda, 1995). Before the advent of government-sponsored programs, however, care to individuals with disabilities was generally provided within the family (Berkson, 1993). Unfortunately, this family-based care was available only to individuals who were fortunate enough to be born to wealthy families. During the 18th century, well-off children with disabilities were educated in their families and often eventually took their place in society when they became adults. Persons who did not have families that could care for them were relegated to life as beggars or in sordid institutions. Society did not view people with disabilities as entitled to the same rights and opportunities as others (Taylor, Knoll, Lehr, & Walker, 1989).

The next century saw dramatic progress in the treatment and education of people with physical and mental disabilities. Dozens of schools for blind, deaf, and mentally retarded children were established in Europe and the United States. Innovative techniques were used, resulting in huge successes. These modern interventions, however, generally involved removing children from their homes, so that they could be educated with others who had similar disabilities and who required similar educational methods (Berkson, 1993). Individuals with disabilities were seen to require specialized and segregated services (Taylor, Knoll, et al., 1989). By the beginning of the 20th century, the vast majority of U.S. children with disabilities were enrolled in special education day schools or long-term residential treatment facilities, although some home-visiting services, influenced by settlement house workers, were also available to children and their families (Levine & Levine, 1970; Roberts, Wasik, Casto, & Ramey, 1991).

The next major shift occurred after World War II, when a movement to "normalize" the lives of children with disabilities occurred. Institutions and segregated special education facilities were dismantled or kept for the most severely disabled. Three main factors contributed to the normalization movement (Berkson, 1993). First, Democratic movements (e.g., the U.S. civil rights movement and the women's movement) paved the way for individuals with disabilities, and their families, to assert their rights to equal access to the benefits of society (Drimmer, 1993). Second, scientific studies demonstrated both that

children with disabilities could be effectively educated (mainstreamed) in the public school system and that children were harmed in their emotional development (young children in particular) by lengthy separations from their parents, particularly their mothers. Finally, it became apparent that educating and caring for children with disabilities in their families [was] far less costly than providing for them in institutions (Bradley, 1992).

Thus, the view that children with disabilities are better off within a family environment is not new. However, only recently has government been willing to provide services without requiring removal or segregation of children with disabilities. Part of this change was prompted by insights generated by social scientific research.

Social Science Perspectives

Three areas of social scientific research are relevant to a discussion of the value of a family environment for children with disabilities: (a) research about general characteristics of families of children with disabilities, (b) evaluation research on family or parent interventions for children with disabilities, and (c) research regarding factors that contribute to institutionalization of children with disabilities.

Characteristics of Families of Children With Disabilities

Historically, it was believed that families of children with disabilities were different in a number of negative ways from comparison families. According to Berkson (1993), the most prevalent beliefs were that families of children with disabilities experienced increased stress, more depression, and more marital difficulties. There is some evidence for these trends. A recent examination of divorce rates and income in a national sample of 25,000 eighth-grade students found that 20% of parents of children with disabilities were divorced or separated, as compared with 15% of other parents, and that the annual income of families of children with disabilities was $4,000–$5,000 less than that of other families (Hodapp & Krasner, 1995). Nonetheless, an overview of controlled studies suggests that many families of children with disabilities adapt quite successfully (Berkson, 1993; Bristol, Gallagher, & Schopler, 1988; Spaulding & Morgan, 1986). Studies that do demonstrate increased stresses for families of children with disabilities do not necessarily suggest debilitating stresses. For example, Breslau and Davis (1986), in a carefully controlled study, found that although 30% of mothers of children with disabilities reported depressive symptoms, compared with only 15% of mothers of children without disabilities, there were no differences in the rates of debilitating diagnosable psychological disorders between the two groups. Further, note that although mothers of children with disabilities may be distressed at a significantly higher rate than other mothers, 70% of these mothers did not report symptoms of such distress.

The best predictor of depressive symptoms in mothers is, not surprisingly, the extent of the child's needs for assistance (Breslau, Staruch, & Mortimer, 1982). Similarly, among parents of children with mental retardation, the parents of the most severely limited children report the highest rates of distress (Pahl & Quine, 1987). Furthermore, the functioning level of the child was the strongest predictor of child-related stress in a large survey of parents of children with disabilities (Boyce, Behl, Mortensen, & Akers, 1991).

As might be expected, the research on siblings of children with disabilities provides a mixed picture. Although some siblings resent or feel burdened by their disabled brother or sister, others feel affection and responsibility for them (Zetlin, 1990). A study that compared 24 preschool-age siblings of children with disabilities with 22 preschoolers with siblings without disabilities found no differences between the groups in self-competence or empathy but found that the children whose siblings had disabilities were more aggressive (Lobato, Barbour, Hall, & Miller, 1987). A longitudinal study of siblings of children with disabilities found that these siblings were, as a group, more unhappy and aggressive than their controls but that there were no differences in rates of diagnosable psychological problems (Breslau & Prabucki, 1987). In contrast, another smaller study that compared children with siblings with disabilities with children with siblings without disabilities found no differences between the groups in behavior problems, social competence, or self-esteem (Bischoff & Tingstrom, 1991).

In addition to the studies that have found some negative effects of a disability in the family, a number of other studies have found positive effects. For example, Abbott and Meredith (1986) found that 55% of their sampled families reported a closer and stronger family and 41% reported personal growth after the birth of a child with mental retardation. Further, Burton and Parks (1994) found that college students who were siblings of individuals with disabilities demonstrated significantly higher locus of control than students with siblings without disabilities. These researchers surmised that siblings of children with disabilities gain psychological strength from their experiences.

Thus, although there may be some evidence of negative effects on parental relationships, sibling relationships, or general family functioning for children with disabilities, there also is evidence of considerable positive impact for families.

Early studies of families of children with disabilities indicated that they experience severe social isolation. However, recent studies that have used more complex models of social support have found that families of children with disabilities are similar to comparison families in their family support networks, although they differ from comparison families in having smaller friendship networks (Kazak, 1987). Families with children with disabilities may not differ from comparison families regarding their help from relatives. However, their need for relative support is considerably greater than comparison families. A recent survey of 92 families of children with disabilities in eight states found that almost a third of the families received no help from relatives outside their household (Knoll, 1992). Thus, many families are clearly not receiving the help they need, even if they may be no more isolated from their relatives than are other families. Perhaps, because of these unmet needs, many families with disabled children develop a rich network of professionals who offer considerable support to them (Kazak, 1987). The availability of support to these families is critical, because social support appears to be positively related to better coping and less stress for families of children with disabilities (Bristol, 1984; Harris, Carpenter, & Gill, 1988).

Unfortunately, the growing recognition that children with disabilities benefit from remaining with their families and that families require both formal and informal support to care for these children has occurred during a period of decreasing resources to families in general (Marcenko & Meyers, 1991). Increased family mobility, smaller family size, more single-parent families, and more families with two working parents create obstacles for all families with children (Hernandez, 1995). Families who have the task of caring for a child who needs extraordinary care are particularly disadvantaged by the changing demographics of our time. Although it may not be obvious, education and income level may be more critical to adaptation than the number of parents in a household. A review of 15 research studies on single parents of children with disabilities found that after education and income were controlled for, the stress and adaptation levels were not different between single mothers and married mothers (Boyce, Miller, White, & Godfrey, 1995). Still, these studies suggested that the vast majority of single mothers had less education and income than their married controls, so the challenges that face these smaller families in managing the care of a child with a disability remain daunting.

Family-Focused Interventions

A variety of interventions directed toward the parents or families of children with disabilities have been demonstrated to be effective in enhancing the child's individual development, helping the parents cope more effectively, and decreasing family stress. Interventions range widely, from informal home visitors to parent behavior modification training, and all appear to yield positive results (Barrera, Rosenbaum, & Cunningham, 1986; Brown-Gorton & Wolery, 1988; Girolametto, 1988;

Harris et al., 1988; Harrold, Lutzker, Campbell, & Touchette, 1992; Resnick, Armstrong, & Carter, 1988). Direct cash subsidies to families that allow them to choose services or support that they might need also appear to be quite successful in reducing family stress (Agosta & Melda, 1995; Melda & Agosta, 1992). Thus, the goal of maintaining children with disabilities within their families appears to be possible, and family-focused interventions are clearly the means to achieve that goal. One study has yielded findings that suggest caution, however. Lower income, single-parent, and socially isolated families apparently are less able to maintain the gains from interventions over the long term, as compared with families with more resources (Harris et al., 1988). Program characteristics, however, seem to play a very significant role in parents' perceptions of personal control, whereas family demographics do not play such a role (Trivette, Dunst, Boyd, & Hamby, 1995). Trivette and her colleagues found that interventions that were family centered, with parents having frequent contact with a caregiver using empowering caregiving practices, resulted in more personal control for all parents. Thus, services to families with few internal resources must be provided over the long term if they can be expected to maintain their effectiveness, and the more family centered the services are, the more likely parents are to feel a sense of control over their situation.

Out-of-Home Placement

There is little research about the factors that contribute to some parents deciding to place their children out of the home. One study of such placements for children with moderate to severe mental retardation suggested that most families make the decision to place their child rather quickly, after a buildup of child-related pressures over time rather than a single precipitating event. About a third of the parents noted child-related reasons for their decision; 23% cited reasons about themselves rather than their children (deteriorating health or change in job, finances, marital status, or marital adjustment; Blacher & Baker, 1994). Another study interviewed 137 randomly selected families from an out-of-home placement waiting list. Caregiver stressors were predictors of feelings of urgency for the out-of-home placement, but behavioral problems of the child were not (Kobe, Rojahn, & Schroeder, 1991).

There is little research directly exploring the link between the availability of family-directed services and decisions to place children out of the home. However, family-focused interventions appear to be successful at increasing the family's commitment to continued care in the home rather than seeking out-of-home placements (Parrott & Herman, 1987). Nonetheless, many parents continue to place their children outside the home despite the evidence supporting in-home care and in spite of professionals encouraging families to care for their children at home (Bromley & Blacher, 1991; Taylor, Lakin, & Hill, 1989).

Summary of Social Scientific Perspectives

Although there are a number of unresearched areas regarding children with disabilities and their families, there are good data that exist. Families of children with disabilities experience more stress than other families, but the majority of these families do not experience debilitating stress. Furthermore, there are positive benefits to families of children with disabilities. Families in which there are children with disabilities—particularly families that have few internal resources due to poverty, single parenthood, or social isolation—appear to have strong needs for help, to enable them to adapt to the difficult circumstances and to care for their child. A variety of intervention programs appear to be quite successful in meeting those needs, as well as directly helping the child's development. These programs do not often result in long-term gains, however, especially for struggling families. Thus, interventions need to be comprehensive, long term, and family centered, if true assistance to these families is to be achieved. The likelihood of out-of-home placement of children appears to be reduced when family support is provided.

Thus, family-focused interventions appear to be necessary to help families with disabled children adapt to the challenges they face. These interventions also help keep children with disabilities in their families.

Keeping children in their homes is an idea that has found support in both international and national legal and policy contexts. Under both U.N.-based policy and legal developments and U.S. policy and legal developments, frameworks have been developed that are supportive of serving children with disabilities in their family environment. We next turn our attention to these legal and policy developments, beginning with the international (i.e., U.N.) activities and then turning to national actions.

U.N. Convention on the Rights of the Child

In 1989, after a decade of deliberation and development, the Convention on the Rights of the Child was adopted by the U.N. General Assembly (see Murphy-Berman & Weisz, 1996). The preamble to the Convention makes it clear that all children have a right to a family environment because the family is the "natural environment" for the growth and well-being of children and that children should grow up in family environments to enable the "full and harmonious development" of their personalities (see Melton, 1996). Furthermore, Article 3 states that the best interests of the child shall be a primary consideration in all actions concerning children.

Article 23 of the U.N. Convention on the Rights of the Child (U.N. General Assembly, 1989) does not explicitly recognize the right of a child with disabilities to a family environment.[1] Article 23 does acknowledge that a child with disabilities has the right to "enjoy a full and decent life, in conditions which . . . facilitate the child's active participation in the community." Because a child's participation in the community typically arises from the child's participation in the family, we believe that Article 23 embodies the idea of a child's right to a family environment.

Further support for this position is found in the deliberations that took place before the final version of Article 23 was settled. The *travaux preparatoires*[2] for Article 23 indicate that the delegation of the United Kingdom did introduce a provision directly acknowledging that the families of children with disabilities were in need of support (Detrick, 1992). This amendment reads as follows:

> The States Parties to the present Convention recognize the right of mentally or physically handicapped children and their families to receive practical advice and support and the provision of a wide range of services to enable them to remain together and for handicapped children to live as independent and normal a life as possible in their community. (Detrick, 1992, p. 332)

The *travaux* does not clarify why this direct statement about children with disabilities and their families being entitled to receive support so that they can stay together was not retained in the further discussions and developments of the U.N. Convention (U.N. General Assembly, 1989). Article 23 does recognize the child's rights for available resources to those responsible for his or her care. This language could be used as a basis for arguments for resources to the parents of children with disabilities. It is unfortunate, however, that the direct statement of a child's need to stay with her or his family never made it into the final version of the Convention.

Still, the Convention (U.N. General Assembly, 1989) does offer considerable support for the notion that children with disabilities are entitled to interventions that keep them in their families. It is most clear in providing that

> ratifying countries [should] acknowledge the right of the [child with disabilities] to special care and . . . extend resources and assistance, free of charge where possible, to the child's family. In particular, State Parties' assistance to [children with disabilities] should ensure effective access to education, training health care and rehabilitative services. (Johnson & McNulty, 1990, p. 229)

U.S. Law Perspectives

In the United States, there are six federal provisions that are relevant to in-home and in-community care for a child with disabilities, that help protect these children from discrimination, and that facilitate access to necessary physical and mental health care (Johnson & McNulty, 1990; see Tomkins & Weisz, 1995, for more details). These are the federal programs and laws that reflect U.S. conformity to Article 23's interest in a disabled child's right to "a full and decent life, in conditions which ensure dignity, promote self-reliance, and facilitate the child's active participation in the community" (Article 23 of the U.N. Convention on the Rights of the Child; U.N. General Assembly, 1989, Paragraph 1; Article 23 is reprinted in its entirety in footnote 1). The six U.S. legal provisions are (a) the Title V Maternal and Child Health Block Grant,[3] (b) Medicaid,[4] (c) Supplemental Security Income (SSI),[5] (d) Section 504 of the Rehabilitation Act of 1973,[6] (e) the 1975 Education for Handicapped Children Act (later amended and renamed the Individuals With Disabilities Education Act; IDEA),[7] and (f) the 1990 Americans with Disabilities Act (ADA).[8]

The Maternal and Child Health Block Grant provides funds for preventive and primary, prenatal and postnatal, health care for low-income mothers and children. Among its aims are the prevention of "handicapping conditions" and the promotion of child health. States are encouraged to establish "home visiting programs" and "related social support services" as part of their care programs (42 U.S.C. § 701 [a] [1]; see, e.g., *Albino v. Chicago*, 1983).

Medicaid provides for prevention, primary, and intervention services for lower income children. It includes, but is not limited to, children with disabilities. One of its most important features is the "early and periodic screening, diagnostic, and treatment services" for children (i.e., anyone under 21 years; 42 U.S.C. § 1396d [a] [4] [B] and § 1396d [r] [5]; see, e.g., *Miller v. Whitburn*, 1993).

SSI provides for direct cash assistance (so that a minimum income level is obtained) to families of children with disabilities (42 U.S.C. § 1381); the cash assistance is in addition to the Medicaid services indicated above. Under the U.S. Supreme Court's interpretation in *Sullivan v. Zebley* (1990), the SSI program is quite flexible in its eligibility criteria: A child is eligible for benefits if a disability interferes with the child's normal daily activities in comparison with a child without such disabilities. Relevant activities for determining eligibility include "speaking, walking, washing, dressing, and feeding oneself, going to school, playing" (*Sullivan v. Zebley* 1990, p. 540).

The Rehabilitation Act of 1973 was the first major Congressional action to combat discrimination against persons with disabilities. The Rehabilitation Act makes it illegal to deny benefits to persons because of their disabilities or to otherwise discriminate against them (see, generally, Rothstein, 1992/1994). Section 504 of the act (29 U.S.C. § 790) is especially important, generally providing persons with disabilities the same rights that are extended to persons without disabilities. Some have suggested that the act is narrow because its jurisdiction only reaches to the context of federally funded programs or activities; nonetheless, it clearly encompasses "education programs; public facilities; transportation; and health and welfare services" implicated (Rothstein, 1992/1994, p. 3). Moreover, the law's "net" is cast even wider because there are so many social programs that receive federal funding (see, e.g., Gittler & Rennert, 1992). Thus, the Rehabilitation Act, both as a matter of history and as a matter of substantive law, is one of the most important pieces of legislation enacted by Congress to aid persons with disabilities.

The 1975 Education for Handicapped Children Act has become even more important. The act was passed in reaction to court decisions that lamented the fact that millions of students with disabilities were not being offered appropriate educational services (see *Mills v. Board of Education*, 1972; *Pennsylvania Association for Retarded Children* [PARC] *v. Pennsylvania*, 1971; see, generally, Rothstein, 1988). The law's name was changed to the IDEA (20 U.S.C. § 1400 [a]); the law also was significantly amended several times in the past decade, most recently in 1994. The IDEA provides for a free and appropriate public education and related services that allow a child to make use of the educational services that are provided (see, e.g., *Board of Education v. Rowley*, 1982; *Irving Independent School District v. Tatro*, 1984). Included among the related services are psychosocial and medical interventions, and they can begin as early as birth (see, e.g., Vincent & Salisbury, 1988).

Especially notable are the IDEA provisions for family-focused services (Hutchins & McPherson, 1991; Vincent & Salisbury, 1988). An Individualized Family Service Plan is provided for in instances in which there is a child with disabilities under the age of 3. The newly enacted amendment to IDEA, the Families of Children With Disabilities Support Act of 1994 (20 U.S.C. § 1491a *et seq.*), is intended to allow children with disabilities to receive in-home (or, at least, in-community) care.

The 1990 ADA has been termed the nation's "most significant disability rights statute" and "the most significant civil rights legislation in 25 years" (Rothstein, 1992/1994, pp. 10 & 18). It is intended to provide persons with disabilities the whole gamut of civil rights available to citizens without disabilities (see, generally, Gostin & Beyer, 1993). Although it is not yet clear what the actual impact of the law will be because it is of such recent vintage, it is possible that it will be extensive. Children with disabilities should be extensive beneficiaries. Under the ADA, "children with disabilities should be protected from the kinds of overt, subtle, and covert forms of discrimination that plague many groups in our society. . . .

The spirit of the ADA seems quite compatible with the kinds of family-friendly policies found in IDEA" (Tomkins & Weisz, 1995, p. 954).

These statutes, especially when considered together, provide a strong foundation in American law for establishing the rights to be free from discrimination and for addressing the needs of children with disabilities (see, e.g., Kramer, 1994, chaps. 26, 31–33; Rothstein, 1992, 1994). Taken together, they also appear to embody the provisions and the spirit of Article 23 of the U.N. Convention on the Rights of the Child (U.N. General Assembly, 1989; see Tomkins & Weisz, 1995).

Conclusion

Current U.S. laws and policies comport with Article 23 of the U.N. Convention on the Rights of the Child (U.N. General Assembly, 1989) in providing financial and programmatic assistance to families of children with disabilities. These national and international legal provisions reflect the social scientific evidence and contemporary public belief that families are the optimum environment for children with disabilities in most instances and that most families do a better job for their children if support is available to them.

There exist sufficient data to argue for the continued support for programs and policies that allow parents to care for their children in their homes. "Millions," wrote Agosta and Melda (1995, p. 279), "are still being spent on out-of-home services" but "relatively little [is] invested in families."

The next several years will quite likely see the responsibility and the costs for providing services to families shifting from the federal government to the states (see Agosta & Melda, 1995). It remains to be seen whether this shift will create opportunities for states to more flexibly and creatively assist families of children with disabilities or whether it will result in the dismantling of programs designed to do so. Safety net policies, which have been put in place over the last two decades, that support the right of a child with disabilities to his or her family environment may be vulnerable.

This vulnerability would be tempered if there were strong legal provisions underscoring the right to a family environment for children, both as a general matter and particularly in the context of children with disabilities. It is unfortunate that as of this writing, the United States has not ratified the U.N. Convention on the Rights of the Child (U.N. General Assembly, 1989). If the Convention were ratified, it could be used as an instrument to protect the gains that have been made in protecting the place of children with disabilities in their family environments. Ratification would give this laudable, international legislation legal status in the United States. Without ratification, the Convention simply serves both as a beacon for what we should stand for and an embarrassment that our nation has not seen fit to join the rest of the world in recognizing it.

Notes

1. Article 23 of the U.N. Convention on the Rights of the Child provides for the following:
   1. States Parties recognize that a mentally or physically disabled child should enjoy a full and decent life, in conditions which ensure dignity, promote self-reliance and facilitate the child's active participation in the community.
   2. States Parties recognize the right of the disabled child to special care and shall encourage and ensure the extension, subject to available resources, to the eligible child and those responsible for his or her care, of assistance for which application is made and which is appropriate to the child's condition and to the circumstances of the parents or others caring for the child.
   3. Recognizing the special needs of a disabled child, assistance extended in accordance with Paragraph 2 shall be provided free of charge, whenever possible, taking into account the financial resources of the parents or others caring for the child, and shall he designed to ensure that the disabled child has effective access to and receives education, training, health care services, rehabilitation services, preparation for employment and recreation opportunities in a manner conducive to the child's achieving the fullest possible social integration and individual development, including his or her cultural and spiritual development.
   4. States Parties shall promote in the spirit of international cooperation the exchange of appropriate information in the field of preventive health care and of medical, psychological and functional treatment of disabled children, including dissemination of and access to information concerning methods of rehabilitation, education and vocational services, with the aim of enabling States Parties to improve their capabilities and skills and to widen their experience in these areas. In this regard, particular account shall be taken of the needs of developing countries.
2. *Travaux preparatoires* are the equivalent of the legislative history of international treaties or agreements.
3. Maternal and Child Health Services Block Grant, Title V of the Social Security Act, 42 U.S.C. §§ 701 *et seq.*
4. 42 U.S.C. § 1396 *et seq.*
5. 42 U.S.C. §§ 1381 *et seq.*
6. 29 U.S.C. §§ 790 *et seq.*
7. 20 U.S.C. §§ 1400 *et seq.*
8. 42 U.S.C. §§ 12101 *et seq.*

References

Abbott, D. A., & Meredith, W. H. (1986). Strengths of parents with retarded children. *Family Relations, 35,* 371–375.

Agosta, J., & Melda, K. (1995). Supporting families who provide care at home for children with disabilities. *Exceptional Children, 62,* 271–282.

Albino v. Chicago, 578 E Supp. 1487 (N.D. III. 1983).

Barrera, M. E., Rosenbaum, P. L., & Cunningham, C. E. (1986). Early home intervention with low-birth-weight infants and their parents. *Child Development, 57,* 20–33.

Berkson, G. (1993). *Children with handicaps: A review of behavioral research.* Hillsdale, NJ: Erlbaum.

Bischoff, L. G., & Tingstrom, D. H. (1991). Siblings of children with disabilities: Psychological and behavioral characteristics. *Counseling Psychology Quarterly 4,* 311–321.

Blacher, J., & Baker, B. L. (1994). Out-of-home placement for children with retardation: Family decisionmaking and satisfaction. *Family Relations, 43,* 10–15.

Board of Education v. Rowley, 458 U.S. 176 (1982).

Boyce, G., Behl, D., Mortensen, L., & Akers, J. (1991). Child characteristics, family demographics and family processes: Their effects on the stress experienced by families of children with disabilities. *Counseling Psychology Quarterly, 4,* 273–288.

Boyce, G., Miller, B. C., White, K. R., & Godfrey, M. K. (1995). Single parenting in families of children with disabilities. *Marriage and Family Review, 20,* 389–409.

Bradley, V. J. (1992). Overview of the family support movement. In V. J. Bradley, J. Knoll, & J. M. Agosta (Eds.), *Emerging issues in family support* (pp. 1–8; Monographs of the American Association on Mental Retardation, No. 18). Washington, DC: American Association on Mental Retardation.

Breslau, N., & Davis, G. C. (1986). Chronic stress and major depression. *Archives of General Psychiatry, 43,* 309–314.

Breslau, N., & Prabucki, K. (1987). Siblings of disabled children: Effects of chronic stress in the family. *Archives of General Psychiatry 44,* 1040–1046.

Breslau, N., Staruch, K. S., & Mortimer, E. A. (1982). Psychological distress in mothers of disabled children. *American Journal of the Disabled Child, 136,* 682–686.

Bristol, M. M. (1984). Family resources and successful adaptation to autistic children. In E. Schopler & G. B. Mesibou (Eds.), *The effects of autism on the family* (pp. 289–310). New York: Plenum.

Bristol, M. M., Gallagher. J. J., & Schopler, E. (1988). Mothers and fathers of young developmentally disabled and nondisabled boys: Adaptation and spousal support. *Developmental Psychology 24,* 441–451.

Bromley, B., & Blacher, J. B. (1991). Parental reasons for out-of-home placement of children with severe handicaps. *Mental Retardation, 29,* 275–280.

Brown-Gorton, R., & Wolery, M. (1988). Teaching mothers to imitate their handicapped children: Effects on maternal demands. *Journal of Special Education, 22,* 97–107.

Burton, S. L., & Parks, A. L. (1994). Self-esteem, locus of control, and career aspirations of college-age siblings of individuals with disabilities. *Social Work Research, 18,* 178–185.

Detrick, S. (Ed.). (1992). *The United Nations Convention on the Rights of the Child: A guide to the "Travaux Preparatoires."* Boston: Martinus Nijhoff.

Drimmer, J. C. (1993). Cripples, overcomers, and civil rights: Tracing the evolution of federal legislation and social policy for people with disabilities. *UCLA Law Review 40,* 1341–1410.

Girolametto, L. E. (1988). Improving the social–conversational skills of developmentally delayed children: An intervention study. *Journal of Speech and Hearing, 53,* 156–167.

Gittler, J., & Rennert, S. (1992). HIV infection among women and children and antidiscrimination laws: An overview. *Iowa Law Review 77,* 1313–1388.

Gostin, L. O., & Beyer, H. A. (Eds.). (1993). *Implementing the Americans with Disabilities Act: Rights and responsibilities of all Americans.* Baltimore: Brookes.

Harris, S. L., Carpenter, L., & Gill, M. (1988). The family. In J. L. Matson & A. Marchetti (Eds.), *Developmental disabilities: A life span perspective* (pp. 47–66). Philadelphia: Grune & Stratton.

Harrold, M., Lutzker, J. R., Campbell. R. V., & Touchette, P. E. (1992). Improving parent–child interactions for families of children with developmental disabilities. *Journal of Behavior Therapy and Experimental Psychiatry 23,* 89–100.

Hernandez, D. J. (1995). Changing demographics: Past and future demands for early childhood programs. In R. E. Behrman (Ed.), *The future of children: Vol. 5. Long term outcomes of early childhood programs* (pp. 145–160). Los Altos, CA: The Center for the Future of Children.

Hodapp, R. M., & Krasner, D. V. (1995). Families of children with disabilities: Findings from a national sample of eighth-grade students. *Exceptionality 5,* 71–81.

Hutchins, V. L., & McPherson, M. (1991). National agenda for children with special health needs: Social policy for the 1990s through the 21st century. *American Psychologist, 46,* 141–143.

Irving Independent School District v. Tatro, 468 U.S. 883 (1984).

Johnson, K. A., & McNulty, M. (1990). Assuring adequate health and rehabilitative care for the child: Articles 6, 23, 34, and 25. In C. Price Cohen & H. A. Davidson (Eds.), *Children's rights in America: U.N. Convention on the Rights of the Child compared with United States law* (pp. 219–237). Chicago: American Bar Association Center on Children and the Law.

Kazak, A. E. (1987). Professional helpers and families with disabled children. A social network perspective. *Marriage and Family Review, 11,* 177–191.

Knoll, J. (1992). Being a family. The experience of raising a child with a disability or chronic illness. In V. J. Bradley, J. Knoll, & J. M. Agosta (Eds.), *Emerging issues in family support* (pp. 9–56, Monographs of the American Association on Mental Retardation, No. 18). Washington, DC. American Association on Mental Retardation.

Kobe, F. H., Rojahn, J., & Schroeder, S. R. (1991). Predictors of urgency of out-of-home placement needs. *Mental Retardation, 29,* 323–328.

Kramer, D. T. (1994). *Legal rights of children* (2nd ed., Vols. 1–3). Colorado Springs, CO: Shepard's/McGraw-Hill.

Levine, M., & Levine, A. (1970). *A social history of the helping services: Clinic, court, school, and community.* New York: Appleton-Century-Crofts.

Lobato, D., Barbour, L., Hall, L. J., & Miller, C. (1987). Psychosocial characters of preschool siblings of handicapped and nonhandicapped children. *Journal of Abnormal Child Psychology 15,* 329–338.

Marcenko, M. O., & Meyers, J. C. (1991). Mothers of children with developmental disabilities: Who shares the burden? *Family Relations, 40,* 186–190.

Melda, K., & Agosta, J. (1992). *Results of a national study of family support: Families do make a difference.* Salem, OR: Human Services Research Institute.

Melton, G. B. (1996). The child's right to a family environment: Why children's rights and family values are compatible. *American Psychologist, 51,* 1234–1238.

Miller v. Whitburn, 10 F.3d 1315 (7th Cir. 1993).

Mills v. Board of Education, 348 F. Supp. 866 (D.D.C. 1972).

Murphy-Berman, V., & Weisz, V. (1996). U.N. Convention on the Rights of the Child: Current challenges. *American Psychologist, 51,* 1231–1233.

Pahl, J., & Quine, L. (1987). Families with mentally handicapped children. In J. Orford (Ed.), *Treating the disorder, treating the family* (pp. 39–61). Baltimore: Johns Hopkins University Press.

Parrott, M. E., & Herman, S. E. (1987). *Report on the Michigan family support subsidy program.* Lansing: Michigan Department of Mental Health.

Pennsylvania Association for Retarded Children (PARC) v. Pennsylvania, 334 F. Supp. 1257 (E.D. Pa. 1971).

Resnick, M. B., Armstrong, S., & Carter, R. L. (1988). Developmental intervention program for high-risk premature infants: Effects on development and parent-infant interactions. *Journal of Developmental and Behavioral Pediatrics, 9,* 73–78.

Roberts, R. N., Wasik, B. H., Casto, G., & Ramey. C. T. (1991). Family support in the home: Programs, policy, and social change. *American Psychologist, 46,* 131–132.

Rothstein, L. F. (1988). Special education malpractice revisited. *Educational Law Reporter, 43,* 1249–1262.

Rothstein, L. F. (1992). *Disabilities and the law.* Colorado Springs, CO: Shepard's/McGraw-Hill.

Rothstein, L. F. (1994). *Disabilities and the law* (Suppl.). Colorado Springs, CO: Shepard's/McGraw-Hill.

Rust v. Sullivan, 500 U.S. 173 (1991).

Spaulding, R., & Morgan, S. B. (1986). Spina bifida children and their parents: A population prone to family dysfunction? *Journal of Pediatric Psychology 11,* 359–374.

Sullivan v. Zebley, 493 U.S. 521 (1990).

Taylor, S. J., Knoll, J. A., Lehr, S., & Walker, P. M. (1989). Families for all children: Value-based services for children with disabilities and their families. In G. H. S. Singer & L. K. Irvin (Eds.), *Support for caregiving families: Enabling positive adaptation to disability* (pp. 41–54). Baltimore: Brookes.

Taylor, S. J., Lakin, K. C., & Hill, B. K. (1989). Permanency planning for children and youth: Out-of-home placement decisions. *Exceptional Children. 55,* 541–549.

Tomkins, A. J., & Weisz, V. (1995). Social science, law, and the interest in a family environment for children with disabilities. *Toledo Law Review 26,* 937–956.

Trivette, C. M., Dunst, C. J., Boyd. K., & Hamby, D. W. (1995). Family-oriented program models, helpgiving practices, and parental control appraisals. *Exceptional Children, 62,* 237–248.

United Nations General Assembly. (1989, November). *Adoption of a convention on the rights of the child* (U.N. Doc. A/Res/44/25). New York: Author.

Vincent, L. J., & Salisbury, C. L. (1988). Changing economic and social influences on family environment. *Topics in Early Childhood Special Education, 8,* 48–59.

Zetlin, A. G. (1990). Mentally retarded adults and their siblings. *American Journal of Mental Deficiency, 91,* 217–225.

Children Who Witness Domestic Violence: The Invisible Victims

Joy D. Osofsky

Children need to be safe and secure at home to develop a positive sense of self necessary to their growing into healthy, productive, caring adults; children need to be safe in their communities to be able to explore and develop relationships with other people; and children need to be safe at school in order to successfully learn.

—Position Statement on Violence in the Lives of Children
(National Association for the Education of Young Children, 1993)

As the incidence of violence in the United States has soared in recent years, so concern has grown about its effects on children. Children are being exposed to violence at an alarming rate—either as direct victims or as witnesses to it. The Children's Defense Fund points out that homicide is now the third leading cause of death among elementary school children (Kochanek & Hudson, 1995). And countless other children whom we never hear about are witness daily to widespread violence in their homes and in their neighborhoods. These latter are the *invisible victims*, the focus of this report.

Background

A Theoretical Framework

A systems approach—i.e., an approach encompassing not just the child but all the interlocking layers that link the child and society—offers a useful theoretical framework for conceptualizing the effects of violence on children. This approach can also inform the prevention and intervention strategies aimed at addressing the problem. We have found in our research that working with people and agencies in the community can effect changes in the system that stand to help children and families traumatized by violence. We have also found that a developmental perspective, including psychoanalytic and social learning principles, provides a helpful background for shaping the skills and techniques needed to counsel children and educate parents, teachers, police, and others about violence.

A developmental approach emphasizes the emergence of trust and empathy as crucial sensitivities. In *Childhood and Society*, Erik Erikson (1963) held that the development of trust is the initial step in forming healthy relationships. Trust develops early and is primarily contingent on the infant's relationship with his or her caregiver. If this first psychosocial stage of trust building is successfully resolved, the infant will learn to trust others, which will then help with later relationship building. Mistrust, in contrast, can result from a single trauma or from chronic environmental stress. If parents are emotionally unavailable, for instance, or are inconsistent, continually negative, or abusive, the infant or child may fail to develop basic trust (Egeland & Erickson, 1987). In light of this theoretical perspective, one must ask how growing up in a neighborhood rife with poverty, drugs, and violence and in a home marked by instability

From *Social Policy Report*, Vol. 9, No. 3, 1995, pp. 1-16. © 1995 by the Society for Research in Child Development, Inc. Reprinted by permission.

and violence may interfere with a child's developing trust. For far too many children, those very relationships on which the development of trust and trusting relationships are built may be limited or changeable.

Social learning theory also informs our understanding of the origins of violent behavior. Children learn and imitate what they see and experience. Considerable evidence indicates that children who are exposed to domestic violence, as well as to violence in their community, are at much higher risk of becoming both perpetrators and victims of violence (Bell, 1995). Imitation and modeling appear to play significant roles in this process.

Exposure to Community Violence

Although exposure to community violence is not the focus of this report, it is instructive to consider the literature on its effects. More is known about it, and it may differ from exposure to domestic violence in important ways (Bell & Jenkins, 1993; Garbarino, 1992; Marans & Cohen, 1993; Pynoos, 1993; Osofsky, 1995; Richters, 1993).

Much of the increase in violence in the United States, which has doubled since the 1950s, has been among adolescents and young adults, ages 15 to 24 years. While homicides decreased slightly in 1995, many criminologists believe this reflects a demographic trend in the adolescent and young-adult population. A recent report estimated that the number of teenagers in the population is expected to increase substantially in the next 6 to 8 years, and that the crime rate will also rise as a consequence (Blumstein, 1995).

Children are being exposed to violence at high rates in many inner-city neighborhoods. In a survey of sixth, eighth, and tenth graders in New Haven in 1992, 40% reported witnessing at least one violent crime in the past year (Marans & Cohen, 1993). Very few of the children escaped some exposure to violence, and almost all of the eighth-grade respondents knew someone who had been killed. In Los Angeles it was estimated that children witness approximately 10% to 20% of the homicides committed in that city (Pynoos & Eth, 1986). In a study of African American children living in a Chicago neighborhood, one-third of the school-aged children had witnessed a homicide and two-thirds had witnessed a serious assault (Bell & Jenkins, 1991). Yet another study showed that children's social and emotional adjustment in the classroom was related to their exposure to community violence. However, the children's adjustment was also positively related to the presence of social support in their lives, regardless of the level of violence in the community or amount of exposure (Hill, 1995).

Two other studies have documented that children are victims of and witnesses to significant amounts of violence. The first (Richters & Martinez, 1993) collected interviews of 165 mothers of children ages 6 to 10 living in a low-income neighborhood in Washington, DC. The second (Osofsky, Wewers, Hann, & Fick, 1993), in an attempt to gather similar data in New Orleans, included interviews with 53 African American mothers of children ages 9 to 12 in a low-income neighborhood, which police statistics showed to have higher violence rates than the Washington neighborhood. Fifty-one percent of the New Orleans fifth graders and 32% of the Washington, DC, children reported being victims of violence; 91% of the New Orleans children and 72% of those in Washington had witnessed some type of violence. Both studies also found a significant relationship between children's reported exposure to community violence and intrafamily conflict as measured by the Conflict Tactics Scale (Straus, 1979).

While few studies make the distinction between domestic and community violence, the Richters and Martinez (1993) and Osofsky et al. (1993) studies highlight the importance of including measures of both to determine how being raised in a violent home versus a violent neighborhood may, separately or in combination, affect children. Some evidence suggests (see the sections below: "A Special Case" and "Protective factors") that witnessing domestic-level violence may have more dire effects.

Exposure to Domestic Violence

While much less is known about children's witnessing of domestic violence, we do know that many homicides and incidents of severe violence occur in the home. It has been estimated that 25% to 30% of American women are beaten at least once in the course of intimate relationships (Pagelow, 1984). Nationwide surveys show that nearly one-eighth of husbands in the U.S. commit one or more acts of physical violence against their wives each year, and one-fifth to one-third of all women are assaulted by a partner or ex-partner during their lifetime (Frieze & Browne, 1989;

Straus & Gelles, 1990). Over half the calls for police assistance in many communities are for domestic disturbances. How much of this violence occurs in the presence of children is unknown, which is why they are considered *invisible victims*. As Judge Cindy Lederman of Miami has poignantly described, unlike most people who can escape violence by simply switching off the TV, some children cannot turn off the real-life violence in their lives (personal communication, November, 1995).

It has been estimated that at least 3.3 million children witness physical and verbal spousal abuse each year, including a range of behaviors from insults and hitting to fatal assaults with guns and knives (Jaffee, Wolfe, & Wilson, 1990). In homes where domestic violence occurs, children are physically abused and neglected at a rate 15 times higher than the national average (Senate Judiciary Committee Hearing 101–939 [as cited in Massachusetts Coalition, 1995]). Several studies have found that in 60% to 75% of families where a woman is battered, children are also battered (Bowker, 1988; McKibben, DeVos, & Newberger, 1989; Straus, Gelles, & Steinmetz, 1980). Although some excellent work is beginning to emerge (e.g., McCloskey, Figueredo, & Koss, 1995; Zuckerman, Augustyn, Groves, & Parker, 1995), relatively little research has focused on the effects of domestic violence on children, and public policy initiatives have been almost nonexistent in this crucial area.

What Do We Know about the Effects of Violence Exposure?

Children's Behavioral and Psychological Responses at Different Ages

Very young children. Although very young children may be partially protected from exposure to a traumatic incident because they do not fully appreciate the potential danger (Drell, Siegel, & Gaensbauer, 1993; Pynoos, 1993), it is important that we not ignore or de-emphasize their reactions to violence. Numerous studies have documented that even young children are likely to exhibit emotional distress, immature behavior, somatic complaints, and regressions in toileting and language (Bell, 1995; Drell et al., 1993; Jaffe et al., 1990; Margolin, 1995; Osofsky & Fenichel, 1995; Pynoos, 1993; Scheeringa & Zeanah, 1994). Recent reports have even noted the presence of symptoms very similar to post-traumatic stress disorder in adults, including

repeated reexperiencing of the traumatic event, avoidance, numbing of responsiveness, and increased arousal (Drell et al., 1993; Osofsky, Cohen, & Drell, 1995; Osofsky & Fenichel, 1994; Zeanah, 1994).

School-aged children are likely to understand more about the intentions behind an act of violence. They may wonder what they could have done to prevent or stop it (Drell et al., 1993; Pynoos, 1993) and they may also exhibit symptoms akin to post-traumatic stress disorder. Several sources report that school-aged children who witness domestic violence often show a greater frequency of externalizing (aggressive, delinquent) and internalizing (withdrawn, anxious) behavior problems in comparison to children from nonviolent families (American Bar Association, 1994; Bell, 1995; Bell in Atnafou, 1995; Bell & Jenkins, 1991; Margolin, 1995). Overall functioning, attitudes, social competence, and school performance are often affected negatively (Jaffe, Wolfe, Wilson, & Zak, 1986).

For *adolescents*, particularly those who have experienced violence exposure throughout their lives, high levels of aggression and acting out are common, accompanied by anxiety, behavior problems, school problems, truancy, and revenge seeking. Although some adolescents who witness domestic or community violence may be able to overcome the experience, many others suffer considerable scars. Some report giving up hope, expecting that they may not live through adolescence or early adulthood. They may become deadened to feelings and pain, with resultant constrictions in emotional development. Or they may attach themselves to peer groups and gangs as substitute family and incorporate violence as a method of dealing with disputes or frustration (Bell & Jenkins, 1991; Parsons, 1994; Pynoos, 1993; Prothrow-Stith, 1991).

A Special Case: When the Child Knows the Perpetrator or Victim

Whatever protective influence a lack of understanding of violence may afford the very young child, this appears to fail when severe trauma occurs, for example, when the child witnesses the murder of a parent. Post-traumatic–like symptoms, including sleeplessness, disorganized behavior, and agitation, are often observed, although caretakers and others in their environment may tend to deny these problems (Eth & Pynoos, 1994; Pynoos, 1993). Many of these children show a reaction to witnessing violence similar to that of having been abused themselves (Fantuzzo, DePaola, Lambert, & Martino, 1991; Hughes, 1988; Hurley & Jaffe, 1990; Kashani, Daniel, Kandoy, & Holcomb, 1992).

Young children may be especially vulnerable to domestic violence. Reports based on clinical experience with the Boston City Hospital Child Witness to Violence Project emphasize that domestic violence can be particularly damaging for young children when they are exposed to assaults between people to whom they are emotionally attached (Groves, Zuckerman, Marans, & Cohen, 1993; Zuckerman et al., 1995). This is corroborated by other evidence that children's psychological reactions to trauma are likely to be more intense if they know the victim or perpetrator (Pynoos & Eth, 1986).

In our own work, we have found that both parents and police perceive witnessing violence against a parent to have a much greater impact on a child than violence against a stranger. Our data show further that children are likely to show the strongest negative reactions when violence involves a parent or caregiver (Osofsky, Fick, Flowers, & Lewis, 1995).

Effects on Parents' Ability to Parent

The child's vulnerability to violence exposure may be compounded by the parent's own response to violence—as witness or victim. The parent-child relationship can be deeply affected when a mother must cope with the physical and mental health aspects of having been battered (Wolfe, Jaffe, Wilson, & Zak, 1985). She must fear for her own safety as well as that of her children. In addition, parents who realize they may not be able to protect their children from violence are likely to feel anxious, frustrated, and helpless (Osofsky & Fenichel, 1994).

Such parents, who are constantly fearful, may well have difficulty being emotionally available and responsive to their children (Augustyn, Parker, Groves, & Zuckerman, 1995; Zuckerman et al., 1995). As a victim of domestic violence, for example, a mother may become so preoccupied with safety and survival that she cannot be mindful of her child's needs. She may become depressed or numb to the violence around her, so that she is unable to be empathic toward her child. Other parents may become overprotective or, if extremely traumatized themselves, they may expect their children to protect them. Unfortunately, children raised by

such parents may fail to develop the sense of basic trust and security that is the foundation of healthy emotional development. Because domestic violence most often affects mothers, the goal of ending violence against women has important implications for protecting children.

Long-Term Sequelae of Violence Exposure

Consequences over the life-span. The long-term implications of childhood exposure to domestic violence are substantial. Children learn from witnessing violence in their homes, and what they learn may become precursors of later violent adolescent and adult behaviors. Clinical evidence suggests that exposure to violence may lead to more high-risk behaviors in adolescence (Bell, 1995). It is not just that the child sees aggression; it is that he or she is learning about "conditions under which aggression may be applied in intimate relationships" (Margolin, 1995, p. 34). Thus, children may come to view violence as an acceptable way, perhaps the only way, to resolve conflicts and they may learn to rationalize the use of violence—they know nothing else.

Our clinical work with young children exposed to repetitive violence has led us to speculate about the effects of exposure on later development. How, for instance, do these experiences relate to subsequent disturbances in school behavior, to mixed feelings toward parents when positive affect is mingled with anger, and to difficulties in forming relationships? In the case of severe violence, including death, how will these children deal with the meaning of death when they come to understand it more fully during preadolescence? How will they handle aggression, sexuality, and intimacy when they reach adolescence? And how will they relate to significant others and their own children during adulthood?

What Children Learn from Witnessing Domestic Violence

- Violence is an appropriate way to resolve conflicts.
- Violence is a part of family relationships.
- The perpetrator of violence in intimate relationships often goes unpunished.
- Violence is a way to control other people.

(Adapted from *The Children of Domestic Violence*, a report by the Massachusetts Coalition of Battered Women Service Groups and the Children's Working Group, 1995)

Intergenerational "transmission." Learned violent behaviors may be repeated. One of the most chilling aspects of domestic violence is that it can become part of an intergenerational cycle of violence (Bell, 1995). In a study of 10,036 elementary and high school children in inner-city Chicago, it was found that children and adolescents who witnessed violence and experienced personal victimization were more likely to become perpetrators of violence than those who were not exposed (Shakoor & Chalmers, 1991). Another study of 536 children in grades 2, 4, 6, and 8 linked children's physical aggression with witnessing family violence, primarily spouse abuse (Jenkins & Thompson, 1986).

This issue was recently brought to the forefront in the media, in an editorial in the *New York Times* entitled "Learning to batter women" (Staples, 1995). "We kid ourselves that we can dismiss the past and create ourselves anew. . . . Then comes the spectral recognition that the past is never really gone. *What we learn as children speaks through us indefinitely often in dramatic fashion. Wife-battering may be just such a thing*" (present author's emphasis). The editorial goes on to tell a story of a recent incident about a young man who had been jailed for pistol whipping his wife. Women were property, according to his religious tradition, and he considered wife-beating his right. He was continuing an old family theme. The article went on to note that when he was a child, his own father went to jail for badly beating a woman. The young man's grandfather had also been a public batterer, a habit he may have learned the way his sons did. One concludes that violence is handed down and essentially woven into the social fabric. Thus, "the fist that breaks and smashes travels through time, destroying more lives and bodies as it goes" (Staples, 1995). At this point, the field lacks objective data supporting the idea of intergenerational transmission of family violence, but evidence from both clinical and personal experience provides important leads to the systematic study of this phenomenon.

What Is the Status of Research on Domestic Violence Exposure?

Further Studies Needed

Most of the research on domestic violence exposure to date is descriptive, consisting of studies like those cited in this report that have documented the behavioral and psychological symptoms associated with exposure. But it is generally agreed that more work is needed (Groves & Zuckerman, in press; Margolin, 1995; Osofsky, 1995; Zuckerman et al., 1995): studies, for example, that would sharpen the conceptualization of violence exposure in general, and domestic violence exposure in particular, investigate possible causal mechanisms at different developmental stages, identify possible protective factors, and evaluate different approaches to intervention.

Conceptualization. Response to violence exposure, as a construct, needs further definition. For instance, although children's symptoms are likened to those associated with post-traumatic stress disorder (Augustyn et al., 1995; Burman & Allen-Meares, 1994; Osofsky, Cohen, et al., 1995; Pynoos, 1993; Richters & Martinez, 1993), "we have not fully conceptualized the impact of exposure to violence on children compared with other groups such as veterans of the Korean and Vietnam Wars" (Bell in Atnafou, 1995, p. 8).

Causal mechanisms. A series of experimental studies have investigated children's response to parental anger, with interesting results (Cummings, Hennessy, Rabideau, & Cicchetti, 1994; Cummings & Zahn-Waxler, 1992). It was shown that even expressions of anger between parents negatively affect children's emotions and behavior. Children exposed to more anger showed increased negative behaviors and affect, and exposure led to more aggressive responses in boys and more withdrawal in girls. Such studies can provide important clues to the study of violence exposure in real-world settings.

Descriptive studies have established that children's response to violence changes with increasing age. What is needed now are more precise demonstrations of the interaction of exposure to domestic violence with development, e.g., with changes in cognitive or socioemotional capacities.

Protective factors. Is exposure to domestic violence universally devastating, or do some children fare better than others? Growing interest in the study of resiliency—the process of surmounting adversity—may be helpful in exploring protective factors that mitigate the effects of violence exposure (Garmezy, 1993; Hawkins, 1995; Zimmerman, 1994). As mentioned earlier, the presence of social support appears to be an important protective factor for children exposed to community violence (Hill, 1995). A recent study of consequences of domestic violence, however, found that while it had been hypothesized that a positive relationship between parent and child might buffer children, this was not borne out (McCloskey et al., 1995).

Interventions. Early referral of the child to clinical services may well be one example of a protective factor against the worst ravages of violence exposure, but little research has been conducted in this area. In one study of 28 child witnesses (aged 1½ to 14 years) from 14 families in which the father killed the mother, delays in referrals for treatment for the children ranged from 2 weeks to 11 years (Black & Kaplan, 1988). In another study, delays ranged from 1 month to several years, with those children whose referral came after a year often showing a more serious diagnostic picture (Eth & Pynoos, 1994). Our clinical experience has been consistent with these reports; we have observed delays in referral, few preventive intervention programs, and children frequently receiving treatment only after serious behavior problems have been identified.

Problems of Methodology

While laboratory studies afford greater control, they cannot duplicate real-life circumstances, and therefore special care must be taken in generalizing from the findings of experimental studies. On the other hand, studies in real-life settings—especially of a phenomenon like domestic violence exposure, which cannot be manipulated—are plagued with a variety of methodological problems.

Much of what we know about domestic violence has been obtained from interviews of parents or sometimes older children living in shelters (Jouriles & O'Leary, 1985; Margolin, 1995; O'Brien, John, Margolin, & Erel, 1994). More often than not, violence exposure is just one of multiple traumas experienced by the child, so that findings on exposure per se are confounded. Most of such children, for example, have just undergone significant loss; they may be living in a new situation with a traumatized parent or with other traumatized children and parents.

Problems with the accuracy of reports of family violence must also be taken into account. Agreement between parents about whether or not violence has occurred tends to be low, and reliability drops even lower when parents are asked if their child has been a witness (Jouriles & O'Leary, 1985; Margolin, 1987; O'Brien et al., 1994).

Interrater agreement between children and parents about whether the child has wit-

nessed domestic violence is also low. Children who are living in families where violence has been documented can often give detailed reports about the violence that their parents assumed went unnoticed (Jaffe et al., 1990; Rosenberg, 1987). Parents tend to underestimate the extent to which their children have been witness to domestic violence—which may not be surprising. Children, out of fear, may try to be unseen while observing; and parents, wishing that their children were not exposed, may be reluctant to acknowledge it. When older children, who tend to be more reliable reporters, are questioned, they are likely to report higher levels of exposure than do parents. To determine the effects on children, more reliable data are needed on both actual exposure and children's perceptions of family violence (Grych, Seid, & Fincham, 1992; Margolin, 1995; O'Brien et al., 1994).

How Can Communities Help the Invisible Victims of Violence Exposure?

Law Enforcement

Beyond the violence perpetrated by people children love and trust, what additional impact do authority figures, such as police officers or protective service workers, have when they come into the home to investigate or defuse a domestic dispute? What does it mean, for instance, for a young child to see his or her father being treated harshly or taken away? What happens when children feel they cannot make their mother safe?

While much has been written about the role of protective services, the response of police, who so often are the first to arrive on the scene, has received much less attention. Yet education and preventive intervention programs involving the police are greatly needed (see Bell, 1995; Bell in Atnafou, 1995; Bell & Jenkins, 1991; Eth & Pynoos, 1994; Garbarino, 1992; Groves & Zuckerman, in press; Lewis, Osofsky, & Fick, 1995; Marans & Cohen, 1993; Osofsky, 1995; Osofsky & Fenichel, 1994; Perry, Pollard, Blakley, Baker, & Vigilante, 1995; Pynoos, 1993).

In an effort to develop a better system of referrals for children exposed to violence and to stimulate community-based intervention programs, my colleagues and I have been involved in a collaborative effort with the local police in New Orleans; similar efforts are underway in New Haven, Boston, and Los Angeles. These programs involve educating police officers about the effects of violence on children and providing mental health consultation and services for the children and their families. Although these programs share a similar philosophy, each is tailored to the needs of the particular city, based on level of violence and availability of resources and support systems. Intervention programs with the police tend to address both community and domestic violence, making it difficult to separate effects by setting.

In New Orleans. We have developed a program model in one of the two police districts with the highest level of violence in the city. It provides an educational component for new recruits in the police academy and patrol and ranking officers in the districts on the effects of violence on children. Also provided is a 24-hour mental health crisis referral and consultation service for children in collaboration with other community agencies. Through the program, we are supporting the development of greater understanding between the police and the children and families who live in high-violence areas of the city.

As part of the program, we carried out a needs assessment related to violence, including domestic violence and neighborhood safety, with 353 police officers, 250 elementary school children, 60 parents, and 68 teachers (Fick, Osofsky, & Lewis, in press; Lewis et al., 1995). Because the police have frequently reported that adolescents from such locations are quite explicit in stating and showing their mistrust of the police, the findings of the study were somewhat unexpected. The children's responses were more positive than either their parents or the police expected. The majority, ages 8 to 12, reported that they trusted police officers as the first people they would go to if they were lost or needed help. We are now gathering empirical data to investigate if and when the level of trust shifts and what factors may influence changes over the course of development (Osofsky, Fick, et al., 1995).

The police respondents showed strong beliefs about domestic violence. Overwhelmingly, law enforcement officers in this study reported that domestic disputes are the most dangerous, unpredictable situations they face in the community. And many officers reported believing that women are just as problematic as men in this situation (Jenkins, Seydlitz, Osofsky, Fisk, & Lewis, 1995; Lewis et al., 1995). They reported that learning more about

family dynamics, children's development, and conflict resolution strategies has helped them feel more comfortable and supported when they have to intervene. Having available an emergency crisis and referral service, staffed by familiar professionals, has given them greater security.

The findings from this developmentally grounded study have been useful in our intervention work with the police and the community. Parents and police have been able to discuss and deal with issues concerning trust and mistrust—both how to improve relationships and how to strengthen children's positive attitudes. With increased education on alternative ways to respond, the police may have the opportunity to develop more proactive and helpful strategies for interacting with the community and dealing with children who witness domestic disputes. As funding becomes available, with the encouragement of the police department, we plan to expand the training throughout the city.

What effects the project may have on referrals is yet to be determined. We plan to assess referral patterns and then consequences, e.g., child and family adjustment following referral.

In New Haven. The Yale Child Study Center Program on Child Development and Community Policing is one of the first programs to link the police with the mental health community (Marans & Cohen, 1993). Started in New Haven in the early 1990s, this collaborative program facilitates the response of mental health professionals and police to children and families exposed to violence. It attempts to change police officers' orientation in their interactions with children toward optimizing their role as providers of a sense of security and positive authority and as models to be emulated. The three major components of the program are (1) training of all incoming police recruits about principles of child and adolescent development; (2) clinical fellowships for veteran officers who have field supervisory roles; and (3) a 24-hour consultation service for officers responding to calls in which children are either the direct victims or witnesses of violence.

The Yale program is designed to increase the effectiveness of the outreach force of police officers who have the most immediate and sustained contact with families touched by community violence. This expanded role of police officers focuses their attention on the child's experience of violence and on the caregiver's capacity to attend to his or her child's needs. Because the city is smaller, the relative level of violence lower, and the community and mental health resources more available (compared with Boston, Los Angeles, and New Orleans), the team has been able to implement the program throughout the city.

In Boston. The Massachusetts attorney general's office has sponsored an initiative in Boston that builds on the city's community policing efforts; the initiative is targeted at the community with the second highest level of violence in the city. The collaboration includes police, the district attorney's office, the courts, community business leaders, youth agencies, community health centers, and a hospital. With so many agencies and systems working together, neighborhood crime is responded to more broadly. Criminal justice professionals are linked with child health and mental health professionals who hold seminars for the police on child development and mental health issues. Child mental health specialists and court professionals also collaborate, especially in domestic violence cases. This initiative follows the earlier establishment at Boston City Hospital of the Child Witness to Violence Project, which developed in response to the urgent need to help children and families who witness violence (Groves & Zuckerman, in press). One of every 10 children attending the Pediatric Primary Care Clinic at this inner-city hospital has witnessed a shooting or stabbing before the age of 6, half of these in their homes and half on the street (Taylor, Zuckerman, Harik, & Groves, 1994). More detail on this program and its focus on the "silent victims" of violence follows in the section on health and mental health care.

In Los Angeles. Researchers have been working with the Inglewood police department in establishing a Community Policing Agency (Pynoos, in press). The goals of this community policing effort are somewhat different from the other programs described thus far. The Inglewood chief of police decided to station some of the community-based police officers at the elementary schools as a way of promoting a relationship between the officers and neighborhood children who were to become involved in a school-based intervention program. The officers assigned to the schools are given training in child development and mental health and are encouraged to interact with the children in two main areas: The first is as part of a regular psychotherapy group where the child can learn more about the officer's action or inaction with regard to the

child's traumatic experience. The second is as part of a crisis intervention module in which the children and the police, along with a clinician, discuss concerns about exposure to violent incidents, fears of retaliation, feelings of revenge, confidentiality issues with the police, etc. These interactions build a different type of relationship between children and police officers that can lead to more effective prevention and intervention efforts for children exposed to violence.

Health Care and Mental Health Care Systems

Helpers in the health and mental health fields have important roles to play with children exposed to violence. Yet they may not always fully appreciate the distress of children who witness domestic violence and may, therefore, miss the opportunity to provide needed help. In a paper addressed to pediatricians, Wolfe and Korsch (1994) point out that exposure to domestic conflict and violence can affect how children learn to relate to others, how they develop their self-concepts and self-control, and how they interact with dating and marital partners in the future. Thus, what needs to be recognized by mental health and other health care providers is that it is not just diagnosable outcomes that are important, but also the broader range of social and behavioral outcomes resulting from violence exposure.

Along with their work at Boston City Hospital with law enforcement and the judicial system, Zuckerman et al. (1995) emphasize that because the scars of children who witness violence are invisible, because these are "silent victims," pediatricians and other primary care clinicians must be consciously alert, even in regular office visits, to the possibility of exposure and victimization and be proactive in providing help. They suggest a pattern of nonintrusive inquiry that can be used by the pediatrician or nurse as a tool for uncovering problems that can then be addressed by the physician or handled through referral to a mental health professional—in those situations of extreme trauma or when post-traumatic or depressive symptoms are present.

A range of counseling and treatment options are relevant for mental health professionals, including 24-hour crisis intervention, brief counseling for children and families, parental guidance, longer-term therapy, and follow-up. Because the treatment of traumatized children and families can be particularly distressing and taxing for the mental health professionals, working as a team or with colleagues can be especially helpful. Creating a safe environment, which can be difficult to accomplish, is the sine qua non for successful treatment of trauma cases (Pynoos, 1993; Zeanah, 1994). Systems changes are aided by individual efforts to promote better community-based services and health and mental health care for children and families. Initiatives in these areas are crucial for effective violence prevention efforts.

Public Policy Initiatives for Children Living with Domestic Violence

The problem of children's exposure to violence is well recognized by both the research and policymaking communities. And many different groups, including the American Psychological Association (1993), the Children's Defense Fund (1994), the Carnegie Corporation of New York (1994), the National Research Council (1993), and Zero to Three/National Center for Clinical Infant Programs (Osofsky & Fenichel, 1994), have recommended policy initiatives to address the problem and its solution.

In 1993 the National Research Council's Commission on Behavioral and Social Sciences and Education and the Institute of Medicine established the Board on Children and Families. The following year the newly formed Board on Children and Families convened the Committee on the Assessment of Family Violence Interventions to examine the state of knowledge about efforts to treat, control, and prevent different forms of family violence. Over the course of 30 months, the 18-member committee has been meeting, taking part in site visits, and organizing workshops to develop findings and recommendations. Interim workshop reports will be published, and the final report is expected in fall 1996. The objectives of the committee are

- to document the costs of family violence interventions to public- and private-sector services;
- to synthesize the relevant research literature and develop a conceptual framework for clarifying what is known about risk and protective factors associated with family violence;
- to characterize what is known about selected interventions in dealing with family violence;
- to identify policy and program elements that appear to improve or inhibit the de-

velopment of effective responses to family violence; and

- to provide a set of criteria and principles that can guide the development of future evaluation of family violence intervention programs.

This work is being sponsored by the Carnegie Corporation of New York and six federal agencies in the U.S. Department of Health and Human Services and the U.S. Department of Justice.

In 1987 the American Psychological Association established the Public Interest Directorate to support and promote members' efforts to apply the study of psychology to the advancement of human welfare. The Public Interest Directorate has taken several initiatives regarding the effects of violence on children and youth. APA's press published a volume, *Reason to Hope: A Psychosocial Perspective on Violence and Youth,* based on work of the Commission on Violence and Youth (Eron et al., 1994). APA President Ronald Fox appointed a 10-member Task Force on Violence and the Family as part of the 1994–95 focus on families. The task force was directed to summarize a broad range of research on the psychological aspects of family violence, its incidence, the scope of the problem, its causes, the risk factors, and interventions. The group's primary goal is to increase public awareness of family violence and to explore what role psychology can play in ameliorating it. The task force report is scheduled for release in December 1995. Finally, the Public Interest Initiatives Office of APA, in collaboration with the American Academy of Pediatrics, has completed a public education brochure, *Raising Children to Resist Violence: What You Can Do,* for parents and others who care for children. The work of the American Psychological Association on children and youth violence is very informative both in terms of how violence affects children and possible directions for public policy initiatives.[1]

In order to prevent and alleviate the effects of witnessing domestic violence on children, it is recommended (see Osofsky, 1995[2]) that we band together

. . . to launch a national campaign to change attitudes toward domestic violence.

Policymakers, media leaders, child development specialists, and citizens at-large must work together to change the image of violence, in general, and domestic violence, in particular, from something we view as acceptable, even admirable, to something disdained. The media, with their glamorizing of violence, have a crucial role to play in reshaping this image. But to the extent the media reflect societal values, the responsibility for change falls to all of us.

... to foster prevention and intervention approaches that build on family and community strengths.

Children, families, and communities bring a variety of strengths to combat domestic violence. They require support, but the most effective strategies seek to empower local forces, such as neighborhood schools and church groups, and encourage self-determining efforts with family and community.

... to provide education to parents, educators, law enforcement officials, and health and mental health professionals (1) about the effects of children's witnessing of domestic violence, and (2) about alternative approaches to resolving conflict.

All individuals who come into contact with children, including those working in daycare centers, schools, law enforcement agencies, and parenting education groups, should be well-informed about all aspects of domestic and other violence exposure and children, from its precursors to its detection and treatment, and also be versed in alternative conflict resolution strategies.

... to promote research that will (1) expand our understanding of domestic violence exposure and (2) contribute to the development of prevention and intervention strategies.

Although we have considerable understanding of some aspects of violence exposure, more research and program evaluation are needed to fill in the knowledge gaps in this field and to assist in planning more effective interventions that can both reduce domestic violence and aid its innocent victims.

Notes

1. For more information, contact the Public Interest Directorate, (202) 336–6050.
2. These recommendations relate specifically to domestic violence. They are drawn from an earlier set of recommendations that address societal violence more broadly (Osofsky, 1995).

References

American Bar Association. (1994). *Report to the President: The impact of domestic violence on children.* Chicago: Author.

American Psychological Association Commission on Violence and Youth. (1993). *Violence and youth: Psychology's response* (vol. 1). Washington, DC: Author.

Atnafou, R. (1995). Children as witnesses to community violence. *Options* (newsletter of the Adolescent Violence Resource Center, Educational Development Center, Inc.), 2, 7–11.

Augustyn, M., Parker, S., Groves, B. M., & Zuckerman, B. (1995). Children who witness violence. *Contemporary Pediatrics, 12,* 35–57.

Bell, C. (1995, January 6). Exposure to violence distresses children and may lead to their becoming violent. *Psychiatric News,* pp. 6–8, 15.

Bell, C., & Jenkins, E. J. (1991). Traumatic stress and children. *Journal of Health Care for the Poor and Underserved, 2,* 175–185.

Bell, C., & Jenkins, E. (1993). Community violence and children on Chicago's Southside. *Psychiatry, 56,* 46–54.

Black, D., & Kaplan, T. (1988). Father kills mother: Issues and problems encountered by a child psychiatric team. *British Journal of Psychiatry, 153,* 624–630.

Blumstein, A. (August, 1995). Why the deadly nexus? *National Institute of Justice Journal,* No. 229, 2–9.

Bowker, L. H. (1988). On the relationship between wife beating and child abuse. In K. Yllo & M. Bograd (Eds.), *Feminist perspectives on wife abuse.* Newbury Park, CA: Sage Publications.

Burman, S., & Allen-Meares, P. (1994). Neglected victims of murder: Children witness to parental homicide. *Social Work, 39,* 28–34.

Carnegie Corporation of New York. (1994). *Starting points: Meeting the needs of our youngest children.* New York: Author.

Children's Defense Fund. (1994, October). *Children's Defense Fund and religious leaders launch crusade to protect children against violence* (press release). Washington, DC: Author.

Cummings, E. M., Hennessy, K., Rabideau, G., & Cicchetti, D. (1994). Responses of physically abused boys to interadult anger involving their mothers. *Development and Psychopathology, 6,* 31–41.

Cummings, E. M., & Zahn-Waxler, C. (1992). Emotions and the socialization of aggression: Adults' angry behavior and children's arousal and aggression. In A. Fraczek & H. Zumley (Eds.), *Socialization and Aggression* (pp. 61–84). New York: Springer-Verlag.

Drell, M., Siegel, C., & Gaensbauer, T. (1993). Post traumatic stress disorders. In C. Zeanah (Ed.), *Handbook of infant mental health* (pp. 291–304). New York: Guilford Press.

Egeland, B., & Erickson, N. F., (1987). Psychologically unavailable caregiving. In M. R. Brassard, R. Germain, & S. N. Hart (Eds.), *Psychological maltreatment of children and youth* (pp. 110–120). New York: Pergamon Press.

Erikson, E. (1963). *Childhood and society* (2nd ed.). New York: Norton.

Eron, L. D., Gentry, J. H., & Schlegel, P. (Eds.). (1994). *Reason to hope: A psychosocial perspective on violence and youth.* Washington, DC: American Psychological Association.

Eth, S., & Pynoos, R. (1994). Children who witness the homicide of a parent. *Psychiatry, 57,* 287–306.

Fantuzzo, J., DePaola, L., Lambert, L., & Martino, T. (1991). Effects of interparental violence on the psychological adjustment and competencies of young children. *Journal of Consulting and Clinical Psychology, 59,* 258–265.

Fick, A. C., Osofsky, J. D., & Lewis, M. L. (in press). Police and parents' preceptions and understanding of violence. In J. D. Osofsky (Ed.), *Children and youth violence: Searching for solutions.* New York: Guilford Press.

Frieze, I. H., & Browne, A. (1989). Violence in marriage. In L. Ohlin & M. Tonry (Eds.), *Family violence* (pp. 163–218). Chicago: University of Chicago Press.

Garbarino, J. (1992). *Children in danger: Coping with the consequences of community violence.* San Francisco: Jossey-Bass Publishers.

Garmezy, N. (1993). Children in poverty: Resilience despite risk. In D. Reiss, J. E. Richters, M. Radke-Yarrow, & D. Scharf (Eds.), *Children and violence* (pp. 127–136). New York: Guilford Press.

Groves, B., & Zuckerman, B. (in press). Interventions with parents and community caregivers. In J. D. Osofsky (Ed.), *Children and youth violence: Searching for solutions.* New York: Guilford Press.

Groves, B., Zuckerman, B., Marans, S., & Cohen, D. (1993). Silent victims: Children who witness violence. *Journal of the American Medical Association, 269,* 262–264.

Grych, J. H., Seid, M., & Fincham, R.D. (1992). Assessing marital conflict from the child's perspective: The children's perception of interparental conflict scale. *Child Development, 63,* 558–572.

Hawkins, J. D. (1995). Controlling crime before it happens: Risk-focused prevention. *National Institute of Justice Journal, 229,* 10–18.

Hill, H. (1995, April). *Community violence and the social and emotional adjustment of African American children.* Poster presented at the biennial meeting of the Society for Research in Child Development, Indianapolis, IN.

Hughes, H. M. (1988). Psychological and behavioral correlates of family violence in child witnesses and victims. *American Journal of Orthopsychiatry, 58,* 77–90.

Hurley, D. J., & Jaffe, P. (1990). Children's observations of violence: II. Clinical implications for children's mental health professionals. *Canadian Journal of Psychiatry, 35,* 471–476.

Jaffe, P. G., Wolfe, D. A., & Wilson, S. K. (1990). *Children of battered women.* Newbury Park, CA: Sage.

Jaffe, P. G., Wolfe, D. A., Wilson, S. K., & Zak, L. (1986). Similarities in behavioral and social maladjustment among child victims and witnesses to family violence. *American Journal of Orthopsychiatry, 56,* 142–146.

Jenkins, P., Seydlitz, R., Osofsky, J. D., Fick, A. C., & Lewis, M. L. (1995, April). *Police perceptions of domestic violence.* Paper presented at the biennial meeting of the Society for Research in Child Development, Indianapolis, IN.

Jenkins, E., & Thompson, B. (1986). *Children talk about violence: Preliminary findings from a survey of black elementary children.* Paper presented at the Nineteenth Annual Convention of the Association of Black Psychologists, Oakland, CA.

Jouriles, E. N., & O'Leary, K. D. (1985). Interspousal reliability of reports of marital violence. *Journal of Consulting and Clinical Psychology, 53,* 419–421.

Kashani, J., Daniel, A. E., Dandoy, A. C., & Holcomb, W. R. (1992). Family violence: Impact on children. *Journal of the American Academy of Child and Adolescent Psychiatry, 31,* 181–182.

Kochanek, K. D., & Hudson, B. L. (1995). *Advance report of final mortality statistics, 1992* (Monthly Vital Statistics Report, 43, 6, suppl.). Hyattsville, MD: National Center for Health Statistics.

Lewis, M. L., Osofsky, J. D., & Fick, A. C. (1995, April). *The New Orleans Violence and Children Intervention Project: Development of a police education curriculum on the effects of violence on children.* Poster presented at the biennial meeting of the Society for Research in Child Development, Indianapolis, IN.

Marans, S., & Cohen, D. (1993). Children and inner-city violence: Strategies for intervention. In L. Leavitt & N. Fox (Eds.), *Psychological effects of war and violence on children* (pp. 281–302). Hillsdale, NJ: Erlbaum.

Margolin, G. (1987). The multiple forms of aggressiveness between marital partners: How do we identify them? *Journal of Marriage and Family Therapy, 13,* 77–84.

Margolin, G. (1995, January). *The effects of domestic violence on children.* Paper presented at the Conference on Violence against Children in the Family and Community, Los Angeles.

Massachusetts Coalition of Battered Women Service Groups. (1995, December). *Children of domestic violence* (working report of the Children's Working Group). Boston: Author.

McCloskey, L. A., Figueredo, A. J., & Koss, M. P. (1995). The effects of systemic family violence on children's mental health. *Child Development, 66,* 1239–1261.

McKibben, L., DeVos, E., & Newberger, E. (1989). Victimization of mothers of abused children: A controlled study. *Pediatrics, 84,* 531–535.

National Association for the Education of Young Children, Position Statement on Violence in the Lives of Young Children. (1993, September). *Young Children,* 81–84.

National Research Council. (1993). *Understanding child abuse and neglect.* Washington, DC: National Academy Press.

O'Brien, M., John, R. S., Margolin, G., & Erel, O. (1994). Reliability and diagnostic efficacy of parents' reports regarding children's exposure to marital aggression. *Violence and Victims, 9,* 45–62.

Osofsky, J. D. (1995). The effects of violence exposure on young children. *American Psychologist, 50,* 782–788.

Osofsky, J. D., Cohen, G., & Drell, M. (1995). The effects of trauma on young children: A case of 2-year-old twins. *International Journal of Psychoanalysis, 76,* 595–607.

Osofsky, J. D., & Fenichel, E. (Eds.). (1994). *Hurt, healing, and hope: Caring for infants and toddlers in violent environments.* Arlington, VA: Zero to Three/National Center for Clinical Infant Programs.

Osofsky, J. D., Fick, A. C., Flowers, A. L., & Lewis, M. L. (1995, April). *Trust in children living with violence.* Poster presented at the biennial meeting of the Society for Research in Child Development, Indianapolis, IN.

Osofsky, J. D., Wewers, S., Hann, D., & Fick, A. C. (1993). Chronic community violence: What is happening to our children? *Psychiatry, 56,* 36–45.

Pagelow, M. D. (1984). *Family violence.* New York: Praeger.

Parsons, E. R. (1994). Inner city children of trauma: Urban violence traumatic stress syndrome (U-VTS) and therapists' responses. In J. Wilson & J. Lindy (Eds.), *Countertransference in the treatment of post-traumatic stress disorder* (pp. 151–178). New York: Guilford Press.

Perry, B., Pollard, R. A., Blakley, T. L., Baker, W. L., & Vigilante, D. (1995). Childhood trauma, the neurobiology of adaptation and "use-dependent" development of the brain: How states become traits. *Infant Mental Health Journal, 16,* 271–291.

Prothrow-Stith, D. (1991). *Deadly consequences.* New York: Harper-Collins.

Pynoos, R. S. (1993). Traumatic stress and developmental psychopathology in children and adolescents. In J. M. Oldham, M. B. Riba, & A. Tasman (Eds.), *American Psychiatric Press Review of Psychiatry,* vol. 12 (pp. 205–238). Washington, DC: American Psychiatric Press.

Pynoos, R. S. (in press). Trauma/grief focused group psychotherapy in an elementary school-based violence prevention intervention program. In J. D. Osofsky (Ed.), *Children and youth violence: Searching for solutions.* New York: Guilford Press.

Pynoos, R. S., & Eth, S. (1986). Witness to violence: The child interview. *Journal of the American Academy of Child and Adolescent Psychiatry, 25,* 306–319.

Richters, J. E. (1993). Community violence and children's development: Toward a research agenda for the 1990's. In D. Reiss, J. E. Richters, M. Radke-Yarrow, & D. Scharf (Eds.), *Children and violence* (pp. 3–6). New York: Guilford Press.

Richters, J. E., & Martinez, P. (1993). The NIMH Community Violence Project: Children as victims of and witnesses to violence. In D. Reiss, J. E. Richters, M. Radke-Yarrow, & D. Scharf (Eds.), *Children and violence* (pp. 7–21). New York: Guilford Press.

Rosenberg, M. S. (1987). The children of battered women: The effects of witnessing violence on their social problem-solving abilities. *Behavior Therapist, 4,* 85–89.

Scheeringa, M., & Zeanah, C. (1994). Two approaches to the diagnosis of posttraumatic stress disorder in infancy and early childhood. *American Academy of Child and Adolescent Psychiatry, 34,* 191–200.

Shakoor, B., & Chalmers, D. (1991). Co-victimization of African American children who witness violence and the theoretical implications of its effect on their cognitive, emotional, and behavioral development. *Journal of the National Medical Association, 83,* 233–238.

Staples, B. (1995, February 12). Learning how to batter women: Wife-beating as "inherited" behavior. *New York Times,* A14.

Straus, M. A. (1979). Measuring intrafamilial conflict and violence: The Conflict Tactics Scales. *Journal of Marriage and Family, 41,* 75–88.

Straus, M. A., & Gelles, R. J. (1990). How violent are American families? Estimates from the National Violence Survey and other studies. In M. A. Straus & R. J. Gelles (Eds.), *Physical violence in American families* (pp. 95–112). New Brunswick, NJ: Transaction.

Straus, M. A., Gelles, R. J., & Steinmetz, S. (1980). *Behind closed doors.* New York: Anchor.

Taylor, L., Zuckerman, B., Harik, V., Groves, B. M. (1994). Witnessing violence by young children and their mothers. *Journal of Developmental and Behavioral Pediatrics, 15,* 120.

Wolfe, D., Jaffe, P., Wilson, S., & Zak, L. (1985). Children of battered women: The relation between child behavior, family violence, and maternal stress. *Journal of Consulting and Clinical Psychology, 53,* 657–665.

Wolfe, D. A., & Korsch, B. (1994). Witnessing domestic violence during childhood and adolescence: Implications for pediatric practice. *Pediatrics, 94,* 594–599.

Zeanah, C. H. (1994). The assessment and treatment of infants and toddlers exposed to violence. In J. D. Osofsky & E. Fenichel (Eds.), *Caring for infants and toddlers in violent environments: Hurt, healing, and hope* (pp. 29–37). Arlington, VA: Zero to Three/National Center for Clinical Infant Programs.

Zimmerman, M. A. (1994). Resiliency research: Implications for schools and policy. *Social Policy Report, 8*(4), 1–18.

Zuckerman, B., Augustyn, M., Groves, B. M., Parker, S. (1995). Silent victims revisited: The special case of domestic violence. *Pediatrics, 96,* 511–513.

About the Author

Joy D. Osofsky, Ph.D., is professor of pediatrics and psychiatry at Louisiana State University Medical Center in New Orleans and adjunct professor of psychology at University of New Orleans. She is coeditor of *Hurt, Healing and Hope: Caring for Infants and Toddlers in Violent Environments* and is editing another book, *Children and Youth Violence: Searching for Solutions.* She is on the National Research Council Committee on the Assessment of Family Violence Interventions and also co-chairs the Louisiana Violence Prevention Task Force. She is promoting an initiative within SRCD concerned with children's exposure to violence.

Acknowledgments

I want to express special appreciation to Nancy Thomas for her untiring efforts and her consistent availability and support during the preparation of this report. Support for the author's work reported in this paper has been provided by the Entergy Corporation, Institute of Mental Hygiene, the Booth-Bricker Fund, the Brown Foundation, the Greater New Orleans Foundation, the Frost Foundation, Bell South Mobility, the Jones Family Foundation, and anonymous donors.

THE LASTING EFFECTS OF CHILD MALTREATMENT

Raymond H. Starr, Jr.

Raymond H. Starr, Jr., is a developmental psychologist on the faculty of the University of Maryland, Baltimore County. He has been conducting research with maltreated children and their families for more than sixteen years and was also a founder and first president of the National Down Syndrome Congress.

Every day, the media contain examples of increasingly extreme cases of child abuse and neglect and their consequences. The cases have a blurring sameness. Take, for example, the fourteen-year-old crack addict who lives on the streets by selling his body. A reporter befriends him and writes a vivid account of the beatings the boy received from his father. There is the pedophile who is on death row for mutilating and murdering a four-year-old girl. His record shows a sixth-grade teacher threatened to rape and kill him if he told anyone what the teacher had done to him. There is the fifteen-year-old girl who felt that her parents didn't love her. So she found love on the streets and had a baby she later abandoned in a trash barrel. And there are the prostitutes on a talk show who tell how the men their mothers had trusted sexually abused them as children. These and hundreds more examples assault us and lead us to believe that abused children become problem adolescents and adults.

Are these incidents the whole story? Case examples are dramatic, but have you ever wondered how such maltreatment changes the course of a child's life? In this sound-bite era, most of us rarely stop to think about this important question. We seldom ask why trauma should play such an important role in shaping the course of a child's life.

To examine these questions, we need to understand what psychologists know about the course of lives and how they study them—the subject of the field of life-span developmental psychology.

LIFE-SPAN DEVELOPMENT

Understanding why people behave the way they do is a complex topic that has puzzled philosophers, theologians, and scientists. The course of life is so complex that we tend to focus on critical incidents and key events.

Most of us can remember a teacher who played an important role in our own development, but we have to consider that other teachers may have been important. If his seventh-grade civics teacher, Ms. Jones, is the person Bill says showed him the drama of the law, leading him to become a lawyer, does this mean that his sixth-grade English teacher, Ms. Hazelton, played no role in his career choice? An outside observer might say that Ms. Hazelton was the key person because she had a debate club and Bill was the most able debater in his class.

Case descriptions fascinate us, but it is hard to divine the reasons for life courses from such examples. It is for this reason that scientists studying human behavior prefer to use prospective studies. By following people from a certain age, we can obtain direct evidence about the life course and factors that influence it. However, most of our information comes from retrospective studies in which people are asked what has happened to them in the past and how it relates to their present functioning.

Life-span developmental theory seeks to explain the way life events have influenced individual development. Of necessity, such explanations are complex; lives themselves are complex. They are built on a biological foundation, shaped by genetic characteristics, structured by immediate events, and indirectly influenced by happenings that are external to the family. As if this were not complex enough, contemporary theory holds that our interpretation of each event is dependent on the prior interactions of all these factors.

Hank's reaction to the loss of his wife to cancer will differ from George's reaction to his wife's death from a similar cancer. Many factors can contribute to these differing reactions. Hank may have grown up with two parents who were loving and attentive, while George may never have known his father. He may have had a mother who was so depressed that from the time he was two, he had lived in a series of foster homes, never knowing a secure, loving, consistent parent.

MALTRATED CHILDREN AS ADULTS

Research has shown that there is a direct relation between a child's exposure to negative emotional, social, and environmental events and the presence of problems during adulthood. Psychiatrist Michael Rutter compared young women who were removed from strife-filled homes and who later came back to live with their parents to women from more harmonious homes.[1] The women from discordant homes were more likely to become pregnant as teens, were less skilled in parenting their children, and had unhappy marriages to men who also had psychological and social problems. Adversity begat adversity.

Do the above examples and theoretical views mean that abused and neglected children will, with great certainty, become adults with problems? Research on this issue has focused on three questions: First, do

maltreated children grow up to maltreat their children? Second, are yesterday's maltreated children today's criminals? Third, are there more general effects of abuse and neglect on later psychological and social functioning? A number of research studies have examined these questions.

The cycle of maltreatment. It makes logical sense that we tend to raise our own children as we ourselves were raised. Different theoretical views of personality development suggest that this should be the case. Psychoanalytic theorists think that intergenerational transmission of parenting styles is unconscious. Others, such as learning theorists, agree that transmission occurs but differ about the mechanism. Learning parenting skills from our parents is the key mode by which child-rearing practices are transmitted from one generation to the next, according to members of the latter group of theorists.

Research suggests that the correspondence between being maltreated as a child and becoming a maltreating adult is far from the one-to-one relationship that has been proposed. Studies have focused on physical abuse; data are not available for either sexual abuse or neglect. In one recent review, the authors conclude that the rate of intergenerational transmission of physical abuse is between 25 percent and 35 percent.[2] Thus, it is far from certain that an abused child will grow up to be an abusive parent. Physical abuse should be seen as a risk factor for becoming an abusive adult, not as a certainty. Many abusive adults were never abused when they were children.

Researchers have also taken a broader approach by examining the cycle of family violence. Sociologist Murray Straus surveyed a randomly selected national sample of families about the extent of violence between family members.[3] Members of the surveyed families were asked about experiences of violence when they were children and how much husband-wife and parent-child violence

there had been in the family in the prior year.

Straus concluded that slightly fewer than 20 percent of parents whose mothers had been violent toward them more than once a year during childhood were abusive toward their own child. The child abuse rate for parents with less violent mothers was less than 12 percent. Having or not having a violent father was less strongly related to whether or not fathers grew up to be abusive toward their own children. Interestingly, the amount of intergenerational transmission was higher if a parent was physically punished by his or her opposite-sex parent.

Straus also found that the abusive adults in his study did not have to have been abused in childhood to become abusive adults. A violent home environment can lead a non-abused child to become an abusive adult. Boys who saw their fathers hit their mothers were 38 percent more likely to grow up to be abusive than were boys who never saw their father hit their mother (13.3 vs. 9.7 percent). Similarly, mothers who saw their mothers hit their fathers were 42 percent more likely to become abusive mothers (24.4 vs. 17.2 percent). Straus views seeing parents fight as a training ground for later child abuse.

To summarize, this evidence suggests that maltreatment during childhood is but one of many factors that lead to a person's becoming an abusive parent. Being abused as a child is a risk marker for later parenting problems and not a cause of such difficulties. It accounts for, at most, less than a third of all cases of physical abuse. Research suggests that a number of other factors, such as stress and social isolation, also play a role as causes of child abuse.[4]

Maltreatment and later criminality. Later criminal behavior is one of the most commonly discussed consequences of child abuse. Research on this subject has examined the consequences of both physical abuse and sexual abuse. Maltreatment has been linked to both juvenile delinquency and adult criminality.

It is difficult to do research on this topic. Furthermore, the results of studies must be carefully interpreted to avoid overstating the connection between maltreatment and criminality. For example, researchers often combine samples of abused and neglected children, making it hard to determine the exact effects of specific forms of maltreatment.

Two types of study have typically been done. Retrospective studies examine the family backgrounds of criminals and find the extent to which they were maltreated as children. It is obvious that the validity of the results of such studies may be compromised by the criminals' distortion of or lack of memory concerning childhood experiences. Prospective studies, in which a sample of children is selected and followed through childhood and into adolescence or adulthood, are generally seen as a more valid research strategy. Such studies are expensive and time-consuming to do.

One review of nine studies concluded that from 8 to 26 percent of delinquent youths studied retrospectively had been abused as children.[5] The rate for prospective studies was always found to be less than 20 percent. In one of the best studies, Joan McCord analyzed case records for more than 250 boys, almost 50 percent of whom had been abused by a parent.[6] Data were also collected when the men were in middle age. McCord found that 39 percent of the abused boys had been convicted of a crime as juveniles, adults, or at both ages, compared to 23 percent of a sample of 101 men who, as boys, had been classified as loved by their parents. The crime rate for both sets of boys is higher than would be expected because McCord's sample lived in deteriorated, urban areas where both crime and abuse are common.

Researchers have also examined the relationship between abuse and later violent criminality. Research results suggest that there is a weak relationship between abuse and later

violence. For example, in one study, 16 percent of a group of abused children were later arrested—but not necessarily convicted—as suspects in violent criminal cases.[7] This was twice the arrest rate for nonabused adolescents and adults. Neglected children were also more likely to experience such arrests. These data are higher than would be the case in the general population because the samples contained a disproportionately high percentage of subjects from low-income backgrounds.

The connection between childhood sexual abuse and the commission of sex crimes in adolescence and adulthood is less clear. Most of the small number of studies that have been done have relied upon self-reports of childhood molestation made by convicted perpetrators. Their results show considerable variation in the frequency with which childhood victimization is reported. Incidence figures rang from a low of 19 percent to a high of 57 percent. However, we should look at such data with suspicion. In an interesting study, perpetrators of sex crimes against children were much less likely to report that they had been sexually abused during their own childhood when they knew that the truthfulness of their answers would be validated by a polygraph examination and that lies were likely to result in being sent to jail.[8] Thus, people arrested for child sexual abuse commonly lie, claiming that they were abusing children because they themselves had been victims of sexual abuse as children.

To summarize, there is a link between childhood abuse and later criminality. Although some studies lead to a conclusion that this relationship is simple, others suggest that it is really quite complex. The latter view is probably correct. The case of neglect is an example of this complexity. Widom, in her study discussed above, found that 12 percent of adolescents and adults arrested for violent offenses were neglected as children and 7 percent experienced both abuse and neglect

(compared to 8 percent of her non-maltreated control adolescents and adults).

These data raise an interesting question: Why is neglect, typically considered to be a nonviolent offense, linked to later criminality? Poverty seems to be the mediating factor. Neglect is more common among impoverished families. Poor families experience high levels of frustration, known to be a common cause of aggression. Similarly, we know that lower-class families are, in general, more violent.[9] For these reasons, all the forms of maltreatment we have considered make it somewhat more likely that a maltreated child will grow up to commit criminal acts.

Maltreatment in context. Research suggests that maltreatment during childhood has far-reaching consequences. These are best seen as the results of a failure to meet the emotional needs of the developing child. Indeed, in many cases, the trust the child places in the parent is betrayed by the parent.

This betrayal has been linked to many and varied consequences. The greatest amount of research has focused on the long-term effects of sexual abuse. Studies have looked at samples that are representative of the normal population and also at groups of adults who are seeking psychotherapy because of emotional problems. The most valid findings come from the former type of study. One review of research concluded that almost 90 percent of studies found some lasting effect of sexual abuse.[10]

Sexual abuse has been linked to a wide variety of psychological disturbances. These include depression, low self-esteem, psychosis, anxiety, sleep problems, alcohol and drug abuse, and sexual dysfunction (including a predisposition to revictimization during adulthood). As was true for the research reviewed in the preceding two sections of this article, any particular problem is present in only a minority of adult survivors of childhood sexual victimization.

We know less about the long-term effects of physical abuse. Most of the limited amount of available research has used data obtained from clinical samples. Such studies have two problems. First, they rely on retrospective adult reports concerning events that happened during childhood. Second, the use of such samples results in an overestimate of the extent to which physical abuse has long-term consequences. Compared with a random sample of the general population, clinical samples contain individuals who are already identified as having emotional difficulties, regardless of whether or not they have been abused.

Researchers in one study found that more than 40 percent of inpatients being treated in a psychiatric hospital had been sexually or physically abused as children, usually by a family member.[11] Also, the abuse was typically chronic rather than a onetime occurrence. The abused patients were almost 50 percent more likely to have tried to commit suicide, were 25 percent more likely to have been violent toward others, and were 15 percent more likely to have had some involvement with the criminal justice system than were other patients at the same hospital who had not experienced childhood maltreatment.

Much research remains to be done in this area. We know little about the long-term consequences of particular forms of abuse. The best that we can say is that many victims of physical and sexual abuse experience psychological trauma lasting into adulthood.

The lack of universal consequences. The above analysis suggests that many victims of childhood maltreatment do *not* have significant problems functioning as adults. Researchers are only beginning to ask why many adult victims apparently have escaped unsullied. Factors that mediate and soften the influence of abuse and neglect are called buffers.

The search for buffers is a difficult one. Many of the negative outcomes that have been discussed in the preceding sections may be the result of a number of factors other than maltreatment itself. For example, abused children commonly have behavior problems that are similar to those that have been reported in children raised by drug addicts or adults suffering from major psychological disturbances. Abused children do not exhibit any problems that can be attributed only to abuse. A given behavior problem can have many causes.

One view of the way in which buffers act to limit the extent to which physical abuse is perpetuated across succeeding generations has been proposed by David Wolfe.[12] He believes that there is a three-part process involving the parent, the child, and the relationships between the two. In the first stage, factors predisposing a parent to child abuse (including stress and a willingness to be aggressive toward the child) are buffered by such factors as social support and an income adequate for the purchase of child-care services. Next, Wolfe notes that children often do things that annoy parents and create crises that may lead to abuse because the parent is unprepared to handle the child's provocative behavior. Ameliorating factors that work at this level include normal developmental changes in child behavior, parental attendance at child management classes, and the development of parental ability to cope with the child's escalating annoying actions. Finally, additional compensatory factors work to limit the ongoing use of aggression as a solution to parenting problems. Parents may realize that researchers are indeed correct when they say that physical punishment is an ineffective way of changing child behavior. In addition, children may respond positively to parental use of nonaggressive disciplinary procedures and, at a broader level, society or individuals in the parents' circle of friends may inhibit the use of physical punishment by making their disapproval known. Parents who were abused as children are therefore less likely to abuse their own children if any or all of these mediating factors are present.

Research suggests that the factors mentioned by Wolfe and other influences all can work to buffer the adult effects of childhood maltreatment. These include knowing a nurturing, loving adult who provides social support, intellectually restructuring the maltreatment so that it is not seen so negatively, being altruistic and giving to others what one did not get as a child, having good skills for coping with stressful events, and getting psychotherapy.

One study compared parents who broke the cycle of abuse to those who did not.[13] Mothers who were not abusive had larger, more supportive social networks. Support included help with child care and financial assistance during times of crisis. Mothers who did not continue the abusive cycle also were more in touch with their own abuse as children and expressed doubts about their parenting ability. This awareness made them more able to relive and discuss their own negative childhood experiences.

To summarize, investigators have gone beyond just looking at the negative consequences of childhood maltreatment. They are devoting increasing attention to determining what factors in a child's environment may inoculate the child against the effects of maltreatment. While research is starting to provide us with information concerning some of these mediating influences, much more work needs to be done before we can specify the most important mediators and know how they exert their influences.

CONCLUSIONS

We know much about the intergenerational transmission of childhood physical and sexual abuse. Research suggests that abused children are (1) at an increased risk of either repeating the acts they experienced with their own children or, in the case of sexual abuse, with both their own and with unrelated children; (2) more likely to be involved with the criminal justice system as adolescents or adults; and (3) likely to suffer long-lasting emotional effects of abuse even if they do not abuse their own children or commit criminal acts.

This does not mean that abused children invariably grow up to be adults with problems. Many adults escape the negative legacy of abuse. They grow up to be normal, contributing members of society. Their escape from maltreatment is usually related to the presence of factors that buffer the effects of the physical blows and verbal barbs.

The knowledge base underlying these conclusions is of varied quality. We know more about the relationship of physical and sexual abuse to adult abusiveness and criminality, less about long-term psychological problems and buffering factors, and almost nothing about the relationship of neglect to any of these outcomes. Almost no research has been done on neglect, a situation leading to a discussion of the reasons behind our "neglect of neglect."[14] Our ignorance is all the more surprising when we consider that neglect is the most common form of reported maltreatment.

The issues involved are complex. We can no longer see the development of children from a view examining such simple cause-effect relationships as exemplified by the proposal that abused children grow up to be abusive adults. Contemporary developmental psychology rec-

ognizes that many interacting forces work together to shape development. Children exist in a context that contains their own status as biological beings, their parents and the background they bring to the task of child-rearing, the many and varied environments such as work and school that exert both direct and indirect influences on family members, and the overall societal acceptance of violence.

Advances in research methods allow us to evaluate the interrelationships of all the above factors to arrive at a coherent view of the course of development. Appropriate studies are difficult to plan and expensive to conduct. Without such research, the best that we can do is to continue performing small studies that give us glimpses of particular elements of the picture that we call the life course.

Research is necessary if we are to develop and evaluate the effectiveness of child maltreatment prevention and treatment programs. Our existing knowledge base provides hints that are used by program planners and psychotherapists to find families where there is a high risk of maltreatment and to intervene early. But when such hints are all we have to guide us in working to break the cycle of maltreatment, there continues to be risk of intergenerational perpetuation.

---

1. Michael Rutter, "Intergenerational Continuities and Discontinuities in Serious Parenting Difficulties," in *Child Maltreatment: Theory and Research on the Causes and Consequences of Child Abuse and Neglect*, ed. Dante Cicchetti and Vicki Carlson (New York: Cambridge University Press, 1989), 317–348.

2. Joan Kaufman and Edward Zigler, "Do Abused Children Become Abusive Adults?" *American Journal of Orthopsychiatry* 57 (April 1987): 186–192.

3. Murray A. Straus, "Family Patterns and Child Abuse in a Nationally Representative American Sample," *Child Abuse and Neglect* 3 (1979): 213–225.

4. Raymond H. Starr, Jr., "Physical Abuse of Children," in *Handbook of Family Violence* ed. Vincent B. Van Hasselt, et al. (New York: Plenum Press, 1988): 119–155.

5. Cathy Spatz Widom, "Does Violence Beget Violence? A Critical Examination of the Literature," *Psychological Bulletin* 106 (1989): 3–28.

6. Joan McCord, "A Forty-year Perspective on Effects of Child Abuse and Neglect," *Child Abuse and Neglect* 7 (1983): 265–270. Joan McCord, "Parental Aggressiveness and Physical Punishment in Long-term Perspective," in *Family Abuse and Its Consequences*, ed. Gerald T. Hotaling, et al. (Newbury Park, Calif.: Sage Publishing, 1988): 91–98.

7. Cathy Spatz Widom, "The Cycle of Violence," *Science*, 14 April 1989.

8. Jan Hindman, "Research Disputes Assumptions about Child Molesters," *National District Attorneys' Association Bulletin* 7 (July/August 1988): 1.

9. Murray A. Straus, Richard J. Gelles, and Suzanne K. Steinmetz, *Behind Closed Doors: Violence in the American Family* (New York: Anchor Press, 1980).

10. David Finkelhor and Angela Browne, "Assessing the Long-term Impact of Child Sexual Abuse: A Review and Conceptualization," in *Family Abuse and Its Consequences*, ed. Gerald T. Hotaling, et al.: 270–284.

11. Elaine (Hilberman) Carmen, Patricia Perri Rieker, and Trudy Mills, "Victims of Violence and Psychiatric Illness," *American Journal of Psychiatry* 141 (March 1984): 378–383.

12. David A. Wolfe, *Child Abuse: Implications for Child Development and Psychopathology* (Newbury Park. Calif.: Sage Publishing, 1987).

13. Rosemary S. Hunter and Nancy Kilstrom, "Breaking the Cycle in Abusive Families," 136 (1979): 1320–22.

14. Isabel Wolock and Bernard Horowitz, "Child Maltreatment as a Social Problem: The Neglect of Neglect," *American Journal of Orthopsychiatry* 54 (1984): 530–543.

Why kids have a lot to cry about

David Elkind, Ph.D.

David Elkind, Ph.D., professor of child study at Tufts University, is the author of more than 400 articles. He is perhaps best known for his books The Hurried Child; All Grown Up and No Place to Go *and* Ties That Stress: Childrearing in a Postmodern Society. *He is an active consultant to government agencies, private foundations, clinics, and mental-health centers.*

"MOMMY," THE FIVE-YEAR-OLD GIRL asked her mother, "why don't you get divorced again?" Her thrice-married mother was taken aback and said in return, "Honey, why in the world should I do that?" To which her daughter replied, "Well, I haven't seen you in love for such a long time."

This young girl perceives family life and the adult world in a very different way than did her counterpart less than half a century ago. Likewise, the mother perceives her daughter quite differently than did a mother raising a child in the 1940s. Although this mother was surprised at her daughter's question, she was not surprised at her understanding of divorce, nor at her familiarity with the symptoms of romance.

As this anecdote suggests, there has been a remarkable transformation over the last 50 years in our children's perceptions of us, and in our perceptions of our children. These altered perceptions are a very small part of a much larger tectonic shift in our society in general and in our families in particular. This shift is nothing less than a transformation of the basic framework, or paradigm, within which we think about and thus perceive our world. To understand the changes in the family, the perceptions of family members, and of parenting that have been brought about, we first have to look at this broader "paradigm shift" and what it has meant for family sentiments, values, and perceptions.

FROM MODERN TO POSTMODERN

Without fully realizing it perhaps, we have been transported into the postmodern era. Although this era has been called "postindustrial" and, alternatively, "information age," neither of these phrases is broad enough to encompass the breadth and depth of the changes that have occurred. The terms modern and postmodern, in contrast, encompass all aspects of society and speak to the changes in science, philosophy, architecture, literature, and the arts—as well as in industry and technology—that have marked our society since mid-century.

THE MODERN AND THE NUCLEAR FAMILY

The modern era, which began with the Renaissance and spanned the Industrial Revolution, was based upon three related assumptions. One was the idea of *human progress*—the notion that the natural direction of human and societal development is toward a more equitable, peaceful, and harmonious world in which every individual would be entitled to life, liberty, and the pursuit of happiness. A second assumption is *universality*. There were, it was taken as given, universal laws of nature of art, science, economics, and so on that transcended time and culture. The third basic assumption was that of *regularity*—the belief that the world is an orderly place, that animals and plants, geological layers and chemical elements could be classified in an orderly hierarchy. As Einstein put it, "God does not play dice with the universe!"

These assumptions gave a unique character and distinctiveness to modern life. Modern science, literature, architecture, philosophy, and industry all embodied these premises. And they were enshrined in the Modern Family as well. The modern nuclear family, for example, was seen as the end result of a progressive evolution of family forms. Two parents, two or three children, one parent working and one staying home to rear the children and maintain the home was thought to be the ideal family form toward which all prior "primitive" forms were merely preliminary stages.

SENTIMENTS OF TNE NUCLEAR FAMILY

The Modern Family was shaped by three sentiments that also reflected the underlying assumptions of modernity. One of these was Romantic Love. In premodern times, couples married by familial and community dictates. Considerations of property and social position were paramount. This community influence declined in the modern era, and couples increasingly came to choose one another on the basis of mutual attraction. This attraction became idealized into the notion that "Some enchanted evening, you will meet a stranger" for whom you and only you were destined ("You were meant for me, I was meant for you"), and that couples would stay together for the rest of their lives, happily "foreveraftering."

A second sentiment of the Modern Family was that of Maternal Love—the idea that women have a maternal "instinct" and a need to care for children, particularly when they are small. The idea of a maternal instinct was a thoroughly modern invention that emerged only after modern medicine and nutrition reduced infant mortality. In premodern times, infant mortality was so high that the young were not even named until they were two years old and stood a good chance of surviving. It was also not uncommon for urban parents to have their infants "wet-nursed" in the country. Often these infants died because the wet-nurse fed her own child before she fed the stranger, and there was little nourishment left. Such practices could hardly be engaged in by a mother with a "maternal instinct."

The third sentiment of the Modern Family was Domesticity, a belief that relationships within the family are always more powerful and binding than are those outside it. The family was, as Christopher Lasch wrote, "a haven in a heartless world." As a haven, the nuclear family shielded and protected its members from the evils and temptations of the outside world. This sentiment also extended to the family's religious, ethnic, and social-class affiliations. Those individuals who shared these affiliations were to be preferred, as friends and spouses, over those with different affiliations.

PARENTING THE INNOCENT

The modern perceptions of parenting, children, and teenagers grew out of these family sentiments. Modern parents, for example, were seen as intuitively or instinctively knowledgeable about child-rearing. Professional help was needed only to encourage parents to do "what comes naturally." In keeping with this view of parenting was the perception of children as innocent and in need of parental nurturance and protection. Teenagers, in turn, were seen as immature and requiring adult guidance and direction. Adolescence, regarded as the age of preparation for adulthood, brought with it the inevitable "storm and stress," as young people broke from the tight nuclear family bonds and became socially and financially independent.

These modern perceptions of parenting and of children and youth were reinforced by the social mirror of the media, the law and the health professions. Motion pictures such as the Andy Hardy series (starring Mickey Rooney) depicted a teenage boy getting into youthful scrapes at school and with friends from which he was extricated by his guardian the judge, played by Harlan Stone. Fiction similarly portrayed teenagers as immature young people struggling to find themselves. Mark Twain's Huck Finn was an early version of the modern immature adolescent, while J. D. Salinger's Holden Caulfield is a modern version.

Modern laws, such as the child-labor laws and compulsory-education statutes were enacted to protect both children and adolescents. And the health professions attributed the mental-health problems of children and youth to conflicts arising from the tight emotional bonds of the nuclear family.

POSTMODERNITY AND THE POSTMODERN FAMILY

The postmodern view has largely grown out of the failure of modern assumptions about progress, universality, and regularity. Many of the events of this century have made the idea of progress difficult to maintain. Germany, one of the most educationally, scientifically, and culturally advanced countries of the world, engaged in the most heinous genocide. Modern science gave birth to the atomic bomb that was dropped on Hiroshima and Nagasaki. Environmental degradation, pollution, population explosions, and widespread famine can hardly be reconciled with the notion of progress.

Secondly, the belief in universal principles has been challenged as the "grand" theories of the modern era—such as those of Marx, Darwin, and Freud—are now recognized as limited by the social and historical contexts in which they were elaborated. Modern theorists believed that they could transcend social-historical boundaries; the postmodern worker recognizes that he or she is constrained by the particular discourse of narrative in play at the time. Likewise, the search for abiding ethical, moral, and religious universals is giving way to a recognition that there are many different ethics, moralities, and religions, each of which has a claim to legitimacy.

Finally, the belief in regularity has given way to a recognition of the importance of irregularity, indeterminacy, chaos, and fuzzy logic. There is much in nature, such as the weather, that remains unpredictable—not because it is perverse, bud only because the weather is affected by non-regular events. Sure regularity appears, but irregularity is now seen as a genuine phenomenon in its own right. It is no longer seen, as it was in the modern era, as the result of some failure to discover an underlying regularity.

In place of these modern assumptions, a new, postmodern paradigm with its own basic premises has been invented. The assumption of progress, to illustrate, has given way to the presumption of *difference*. There are many different forms and types of progress, and not all progressions are necessarily for the better. Likewise, the belief in universals has moved aside for the belief in *particulars*. Different phenomena may have different rules and principles that are not necessarily generalizable. For example, a particular family or a particular class of children is a nonreplicable event that can never be exactly duplicated and to which universal principles do not apply. Finally, the assumption of regularity moved aside to make room for the principle of *irregularity*. The world is not as orderly and as logically organized as we had imagined.

As the societal paradigm has shifted, so has the structure of the family. The ideal nuclear family, thought to be the product of progressive social evolution, has given way to what might be called the *Permeable Family* of the postmodern era. The Permeable Family encompasses many different family forms: traditional or nuclear, two-parent working, single-parent, blended, adopted child, test-tube, surrogate mother, and co-parent families. Each of these is valuable and a potentially successful family form.

The family is permeable in other ways as well. It is no longer isolated from the larger community. Thanks to personal computers, fax and answering machines, the workplace has moved into the homeplace. The homeplace, in turn, thanks to child-care facilities in office buildings and factories, has moved into the workplace. The home is also permeated by television, which brings the outside world into the living room and bedrooms. And an ever-expanding number of TV shows (*Oprah*,

Donahue, Geraldo, and *Sally Jessy Raphael*), all detailing the variety of family problems, brings the living room and the bedroom into the outside world.

Quite different sentiments animate the postmodern Permeable Family than animated the modern nuclear family. The transformation of family sentiments came about in a variety of ways, from the civil-rights movement, the women's movement, changes in media, and laws that were part of the postmodern revolution. Because there is a constant interaction between the family and the larger society, it is impossible to say whether changes in the family were brought about by changes in society or vice versa. Things moved in both directions.

For a number of reasons, the Modern Family sentiment of Romantic Love has been transformed in the Postmodern era into the sentiment of *Consensual Love.* In contrast to the idealism and perfectionism of Romantic Love, consensual love is realistic and practical. It recognizes the legitimacy of premarital relations and is not premised on long-term commitment. Consensual Love is an agreement or contract between the partners; as an agreement it can be broken. The difference between Romantic Love and Consensual Love is summed up in the prenuptial agreement, which acknowledges the possible rupture of a marriage—before the marriage actually occurs. The current emphasis upon safe sex is likewise a symptom of consensual, not romantic, love.

The Modern Family sentiment of maternal love has yielded to other changes. Today, more than 50 percent of women are in the workforce, and some 60 percent of these women have children under the age of six. These figures make it clear that non-maternal and non-parental figures are now playing a major role in child-rearing. As part of this revision of child-rearing responsibilities, a new sentiment has emerged that might be called *shared parenting.* What this sentiment entails is the understanding that not only mothers, but fathers and professional caregivers are a necessary part of the child-rearing process. Child-rearing and childcare are no longer looked upon as the sole or primary responsibility of the mother.

The permeability of the Postmodern Family has also largely done away with the Modern Family sentiment of domesticity. The family can no longer protect individuals from the pressures of the outside world. Indeed, the impulse of the Permeable Family is to move in the other direction. Permeable Families tend to thrust children and teenagers forward to deal with realities of the outside world at ever earlier ages. This has resulted in what I have called the "hurrying" of children to grow up fast. Much of the hurrying of children and youth is a well-intentioned effort on the part of parents to help prepare children and youth for the onrush of information, challenges, and temptations coming at them through the now-permeable boundaries of family life.

POSTMODERN PARENTS OF KIDS WITHOUT INNOCENCE

These new, postmodern sentiments have given rise to new perceptions of parenting, of children, and of adolescents. Now that parenting is an activity shared with nonparental figures, we no longer regard it as an instinct that emerges once we have become parents; it is now regarded as a matter of learned *technique.*

Postmodern parents understand that doing "what comes naturally" may not be good for children. There are ways to say things to children that are less stressful than others. There are ways of disciplining that do not damage the child's sense of self esteem. The problem for parents today is to choose from the hundreds of books and other media sources bombarding them with advice on child-rearing. As one mother said to me, "I've read your books and they sound okay, but what if you're wrong?"

With respect to children, the perception of childhood innocence has given way to the perception of childhood competence. Now that children are living in Permeable Families with—thanks to television—a steady diet of overt violence, sexuality, substance abuse, and environmental degradation, we can no longer assume they are innocent. Rather, perhaps to cover our own inability to control what our children are seeing, we perceive them as competent to deal with all of this material. Indeed, we get so caught up in this perception of competence that we teach four- and five-year-olds about AIDS and child abuse and provide "toys" that simulate pregnancy or the dismemberment that accidents can cause unbuckled-up occupants. And the media reinforce this competence perception with films such as *Look Who's Talking* and *Home Alone.*

If children are seen as competent, teenagers can no longer be seen as immature. Rather they are now seen as sophisticated in the ways of the world, knowledgeable about sex, drugs, crime, and much more. This is a convenient fiction for parents suffering a time-famine. Such parents can take the perception of teenage sophistication as a rationale to abrogate their responsibility to provide young people with limits, guidance, and supervision. Increasingly, teenagers are on their own. Even junior and senior high schools no longer provide the social programs and clubs they once did.

This new perception of teenagers is also reflected in the social mirror of media, school and law. Postmodern films like *Risky Business* (in which teenager runs a bordello in the parents' home) and *Angel* (demure high school student by day, avenging hooker by night) are a far cry from the Andy Hardy films. Postmodern TV sitcoms such as *Married with Children* and *Roseanne* present images of teenage sophistication hardly reconcilable with the teenagers portrayed in modern TV shows such as *My Three Sons* or *Ozzie and Harriet.* Postmodern legal thinking is concerned with protecting the *rights* of children and teenagers, rather than protecting children themselves. Children and teenagers can now sue their parents for divorce, visitation rights, and for remaining in the United States when the family travels overseas.

REALITY IS HERE TO STAY

The postmodern perceptions of children as competent and of teenagers as sophisticated did not grow out of any injustices nor harm visited upon children and youth. Rather they grew out of a golden era for young people that lasted from the end of the last century to the middle of this one. Society as a whole was geared to regard children as innocent and teenagers as immature, and sought to protect children and gradually inculcate teenagers into the ways of the world.

In contrast, the perceptions of childhood competence and teenage sophistication have had detrimental effects upon children and youth. Indeed, these perceptions have placed children and teenagers under inordinate stress. And it shows. On every measure that we have, children and adolescents are doing less well today than they did a quarter century ago, when the new postmodern perceptions were coming into play. While it would be unwise to attribute all of these negative effects to changed perceptions alone—economics and government policy clearly played a role—it is also true that government policy and economics are affected by the way young people are perceived.

The statistics speak for themselves. There has been a 50-percent increase in obesity in children and youth over the past two decades. We lose some ten thousand teenagers a year in substance-related accidents, not including injured and maimed. One in four teenagers drinks to excess every two weeks, and we have two million alcoholic teenagers.

Teenage girls in America get pregnant at the rate of one million per year, twice the rate of the next Western country, England. Suicide has tripled among teenagers in the last 20 years, and between five and six thousand teenagers take their own lives each year. It is estimated that one out of four teenage girls manifests at least one symptom of an eating disorder, most commonly severe dieting. The 14- to 19-year-old age group has the second-highest homicide rate of any age group.

These are frightening statistics. Yet they are not necessarily an indictment of the postmodern world, nor of our changed perceptions of children and youth. We have gone through enormous social changes in a very brief period of time. No other society on Earth changes, or can change, as rapidly as we do. That is both our strength and our weakness. It has made us, and will keep us, the leading industrial nation in the world because we are more flexible than any other society, including Japan.

But rapid social change is a catastrophe for children and youth, who require stability and security for healthy growth and development. Fortunately, we are now moving toward a more stable society. A whole generation of parents was caught in the transition between Modern and Postmodern Family sentiments; among them, divorce, open marriage, and remarriage became at least as commonplace as the permanent nuclear family. The current generation of parents have, however, grown up with the new family sentiments and are not as conflicted as their own parents were.

As a result, we are slowly moving back to a more realistic perception of both children and teenagers, as well as toward a family structure that is supportive of all family members. We are moving towards what might be called the *Vital Family*. In the Vital Family, the modern value of togetherness is given equal weight with the Postmodern Family value of autonomy. Children are seen as *growing into competence* and as still needing the help and support of parents. Likewise, teenagers are increasingly seen as *maturing into sophistication,* and able to benefit from adult guidance, limits, and direction.

These new perceptions pop up in the media. Increasingly, newspapers and magazines feature articles on the negative effects pressures for early achievement have upon children. We are also beginning to see articles about the negative effects the demands for sophistication place upon teenagers. A number of recent TV shows (such as *Beverly Hills 90210*) have begun to portray children and youth as sophisticated, but also as responsible and accepting of adult guidance and supervision. There is still much too much gratuitous sex and violence, but at least there are signs of greater responsibility and recognition that children and adolescents may not really be prepared for everything we would like to throw at them.

After 10 years of traveling and lecturing all over the country, I have an impression that the American family is alive and well. It has changed dramatically, and we are still accommodating to the changes. And, as always happens, children and youths are more harmed by change than are adults. But our basic value system remains intact. We do have a strong Judeo-Christian heritage; we believe in hard work, democracy, and autonomy. But our sense of social and parental responsibility, however, was temporarily deadened by the pace of social change. Now that we are getting comfortable in our new Permeable Family sentiments and perceptions, we are once again becoming concerned with those who are young and those who are less fortunate.

As human beings we all have a need to become the best that we can be. But we also have a need to love and to be loved, to care and to be cared for. The Modern Family spoke to our need to belong at the expense, particularly for women, of the need to become.

The Permeable Family, in contrast, celebrates the need to become at the expense of the need to belong, and this has been particularly hard on children and youth. Now we are moving towards a Vital Family that ensures both our need to become and our need to belong. We are not there yet, but the good news is, we are on our way.

TV VIOLENCE
Myth and Reality

MARY A. HEPBURN

Mary A. Hepburn is professor of social science education and head of the Citizen Education Division at the Carl Vinson Institute of Government, University of Georgia, Athens.

With an average national TV viewing time of 7¼ hours daily, the prevalence of violence in broadcasts is a serious concern. Television programming in the United States is considered the most violent in advanced industrialized nations. Violence is common in TV entertainment—the dramas that portray stories about crime, psychotic murderers, police cases, emergency services, international terrorism, and war. The dramas are played out in highly realistic scenes of violent attacks accompanied by music and other sounds that churn up emotions.

As the realism and gore in the screen images of TV entertainment have intensified, local news cameras have also increasingly focused directly on the bloody violence done to individuals in drive-by shootings, gang attacks, and domestic beatings. Why must these visual details be presented in the news? Why does a typical television evening include so many beatings, shootings, stabbings, and rapes in dramas designed for "entertainment"?

Producers of programming ascertain that scenes of violent action with accompanying fear-striking music can be counted on to hold viewers' attention, keep them awake and watching, and make them less likely to switch channels. The purpose is to gain and maintain a large number of viewers—the factor that appeals to advertisers. The generations of younger adults who have grown up with daily viewing of violence in entertainment are considered to be "hooked." A program has more commercial value if it can hold more viewers, and programmers attempt to ensure high viewer attention with doses of violent action in the program. How does all of this violence affect young people?

The Results of Research

Several decades ago, a few psychologists hypothesized that viewing violence in the unreal television world would have a cathartic effect and thus reduce the chances of violent behavior in the real world. But other psychologists began to doubt this notion when their research with children revealed that much action on the TV screen is perceived as real by children. Huesmann and Eron (1986), who studied the effects of media violence on 758 youngsters in grades 1 through 3, found that children's behavior was influenced by television, especially if the youngsters were heavy viewers of violent programming. Television violence, according to the researchers, provided a script for the children to act out aggressive behavior in relationships with others. The most aggressive youngsters strongly identified with aggressive characters in the TV story, had aggressive fantasies, and expressed the attitude that violent programs portrayed life as it is. These children were also likely to perform poorly in school and often were unpopular with their peers.

Huesmann and Eron state that television is not the *only* variable involved, but their many years of research have left them with no doubt that heavy exposure to media violence is a highly influential factor in children and later in their adult lives (see also Institute for Social Research 1994 and medical research by Zuckerman and Zuckerman 1985 and by Holroyd 1985).

Research in the field of public communications also supports the conclusion that exposure to television violence contributes to increased rates of aggression and violent behavior. Centerwall (1989, 1993) analyzed crime data in areas of the world with and without television and, in addition, made comparisons in areas before and after the introduction of TV. His studies determined that homicide rates doubled in ten to fifteen years after TV was introduced for the first time into specified areas of the United States and Canada. Observing that violent television programming exerts its aggressive effects primarily on children, Centerwall noted that the ten- to fifteen-year lag time can be expected before homicide rates increase. Acknowledging that other factors besides TV do have some influence on the quantity of violent crimes, Centerwall's careful statistical analysis indicated, nevertheless, that when the negative effects of TV were removed, quantitative evidence showed "there would be 10,000 fewer homicides, 70,000 fewer rapes, and 700,000 fewer injurious assaults" (1993, 64).

Centerwall (1993) has also brought to light important research literature that has been little known among social scientists and educators concerned about television violence. In the late sixties, as a result of public hearings and a national report implying that exposure to TV increases physical aggression, the large television networks decided to commission their own research projects. NBC appointed a team of four researchers, three of whom were NBC employees, to observe more than two thousand school children up to three years to determine if watching television programs increased their physical aggressiveness. NBC reported no effect. Centerwall points out, however, that every independent researcher who has analyzed the same data finds an increase in levels of physical aggression.

In the study commissioned by the ABC network, a team at Temple University surveyed young male felons who had been imprisoned for violent crimes. Results of these interviews showed that 22 to 34 percent of the young felons, especially those who were the most violent, said they had consciously imitated crime techniques learned from television programs. It was learned that, as children, felons in the study had watched an average of six hours of TV per day,

about twice as much as children in the general population at that time. Research results were published privately by ABC and not released to the general public or to scientists (Centerwall 1993, 65).

CBS commissioned a study to be conducted in London and ultimately published in England (Belson 1978). In the study, 1,565 teenaged boys were studied for behavioral effects of viewing violent television programs, many of which were imported from the United States. The study (Belson 1978) revealed that those who watched above average hours of TV violence before

adolescence committed a 49 percent higher rate of serious acts of violence than did boys who had viewed below average quantities of violence. The final report was "very strongly supportive of the hypothesis that high exposure to television violence increases the degree to which boys engage in serious violence" (Belson 1978, 15).

Five types of TV programming were most powerful in triggering violent behavior in the boys in the London study: (1) TV plays or films in which violence is demonstrated in close personal relationships; (2) programs where violence

Student Activities to Develop Critical Media Skills

1. Our Favorite Programs. Take a poll of students in your class to find out what their favorite weekday prime time (8–11 p.m.) programs are, and also their favorite programs on Saturday and Sunday. Favorite programs can be summarized by type (e.g., movies, cartoons, police dramas) on a poster for a later study of contents. If each student has a notebook for the study of mass media, the results of this poll could be the first entry.

2. What's on the Air? Assign each student a different TV channel (include local, regular network, public TV, and pay cable network channels), and ask each to use TV listings in newspapers or magazines to determine how many minutes on a specified day are designated for (1) young children's entertainment, (2) special programs for teenagers, (3) public affairs information and discussion programs, (4) adult entertainment programs (dramas, sitcoms, quiz shows, science fiction, detective series, love stories), (5) religious programs, and (6) cooking and household repair programs.

3. What Are the Rules and Obligations? The airwaves are publicly owned. Licensing and oversight of the use of the airwaves is conducted by the Federal Communications Commission (FCC). To obtain guidelines and legal explanation of the responsibilities of all broadcasters to consider community needs and interests in their programming, write or call the FCC, 1919 M Street, NW, Washington, DC 10554; phone 202–418–0200. Reference books and government books in the school library will help clarify the legal framework for radio and television broadcasting.

4. How Much Violence Is in Our Entertainment? Discuss the kinds of violent acts and language in television programs and movies to prepare students to monitor "violence" in TV programs. From the list of "favorite programs" (no. 1 above), prepare slips of paper with program titles, so students can randomly draw a program title and plan to monitor the program for violent action, language, or threats. Students should take notes on the name, time, station, and advertisers for each program, and describe the violence discussed or shown in the program. This monitoring activity can be extended to other programs over a weekend or over several evenings. Students can invite their parents to join them in noting how much violence is depicted, suggested, or threatened.

Following a period of collecting data, student groups can share their findings: Which programs contained the most violence? Is violence common in prime time programs and/or at other times? On cable? On regular network channels? On public channels? Which advertisers support programs with heavy violence? Finally, prepare a class summary listing of the most violent and least violent programs.

5. How Does TV Violence Affect Us? Discussion: Using notes from program monitoring and recollections or videotape of violent scenes, analyze the images, sounds, and dialogue that hold the viewer's attention. Which are the most frightening, hard to forget, or likely to give people nightmares? Why are some viewers fascinated by scenes of beating, killing, and hurting people? Would these scenes and sounds encourage similar behavior by young viewers? Why or why not?

6. How Do Music and Sounds Affect Our Emotions? To further analyze the contents and affects of violent programming, have students return to a selected program that is usually violent and scary. Have them experiment with turning down the sound in dramatic scenes without dialogue. Ask them to observe how pulsating, eerie, pounding music and sounds of howling wind, roaring cars, squealing cats, and other noises can arouse excitement or fear. In turn, they can observe programs where soothing music, laughing children, and cheerful sounds help to make the viewer feel at ease.

7. Why Would Advertisers Select Programs with Violence? Discuss with students the fascination that violence and fast action have for some viewer groups, including youngsters, uncritical adults, and less educated individuals. Discuss how people can be mesmerized and fascinated by images of violent conflict, especially if they watch violence daily and begin to see it as a way of life. (References to writings by psychologists and sociologists in the article above will lead you to books and readings about the appeal of violent scenes and the high vulnerability of certain groups of people.) Students can reflect on how advertisers look for programs with large numbers of viewers. In turn, discuss how critical viewers might influence advertisers to select better quality programs for their ads.

8. TV Consumer Power. Discuss the power potential of viewers to select quality programs. Students can learn about "market share" and Nielsen ratings from magazines and newspapers. A local TV station or radio station manager can explain how "market share" affects program selection.

was not necessary to the plot but just added for its own sake; (3) fictional violence of a very realistic kind; (4) violent "Westerns"; and (5) programs that present violence as being for a good cause. In summarizing the implications of the study, the research director made it clear that the results also applied to boys in U.S. cities with the same kind of violence in TV programming (ibid. 528).

For about fifteen years, these studies have received little attention. Each was either filed away or distributed to a very limited audience—not to the general public, the research community, or the press. Today, that seems eerily similar to the fate of tobacco company research on the ill effects of smoking, the results of which were also disseminated only to a small select group. The Commission on Violence and Youth of the American Psychological Association recently communicated the above-mentioned and other supporting research to its members. It concluded that evidence clearly reveals that viewing and hearing high levels of violence on television, day after day, were correlated with increased acceptance of aggression and more aggressive behavior. The commission noted that the highest level of consumption of television violence is by those most vulnerable to the effects, those who receive no moderating or mediating of what is seen on the screen. (Slaby 1994, Institute for Social Research 1994; see also Holroyd 1985; Zuckerman and Zuckerman 1985).

This information is of great significance to social studies educators. Yet it is only in the last two years that the network-funded studies of the seventies and eighties have been gaining some attention in journals that reach educational professionals. In January 1994, an article in the *Chronicle of Higher Education* pointed up the huge "education gap" that exists between the effects of television violence that have been conclusively documented by psychological and medical researchers and what the general public knows. According to the article, "Until recently, researchers' voices have been drowned out in the din of denial and disinformation coming from executives of the television and movie industries, whose self-serving defense of violent programming has prevailed" (Slaby 1994).

TV industry spokespersons argue that violent programs are a mere reflection of the society, and that any effort to modify programming would interfere with First Amendment guarantees of freedom of the press. Others claim to be giving the public "what they want" and take no responsibility for the effects on viewers. Another response from the networks is that parents or families must take the responsibility for preventing viewing of violent programs. In none of these defenses are the networks willing to recognize research information that shows that an appetite for violence has been stimulated by the glorification of violence and a daily diet of violent programs broadcast into every home in America.

History and Social Science Content
The issue of the influence of electronic media on the American life-style is of direct concern to social studies (Hepburn 1990). The curriculum must include study of the influence of the media. Students should be aware of how persistent viewing of violent acts and violent language and music can motivate violent behavior. A number of suggestions for media-related student activities accompany this article.

Although readings about the influence of media are hard to find in school textbooks, at last, magazines, newspapers, public television, and CNN have begun to examine the role of the mass media in the decline of civility and the loss of community. Commercial television networks have been compared with individuals who seek only their own profit, lack respect for others, and feel no sense of public trust. Are these fair conclusions? Social studies can pick up the debate.

Could a media-literate public demand and get better news presentation and more depth in the discussion of alternative social and economic policies? Is there a parallel between the decades in which the public lacked information about the lethal effects of cigarette smoking and the two decades in which the public has been unaware of the effects of heavy doses of television violence on youngsters? Can the reduction of violence in mass media be accomplished by means of increased citizen knowledge and action? Are First Amendment rights of the broadcast industry threatened by public pressures? Will television and radio respond to public discourse and a changed perception of the public market? These are social studies issues of interest to students.

From many passive hours in front of television, what life roles are instilled in viewers, especially more impressionable young viewers? From TV and radio, what values and visions of family life, leadership, friendship, personal relationships, heroism, and public responsibility are absorbed from the images and voices they see and hear? A discussion of role models, of both the norms and realities, can greatly stimulate the awareness and interest of young citizens. This is the stuff of social studies.

Sources
Belson, W. A. *Television Violence and the Adolescent Boy*. Westmead, England: Saxon House, 1978.

Bowen, Wally. "Media Violence." *Education Week* (March 16, 1994): 60ff.

Centerwall, B. S. "Exposure to Television as a Cause of Violence." In *Public Communication and Behavior*. volume 2, edited by G. Comstock. San Diego: Academic Press, 1989.

——. "Television and Violent Crime." *The Public Interest* 3 (1993): 56–71.

Gamson, W. A., D. Croteau, W. Hoynes, and T. Sasson. "Media Images and the Social Construction of Reality." *Annual Review of Sociology* 18 (1992): 373–393.

Hepburn, M. A. "Americans Glued to the Tube: Mass Media, Information, and Social Studies." *Social Education* 54, no. 4 (April/May 1990): 233–237.

Holroyd, H. J. "Children, Adolescents, and Television." *American Journal of Diseases in Children* 139, no. 6 (1985): 549–550.

Huesmann, L. R., and L. D. Eron. "The Development of Aggression in American Children as a Consequence of Television Violence Viewing." In *Television and the Aggressive Child: A Cross-National Comparison*, edited by L. R. Huesmann and L. D. Eron. Hillsdale, New Jersey: Erlbaum Associates, 1986.

Institute for Social Research. "Televised Violence and Kids: A Public Health Problem?" *ISR Newsletter* 18 (1994): 1.

National Association of Broadcasters. *America's Watching—Public Attitudes Toward Television 1993*. New York: The Network Television Association and the National Association of Broadcasters.

Nielson Media Research. *1992–1993 Report on Television*. New York: A. C. Nielsen Co., 1993.

Postman, N. *The Disappearance of Childhood*. New York: Delacorte Press, 1982.

Roper Organization. *Public Attitudes Toward Television and Other Media in a Time of Change*. New York: Television Information Office, 1985.

Slaby, R. G. "Combating Television Violence." *The Chronicle of Higher Education* 40, no. 18 (January 5, 1994): B1–2.

Zuckerman, D. M., and B. S. Zuckerman. "Television's Impact on Children." *Pediatrics* 75, no. 2 (1985): 233–240.

The biology of soul murder

Fear can harm a child's brain. Is it reversible?

By their appearances, the three little girls sitting quietly in molded plastic chairs in the psychiatric clinic of Texas Children's Hospital in Houston betray nothing of the mayhem they have experienced. No one would know that the night before, two armed men broke into their apartment in a drug-ravaged part of the city. That the children were tied up and the youngest, only 3, was threatened with a gun. Or that the men shot the girls' teenage sister in the head before leaving (she survived).

Yet however calm the girls' appearances, their physiology tells a different story. Their hearts are still racing at more than 100 beats per minute, their blood pressure remains high and, inside their heads, the biological chemicals of fear are changing their brains. "People look at kids who seem so normal after these experiences and say, 'All they need is a little love,'" says Bruce Perry, a child psychiatrist at Children's Hospital and at Baylor College of Medicine. But as Perry and other researchers are finding, trauma, neglect, and physical and sexual abuse can have severe effects on a child's developing brain.

Tangled chemistry. Once viewed as genetically programmed, the brain is now known to be plastic, an organ molded by both genes and experience throughout life. A single traumatic experience can alter an adult's brain: A horrifying battle, for instance, may induce the flashbacks, depression and hair-trigger response of post-traumatic stress disorder (PTSD). And researchers are finding that abuse and neglect early

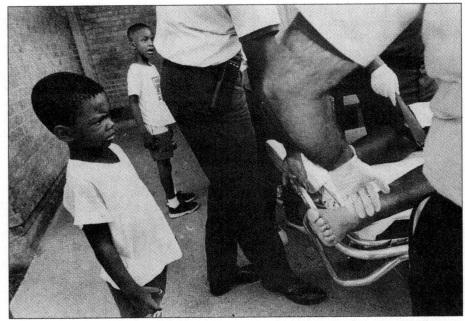

STEPHEN SHAMES—MATRIX

WORLD WITHOUT COMFORT. Living with fear puts children at high risk for problems later in life. Above, two boys watch as medics treat the victim of a gunshot in Houston.

in life can have even more devastating consequences, tangling both the chemistry and the architecture of children's brains and leaving them at risk for drug abuse, teen pregnancy and psychiatric problems later in life.

Yet the brain's plasticity also holds out the chance that positive experiences—psychotherapy, mentoring, loving relationships—might ameliorate some of the damage. Much remains unknown. But if scientists can understand exactly how trauma harms the brain, they may also learn much about healing broken lives.

Trauma's toll on a child's brain begins with fear. Faced with a threat, the body embarks on a cascade of physiological reactions. Adrenalin surges, setting the heart pounding and blood pressure soaring and readying the muscles for action, a response called "fight or flight." At the same time, a more subtle set of changes, called the stress response, releases the hormone cortisol, which also helps the body respond to danger.

Increasing evidence suggests that in abused or neglected children, this system somehow goes awry, causing a

From *U.S. News & World Report*, November 11, 1996, pp. 71-73. © 1996 by U.S. News & World Report. Reprinted by permission.

harmful imbalance of cortisol in the brain. In a study of children in Romanian orphanages, for example, Megan Gunnar, a University of Minnesota developmental psychobiologist, is finding that cognitive and developmental delays correlate with irregular cortisol levels.

Gunnar and others believe that excess cortisol leads to damage in a brain region known as the hippocampus, causing memory lapses, anxiety and an inability to control emotional outbursts. Cortisol and other brain chemicals also can alter brain centers that regulate attention, affecting a child's capacity to attend to words on the blackboard instead of a jackhammer banging outside.

Many of the brain abnormalities seen in abused and neglected children are localized in the brain's left hemisphere, where language and logical thought are processed. Martin Teicher, a psychiatrist at McLean Hospital in Belmont, Mass., compared recordings of brain electrical activity in abused and normal children. His finding: In abused kids, the left hemisphere has fewer nerve-cell connections between different areas. The electrical traces also revealed that tiny seizures, similar to those of epileptics, crackled through various sectors of abused children's brains. Children with the most abnormal recordings were the most likely to be self-destructive or aggressive.

Scanning for danger. Abused children also show a variety of other disturbances in physiology, thinking and behavior. Many have elevated resting heart rates, temperature and blood pressure. Hypervigilance is common. Abused kids continually scan their surroundings for danger and overinterpret the actions of others: An innocent playground bump may be seen as a direct threat. And as many as half of children from some violent neighborhoods show symptoms of Attention Deficit Hyperactivity Disorder (ADHD), compared with about 6 percent of the general population.

"Children who are aroused [from fear] can't take in cognitive information," says Perry. "They're too busy watching the teacher for threatening gestures, and not listening to what she's saying." Such behavior makes sense, given the constant threats in the child's world. His brain has become exquisitely tuned to emotional and physical cues from other people. At the same time, he may be failing to develop problem solving and language skills. Perry has found that in a group of neglected children, the cortex, or thinking part of the brain, is 20 percent smaller on average than in a control group.

Studies now indicate that abused and neglected children run a high risk of developing mental illnesses. Since 1987, National Institute of Mental Health child psychiatrist Frank Putnam has tracked 90 sexually abused girls, comparing them to a control group who were not abused. The abused girls were more likely to evidence depression and suicide attempts, and many showed the beginnings of PTSD, including anxiety attacks and abnormal levels of cortisol, which are also seen in combat veterans. Putnam also found a decline in the abused girls' IQ over time. Saddest of all, the abused girls are rated by their teachers as not very likable. "That's tragic," says Putnam, "because the one place where they might find some support is at school."

Indeed, for some children, a loving adult can serve as a powerful antidote to abuse and neglect. Infants and young children normally learn from a comforting caretaker how to soothe themselves, thereby regulating their stress response and cortisol levels. Researchers now believe loving relationships also can help older children reset their response to stress when it has been derailed by abuse. Says Gunnar: "We don't know when the door to the brain's plasticity closes."

Unfortunately, loving damaged children can be tough. One minute they are hostile, the next withdrawn. In class, they escape their feelings by daydreaming. When the teacher confronts them, they retreat even further. Then, says Perry, "the teacher touches the kid. When you touch them, that's incredibly threatening, and the child has a tantrum."

The growing understanding of what's going on in an abused and neglected child's brain has begun to yield new treatments. In addition to psychotherapy, Perry gives some of his young patients clonidine, a drug that helps check the fight-or-flight response. Clonidine, and other drugs that interfere with the release of cortisol, may decrease the chances a child will go on to develop PTSD. Perry also hands out devices that allow teachers and foster parents to monitor a child's heart rate from a distance, so they can refrain from making demands on him when he's frightened.

For every child who finds help at a clinic like Perry's, there are dozens who fall through the cracks. Only a fraction of the millions of children who are mistreated each year receive the kind of help that can reverse the underlying physiological changes they suffer. Ultimately, says McLean's Teicher, failing these kids may be shortsighted. They are less likely to live up to their economic potential, and more likely to wind up in prison, on drugs or in psychiatric units, he says. "The cost on society of having a child who has gone through abuse is enormous."

BY SHANNON BROWNLEE

CHILDREN AT RISK:

Fostering Resilience and Hope

Robert B. Brooks, Ph.D.

A number of children, many with ADHD and learning disabilities, are at high risk for developing long-lasting problems affecting many areas of their lives, including their social relationships, academic and later professional success, tolerance of frustration and failure, and self-esteem. Factors that contribute to resiliency in these high-risk children are examined, and implications for interventions to enhance their lives are discussed.

Many children are at risk for developing cognitive, emotional, and behavioral problems that can affect almost all areas of their lives. A number of these children have diagnoses of attention-deficit disorder (ADD) or attention-deficit hyperactivity disorder (ADHD) and, not infrequently, these diagnoses are found in association with other symptoms representing mood, anxiety, learning, or conduct disorders (Biederman, Faraone, & Lapey, 1992). Researchers and clinicians continue to refine diagnostic instruments with the goal of articulating and assessing the characteristics of these children more precisely (Herrero, Hechtman, & Weiss, 1994).

As more is learned about the disorders of childhood, there has been an increased effort to understand not only the risk factors that contribute to the emergence and maintenance of these disorders, but the protective factors that serve to fortify the resources of children and help them to become more resilient (Beardslee, 1989; Beardslee & Podorefsky, 1988; Katz, 1994; Luthar & Zigler, 1991; Masten, Best, & Garmezy, 1990; Rutter, 1985, 1987; Werner,

1993; Werner & Smith, 1992). This article will examine several important factors that provide the nutriments for children to overcome adversity and will describe interventions that are guided by an appreciation of these factors.

DOMAINS OF RESILIENCE

Hechtman (1991), in reviewing the findings of researchers, noted that three interrelated domains influence the presence of resilience, namely, the child, the family, and the larger social environment.

Internal Resources

Temperament. Grizenko and Pawliuk (1994) have observed that having a happy temperament as an infant serves as a protective factor. Resilient children have often been found to have easy temperaments from birth, eliciting more positive responses from their caregivers; in addition, they appear to have higher intelligence, and more advanced problem-solving skills, cognitive-integrative abilities, social skills, and coping strategies (Hechtman, 1991; Mantzicopoulos & Morrison, 1994; Werner, 1993). In contrast, children with so-called "difficult" temperaments typically prompt more

This paper was invited by the Editor for inclusion in this special section. Author is at McLean Hospital and Harvard Medical School, Belmont, Mass.

angry and less empathic responses from care-givers, so that a negative cycle is triggered.

Self-esteem. Most importantly, resilient children appear to maintain a high level of self-esteem, a realistic sense of personal control, and a feeling of hope. In describing the significance of self-esteem as part of the foundation for resilience, Rutter (1985) noted that

> ...a sense of self-esteem and self-efficacy makes successful coping more likely while a sense of helplessness increases the likelihood that one adversity will lead to another. (p. 603)

Similarly, Werner (1993) wrote that

> ...the central component in the lives of the resilient individuals...that contributed to their effective coping in adulthood appeared to be a feeling of confidence that the odds can be surmounted. (p. 512)

Rutter and Werner's observations raise questions about the kinds of interventions that might be used to foster a child's self-esteem and hopefulness.

Family Climate

Not unexpectedly, resilient children are more likely to come from home environments characterized by warmth, affection, emotional support, and clear-cut and reasonable structure and limits (Rutter, 1985; Werner, 1993). If parents are not able to provide this kind of positive climate, the presence of other family members can serve this function. Homes riddled with family discord, hostility, and a lack of warmth and understanding are less likely to produce resilient children.

Social Environment

Grandparents, other extended family members, friends, and community groups and agencies can provide support that is absent in the home (Grizenko & Pawliuk, 1994; Herrenkohl, Herrenkohl, & Egolf, 1994; Katz, 1994; Rutter, 1987; Werner, 1993). Werner (1993) observed that

> ...most of all, self-esteem and self-efficacy were promoted through supportive relationships. The resilient youngsters in our study all had at least one person in their lives who accepted them unconditionally, regardless of temperamental idiosyncrasies, physical attractiveness, or intelligence. (p. 512)

Similarly, when young adults with ADHD were asked what they believed was most helpful to them as they were growing up, the most frequent reply was that there was someone—a parent, teacher, or other significant adult—who believed in them (Weiss & Hechtman, 1993).

Schools have been highlighted as institutions that can offer children experiences that enhance their self-esteem and competence, thereby reinforcing resilience (Brooks, 1991, 1992; Curwin, 1992; Rutter, 1980, 1985; Zunz, Turner, & Norman, 1993). Rutter (1985) noted that

> ...the long-term educational benefits from positive school experiences probably stem less from what children are specifically taught than from effects on children's attitude to learning, on their self-esteem, and on their task orientation and work strategies. (p. 607)

Segal (1988), in describing resilient children, has written:

> From studies conducted around the world, researchers have distilled a number of factors that enable such children of misfortune to beat the heavy odds against them. One factor turns out to be the presence in their lives of a charismatic adult—a person with whom they identify and from whom they gather strength. And in a surprising number of cases, that person turns out to be a teacher. (p. 2)

A Massachusetts Department of Education (1988) report about at-risk students also captured the significant role an educator can play:

> Possibly the most critical element to success within school is a student developing a close and nurturing relationship with at least one caring adult. Students need to feel that there is someone within school whom they know, to whom they can turn, and who will act as an advocate for them. (p. 17)

It is obvious that many factors residing within the child, in the family, and in the larger social environment interact in an ongoing and dynamic way to determine whether early vulnerabilities give way to a life of productivity, success, and happiness—a life truly characterized as resilient—or whether these vulnerabilities intensify, resulting in a life punctured with disappointment, despair, envy, underachievement, and ongoing failure. As these factors are articulated more precisely, increasingly effective programs can be developed and implemented for harnessing the unique strengths of individual children.

SELF-ESTEEM

As noted, most researchers and clinicians have emphasized self-esteem as a key variable in determining resilience. Given its apparent prominence, it may be fruitful to examine the concept of self-esteem more closely and then to describe strategies that have proved useful in fostering a child's self-esteem and, thus, resilience.

Definition

Self-esteem has been defined in various ways (Branden, 1971; Brooks, 1991; Coopersmith, 1975; Evans, Noam, Wertlieb, Paget, & Wolf, 1994; Harter, 1990). The California Task Force to Promote Self-Esteem and Personal and Social Responsibility (1990) developed a definition that, while somewhat broad, captures several key aspects of self-esteem:

> Appreciating my own worth and importance and having the character to be accountable for myself and to act responsibly toward others. (p. 1)

This definition thus proposes that a fundamental ingredient of self-esteem involves respect and caring for others.

Self-esteem may be understood as including the feelings and thoughts that individuals have about their competence and worth, about their abilities to make a difference, to confront rather than retreat from challenges, to learn from both success and failure, and to treat themselves and others with respect. Self-esteem guides and motivates actions and the outcome of the actions in turn affects self-esteem, so that a dynamic, reciprocal process is continuously in force (Brooks, 1992).

Low Self-Esteem

The signs of low self-esteem vary considerably from one child to the next and even from one situation to the next. Children may display low self-esteem in situations in which they do not feel successful but not in those situations in which they feel more competent. For instance, children with ADD or learning disabilities may feel "dumb" in the classroom, but may engage in particular sports or a Nintendo game with self-assurance. For some children, a sense of low self-esteem is perva-

sive, so that there are few situations in which it is not evident; such children are often labeled "at risk."

Some children leave little doubt of their low self-esteem, conveying messages of despair and of lack of confidence and hope such as, "I'm stupid," "I always do things wrong," "I'm so ugly," "I was born with half a brain." Other children are not so direct and their level of self-esteem is to be inferred from their coping strategies for stress and pressure (Brooks, 1992).

While children with high self-esteem display adaptive strategies that promote growth (e.g., requesting help with reading difficulties and spending more time learning this skill), children with low self-esteem frequently rely on coping behavior that is counterproductive and actually intensifies difficulties. Such behavior as quitting, avoiding, cheating, clowning, bullying, denying, or making excuses often signals that a child is feeling vulnerable and is attempting to escape from challenging situations he or she believes will lead to failure. All children show self-defeating behavior at times, but its regular appearance strongly suggests low self-esteem.

Identification of Variables

Recognition of the importance of self-esteem in a child's development and capacity for resilience has stimulated efforts to identify the main variables associated with self-esteem with a view to designing interventions likely to reinforce a child's sense of competence and self-worth.

Attribution theory. Initially proposed by Weiner (1974) and applied by many clinicians and researchers (Canino, 1981; Licht, 1983), attribution theory is a promising approach in that it provides a framework within which variables associated with self-esteem may be located. It examines the reasons that people offer for their success or failure in a task or situation, and their explanations have been found to be directly linked to their self-esteem.

So far as successes are concerned, children with high self-esteem apparently perceive them as predicated in large part on their own efforts, resources, and abilities. These children assume realistic ownership for their achievements and possess a sense of personal control over what is transpiring in their lives. In contrast, children who are not resilient, who do not easily bounce back, often believe that their successes are a result of luck or chance, that is, factors outside their control. Not surprisingly, such a self-perception lessens confidence of success in the future.

In terms of mistakes and failure, children with high self-esteem typically believe that mistakes are experiences from which to learn rather than occasions of defeat. They attribute mistakes to factors that can be changed, such as a lack of adequate effort or an unrealistic goal. Children with low self-esteem, on the other hand, are prone to believe that they cannot correct the situation. They believe that mistakes are a consequence of factors that are not modifiable, such as a lack of ability or intelligence, and this belief breeds a feeling of helplessness and hopelessness. Future success becomes less likely because these children expect to fail and, in response, they retreat from age-expected demands, resorting to self-defeating coping strategies that exacerbate their situation.

Attribution theory holds important implications for interventions to foster self-esteem in at-risk children. It provides a blueprint for the following questions:

1. How to create an environment at home and school that reinforces the probability that a child will be successful and will experience that success as largely due to his or her own abilities and efforts. This entails empowering children, and reinforcing their sense of personal control to increase their sense of ownership and responsibility for their own lives. The importance of personal control and empowerment as the basic scaffolding for self-esteem, motivation, and resilience has been emphasized by a number of clinicians and researchers (*Adelman & Taylor, 1983; Brendtro, Brokenleg, & Van Bockern, 1990; Curwin & Mendler, 1988; Deci & Chandler, 1986; Glasser, 1984*).

2. How to create an environment that reinforces a child's belief that mistakes and failure are not only acceptable, but also to be expected, and are best seen as ways of learning. In particular, can at-risk children, many of whom feel defeated by years of frustration and failure, be convinced that their failures can lead to success?

FOSTERING RESILIENCE

Strategies predicated on the basic tenets of attribution theory or similar frameworks can be applied in every domain of a child's life.

Obviously, the specific form of the intervention should be guided by knowledge of the child's temperament, interests, strengths, vulnerabilities, cognitive skills, and types of coping behavior. Interventions that do not take a child's unique qualities into account will be less effective.

Too often the same approach is used for all children and those who do not fit that approach are likely to fail. For example, hyperactive children typically require more physical activity in their school programs than do children who are less active. As Mantzicopoulos (*1994*) noted,

> . . . children with characteristics similar to those of the [at-risk] group are more likely to profit from programs that emphasize developmentally appropriate, child-centered instructional practices that build on children's strengths and interests. . . . These practices also tend to build an intrinsic interest in learning . . . and are associated with fewer behavior problems and a more positive overall school adjustment. (*p. 532*)

Adult Attitudes

The impact that a single adult can have on the life of a child should never be underestimated, and care must be taken not to increase the child's burden. For successful intervention with at-risk children, the adults involved must convey their own optimism and caring about the children. In such an atmosphere, the children may come to believe, regardless of the hardships they have experienced, that they can replace self-defeating coping behavior with behavior that promotes growth. Empathy with these children is essential to understanding of how they experience communications from the adults in their lives (*Brooks, 1991*).

For example, far too many children with ADHD still receive report cards with such comments as, "If only you tried harder and put in more of an effort you would do better" or "If you paid attention more consistently you would succeed more often." They hear similar exhortations from parents. Many of these children experience such remarks as accusations that serve only to heighten their defensiveness, frustration, and anger. Until reliable instruments are developed for its measurement, it may be best not to impugn a child's lack of effort, remembering that an apparent lack of effort may signal a feeling of hopelessness. It is far more effective to say to children with ADHD, "I think you're trying, but I think the problem may be that the strategies you're using to learn or the strategies the teachers are using to teach you are not the best strategies." At the very least, such a comment will not immediately raise the child's defensive hackles; often it can lead a child to ask what exactly a "strategy" is, prompting further discussion about developing and using more effective techniques for learning.

Areas of Competence

Because of their low self-esteem, many at-risk children seem to find themselves drowning in an ocean of inadequacy. However, every child has "islands of competence," areas that are (or could be) sources of pride and accomplishment. As part of the intervention strategy, parents, teachers, and other significant adults in the child's life can identify and reinforce these islands of competence; doing so may create a ripple effect, motivating the child to venture forth and confront the tasks that have been difficult.

Rutter *(1985),* too, in discussing resilient individuals, noted that:

> . . . experience of success in one arena of life led to enhanced self-esteem and a feeling of self-efficacy, enabling them to cope more successfully with the subsequent life challenges and adaptations. *(p. 604)*

According to Katz *(1994):*

> . . . being able to showcase our talents, and to have them valued by important people in our lives, helps us define our identities around that which we do best. *(p. 10)*

Werner *(1993),* studying a high-risk group of children, observed:

> . . . most of the resilient children . . . were not unusually talented, but they took great pleasure in hobbies that brought them solace when things fell apart in their homes. *(p. 511)*

Similarly, Grizenko and Pawliuk *(1994)* commented that

> . . . after-school programs can be utilized to encourage outside activities, build friendships, and develop hobbies, all of which may serve as an escape from stressful home situations, and provide the child with experiences of success or mastery. *(p. 541)*

INTERVENTION STRATEGIES

Guided by attribution theory, a number of interventions can make initial use of a child's islands of competence to build a solid foundation from which to move to the less secure territories of the child's life. Several are described below. A more detailed description of these, and others, is available elsewhere *(Brooks, 1991).*

Encouraging Contributions

If children are to develop a sense of ownership and pride, it is essential to provide them with ample opportunities for assuming responsibilities, especially those that help them to feel they are making a contribution to their home, school, or community environments *(Brooks, 1988, 1990).*

Making a contribution to the school milieu gives children a more positive attachment to school and more motivation to learn, an especially important tactic for students with ADHD or learning disabilities *(Brooks, 1991; Rutter, 1980; Werner, 1993).* The experience of making a positive difference in the lives of others builds self-respect and hopefulness and serves as a powerful antidote to feelings of defeat and despair. The following vignettes illustrate ways of encouraging contributions from at-risk children:

> An elementary school child, who had no use for school and whose self-perceived island of competence was taking care of his pet dog, was enlisted as the "pet monitor" of the school. The position involved taking care of various pets in the school, writing a brief manual about pet care that was eventually bound and placed in the school library, and speaking to all the classes about the care of pets. Until the manual was proposed, this boy had disliked writing, but with the encouragement and assistance of his teacher he wrote the manual because he believed he had a message of value to offer.

> A sixth-grade girl with low self-esteem, who enjoyed interacting with younger children, was enlisted to tutor first and second graders in school and to be a babysitter in her neighborhood. The tutoring, besides directly enhancing her self-esteem, increased her motivation to learn, which also added to her self-esteem.

These kinds of "contributory activities" provide concrete proof to at-risk children that they can be successful, that they are capable, and that they can earn respect. As Werner (1993) has written:

> Self-esteem and self-efficacy also grew when youngsters took on a responsible position commensurate with their ability, whether it was part-time paid work, managing the household when a parent was incapacitated, or, most often, caring for younger siblings. At some point in their young lives, usually in middle childhood and adolescence, the youngsters who grew into resilient adults were required to carry out some socially desirable task to prevent others in their family, neighborhood, or community from experiencing distress or discomfort. *(p. 511)*

Enhancing Decision-Making Skills

An essential ingredient of high self-esteem is the belief that one has some control over what is occurring in one's life. To acquire this attitude, children need opportunities to learn the skills necessary for making sound choices and decisions and for solving problems. They also need opportunities to apply and refine these skills, especially in situations that have an impact on their lives *(Adelman & Taylor, 1983; Deci & Chandler, 1986; Deci, Hodges, Pierson, & Tomassone, 1992; Kohn, 1993; Spivack & Shure, 1982)*. Rutter *(1985)* has described some of these skills under the rubric of "planning," highlighting the importance of social problem-solving techniques in reinforcing resilience.

How decision-making and problem-solving skills may be taught can be seen in the following examples:

> A group of students was engaged in conducting research about existing charities. They used their findings to decide the most effective ways of raising money and to choose which charity to support.

> Parents of a fussy eater permitted the child to choose the food for the family dinner once each month; eventually the child helped prepare the dinner.

> A junior-high-school girl, who often engaged in struggles with her parents about her bedtime, was permitted to select one evening each week when she could stay up 30 minutes later than usual.

These kinds of activities help children to feel in control and, in the process, they increase the children's sense of ownership and empowerment—important ingredients in strengthening resilience.

Encouragement and Positive Feedback

Self-esteem and resilience are nurtured when caregivers communicate realistic appreciation and encouragement to children. This kind of communication is often absent, however, because too great a focus is placed on negative behavior. Words and actions that help children to feel genuinely special in a positive way are energizing and demonstrate the existence of people who accept and believe in them.

Even a small gesture of appreciation can have a life-long impact; for example, a brief note written by a teacher on a child's paper that acknowledges the child's efforts, a school assembly in which the achievements and contributions of all the students are recognized, or a special time (perhaps 15–30 minutes) set aside each week by a parent to spend with each child individually. The effect that special time with parents can have is shown in the following vignette:

> A five-year-old patient with a diagnosis of ADHD believed (correctly) that his father was disappointed and angry with him. During the course of treatment, the father scheduled a "private time" once a week with his son, going with him to a local donut shop for breakfast before school. This action contributed to a significant improvement in their relationship.

The emotional support and encouragement offered by significant adults in a child's life are crucial for promoting self-worth and resilience.

Developing Self-Discipline

It is difficult to conceive of children developing high self-esteem if they do not possess a comfortable sense of self-discipline—that is, a realistic ability to reason about one's behavior and its impact on others, and then change it if necessary. One of the reasons that temperamentally difficult children are so labeled is because of their problems in developing self-discipline; they are frequently described as "acting before they think." Unfortunately, although they need limits and structure, these children are quick to experience them as unfair impositions. It is often a Herculean effort to establish rules that they will not immediately reject as arbitrary.

In teaching children to develop self-discipline, it is important not to humiliate or intimidate them *(Curwin & Mendler, 1988; Mendler, 1992)*. If children are to assume responsibility for their actions and perceive rules as being fair, they must understand the purpose of the rules and contribute within reason to their formation, along with guidelines and consequences. Caregivers must maintain a delicate balance between rigidity and permissiveness, striving to blend warmth, nurturance, and acceptance with realistic expectations, clear-cut regulations, and logical and natural consequences.

When a child constantly challenges rules, the nature and appropriateness of those rules for this particular child should be examined. A child who perceives the demands as unfair may react with resentment and a reduced sense of autonomy, hence the misbehavior (Adelman & Taylor, 1990).

The following vignettes illustrate some effective uses of discipline:

> A child who had ridden his bicycle on a dangerous street that was off-limits, was forbidden by his parents to use the bike for a couple of days (an instance of the use of logical consequences).

> A teacher asked her students at the start of the school year for suggestions about classroom rules, and discussed with them why the rules were necessary and what the consequences should be for infraction (rules related to safety, of course, were not negotiable).

If they are skillfully involved, students will better understand the necessity for rules and be more motivated to follow them.

> More physical activity during the school day was scheduled for hyperactive children, thereby lessening the probability of disruptive behavior (an example of preventative discipline).

Dealing with Mistakes and Failure

For at-risk children, the fear of making mistakes and feeling embarrassed is a formidable obstacle to facing and overcoming problems and challenges. These children are often easily defeated and thus readily retreat from tasks that threaten failure and humiliation. Since self-esteem and resilience are intimately tied to children's experience of failure, children must be helped to realize that mistakes are an important ingredient in the process of learning.

To help children deal more comfortably and effectively with mistakes, adults must avoid reacting to a child's mistakes with such humiliating remarks as: "Why don't you use your brain!" or "I told you it wouldn't work!"

or "You always fail at things!" The following vignette is an example of openly acknowledging the fear of failure in order to vitiate its potency and strengthen children's courage to face new challenges:

> At the beginning of the school year, the teacher asked which of the students thought they would probably make a mistake or not understand something in class that year. Before any of the children could respond, the teacher raised his own hand. Then the teacher asked the students why they thought he had asked the question. He used their answers as the starting point for a discussion of the ways in which the fear of mistakes and embarrassment limits the freedom to offer opinions and learn.

Emphasizing what children can accomplish, rather than placing the spotlight exclusively on what they cannot do, also helps to reduce the dread of making mistakes:

> Teachers graded tests in their classes by adding points for correct answers instead of subtracting them for incorrect responses.

CONCLUSIONS

More attention must be given to defining those variables within the child, family, and larger social community that provide the means with which at-risk children can overcome adversity and lead more productive and successful lives. Support for parents, teachers, and other adults to learn effective caregiving skills is essential.

A basic feature of resilient children is that their self-esteem and sense of competence have been maintained or, if damaged, have been repaired. Resilient children feel optimism, ownership, and personal control. Such feelings are nurtured by "charismatic adults" who believe in them, and who provide experiences that reinforce the children's islands of competence and feelings of self-worth. If the goal for these children is the development of self-esteem, self-respect, self-discipline, and compassion, the adults influential in their lives must display the same qualities. If we do, all our lives will be enriched.

REFERENCES

Adelman, H., & Taylor, L. (1983). Enhancing motivation for overcoming learning and behavior problems. *Journal of Learning Disabilities, 16,* 384–392.

Adelman, H., & Taylor, L. (1990). Intrinsic motivation and school misbehavior: Some intervention implications. *Journal of Learning Disabilities, 16,* 384–392.

Beardslee, W.R. (1989). The role of self-understanding in resilient individuals: The development of a perspective. *American Journal of Orthopsychiatry, 59,* 266–278.

Beardslee, W.R., & Podorefsky, D. (1988). Resilient adolescents whose parents have serious affective and other psychiatric disorders: importance of self-understanding and relationships. *American Journal of Psychiatry, 145,* 63–69.

Biederman, J., Faraone, S.V., & Lapey, K. (1992). Comorbidity of diagnosis in attention-deficit hyperactivity disorder. *Child and Adolescent Psychiatric Clinics of North America, 1,* 335–360.

Branden, N. (1971). *The psychology of self-esteem.* New York: Bantam.

Brendtro, L.K., Brokenleg, M., & Van Bockern, S. (1990). *Reclaiming youth at risk: Our hope for the future.* Bloomington, IN: National Educational Service.

Brooks, R.B. (1988). Fostering self-esteem and caring: The taming of anger. In P. Vesin (Ed.), *Proceedings of the International Conference on Children and the Media: Channeling Children's Anger* (pp. 127–136). Paris: International Children's Center.

Brooks, R.B. (1990). Indelible memories of school: Of contributions and self-esteem. *School Field, 1,* 121–129.

Brooks, R.B. (1991). *The self-esteem teacher.* Circle Pines, MN: American Guidance Service.

Brooks, R.B. (1992). Self-esteem during the school years: Its normal development and hazardous decline. *Pediatric Clinics of North America, 39,* 537–550.

California State Department of Education. (1990). *Toward a state of esteem: The final report of the Task Force to Promote Self-Esteem and Personal and Social Responsibility.* Sacramento, CA: Author.

Canino, F.J. (1981). Learned-helplessness theory: Implications for research in learning disabilities. *Journal of Special Education, 15,* 471–484.

Coopersmith, S. (1975). *Developing motivation in young children.* San Francisco: Albion.

Curwin, R.L. (1992). *Rediscovering hope: Our greatest teaching strategy.* Bloomington, IN: National Educational Service.

Curwin, R.L., & Mendler, A.N. (1988). *Discipline with dignity.* Reston, VA: Association for Supervision and Curriculum Development.

Deci, E.L., & Chandler, C. (1986). The importance of motivation for the future of the LD field. *Journal of Learning Disabilities, 19,* 587–594.

Deci, E.L., Hodges, R., Pierson, L., & Tomassone, J. (1992). Autonomy and competence as motivational factors in students with learning disabilities and emotional handicaps. *Journal of Learning Disabilities, 25,* 457–471.

Evans, D.W., Noam, G., Wertlieb, D., Paget, K., & Wolf, M. (1994). Self-perception and adolescent psychopathology: A clinical-developmental perspective. *American Journal of Orthopsychiatry, 64,* 293–300.

Glasser, W. (1984). *Control theory: A new explanation of how we control our lives.* New York: Harper & Row.

Grizenko, N., & Pawliuk, N. (1994). Risk and protective factors for disruptive behavior disorders in children. *American Journal of Orthopsychiatry, 64,* 534–544.

Harter, S. (1990). Developmental differences in the nature of self-representations: Implications for the understanding, assessment and treatment of maladaptive behavior. *Cognitive Therapy and Research, 14,* 113–142.

Hechtman, L. (1991). Resilience and vulnerability in long term outcome of attention deficit hyperactivity disorder. *Canadian Journal of Psychiatry, 36,* 415–421.

Herrenkohl, E.C., Herrenkohl, R.C., & Egolf, B. (1994). Resilient early school-age children from maltreating homes: Outcomes in late adolescence. *American Journal of Orthopsychiatry, 64,* 301–309.

Herrero, M.E., Hechtman, L., & Weiss, G. (1994). Antisocial disorders in hyperactive subjects from childhood to adulthood: Predictive factors and characterization of subgroups. *American Journal of Orthopsychiatry, 64,* 510–521.

Katz, M. (1994, May). From challenged childhood to achieving adulthood: Studies in resilience. *Chadder,* pp. 8–11.

Kohn, A. (1993). Choices for children: Why and how to let students decide. *Phi Delta Kappan, 75,* 8–20.

Licht, B.G. (1983). Cognitive-motivational factors that contribute to the achievement of learning-disabled children. *Journal of Learning Disabilities, 16,* 483–490.

Luthar, S.S., & Zigler, E. (1991). Vulnerability and competence: A review of research on resilience in childhood. *American Journal of Orthopsychiatry, 61,* 6–22.

Mantzicopoulos, P.Y., & Morrison, D. (1994). A comparison of boys and girls with attention problems: Kindergarten through second grade. *American Journal of Orthopsychiatry, 64,* 522–533.

Massachusetts Department of Education, Office of Student Services. (1988). *Systemic school change: A comprehensive approach to dropout prevention.* Boston: Author.

Masten, A.S., Best, K.M., & Garmezy, N. (1990). Resilience and development: Contributions from the study of children who overcome adversity. *Development and Psychopathology, 2,* 425–444.

Mendler, A.N. (1992). *What do I do when...? How to achieve discipline with dignity in the classroom.* Bloomington, IN: National Educational Service.

Rutter, M. (1980). School influences on children's behavior and development. *Pediatrics, 65,* 208–220.

Rutter, M. (1985). Resilience in the face of adversity: Protective factors and resistance to psychiatric disorder. *British Journal of Psychiatry, 147,* 598–611.

Rutter, M. (1987). Psychosocial resilience and protective mechanisms. *American Journal of Orthopsychiatry, 57,* 316–331.

Segal, J. (1988). Teachers have enormous power in affecting a child's self-esteem. *Brown University Child Behavior and Development Newsletter, 4,* 1–3.

Spivack, G., & Shure, M.B. (1982). Interpersonal cognitive problem-solving and clinical theory. In B. Lahey & A.E. Kazdin (Eds.), *Advances in child clinical psychology* (Vol. 5, pp. 323–372). New York: Plenum.

Weiner, B. (1974). *Achievement motivation and attribution theory.* Morristown, NJ: General Learning Press.

Weiss, G., & Hechtman, L.T. (1993). *Hyperactive children grown up: ADHD in children, adolescents, and adults.* New York: Guilford Press.

Werner, E.E. (1993). Risk, resilience, and recovery: Perspectives from the Kauai Longitudinal Study. *Development and Psychopathology, 5,* 503–515.

Werner, E.E., & Smith, R.S. (1992). *Overcoming the odds: High risk children from birth to adulthood.* Ithaca, NY: Cornell University Press.

Zunz, S.J., Turner, S., & Norman, E. (1993). Accentuating the positive: Stressing resiliency in school-based substance abuse prevention programs. *Social Work in Education, 15,* 169–176.

For reprints: Robert B. Brooks, Ph.D., Department of Psychology, McLean Hospital, 115 Mill Street, Belmont, MA 02178

Development during Adolescence and Young Adulthood

Adolescence (Articles 30–34)
Young Adulthood (Articles 35–38)

The amount of time people spend in the limbo between childhood and adulthood is collectively known as adolescence. This term was coined in 1904 by G. Stanley Hall, one of the world's first psychologists. He saw adolescence as a discrete stage of life bridging the gap between sexual maturity (puberty) and socioemotional and cognitive maturity. At the turn of the twentieth century, it was typical for young men to begin working in middle childhood (there were no child labor laws) and for young women to become wives and mothers as soon as they were fertile and/or spoken for. The beginning of adolescence today is often marked by the desire to be independent of parental control as much as by the beginning of sexual maturation. The end of adolescence, which at the turn of the century coincided with the age of legal maturity (usually 16 or 18 depending on local laws), has now been extended upwards. Although legal maturity is now usually age 18 (voting, enlisting in the armed services, owning property, marrying without permission are all possible), the social norm is to consider persons in their late teens as adolescents, not as adults. Even college students, or students in post-degree programs (e.g., graduate schools, medical schools, law schools), are usually not considered "mature" until they have reached their final or desired educational attainments. "Maturity" is usually reserved for those who have achieved full independence as adults.

The first article in the adolescence section speaks about the phenomena of extending the period of limbo between childhood and adulthood through the early twenties or beyond. Cynthia Crossen reviews the milestones of the history of adolescence with a pictorial time line. She presents reasons for the lengthening of time it takes to "grow up" in a technologically complicated and affluent society. She quotes several experts on adolescent psychology with their explanations for the behavioral changes seen in the youth of the 1990s.

As adolescence has been extended, so too has young adulthood. One hundred years ago, life expectancy did not extend too far beyond menopause for women and retirement for men. Chronic and/or debilitating illnesses made people in their sixties feel old. Today life expectancy

has been extended into the mid-seventies, and it is not unusual for persons to live for 100 years. Improved health care, diet, exercise, and a safer food and water supply have allowed persons in their sixties and seventies to enjoy vigorous good health. One hundred years ago, young adulthood ended when children reached puberty. Parents of teenagers were middle-aged between 35 and 55. With the passage of the Social Security Act in 1935, the end of middle age and the beginning of old age was redefined as age 65. Today retirement is usually postponed until age 70, which has again redefined the line between middle age and old age. Later marriages and delayed childbearing have, concurrently, redefined the line between young adulthood and middle age. Many people today do not appreciate or agree to the label "middle-aged" until they are closer to 50.

Adolescence, by anyone's description, is a time of accelerated growth and change. A child becomes an adult through a series of profound physical changes, including becoming capable of sexual reproduction. Accompanying the physical and physiological alterations in the child's body are stupendous changes in emotions, in cognitions, and in a desire for social freedoms.

The second article included in this section is an excellent description of some of the repercussions of the transformation from child to adult. Virginia Rutter asks and answers the question "Whose Hell Is It?" She provides several quotes from teenagers about their worries: parents, school, peers, guns, gangs, drugs, AIDS. She discusses, in turn, parents' worries: adolescents, jobs, peers, guns, gangs, drugs, AIDS. She advises parents to continue parenting through these turbulent years.

The third article in the adolescent section deals with emotionally sensitive young people who are prone to internalizing their problems (depression) and/or externalizing them (violence). Many youth with extreme emotional sensitivity are highly creative. They may also be difficult to live with and difficult to teach. The authors of this article describe how to recognize emotional sensitivity, what causes it, and what concerns and gifts are common to this diverse group of adolescents. They give suggestions

UNIT 5

for parenting, teaching, and counseling emotionally sensitive youth.

The fourth article in the adolescence section looks at cross-cultural views of adolescent behaviors. The behaviors most frequently associated with a "bad kid" were lack of self-control (American), acts against society (Chinese), and disruptions of interpersonal harmony (Japanese). Do these responses reflect different cultural values? What do they mean for a world with increased multicultural interactions?

The last article in this section is an essay by an HIV-infected youth. It will have an emotional impact on all readers. It deals with many topics: child abuse, rape, drug abuse, and AIDS. It depicts a slice of the all-too-real life of one adolescent turned young adult. The author pleads for support and health care for persons like himself.

Erik Erikson, the personal/social personality theorist, marked the passage from adolescence to young adulthood by a change in the nuclear conflicts of the two life stages. Adolescents struggle to answer the question "Who am I?" Young adults struggle to answer questions about their commitments to partnerships and intimate relationships. They struggle to find a place within the existing social order where they can feel propinquity rather than isolation. In the 1960s, Erikson wrote that some females resolve both their conflicts of identity and intimacy by living vicariously through their husbands. He did not comment, however, on whether or not some males resolve

their conflicts of identity and intimacy by living vicariously through their wives. He felt that true intimacy was difficult to achieve if the person seeking it had not first become a trusting, autonomous, self-initiating, industrious, and self-knowledgeable human being. Role confusion and isolation were what Erikson predicted for adolescents and young adults who remain immature.

The first article in the young adult section of this unit deals with the problems inherent in developing a mature, self-identified, intimate orientation toward life in the 1990s. The author discusses what he calls "psychotrends" (e.g., greater sexual equality, a new masculinity, diversity of sexual expression, a more forgiving religious attitude, expanding sexual entertainment) and the impact that these trends are having on relationships. He also scrutinizes divorce rates, cohabitation, single-parenting, childless families, interracial families, same-sex families, and multiadult households as trends that are affecting the way young adults resolve their crisis of intimacy versus isolation.

The second article about young adulthood asks "Who Stole Fertility?" It considers the impact of reproductive technology on the lives of young couples.

The next selection addresses the possible biological correlates of drug addiction. Many young people experiment with drugs. Only a small percentage of experimenters become addicted. Addiction has long-lasting repercussions on the attainment of maturity. Drug use tends to keep a person in an immature holding pattern, unable to proceed to self-identity, intimacy, and procreating. J. Madeleine Nash reviews research that suggests that the neurotransmitter dopamine may be involved in addiction. If this hypothesis is correct, treatment for drug dependence will change dramatically.

The last selection included in this section addresses the issue of spousal abuse. The author recounts the experience of a professional women who has been on the receiving end of a fist. The manuscript communicates not only why abused persons stay in abusive relationships but also takes notice of what legal and societal changes are necessary to protect victims and reduce domestic violence.

Looking Ahead: Challenge Questions

Why is adolescence going on and on and on?
Why is adolescence difficult for both parents and kids?
How can adults help emotionally sensitive adolescents?
Describe some cultural differences in what is considered "bad" behavior?
What can we offer adolescents who are HIV-positive?
Where are psychotrends taking young adults?
Who stole fertility?
Why do people get hooked on drugs?
What can be done to reduce spousal abuse?

Growing Up Goes On and On and On

By CYNTHIA CROSSEN

Staff Reporter of THE WALL STREET JOURNAL

THERE'S GOOD NEWS and bad news about adolescence, and it's the same: The amount of time Americans spend in limbo between childhood and adulthood is the longest it has ever been—and getting longer.

On the early side, puberty, the physical changes that kick off adolescence, now begins for girls a good two years earlier than it did in the early part of this century. That means the precursors of puberty, the secondary sex characteristics, now appear in girls as young as eight or nine. At the late end, the age of separating from parents—the last and most important task of adolescence—has steadily risen from 16 to 18 to 21 and now often well beyond.

"Alligators drop their eggs, the egg is ready to roll," says David Murray, an anthropologist by training and now director of a statistical research center in Washington, D.C. "We hold on to youth more than any other species."

If you think of adolescents as hormones with feet, as some do, this is troubling news. The baby boom's children are marching toward their teen years; when they arrive, there will be more teenagers than in two decades. Adolescence means drugs, violence and unwed pregnancies, not to mention bad haircuts, big clothes, loud music and pierced everything. Surges of hormones make adolescents emotionally unsteady, and creating their own identities is a mandate to annoy adults, especially their parents. "I think some adults are scared because the bad teenagers are getting 'badder,'" says 14-year-old Sylvia Indyk of Fairway, Kan. Indeed, some experts believe the fact that guns have replaced fists and knives as the weapon of choice among some teens is the single most significant change in adolescence today.

But today's powerful adolescent culture adds zest to a society that is otherwise getting creakier. With the extraordinary increase in life expectancy in this century, every stage of life is longer, and the baby boom will soon begin a very long old age. "Adolescents are delightfully fun, creative and unconstrained people," says Susan Mackey, a clinical psychologist at the Family Institute at Northwestern University. "There's nothing funnier than their sense of humor. They can laugh hysterically for a half hour over one phrase."

Fortunately, youth isn't always wasted on the young. "I enjoy being a teenager," says 16-year-old Jeannie Gardiner of Dayville, Conn. "I get to hang out with my friends, and I don't have to think about major expenses and bills, like house payments and children."

That does sound like a good deal. Which is why a long adolescence is a luxury enjoyed only by societies with money and leisure. In the earliest cultures, where boys and girls could do most adult tasks by their early teens, adolescence was a brief rite of passage: A boy would go away for a few weeks and return a man; girls simply found a mate and began bearing children. Even in early, rural America, few farm families could afford to give their children much in the way of adolescence. In 1879, Henry Ford left his family's farm at the age of 15 to start apprenticing in Detroit machine shops.

In fact, it wasn't until 1904 that adolescence became a recognized and discrete stage of life, instead of simply a brief transition between child and adult. That year G. Stanley Hall, a psychologist and the president of Clark University, declared that youths' minds were too tender to be exposed to the real world's severity—the so-called early ripe, early rot philosophy. Many scholars note the coincidence between Dr. Hall's widely accepted theories and the fact that the industrial economy couldn't absorb as many workers as the rural economy.

The problem of warehousing these able-bodied but impressionable young people was solved by state laws making education compulsory to the age of 16 or 17. In 1900, only 11% of America's high-school age youth were in high school. Today, that figure is over 90%. Some people believe high schools exacerbate the problems of adolescents, confining them to an overcharged world where they are permitted to do far less than they could.

"We now so believe teenagers are . . . irresponsible, incapable, can't be trusted, can't be left alone that trying to think about what they might do that's productive is really hard," says Nancy Lesko, an associate professor of education at Indiana University.

That's exactly how many teenagers feel. "I feel like I'm mature enough to have more privileges," says Tara Conte, 15, of Haverhill, Mass. Such as? "Like being able to work part time and drive, but I have to wait until the law says I can do these things. And I think I'm mature enough to make most decisions on my own, but my parents have a difference of opinion."

Others say with the world becoming more technological and complicated, it takes longer to train children for adult responsibilities. "The age at which you are truly established and can support yourself keeps lengthening," says Joseph P. Allen, associate professor of clinical and development psychology at the University of Virginia. "I have graduate students who are in their late 20s and are still a ways away from being able to support themselves." Bob Enright, a professor at the University of Wisconsin with a specialty in adolescent psychology, agrees that "part of the reason we have adolescence is to educate people for an increasingly complex society." But, he adds, "there's also only so much room in a work force that is being downsized."

For many people, the lengthening of adolescence today is less worrisome than the fact that it is starting so early for girls. Earlier menstruation is associated with heavier body weight, so girls may not only be sexual before their minds and hearts are ready, but also out of step with the culture of leanness. Meanwhile, puberty is accelerating the growth process at a time when most of the boys are still shrimps. "For a boy, getting taller and larger is good," says Joan Jacobs Brumberg, a historian and author of the forthcoming "The Body Project: An Intimate History of American Girls." "For girls, it's problematic."

Psychologists who work with teenagers say there is no question that girls are

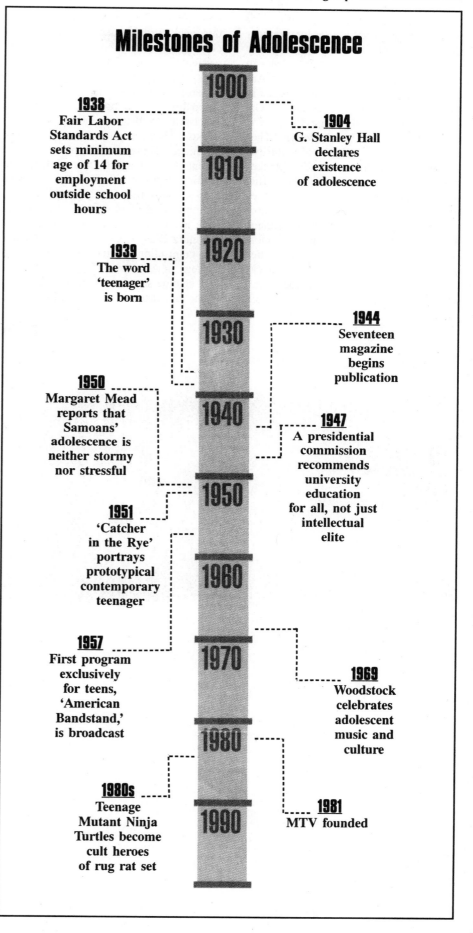

Milestones of Adolescence

1900

1904 G. Stanley Hall declares existence of adolescence

1910

1938 Fair Labor Standards Act sets minimum age of 14 for employment outside school hours

1920

1939 The word 'teenager' is born

1930

1944 Seventeen magazine begins publication

1950 Margaret Mead reports that Samoans' adolescence is neither stormy nor stressful

1940

1947 A presidential commission recommends university education for all, not just intellectual elite

1950

1951 'Catcher in the Rye' portrays prototypical contemporary teenager

1960

1957 First program exclusively for teens, 'American Bandstand,' is broadcast

1970

1969 Woodstock celebrates adolescent music and culture

1980

1980s Teenage Mutant Ninja Turtles become cult heroes of rug rat set

1981 MTV founded

1990

having sex earlier, usually with older males. "Kids have sex a lot younger than they used to, and they're really very young to be doing something that can have the consequences it has," says Anthony E. Wolf, a clinical psychologist in Longmeadow, Mass., and author of "Get Out of My Life, But First Could You Drive Me and Cheryl to the Mall?" "They just don't have the emotional maturity."

The Family Institute's Dr. Mackey cites research showing that the earlier girls hit puberty, the more likely they are to have poor body images, more problems in school, more depression and more drug use; they are also more likely to become sexually active earlier.

Furthermore, early development can exact a psychological price from a girl at home, where some parents back off, both physically and emotionally, from this new sexual person living in such close quarters. Psychologists say this is particularly true of fathers and daughters. "We can maintain the fiction of nonerotic children, but when girls develop breasts and boys get facial hair, we can't do that anymore," says Dr. Lesko. "They're right in our face. That's a trigger of major discomfort." When parents stop hugging their children or holding them on their laps, "the kid thinks, 'Now that I'm a sexual person, the only kind of physical contact I can have is sexual,' " says Dr. Mackey.

Linda Bips, a psychologist who runs the counseling center at Muhlenberg College in Allentown, Pa., says the biggest change she sees among adolescents is the increased intensity of their psychological problems. "In the '80s you'd see kids who had a kind of mild, everyday depression that rattled them; it was supportive therapy," she says. "Today they don't get out of bed. They end up eventually needing medication. I almost never used to refer out to medication. Now it's become more of a necessity."

Despite all this, many teenagers say the 1990s are a great time to be an adolescent. "We've got the Internet, the greatest thing to happen to education in a long time," says Daniel Snow, 18, of Tulsa, Okla. And they've always got their hormones. "Some days you can feel on top of the world, and on other days you feel hopeless, you wonder why you're here," says Mr. Snow. "Our emotions go to extremes, so when we have hope, we can do great things."

Adolescence

Whose Hell Is It?

The image of teenagers as menacing and rebellious is a big fiction that's boomeranging on kids. We've mythologized adolescence to conceal a startling fact: It is indeed a difficult and turbulent time—for parents. The trouble is, kids look like adults much sooner than ever before. Kids wind up feeling abandoned—and angry at the loss of their safety net. If we haven't got adolescence exactly figured out yet, there's some consolation in the fact that it's a brand-new phenomenon in human history.

Virginia Rutter

I recently spent the weekend with a friend's 13-year-old son. In contrast to the tiny tots most of my friends have, Matthew seemed much more like an adult. The time spent with him wasn't so much like baby-sitting; it was like having company. It was impressive to see how self-sufficient he was. Simple matters struck me: he didn't need someone to go to the bathroom with him at the movies; he could help himself to ice cream; he was actually interested in following the O. J. Simpson story, and we discussed it.

He was polite, thoughtful, and interesting. While the intensive caretaking necessary for smaller children has its own rewards (I suppose), Matthew's contrasting autonomy was pleasant to me. And so I imagined it would be for parents of adolescents. But then, I am not a parent. And most parents report not feeling pleasant about their adolescents.

The weekend reminded me of how easy it is to think of these youngsters as adults. Compared to an eight-year-old, an adolescent is a lot like an adult. Can't reason like an adult, but doesn't think like a child anymore, either. Some parents are tempted to

cut 'em loose rather than adjust to the new status of their teenager. Others fail to observe their adolescent's new adultlike status, and continue monitoring them as closely as a child. But it's obvious that adolescents aren't miniature adults. They are individuals on their way to adulthood; their brains and bodies—to say nothing of

---

A couple of teachers are my heroes. My history teacher is great because he listens to what everybody has to say and never judges.
—Chelsea, 14, Bakersfield, California

---

their sexuality—stretching uneasily toward maturity.

Yet the sight of kids reaching for some form of adult status commonly evokes contempt rather than curiosity. Negative feelings about teenagers have a strong grip on American culture in general, and on surprising numbers of parents in particular. It's not uncommon for parents to anticipate their child's adolescence with fear and trepidation even before they've gotten out of diapers. They expect a war at home.

"It becomes a self-fulfilling prophesy that adolescence is seen as this bizarre, otherworldly period of development, complete with a battleground set for World War III," says Tina Wagers, Psy.D., a psychologist who treats teens and their families at Kaiser Permanente Medical Center in Denver.

We were all once 13, but it seems we can no longer imagine what kind of parenting a 13-year-old needs. Perhaps it's gotten worse with all the outside opportunities for trouble kids have—gangs, guns, drugs. Families used to extend their turf into their children's schools, friends, and athletic activities. But kids now inhabit unknown territory, and it is scary for parents. "I think

Reprinted with permission from *Psychology Today*, January/February 1995, pp. 54–60, 62, 64, 66, 68. © 1995 by Sussex Publishers, Inc.

this fear and lack of understanding makes some parents more likely to back off and neglect teenagers," reports Wagers. "There is an expectation that you can't influence them anyhow."

This skeptical, sometimes hostile view of teens, however, was countered by my experience with Matthew. I found him hardly a "teenager from hell." Like most teens, Matthew prefers to be with his own friends more than with family or other grown-ups. He's not good with time, and music, basketball, and girls are more central to him than achievement, responsibility, and family. (Despite his tastes, he does very well in school.) At home there is more conflict than there has been in the past, though not less love and commitment to his mom, with whom he lives in eastern Washington.

The story of Matthew falls in line with new research on adolescents, and it's causing psychologists to totally revise conventional wisdom on the subject. According to psychologist Laurence Steinberg, Ph.D., of Temple University, the majority of adolescents are not contentious, unpleasant, heartless creatures. They do not hate their parents—although they do fight with them (but not as much as you might think). "In scrutinizing interviews with adolescents and their families, I reaffirmed that adolescence is a relatively peaceful time in the house." Kids report continued high levels of respect for their parents, whether single, divorced, or together, and regardless of economic background.

When fighting does occur, it's in families with younger teenagers, and it has to do at least in part with their burgeoning cognitive abilities. Newly able to grasp abstract ideas, they can become absorbed in pursuing hypocrisy or questioning authority. In time, they learn to deploy relativistic and critical thinking more selectively.

NOT A DISEASE

If adolescents aren't the incorrigibles we think—then what to make of the endless stream of news reports of teen sexism, harassment, drug abuse, depression, delinquency, gangs, guns, and suicide?

Any way you measure it, teens today are in deep trouble. They face increasing rates of depression (now at 20 percent), suicide (12 percent have considered it, 5 percent attempted), substance abuse (20 percent of high school seniors), delinquency (1.5 million juvenile arrests—about 1 percent of teens—in 1992), early sexual activity (29 percent have had sexual relations by age 15), and even an increased rate of health problems (20 percent have conditions that will hamper their health as adults). And kids' problems appear to be getting worse.

How to reconcile the two parts of the story: adolescents aren't so bad, but a grow-

ing number are jeopardizing their future through destructive behavior? Though we look upon teenagers as time bombs set to self-destruct at puberty, in fact the problems teens face are not encoded in their genes. Their natural development, including a surge of hormonal activity during the first few years of adolescence, may make them a little more depressed or aggressive—but how we treat them has much more to do with teenagers' lives today. From the look of it, we aren't treating them very well.

A CRISIS OF ADULTS

If what goes on in adolescence happens largely in the kids, what goes wrong with adolescence happens primarily in the parents. "It wasn't until I turned to the parents' interviews that I really got a sense that something unusual was going on," reports Steinberg of his ongoing studies of over 200 adolescents and their families. As he details in his recent book, *Crossing Paths:*

Teenagers say that parents are not understanding and I don't think it is always that way.
—Gabriel, 16, Alburquerque, New Mexico

How Your Child's Adolescence Triggers Your Own Crisis (Simon & Schuster), Steinberg finds that adolescence sets off a crisis for parents.

Parents do not have positive feelings during the time their kids go through adolescence, and it isn't simply because they expect their kids to be bad (although that's part of it). Scientists have studied the behavior and emotions of parents as well as their adolescent children, and found that when children reach puberty, parents experience tremendous changes in themselves. What's more, they shift their attitudes toward their children. It isn't just the kids who are distressed. Parents are too. Consider the following:

• Marital satisfaction, which typically declines over the course of marriage, reaches its all-time low when the oldest child reaches adolescence. Married parents of adolescents have an average of seven minutes alone with each other

every day. For the marriages that don't pass the point of no return during their kids' teen years, there is actually an increase in satisfaction after the kids complete adolescence.

• Happily married parents have more positive interactions with their kids than unhappy parents. In single-parent families, parental happiness also influences their response to adolescence.

• In a surprising finding, the marital satisfaction of fathers is directly affected

---

Adults want kids to learn to take care of themselves. Kids need guides and advice. That is how you help people mature—not by leaving them alone.
—Michelle, 16, Clackamas, Oregon

---

by how actively their adolescents are dating. Especially when sons are busy dating, fathers report a marked decline in interest in their wives. Dads aren't lusting for the girls Johnny brings home, they just miss what now seem like their own good old days.

• In family discussions, parents become increasingly negative toward their adolescents—there's more criticism, whining, frustration, anger, and defensiveness expressed verbally or in grimaces. While the kids are always more negative than their parents (it comes with increasing cognitive ability, in part), the parents are actually increasing the amount of negativity toward their children at a higher rate.

• Working mothers don't spend less time at home with their teenagers than nonworking moms do, but they do risk higher levels of burnout, because they continue to cover the lioness' share of work at home. On the other hand, a mother's employment makes her less vulnerable to the ups and downs of parenting an adolescent. Maternal employment also benefits kids, especially teen daughters, who report higher levels of self-esteem.

• Despite their fulfillment, mothers' self-esteem is actually lower while they are with their adolescents than when they are not. After all, a mother's authority is constantly being challenged, and she is being shunted to the margins of her child's universe.

- Teenagers turn increasingly to their friends, a distancing maneuver that feels like an emotional divorce to parents. Since mothers are generally more emotionally engaged with their children than are fathers, the separation can feel most painful to them. In fact, mothers typically report looking forward to the departure of their kids after high school. After the kids leave, mothers' emotional state improves.
- Fathers' emotional states follow a different course. Fathers have more difficulty launching their adolescents, mostly because they feel regret about the time they didn't spend with them. Fathers have more difficulty dealing with their kids growing into adolescence and adulthood; they can't get used to the idea that they no longer have a little playmate who is going to do what daddy wants to do.

Add it all up and you get a bona fide midlife crisis in some parents, according to Steinberg. All along we've thought that a midlife crisis happens to some adults around the age of 40. But it turns out that midlife crisis has nothing to do with the age of the adult—and everything to do with the age of the oldest child in a family. It is set off by the entry of a family's first-born into adolescence.

Once the oldest child hits adolescence, parents are catapulted into a process of life review. "Where have I been, where am I now, where am I going?" These questions gnaw at parents who observe their children at the brink of adulthood.

It hits hardest the parent who is the same sex as the adolescent. Mothers and daughters actually have more difficulty than fathers and sons. In either case, the children tend to serve as a mirror of their younger lost selves, and bear the brunt of parents' regrets as parents distance themselves.

Steinberg tracks the psychological unrest associated with midlife crisis in parents:

- The onset of puberty is unavoidable evidence that their child is growing up.
- Along with puberty comes a child's burgeoning sexuality. For parents, this can raise doubts about their own attractiveness, their current sex life, as well as regrets or nostalgia for their teenage sexual experiences.
- The kids' new independence can make parents feel powerless. For fathers in particular this can remind them of the powerlessness they feel in the office if their careers have hit a plateau.
- Teens also become less concerned with their parents' approval. Their peer group approval becomes more impor-

tant. This hits mothers of daughters quite hard, especially single mothers, whose relationship to their daughters most resembles a friendship.

- Finally, de-idealization—kids' often blunt criticism of their parents—is a strong predictor of decline in parental mental health. Parents who used to be the ultimate expert to their kids are now reduced to debating partner for kids who have developed a new cognitive skill called relativism.

A clear picture begins to emerge: parents of a teenager feel depressed about their own life or their own marriage; feel the loss of their child; feel jealous, rejected, and confused about their child's new sexually mature looks, bad moods, withdrawal into privacy at home, and increasing involvement with friends. The kid is tied up in her (or his) own problems and wonders what planet mom and dad are on.

EMOTIONAL DIVORCE

The sad consequence is that parents who experience a midlife crisis begin avoiding their adolescent. Although a small proportion of parents are holding on to their teens too closely—usually they come from traditional families and have fundamentalist religious beliefs—more parents are backing off. The catch is that these teenagers want

---

Adults need to understand that it is very difficult to be a teenager nowadays. It takes a lot of understanding with so many problems like guns, drugs, AIDS, and gangs.
—Melissa, 14, Dallas, Texas

---

their parents' guidance. But more and more they just aren't getting it.

Some parents back away not out of their own inner confusion but because they think it's hip to do so. Either way, letting go causes confusion in the kids, not help in making their way into adulthood. Even if they are irritating or irritable, or just more withdrawn than they used to be, teens are seeking guidance.

"I have this image of a kid groping through adolescence, kind of by himself,"

confides therapist Wagers, who sees a lot of parents out of touch with their kids. "The parents swarm around him, but don't actually talk to him, only to other people about him."

The mantra of therapists who work with adolescents and their families is "balance." Parents have to hold on, but not too tightly. They need to stay involved, even when their kids are ignoring them. Roland Montemayor, Ph.D., professor of psychology at Ohio State, finds it is not so different from learning how to deal with a two-year-old. You must stay within earshot, and be available whenever they falter or get themselves into trouble.

With a two-year-old, trouble means experimenting with mud pies or bopping a playmate; with a 14-year-old, it means experimenting with your car keys or sex. The task is the same—keep track of them and let them know what the rules are. Parents unfortunately taken up with their own midlife concerns may not embrace the task. God knows, it isn't easy. But it is vital.

Among parents who have gone through a real divorce, the emotional divorce that occurs between adolescents and their parents can heighten difficulty. It may reawaken feelings of sadness. Parents who don't have many interests outside the family are also vulnerable. Their kids are telling them to "Get a life!"—and that is exactly what they need to do.

DROPOUT PARENTS

As an adolescent reaches age 13, the time she is spending with parents is typically half that before age 10. "Teens come home and go into their bedrooms. They start to feel more comfortable by themselves than with siblings or parents around. They talk on the phone with friends, and their biggest worry usually has to do with a romantic interest," explains Reed Larson, Ph.D., who studies families and adolescents at the University of Illinois, Champaign-Urbana. Larson, coauthor of the recent book, *Divergent Realities: The Emotional Lives of Mothers, Fathers, and Adolescents*, studied 55 families who recorded their feelings and activities for one week, whenever prompted at random intervals by a beeper. He surveyed another 483 adolescents with the beeper method.

The families' reports revealed that a mutual withdrawal occurs. "When kids withdraw, parents get the message. They even feel intimidated. As a result they don't put in the extra effort to maintain contact with their kids," observes Larson. The kids feel abandoned, even though they're the ones retreating to their bedroom. The parents, in effect, cut their kids loose, just when they dip their toes in the waters of autonomy.

Separation is natural among humans as well as in the animal kingdom, Larson notes. Yet humans also need special care during this life transition—and suffer from reduced contact with parents and other adults. They still need to be taught how to do things, how to think about things, but above all they need to know that there is

> *I don't think adults understand how complicated kids' minds are today, how much they think; they don't just accept something but wonder why it is.*
> —Adam, 14, Bethesda, Maryland

a safety net, a sense that their parents are paying attention and are going to jump in when things go wrong. The kids don't need the direct supervision they received at age two or eight, but they benefit emotionally and intellectually from positive contact with their parents.

Despite the tensions in family life, studies continue to confirm that the family remains one of the most effective vehicles to promote values, school success, even confidence in peer relationships. When it works, family functions as what Larson calls a "comfort zone," a place or a relationship that serves as a home base out of which to operate. Kids feel more secure, calm, and confident than those without a comfort zone. Similarly, Steinberg finds, the one common link among the many successful adolescents in his studies is that they all have positive relationships with their parents. Without positive relationships, the kids are subject to depression and likely to do poorly in school.

Parental withdrawal is a prime characteristic of families where adolescents get into trouble. It often catapults families into therapy. Wagers tells the story of a single parent who wasn't simply withdrawn, her head was in the sand: "I was seeing a mother and her 12-year-old son, who had depression and behavior problems. The mother called me up one time to say she had found all this marijuana paraphernalia in her son's room, in his pocket. She said she wasn't sure what it means. When I said 'it means that he's smoking pot,' she was very reluctant to agree. She didn't want to talk to her son about why he was getting

into trouble or smoking pot. She wanted me to fix him." (Eventually, in therapy, the mother learned how to give her son a curfew and other rules, and to enforce them. He's doing much better.)

Marital problems also enter into the distancing equation. Although the marital decline among teens' parents is part of the normal course of marriage, the adolescent can exacerbate the problem. "Here is a new person challenging you in ways that might make you irritable or insecure," explains Steinberg. "That can spill over into the marriage. The standard scenario involves the adolescent and the mother who have been home squabbling all afternoon. Well, the mom isn't exactly going to be in a terrific mood to greet her husband. It resembles the marital problems that occur when

> *Teenagers know what is happening around them in school but adults hide things. Parents should shield their kids from some things but not so much that kids are afraid to go out into the world.*
> —Sarah, 17, Hanover, NH

a couple first has a new baby." Trouble is, when the parents' marriage declines, so does the quality of the parenting—at a time when more parental energy is needed.

As if there are not enough psychological forces reducing contact between parents and adolescents today, social trends add to the problem, contends Roland Montemayor. Intensified work schedules, increased divorce and single parenthood, and poverty—often a result of divorce and single parenthood—decrease parent-child contact. A fourth of all teenagers live with one parent, usually their mother. Families have fewer ties to the community, so there are fewer other adults with whom teens have nurturing ties. The negative images of teenagers as violent delinquents may even intimidate parents.

ALONE AND ANGRY

Whatever the source, parental distancing doesn't make for happy kids. "The kids I work with at Ohio State are remarkably in-

dependent, yet they are resentful of it," says Montemayor. "There is a sense of not being connected somehow." Kids are angry about being left to themselves, being given independence without the kind of mentoring from their parents to learn how to use their independence.

Adult contact seems to be on teenagers' minds more than ever before. Sociologist Dale Blythe, Ph.D., is an adolescence researcher who directs Minneapolis' noted Search Institute, which specializes in studies of youth policy issues. He has surveyed teens in 30 communities across the country, and found that when you ask teens, they say that family is not the most important thing in their lives—peers and social activities are. Nevertheless a large proportion of them say that they want more time with adults—they want their attention and leadership. They want more respect from adults and more cues on how to make it in the adult world. What a shift from 25 years ago, when the watchword was "never trust anyone over 30"!

So it's up to parents to seek more contact with their kids—despite the conflict they'll encounter. "The role of parents is to socialize

> *I am insecure about my future. The main view toward people in my generation is that we are all slackers and it's kind of disturbing. We are actually trying to make something of ourselves.*
> —Jasmine, 16, Brooklyn, New York

children, to help them become responsible adults, to teach them to do the right thing. Conflict is an inevitable part of it," says Montemayor. He notes that one of the biggest sources of conflict between parents and teens is time management. Teens have trouble committing to plans in advance. They want to keep their options wide open all the time. The only surefire way to reduce conflict is to withdraw from teenagers—an equally surefire way to harm them.

"In other countries parents don't shy away from conflict. In the United States we have this idea that things are going to be hunky-dory and that we are going to go

The Invention of Adolescence

Are Romeo and Juliet the Quintessential adolescents? On the yes side, they were rebelling against family traditions, in the throes of first love, prone to melodrama, and engaged in violent and risky behavior. But the truth is that there was no such thing as adolescence in Shakespeare's time (the 16th century). Young people the ages of Romeo and Juliet (around 13) were adults in the eyes of society—even though they were probably prepubescent.

Paradoxically, puberty came later in eras past while departure from parental supervision came earlier than it does today. Romeo and Juliet carried the weight of the world on their shoulders—although it was a far smaller world than today's teens inhabit.

Another way to look at it is that in centuries past, a sexually mature person was never treated as a "growing child." Today sexually mature folk spend perhaps six years—ages 12 to 18—living under the authority of their parents.

Since the mid-1800s, puberty—the advent of sexual maturation and the starting point of adolescence—has inched back one year for every 25 years elapsed. It now occurs on average six years earlier than it did in 1850—age 11 or 12 for girls; age 12 or 13 for boys. Today adolescents make up 17 percent of the U.S. population and about a third of them belong to racial or ethnic minorities.

It's still not clear exactly what triggers puberty, confides Jeanne Brooks-Gunn, Ph.D., of Columbia University Teachers College, an expert on adolescent development. "The onset of puberty has fallen probably due to better nutrition in the prenatal period as well as throughout childhood. Pubertal age—for girls, when their first period occurs—has been lower in the affluent than the nonaffluent classes throughout recorded history. Differences are still found in countries where starvation and malnutrition are common among the poor. In Western countries, no social-class differences are found." Although adolescence is a new phenomenon in the history of our species, thanks to a stable and abundant food supply, we've already hit its limits—it's not likely puberty onset will drop much below the age of 12.

If kids look like adults sooner than ever before, that doesn't mean they are. The brain begins to change when the body does, but it doesn't become a grown-up thinking organ as quickly as other systems of the body mature. The clash between physical maturity and mental immaturity not only throws parents a curve—they forget how to do their job, or even what it is—it catapults teens into some silly situations. They become intensely interested in romance, for example, only their idea of romance is absurdly simple, culminating in notes passed across the classroom: "Do you like me? Check yes or no."

Puberty isn't the only marker of adolescence. There's a slowly increasing capacity for abstract reasoning and relative thinking. Their new capacity for abstraction allows teens to think about big things—Death, Destruction, Nuclear War—subjects that depress them, especially since they lack the capacity to ameliorate them.

The idea that everything is relative suddenly makes every rule subject to debate. As time passes, teens attain the ability to make finer abstract distinctions. Which is to say, they become better at choosing their fights.

Teens also move toward autonomy. They want to be alone, they say, because they have a lot on their minds. Yet much of the autonomy hinges on the growing importance of social relationships. Evaluating the ups and downs of social situations indeed requires time alone. Family ties, however, remain more important than you might expect as teens increase identification with their peers.

Whatever else turns teens into the moody creatures they are, hormones have been given far too much credit, contends Brooks-Gunn. In fact, she points out, the flow of hormones that eventually shapes their bodies actually starts around age seven or eight. "Certain emotional states and problems increase between ages 11 and 14, at the time puberty takes place. These changes are probably due to the increased social and school demands, the multiple new events that youth confront, their own responses to puberty, and to a much lesser extent hormonal changes themselves."

The nutritional abundance that underlies a long adolescence also prompted the extension of education, which has created a problem entirely novel in the animal kingdom—physically mature creatures living with their parents, and for more years than sexually mature offspring ever have in the past. College-bound kids typically depend on their parents until at least age 21, a decade or more after hitting puberty.

Historically, children never lived at home during the teen years, points out Temple University's Laurence Steinberg. Either they were shipped out to apprenticeships or off to other relatives.

Among lower primates, physically mature beasts simply are not welcome in the family den; sexual competition makes cohabiting untenable. But for animals, physical maturity coincides with mental acuity, so their departure is not a rejection.

The formal study of adolescence began in the 1940s, just before James Dean changed our perception of it forever. There is a long-standing tradition of professional observers looking at adolescence as a pathology—and this one really did start with Freud. It continues still.

A 1988 study reported that although the under-18 population actually declined from 1980 to 1984, adolescent admissions to private psychiatric hospitals increased—450 percent! The study suggests a staggering cultural taste for applying mental health care to any problem life presents. It also hints at the negative feelings Americans have toward adolescence—we consider it a disease.

The study of adolescence has come with a context—a culture of, by, and for youth, arising in the postwar boom of the 1950s and epitomized by James Dean. Once the original badass depressive teenager from hell, Dean seems quaintly tame by today's standards. But the fear and loathing he set in motion among adults is a powerful legacy today's teens are still struggling to live down.—V.R.

Many times teenagers are thought of as a problem that no one really wants to deal with. People are sometimes intimidated and become hostile because teenagers are willing to challenge their authority. It is looked at as being disrespectful. Teenagers are, many times, not treated like an asset and as innovative thinkers who will be the leaders of tomorrow. Adults have the power to teach the younger generation about the world and allow them to feel they have a voice in it.—**Zula, 16, Brooklyn, NY**

A postpubescent child introduces a third sexually mature person into the household, where once sex was a strictly private domain restricted to the older generation. It's difficult for everyone to get used to.

No matter how you slice it, sex can be an awkward topic. For parents, there's not only the feeling of powerlessness, there's discomfort. Most parents of adolescents aren't experiencing much sexual activity—neither the mechanics of sex nor its poetry—in this stage of the marriage (though this eventually improves).

The fact that fathers' marital satisfaction decreases when their kids start to date suggests the power of kids' sexuality, no matter how silenced, to distort parental behavior. Sex and marital therapist David Schnarch, Ph.D., points out that families, and the my-

I think Al Gore is a super environmentalist. With no ozone layer, the world is just going to melt. It's hard not to worry. The environment is really messed up and with no environment there will be no economy, no education, nothing. I hate it when people throw six-pack rings in the lake. We need to think about the environment because we need to get on with the rest of our lives. I don't think adults generally look to kids for opinions.—**Sam, 13, New York City**

bowling and have fun together. Most people in the world would find that a pretty fanciful idea. There is an inevitable tension between parents and adolescents, and there's nothing wrong with that."

SILENCED SEX

Who can talk about teens without talking about sex? The topic of teenage sexuality, however, heightens parents' sense of powerlessness. Adults hesitate to acknowledge their own sexual experience in addressing the issue. They resolve the matter by pretending sex doesn't exist.

Sexuality was conspicuous by its absence in all the family interviews Steinberg,

Doing the right thing and being good at what you're doing is important to me.

As teenagers we have a lot of things on our back, a lot of people are looking for us to do many great things. We also take in a lot of things and we know a lot of things. I care about the environment because it's a place that we all have to live in, not just us but our families and children. Even though I'm 15, I still have to keep those things in mind because it's serious. As for my own future, I've had a good upbringing and I see all open doors.—**Semu, 15, New York City**

model of sexuality, we imply to the kids 'we know you can't delay. We think these are the best years of your life.'"

Parents can help their children by letting them know that they understand sex and have valuable experience about decisions related to sex; that they know it isn't just a mechanical act; that they recognize that teens are going to figure things out on their own with or without guidance from their parents; and that they are willing to talk about it. But often, the experience or meaning of sex gets lost.

I asked a woman whose parents had handed her birth control pills at age 15 how she felt about it now, at age 30. "I

I think there is going to be a lot of destruction and violence. There are all these peace treaties, but I don't think they are going to work out.
—Julia, 12, Albuquerque, NM

thology of the culture, worship teen sexuality, mistakenly believing adolescence is the peak of human sexuality. Boys have more hard-ons than their dads, while the girls have less cellulite than their moms.

These kids may have the biological equipment, says Schnarch, but they don't yet know how to make love. Sex isn't just about orgasms, it is about intimacy. "All of our sex education is designed to raise kids to be healthy, normal adults. But we are confused about what we believe is sexually normal. Textbooks say that boys reach their sexual peak in late adolescence; girls, five to 10 years later. The adolescent believes it, parents believe it, schools believe it. In the hierarchy dictated by this narrow biological model of sexuality, the person with the best sex is the adolescent. On the one hand we are telling kids, 'we would like you to delay sexual involvement.' But when we teach a biological

The future sounds alright. It is probably going to be more modern and really scientific. Things will be run by computers and computers will do more for people.
—Emily, 13, New York City

wish sex had been a little more taboo than it was. I got into a lot more sexual acting out before I was 20, and that didn't go very well for me. Even though my parents talked about the health consequences of sex, they did not mention other consequences. Like what it does to your self-esteem when you get involved in a series of one-night stands. So I guess I wish they had been more holistic in their approach to sex. Not just to tell me about the pill when I was 15, but to understand the dif-

Montemayor, or Larson observed. Calling sex a hidden issue in adolescence verges on an oxymoron. Sprouting pubic hair and expanding busts aren't particularly subtle phenomena. But adolescent sexuality is only heightened by the silence.

ferent issues I was struggling with. In every other aspect of my life, they were my best resource. But it turns out sex is a lot more complicated than I thought it was when I was 15. At 30, sex is a lot better than it was when I was a teenager."

The distortions parents create about teen sexuality lead directly to events like the "Spur Posse," the gang of teenage football stars in Southern California who systematically harassed and raped girls, terrorizing the community in the late 80s. The boys' fathers actually appeared on talk shows—to brag about their sons' conquests. "The fathers were reinforcing the boys' behavior. It was as if it were a reflection on their own sexuality," observes Schnarch.

By closing their eyes to teen sexual behavior, parents don't just disengage from their

---

I don't feel any pressure about sex. It's a frequent topic of conversation, but we talk about other things, too—when I'm going to get my history paper done, movies, music. I listen to classical music a lot. I think about my maturity a lot, because I have recently had losses in my immediate family and it feels like I am maturing so fast. But then sometimes I feel so young compared to everything out there. I think adults have always felt that teens were more reckless.—**Amanda, 16, New York City**

Teenagers, like adults, are all different. One has a job that is hard, another has more money and more education, and one just gets by. It is unfair to look at all teens the same way. You have maturity in you, but you just don't want to show it because it's no fun. We've got problems, but not really big ones like my uncle who came over from China when he was 16, or going to war when you're 18. If teenagers make it through this era, adults will just bash the next generation of teenagers.—**Mike, 14, Brooklyn, New York**

---

kids. They leave them high and dry about understanding anything more than the cold mechanics of sex. Kids raised this way re-

---

Jackie Joyner-Kersee, the Olympic track star, is my hero because she has accomplished so much and she is one of the main female athletes.
—Kristy, 12, Woodbridge, New Jersey

---

port feeling very alone when it gets down to making intimate decisions for the first time. They feel like they haven't been given any help in what turns out to be the bigger part of sex—the relationship part of it.

Returning to the authoritarian, insular family of Ward, June, Wally, and the Beaver

---

My hero is Queen Latifah. She is herself and doesn't try to be somebody else. My mother is also my hero because she raises me as well as she can and she is a single parent.
—Maria, 15, Bronx, New York

---

is not the solution for teenagers any more than it is for their parents. But teenagers do need parents and other responsible adults actively involved in their lives, just as younger children do. Only when it comes to teenagers, the grown-ups have to tolerate a lot more ambiguity—about authority, safety, responsibility, and closeness—to sustain the connection. If they can learn to do that, a lot of young people will be able to avoid a whole lot of trouble.

Working with the Emotionally Sensitive Adolescent

Michael F. Shaughnessy, Fred Cordova, Joe Strickland, Cam Smith

Eastern New Mexico University, Psychology Department, Portales, New Mexico 88130 U.S.A.

Russell Eisenman

Department of Psychology, McNeese State University, Lake Charles, Louisiana 70609-1895, U.S.A.

ABSTRACT

Emotionally sensitive adolescents are difficult to teach, to live with, and to counsel. The incidence of the overly sensitive adolescent seems to be increasing. This paper explores this syndrome, relevant issues, causes, symptoms and basic counseling concerns. Emotional sensitivity can lead to such different outcomes as crime, creativity, substance abuse or extreme withdrawal. Implications for teachers, counselors and parents are discussed.

Teachers, parents, counselors and other adult figures are reporting an increase in what may be termed 'emotionally sensitive' adolescents. These teenagers manifest a number of different problems in varying situations (school, home, athletics, part time work) in varying degrees. This paper will attempt to address this issue and to focus on possible causal factors.

RECOGNIZING THE EMOTIONALLY SENSITIVE CHILD

The emotionally sensitive adolescent can be recognized by some of the following behaviors. Some adolescents tend to manifest a 'clinging' type of behavior. They seek out inordinate amounts of teacher, and parental attention and are seen as dependent by coaches and adults.

There is also a tendency to withdraw, particularly after they have been chastised or criticized by adult figures. Some are simply characterized as 'shy' and inhibited. Many of these adolescents tend to repress feelings and do not often verbalize what is on their minds. On the other hand, many, do not have the verbal skills to verbalize their feelings and emotional concerns.

One hallmark of the emotionally sensitive adolescent is the fact that they do not react at all well to criticism. They may make self disparaging statements. In general, low self esteem and low self worth is apparent. They have a low self concept which tends to become even more frail and fragile after being criticized. Some respond negatively after being simply talked to by an adult. Some are seen as emotionally volatile. They may become verbally hostile when criticized. This may later revert to depression. They have difficulty forgiving themselves when they have made a mistake or error. Their thoughts tend to linger on their transgressions. They may

From *International Journal of Adolescence and Youth*, Volume 6, 1995, pp. 47-55. © 1995 by A B Academic Publishers. Reprinted by permission.

make very negative statements such as 'It's all my fault' and 'I'll never be any good'. Often, there is minimal or even poor peer interaction. In extreme cases, there may be blow ups or verbal tirades.

CAUSES OF EMOTIONAL SENSITIVITY

There are many theoretical causes as to emotional sensitivity. Some believe that the fault lies in the family unit. These children may come from a dysfunctional family where there is verbal abuse and lack of love and nurturance. Some of the parents may be adult children of alcoholic parents. Susan Forward (1989) often refers to these types of parents as 'toxic parents'. In some cases, a new step parent may have been a beginning factor.

In other cases, parents have unrealistic expectations for their sons or daughters. The adolescent however, simply does not have the intellectual capacity to support a drive toward medical or dental school. Parents simply may expect too much in other realms—sports, music, drama or whatever.

In many homes in America, there are children and adolescents who are being emotionally, physically, sexually abused and neglected. There may or may not be any physical abuse, but the child is subjected to verbal tirades and verbal harassment from parents who have anger problems or low frustration tolerance. The scars are internal and psychological. Substance abuse, anger or extreme isolation are common outcomes.

In still other homes, children are given inordinate responsibilities which are not age appropriate. They are expected to 'parent' their younger brothers and sisters and care for the house, the laundry and other housekeeping duties. Often, the first born child is, in effect, a surrogate parent, given too much responsibility for raising or caring for the younger siblings (Eisenman, 1991, 1994)

GIFTED CHILDREN

Often, gifted children are very prone to the 'emotionally sensitive child' syndrome. Gifted adolescents tend to think too much and repress their feelings. They often have a great desire to please and have certain needs for approval and recognition that other children do not have. In addition, gifted children often have emotional/social needs which may not be met in school, or in the home. These needs may be neglected for academic subjects.

Cobb (1992) suggests that cognitive and emotional immaturity may be a factor that influences how adolescents may perceive and think of themselves in social situations. Elkind (1978) describes the phenomenon of the imaginary audience, where early adolescents tend to think that others are as interested in what they are thinking or doing as they are themselves. Imagining that others are aware of their feelings, thoughts, or activities can magnify and possibly distort the meaning and intention of social interactions for the adolescent. This could especially be the situation for the emotionally sensitive adolescent. A related concept, the personal fable, may also provide the basis for the adolescent to feel that they are special and unique (Lapsley, Fitzgerald, Rice, and Jackson, 1989). These related concepts, the imaginary audience and the personal fable, could, in part, explain some of the emotional sensitivity that these particular adolescents experience. Furthermore, unlike children, adolescents relate their feelings to their experience of themselves as well as to the interactions and situations that may prompt the feelings. Thus, this adds an extra level of magnification to their perception of the world (Cobb, 1992).

PARENTING THE EMOTIONALLY SENSITIVE ADOLESCENT

Parents who have a child who is highly sensitive may want to consult a professional mental health specialist if needed. They need to be careful of comparative statements—such as 'Your brother has always done better'. Parents need to be aware that adolescents, in general, are very sensitive to criticism. Parents should try to schedule 'quality time' if at all possible with their children. Dealing with these emotional sensitivity issues should be done in a patient, gentle manner.

Some parents should recognize that their children may have special specific skills, talents and abilities. Some emotionally sensitive individuals should be encouraged to read. Some escape in this manner. For others, it is a welcome diversion. A hobby may also divert energy and may serve as a therapeutic distraction.

Parents may want to talk to the teacher to find out what their child's behavior is like in the classroom situation. Consulting with teachers can be very beneficial and can offer some real insights into problem areas.

The parents should be supportive and caring if at all possible. There may have been a lack of this support in the past. Parents can model a certain type of appropriate response style. We are all criticized, fairly or unfairly, justly or unjustly, at some point in our lives. We can role model how to deal with this and demonstrate coping with this in a reasonable manner. Active listening to the child can also facilitate growth. Parents must provide a consistent, safe home environment. If one parent is not consistent, then it is incumbent upon the other to articulate and verbalize the need for consistency. Parents can also verbalize choices rather than simply criticize. Although the term 'constructive criticism' has been overused, we may need to look at it more closely. Criticism should have a valid constructive purpose that will help the child, not simply make the parents feel better by expressing anger. Parents need to share the parenting duties and responsibilities for their child with their spouse. Lastly, parents need to allow the adolescent to have their privacy and to respect their boundaries. Opening the child's mail or reading the child's diary is inappropriate parental behavior. The only exception would be in extreme cases, e.g. if there were indicators that the child was contemplating suicide.

TEACHING THE EMOTIONALLY SENSITIVE ADOLESCENT

The classroom teacher may have a good deal of difficulty relating to, and teaching an emotionally sensitive student. Patience is one of the most needed crucial skills. These students may need to proceed at their own rate and to follow their own interests. Teachers must let students proceed at their own rate and follow their own interests.

Teachers need to be sensitive to male and female differences and the amount of type of feedback which they provide to students. Teachers should also be aware of the issue of 'personal space'. Some students need more of it than others. In extreme cases, a parent teacher conference may be needed. Parents may, or may not be aware of the child's behavior or reaction in the school setting.

Obviously, teachers should not mock, insult, ridicule, make fun of, or tease the emotionally sensitive child. Teachers should also be aware of developmental sequences and stages. Some students are 'emotionally sensitive' simply by dint of the fact that they are in adolescence. Others are sensitive because of other factors. They may have been rejected by a peer of the opposite sex or by a friend.

Teachers, coaches and counselors need to be supportive of students. Such support can come about in a variety of ways. Teachers must be patient, and allocate extra time for the adolescent. Teachers must practice the genteel art of diplomacy and tact. A cordial, congenial approach and a friendly manner may be helpful. Global statements are good 'ice breakers'. Teachers should proceed in slow incremental steps and be gentle.

Teachers can also validate the fact that it is difficult for individuals to receive negative comments from others. Often much time, effort and energy does go into one's endeavors.

COUNSELING THE EMOTIONALLY SENSITIVE CHILD

The first step is to form a nonthreatening, nonjudgmental relationship with the child. The counselor should work at building rapport with this child. Patience will be necessary. As counseling progresses, the adolescent will recognize their particular past traumatic events and their sensitivity. Pressure should be minimized if at all possible. The counselor should recognize that more time will be needed for this type of counseling. The counselor should see the positives in this type of personality—the emotionally sensitive child is often insightful, tender, caring, empathic and sympathetic to others.

These are positive traits which our society does not always reward or reinforce. The counselor may want to check to see if they are in touch with their feelings and examine and explore the specificity of their feelings. Listening to nonverbals may also be helpful. The counselor may want to form hunches, opinions, and guesses regarding their feelings and internal thoughts. Students may be asked if they can identify the 'triggers' which upset them and discuss these antecedents.

The counselor must be able to teach coping skills to these students in a supportive way. For adolescents whose parents are alcoholic, ALATEEN, or some other support group for children of alcoholics may be helpful if that is the reason for their sensitivity.

CONCERNS OF THE EMOTIONALLY SENSITIVE CHILD

The emotionally sensitive adolescent may feel that their teachers are making inordinate demands on them. The teacher may be a martinet or a very strict disciplinarian. On the other hand, a teacher may be perceived by the adolescent as being an intimidating, loud imposing figure. The truth or reality may be somewhat in-between.

The emotionally sensitive child may be dealing with a wide variety of issues. They may feel inferior or inadequate, and may also fear the loss of parental love.

Often, the death of a pet, a parent, a grandparent or a significant other can trigger emotionally sensitive behaviors or feelings. Coming to grips with their own mortality may be difficult for many adolescents.

Rejection may also bring about a number of adolescent concerns. This is true whether the rejection is from a friend or is in the form of an idea being rejected by a teacher. Things that would make most of us somewhat unhappy can have devastating effects on the emotionally sensitive youth.

Any type of significant change in one's environment can bring about feelings of sensitivity. Friends may move away, a teacher or mentor may leave the school or area, a coach may be reassigned or a teenager may move from an urban to a rural area. Even the presence of a 'school bully' can trigger certain behaviors.

In adolescence, there are a number of age appropriate concerns which may be seen. These issues are familiar to those who study adolescence—acne, body size and weight, feelings of being 'ugly', the need for glasses, and breasts (or the lack thereof).

The approval of the peer group, boy friend and girl friend difficulties, parental divorce, clothing, and car concerns may all preoccupy the thoughts of the adolescent.

In addition to the identity crisis of adolescence, other pressures such as the need for a part time job, concerns about which college to apply to, the need for a date for the prom or even for this coming weekend may overwhelm some adolescents.

OVERINVESTMENT

The greater the investment in self, clothes, sports, work, or whatever, the more sensitive the child may be to criticism in that area (Baumeister, 1991). The more important an individual is to the adolescent, the more sensitive that child will be to criticism or feedback from that individual. If the adolescent is overly invested in his or her music, there will be a heightened sensitivity to comments from adults in that area. If the teenager feels that they can only do one thing well, they will obviously be highly sensitive to feedback from significant others relative to that area.

LACK OF REINFORCEMENT

It is thought that the 'emotional sensitivity' may come about due to a lack of praise, positive comments, rewards, statements and overall lack of positive feedback. If one examines teacher and parent interactions with children and adolescents, there is often a lack of positive feedback and reinforcement—both in terms of quality, and quantity. In most schools and homes in America, children are criticized, yelled at, hassled, pressured, and put down. In those cases where the above is not occurring, children and adolescents are often ignored. They are not given any feedback at all. They receive no positive OR negative feedback. Thus, when they are criticized, they may be less well prepared to deal with it.

QUALITY OF FEEDBACK

On a scale of 1 to 100, children can receive a wide variety of emotional feedback. The quality of feedback can range from being very positive (100) to about 70 (wherein the child is rewarded, receives praise, attention and positive strokes from parents, teachers, coaches and others) to about 50 (wherein there is either non existent or minimal feedback or the child is simply ignored).

These adolescents and middle schoolers find life difficult and they have few coping skills. Ranging down from 50 to 1, we have children who are emotionally abused, neglected, disturbed, and who receive very negative feedback. There are at the proverbial 'bottom of the barrel' children who are physically abused, sexually abused, and exploited. These children are the most emotionally sensitive individuals. Some will become sex offenders, repeating to others what was done to them (Eisenman and Kritsonis, 1995)

CLINICAL CONCERNS

There are some emotionally sensitive individuals who present real clinical concerns for mental health counselors. Some children do not seem to experience emotions and are termed 'alexithymia'. For these adolescents, their emotions are expressed through ulcers, high blood pressure, anorexia, bulimia and migraine headaches.

For some of these individuals, clinical testing may be in order. Projective tests can offer a wealth of material to assist the clinician in discerning the underlying concerns. The Thematic Apperception Test or the Children's Apperception Test as well as Incomplete Sentences and the Draw a Person may provide important data and information.

PROGNOSIS FOR THE EMOTIONALLY SENSITIVE INDIVIDUAL

In general, the prognosis for the emotionally sensitive individual is good if he or she receives adequate support from parents (or perhaps even from the peer group if parental support is not forthcoming). Those working with these adolescents need to look for strengths and comment positively. Often, many adolescents have creative artistic skills, talents and abilities that have gone unrecognized. Self determination, often seen in these children can facilitate creativity (Sheldon, 1995). If possible, the adolescent may benefit from a mentor.

Parents, teachers and counselors should avoid stereotypes and generalizations. While emotional sensitivity is not always a pervasive issue or concern in adolescence, it does appear to be increasing, as we expect more from students and fail to praise, reinforce and reward in earlier years. Much more in depth investigation of a longitudinal nature is warranted into this phenomenon to ascertain it's course, and etiology. It is hoped that this article will sensitize teachers, parents and others to this issue in adolescence, and youth.

REFERENCES

Baumeister, R.F. (1991). *Escaping the self*. Basic Books; New York.

Cobb, N.J. (1992), *Adolescence: Continuity, change and diversity*. Mayfield Publishing Company; Mountain View, CA.

Eisenman, R. (1991). *From crime to creativity: Psychological and social factors and deviance*. Kendall/Hunt; Dubuque, IA.

Eisenman, R. (1994). *Contemporary social issues. Drugs, crime, creativity and education*. Book Masters; Ashland, OH.

Eisenman, R. & Kritsonis, W. (1995). How children learn to become sex offenders. *Psychology: A Journal of Human Behavior*, **32**, 25–29.

Elkind, D. (1978). Understanding the young adolescent. *Adolescence*, **13**, 127–134.

Lapsley, D.K., Fitzgerald, D.P., Rice, K.G. & Jackson, S. (1989). Separation-individuation and the 'new look' at the imaginary audience and personal fable: A test of an integrative model. *Journal of Adolescent Research* **4**, 483–505.

Forward, S. (1989). *Toxic Parents*. Bantam; New York.

Sheldon, K.M. (1995). Creativity and self determination in personality. *Creativity Research Journal*, **8**, 25–36.

What Is a Bad Kid? Answers of Adolescents and Their Mothers in Three Cultures

David S. Crystal and
Harold W. Stevenson

University of Michigan

This study examined the behaviors and personality traits attributed to a "bad kid" by a cross-national sample of 204 American high-school students and 204 American mothers, 237 Chinese students and 224 Chinese mothers, and 157 Japanese students and 167 Japanese mothers. Correlates of students' responses were also examined, including the degree of valuing academics, level of academic achievement, level of psychological adjustment, and quality of social relationships. The behaviors most frequently associated with a bad kid were lack of self-control (American), acts against society (Chinese), and disruptions of interpersonal harmony (Japanese). In addition, American students mentioned substance abuse as a feature of a bad kid more often than did their Chinese and Japanese peers. Disturbances in interpersonal harmony received the highest frequency of response from Chinese and Japanese students and second highest frequency of response from American students. Adolescents and their mothers differed significantly in the frequency with which they mentioned the types of conduct attributed to a bad kid. Few associations were found between students' own characteristics and their descriptions of a bad kid.

Over the past 30 years, due, in large part, to the influence of the labelling theorists (e.g., Becker, 1964; Scheff, 1974), a growing number of social scientists have come to view deviance not as an objective quality but, rather, as a subjective definition made by a particular audience. From this perspective, a behavior is bad, wrong, or abnormal because it is defined that way by members of a particular society (Newman, 1976). Based on this premise, there is an increasing interest among psychologists and sociologists in identifying cross-cultural differences in perceptions of deviance and

in understanding how these perceptions reflect the characteristics of the society or culture from which they derive.

One way of understanding the process by which cultural characteristics come to express themselves through perceptions of deviance may be seen in a paradigm put forth by LeVine (1973). According to the paradigm, the environment influences child rearing practices which, in turn, affect the nature of child and adult personality, as well as important facets of group life, including perceptions of good and bad. These latter products of culture may be seen as reflected in what Robin and Spires (1983) called the individual's "projective system" (p. 109) that guides a person's social and moral behavior. Because children and adults are socialized to be able to function within the existing cultural environment, looking at certain aspects of the projective system of children and adults, such as perceptions of deviance, may tell us important

Requests for reprints should be sent to David S. Crystal, Center for Human Growth and Development, 300 North Ingalls, 10th Level, University of Michigan, Ann Arbor, MI 48109-0406.

From the *Journal of Research on Adolescence*, Vol. 5, No. 1, 1995, pp. 71–91. © 1995 by Lawrence Erlbaum Associates, Inc. Reprinted by permission.

things about how adaptation within a specific culture takes place.

Cross-cultural studies on perceptions of deviance fall into two basic categories: those that examine expressions of psychological deviance such as mental illness (e.g., Hardy, Cull, & Campbell, 1987; Wilson & Young, 1988) and those that examine expressions of social deviance such as crime and juvenile delinquency (e.g., Newman, 1976; Rivers, Sarata, & Anagnostopulos, 1986). Although the literature contains numerous studies on perceptions of psychological deviance, we found relatively few investigations that examined cultural variations in the perception of social deviance and, of these, none that focused on adolescents.

This gap in the literature is surprising given that adolescents, who are in transition to adult society, should be a particularly rich source of information about perceptions of deviance. Some theories suggest that discrepancies that exist between the definitions of deviance of adolescent peer groups and those of adult society may explain, in part, the increase in antisocial behavior that occurs during the adolescent period (e.g., Sutherland, 1947). Even so, we have found no studies in which adolescents were directly asked what they consider to be deviant and none in which comparisons were made of the responses of adolescents and their parents or other adults.

We responded to this gap by exploring the concept of a "bad kid" among samples of high school students and their mothers in three cultures: American, Chinese, and Japanese. Our goals were threefold:

First, we wished to examine cross-cultural differences in perceptions of deviance as expressed in the image of a bad kid. As mentioned earlier, notions of *good* and *bad* represent fundamental aspects of culture that may be reflected in various projective systems. For example, Funkhouser (1991) studied stereotypes of good and evil by asking college students in five countries to complete a questionnaire while imagining themselves to be, first, a very good person and, then, a very bad person. Ekstrand and Ekstrand (1986) had 9- to 13-year-old Swedish and Indian children and their parents describe what they regarded as good and bad behavior and the sanctions they expected for the latter. None of these studies focused primarily on adolescents and none of them directly compared American respondents with those from East Asian cultures.

We purposefully selected two East Asian cultures for comparison because of their widely diverse histories and cultural traditions and because other investigators have described distinctive attributes of what members of an East Asian society (i.e., Japan) considered a good child (White & LeVine, 1986). Because perceptions of deviance, like perceptions of normalcy, are assumed to be influenced by social values, the description of a bad kid was anticipated to be very different in Japan, Taiwan, and the United States. For example, the high value that Asian cultures traditionally place on education and academic achievement suggests that members of Japanese and Chinese societies would be likely to define a bad kid as someone who disrupts schoolwork and learning. The emphasis on group participation and social cooperation in Japan (e.g., Kojima, 1989; Reischauer, 1977) may also lead Japanese individuals to express more concern about disturbances in interpersonal and other social relationships than would their peers from an individualistic society such as the United States. Similarly given the overriding importance that Asian cultures, especially the Chinese, place on maintaining order in society and in the family, individuals from these cultures would, to a greater degree than Americans, be expected to associate a bad kid with behavior that disrupts the social order or damages family ties. Finally the strongly individualistic nature of American culture (Bellah, Madsen, Sullivan, Swidler, & Tipton, 1985), in addition to the high incidence of aggressive and externalizing problem behaviors among adolescents in the United States (Weisz, Suwanlert, Chaiyasit, & Walter, 1987), implies that Americans may define a bad kid in terms of individual psychological characteristics, such as lack of self-control.

A second goal was to examine variables other than culture that might affect definitions of deviance. Perceptions of a bad kid are influenced not only by social values but also by the characteristics of the individuals themselves. We were interested in looking at three characteristics of heightened importance during the adolescent years: success in school, general adjustment, and social skills. For example, students within each culture who value academics or are successful in school may be more disturbed by a peer who disrupts activities at school than would students for whom school plays a less important role. Second, students who report good psychological adjustment may be more likely to consider behaviors related to lack of self-control as being characteristic of a bad kid than students who have less satisfactory adjustment. Third, adolescents who get along well with their peers may be more likely than those who are less adept at social relationships to see disturbances in interpersonal harmony as features of a bad kid.

A final goal was to gain a better understanding of the process by which cultural values and behavioral standards regarding deviance are transmitted to children in the different societies. To do this, we compared adolescents' ideas of a bad kid with those of their mothers. Given the emphasis on individualism in the United States, in contrast to the collectivistic orientation of East Asian cultures (e.g., Triandis, 1987) and the fact that parent-adolescent conflict appears to be less extreme and more subtle in Asian than in American families (Rohlen, 1983; White, 1993), we expected to find a greater degree of concordance in perceptions of deviance among Japanese and Chinese adolescents and mothers than among their American counterparts.

METHOD

Subjects

Data were collected in 1990 and 1991 in three large metropolitan areas: Minneapolis; Taipei, Taiwan; and Sendai, Japan. Respondents included 204 American eleventh-grade students and 204 American mothers, 237 Chinese students and 224 Chinese mothers, and 157 Japanese students and 167 Japanese mothers. Although the intent was to interview both students and their mothers, there were some cases in which students were interviewed but their mothers could not be interviewed and vice versa. In addition, some students and some mothers did not respond to the question about the bad kid. The students, who were selected to constitute a representative sample of children in each city, were part of a longitudinal study that was begun in 1980, when they were in first grade (see Stevenson, Stigler, & Lee, 1986, for a detailed description of sampling procedures and subject selection). The percentages of girls from Minneapolis, Taipei, and Sendai in the present samples were 55%, 49%, and 49%, respectively.

In Minneapolis, consent to participate in the study was obtained directly from the students themselves. In Taipei and Sendai, school authorities were responsible for giving consent. We first obtained permission from the school principal and then sought the cooperation of the teachers. After each teacher's permission was granted, participation from the students was obligatory and universal. Such procedures to obtain consent were those approved by the sponsoring agencies and the relevant authorities in each city.

The families represented the full range of socioeconomic levels existing in each metropolitan area; however, the occupational and educational status of the families differed. Skilled workers in Japan (51%) and Taiwan (38%) accounted for the largest percentage of fathers' occupations. In the United States, semiprofessional (40%) was the most frequently indicated level of occupation among fathers. The fathers' average number of years in school was 15 in Minneapolis, 11 in Taipei, and 13 in Sendai. Occupational level of the mothers who worked was similar to that of their husbands, but their average number of years of education was lower: 14 in Minneapolis, 9 in Taipei, and 13 in Sendai.

Measures

We took great care in constructing the measures to ensure that the wording of the questions conveyed the same meaning in each language. Members of our research group included bilingual native speakers of Chinese, Japanese, and English. In contrast to the common procedure of translation and back translation, we devised all the items simultaneously in the three languages. Consensus on item selection and wording of the instruments was arrived at through further discussion with bilingual and trilingual colleagues in the United States, Taiwan, and Japan. We believe this process of simultaneous construction of the questions considerably reduced the inconsistencies in nuance that often arise when items are initially written in English and then translated into unrelated languages, such as Chinese and Japanese. Rather than trying to find appropriate words and questions in a second language after the questions have been constructed, simultaneous composition allows discussion of terms by psychologists familiar with the languages before items are selected.

The items regarding a "bad kid" were part of a questionnaire that was given to students in all three locations.

Bad kid. In line with prior studies defining a good child (e.g., White & LeVine, 1986), we asked both students and their mothers the following question about a bad child: "Think of someone your (child's) age who you would consider to be a 'bad kid.' Describe what kind of person that would be." We also asked whether respondents were thinking of a boy girl, or someone of no specific gender in answering the question about a bad kid.

It is not difficult to find equivalents for the phrase *bad kid* in Japanese and Chinese. We used the term *warui ko* in the Japanese version of the question, and *huai haizi* in the Chinese. The phrases are simple and straightforward and have approximately the same connotations in each language. For example, in a standard Japanese-English dictionary examples of the word *warui* (bad) were given in sentences such as "He is a very bad boy—always up to mischief" (Kondo & Takano, 1986, p. 1897). Similarly, the Chinese word for *bad*—*huai*—was illustrated in a Chinese-English dictionary in the following way: "Bad elements held sway while good people were pushed around" (*Modern Chinese-English Dictionary*, 1988, p. 376).

We developed the coding scheme for the open-ended questions based on an analysis of the answers from subsamples of respondents in each culture. We were able to sort responses into 12 domains of behavior. We have concentrated our attention on the five major domains that appeared to us to be most likely to yield cross-cultural differences: *society, family, school, interpersonal harmony,* and *self-control*. In addition, two more major domains emerged in the analysis of the results: *substance abuse* and *crime*. (Examples of statements included in each domain are given later.) The seven major domains, including substance abuse and crime, accounted for 81% of American, 67% of Chinese, and 89% of Japanese students' responses. The remaining five domains dealt with *religion, sexual behavior, physical appearance, self-destructive behavior* and *physical aggression*. None of these do-

TABLE 1
Means and Standard Deviations of Measurements of Students' Personal Characteristics

Measure	USA[e]		Taiwan[f]		Japan[g]	
	M	SD	M	SD	M	SD
Value of academics[a]	6.2	1.0	5.5	1.2	5.2	1.3
How important is it to you: (a) that you go to college? (b) that you get good grades? (c) to study hard to go to college? (d) to study hard to get good grades?						
Social relationships[b]	5.5	0.8	4.9	1.0	4.6	1.0
How would you rate yourself in comparison to other persons your age: (a) in getting along with other young people? (b) in working out everyday problems on your own? (c) in caring about others?						
Psychological adjustment[c]						
Stress: How often do you feel stressed (under pressure)?	3.7	1.0	3.4	1.2	2.9	1.3
Depression: How often do you feel depressed?	3.0	1.0	3.3	1.1	2.8	1.2
Aggression: In the past month, how often have you: (a) felt like hitting someone? (b) felt like destroying something (c) gotten into serious arguments or fights with other students? (d) felt angry at your teacher?	2.1	0.8	1.8	0.8	1.8	0.7
Achievement[d]	12.1	7.6	21.8	10.4	20.1	6.6

Note. All $dfs = (2,557–572)$, $Fs = 6.93–75.10$, $ps < .001$.
[a]Answers ranged from *not at all important* (1) to *very important* (7). Cronbach alphas ranged from .67 to .71. [b]Questions used 7-point scales ranging from *much below average* (1) to *much above average* (7). Cronbach alphas ranged from .65 to .74. [c]Students rated the frequency with which they experienced these feelings on 5-point scales ranging from *never* (a) to *almost every day* (5). Cromback alphas for the aggression ratings ranged from .72 to .77. [d]The test of mathematics achievement (Stevenson, Chen, & Lee, 1993) contained 47 open-ended items covering a broad range of mathematical topics. The Cronback alphas ranged from .92 to .95. [e]$n = 190–199$. [f]$n = 221–228$. [g] = $n = 147–154$.

mains encompassed as many as 10% of the students' responses in each culture and yielded no significant cross-cultural differences. Five percent of American, 4% of Chinese, and 6% of Japanese students' responses were idiosyncratic and could not be categorized under one of the 12 domains.

The domains of behavior were coded according to a common scheme for the three languages and cultures. Responses were coded independently by two native speakers of each language. Each pair resolved any disagreements in coding through discussion between themselves and, if necessary through group discussion among the coders from all three locations. The percentage of agreement among coders before resolution was 87% (United States), 87% (Taiwan), and 84% (Japan).

Respondents were allowed to give as many characteristics of a bad kid as they wished; however, we coded only the first six responses from each subject. Within the six responses, only one mention of each domain was counted, regardless of the number of examples given by a subject for a particular domain. Thus, we sought to determine the number of respondents in each culture who mentioned each domain, rather than the number of responses given by subjects within each of the domains.

Students also rated themselves on a number of variables, including the degree to which they valued academics, their social relationships, and their psychological adjustment (see Table 1).

RESULTS

Students' Responses

There was little concordance between the responses of the American and the Japanese or Chinese students or between the Chinese and Japanese students (see Table 2). Whereas interpersonal harmony predominated in the responses of the Japanese students, the responses of the American and Chinese students were much more evenly distributed across the five domains (see Figure 1). Consistent with the importance to adolescents of having satisfactory relations with their peers, the highest frequency of response of Chinese and Japanese students and the second highest of American students was interpersonal harmony. More than one third of the American students, however, also mentioned behaviors related to self-control, and more than one third of the Chinese students mentioned school and society. Additionally, American students noted substance abuse more frequently than Chinese and Japanese students, but Japanese students noted crime more frequently than did students in the other two groups. Cross-cultural differences in the percentages of students who mentioned a particular behavioral domain were evaluated by computing chi-square values. When they were found to be significant, a series of pairwise comparisons was conducted to identify possible sources of difference. Alpha levels for these pairwise tests were lowered to $p < .016$, according to the Bonferroni Correction (Neter, Wasserman, & Kutner, 1985).

Society-related behavior. Nearly one and a half times as many Chinese as American adolescents and three times as many Chinese as Japanese adolescents mentioned society-related conduct (i.e., "rebels against society" "makes trouble for society" and "is a member of a street gang") as characteristic of a bad kid. Because of the importance placed in Japan on identifying with the social world, we had anticipated that many more Japanese students would mention society-related behavior.

Family-related behavior. The family-related domain contained responses that referred to behavior such as being disrespectful of or disobedient toward one's parents, running away from home, or physically attacking family members. Contrary to our expectation, Chinese students were no more likely than American students to cite family-related behaviors as being a feature of their image of a bad kid. Both groups mentioned family-related behaviors more frequently than their Japanese peers.

School. Chinese and Japanese students were not more likely, as we had initially posited, than American students to mention behaviors related to school. In fact, nearly three times as many American as Japanese students mentioned misconduct dealing with school as characteristic of a bad kid.

Four major categories of response fell within the domain of school-related behaviors. Two—"skips school" and "having low motiva-tion"—yielded no significant differences. The other two categories were "breaks rules" and teacher-related responses ("disrespectful to the teacher," "scolded by the teacher," and "badmouthing the teacher"). Among the 82 American, 92 Chinese, and 25 Japanese students giving school-related responses, more Japanese (28%) students mentioned breaking rules than did their Chinese (4%) or American (11%) peers, $\chi^2(1, N = 117) = 12.91$, $p < .05$ and $\chi^2(1, N = 107) = 4.37$, $p < .05$, respectively. Chinese (25%) and Japanese (12%) students were more likely, in turn, than American (2%) students to perceive disrespect for teachers as indicative of a bad kid, $\chi^2(1 N = 174) = 17.94$ $p < .05$ and $\chi^2(1, N = 107) = 3.93$, $p < .05$, respectively.

Interpersonal harmony. As anticipated, Japanese students were much more likely than American or Chinese students to view behaviors disruptive of interpersonal harmony ("hurting other people's feelings," "being argumentative and starting fights," "speaking badly of other people," and "not caring about others") as features of a bad kid.

Self-control. Responses that described a bad kid as "weak-willed," "goes to extremes," "childish," or "immature" were included in the domain of self-control. As anticipated, more American than Chinese or Japa-nese students associated a bad kid with problems in self-control.

Substance abuse. The domain of substance abuse primarily contained references to the use of drugs and alcohol. In the United States, the major type of substance abuse mentioned was drugs (81%), whereas in Taiwan and Japan it was alcohol (76% and 80%, respectively). American students were more likely than Chinese students, who, in turn were more likely than Japanese students, to perceive substance abuse as characterizing a bad kid.

Crime. Responses coded in the crime domain mentioned acts ranging from milder crimes, such as stealing and destruction of property, to serious crimes, such as rape and murder. Japanese students noted crime as a feature of a bad kid significantly more often than did Chinese students. There were no significant differences in the percentages of American and Asian students who mentioned crime.

To determine whether disparities within each culture in the socioeconomic status of the families might have had a significant effect on cross-cultural differences in adolescents' perceptions of a bad kid, log linear analyses were performed on the data. Each behavioral domain served as the dependent variable, with location and occupational level comprising the independent variables. No significant interactive or main effects of occupational level were found for any behavioral domain mentioned by the students in analyses involving either mothers' or fathers' occupation.

In summary, relative to their peers in the other two locations, American students emphasized problems with self-control, Chinese students emphasized disturbances of the social order, and Japanese students emphasized disruptions in interpersonal harmony in their descriptions of a bad kid. Students in the United States were as likely as Chinese and more likely than Japanese students to mention school-related responses. In addition, American students noted substance abuse

TABLE 2

Percentages and Chi-Square Values for United States, Taiwan, and Japan for Analysis of Students' Responses Falling in Various Behavioral Domains

Domain	Percentage of Students			χ^2			
	U	T	J	U-T-J[ae]	U-T[bf]	U-J[cf]	T-J[df]
Society	29	40	14	29.63	7.28*	8.58	28.91
Family	17	24	5	25.01	ns	11.99	25.11
School	43	42	17	32.79	ns	28.77	25.92
Interpersonal harmony	53	50	84	53.19	ns	39.47	48.31
Self-control	38	24	24	13.00	9.44	9.00	ns
Substance abuse	62	40	12	8.90	19.60	89.16	36.54
Crime	10	8	19	10.80	11.5	11.5	9.75*

Note. All $ps < .001$, except where noted. U = United States. T = Taiwan. J = Japan.
[a]$n = 563$. [b]$n = 411$. [c]$n = 340$. [d]$n = 375$. [e]$df = 2$. [f]$df = 1$.
*$p < .01$.

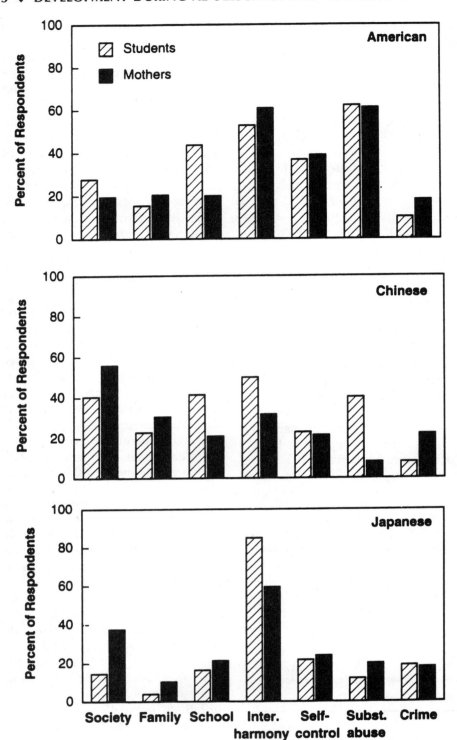

FIGURE 1 Mentions by students and mothers in each culture of the seven behavioral domains

mothers' responses were most frequently related to society. Japanese mothers gave primary emphasis to disruptions in interpersonal harmony. A relatively high proportion of mothers in the United States and Taiwan mentioned substance abuse. References to crime, however, were mentioned with similar frequencies across the three cultures.

Cross-cultural comparisons. With only two exceptions, cross-national differences in mothers' views of a bad kid were similar to those found for their children. First, the mothers in the three cultures displayed a surprising similarity in the low proportion of their responses that were related to school. Second, American mothers were as likely as Japanese, and twice as likely as Chinese mothers, to include disruptions of interpersonal harmony in their descriptions of a bad kid. In line with expectations, American mothers, like their children, tended to perceive lack of self-control as being characteristic of a bad kid more frequently than did their Chinese or Japanese counterparts. Also, Chinese mothers associated a bad kid with behaviors in the domains of society and family. In addition, American mothers were more likely than Chinese mothers, who, in turn, were more likely than Japanese mothers, to mention substance abuse in their descriptions of a bad kid. There were no significant differences in the percentages of mothers in the three cultures who perceived a bad kid as engaging in criminal behavior.

Log linear analyses were conducted to assess the possible influence of socioeconomic status on cross-cultural differences in mothers' perceptions of deviance. Results indicated that neither fathers' nor mothers' occupational level had any significant interactive or main effects on mothers' definitions of a bad kid.

Comparison of Students and Mothers

We next examined the domains in which adolescents' ideas about a

behaviors more frequently than did students in the other two locations. Japanese students mentioned crime significantly more often than Chinese students. For the most part, these emphases were in accord with the cultural orientations in each location.

Mothers' Responses

We next examined the mothers' impressions of a bad kid (see Figure 1 and Table 3). The most frequent responses of American mothers fell into the domain of interpersonal harmony and self-control. Chinese

TABLE 3

Chi-Square Values for United States, Taiwan, and Japan for Analysis of Frequency of Mothers' Responses Falling in Various Behavioral Domains

Domain	Percentage of Mothers			χ^2			
	U	T	J	U-T-J[ae]	U-T[bf]	U-J[f]	T-J[df]
Society	19	56	37	57.46	57.38	14.33	12.01
Family	20	31	10	21.79	ns	6.61*	21.24
School	20	21	21	ns	ns	ns	ns
Interpersonal harmony	61	32	59	42.64	34.79	ns	27.82
Self-control	39	21	24	17.33	14.75	8.93*	ns
Substance abuse	61	40	20	61.37	17.78	60.50	16.86
Crime	18	22	18	ns	ns	ns	ns

bad kid differed from those of the mothers. As can be seen in Table 4, culture played a major role in determining the nature of the differences. Among the three cultures, American students and mothers evidenced the highest degree of similarity in their perceptions of a bad kid. Only in the school-related domain did the frequency of responses differ between American mothers and students. Adolescents, more than mothers, viewed a bad kid as someone who disrupts activities in school. Chinese students were more likely than Chinese mothers to perceive a bad kid as disturbing school-related activities and interpersonal harmony. Chinese mothers, however, were more likely than students to cite behaviors related to society. Like their Chinese peers, adolescents in Japan referred to interpersonal harmony more often than did the mothers. In contrast, more Japanese mothers than students gave responses that fell in the domains of society and family. There were no significant differences in any of the three cultures in the percentages of responses of students and mothers that referred to substance abuse. Chinese mothers were, however, more likely than Chinese students to include the commission of crimes in their descriptions of a bad kid.

In addition to cross-generational group differences, we also compared the degree of within-family concordance in ideas about a bad kid across the three cultures (see Table 5). *Concordance* was defined as the number of agreements between adolescents and their mothers regarding a specific domain of bad kid behavior divided by the total number of adolescent-mother pairs in a particular culture. We then calculated T values to determine the significance of cross-cultural differences in the percentages of concordance.

Cross-national differences in the pattern of within-family concordance regarding notions of a bad kid were less consistent than those found in the cross-generational group comparisons. American and Chinese students and their mothers exhibited higher concordance in their view of a bad kid as disrupting school-related activities than did their Japanese counterparts. Adolescents and their mothers in the United States were more likely to agree that a bad kid lacked self-control than were their peers in Taiwan and Japan. Similarly, Chinese students and their mothers were in greater agreement than American and Japanese students and their mothers that disruptive behaviors related to family and society characterized a bad kid. In perceiving a bad kid as someone who disturbs interpersonal harmony, Japanese students and their mothers demonstrated a significantly higher degree of concordance than did their American and Chinese peers. Additionally, American students and their mothers demonstrated a much higher degree of concordance than their Chinese and Japanese counterparts in their mention of substance abuse as a feature of a bad kid. There were no significant cross-cultural differences in the degree of concordance with which students and their mothers described a bad kid as someone who commits a crime.

TABLE 4

Percentages and Chi-Square Values for Evaluating the Similarity of Students' and Mothers' Responses Regarding Domains of Bad Kid Behavior

Domain	USA[a]			Taiwan[b]			Japan[c]		
	Percentage			Percentage			Percentage		
	Students	Mothers	χ^2	Students	Mothers	χ^2	Students	Mothers	χ^2
Society	28	19	ns	40	56	9.66*	15	37	19.80
Family	15	20	ns	23	31	ns	4	10	ns
School	44	20	24.29	41	21	19.69	16	21	ns
Interpersonal harmony	53	61	ns	50	32	13.95	85	59	23.52
Self-control	37	39	ns	23	21	ns	22	24	ns
Substance abuse	62	61	ns	40	40	ns	12	20	ns
Crime	10	18	ns	8	22	17.06	19	18	ns

Note. All *p*s < .001, except where noted.
[a]*n* = 389. [b]*n* = 429. [c]*n* = 307.
*p < .01.

In general, adolescents and mothers differed significantly in the frequency with which they mentioned behaviors falling under the five major behavioral domains, but within-family comparisons yielded even less concordance between students and their mothers. The domains in which significant discrepancies emerged were those that apparently were the most crucial to students in each of the cultures: school-related behavior in the United States and interpersonal harmony and society-related behavior in Taiwan and Japan. The direction of these differences—students emphasizing school and interpersonal harmony, mothers emphasizing society—suggests the broader, more conventional perspective of the mothers, in contrast to the more personal viewpoint of the students.

In terms of within-family concordance, American students and their mothers were in greater agreement that a bad kid lacked self-control, Chinese students and their mothers that a bad kid disrupted society and family, and Japanese students and their mothers that a bad kid disturbed interpersonal harmony, than were their counterparts in the other two cultures. In addition, American adolescents and their mothers exhibited a much greater degree of concordance regarding the mention of substance abuse than did their Chinese and Japanese peers. Generally, the domains in which cross-national differences in within-family concordance were the greatest appeared to conform to the social values that are emphasized in each of the cultures.

Correlates of Student Mentions of Bad-Kid Behaviors

Finally, we sought to determine whether the personal characteristics of the adolescents themselves were related to ones they associated with a bad kid. To evaluate whether these characteristics were related to the likelihood that a student would mention behavior in a specific domain, we formed high and low groups on each of the six measures described in Table 1. Students were included in a high group if their ratings on the measures or mathematics test scores fell within the upper third of the students in their respective cultures. Students in the lower third constituted the low group.

We performed log linear analyses using location and one of the student characteristics as the independent variables and each behavioral domain as the dependent variable. To test for significant effects, factors in the model were systematically omitted over successive analyses, and differences in the -2 log likelihood statistics, which are distributed as chi-square values, were examined. We report these chi-square values in describing main and interaction effects.

There was little relation between the characteristics of the students and their descriptions of a bad kid. Only one main effect was significant. Students who held a high value for academics mentioned deviant behavior in school as characterizing a bad kid more often than did students who did not value academics (44% vs. 25%), $\chi^2(1, N = 384) = 8.36$, $p < .01$.

Gender Differences

Log linear analyses were also used to assess the effects of gender on the likelihood that students in different cultures would include a certain domain of behavior in their concept of a bad kid. Main effects of gender were found in the domains of school and family $\chi^2(1, N = 563) = 7.59$, $p < .01$ and $\chi^2(1, N = 563) = 8.40$, $p < .01$. Girls were more likely than boys to view a bad kid as someone who disrupted school activities (41% vs. 29%) and damaged family ties (19% vs. 11%). No significant gender × country interactions emerged.

When asked whether they were thinking of a boy, girl, or someone of no specific gender in answering the question about the bad kid, the majority of students in all three countries reported that they were thinking of someone of no specific gender (see Figure 2). Furthermore, there were significantly more students in the United States and Taiwan who said they thought of a boy than those who said they thought of a girl, $\chi^2(1, N = 347)$ 22.82, $= p < .01$ and $\chi^2(1, N = 396) = 9.46$, $p < .01$, respectively. In contrast, Japanese students were far more likely than their American and Chinese peers to think of a girl, $\chi^2(1, N = 347) = 21.42$, $p < .001$ and $\chi^2(1, N = 396) = 22.40$, $p < .001$, respectively. Boys in all three countries more often thought of a bad kid as someone of their own gender than did girls (United States:

TABLE 5
Correlations of Mothers' and Their Children's Conceptions of Bad Kid Behavior (Percentage of Pairs in Which Both Mother and Child Mentioned Some Item Falling Within Each Domain)

Domain	Country			t		
	U^a	T^b	J^c	U-T	U-J	T-J
Society	.03	.21	.07	5.81	ns	4.06
Family	.04	.09	.01	2.11*	ns	4.82
School	.12	.11	.03	ns	3.23	3.10
Interpersonal harmony	.35	.17	.51	6.32	3.74	6.95
Self-control	.18	.04	.03	4.67	5.00	ns
Substance abuse	.41	.02	.02	10.26	10.26	ns
Crime	.02	.01	.03	ns	ns	ns

Note. U = United States. T = Taiwan. J = Japan. All $ps < .001$, except where noted.
[a]$n = 182$. [b]$n = 204$. [c]$n = 146$.
*$p < .05$.

56% versus 35%, $\chi^2[1, N = 190] = 8.71, p < .01$; Taiwan: 49% versus 20%, $\chi^2[1\ N = 239] = 22.08, p < .001$; Japan: 34% versus 7%, $\chi^2[1, N = 157] = 17.36, p < .001$). American (9% vs. 0%) and Japanese (33% vs. 8%), but not Chinese (9% vs 2%), girls thought of a girl significantly more often than did their male peers (United States: $\chi^2[1, N = 190] = 7.98, p < .01$; Japan, $\chi^2[1, N = 157] = 15.28, p < .001$).

DISCUSSION

When we began this study, we focused on five domains of behavior that we believed would lead to different definitions of a bad kid in American, Chinese, and Japanese cultures. Although our analyses yielded 12 different domains of behavior, 7 were sufficient to encompass the vast majority of the behaviors mentioned. Although there were differences in the degree to which these broad domains were represented among the three cultures, we also found commonalities across the cultures. For example, *disruptions in interpersonal harmony* was a dominant response in all three locations, reflecting the common pattern of adapting to the peer group and to the cultural demands faced by adolescents in all societies.

Interesting cross-cultural differences did emerge. Adolescents and mothers differed significantly in the frequency with which they mentioned behaviors falling under the five major behavioral domains. Students seemed to conceive of deviance from a more personal, circumscribed perspective, in contrast to the mothers, whose descriptions of a bad kid more consistently suggested broader conventional concerns, a finding that agrees with that of Smetana (1988). In other words, students' perceptions of a bad kid tended to deviate more from expected cultural values than did those of the mothers, apparently reflecting the transitional nature of the socialization process that characterizes the adolescent period in the

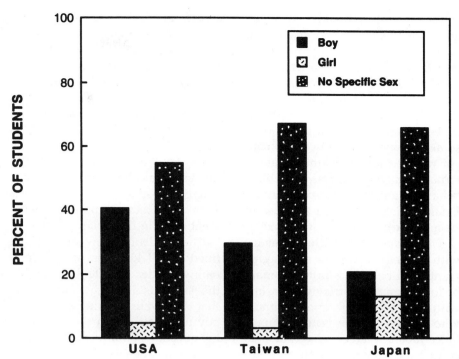

FIGURE 2 Percentages of students thinking of a boy, girl, or someone of no specific gender when describing a bad kid.

three societies (e.g., Chang, 1989; White, 1993).

Cross-cultural differences in the degree of within-family concordance in perceptions of a bad kid were generally found in those domains that appear to represent the most prominent social values in each culture. American adolescents and their mothers exhibited higher concordance in the domain of self-control; Chinese adolescents and their mothers showed a greater level of agreement in the domains of society and family; and Japanese adolescents and their mothers were most likely to agree about the domain of interpersonal harmony. These results suggest that the nature of the socialization process by which perceptions of deviance are transmitted from mothers to children is basically similar in the three cultures. That is, in all three locations, the criteria that mothers deemed as being most important in defining an individual as bad were generally reflected in the responses of their adolescent children.

The concept of a bad kid found among American, Chinese, and Japanese high school students and their mothers, although generally

consistent with the social values espoused in the three cultures, did not necessarily accord with the actual prevalence of deviant behavior in each of the cultures. For example, a higher percentage of Chinese than American students mentioned society-related behavior, despite the fact that Taiwan has a much lower incidence of antisocial behavior than does the United States (Federal Bureau of Investigation, 1990; Ministry of the Interior, Republic of China, 1989). Similarly, a much larger percentage of Japanese than American students cited disruptions in interpersonal harmony in their descriptions of a bad kid, even though interstudent conflict in Japan is not more pervasive or serious than it is in the United States (Federal Bureau of Investigation, 1990; Headquarters of the Youth and Children Program, General Affairs Division, 1989).

The tendency of American students to define a bad kid in terms of lack of self-control is consonant with the work of Tropman (1986) who pointed out the fundamental conflict between control and permissiveness in American culture. A focus on self-control is also compatible with the greater tendency toward an internal locus of control orientation that has been found among American, relative to Chinese and Japanese, individuals (e.g., Chiu, 1986; Evans, 1981). In addition, American adolescents' descriptions of a bad kid as someone lacking in self-control concur with the higher frequency of externalizing and aggressive problem behaviors among adolescents in the United States compared to those in Asian countries (Weisz et al., 1987).

The remarkably high frequency with which Japanese adolescents mentioned behaviors in the domain of interpersonal harmony is in line with the writings of various authors who emphasize the central importance Japanese give to interpersonal consensus and cooperation (e.g., Kojima, 1989; Reischauer, 1977).

The importance of maintaining order and tranquility in the society and in family relationships is a cornerstone of Confucian philosophy upon which much of Chinese culture is based. This traditional emphasis is reflected in the frequent mention of society- and family-related behaviors among the Chinese respondents in our study. (The Chinese culture in Taiwan, it should be noted, tends to be more traditional in terms of customs and values than that in Hong Kong or Mainland China.)

In some cases, the students' responses departed greatly from what we expected on the basis of presumed cultural values. For example, students in the United States mentioned disruptive behaviors at school as characteristic of a bad kid more frequently than did students in Japan. One explanation is that American students place a higher value on school and academic achievement than do their counterparts in Japan, where education and learning are thought to be held in especially high esteem. In support of this explanation, we found that American adolescents indicated significantly higher ratings than did their Japanese peers on our measure

assessing the value students gave to academic achievement.

Of special interest was the high frequency of substance abuse, particularly drug-related, mentions in the United States. In Taiwan and Japan, possession of drugs is considered to be a serious felony punishable by imprisonment; the consequences in the United States are less severe. The use of alcohol, which is not considered a serious crime, was the form of substance more frequently mentioned in the Asian countries.

The students' view of what defined a bad kid was not predominantly gender-specific: Over 50% of the students in each country said that they were thinking of neither a boy nor a girl when they answered the question about the bad kid. Nevertheless, when students did reply that they were thinking of a person of a specific gender, boys more than girls said that they were thinking of someone of their own gender. These findings are consistent with statistics showing that adolescent boys are more likely to engage in deviant behavior than are adolescent girls (Federal Bureau of Investigation, 1990).

Just as efforts to describe a good kid (White & Levine, 1986) have yielded interesting insights into cultural differences, this exploratory study of the definitions of a bad kid given by adolescents and their mothers adds to our understanding of the socialization of cultural values in American and East Asian societies. These high school students' responses differed according to culture, as did those of their mothers; but adolescents and mothers were not always in agreement as to which behaviors defined a bad kid.

ACKNOWLEDGMENTS

This study was supported by National Science Foundation Grant MDR 89564683 to Harold W. Stevenson. The collection of the data in Taiwan was supported by National Science Council of R.O.C. Grants No. NSC 79-80-81-0301-H-006-08Y to Chen-Chin Hsu and Huei-Chen Ko.

We thank our colleagues, Shin Ying Lee and Kazuo Kato, and all the other people who have participated in this study. We are indebted to Yann-Yann Shieh, Kathy Kolb, Susan Fust, Heidi Schweingruber, and Etsuko Horikawa, to our research coordinators, and to the teachers and students for their cooperation. We also thank Chuansheng Chen for his helpful comments on the manuscript.

REFERENCES

Becker, H. (1964). *Outsiders*. Glencoe, IL: Free Press.

Bellah, R. N., Madsen, R., Sullivan, W. M., Swidler, A., & Tipton, S. M. (1985). *Habits of the heart: Individualism and commitment in American life*. Berkeley: University of California Press.

Chang, C. (1989). The growing generation in a changing Chinese society: Youth problems and strategies. *Bulletin of Educational Psychology, 22*, 243–254.

Chiu, L.-H. (1986). Locus of control in intellectual situations in American and Chinese schoolchildren. *International Journal of Psychology, 21*, 167–176.

Evans, H. M. (1981). Internal-external locus of control and work association: Research with Japanese and American students. *Journal of Cross-Cultural Psychology, 12*, 372–382.

Ekstrand, G., & Ekstrand, L. H. (1986). How children perceive parental norms and sanctions in two different cultures. *Educational and Psychological Interactions, 88*, p. 28.

Federal Bureau of Investigation. (1990). *Uniform crime reports for the United States*. Washington, DC: United States Government Printing Office.

Funkhouser, G. R. (1991). Cross-cultural similarities and differences in stereotypes of good and evil: A pilot study. *Journal of Social Psychology, 131*, 859–874.

Hardy, R. E., Cull, J. G., & Campbell, M. E. (1987). Perception of selected disabilities in the United States and Portugal: A cross-cultural comparison. *Journal of Human Behavior and Learning 4*, 1–12.

Headquarters of the Youth and Children Program, General Affairs Division (1989) Seishonen hakusho, heisei gannenpan [Adolescent white paper, 1989]. Tokyo, Japan: Okurasho.

Kondo, I., & Takano, F. (Eds.). (1986). *Progressive Japanese-English dictionary*. Tokyo: Shogakkan.

Kojima, H. (1989). *Kosodate no dento o tazunete* [Inquiring into the tradition of childrearing]. Tokyo, Japan: Shinyosha.

LeVine, R. A. (1973). *Culture, behavior and personality*. Chicago: Aldine.

Modern Chinese-English Dictionary. (1988). Beijing, People's Republic of China: Foreign Language and Teaching Research Press.

Ministry of the Interior, Republic of China (1989). *Crime statistics.* Taipei, Taiwan: Ministry of the Interior.

Neter, J., Wasserman, W., & Kutner, M. (1985). *Applied linear statistical models.* Homewood, IL: Irwin.

Newman, G. (1976). *Comparative deviance: Perception and law in six cultures.* New York: Elsevier.

Reischauer, E. O. (1977). *The Japanese.* Cambridge, MA: Harvard University Press.

Rivers, P C., Sarata, B. P., & Anagnostopulos, M. (1986). Perceptions of deviant stereotypes by alcoholism, mental health, and school personnel in New Zealand and the United States. *International Journal of the Addictions, 21,* 123–129.

Robin, M. W., & Spires, R. (1983). Drawing the line: Deviance in cross-cultural perspective. *International Journal of Group Tensions, 13,* 106–131.

Rohlen, T. (1983). *Japanese high schools.* Berkeley: University of California Press.

Scheff, T. S. (1974). The labelling theory of mental illness. *American Sociological Review, 39,* 444–452.

Smetana, J. G. (1988). Adolescents' and parents' conceptions of parental authority. *Child Development, 59,* 321–335.

Stevenson, H. W, Chen, C., & Lee, S. Y (1993). Mathematics achievement. Chinese, Japanese, and American children: Ten years later. *Science, 259,* 53–58.

Stevenson, H. W., Lee, S. Y., & Stigler, J. W. (1986). Mathematics achievement of Chinese, Japanese, and American children. *Science, 231,* 693–699.

Sutherland, E. (1947). *Principles of criminology.* Philadelphia, PA: Lippincott.

Triandis, H. C. (1987). Collectivism vs. individualism: A reconceptualization of a basic concept in cross-cultural social psychology. In C. Bagley & G. K. Verma (Eds.), *Personality, cognition and values: Cross-cultural perspectives of childhood and adolescence.* London: MacMillan.

Tropman, J. E. (1986). *Conflict in culture: Permissions versus controls and alcohol use in American society.* Lanham, MD: University Press of America.

Weisz, J. R., Suwanlert, S., Chaiyasit, W., & Walter, B. R. (1987). Over- and undercontrolled referral problems among children and adolescents from Thailand and the United States: The *wat* and *wai* of cultural differences. *Journal of Consulting and Clinical Psychology, 55,* 719–726.

White, M. (1993). *The material child: Coming of age in Japan and America.* New York: Free Press.

White, M. I., & LeVine, R. A. (1986). What is an *ii ko* (good child)? In H. Stevenson, H. Azuma, & K. Hakuta (Eds.), *Child development and education in Japan.* New York: Freeman.

Wilson, L. G., & Young, D. (1988). Diagnosis of severely ill inpatients in China: A collaborative project using the Structured Clinical Interview for DSM-III (SCID). *Journal of Nervous and Mental Disease, 176,* 585–592.

Received August 14, 1993
Revision received June 14, 1993
Accepted November 18, 1993

HIV Infected Youth Speaks About Needs for Support and Health Care

Wayne Davis is a 24-year-old, HIV positive youth from Oregon who became infected when he was 17. He currently lives in San Francisco and is the coordinator of the HIV Positive Youth Speakers Bureau, sponsored by Health Initiatives for Youth. He recently shared his personal experiences with the editor of Target 2000, stating that it sounded important to have the opportunity to let adolescent health care providers know about the needs of HIV infected youth. The following is his story.

Early Lessons in Life

I think in order to explain how I got where I am today, I have to go back a little earlier than when I actually tested positive for the virus. Most of my life from birth to the age of 9, I was with my mother and she was very abusive. Every day she beat me. As she beat me she would say things like "this is your fault" and "if only you were a better child I wouldn't beat you like this. I would be a better mother if you were a better child." That taught me that things were my fault. It taught me guilt. It taught me to really feel bad about myself.

I had an uncle who was sexually abusive. He molested my brother and me. That taught me that my body wasn't mine and that other people had the right to do to me whatever they wanted to do. All of my messages growing up were very unhealthy. When I was 9, my mother left and joined

 From *Target 2000*, Summer 1995, pp. 8-10. © 1995 by the American Medical Association. Reprinted by permission.

the Hare Krishnas. Mental illness runs in my family, my grandmother was really strange and my mother is unstable mentally. She needed other people to run her life. She went through churches and different places to do this. When she joined the Hare Krishnas, I was in a foster home. She wrote us and said "some day you will understand but I have to leave." You know your mother is supposed to be there no matter what. It's a given. It's a very solid form of support. It's fundamental, regardless of how messed up she is, she is supposed to be there. So, her leaving taught me that I can't trust people, I can't trust my environment, I can't trust people to be there. That made me kind of bitter.

I started running away. I had run away before but I started running away to the streets. This was different because before I was running away from the beatings. When I went to the streets I found a real community. I found people who were willing to take care of me, be my friend, and treat me like I had decisions to make. That was really important to me. So I started to run away "to" things instead of "from" things. I started running away to my family on the streets.

Life on the Streets

There are few things that you can do on the streets to survive and being 9 years old there are even fewer things. You could rob people but I was too little. You could do burglaries but I got caught doing that. I couldn't deal drugs because I didn't have the heart for it. There was only one thing left that I could do. That was to sell myself. It made perfect sense to me because all I had known was hurt and that my body wasn't mine. All I had known was that I should feel bad about myself. That just fit right in. I started doing that and it's hard selling yourself on the streets. It really takes something out of you.

The only way that I could live with myself or the only way that I could deal with the pain that I was putting myself through was to do drugs. So I started shooting up speed when I was about 10, which for the first time in my life, I remember clearly I felt like I was in control. I felt that nobody could hurt me or do anything to me. No matter what anybody did I could deal with it. That was a really good feeling. It took foreign substances to make me feel like that but I didn't care. I felt like it and that's what's important. So, that was pretty much my life.

I would run away to the streets and stay gone from the juvenile system for anywhere from a couple of days to a couple of months. I would get caught and, since I was on probation for stealing, they would hold me for 8 days in juvenile hall and then place me into a foster home or group home. I would be there for all of about 3 hours and I would leave. I did that over and over again. All together I've been in 18 different group homes

and 26 different foster homes. Finally they didn't have anywhere to send me. They ran out of places to put me so they committed me to the juvenile jail.

One Foster Home

I met a security guard at the juvenile jail who helped me to run away. He befriended me and treated me nice but while I was a runaway, he abused me. He pedophiled me. I remember at one point we were on the lake shooting at bottles and he turned to me and said, "what would stop me from raping you and killing you right now?" I remember I was thinking really hard about what I could say. I told him that I had called my sister and told her where I was and gave her his license plate number. He said, oh that's a good answer. I turned myself in to him and then went back to juvenile hall. They released me and I was back on the streets for awhile. I was about 14 then.

I was doing drugs for a while and I woke up one morning in a pair of shorts. I was in Portland, Oregon, in the middle of winter which was really cold. I had the phone number of this security guard in my pocket so I called him up and he came and got me. I lived with him for about 1½ years. I became a foster child of his and I received some really mixed messages from him. On the one hand, he was a real father figure which I had never had. He taught me how to hunt, how to fish, how to farm, and how to be what I felt was a man. On the other hand, at night time I was going to his room and he was having sex with me. It was really a mixed up time of my life. Then he started getting other foster children and ended up getting 6 or 7 other foster children ranging from the age of 9 to 14. I figured out that he was messing with them too and he kicked me out. So I went back to the streets. I felt so bad about myself because I knew what was going on in his home and I just did my best to block it out of my mind by using a lot of drugs.

Down and Out—With HIV

I had heard about HIV. What I was hearing was that if you get it you die and that older gay men get it. I figured out that there was a lot [of] attention that went along with HIV. I was hanging out with this guy who was HIV positive. He was young. He was 23 and he had access to money and to drugs. I did a pile of coke about the size of my fist for about a period of a day with him one time. At the end of it, I was coming down and feeling really bad. I looked at him and realized that he had my way out. I was hurting so bad that I just realized that he could help me out. He could stop my hurting. So I told

him to give me his blood and he came over and he did.

So, October 16, 1988, I infected myself. It was strange because when I took the needle out of my arm, I didn't feel any different. For some reason I thought I would feel better. I thought something would change like some sparks would go off or I would become animated or feel better. I didn't. I was still here. I had been tested before that and I had tested negative. A couple days after this incident, I got really sick and went into the hospital. About 6 months later, I tested positive.

I remember when I tested, it was a confidential test. It was the type of place where you had to give a name. It didn't necessarily have to be yours. For some reason I gave them my real name. They called me back and told me to come in and get my results. So there was this woman from the Salvation Army Greenhouse named Margie who was really supportive of me. She is one of the few solid influences I had in my life. I asked her to go with me and she did. She had been diagnosed with cancer before. She had gone into remission and she knew what it was like to be told that you have a life threatening illness. She told me it was good idea to take somebody to hear what was being said because I wouldn't hear anything if I tested positive. She was right. She went in with me and we sat down and they told me that I tested positive to the HIV virus and all I could hear was mumbling and I was kind of just nodding my head. I think I was doing it at the right time.

For the next four years, all I did was get loaded. I don't really remember a lot about it. The things I do remember were really traumatic. I know I hurt a lot of people and myself a lot. I slept with a lot of people. Most of them I used condoms with and a lot of times I didn't. I didn't care. People were items, commodities, things. I was only a thing and that was as deep as people went.

A Move to San Francisco and to Medical Care

When I was 19, I ended up coming down to San Francisco because I was shot at in Portland. When I got here the drugs were better and so I decided to live here. Somebody from Portland told me to go to the Larkin Street Youth Center and get myself "hooked up." I went to Larkin Street and talked with Mike Kennedy. I dressed up to go there. I was trying to show everybody how together I was. When I first meet people, I am really good at being presentable. Somehow or another they knew that I needed to be there. They hooked me up with medical care.

This was the first point in my whole life that I ever had solid medical care. It was a real strange adjustment. There was a woman there named Susan Wayne, a nurse practitioner, who is really awesome. Every time she saw me, she was really supportive. She wasn't pushy, just supportive. She found the right balance with me. I started seeing her and developed a trust with her. So I started going in for my medical care. When I first started going I went when I was feeling really sick or when I had crabs or whatever. Slowly I went into this phase where I went every couple of weeks to check in. That was cool too. She gave me a little examination and then just sat down and talked with me a couple of minutes. It made me feel like I could be there and didn't have to have a reason. Then I started going when I needed to or just for regular check ups.

I realized during that time how much I was hurting myself. I was trying to find a way to not be hurting myself anymore. I had taken 175 Elavil to overdose and went into a coma. I just wanted to die. I realized that no matter what I tried I wasn't going to die and that I couldn't live the way I was living. So I decided that I needed to change my life. And that's what I did.

At Larkin Street, I was also hooked up with a case manager who was really helpful. When I went into the coma, the case manager was the first person I saw when I woke up. In a lot of ways I found a family. They all gave me the opportunity to try time and time again to help myself. They didn't try to push it on me. That was the key. It was like I picture myself in this room surrounded by doors. Every time a door opens up, it is an opportunity. I have to be looking at the door and get up. I have to have the motivation to walk over to the door, walk through it, and stay through it for the opportunities to happen. All the time I'm sittin there, all of these doors are opening and closing and people are crawling from the doors. It makes a combination of everything being set up at once for a person to be able to change in any direction. At the clinic, they just kept opening the doors. The opportunities empowered me and got me to the clinic when

I was sick. More than once, people from the clinic came and got me and took me to where I needed to go—to the clinic or detox or wherever. There were opportunities for drug and alcohol abuse treatment and getting me to the hospital.

A New Life With Help From a Treatment Program

My case manager helped me check into a program called Walden House. It is a behavior modification program. I started learning the fundamental ways to deal with life that I had missed out on while growing up. Life is a rough thing to live in. If you miss out when you are young on how to deal with life, you have a really hard time. That's what they taught me. They taught me how to deal with life. Because I was leaving the streets, I switched my care from Larkin Street to the Cole Street Clinic. I saw the same nurse practitioner. That was really good because I had established a real trust with her.

Deciding What Is Important in Primary Care

I don't go to the Cole Street Clinic anymore. The nurse practitioner moved away and I was getting to the age anyway, where I decided to change my primary care. I found a nurse practitioner who isn't necessarily the most educated person on HIV but when I asked her about it she said that she was really willing to learn. She is a part of the UCSF hospital and they have special HIV services there. I really trust her so I decided this was the right choice.

When I went searching for health care providers, I decided that I wanted a nurse practitioner instead of a doctor. I have found in general, though this isn't always the case,

but my experience is that the doctors think they really know everything. But HIV is something that nobody knows everything about. It is important for me to be in the driver's seat regarding what I'm going to do to take care of myself. There are so many different therapies, if I say I don't want to take AZT, I don't want some doctors telling me that I am going to die if I don't. I do a lot of research and need to be in control of my health. I need to work with the provider and have the provider work with me, instead of being told what to do. My experience has been that nurse practitioners are more education oriented and present me with options.

A Better Life

I've been in a relationship now for about 2½ years. We're moving in together in about a month. She's negative. Sex is really hard to deal with in the relationship. If she isn't afraid, I am. If I'm not afraid, she's afraid. There are a lot of other issues to worry about, like what if I die. What if I get sick? So there is a lot more to deal with in this relationship besides the regular issues of being in a relationship. There are a lot of things that go along with one partner being HIV positive and one being negative.

Since I entered the treatment program I've been working with young people at risk. I've been trying to spread the word where I can. I go to schools to speak. I am the coordinator for the speakers bureau now, which is really a big step for me. My life is about healing people, healing myself, and about teaching people some of the things that I've learned along the way. Today I know that I don't have to hurt myself. I know that I don't have to let anybody touch me that I don't want to. I don't have to lie to somebody or do what it was that I used to do just to survive. Today I know that there is a different way. And that's pretty much my story.

PSYCHOTRENDS

Taking Stock of Tomorrow's Family and Sexuality

Where are we going and what kind of people are we becoming? Herewith, a road map to the defining trends in sexuality, family, and relationships for the coming millenium as charted by the former chair of Harvard's psychiatry department. From the still-rollicking sexual revolution to the painful battle for sexual equality to the reorganization of the family, America is in for some rather interesting times ahead.

Shervert H. Frazier, M.D.

Has the sexual revolution been sidetracked by AIDS, and the return to traditional values we keep hearing about? In a word, no. The forces that originally fueled the revolution are all still in place and, if anything, are intensifying: mobility, democratization, urbanization, women in the workplace, birth control, abortion and other reproductive interventions, and media proliferation of sexual images, ideas, and variation.

Sexuality has moved for many citizens from church- and state-regulated behavior to a medical and self-regulated behavior. Population pressures and other economic factors continue to diminish the size of the American family. Marriage is in sharp decline, cohabitation is growing, traditional families are on the endangered list, and the single-person household is a wave of the future.

AIDS has generated a great deal of heat in the media but appears to have done little, so far, to turn down the heat in the bedroom. It is true that in some surveys people *claimed* to have made drastic changes in behavior—but most telling are the statistics relating to marriage, divorce, cohabitation, teen sex, out-of-wedlock births, sexually transmitted diseases (STDs), contraception, and adultery. These are far more revealing of what we *do* than what we *say* we do. And those tell a tale of what has been called a "postmarital society" in continued pursuit of sexual individuality and freedom.

Studies reveal women are more sexual now than at any time in the century.

Arguably there are, due to AIDS, fewer visible sexual "excesses" today than there were in the late 1960s and into the 1970s, but those excesses (such as sex clubs, bathhouses, backrooms, swinging singles, group sex, public sex acts, etc.) were never truly reflective of norms and were, in any case, greatly inflated in the media. Meanwhile, quietly and without fanfare, the public, even in the face of the AIDS threat, has continued to expand its interest in sex and in *increased*, rather than decreased, sexual expression.

Numerous studies reveal that women are more sexual now than at any time in the century. Whereas sex counselors used to deal with men's complaints about their wives' lack of "receptivity," it is now more often the women complaining about the men. And women, in this "postfeminist" era, are doing things they never used to believe were "proper." Fellatio, for example, was seldom practiced (or admitted to) when Kinsey conducted his famous sex research several decades ago. Since that time, according to studies at UCLA and elsewhere, this activity has gained acceptance among women, with some researchers reporting that nearly all young women now practice fellatio.

Women's images of themselves have also changed dramatically in the past two decades, due, in large part, to their movement into the workplace and roles previously filled exclusively by men. As Lilian Rubin, psychologist at the University of California Institute for the Study of Social Change and author of *Intimate Strangers*, puts it, "Women feel empowered sexually in a way they never did in the past."

Meanwhile, the singles scene, far from fading away (the media just lost its fixation on this subject), continues to grow. James Bennett, writing in *The New Republic*, characterizes this growing population of no-reproducers thusly: "Single adults in America display a remarkable tendency to multiply without being fruitful."

From *Psychology Today*, January/February 1994, pp. 32–37, 64, 66. Excerpted from *Psychotrends: What Kind of People Are We Becoming?* by Shervert H. Frazier, M.D. © 1994 by Shervert H. Frazier, M.D. Reprinted by permission of Simon & Schuster, Inc.

Their libidos are the target of million-dollar advertising budgets and entrepreneurial pursuits that seek to put those sex drives on line in the information age. From video dating to computer coupling to erotic faxing, it's now "love at first byte," as one commentator put it. One thing is certain: the computer is doing as much today to promote the sexual revolution as the automobile did at the dawn of that revolution.

Political ideologies, buttressed by economic adversities, *can* temporarily retard the sexual revolution, as can sexually transmitted diseases. But ultimately the forces propelling this revolution are unstoppable. And ironically, AIDS itself is probably doing more to promote than impede this movement. It has forced the nation to confront a number of sexual issues with greater frankness than ever before. While some conservatives and many religious groups have argued for abstinence as the only moral response to AIDS, others have lobbied for wider dissemination of sexual information, beginning in grade schools. A number of school districts are now making condoms available to students—a development that would have been unthinkable before the outbreak of AIDS.

Despite all these gains (or losses, depending upon your outlook) the revolution is far from over. The openness that it has fostered is healthy, but Americans are still ignorant about many aspects of human sexuality. Sexual research is needed to help us deal with teen sexuality and pregnancies, AIDS, and a number of emotional issues related to sexuality. Suffice it to say for now that there is still plenty of room for the sexual revolution to proceed—and its greatest benefits have yet to be realized.

THE REVOLUTION AND RELATIONSHIPS

The idea that the Sexual Revolution is at odds with romance (not to mention tradition) is one that is widely held, even by some of those who endorse many of the revolution's apparent objectives. But there is nothing in our findings to indicate that romance and the sexual revolution are inimical—unless one's defense of romance disguises an agenda of traditional male dominance and the courtly illusion of intimacy and communication between the sexes.

The trend now, as we shall see, is away from illusion and toward—in transition, at least—a sometimes painful reality in which the sexes are finally making an honest effort to *understand* one another.

But to some, it may seem that the sexes are farther apart today than they ever have been. The real gender gap, they say, is a communications gap so cavernous that only the most intrepid or foolhardy dare try to bridge it. Many look back at the Anita Hill affair and say that was the open declaration of war between the sexes.

The mistake many make, however, is saying that there has been a *recent* breakdown in those communications, hence all this new discontent. This conclusion usually goes unchallenged, but there is nothing in the data we have seen from past decades to indicate that sexual- and gender-related communication were ever better than they are today. On the contrary, a more thoughtful analysis makes it very clear they have always been *worse*.

What has changed is our *consciousness* about this issue. Problems in communication between the sexes have been masked for decades by a rigid social code that strictly prescribes other behavior. Communication between the sexes has long been preprogrammed by this code to produce an exchange that has been as superficial as it is oppressive. As this process begins to be exposed by its own inadequacies in a rapidly changing world, we suddenly discover that we have a problem. But, of course, that problem was there for a long time, and the discovery does not mean a decline in communication between the sexes but, rather, provides us with the potential for better relationships in the long run.

Thus what we call a "breakdown" in communications might more aptly be called a *breakthrough*.

Seymour Parker, of the University of Utah, demonstrated that men who are the most mannerly with women, those who adhere most strictly to the "code" discussed above, are those who most firmly believe, consciously or unconsciously, that women are "both physically and psychologically weaker (i.e.,less capable) than men." What has long passed for male "respect" toward women in our society is, arguably, *disrespect*.

Yet what has been learned can be unlearned—especially if women force the issue, which is precisely what is happening now. Women's views of themselves are changing and that, more than anything, is working to eliminate many of the stereotypes that supported the image of women as weak and inferior. Women, far from letting men continue to dictate to them, are making it clear they want more *real* respect from men and will accept nothing less. They want a genuine dialogue; they want men to recognize that they speak with a distinct and equal voice, not one that is merely ancillary to the male voice.

The sexual revolution made possible a serious inquiry into the ways that men and women are alike and the ways that each is unique. This revolutionary development promises to narrow the gender gap as nothing else can, for only by understanding the differences that make communication so complex do we stand any chance of mastering those complexities.

SUBTRENDS
Greater Equality Between the Sexes

Despite talk in the late 1980s and early 1990s of the decline of feminism and declarations that women, as a social and political force, are waning, equality between the sexes is closer to becoming a reality than ever before. Women command a greater workforce and wield greater political power than they have ever done. They are assuming positions in both public and private sectors that their mothers and grandmothers believed were unattainable (and their fathers and grandfathers thought were inappropriate) for women. Nonethe-

---

All this will surely pale alongside the brave new world of virtual reality.

---

less, much remains to be achieved before women attain complete equality—but movement in that direction will continue at a pace that will surprise many over the next two decades.

Women voters, for example, who have long outnumbered male voters, are collectively a sleeping giant whose slumber many say was abruptly interrupted during the Clarence Thomas–Anita Hill hearings in 1991. The spectacle of a political "boy's club" raking the dignified Hill over the coals of sexual harassment galvanized the entire nation for days.

On another front, even though women have a long way to go to match men in terms of equal pay for equal work, as well as in equal opportunity, there is a definite *research* trend that shows women can match men in the skills needed to succeed in business. This growing body of data will make it more difficult for businesses to check the rise of women into the upper echelons of management and gradually help to change the corporate consciousness that still heavily favors male employees.

As for feminism, many a conservative wrote its obituary in the 1980s, only to find it risen from the dead in the 1990s. Actually, its demise was always imaginary. Movements make headway only in a context of dissatisfaction. And, clearly, there is still plenty for women to be dissatisfied about, particularly in the wake of a decade that tried to stifle meaningful change.

The "new feminism," as some call it, is less doctrinaire than the old, less extreme in the sense that it no longer has to be outrageous in order to call attention to itself. The movement today is less introspective, more goal oriented and pragmatic. Demands for liberation are superseded—and subsumed—by a well-organized quest for power. Women no longer want to burn bras, they want to manufacture and market them.

The New Masculinity

To say that the men's movement today is confused is to understate mercifully. Many men say they want to be more "sensitive" but also "less emasculated," "more open," yet "less vulnerable." While the early flux of this movement is often so extreme that it cannot but evoke guffaws, there is, nonetheless, something in it that commands some respect—for, in contrast with earlier generations of males, this one is making a real effort to examine and redefine itself. The movement, in a word, is *real*.

Innumerable studies and surveys find men dissatisfied with themselves and their roles in society. Part of this, undoubtedly, is the result of the displacement men are experiencing in a culture where *women* are so successfully transforming themselves. There is evidence, too, that men are dissatisfied because their own fathers were so unsuccessful in their emotional lives and were thus unable to impart to their sons a sense of love, belonging, and security that an increasing number of men say they sorely miss.

The trend has nothing to do with beating drums or becoming a "warrior." It relates to the human desire for connection, and this, in the long run, can only bode well for communications between humans in general and between the sexes in particular. Many psychologists believe men, in the next two decades, will be less emotionally closed than at any time in American history.

More (and Better) Senior Sex

People used to talk about sex after 40 as if it were some kind of novelty. Now it's sex after 60 and it's considered not only commonplace but healthy.

Some fear that expectations among the aged may outrun physiological ability and that exaggerated hopes, in some cases, will lead to new frustrations—or that improved health into old age will put pressure on seniors to remain sexually active beyond any "decent" desire to do so.

But most seem to welcome the trend toward extended sexuality. In fact, the desire for sex in later decades of life is *heightened*, studies suggest, by society's growing awareness and acceptance of sexual activity in later life.

Diversity of Sexual Expression

As sex shifts from its traditional reproductive role to one that is psychological, it increasingly serves the needs of the individual. In this context, forms of sexual expression that were previously proscribed

are now tolerated and are, in some cases increasingly viewed as no more nor less healthy than long-accepted forms of sexual behavior. Homosexuality, for example, has attained a level of acceptance unprecedented in our national history.

More Contraception, Less Abortion

Though abortion will remain legal under varying conditions in most, if not all, states, its use will continue to decline over the next two decades as more—and better—contraceptives become available. After a period of more than two decades in

---

Our longing for sources of nurturance has led us to redefine the family.

---

which drug companies shied away from contraceptive research, interest in this field is again growing. AIDS, a changed political climate, and renewed fears about the population explosion are all contributing to this change.

Additionally, scientific advances now point the way to safer, more effective, more convenient contraceptives. A male contraceptive that will be relatively side-effect free is finally within reach and should be achieved within the next decade, certainly the next two decades. Even more revolutionary in concept and probable impact is a vaccine, already tested in animals, that some predict will be available within 10 years—a vaccine that safely stops ovum maturation and thus makes conception impossible.

Religion and Sex: A More Forgiving Attitude

Just a couple of decades ago mainstream religion was monolithic in its condemnation of sex outside of marriage. Today the situation is quite different as major denominations across the land struggle with issues they previously wouldn't have touched, issues related to adultery, premarital sex, homosexuality, and so on.

A Special Committee on Human Sexuality, convened by the General Assembly of the Presbyterian Church (USA), for example, surprised many when it issued a report highly critical of the traditional "patriarchal structure of sexual relations," a structure the committee believes contributes, because of its repressiveness, to the proliferation of pornography and sexual violence.

The same sort of thing has been happening in most other major denominations. It is safe to say that major changes are coming. Mainstream religion is beginning to

perceive that the sexual revolution must be acknowledged and, to a significant degree, accommodated with new policies if these denominations are to remain in touch with present-day realities.

Expanding Sexual Entertainment

The use of sex to sell products, as well as to entertain, is increasing and can be expected to do so. The concept that "sex sells" is so well established that we need not belabor the point here. The explicitness of sexual advertising, however, may be curbed by recent research finding that highly explicit sexual content is so diverting that the viewer or reader tends to overlook the product entirely.

Sexual stereotyping will also be less prevalent in advertising in years to come. All this means, however, is that women will not be singled out as sex objects; they'll have plenty of male company, as is already the case. The female "bimbo" is now joined by the male "himbo" in ever-increasing numbers. Sexist advertising is still prevalent (e.g., male-oriented beer commercials) but should diminish as women gain in social and political power.

There's no doubt that films and TV have become more sexually permissive in the last two decades and are likely to continue in that direction for some time to come. But all this will surely pale alongside the brave (or brazen) new world of "cybersex" and virtual reality, the first erotic emanations of which may well be experienced by Americans in the coming two decades. Virtual reality aims to be just that—artificial, electronically induced experiences that are virtually indistinguishable from the real thing.

The sexual revolution, far from over, is in for some new, high-tech curves.

FROM BIOLOGY TO PSYCHOLOGY: THE NEW FAMILY OF THE MIND

Despite recent pronouncements that the traditional family is making a comeback, the evidence suggests that over the next two decades the nuclear family will share the same future as nuclear arms: there will be fewer of them, but those that remain will be better cared for.

Demographers now believe that the number of families consisting of married couples with children will dwindle by yet another 12 percent by the year 2000. Meanwhile, single-parent households will continue to increase (up 41 percent over the past decade). And household size will continue to decline (2.63 people in 1990 versus 3.14 in 1970). The number of households maintained by women, with no males present, has increased 300 percent since 1950 and will continue to rise into the 21st century.

Particularly alarming to some is the fact that an increasing number of people are choosing *never* to marry. And, throughout the developed world, the one-person household is now the fastest growing household category. To the traditionalists, this trend seems insidious—more than 25 percent of all households in the United States now consist of just one person.

There can be no doubt: the nuclear family has been vastly diminished, and it will continue to decline for some years, but at a more gradual pace. Indeed, there is a

---

We need to realize the "traditional family" is not particularly traditional.

---

good chance that it will enjoy more stability in the next two decades than it did in the last two. Many of the very forces that were said to be weakening the traditional family may now make it stronger, though not more prevalent. Developing social changes have made traditional marriage more elective today, so that those who choose it may, increasingly, some psychologists believe, represent a subpopulation better suited to the situation and thus more likely to make a go of it.

As we try to understand new forms of family, we need to realize that the "traditional" family is not particularly traditional. Neither is it necessarily the healthiest form of family. The nuclear family has existed for only a brief moment in human history. Moreover, most people don't realize that no sooner had the nuclear family form peaked around the turn of the last century than erosion set in, which has continued ever since. For the past hundred years, reality has chipped away at this social icon, with increasing divorce and the movement of more women into the labor force. Yet our need for nurturance, security, and connectedness continues and, if anything, grows more acute as our illusions about the traditional family dissipate.

Our longing for more satisfying sources of nurturance has led us to virtually redefine the family, in terms of behavior, language, and law. These dramatic changes will intensify over the next two decades. The politics of family will be entirely transformed in that period. The process will not be without interruptions or setbacks. Some lower-court rulings may be overturned by a conservative U.S. Supreme Court, the traditional family will be revived in the headline from time to time, but the economic and psychological forces that for decades

have been shaping these changes toward a more diverse family will continue to do so.

SUBTRENDS
Deceptively Declining Divorce Rate

The "good news" is largely illusory. Our prodigious national divorce rate, which more than doubled in one recent 10-year period, now shows signs of stabilization or even decline. Still, 50 percent of all marriages will break up in the next several years. And the leveling of the divorce rate is not due to stronger marriage but to *less* marriage. More people are skipping marriage altogether and are cohabiting instead.

The slight dip in the divorce rate in recent years has caused some prognosticators to predict that younger people, particularly those who've experienced the pain of growing up in broken homes, are increasingly committed to making marriage stick. Others, more persuasively, predict the opposite, that the present lull precedes a storm in which the divorce rate will soar to 60 percent or higher.

Increasing Cohabitation

The rate of cohabitation—living together without legal marriage—has been growing since 1970 and will accelerate in the next two decades. There were under half a million cohabiting couples in 1970; today there are more than 2.5. The trend for the postindustrial world is very clear: less marriage, more cohabitation, easier and—if Sweden is any indication—less stressful separation. Those who divorce will be less likely to remarry, more likely to cohabit. And in the United States, cohabitation will increasingly gather about it both the cultural acceptance and the legal protection now afforded marriage.

More Single-Parent Families and Planned Single Parenthood

The United States has one of the highest proportions of children growing up in single-parent families. More than one in five births in the United States is outside of marriage—and three quarters of those births are to women who are not in consensual unions.

What is significant about the single-parent trend is the finding that many single women with children now *prefer* to remain single. The rush to the altar of unwed mothers, so much a part of American life in earlier decades, is now, if anything, a slow and grudging shuffle. The stigma of single parenthood is largely a thing of the past—and the economic realities, unsatisfactory though they are, sometimes favor single parenthood. In any case, women have more choices today than they had even 10 years ago; they are choosing the

psychological freedom of single parenthood over the financial security (increasingly illusory, in any event) of marriage.

More Couples Childless by Choice

In the topsy-turvy 1990s, with more single people wanting children, it shouldn't surprise us that more married couples *don't* want children. What the trend really comes down to is increased freedom of choice. One reason for increasing childlessness among couples has to do with the aging of the population, but many of the reasons are more purely psychological.

With a strong trend toward later marriage, many couples feel they are "too old" to have children. Others admit they like the economic advantages and relative freedom of being childless. Often both have careers they do not want to jeopardize by having children. In addition, a growing number of couples cite the need for lower population density, crime rates, and environmental concerns as reasons for not wanting children. The old idea that "there must be something wrong with them" if a couple does not reproduce is fast waning.

The One-Person Household

This is the fastest growing household category in the Western world. It has grown in the United States from about 10 percent in the 1950s to more than 25 percent of all households today. This is a trend that still has a long way to go. In Sweden, nearly *40 percent* of all households are now single person.

"Mr. Mom" a Reality at Last?

When women began pouring into the work force in the late 1970s, expectations were high that a real equality of the sexes was at hand and that men, at last, would begin to shoulder more of the household duties, including spending more time at home taking care of the kids. Many women now regard the concept of "Mr. Mom" as a cruel hoax; but, in fact, Mr. Mom is slowly emerging.

Men *are* showing more interest in the home and in parenting. Surveys make clear there is a continuing trend in that direction. Granted, part of the impetus for this is not so much a love of domestic work as it is a distaste for work outside the home. But there is also, among many men, a genuine desire to play a larger role in the lives of their children. These men say they feel "cheated" by having to work outside the home so much, cheated of the experience of seeing their children grow up.

As the trend toward more equal pay for women creeps along, gender roles in the home can be expected to undergo further change. Men will feel less pressure to take on more work and will feel more freedom to spend increased time with their families.

More Interracial Families

There are now about 600,000 interracial marriages annually in the United States, a third of these are black-white, nearly triple the number in 1970, when 40 percent of the white population was of the opinion that such marriages should be illegal. Today 20 percent hold that belief. There is every reason to expect that both the acceptance of and the number of interracial unions will continue to increase into the foreseeable future.

Recognition of Same-Sex Families

Family formation by gay and lesbian couples, with or without children, is often referenced by the media as a leading-edge signifier of just how far society has moved in the direction of diversity and individual choice in the family realm. The number of same-sex couples has steadily increased and now stands at 1.6 million such couples. There are an estimated 2 million gay parents in the United States.

And while most of these children were had in heterosexual relationships or marriages prior to "coming out," a significant number of gay and lesbian couples are hav-ing children through adoption, cooperative parenting arrangements, and artificial insemination. Within the next two decades, gays and lesbians will not only win the right to marry but will, like newly arrived immigrants, be some of the strongest proponents of traditional family values.

The Rise of Fictive Kinships

Multiadult households, typically consisting of unrelated singles, have been increasing in number for some years and are expected to continue to do so in coming years. For many, "roommates" are increasingly permanent fixtures in daily life.

In fact housemates are becoming what some sociologists and psychologists call "fictive kin." Whole "fictive families" are being generated in many of these situations, with some housemates even assigning roles ("brother," "sister," "cousin," "aunt," "mom," "dad," and so on) to one another. Fictive families are springing up among young people, old people, disabled people, homeless people, and may well define one of the ultimate evolutions of the family concept, maximizing, as they do, the opportunities for fulfillment of specific social and economic needs outside the constraints of biological relatedness.

THE BREAKUP OF THE NUCLEAR FAMILY

It's hard to tell how many times we've heard even well-informed health professionals blithely opine that "the breakup of the family is at the root of most of our problems." The *facts* disagree with this conclusion. Most of the social problems attributed to the dissolution of the "traditional" family (which, in reality, is *not* so traditional) are the product of other forces. Indeed, as we have seen, the nuclear family has itself created a number of economic, social, and psychological problems. To try to perpetuate a manifestly transient social institution beyond its usefulness is folly.

What *can* we do to save the nuclear family? Very little.

What *should* we do? Very little. Our concern should not be the maintenance of the nuclear family as a *moral* unit (which seems to be one of the priorities of the more ardent conservative "family values" forces), encompassing the special interests and values of a minority, but, rather, the strengthening of those social contracts that ensure the health, well-being, and freedom of individuals.

Who Stole Fertility?

CONTRARY TO POPULAR BELIEF, THERE IS NO INFERTILITY CRISIS SWEEPING THE NATION. WE'VE JUST LOST ALL CONCEPTION OF WHAT IT TAKES TO CONCEIVE. REPRODUCTIVE TECHNOLOGY HAS MADE US IMPATIENT WITH NATURE. SO FOR INCREASING NUMBERS OF COUPLES THE CREATION OF A NEW HUMAN BEING HAS BECOME A STRANGELY DEHUMANIZING PROCESS.

VIRGINIA RUTTER

My great-aunt Emily and great-uncle Harry never had kids, and nobody in our family talked about it. Growing up, I knew not to ask. It would have been impolite, as crass as asking about their income or their weight. The message was clear: If they didn't have kids, they couldn't have them, and talking about it would only be humiliating.

How times have changed. Today, a couple's reproductive prospects—or lack of them—are not only apt to be a conversation topic at your average dinner party, they're the subject of countless news stories illustrating our nationwide infertility "crisis."

In an infertility cover story last year, *Newsweek* reported that more than 3 million American couples would seek procreative help in 1995. Diagnostic tests, hormone treatments, fertility drugs, and assisted-reproduction techniques with names like in vitro fertilization (IVF), gamete intrafallopian transfers (GIFT), intrauterine insemination (IUI), zygote intrafallopian transfer (ZIFT), intracytoplasmic sperm injection (ICSI)—to name the top five procedures—have become as much a part of the reproductive process as the more poetic aspects of family making. While some of those 3 million-plus couples were legitimate candidates for the host of high-tech options now available to them, most wound up needing only low-tech assistance, such as boxer shorts instead of briefs.

Earlier this year, in a four-part series, the *New York Times* reported on the fertility industry's growth and the increased competition among clinics.

And that's how an infertility crisis is created and perpetuated. For contrary to popular belief, infertility rates are not on the rise. Creighton University sociologist Shirley Scritchfield, Ph.D., says that American infertility rates have not increased during the past three decades: in 1965, the infertility rate for the entire U.S. population was around 13.3 percent; in 1988, it was 13.7 percent. According to the U.S. Office of Technology Assessment, infertility rates for married women have actually *decreased* from 11.2 percent in 1965 to a little less than eight percent in 1988. These rates even include the "subfecund," the term used to describe people who have babies, just not as many as they want as quickly as they want. This means that more than 90 percent of couples have as many babies—or more than as many babies—as they want.

LETTING NATURE TAKE ITS COURSE

Rather than an infertility crisis, what we have is a society that's allowed technology to displace biology in the reproductive process, in effect dehumanizing the most human of events. At the very least, this means stress replaces spontaneity as women become tied to thermometers—constantly checking to see when they're ovulating—while men stand by waiting to give command performances. At the most, it involves women and men subjecting themselves to invasive procedures with high price tags. Whatever happened to love and romance and the idea of letting nature take its course? Instead, we seem to have embraced the idea that science, not sex, provides the best chance for producing biological children. Technicians have stolen human reproduction. And there are some 300 fertility clinics—with annual revenues of $2 billion—to prove it.

Infertility has become big business, one that's virtually exempt from government regulation. And it's not for the faint of heart—or pocketbook (see "Bucks for Babies"). But all the hype has made us lose sight of what it really takes to make a baby. Conception takes time. Infertility is classically defined as the inability to conceive or carry a baby to term after one year of unprotected sex two to three times a week. On average, it takes less time for younger (in their 30s) ones; as couples move through their 30s, experts suggest staying on the course for two years. But even couples in their reproductive prime—mid- to late 20s—need around eight months of sex two to three times a week to make a baby. (Last December, the New England Journal of Medicine reported that healthy women

Reprinted with permission from *Psychology Today*, March/April 1996, pp. 46–49, 65–69. © 1996 by Sussex Publishers, Inc.

are most fertile, and therefore most likely to conceive, when they have intercourse during the six-day period leading up to ovulation.)

The correlation between how often a couple has sex and the speed with which they succeed in conceiving may seem obvious. But psychologist and University of Rochester Medical School professor Susan McDaniel, Ph.D., says she counseled one infertile couple for six months before discovering they had only been having sex once or twice a month!

Of course, these days the one thing many prospective parents feel they don't have is time. During the baby boom, couples began having children at about age 20. But by 1980—when women were in the workforce in record numbers and putting off motherhood—10.5 percent of first births were to women age 30 and older. By 1990, 18 percent of first births were to women age 30 and up. Because more would-be parents are older and hear their biological clocks ticking, they're more likely to become impatient when they don't conceive instantly. But how much of a factor is age in the conception game? Men have fewer age-related fertility problems than women do. The quality of their sperm may diminish with age; when they reach their 50s, men may experience low sperm motility (slow-moving sperm are less likely to inseminate).

After about age 37, women's eggs tend to show their age and may disintegrate more easily. This makes it increasingly difficult for women to conceive or maintain a pregnancy. That's not to say there's anything unusual about a 40-year-old woman having a baby, however. Older women have been having children for eons—just not

The confidence we have in preventing pregnancies has given us a false sense of control over our fertility.

their first ones. In many cultures, the average age of a last child is around age 40.

Some older women may even be as fertile as their younger sisters. A 40-year-old woman who has been taking birth control pills for a good part of her reproductive life—thus inhibiting the release of an egg each month—may actually benefit from having conserved her eggs, says Monica Jarrett, Ph.D., a professor of nursing at the University of Washington. She may even have a slight edge over a 40-year-old mother with one or two children trying to conceive.

"Focusing on aging as the primary source of infertility is a distraction," says Scritchfield. "Age becomes a factor when women have unknowingly always been infertile. These are women who, even if they'd tried to get pregnant at age 20 or 27, would have had difficulty despite the best technology."

GENDER POLITICS AND INFERTILITY

Some feminists suggest all this talk of infertility is part of a backlash, an effort to drive women out of the boardroom and back into the nursery. While there may be some truth to this, it's only part of the story. The fertility furor is also a result of increasing expectations of control over nature by ordinary men and women.

Ironically, the growing intolerance for the natural course of conception stems from technological advances in contraception. Birth control is more reliable than ever. The confidence we have in preventing pregnancies has given us a false sense of control over our fertility. "People have the idea that if they can prevent conception, then they should also be able to conceive when they want to," says McDaniel.

This illusory sense of control, says Judith Daniluk, Ph.D., a University of British Columbia psychologist and fertility researcher, weighs most heavily on women. "Women are told that if they miss taking even one birth control pill, they risk becoming pregnant. This translates into feeling extremely responsible when it comes to getting pregnant, too."

If we've let technicians steal fertility from us, perhaps it's because it was up for grabs. Until recently, infertility was considered a woman's problem rather than a couple's problem. In the 1950s, physicians and psychologists believed that women whose infertility couldn't be explained were "suppressing" their true femininity. Of course, in those days men were rarely evaluated; the limited technology available focused mostly on women.

When a couple steps into the infertility arena today, both partners receive full evaluations—in theory. In practice, however, this doesn't always happen because technology is such that even a few sperm from an infertile man are enough for high-tech fertilization. About 40 percent of in-

Who Is Infertile?

Although infertility rates are not on the rise overall, Creighton University sociologist Shirley Scritchfield, Ph.D., points out that they are rising among some subgroups of the population: all young women between the ages of 20 and 24 and women of color. She says this is due to an increase in sexually transmitted diseases (STDs) among the young. STDs, including chlamydia, gonorrhea, and genital warts, can permanently harm reproductive organs. Pelvic inflammatory disease, which women can develop as a consequence of other STDs, is perhaps most responsible for infertility in young women, in part because it—as well as other STDs—often goes undetected.

With few records having been kept, it's difficult to determine whether male infertility is on the rise. A 1992 study by Norwegian scientists looked at semen quality over the past 50 years by pooling the evidence available from earlier research. They concluded that, in general, sperm counts had decreased.

Rebecca Sokol, M.D., professor of medicine and obstetrics/gynecology at the University of Southern California, says that while the Norwegian study reports a significant reduction in sperm counts over half a century, the reductions are not "clinically significant." That is, if sperm counts have decreased over time—and many scientists do not agree that they have—they've simply gone from a very high count to moderate levels.

"We're exposed to higher levels of estrogens than ever before; we inject cows and other animals with estrogens and estrogen-like hormones to keep them healthy. There isn't any data that directly proves this alters sperm counts, but we know an increase in estrogens in men is toxic to sperm. The theory is that in some way, this low-grade constant exposure to estrogen is ultimately altering sperm."

fertility is the result of "female factors"—problems with hormones, eggs, or reproductive organs. Another 40 percent is explained by "male factors"—problems with low sperm count or slow-moving sperm. The remaining 20 percent is unexplained or due to factors in both partners. There may be an immune problem, where the sperm and egg are "allergic" to each other. Advances—such as ICSI, a way of injecting a single sperm into an egg during IVF—have been made to get around this immune system clash. Advances have also been made in understanding male infertility, including treatments for low sperm motility that involve extracting sperm directly from the testes. But the bulk of fertility treatments still focus on women.

Women also tend to "carry" the issue for a couple, says McDaniel. "As much as men are invested in having children, they don't have to think about it, or perhaps be as conscious of it—because women are so focused on the problem. It makes sense, then, that when it comes to an infertility workup, men will often be the ones to put on the brakes. If both partners were running headlong onto the conveyor belt of technology, there'd be a mess. So what happens—largely because of sex roles—is women become advocates of the process, and men, who may be more ambivalent, question it and wonder whether it's time to stop."

Women will go so far as to protect their partner from the diagnostic process, as well as treatment, observes Daniluk. She says they'll even shield their partner from blame when he's the infertile one.

COMPELLED TO PRODUCE

Regardless of its cause, infertility is a profound blow to people's sense of self, who they are, and who they think they should be. To understand just how devastating infertility is, it helps to know why we want babies in the first place.

"The most essential thing the human animal does is reproduce," insists anthropologist Helen Fisher, Ph.D., author of *Anatomy of Love*. Citing survival of the spe-

An overestimation of success rates by the technofertility industry hooks couples in.

cies as the reason why our drive to reproduce is so strong, Fisher says it's not surprising that couples will go to great emotional and financial lengths to conceive. "The costs of reproducing have always been great. The time-consuming and costly procedures a modern couple uses to pursue their reproductive ends may never be as costly as it was on the grasslands of Africa, when women regularly died in childbirth."

Fisher says men, too, feel obliged to plant their seed or die out, so they'll work very hard to sire and raise their own kids. They aren't exempt from social pressures either. "Male sexuality has always been tied to potency," says William Doherty, Ph.D., a professor of family social science at the University of Minnesota. "The slang term for male infertility is 'shooting blanks.' After all, what good is a man if he can't reproduce? That's probably why we've blamed women for infertility for millennia. It's too humiliating for men."

Animal instincts may provide the primal motivation for having kids. But notions of masculinity and femininity are another big influence. Infertility taps into our deepest anxieties about what it is to be a man or a woman, a core part of our identity. McDaniel says many of the infertile women she sees speak of feeling incomplete. They also talk of a loss of self-confidence and a sense of helplessness and isolation.

Women still get the message that much of their femaleness is derived from motherhood—more so than men are taught their maleness is tied to fatherhood. Losing the dream of motherhood may fill a woman with such grief that she'll consciously avoid the places kids populate. It's a loss that can be difficult to share because it's the death of something that never was.

Infertile men also experience a loss, says McDaniel. They, too, may insulate themselves from the world of kids. They may be even less likely than women, says Doherty, to talk about their sad feelings. "Men feel if they're not able to pass on their seed, they're not living up to what's expected of them as men," says Andrew McCullough, M.D., director of the Male Sexual Health and Fertility Clinic at New York University Medical Center.

Parental expectations are yet another powerful reason people feel the procreational pull. "When it comes to having kids," says McDaniel, "there can be a lot of familial pressure. If you don't have them, everybody wonders why."

TECHNOFERTILITY TAKES OVER

With all of these pressures to produce, is it any wonder couples get caught up in the technofertility maze? Seduced by well-meaning doctors who hold out hope and the availability of all kinds of treatments, two vulnerable people—alone—are left to decide how much reproductive assistance they will or won't accept. There are no guidelines.

It wasn't until about their seventh year of fertility treatments that a physician finally sat Steve and Lori down and told them that their chances of having a baby were slim, given their ages—37 and 32—and their efforts until that point. Steve had had a varicocele, a twisting of veins in the testicles, and Lori had had various explorations of her ovaries by endoscopy in search of ovarian cysts, plus two failed IVFs.

"It turned out that my wife's gynecologist wasn't really competent to tell us about fertility treatments," Steve says. "It ended

Bucks for Babies

The fertility industry may boast of its dedication to bringing healthy babies into the world, but in reality, it appears to be interested in producing only *wealthy* ones.

A thorough fertility workup to diagnose the source of a couple's problem can take up to two months and cost from $3,000 to $8,000. That's just for starters. For a simple procedure, like hormone shots to stimulate egg production, it's $2,300 per cycle. Expect to pay $10,000 for one round of in vitro fertilization (IVF). About 30,000 women a year attempt pregnancy via IVF.

Intracytoplasmic sperm injection, where doctors inject a single sperm into an egg, adds $1,000 to the price of IVF. A procedure requiring an egg donor (in demand among older mothers) runs from $8,500 to $16,000—per cycle. A varicocelectomy, to correct varicose veins around the testicles, costs $3,500. Few health plans include coverage for fertility treatment. Even when insurance does kick in, it doesn't cover all of the direct costs, to say nothing of the many indirect costs, including lost income from missed work and child care expenses.

How Couples Cope with Infertility

In general, couples without children are more likely to split up than partners with children, reports demographer Diane Lye, Ph.D., a professor of sociology at the University of Washington. What about mates who can't have kids, or who want them but encounter difficulties? Researchers don't know about the ones who don't seek fertility treatment—and who tend to be poor. But Lauri Pasch, Ph.D., a psychologist and fertility researcher at the University of California at San Francisco, did study 50 couples who, on average, had been trying to get pregnant for two years. She says infertile couples going for fertility treatment tend to have higher rates of marital satisfaction than the rest of the population.

"Most couples who seek fertility treatment are committed enough to their relationship that they will go through pain and suffering to have a child together," says Pasch. And if they have the skills to address their problem, their relationships tend to become stronger—even if they never have a baby."

So what kind of skills does a couple comfronting infertility need? Mates with matching coping styles do best, says Pasch, who points out that infertility, like other major stressors, tends to bring out people's natural ways of coping. "Couples who have similar ways of living with problems and relieving their distress are better off than those with different styles," says Pasch. "Both might be support seekers, or both might be private and keep to themselves. So long as they both go about things in the same way."

Pasch finds that spouses who rely on emotional expression can do harm to their relationship. That's because they tend to let their feelings out *at* their partner rather than sharing them *with* him or her. (So much for the old saw that talking things out always makes them better.) "In this destructive communication pattern, one person eventually demands and one withdraws," says Pasch. "One member of the couple pressures for change, while the other one withdraws, refusing to discuss the problem."

Though which partner demands and which one withdraws can shift, typically women are the ones who demand more, and men are the ones who withdraw. In the case of an infertile couple, the woman may get alarmed sooner than her husband about not being able to have children. But they may switch roles, and she may become more resigned to it while he becomes more concerned and wants to start treatment. Either way, the couple is at odds.

Tammy and Dan, the parents of two children—the products of five IVFs and eight years of fertility treatments—were just such a couple. "I was the leader, taking care of everything," says Tammy. Her daily routine included being at the fertility clinic at 6:30 every morning for blood tests, and returning every afternoon for more exams. Once she became pregnant, she had to stay in bed practically from the day she conceived until the day her children were born.

"When you're trying to get pregnant, it becomes your whole focus. Everything you do is planned around it. You are told what to do every day, and you can't do very much. Then, all of a sudden, you realize you have focused your whole life on getting pregnant and not on your relationship. After our second child was born, and we didn't have a crisis to deal with every day, it was difficult being normal."

The emotional climate becomes even more difficult when one partner chooses to withdraw from the entire fertility process. Psychologist Susan McDaniel, Ph.D., of the University of Rochester School of Medicine, saw one couple where the wife underwent extensive tests to see whether she was infertile. Her husband, meanwhile, could never seem to make it to the urologist to be tested. He couldn't tolerate the idea that his sperm count might be low. Of course, his wife was furious. She had gone through painful and stressful—not to mention expensive—workups. When her husband finally went to the urologist, he couldn't produce a sperm sample. When he finally did, it turned out he was the infertile one. Both partners had trouble understanding what the prospect of infertility was like for the other one. Eventually, they decided to get a divorce.

up being like going to the Motor Vehicle Bureau. First, they tell you to take care of one thing, but it turns out you need to take care of something else. Then they tell you to go do a third thing. You wind up moving from place to place with no particular plan. It's rare that you get a doctor who explains in plain English what's going on and helps you evaluate your choices. Instead of talking with Lori and me and asking us what was in our hearts, they were saying, 'Okay, you want a baby, how can we make one for you?' "

Even as they went through test after test, procedure after procedure, it seemed at least semicomical to them: drives at the crack of dawn to a distant clinic, painful shots Steve was obliged to administer to Lori, even a "hamster penetration" test that involved Steve producing a sperm sample to see whether his sperm could penetrate a hamster's egg. All of it was very difficult to resist. "I think it was partly the adventure that kept us going," Steve says. "Once you commit and say you're going to give

it a go, you don't want to stop midstream. There's always the chance that it might work. I mean, medicine is fantastic; you take some pills, stick some stuff in you, and maybe you get a baby."

Fertility treatments are so technically focused, says McDaniel, that people's feelings get left behind. She advocates a more human "biopsychosocial" approach. "Couples' emotional needs should dictate the pacing and decision making as they move up the pyramid of technological possibilities. But in some, maybe even most clinics, little or no attention is paid to the process, only the possible product. As a result, the patients suffer."

Even under normal circumstances, conception is immaculate—it tends to clean all else out of the mind. Whenever people begin to plan a family, says McDaniel, their world-view narrows. But with technofertility, a couple's worldview can narrow to the exclusion of all else. Because the outcome is the entire focus, fertility treatments intensify our in-

stincts to give birth and nurture a baby. So the very technology that disregards couples' emotions also heightens their desire to nurture. For women, especially, maternal instincts are intensified by all-consuming fertility treatments that leave little time for anything else and cause women to define themselves solely as mothers.

Indeed, as soon as prospective parents seek help, statistics and biology become the focus. Before long, they're up on the latest research and talking in terms of "control groups," "statistical significance," and "replication." The walls of fertility clinics are plastered with pictures of newborns, and staffers and customers alike speak endlessly about "take-home baby rates," the bottom line when it comes to success. But take-home baby rates are more than numbers. They represent people's hopes for a family.

As a result, couples undergoing intensive fertility treatments lose their wide-angle perspective on life. They may fall behind in their careers and cut themselves off from friends and family, all in the narcissistic pursuit of cloning their genes. Technology may provide us with the illusion that it's helping us control our reproductive fate, but in reality, it just adds to the narcissism. "The higher tech the treatment, the more inwardly focused couples become," says Doherty.

"Biological connections are so strongly emphasized in our culture that it's hard not to become self-absorbed," Steve explains. "You even see it in the adoption process. Couples are often concerned that the kids they adopt have similar characteristics to their own. But the truth is, kids are kids." (Steve and Lori have since adopted a baby.)

An overestimation of success rates by the technofertility industry hooks couples in and fuels the narcissism. Fertility clinics typically report about a 25 percent success rate. But this rate is usually calculated after clinics have screened out the most hopeless cases. The true rate—which counts everyone who has sought reproductive help and which considers live births rather than pregnancies as success—is closer to half, Scritchfield says. "Unfortunately, this isn't what the public hears. If we were really concerned about infertility, we would be working on preventive measures. That's not addressed by biomedical entrepreneurs because they don't deal with people, just body parts."

Yet technofertility can create such stress in a couple that it can come close to undoing their relationship—the raison d'être for baby making. McDaniel remembers one couple who were at complete odds, having come to see her a year after having undergone five years of unsuccessful fertility treatments. The woman still hoped technology could help them, but the man felt his wife had gone too far; the procedures were invasive and the lack of results too painful. Attempting to protect both of them from any more disappointment, he insisted they stop.

The husband questioned why they'd ever gotten involved in the first place, and the wife felt unsupported by his reaction. No one at the fertility clinic had helped them work through any of their reactions. In therapy with McDaniel, they ultimately admitted to themselves—and to each other—what their expectations had been and the anxiety and grief they felt over the loss of an early pregnancy. Then they decided to adopt.

Given the single-mindedness of baby making, adding infertility and technology to the mix creates the perfect recipe for obsession. But it's an obsession only for the rich. Which means having a baby becomes a luxury that many truly infertile couples, who might otherwise make wonderful parents, will never be able to afford.

ADDICTED

Why do people get hooked? Mounting evidence points to a powerful brain chemical called dopamine

By J. MADELEINE NASH

IMAGINE YOU ARE TAKING A SLUG OF WHISKEY. A puff of a cigarette. A toke of marijuana. A snort of cocaine. A shot of heroin. Put aside whether these drugs are legal or illegal. Concentrate, for now, on the chemistry. The moment you take that slug, that puff, that toke, that snort, that shot, trillions of potent molecules surge through your bloodstream and into your brain. Once there, they set off a cascade of chemical and electrical events, a kind of neurological chain reaction that ricochets around the skull and rearranges the interior reality of the mind.

Given the complexity of these events—and the inner workings of the mind in general—it's not surprising that scientists have struggled mightily to make sense of the mechanisms of addiction. Why do certain substances have the power to make us feel so good (at least at first)? Why do some people fall so easily into the thrall of alcohol, cocaine, nicotine and other addictive substances, while others can, literally, take them or leave them?

The answer, many scientists are convinced, may be simpler than anyone has dared imagine. What ties all these mood-altering drugs together, they say, is a remarkable ability to elevate levels of a common substance in the brain called dopamine. In fact, so overwhelming has evidence of the link between dopamine and drugs of abuse

become that the distinction (pushed primarily by the tobacco industry and its supporters) between substances that are addictive and those that are merely habit-forming has very nearly been swept away.

The Liggett Group, smallest of the U.S.'s Big Five cigarette makers, broke ranks in March and conceded not only that tobacco is addictive but also that the company has known it all along. While RJR Nabisco and the others continue to battle in the courts—insisting that smokers are not hooked, just exercising free choice—their denials ring increasingly hollow in the face of the growing weight of evidence. Over the past year, several scientific groups have made the case that in dopamine-rich areas of the brain, nicotine behaves remarkably like cocaine. And late last week a federal judge ruled for the first time that the Food and Drug Administration has the right to regulate tobacco as a drug and cigarettes as drug-delivery devices.

Now, a team of researchers led by psychiatrist Dr. Nora Volkow of the Brookhaven National Laboratory in New York has published the

strongest evidence to date that the surge of dopamine in addicts' brains is what triggers a cocaine high. In last week's edition of the journal *Nature* they described how powerful brain-imaging technology can be used to track the rise of dopamine and link it to feelings of euphoria.

Like serotonin (the brain chemical affected by such antidepressants as Prozac), dopamine is a neurotransmitter—a molecule that ferries messages from one neuron within the brain to another. Serotonin is associated with feelings of sadness and well-being, dopamine with pleasure and elation. Dopamine can be elevated by a hug, a kiss, a word of praise or a winning poker hand—as well as by the potent pleasures that come from drugs.

The idea that a single chemical could be associated with everything from snorting cocaine and smoking tobacco to getting good

PRIME SUSPECT

They don't yet know the precise mechanism by which it works, but scientists are increasingly convinced that dopamine plays a key role in a wide range of addictions, including those to heroin, nicotine, alcohol and marijuana

DOPAMINE MAY BE LINKED TO GAMBLING, CHOCOLATE AND EVEN SEX

grades and enjoying sex has electrified scientists and changed the way they look at a wide range of dependencies, chemical and otherwise. Dopamine, they now believe, is not just a chemical that transmits pleasure signals but may, in fact, be the master molecule of addiction.

This is not to say dopamine is the only chemical involved or that the deranged thought processes that mark chronic drug abuse are due to dopamine alone. The brain is subtler than that. Drugs modulate the activity of a variety of brain chemicals, each of which intersects with many others. "Drugs are like sledgehammers," observes Dr. Eric Nestler of the Yale University School of Medicine. "They profoundly alter many pathways."

Nevertheless, the realization that dopamine may be a common end point of all those pathways represents a signal advance. Provocative, controversial, unquestionably incomplete, the dopamine hypothesis provides a basic framework for understanding how a genetically encoded trait—such as a tendency to produce too little dopamine—might intersect with environmental influences to create a serious behavioral disorder. Therapists have long known of patients who, in addition to having psychological problems, abuse drugs as well. Could their drug problems be linked to some inborn quirk? Might an inability to absorb enough dopamine, with its pleasure-giving properties, cause them to seek gratification in drugs?

Such speculation is controversial, for it suggests that broad swaths of the population may be genetically predisposed to drug abuse. What is not controversial is that the social cost of drug abuse, whatever its cause, is enormous. Cigarettes contribute to the death toll from cancer and heart disease. Alcohol is the leading cause of domestic violence and highway deaths. The needles used to inject heroin and cocaine are spreading AIDS. Directly or indirectly, addiction to drugs, cigarettes and alcohol is thought to account for a third of all hospital admissions, a quarter of all deaths and a majority of serious crimes. In the U.S. alone the combined medical and social costs of drug abuse are believed to exceed $240 billion.

biological basis. "Addiction," declares Brookhaven's Volkow, "is a disorder of the brain no different from other forms of mental illness."

That new insight may be the dopamine hypothesis' most important contribution in the fight against drugs. It completes the loop between the mechanism of addiction and programs for treatment. And it raises hope for more effective therapies. Abstinence, if maintained, not only halts the physical and psychological damage wrought by drugs but in large measure also reverses it.

Genes and social forces may conspire to turn people into addicts but do not doom them to remain so. Consider the case of Rafael Rios, who grew up in a housing project in New York City's drug-infested South Bronx. For 18 years, until he turned 31, Rios, whose father died of alcoholism, led a double life. He graduated from Harvard Law School and joined a prestigious Chicago law firm. Yet all the while he was secretly visiting a shooting gallery once a day. His favored concoction: heroin spiked with a jolt of cocaine. Ten years ago, Rios succeeded in kicking his habit—for good, he hopes. He is now executive director of A Safe Haven, a Chicago-based chain of residential facilities for recovering addicts.

How central is dopamine's role in this familiar morality play? Scientists are still trying to sort that out. It is no accident, they say, that people are attracted to drugs. The major drugs of abuse, whether depressants like heroin or stimulants like cocaine, mimic the structure of neurotransmitters, the most mind-bending chemicals nature has ever concocted. Neurotransmitters underlie every thought and emotion, memory and learning; they carry the signals between all the nerve cells, or neurons, in the brain. Among some 50 neurotransmitters discovered to date, a good half a dozen, including dopamine, are known to play a role in addiction.

The neurons that produce this molecular messenger are surprisingly rare. Clustered in loose knots buried deep in the brain, they number a few tens of thousands of nerve cells out of an estimated total of 100 billion.

But through long, wire-like projections known as axons, these cells influence neurological activity in many regions, including the nucleus accumbens, the primitive structure that is one of the brain's key pleasure centers. At a purely chemical level, every experience humans find enjoyable—whether listening to music, embracing a lover or savoring chocolate—amounts to little more than an explosion of dopamine in the nucleus accumbens, as exhilarating and ephemeral as a firecracker.

Dopamine, like most biologically important molecules, must be kept within strict bounds. Too little dopamine in certain areas of the brain triggers the tremors and paralysis of Parkinson's disease. Too much causes the hallucinations and bizarre thoughts of schizophrenia. A breakthrough in addiction research came in 1975, when psychologists Roy Wise and Robert Yokel at Concordia University in Montreal reported on the remarkable behavior of some drug-addicted rats. One day the animals were placidly dispensing cocaine and amphetamines to themselves by pressing a lever attached to their cages. The next they were angrily banging at the lever like someone trying to summon a stalled elevator. The reason? The scientists had injected the rats with a drug that blocked the action of dopamine.

In the years since, evidence linking dopamine to drugs has mounted. Amphetamines stimulate dopamine-producing cells to pump out more of the chemical. Cocaine keeps dopamine levels high by inhibiting the activity of a transporter molecule that would ordinarily ferry dopamine back into the cells that produce it. Nicotine, heroin and alcohol trigger a complex chemical cascade that raises dopamine levels. And a still unknown chemical in cigarette smoke, a group led by Brookhaven chemist Joanna Fowler reported last year, may extend the activity of dopamine by blocking a mopping-up enzyme, called MAO B, that would otherwise destroy it.

The evidence that Volkow and her colleagues present in the current issue of *Nature* suggests that dopamine is directly responsible for the exhilarating rush that reinforces the desire to take drugs, at least in cocaine addicts. In all, 17 users participated in the study, says Volkow, and they experienced a high whose intensity was directly related to how extensively cocaine tied up available binding sites on the molecules that transport dopamine around the brain. To produce any high at all, she and her colleagues found, cocaine had to occupy at least 47% of these sites; the "best" results occurred when it took over 60% to 80% of the sites, effectively preventing the transporters from latching onto dopamine and spiriting it out of circulation.

F OR NEARLY A QUARTER-CENTURY the U.S. has been waging a war on drugs, with little apparent success. As scientists learn more about how dopamine works (and how drugs work on it), the evidence suggests that we may be fighting the wrong battle. Americans tend to think of drug addiction as a failure of character. But this stereotype is beginning to give way to the recognition that drug dependence has a clear

WHAT ELSE?

Preliminary evidence suggests that dopamine may be involved even when we form dependencies on things—like coffee or candy—that we don't think of as drugs at all

SCIENTISTS BELIEVE THE DOPAMINE system arose very early in the course of animal evolution because it reinforces behaviors so essential to survival. "If it were not for the fact that sex is pleasurable," observes Charles Schuster of Wayne State University in Detroit, "we would not engage in it." Unfortunately, some of the activities humans are neurochemically tuned to find agreeable—eating foods rich in fat and sugar, for instance—have backfired in modern society. Just as a surfeit of food and a dearth of exercise have conspired to turn heart disease and diabetes into major health problems, so the easy availability of addictive chemicals has played a devious trick. Addicts do not crave heroin or cocaine or alcohol or nicotine per se but want the rush of dopamine that these drugs produce.

Dopamine, however, is more than just a feel-good molecule. It also exercises extraordinary power over learning and memory. Think of dopamine, suggests P. Read Montague of the Center for Theoretical Neuroscience at Houston's Baylor College of Medicine, as the proverbial carrot, a reward the brain doles out to networks of neurons for making survival-enhancing choices. And while the details of how this system works are not yet understood, Montague and his colleagues at the Salk Institute in San Diego, California, and M.I.T. have proposed a model that seems quite plausible. Each time the outcome of an action is better than expected, they predicted, dopamine-releasing neurons should increase the rate at which they fire. When an outcome is worse, they should decrease it. And if the outcome is as expected, the firing rate need not change at all.

As a test of his model, Montague created a computer program that simulated the nectar-gathering activity of bees. Programmed with a dopamine-like reward system and set loose on a field of virtual "flowers," some of which were dependably sweet and some of which were either very sweet or not sweet at all, the virtual bees chose the reliably sweet flowers 85% of the time. In laboratory experiments real bees behave just like their virtual counterparts. What does this have to do with drug abuse? Possibly quite a lot, says Montague. The theory is that dopamine-enhancing chemicals fool the brain into thinking drugs are as beneficial as nectar to the bee, thus hijacking a natural reward system that dates back millions of years.

The degree to which learning and memory sustain the addictive process is only now being appreciated. Each time a neurotransmitter like dopamine floods a synapse, scientists believe, circuits that trigger thoughts and motivate actions are etched onto the brain. Indeed, the neurochemistry supporting addiction is so powerful that the people, ob-

jects and places associated with drug taking are also imprinted on the brain. Stimulated by food, sex or the smell of tobacco, former smokers can no more control the urge to light up than Pavlov's dogs could stop their urge to salivate. For months Rafael Rios lived in fear of catching a glimpse of bare arms—his own or someone else's. Whenever he did, he remembers, he would be seized by a nearly unbearable urge to find a drug-filled syringe.

Indeed, the brain has many devious tricks for ensuring that the irrational act of taking drugs, deemed "good" because it enhances dopamine, will be repeated. PET-scan images taken by Volkow and her colleagues reveal that the absorption of a cocaine-like chemical by neurons is profoundly reduced in cocaine addicts in contrast to normal subjects. One explanation: the addicts' neurons, assaulted by abnormally high levels of dopamine, have responded defensively and reduced the number of sites (or receptors) to which dopamine can bind. In the absence of drugs, these nerve cells probably experience a dopamine deficit, Volkow speculates, so while addicts begin by taking drugs to feel high, they end up taking them in order not to feel low.

PET-scan images of the brains of recovering cocaine addicts reveal other striking changes, including a dramatically impaired ability to process glucose, the primary energy source for working neurons. Moreover, this impairment—which persists for up to 100 days after withdrawal—is greatest in the prefrontal cortex, a dopamine-rich area of the brain that controls impulsive and irrational behavior. Addicts, in fact, display many of the symptoms shown by patients who have suffered strokes or injuries to the prefrontal cortex. Damage to this region, University of Iowa neurologist Antonio Damasio and his colleagues have demonstrated, destroys the emotional compass that controls behaviors the patient knows are unacceptable.

Anyone who doubts that genes influence behavior should see the mice in Marc Caron's lab. These tireless rodents race around their cages for hours on end. They lose weight because they rarely stop to eat, and then they drop from exhaustion because they are unable to sleep.

Why? The mice, says Caron, a biochemist at Duke University's Howard Hughes Medical Institute laboratory, are high on dopamine. They lack the genetic mechanism that sponges up this powerful stuff and spirits it away. Result: there is so much dopamine banging around in the poor creatures' synapses that the mice, though drug-free, act as if they were strung out on cocaine.

For years scientists have suspected that genes play a critical role in determining who will become addicted to drugs and who will not. But not until now have they had molecular tools powerful enough to go after the prime suspects. Caron's mice are just the most recent example. By knocking out a single gene—the so-called dopamine-transporter gene—Caron and his colleagues may have created a strain of mice so sated with dopamine that they are oblivious to the allure of cocaine, and possibly alcohol and heroin as well. "What's exciting about our mice," says Caron, "is that they should allow us to test the hypothesis that all these drugs funnel through the dopamine system."

Several dopamine genes have already been tentatively, and controversially, linked to alcoholism and drug abuse. Inherited vari-

ations in these genes modify the efficiency with which nerve cells process dopamine, or so the speculation goes. Thus, some scientists conjecture, a dopamine-transporter gene that is superefficient, clearing dopamine from the synapses too rapidly, could predispose some people to a form of alcoholism characterized by violent and impulsive behavior. In essence, they would be mirror images of Caron's mice. Instead of being drenched in dopamine, their synapses would be dopamine-poor.

The dopamine genes known as D2 and D4 might also play a role in drug abuse, for similar reasons. Both these genes, it turns out, contain the blueprints for assembling what scientists call a receptor, a minuscule bump on the surface of cells to which biologically active molecules are attracted. And just as a finger lights up a room by merely flicking a switch, so dopamine triggers a sequence of chemical reactions each time it binds to one of its five known receptors. Genetic differences that reduce the sensitivity of these receptors or decrease their number could diminish the sensation of pleasure.

The problem is, studies that have purported to find a basis for addiction in vari-

COKE'S HIGH IS DIRECTLY TIED TO DOPAMINE LEVELS

A.A.'S PATH TO RECOVERY STILL SEEMS THE BEST

ations of the D2 and D4 genes have not held up under scrutiny. Indeed, most scientists think addiction probably involves an intricate dance between environmental influences and multiple genes, some of which may influence dopamine activity only indirectly. This has not stopped some researchers from promoting the provocative theory that many people who become alcoholics and drug addicts suffer from an inherited condition dubbed the reward-deficiency syndrome. Low dopamine levels caused by a particular version of the D2 gene, they say, may link a breathtaking array of aberrant behaviors. Among them: severe alcoholism, pathological gambling, binge eating and attention-deficit hyperactivity disorder.

The more science unmasks the powerful biology that underlies addiction, the brighter the prospects for treatment become. For instance, the discovery by Fowler and her team that a chemical that inhibits the mopping-up enzyme MAO B may play a role in cigarette addiction has already opened new possibilities for therapy. A number of well-tolerated MAO B inhibitor drugs developed to treat Parkinson's disease could find a place in the antismoking arsenal. Equally promising, a Yale University team led by Eric Nestler and David Self has found that another type of compound—one that targets the dopamine receptor known as D1—seems to alleviate, at least in rats, the intense craving that accompanies withdrawal from cocaine. One day, suggests Self, a D1 skin patch might help cocaine abusers kick their habit, just as the nicotine patch attenuates the desire to smoke.

Like methadone, the compound that activates D1 appears to be what is known as a partial agonist. Because such medications stimulate some of the same brain pathways as drugs of abuse, they are often addictive in their own right, though less so. And while treating heroin addicts with methadone may seem like a cop-out to people who have never struggled with a drug habit, clinicians say they desperately need more such agents to tide addicts—particularly cocaine addicts—over the first few months of treatment, when the danger of relapse is highest.

REALISTICALLY, NO ONE BELIEVES better medications alone will solve the drug problem. In fact, one of the most hopeful messages coming out of current research is that the biochemical abnormalities associated with addiction can be reversed through learning. For that reason, all sorts of psychosocial interventions, ranging from psychotherapy to 12-step programs, can and do help. Cognitive therapy, which seeks to supply people with coping skills (exercising after work instead of going to a bar, for instance), appears to hold particular promise. After just 10 weeks of therapy, before-and-after PET scans suggest, some patients suffering from obsessive-compulsive disorder (which has some similarities with addiction) manage to resculpt not only their behavior but also activity patterns in their brain.

In late 20th century America, where drugs of abuse are being used on an unprecedented scale, the mounting evidence that treatment works could not be more welcome. Until now, policymakers have responded to the drug problem as though it were mostly a criminal matter. Only a third of the $15 billion the U.S. earmarks for the war on drugs goes to prevention and treatment. "In my view, we've got things upside down," says Dr. David Lewis, director of the Center for Alcohol and Addiction Studies at Brown University School of Medicine. "By relying so heavily on a criminalized approach, we've only added to the stigma of drug abuse and prevented high-quality medical care."

Ironically, the biggest barrier to making such care available is the perception that efforts to treat addiction are wasted. Yet treatment for drug abuse has a failure rate no different from that for other chronic diseases. Close to half of recovering addicts fail to maintain complete abstinence after a year—about the same proportion of patients with diabetes and hypertension who fail to comply with their diet, exercise and medication regimens. What doctors who treat drug abuse should strive for, says Alan Leshner, director of the National Institute on Drug Abuse, is not necessarily a cure but long-term care that controls the progress of the disease and alleviates its worst symptoms. "The occasional relapse is normal," he says, "and just an indication that more treatment is needed."

Rafael Rios has been luckier than many. He kicked his habit in one lengthy struggle that included four months of in-patient treatment at a residential facility and a year of daily outpatient sessions. During that time, Rios checked into 12-step meetings continually, sometimes attending three a day. As those who deal with alcoholics and drug addicts know, such exertions of will power and courage are more common than most people suspect. They are the best reason yet to start treating addiction as the medical and public health crisis it really is.

—With reporting by Alice Park/New York

Why They Stay: A Saga of Spouse Abuse

Whatever else American culture envisions of petite blondes, it doesn't expect them to end up as social revolutionaries. But just that turn of fate has brought Sarah Buel to Williamsburg, Virginia, from suburban Boston, where she is assistant district attorney of Norfolk County. To a gathering of judges, lawyers, probation and police officers, victim advocates, and others, she has come to press an idea that meets persistent resistance—to explain why and, perhaps more importantly, precisely how domestic violence should be handled, namely as the serious crime that it is, an assault with devastating effects against individuals, families, and communities, now and for generations to come.

Hara Estroff Marano

Hara Estroff Marano is an author living in Brooklyn Heights, NY. She is currently Editor at Large of *Psychology Today,* contributor to many national publications, and working on a book about the social development of children.

Buel, 41, a speed talker—there is, after all, so much to say—tells them what Los Angeles prosecutors failed to explain in the O. J. Simpson case: how batterers cannily dodge responsibility for their own actions, as if other people sneak into their brains and ball their fingers into fists; how they are deft at shifting the blame to others, especially their mates; how they watch and stalk partners, even those under the protection of the court, and especially those who have separated or divorced. Instead of holding up Simpson as the poster boy for domestic violence, the California trial let him get away with doing what batterers almost always do—put on a great public face and portray themselves as victims.

The judges and cops and court officers pay attention to Buel because domestic violence is a daily hassle that takes a lot out of them. And if there's one thing Buel knows,

it's how batterers manipulate the law enforcement system. They listen because Buel has that most unassailable credential, an honors degree from Harvard Law School. But mostly they listen because Buel has been on the receiving end of a fist.

"Sometimes I hate talking about it," she confides. "I just want people to see me as the best trial lawyer." But, as Deborah D. Tucker says, "she grabs them by the heart." Tucker, head of the Texas Council on Family Violence and chairman of the national committee that pushed the Violence Against Women Act into the 1994 Omnibus Crime Bill, explains: "She gets people to feel what they need to feel to be vulnerable to the message that domestic violence is not we/they. Any of us can become victimized. It's not about the woman. It's about the culture."

Certainly Buel never had any intention of speaking publicly about her own abuse. It started accidentally. She was in a court hallway with some police officers on a domestic violence case. "See, a smart woman like you would never let this happen," the chief said, gesturing her way. And in an in-

stant Buel made a decision that changed her life irrevocably, and the lives of many others. "Well, it did happen," she told him, challenging his blame-the-victim tone. He invited her to train his force on handling domestic violence. "It changed things completely. I decided I had an obligation to speak up. It's a powerful tool."

It has made her a star, says psychologist David Adams, Ed.D. By speaking from her own experience, Buel reminds people that law can be a synonym for justice. In conferences and in courts, she has gotten even the most cynical judges to listen to battered women—instead of blaming them. "I am amazed at how often people are sympathetic as long as the victim closely resembles Betty Crocker. I worry about the woman who comes into court who doesn't look so pretty. Maybe she has a tattoo or dreadlocks. I want judges to stop wondering, 'What did she do to provoke him?'" Sarah Buel is arguably the country's sharpest weapon against domestic violence.

Buel finishes her talk, and in the split second before the audience jumps to its feet cheering, you can hear people gasp "Whew!" Not because they're tired of sitting, but because in her soft but hurried tones, the prosecution of batterers takes on a passionate, even optimistic, urgency. It's

From *Psychology Today,* May/June 1996, pp. 56–60, 62, 66, 68, 70, 74, 76, 78. © 1996 by Hara Estroff Marano. Reprinted by permission.

possible, she feels, to end domestic violence, although not by prosecution alone. Buel does not dwell on herself as victim but transmutes her own experience into an aria of hope, a recipe for change, "so that any woman living in despair knows there's help."

Not like she knew. She herself was clueless.

One of five children, Buel was born in Chicago but moved endlessly with her family from the age of four. Her father, an auto mechanic fond of drink, always felt success lay elsewhere. Her mother, a Holocaust refugee who fled Austria as a child, went along selflessly—"she didn't know how to speak up," says Buel, which fueled her own desire to do so.

In the seventh grade, Buel was put on a secretarial track. "I was told I wasn't smart enough. So I refused to learn how to type." When she was 14, her parents divorced. Rather than choose which one to live with (her siblings split evenly), Buel headed for New York.

She went to school—at first—while working as a governess. For the first time, she saw television and while watching Perry Mason decided "this is what I want to do." The next year Buel bounced around to four different schools and families, including her mother's. "I went home for three months, but it was too different," she recalls.

Buel eventually went back to New York, where she had relatives, and began a very erratic course through high school, cutting class and shoplifting with a cousin. By the time she was 22, Buel was an abused woman. It came completely out of the blue. She was listening to a song on the radio, "Jeremiah Was a Bullfrog." "I bet that makes you think of Jeremy [a boyfriend of hers way back when she was 15]," her partner said. Actually what she was thinking was how stupid the song was. "Admit it," he insisted, "it does, doesn't it?" No, she said, it doesn't. He accused her of lying—and slapped her across the face.

The verbal and psychological abuse proved more damaging than the physical abuse. There was endless criticism. "He always said I looked frumpy and dumpy. He was enraged if I bought the *New York Times*." He read the tabloid *Daily News*. " ' Isn't it good enough for you?' he demanded. He was extremely jealous. If I so much as commented on, say, a man's coat, he'd accuse me of wanting an affair and flirting. If I wanted to take courses, he insisted the only reason was to flirt with other men. I didn't cook like his mother, clean like his mother. By the time I left I thought, 'The only thing I do well is, I'm a good mother.' "

Suddenly, Buel is surprised to find herself revealing this much personal detail. "I never tell other women the details of my own abuse. They'll measure. Was theirs more or less?"

In 1993 and 1994, a coveted Bunting fellowship from Radcliffe College allowed Buel to work only part time as a public prosecutor. Now, in between court appearances, she crisscrosses the country, finally able to accept invitations to train judges and address gatherings such as this, a first-ever assembly of Virginians Against Domestic Violence. She has visited 49 states. She has testified before Congress. She was even asked to introduce the president of the United States at a press conference last spring, when the federal government set up a new Violence Against Women Office.

But no matter who she talks to or what she says about domestic violence, "it always comes down to one thing," says Buel. "They all ask the same question: Why do they [the women] stay."

First she points out that there are half as many shelters for battered women as there are for stray animals—about 1,800—and most do not accept children. For every two women sheltered, five are turned away. For every two children sheltered, eight are turned away.

A Texas study shows that 75 percent of victims calling domestic violence hotlines had left at least five times. Buel herself first went to the Legal Aid Society. There was a three-year wait for help. They never informed her about safety, never told her about alternatives. She did see a counselor at a family center, but her partner wouldn't go; he would only drive her.

Buel left her abuser and got a job in a shoe factory. But the wage was so low she couldn't pay the rent and a babysitter. "I went back because he said he was sorry, it'll never happen again. When I realized it wasn't true, I left again. I told him I was packing to go to my brother's wedding. I took a bus to New Hampshire, where my mother lived. That didn't work out—she was living on a remote farm, I had no car, and my son was allergic to many of the animals—but I never went back. So 18 years ago I stood on a welfare line with three kids, my own son and two foster children I was raising. But you can't live on that amount of money. We trade our safety for poverty. We go back because we don't know what else to do."

Batterers are expert at portraying themselves as the injured party. The first time her batterer threw her against a wall, Buel's son screamed, "Don't hurt my mom." Then the batterer shouted, "See, you're turning the kid against me."

"I used to think, 'Why me? I must have done something terrible.' Women come to think it was their fault. They feel guilty for not doing a good enough job as a mom because they are unable to protect themselves, or their children."

A major obstacle to leaving, says Buel, is battered women's fear of losing their children or of being unable to protect them. "A Massachusetts study documented that in 70 percent of cases where fathers attempted to get custody of their children, they did so successfully. So when the abuser says to her, 'Sure, you can leave, but I've got the money to hire a good lawyer and I'll get the kids,' he may be right.

"We go back because we think we'll figure out a way to stop the violence, the magic secret everybody else seems to know. We don't want to believe that our marriage or relationship failed because we weren't willing to try just a little harder. I felt deeply ashamed, that it must be my fault. I never heard anyone else talking about it. I assumed I was the only one it was happening to."

One of the biggest reasons women stay, says Buel, is that they are most vulnerable when they leave. That's when abusers desperately escalate tactics of control. More domestic abuse victims are killed when fleeing than at any other time.

Buel has a crystal-clear memory of a Saturday morning at the laundromat with her young son, in the small New Hampshire town where she had fled, safely, she thought, far from her abuser. "I saw my ex-partner, coming in the door. There were people over by the counter and I yelled to them to call the police, but my ex-partner said, 'No, this is my woman. We've just had a little fight and I've come to pick her up. Nobody needs to get involved.' Nobody moved. And I thought, as long as I live I want to remember what it feels like to be terrified for my life while nobody even bothers to pick up the phone."

It's time, Buel sighs, to stop asking why they stay and start asking what they need to feel safe. "I'm obsessed with safety now," she confides. "More important than prosecution, more important than anything, is a safety plan, an action plan detailing how to stay alive." And so a first encounter with a victim requires a verbal walk-through of what she'll need to feel safe at her place of work, at home, on the streets, and suggestions about what she'll need for leaving—birth certificates, legal papers, bank accounts—and for dealing with the abuser.

Buel entered Harvard Law in 1987. "I would love to have gone sooner but I had no idea how to get there. I didn't know you had to go to college to go to law school." She imagined you first had to work long enough as a legal secretary. In 1977, after two months on welfare, Buel entered a federally funded job-training program that, despite her awful typing, landed her in a legal services office. Eventually, she became a paralegal aide and began helping domestic violence victims.

In 1980, she started seven years of undergraduate study, first at Columbia University on scholarship, which necessitated "nine horrible months" in a drug-ridden building in New York while on welfare, so that instead of working nights she could spend them with her son. Ultimately she returned to New England and, two nights a week, attended Harvard Extension School, a vastly different world from Harvard Yard. She did well.

Days were spent working as a women's advocate in federal legal services offices, first in New Hampshire, then in grimy Lowell, Massachusetts. Buel started shelters and hotlines for battered women. She helped draft an abuse prevention law. She dreamed about being a voice for the women she represented.

She learned to write. She took classes in public speaking. Toward the end of her undergraduate studies, her bosses asked her where she wanted to go to law school. "Harvard," she replied, "because they're rich and they'll give me money." The lawyers laughed and told her that wasn't how it worked: "They do the choosing, not you." They took pains to point out she just wasn't Harvard material. "You're a single mother. You've been on welfare. You're too old."

Angry and humiliated, Buel began a private campaign that typifies her fierce determination. In the dark after classes, she drove around the law school, shouting at it: "You're going to let me in." Soon she got braver and stopped the car to go inside and look around. Then she had to see what it was like to sit in a classroom. She decided if she ever got accepted, she'd choose one of the orange-colored lockers, because her son was a fan of the Syracuse Orangemen.

Harvard Law not only accepted Buel but gave her a full scholarship. Once there, she was surprised there was nothing in the criminal-law syllabus about family violence—this despite the fact that women are more likely to be the victim of a crime in their own home, at the hands of someone they know, than on the streets. Buel mentioned the oversight to her professor. He told her to take over the class for one hour one day. She thought she'd be educating movers and shakers for the future. "I was amazed when, during the next six weeks, no less than 16 classmates came up to me either because they were in violent relationships or their parents or friends were."

When Boston-area colleagues requested help on an advocacy program for battered women and she couldn't do it alone, Buel put an ad in the student newspaper; 78 volunteers showed up for the first meeting. By year's end there were 215. She started a pro bono legal counseling program. The Bat-

tered Women's Advocacy Project is now the largest student program at Harvard Law; a quarter of the participants are men.

In 1990, at age 36, Buel graduated, cum laude. She sent a copy of her transcript to her old junior-high teacher with a note suggesting that she not judge the future of 12-year-old girls.

At first Buel thought it would be enough to become a prosecutor and make sure that batterers are held accountable for assaulting others. But she has come to see it differently. "That's not enough. My role is not just to make women safe but to see that they are financially empowered and that they have a life plan." So every morning, from 8:30 to 9:15, before court convenes, she sees that all women there on domestic issues are briefed, given a complete list of resources, training options, and more. "We surveyed battered women. We asked them what they needed to know. I wanted everyone to listen to them. Usually no one ever does. Most people tell them what to do. 'Leave him.' 'Do this.' 'Do that.' You can't tell women to leave until you give them—with their children—a place to go, the knowledge how and the resources to get by on their own, and the safety to do so. It's all about options."

What's more, Buel now sees domestic violence as just one arc of a much bigger cycle, intimately connected to all violence, and that it takes a whole coordinated community effort to stop it, requiring the participation of much more than attorneys and judges. It takes everyone; even the locksmith, so that when a woman suddenly needs her locks changed, the call will be heeded.

Rather than drive her own career narrowly forward, Buel has instead broadened her approach, venturing into places few lawyers ever go. She regularly attends community council meetings in Germantown, a dreary outpost of public housing in Quincy, known for its high crime rate. The council—Head Start teachers, the parish priest, two cops who requested duty in the projects, a few community members—celebrates mundane triumphs. A parents dinner at Head Start. A potluck supper at the church.

Buel is absolutely certain that this is the real answer to crime. It is the prevailing fallacy to assume that big problems require big solutions. First a community has to knit itself together—and from the sound of things the best way is on its stomach. "People here hear that some things are unacceptable," says one. A cop reports, remarkably, there has not been a single incident in a month.

Buel tells the assembled that emergency housing funds are available for battered women whose husbands are not paying support. "This is how I get the dirt on what's going on," she tells me. "These of-

ficers will call me when there's a domestic violence problem but the woman isn't ready to enter the legal system. At least we can keep an eye on her, and the children, to make sure she's safe."

Buel is particularly concerned about the children. She knows that children who witness violence become violent themselves. "Some take on the role of killing their mother's batterer," says Buel, who notes that 63 percent of males between ages 11 and 20 who are doing time for homicide have killed their mother's batterer. "We adults have abdicated the role of making the home safe."

Children who witness violence may commit suicide as adolescents, says Buel, pointing to soaring suicide rates among teenagers. Or grow up to soothe the pain with drugs. Or run away from home. A University of Washington study demonstrates that the vast majority of runaway and pregnant teenagers grew up in violent households.

BECAUSE SHE CARES SO MUCH about the kids, in 1992 Buel started the What Is Your Dream Project in an adolescent center in Chelsea, a depressed community. It grew out of her frustration about pregnant teens, the group at highest risk for domestic violence. "Most of them have no person in their life talking to them about the future. That made me angry. That's how I was stereotyped. There was no assumption I'd be college-bound." The program trains at-risk teens to champion younger kids, telling them about educational and job options, about grants for beautician school or training as electricians or computer technicians, for example. "It was a powerful force for me to name going to law school as a dream. It focused my life," Buel recalls.

For her unusually diversified approach to domestic violence, Buel gives full credit to William Delahunt, her boss, the district attorney. "He has allowed me to challenge the conventional notion of what our job is."

"My boss gets complaints about me all the time," Buel says proudly. There was the batterer who, despite divorce and remarriage, was thought to be the source of menacing gifts anonymously sent to his ex-wife—a gun box for Christmas, a bullet box for Valentine's Day, followed by the deeds to burial plots for her and her new husband. The woman repeatedly hauled her ex into court for violating a restraining order; one lawyer after another got him off. "Finally I got him for harassing her in the parking garage where she was going to college; of course he denied it. The lawyer contended she was making up all the stories. But a detective found a videotape from the garage, which corroborated her charge. In the appeals court, his lawyer, a big guy, leaned into my face and hissed, 'You may be a good little advocate for your cause, but you're a terrible lawyer.' " She won the appeal.

Because the students asked for one, Buel teaches a class on domestic violence to 43 students at Boston College Law School. Over a third of them are males.

And she lectures widely to the medical profession. "Doctors see abused women all the time and don't know it," she says. She is especially interested in reaching family doctors and obstetrician/gynecologists, because in over a third of instances, abuse occurs during pregnancy—as it did for her. It is the primary time for the onset of violence. Her goal is to see that all doctors routinely ask every woman at every visit whether she has been hit or threatened since her last visit, explain that they are now routinely asking the question, state that no woman deserves to be abused, and then provide information and referral if she has. This simple question, by exposing abuse to plain daylight, brilliantly erases some of its shame. It is only when shame is gone that abused women can ask for help.

YOU COULD SAY THAT 1994

was the best of times and the worst of times for domestic violence. Spouse abuse was "discovered" by Congress, which passed the Violence Against Women Act. Among its provisions are federal standards that permit enforcement of restraining orders across state lines, the single most important weapon women have to keep abusers from threatening or attacking them or their children.

And spouse abuse was "discovered" by the public at large after O. J. Simpson was arrested for the murder of ex-wife Nicole Brown Simpson and her friend Ronald Goldman. Clear evidence quickly emerged that O. J. Simpson had beaten his wife in the past. To those who know about domestic violence, Simpson fit a well-established pattern—when his partner got serious about leaving him for good, he began a campaign of terror. He began stalking her. He followed her movements. He peeked in her windows. He wouldn't, couldn't, let go.

Despite his ultimate acquittal, O. J., nevertheless, was the answer to some people's prayers. Like Deborah Tucker's. One of those whip-smart, wise-crackin', well-coifed dynamos that Texas seems to breed, who have you howling on the floor while they're stripping your political illusions, Tucker not only heads Texas's Council on Family Violence, she runs the new national Domestic Violence Hotline (1-800-799-SAFE). If the world of action against domestic violence has an axis on which it turns, Tucker is its south pole to Sarah Buel's north.

"Many people worked awfully hard for 20 years to see that violence against women was taken seriously and recognized as a crime. We had seen a law passed, established 1,800 organizations around the country providing services to battered women. We had built an infrastructure to respond to domestic violence and educate about it. Now all that was needed was visibility for the cause. Many of us talked among ourselves that that would happen only when a famous person killed his wife." Of course, no one imagined that person would be black, opening the racial divide. Tucker is now more cautious about what she wishes for.

O. J.'s arrest, says Tucker, "put domestic violence on the map." O. J. and Nicole were wealthy. They were visible. We tend to accept domestic violence in invisible people. We were at a juncture where something like that needed to happen. Social change is slow.

"The murder created a vehicle for common discourse about spouse abuse. The trial was a fiasco. The prosecutor never educated the public about stalking or about patterns of domestic violence. O. J. had followed Nicole and watched her. Everywhere I went, people asked: 'Why would he do that? He was divorced; he even had a girlfriend.' It was a chance to discuss tactics of power and control that do not stop with divorce, a chance to point out that women are in more danger when they leave—though everyone always asks why they stay."

If the Los Angeles D.A.s did little to explain, that is not the case with Buel. She has talked almost nonstop since.

In her travels, Buel has observed firsthand that many jurisdictions have figured out how to reduce violence against women. She sees her mission as spreading the word about them. Buel's considerable charisma stems in no small measure from her conviction that the solutions are out there, if only everyone knew about them. "People are always surprised at my optimism," she says.

"There's no one solution," she insists. "You need a message from the whole community. People point to the policy of mandatory arrest of all batterers in Duluth, Minnesota. But Duluth also has billboards that warn, 'Never hit a child.' " Buel's list of what works includes:

- the end of silence about spouse abuse.
- probation officers sensitive to the safety needs of victims and serious monitoring of offenders.
- mandatory group treatment programs for batterers. Programs must last at least a year, hold them alone accountable, and teach them to respect women.
- sanctions for failure to comply with probation or restraining orders.

- the use of advocates to follow cases.
- training cops in how to investigate and gather complete evidence when answering domestic violence calls.

Buel waves an investigation checklist she got from police in San Diego. If information gathering is done correctly, prosecution can proceed even when the victim refuses to press charges or come to court as a witness. "When a woman refuses to testify, she's not 'failing to cooperate,' " she says. "She's terrified. She's making the statement, 'I want to stay alive.' "

I ask Buel about her working relationships with judges. "In Massachusetts, I'm characterized as too harsh. I simply ask for some mechanism of accountability. Judges here are appointed for life without mandatory training. Many come from the big law firms that represent the batterers. Some do a great job. Others lose sight of the victims and children."

Discrimination against women through the law infuriates Buel. A recent study shows that a batterer who kills his wife typically gets a jail term of two to four years. But a woman who kills her abuser gets 14 to 18 years.

Of course, a great deal of domestic violence never finds its way into the criminal justice system; it's handled by private psychotherapists. "No one wants her husband arrested," especially women from the upper income strata, says Buel. She regrets that she is rarely invited to speak to the mental health community.

"Unfortunately," she charges, "most therapists, including family counselors, have little training in domestic violence. They are often conned by the stories of the batterers, experts at shifting blame. Without realizing it, therapists often put women at greater risk of abuse. There is nothing victims can disclose to them for which there will not be later retaliation. At the very least, therapists don't think in terms of safety plans for the victims.

"Batterers are extraordinarily talented in sucking in therapists, the community, even their wives' families. Their whole M.O. is manipulation. They'll get the priest to testify that they're family-loving men, but the priest isn't there during the abuse. They are notorious liars; they'll say whatever makes them look good. Even if the woman gets a restraining order barring her partner from having any contact with her, these guys will make calls or send flowers. They're not really showing love, just proving they can get around the system, showing who's boss." In the toxic world of domestic violence, simply receiving an unsigned birthday card can be a deadly threat.

Yet domestic violence thrives in the best of zip codes, including the bedroom communities for Boston's medical chiefs. "Two of the worst cases I ever prosecuted involved doctors," says Buel, who finds that domestic violence is increasing in severity among wealthier families. "There's a much greater use of weapons. Ten years ago you would never have heard of a computer executive putting a gun to his wife's head."

BECAUSE TOO MANY VICTIMS stay with their batterers, Buel has begun to radically shift her approach to ending violence. "I'm learning new ways to compromise, reaching out to defense attorneys." In this she is crossing a divide most feminist lawyers shun. The defense attorneys, after all, represent batterers, "because they have the money." But they also have some power over their clients. "Some defense attorneys are willing to change their practices, to agree to take on batterers only if they go to a treatment program and stick with it."

This braving of the breach gives the lie to any suggestion that Buel is motivated by vindictiveness. She rolls her huge eyes at characterizations of activists as man haters. Or as do-gooders blind to the "fact" that people don't change.

There are men in her life. First and foremost is her son; he's away—but not too far away—at college. And there is a serious relationship. "He works in another domain, so there's no sense of competition. He is very emotionally supportive and respects the work I do. I had pretty much given up. Most men say I'm too intimidating."

Not David Adams, who runs the first and arguably best counseling program set up in the United States for men who batter. "It's taken someone like her to move the system forward. Only recently have the courts begun to hear women's concerns; they're more attuned to men's perspectives and complaints. She's a tremendous leader widely respected in the criminal justice system. She's become the conscience of the system, always looking at ways victims can be helped and perpetrators held accountable."

Holding men accountable for their violence is a full-time job for Adams, who sees 300 abusers a week at his Cambridge-based Emerge program. "These guys constantly minimize their own behavior. They'll say, 'She provoked me; if she'd only just shut up or respect me more.' " Excuse number two is "I lost control. I just snapped." Observes Adams: "But their 'snapping' is awfully selective; they snap only with the victim, not with their boss or other people."

Battering, Adams insists, "is primarily an instrument of control. It's not anger, though abusers always claim they're impulsive. It is purposeful, though from the outside it looks as if it's irrational behavior. And there's a logic to it; it enforces social rules. It is a learned behavior that's self-reinforcing—batterers get what they want through violence—and socially reinforced through beliefs about women as the social and sexual caretakers of men." He finds it takes at least nine months in the program just to puncture men's denial.

Returning to Boston from Williamsburg, Buel attends back-to-back meetings. First is the board session of a foundation that funds battered-women's shelters. Next comes the Domestic Violence Council, a regional group of private and public attorneys who share information and strategies. Buel started the council in law school. It has grown exponentially since, and now meets at one of Boston's prestige law firms. Discussions this day focus on:

- Lawyers' safety. Being the barrier between a woman and her batterer sometimes leads to threats, or worse; victims and their attorneys have been murdered—even in the courthouse. A lawyer reports that her tires were punctured.
- A new cultural trend toward what look like organizations for the preservation of fatherhood. Masquerading as involved fathers, members are often batterers who use their kids as a way of stalking or threatening ex-partners. A law student assigned to check out one group's roster reports that 86 percent of the men have restraining orders against them.
- Monitoring the courts. For two years, practicing and student attorneys have been trained to evaluate how the state's judges handle domestic violence cases. Now they're assembling a committee to meet with those doing a bad job—those who, say, don't ask about kids or weapons when considering requests for restraining orders—and inform them how to do better.

The day has no end. Dinner isn't simply a meal, it's an opportunity to give support and advice to two Harvard Law grads who have formed the fledgling Women's Rights Network. Where should they go for funding? Does she know a defense attorney in Edmonton (Canada) for the international information they are putting together on domestic violence?

And Buel whips out some formidable pieces of paper, legal-pad sheets neatly filled with the names and phone numbers of people—73 per side—whose calls she must return. There were, I think, four of them, neatly written, neatly folded, representing two or three days' worth of calls to her office and her home. She keeps her number listed so women in trouble can find her. Somewhere on the list is an Edmonton attorney.

The two young women complain that despite its own budget surplus, Harvard Law has cut funding for law clinics, needed now more than ever as the public sector cuts back. "They'll no doubt use the money to put in more rosewood desks," they scoff.

But all three know it is the very credibility a Harvard Law degree bestows that compels the attention of so many others. And that, says Buel, "also pisses me off. People who wouldn't pay attention to me before suddenly hang on every word."

That seventh-grade teacher, I am certain, the one who almost derailed her for good, is never far from Buel's mind.

Development during Middle and Late Adulthood

Middle Adulthood (Articles 39–41)
Late Adulthood (Articles 42–46)

There is a gradual slowing of the rate of mitosis of cells of all the organ systems with age (except the neurons, which do not undergo mitosis after birth). This gradual slowing of mitosis translates into a slowed rate of repair of cells of all the organs. By the thirties, signs of aging can be seen in skin, skeleton, vision, hearing, smell, taste, balance, coordination, heart, blood vessels, lungs, liver, kidneys, digestive tract, immune response, endocrine functioning, and ability to reproduce. To some extent, moderate use of any body part (as opposed to disuse or misuse) helps it retain its strength, stamina, and repairability. However, by middle and late adulthood, persons become increasingly aware of the aging effects of their organ systems on their total physical fitness. A loss of height occurs as spinal disks and connective tissues diminish and settle. Demineralization, especially loss of calcium, causes weakening of bones. Muscles atrophy, and the slowing of cardiovascular and respiratory responses creates a loss of stamina for exercise. All of this may seem cruel, but it occurs very gradually and need not adversely affect one's enjoyment of life.

Healthful aging, at least in part, seems to be genetically preprogrammed. The females of many species, including humans, outlive the males. The sex hormones of females may protect them from some early aging effects. Males, in particular, experience earlier declines in their cardiovascular systems. Diet and exercise can ward off many of the deleterious effects of aging. A reduction in saturated fat intake coupled with regular aerobic exercise contributes to less bone demineralization, less plaque in the arteries, stronger muscles (including heart and lung muscles), and a general increase in stamina and vitality. An adequate intake of complex carbohydrates, fibrous foods, fresh fruits, fresh vegetables, and water also enhances good health.

Cognitive abilities do not appreciably decline with age in healthy adults. Research suggests that the speed with which the brain carries out problems involving abstract (fluid) reasoning may slow, but not cease. Complex problems may simply require more time to solve with age. On the other hand, research suggests that the memory banks of older people may have more crystallized (accumulated and stored) knowledge. One's ken (range of knowledge) and practical skills (common sense) grow with age and experience. Older human beings become more expert at the tasks they frequently do.

The first article included in the middle adulthood section of this unit examines the speculation about sex differences in the cognitive abilities of adults. Are women better at emotional and linguistic types of reasoning? If so, is their superiority due to brain differences, or does it reflect dissimilar experiences from men? Conversely, men seem to be better at spatial orientating ability. Is this superiority a result of nature or nurture? The research suggests that there are subtle but real differences in adults' cognitive styles related to their sex, which may be due to brain differences.

The second article on middle age deals with the value of a good night's sleep to one's physical, cognitive, and socioemotional functioning during the day. The author, Dr. J. Allen Hobson, suggests that we pay attention to sleep as a major determinant of human behavior.

The third article paints a beautiful/handsome face on the middle-aged adult. Susan Scarf Merrell extols the benefits of living in this interesting and fruitful stage of life. She gives brief snapshots of several people who thoroughly enjoy being middle-aged. She quotes several psychologists who share their views of the positive aspects of the middle years of adulthood.

Erik Erikson suggested that the most important psychological conflict of late adulthood is achieving a sense of ego integrity. This is fostered by self-respect, self-esteem, love of others, and a sense that one's life has order and meaning. The articles in the subsection on late adulthood reflect Erikson's concern with experiencing ego integrity rather than despair.

Daniel Goleman, in the second article in the late adulthood section of this unit, describes the aging brain from a new perspective, that of two imaging techniques, positron emission tomography (PET scans) and magnetic resonance imaging (MRI). Data from healthy seniors in their 80s and 90s reveal that loss of brain tissue is modest and largely confined to selective areas. Intellectual functioning can continue to be robust and may even continue to grow in areas such as vocabulary and overall knowledge.

The third article in this section looks at grandparents and the possibilities for their keeping up with grandchildren and great-grandchildren in areas such as computer skills. The authors describe other educational curricula as well that benefit grandparent development and have a positive impact on family life.

Robert Sapolsky's essay on the patterns of life ends this section and this anthology. He takes a positive view of dying, death, and bereavement. He finds solace in experiencing the human life span as a cycle complete with predictable patterns and stages.

Looking Ahead: Challenge Questions

Do men's and women's brains function differently? Why?

How can paying attention to sleep be a way of paying attention to one's occupational and personal pursuits in middle adulthood?

Does the baby-boom generation relish being middle-aged? Why?

Is the rapid increase in longevity creating a new stage of life? Describe.

Can the resourceful older brain show plasticity and compensate for lost neurons by using other neurons to get the job done? Explain.

How can grandparents join the computer generation?

Why is there solace to be found in predictable patterns of living and dying?

Jack Rosenthal, in "The Age Boom," describes the phenomena of longer life, better health, and greater security in the late years of adulthood in the 1990s. Many elderly people are living life with dignity and elan. The factors that he weighs most heavily as contributors to their longevity and integrity are family, school, and work.

Man's World, Woman's World? Brain Studies Point to Differences

Gina Kolata

Dr. Ronald Munson, a philosopher of science at the University of Missouri, was elated when Good Housekeeping magazine considered publishing an excerpt from the latest of the novels he writes on the side. The magazine eventually decided not to publish the piece, but Dr. Munson was much consoled by a letter from an editor telling him that she liked the book, which is written from a woman's point of view, and could hardly believe a man had written it.

It is a popular notion: that men and women are so intrinsically different that they literally live in different worlds, unable to understand each other's perspectives fully. There is a male brain and a female brain, a male way of thinking and a female way. But only now are scientists in a position to address whether the notion is true.

The question of brain differences between the sexes is a sensitive and controversial field of inquiry. It has been smirched by unjustifiable interpretations of data, including claims that women are less intelligent because their brains are smaller than those of men. It has been sullied by overinterpretations of data, like the claims that women are genetically less able to do everyday mathematics because men, on average, are slightly better at mentally rotating three dimensional objects in space.

But over the years, with a large body of animal studies and studies of humans that include psychological tests, anatomical studies, and increasingly, brain scans, researchers are consistently finding that the brains of the two sexes are subtly but significantly different.

Now researchers have a new noninvasive method, functional magnetic resonance imaging, for studying the live human brain at work. With it, one group recently detected certain apparent differences in the way men's and women's brains function while they are thinking. While stressing extreme caution in draw-

New scanner finds more evidence of how the sexes differ in brain functions.

ing conclusions from the data, scientists say nonetheless that the groundwork was being laid for determining what the differences really mean.

"What it means is that we finally have the tools at hand to begin answering these questions," said Dr. Sally Shaywitz, a behavioral scientist at the Yale University School of

Medicine. But she cautioned: "We have to be very, very careful. It behooves us to understand that we've just begun."

The most striking evidence that the brains of men and women function differently came from a recent study by Dr. Shaywitz and her husband, Dr. Bennett A. Shaywitz, a neurologist, who is also at the Yale medical school. The Shaywitzes and their colleagues used functional magnetic resonance imaging to watch brains in action as 19 men and 19 women read nonsense words and determined whether they rhymed.

In a paper, published in the Feb. 16 issue of Nature, the Shaywitzes reported that the subjects did equally well at the task, but the men and women used different areas of their brains. The men used just a small area on the left side of the brain, next to Broca's area, which is near the temple. Broca's area has long been thought to be associated with speech. The women used this area as well as an area on the right side of the brain. This was the first clear evidence that men and women can use their brains differently while they are thinking.

Men have larger brains; women have more neurons.

Another recent study by Dr. Ruben C. Gur, the director of the brain behavior laboratory at the University of Pennsylvania School of Medicine, and his colleagues, used magnetic resonance imaging to look at the metabolic activity of the brains of 37 young men and 24 young women when they were at rest, not consciously thinking of anything.

In the study published in the Jan. 27 issue of the journal Science, the investigators found that for the most part, the brains of men and women at rest were indistinguishable from each other. But there was one difference, found in a brain structure called the limbic system that regulates emotions. Men, on average, had higher brain activity in the more ancient and primitive regions of the limbic system, the parts that are more involved with action. Women, on average, had more activity in the newer and more complex parts of the limbic system, which are involved in symbolic actions.

Dr. Gur explained the distinction: "If a dog is angry and jumps and bites, that's an action. If he is angry and bares his fangs and growls, that's more symbolic."

Dr. Sandra Witelson, a neuroscientist at McMaster University in Hamilton, Ontario, has focused on brain anatomy, studying people with terminal cancers that do not involve the brain. The patients have agreed to participate in neurological and psychological tests and then to allow Dr. Witelson and her colleagues to examine their brains after they die, to look for relationships between brain structures and functions. So far she has studied 90 brains.

Several years ago, Dr. Witelson reported that women have a larger corpus callosum, the tangle of fibers that run down the center of the brain and enable the two hemispheres to communicate. In addition, she said, she found that a region in the right side of the brain that corresponds to the region women used in the reading study by the Shaywitzes was larger in women than in men.

Most recently Dr. Witelson discovered, by painstakingly counting brain cells, that although men have larger brains than women, women have about 11 percent more neurons. These extra nerve cells are densely packed in two of the six layers of the cerebral cortex, the outer shell of the brain, in areas at the level of the temple, behind the eye. These are regions used for understanding language and for recognizing melodies and the tones in speech. Although the sample was small, five men and four women, "the results are very, very clear," Dr. Witelson said.

Going along with the studies of brain anatomy and activity are a large body of psychological studies showing that men and women have different mental abilities. Psychologists have consistently shown that men, on average, are slightly better than women at spatial tasks, like visualizing figures rotated in three dimensions, and women, on average, are slightly better at verbal tasks.

Dr. Gur and his colleagues recently looked at how well men and women can distinguish emotions on someone else's face. Both men and women were equally adept at noticing when someone else was happy, Dr. Gur found. And women had no trouble telling if a man or a woman was sad. But men were different. They were as sensitive as women in deciding if a man's face was sad—giving correct responses 90 percent of the time. But they were correct about 70 percent of the time in deciding if women were sad; the women were correct 90 percent of the time.

"A woman's face had to be really sad for men to see it," Dr. Gur said. "The subtle expressions went right by them."

Studies in laboratory animals also find differences between male and female brains. In rats, for example, male brains are three to seven times larger than female brains in a specific area, the preoptic nucleus, and this difference is controlled by sex hormones that bathe rats when they are fetuses.

"The potential existence of structural sex differences in human brains is almost predicted from the work in other animals," said Dr. Roger Gorski, a professor of anatomy and cell biology at the University of California in Los Angeles. "I think it's a really fundamental concept and I'm sure, without proof, that it applies to our brains."

But the question is, if there are these differences, what do they mean?

Dr. Gorski and others are wary about drawing conclusions. "What happens is that people overinterpret these things," Dr. Gorski said. "The brain is very complicated, and even in animals that we've studied for many years, we don't really know the function of many brain areas."

This is exemplified, Dr. Gorski said, in his own work on differences in rat brains. Fifteen years ago, he and his colleagues discovered that males have a comparatively huge preoptic nucleus and that the area in females is tiny. But Dr. Gorski added: "We've been studying this nucleus for 15 years, and we still don't know what it does. The most likely explanation is that it has to do with sexual behavior, but it is very, very difficult to study. These regions are very small and they are interconnected with other things." Moreover, he said, "nothing like it has been shown in humans."

And, with the exception of the work by the Shaywitzes, all other findings of differences in the brains or mental abilities of men and women have also found that there is an amazing degree of overlap. "There is so much overlap that if you take any individual man and woman, they might show differences in the opposite direction" from the statistical findings, Dr. Gorski said.

Dr. Munson, the philosopher of science, said that with the findings so far, "we still can't tell whether the experiences are different" when men and women think. "All we can tell is that the brain processes are different," he said, adding that "there is no Archimedean point on which you can stand, outside of experience, and say the two are the same. It reminds me of the people who show what the world looks like through a multiplicity of lenses and say 'This is what the fly sees.'" But, Dr. Munson added, "We don't know what the fly sees." All we know, he explained, is what we see looking through those lenses.

Some researchers, however, say that the science is at least showing the way to answering the ancient mind-body problem, as applied to the cognitive worlds of men and women.

Dr. Norman Krasnegor, who directs the human learning and behavior branch at the National Institute of Child Health and Human Development, said the difference that science made was that when philosophers talked about mind, they "always were saying, 'We've got this black box.'" But now, he said, "we don't have a black box; now we are beginning to get to its operations."

Dr. Gur said science was the best hope for discovering whether men and women inhabited different worlds. It is not possible to answer that question simply by asking people to describe what they perceive, Dr. Gur said, because "when you talk and ask questions, you are talking to the very small portion of the brain that is capable of talking." If investigators ask people to tell them what they are thinking, "that may or may not be closely related to what was taking place" in the brain, Dr. Gur said.

On the other hand, he said, scientists have discovered that what primates perceived depends on how their brains function. Some neurons fire only in response to lines that are oriented at particular angles, while others seem to recognize faces. The world may well be what the philosopher Descartes said it was, an embodiment of the workings of the human mind, Dr. Gur said. "Descartes said that we are creating our world," he said. "But there is a world out there that we can't know."

Dr. Gur said that at this point he would hesitate to boldly proclaim that men and women inhabit different worlds. "I'd say that science might be leading us in that direction," he said, but before he commits himself he would like to see more definite differences in the way men's and women's brains function and to know more about what the differences mean.

Dr. Witelson cautioned that "at this point, it is a very big leap to go from any of the structural or organizational differences that were demonstrated to the cognitive differences that were demonstrated." She explained that "all you have is two sets of differences, and whether one is the basis of the other has not been shown." But she added, "One can speculate."

Dr. Witelson emphasized that in speculating she was "making a very big leap," but she noted that "we all live in our different worlds and our worlds depend on our brains.

"And," she said, "if these sex differences in the brain, with 'if' in big capital letters, do have cognitive consequences, and it would be hard to believe there would be none, then it is possible that there is a genuine difference in the kinds of things that men and women perceive and how these things are integrated. To that extent it may be possible that in some respects there is less of an easy cognitive or emotional communication between the sexes as a group because our brains may be wired differently."

The Shaywitzes said they were reluctant even to speculate from the data at hand. But, they said, they think that the deep philosophical questions about the perceptual worlds of men and women can eventually be resolved by science.

"It is a truism that men and women are different," Dr. Bennett Shaywitz said. "What I think we can do now is to take what is essentially folklore and place it in the context of science. There is a real scientific method available to answer some of these questions."

Dr. Sally Shaywitz added: "I think we've taken a qualitative leap forward in our ability to ask questions." But, she said, "the field is simply too young to have provided more than a very intriguing appetizer."

Sleep
Pays Attention

What Is REM Sleep?

The sleep cycle is a continuous and dynamic process with the deepest sleep stage known as rapid eye movement (REM) sleep. REM sleep typically occurs 4 to 6 times a night and accounts for about one-fourth of the total sleep time. REM sleep is characterized by rapid eye movement, slack skeletal muscles, cerebral activity similar to waking, increased autonomic activity and dreaming. REM sleep is also known as paradoxical sleep because the brain wave activity and cerebral blood flow are similar to when a person is awake. If a person is awakened during REM sleep, vivid dreams are often recalled.

J. ALLAN HOBSON, M.D.

WHENEVER I HAVE MISSED EVEN ONE or two hours of sleep, I have difficulty being attentive the next day. Whether or not I actually feel sleepy, I notice that I have a subtle but definite attention deficit disorder. I just can't seem to keep my mind focused on my work.

Recently my new wife, Lia Silvestri (who is a neurologist and sleep disorders specialist from Messina, Sicily), honored me by delivering twin sons. Because they were born at 34 weeks and were thus premature, they tend to be superb sleepers. But still, like other newborns, they do wake up once or twice a night—and fret a good deal before and after Lia feeds them.

Although I am not losing as much sleep as she is, I am obviously not getting as much as I need to function optimally, especially at age 62. For example, instead of focusing on one of the five papers I am currently writing (like this one), I flit back and forth from one to the other and am often distracted by completely irrelevant stimuli, which I could easily ignore if I had gotten a good, solid night of sleep.

Two questions arise. The first is functional: how might attention benefit from sleep? The second is methodological: how could we actually measure the relationship of attention to sleep? The answers to these two questions have profound scientific and practical implications. They could help us solve the elusive riddle of sleep function. And they could help us avoid always annoying—and sometimes tragic—effects of attentional failures.

Is Sleep a Treatment for Normal Attention Deficit Disorder?

IT CERTAINLY COULD BE. IN MY 25 YEARS AS A prober of the brain stem, one of the most surprising and significant observations I made was that the neurons of the locus coeruleus reduce their output by half at sleep onset and stop firing altogether during REM! Now, the locus coeruleus produces norepinephrine, the brain chemical that is necessary to normal attentiveness. This means that when I dream, my brain is saving norepinephrine, and perhaps even stockpiling it. What a nifty mechanism!

In my dreams I don't need to pay attention. Indeed, I can't pay attention while dreaming. I am so distracted by the kaleidoscopic rush of events and feelings that I don't even know I am dreaming. I am deluded into thinking I am awake. I am psychotic. That's the bad news. The good news is that my brain may thus be conserving its own attention juice.

This is what I mean by "Sleep Pays Attention." Good sleep, especially good REM sleep, gives good attention the next day by enhancing the effects of norepinephrine in the brain. When we realize that the medical treatment of attention deficit disorder depends upon artificially providing norepinephrine-like molecules to the brain, our interest in this theory increases. Of course, there is a lot more to the functional chemistry of sleeping and waking than this one little fact, but it does capture our scientific attention.

Can We Measure Sleep and Attention?

YES, WE CAN. AND, THANKS TO THE NEW NIGHTcap system, we can measure both simultaneously as subjects sleep and wake in normal, real-life settings that are more natural than sleep laboratories. The Nightcap is a simple, portable, self-applied monitoring system that counts the movements of the head and eyelids on a minute-to-minute basis and allows an algorithmic estimate of the stages of sleep (REM and non-REM) and waking. Being compact and battery-operated, it is capable of recording up to 30 nights at a shot. The Nightcap can be used to assess normal and disordered sleep and dreams in the subject's own home and is ideal for research in extreme conditions like mountain tops and space vehicles.

The algorithmic estimation of the sleeping and waking states from the Nightcap movement data is made either on- or off-line by a Macintosh computer. My colleague Robert Stickgold has programmed a bedside Mac to compute the sleep-wake algorithm in real time and to perform voice prompt awakenings, after which the subjects either give reports on what they have been thinking or perform standard cognitive tests of attention. We have already found that attention does vary dramatically over the sleep-wake cycle, and we have also made a surprising new discovery.

Originally developed exclusively for sleep, the Nightcap has recently shown itself to be sensitive to fluctuations in the level of vigilance during waking. By monitoring around the clock, we are able to correlate the goodness of sleep with the goodness of subsequent waking behavior. And we can purposely make sleep worse (or better) and see what happens to performance on specific cognitive tasks that measure attention and vigilance. The still preliminary results of pilot studies on vigilance conducted by Robert Stickgold are eye-opening. Whenever Bob took a test of vigilance after a night of sleep deprivation, he had trouble with it. His attentional lapses could be predicted by drops in counts from the eyelid movement monitor. When he analyzed his data, Bob found a negative linear correlation between eye counts and performance.

To keep our eyelids open—and to keep our brains attentive—we use brain stem reticular and oculomotor neurons that are modulated by norepinephrine. If that chemical is in short supply, the neurons don't function well, our eyelids droop, counts fall in the Nightcap eye channel, and we miss cues on tasks of perception and vigilance.

It is said that professors live by the law of "publish or perish." Thus the cost of attentional failure and vigilance lapses to an intellectual, like me, may be relatively trivial, for example, the stunting of an already bloated bibliography! And even the loss of tenure or one's job can't compare to the risk of attentional failure in an airline pilot, a railroad engineer, or an automobile operator. In those occupations a single failure can be fatal.

The cure? A good night of sleep—especially one with lots of REM sleep, which allows the norepinephrine-making cells of the locus coeruleus to stop firing. This conserves the transmitters already made, and allows more to be synthesized as we sleep and dream. We wake up alert, energetic, and able to write papers, or perform whatever other brain functions our livelihood—and our life itself—may require. I think I'll go home and take a little nap!

Dr. Hobson is Professor of Psychiatry at Harvard Medical School and Director of the Laboratory of Neurophysiology at the Massachusetts Mental Health Center. He is a winner of the prestigious von Humboldt award of the Max Planck Society.

Getting Over

Getting Older

Forget about trying to reverse the process. It's never been a

better time to face up to aging. In fact, getting older truly does mean getting

better. By Susan Scarf Merrell

Baby boomers: We were supposed to be the generation that turned aging into a bedroom act, making it sexy to grow old and gray, and get laugh lines. If 76 million of us wrinkled into middle age with style and verve, well, wow, the entire Western World might rethink the need to search for a fountain of youth. Most of us, however, don't seem to have found that sense of contentment with our aging bodies that we expected to. Instead, baby boomers have both masterminded—and fallen victim to—an anti-aging epidemic far more virulent than the average case of mass hysteria. It isn't simply that we're trying to exercise and eat our way to longer, healthier lives. Sales are up dramatically across the gamut of age-fighting weaponry, from wrinkle creams to collagen injections to cosmetic surgery. Nor are the warriors only women. According to a recent Roper Starch Worldwide survey, six percent of men nationwide actually use such traditionally feminine products as bronzers and foundation to create the illusion of a more youthful appearance.

What is it about aging that makes our sagging skin crawl? Are we frightened of looking and feeling old because it reminds us that we're mortal? That we might become infirm? What, in fact, does older age bring and how will it be different for us boomers than for the generations that came before?

The first surprise is that those of us entering the middle years en masse are truly lucky to be hitting our thirties, forties, and fifties now, in the 1990s. Because the state of a civilization has a very real impact on the inevitable path to getting older, every generation experiences aging differently. According to aging expert Helen Kivnick, Ph.D., a psychologist at the University of Minnesota, the experience of later life is determined partly by biology, partly by history, and partly by society and culture. Never before in history has the phase of later life had the potential to be so long and fruitful. "Old age as we now know it is very new, and doesn't look at all like it used to," Kivnick says. "Because people live longer and with greater independence, they can plan their futures more actively. Elders today [those over 65] are breaking new ground."

OLD AIN'T WHAT IT USED TO BE

If those who are old today are stepping onto untrodden ground, we boomers are about to create a stampede. And chances are we'll be extremely skilled at making old age into an interesting and fruitful time of life. We know how to explore and plumb possibility. We have already been enjoying far fewer societal constraints in our middle years than has ever previously been the norm. Renee Garfinkel, Ph.D., a psychologist and aging expert from Silver Springs, Maryland, says across the board we have fewer age-based limitations to hinder us. "It's not simply that we tend to keep our health longer; it's that we also aren't subject to generational restrictions on behavior, career choices, or clothing." If you decide to go to medical school—or rollerblading—tomorrow, you might just do so. If I pick out similar dresses for my five-year-old daughter and me, neither one of us will seem out of place: She won't be dressed "old," and I won't be dressed "young." Our tastes are actually fairly alike. In blue jeans and sweaters—particularly from the back—one often can't tell a fit 55-year-old from his or her fit adolescent kid.

As recently as twenty or thirty years ago, society was much more hierarchical. When a woman's children left home, she struggled to make sense of a future in which her life's task was done, even though she herself remained healthy and alert and capable of making further—and even greater—contributions. In the 1970s, when women in their thirties and forties ventured out to colleges and universities in large numbers, they were breaking norms and redefining their roles. Certainly, I myself would have been extremely aware of the oddity of an older man or woman—even a person so aged as to be in his or her late twenties—sitting in a lecture hall back when I was in college. Nowadays, that's almost laughable: The student in the next chair in the lecture hall could just as easily be a grandparent as an 18-year-old. In fact, if those "nontraditional" students weren't filling seats, many institutions of higher learning would be struggling to keep their doors open.

Middle age doesn't mean what it used to. Mid-lifers aren't ossified and set in their ways; they tend to be open to new ideas and new experiences; the tastes of childhood have matured but the sense of potential and of discovery is still deep and real. A former newspaper editor, who had her first child at the age of forty and recently completed her doctoral dissertation at the age of forty-five, says, "I know how old I am. I'm not in denial about the fact of the years. I simply reject the fears, stereotypes, and caricatures of aging. If you ask me my age, I'll tell you, but I don't think it's the most relevant fact about me."

"I think young," says a globe-trotting artist in his early eighties. "I won't allow myself to feel old, or act old, until they cart me out in a box." Does attitude make a difference? Are we truly only as old as we feel?

Yes and no, says Garfinkel, who heads Gerontology Service, a consulting practice for institutions that deal with the elderly. She finds that we associate aging with dysfunction. A young person in poor health tends to report feeling old, while an old person in good health feels young and active. "It's a two-way street," says Garfinkel. "If you aren't in good health, it's very hard to think young. But if you think young, have good genes, and take care of yourself, you'll probably feel and seem younger than you are."

Believing yourself to be in better than normal condition for your age is typical for healthy people in general. It's not that we're deluding ourselves, it's simply that the interplay of chronological age and physical health is much stronger than we tend to realize. That's why the following statistical impossibility can exist: According to "The Wrinkle Report," a national survey of more than 1,200 people ages 30 to 50, three in four baby boomers think they look younger than their actual years, and eight in ten say they have fewer signs of facial aging than other people their age. "People in their forties and those in their eighties actually say quite similar things," Garfinkel reports. "It's more an indication of physical health than of anything else. If we don't feel bad, we feel great. We're a little bit like the people in Lake Woebegon, whose children are all above average."

AM I OLD YET?

People tend not to feel downright old, no matter what their age. They just get more and more surprised when they look in the mirror and see the ways in which they're changing physically. The fact is that aging tends to be subtle and most losses come hand in hand with small, new rewards. For example, one's first gray hairs may arrive around the same time one earns a major promotion—somehow the equation of loss and gain nets out in a surprisingly satisfying manner. In some way, we continue to expect that the next milestone will be the one that makes us suddenly feel old.

I'm reminded of a birthday luncheon I went to recently for a friend who's just rounded the hump of thirty. Call her Sally. Sally had anticipated the event with a great deal of fear and anxiety, and was surprised at how little change the actual big day had wrought. I mentioned that I'd felt very few negative changes during my thirties, and said that I felt surer of myself and much happier than I'd been in my twenties. Then Kim, our 43-year-old friend, smiled broadly at both of us and said that the thirties were a wonderful decade. We continued eating for a moment. After a bit, Sally turned to me and said, "How old are you again? Thirty-eight?"

"Thirty-seven," I snapped. Kim's smile drooped—to her, my quick reaction meant that though I was happy to be getting older, I didn't want to be as old as she was. In fact, she's right. I'm enjoying each year far more than I might have imagined possible as a teenager, but that doesn't mean I want my life to pass any more quickly. As much as I like my thirties, I'm not giving up a single year before it's time.

Paradoxically, I do know that, on most levels, the future looks promising. Given all the fear we seem to have of it, the wondrous news is that getting older is a generally positive thing. We don't just accumulate years, we also gain wisdom which enables us to make decisions with less of the fussing and wheel-spinning that marked our teens and twenties. "I often think the excess energy of youth is nature's way of compensating for a lack of wisdom," says Garfinkel. "All that zip means you don't collapse from all the work of chasing your own tail."

As we get older, we know more not only about the world but about ourselves. We have better attention spans and an increased ability to focus. "In general, most non-neurotic older people are content with what they've done with their lives, are happy, have high self-esteem, and a sense of well-being," says clinical psychologist Forrest Scogin, Ph.D., of the University of Alabama. "We become more adaptable and flexible, and have a greater understanding of our own resilience."

Conventional thinking has always emphasized the miserable, crotchety older person, Scogin adds, but in fact unhappiness is far from the norm. Rates of depression tend to decline after the age of 45, for both men and women. (There's a slight—but temporary—blip in men's rates around the time of retirement.) Other research shows that our sense of what we deem most important for happiness tends to alter appropriately as we age, a sign of the true resilience of the human spirit: We may not look as fresh-faced, but we like ourselves more. We actually think fewer negative thoughts. Life becomes simpler.

Our priorities shift in a healthy and adaptive fashion. "We care less about our appearance and more about our emotional well-being, our character, and our involvements in the world at large and with those we love," says clinical psychologist Betsy Stone, Ph.D., of Stamford, Connecticut.

One other rosy aspect to the future is that as physical attributes become a little less stunning, sex roles begin to blur. Men become more accommodating and emotionally expressive; women more assertive and active in meeting their own needs. With a little less passion, a little less division of roles, and an increase in

contentment and openness with one another, relationships in later life tend to become far more important, satisfying, and mutual.

On the down side—and, of course, there had to be one—we begin to slow on all fronts. It becomes increasingly difficult to keep up with the energies of a two-year-old, or to add up a series of numbers in one's head. Memory grows less efficient as well. In fact, it's a process that begins between the ages of 18 and 20 but is so slow and subtle that it doesn't become noticeable until around the age of 35. And when we first face the fact that memorizing what we need to do that day is getting difficult, we adapt. We start making lists and otherwise reorder our approach to retaining information. "You tell yourself it's not so important to remember things," says Garfinkel.

In truth, the worst part of getting older appears to be ageism—the intolerant attitudes of younger people. According to Scogin, "People grow impatient with you for your slowness, even though that decline in speed is appropriate. Think of that driver who makes you crazy when you're trying to get some place. That person isn't being oppositional, as it appears to you. His or her reactions are slower, so it's natural that he or she would drive more cautiously." Of course, older people are as heterogeneous as any other population, Scogin adds: "Some are hot-rodding down the highway, some are doddering along. One can't ever generalize."

BETTER, NOT OLDER

Okay, so if we're supposed to be satisfied with our aging selves, does that mean it's wrong to help nature along, to try and slow down the ravages of time? According to Stone, author of the forthcoming *Happily Ever After: A Guide for Newlyweds*, "Dying your hair or having collagen injections doesn't really have anything to do with avoiding getting older per se; it's about wanting to feel good about yourself and feel attractive. It's like wearing beautiful lingerie: Nobody else knows you're doing it, but you feel indulged and valuable. That's a reasonable thing to do."

But such self-improvement can go too far, Stone explains. For example, if a person values his or her attractiveness to the exclusion of other personal characteristics, then the person is loving him or herself from the outside-in rather than the inside-out. "That's a problem," she says.

According to Kivnick, who researches how the lives of very frail elders can be improved, the most important thing we can do to ensure a comfortable and interesting old age is to plan for one. Not simply financially, although that's obviously important. Most of us will spend a good twenty years or more in healthy, active post-retirement, and just expecting to sit on one's heels and rest is hardly a realistic plan for happiness. Don't just daydream about planting a garden, says Kivnick. Learn about gardening, and be ready for the day you'll be free to spend all afternoon with your hands in the dirt. Plan to stay involved in your community, with your family, with whatever has interested and intrigued you thus far. "Perhaps the most important and neglected aspect of getting older is the need to continue giving to others," Kivnick says. "The most unhappy people in the world are those who use retirement to withdraw from involvements, expecting that using their time to concentrate on themselves alone will make them happy. They end up miserable."

Researchers at the Duke University Center for the Study of Aging and Human Development concur. Having family and friends isn't the answer to a happy life, but engaging actively with them is. And it seems possible that this involvement can help you live even longer.

It's also essential to know yourself. Your personality isn't likely to change so much that it becomes unrecognizable as you get older. Thus you can begin to speculate about the future in practical ways. It's never too early to start considering the basic questions: What's important to me? What life do I most want to live? With whom and where? Would I prefer to stay near my own family or to be in an elder community? Do I want to travel? How will I remain connected to the greater world? What contribution should I make? Once you're no longer bound by the structure of a formal paid job, the whole world can be your oyster.

There's no time better than the present for beginning to imagine an enjoyable, wise, active, and fruitful later life. Such planning can only add richness to the middle years as well. Says Kivnick, "How we are old depends very much on how we are young."

Susan Scarf Merrell is the author of The Accidental Bond: The Power of Sibling Rivalry, *out in paperback this January. She has just completed her first novel.*

The Age Boom

America discovers a new stage of life as many more people live much longer—and better. By Jack Rosenthal

When my father died at 67, leaving my mother alone in Portland, Ore., I thought almost automatically that she should come home with me to New York. Considering her heavy Lithuanian accent and how she shrank from dealing with authority, I thought she'd surely need help getting along. "Are you kidding?" she exclaimed. Managing her affairs became her work and her pride, and it soon occurred to me that this was the first time that she, traditional wife, had ever experienced autonomy. Every few days she would make her rounds to the bank, the doctor, the class in calligraphy. Then, in her personal brand of English, she would make her telephone rounds. She would complain that waiting for her pension check was "like sitting on pins and noodles" or entreat her granddaughter to stop spending money "like a drunken driver." Proudly, stubbornly, she managed on her own for 18 years. And even then, at 83, frustrated by strokes and angry at the very thought of a nursing home, she refused to eat. In days, she made herself die.

Reflecting on those last days, I realize that the striking thing was not her death but those 18 years of later life. For almost all that time, she had the health and the modest income to live on her own terms. She could travel if she chose, or send birthday checks to family members, or buy yet another pair of shoes. A woman who had been swept by the waves of two world wars from continent to continent to continent—who had experienced some of this century's worst aspects—came finally to typify one of its best. I began to understand what people around America are coming to understand: the transformation of old age. We are discovering the emergence of a new stage of life.

The transformation begins with longer life. Increased longevity is one of the striking developments of the century; it has grown more in the last 100 years than in the prior 5,000, since the Bronze Age. But it's easy to misconstrue. What's new is not the number of years people live; it's the number of people who live them. Science hasn't lengthened life, says Dr. Robert Butler, a pioneering authority on aging. It has enabled many more people to reach very old age. And at this moment in history, even to say "many more people" is an understatement. The baby boom generation is about to turn into an age boom.

Still, there's an even larger story rumbling here, and longevity and boomers tell only part of it. The enduring anguish of many elders lays continuing claim on our conscience. But as my mother's last 18 years attest, older adults are not only living longer; generally speaking, they're living better—in reasonably good health and with enough money to escape the anxiety and poverty long associated with aging.

Shakespeare perceived seven ages of man—mewling infant, whining schoolboy, sighing lover, quarrelsome soldier, bearded justice, spectacled wheezer and finally second childhood, "sans teeth, sans eyes, sans taste, sans everything." This special issue of the Magazine examines the emerging new state, a warm autumn that's already altering the climate of life for millions of older adults, for their children, indeed for all society.

Longer Life

In 1900, life expectancy at birth in America was 49. Today, it is 76, and people who have reached 55 can expect to live into their 80's. Improved nutrition and modern medical miracles sound like obvious explanations. But a noted demographer, Samuel Preston of the University of Pennsylvania, has just published a paper in which he contends that, at least until mid-century, the principal reason was neither. It as what he calls the "germ theory of disease" that generated personal health reforms like washing hands, protecting food from flies, isolating sick children, boiling bottles and milk and ventilating rooms.

Jack Rosenthal is the editor of The New York Times Magazine.

Since 1950, he argues likewise, the continuing longevity gains derive less from Big Medicine than from changes in personal behavior, like stopping smoking.

The rapid increase in longevity is now about to be magnified. The baby boom generation born between 1946 and 1964 has always bulged out—population peristalsis—like a pig in a python. Twice as many Americans were born in 1955 as in 1935. Between now and the year 2030, the proportion of people over 65 will almost double. In short, more old people. And there's a parallel fact now starting to reverberate around the world: fewer young people. An aging population inescapably results when younger couples bear fewer children—which is what they are doing almost everywhere.

The fertility news is particularly striking in developed countries. To maintain a stable population size, the necessary replacement rate is 2.1 children per couple. The United States figure is barely 2.0, and it has been below the replacement rate for 30 years. The figure in China is 1.8. Couples in Japan are typically having 1.5 children, in Germany 1.3 and in Italy and Spain, 1.2.

To some people, these are alarming portents of national decline and call for pronatalist policies. That smacks of coarse chauvinism. The challenge is not to dilute the number of older people by promoting more births. It is to improve the quality of life at all ages, and a good place to start is to conquer misconceptions about later life.

Better Health

"This," Gloria Steinem once said famously, "is what 40 looks like." And this, many older adults now say, is what 60, 70, and even 80 look like. Health and vitality are constantly improving, as a result of more exercise, better medicine and much better prevention. I can't imagine my late father in a sweatsuit, let alone on a Stairmaster, but when I look into the mirrored halls of a health-club gym on upper Broadway I see, among the intent young women in black leotards, white-haired men who are every bit as earnest, climbing, climbing, climbing.

Consider the glow that radiates from the faces on today's cover, or contemplate the standards maintained by people like Bob Cousy, Max Roach, Ruth Bernhard and others who speak out in the following pages.

That people are living healthier lives is evident from the work of Kenneth G. Manton and his colleagues at Duke's Center for Demographic Studies. The National Long-Term Care Survey they started in 1982 shows a steady decline in disability, a 15 percent drop in 12 years. Some of this progress derives from advances in medicine. For instance, estrogen supplements substantially relieve bone weakness in older women—and now seem effective also against other dis-

I go out and play 18 holes in the morning and then three sets in the afternoon.
Bob Cousy, 68

Sports Commentator

I still thrive on competition, and when I feel those competitive juices flowing, I've got to find an outlet. Of course, at 68, it's not going to be playing basketball. Basketball's not a sport you grow old with. Sure, I can manage a few from the free-throw line, but being in shape for basketball's something you lose three months after you retire. I stay in shape by doing as little as possible. I play mediocre golf and terrible tennis. My wife calls it my doubleheader days, when I go out and play 18 holes in the morning and then three sets in the afternoon. Now I'm working in broadcasting and schmoozing the corporates. I'm a commentator for the Celtics' away games. I like it because I'm controlling my own destiny. Everything I've done since I graduated from Holy Cross in 1950 has been sports-related, and it's all because I learned to throw a little ball into a hole. A playground director taught me how to play when I was 13. To me it'll always be child's game.

> After 10 weeks of leg-extension exercises, the participants, some as old as 98, typically doubled the strength of the quadriceps, the major thigh muscle. For many, that meant they could walk. Consider what this single change—the ability among other things to go to the bathroom alone—means to the quality and dignity of their lives.

eases. But much of the progress may also derive from advances in perception.

When Clare Friedman, the mother of a New York lawyer, observed her 80th birthday, she said to her son, "You know, Steve, I'm not middle-aged anymore." It's no joke. Manton recalls survey research in which people over 50 are asked when old age begins. Typically, they, too, say "80." Traditionally, spirited older adults have been urged to act their age. But what age is that in this era of 80-year-old marathoners and 90-year-old ice skaters? As Manton says, "We no longer need to accept loss of physical function as an inevitable consequence of aging." To act younger is, in a very real sense, to be younger.

Stirring evidence of that comes from a 1994 research project in which high-resistance strength training was given to 100 frail nursing-home residents in Boston, median age 87 and some as old as 98. Dr. Maria Fiatarone of Tufts University and her fellow researchers found that after 10 weeks of leg-extension exercises, participants typically doubled the strength of the quadriceps, the major thigh muscle. For many, that meant they could walk, or walk without shuffling; the implications for reduced falls are obvious. Consider what this single change—enabling many, for instance, to go to the bathroom alone—means to the quality and dignity of their lives.

Just as old does not necessarily mean feeble, older does not necessarily mean sicker. Harry Moody, executive director of Hunter College's Brookdale Canter on Aging, makes a telling distinction between the "wellderly" and the "illderly." Yes, one of every three people over 65 needs some kind of hospital care in any given year. But only one in 20 needs nursing-home care at any given time. That is, 95 percent of people over 65 continue to live in the community.

Greater Security

The very words "poor" and "old" glide easily together, just as "poverty" and "age" have kept sad company through history. But suddenly that's changing. In the mid-1960's, when Medicare began, the poverty rate among elders was 29 percent, nearly three times the rate of the rest of the population. Now it is 11 percent, if anything a little below the rate for everyone else. That still leaves five million old people struggling below the poverty line, many of them women. And not many of the other 30 million elders are free of anxiety or free to indulge themselves in luxury. Yet most are, literally, socially secure, able to taste pleasures like travel and education that they may have denied themselves during decades of work. Indeed, many find this to be the time of their lives.

Elderhostel offers a striking illustration. This program, begun in 1975, combines inexpensive travel with courses in an array of subjects and cultures. It started as a summer program with 220 participants at six New Hampshire colleges. Last year, it enrolled 323,000 participants at sites in every state and in 70 foreign countries. Older Americans already exercise formidable electoral force, given how many of them vote. With the age boom bearing down, that influence is growing. As a result, minutemen like the investment banker Peter G. Peterson are sounding alarms about the impending explosion in Social Security and Medicare costs. Others regard such alarms as merely alarmist; either way a result is a spirited public debate, joined by Max Frankel in his column* and by the economist Paul Krugman in his appraisal of the future of Medicare and medical costs.**

Politicians respect the electoral power of the senior vote; why is the economic power of older adults not understood? Television networks and advertisers remain oddly blind to this market, says Vicki Thomas of Thomas & Partners, a Westport, Conn., firm specializing in the "mature market." One reason is probably the youth of copywriters and media buyers. Another is advertisers' desire to identify with imagery that is young, hip, cool. Yet she cites a stream of survey data showing that householders 45 and over buy half

of all new cars and trucks, that those 55 and over buy almost a third of the total and that people over 50 take 163 million trips a year and a third of all overseas packaged tours.

How much silver there is in this "silver market" is Jerry Della Femina's subject.*** It is also evident from Modern Maturity magazine, published by the American Association of Retired Persons. Its bimonthly circulation is more than 20 million; a full-page ad costs $244,000.

All this spending by older adults may not please everyone. Andrew Hacker, the Queens College political scientist, observes that the longer the parents live, the less they're likely to leave to the children—and the longer the wait. He reports spotting a bumper sticker to that effect, on a passing Winnebago: "I'm Spending My Kids' Inheritance!" Even so, the net effect of generational income transfers remains highly favorable to the next generation. For one thing, every dollar the public spends to support older adults is a dollar that their children won't be called on to spend. For another, older adults sooner or late engage in some pretty sizable income transfers of their own. As Hacker observes, the baby boomers' children may have to wait for their legacies, but their ultimate inheritances will constitute the largest income transfer to any generation ever.

Longer years, better health, comparative security: this new stage of life emerges more clearly every day. What's less clear is how older adults will spend it. The other stages of life are bounded by expectations and institutions. We start life in the institution called family. That's soon augmented for 15 or 20 years by school, tightly organized by age, subject and social webs. Then follows the still-more-structured world of work, for 40 or 50 years. And then—fanfare!—what? What institutions then give shape and meaning to everyday life?

Some people are satisfied, as my mother was, by managing their finances, by tending to family relationships and by prayer, worship and hobbies. Others, more restless, will invent new institutions, just as they did in Cleveland in the 1950's with Golden Age Clubs, or in the 1970's with Elderhostel. For the moment, the institutions that figure most heavily for older adults are precisely those that govern the other stages of life—family, school and work.

FAMILY: The focus on family often arises out of necessity. In a world of divorce and working parents, grandparents are raising 3.4 million children; six million families depend on grandparents for primary child care. And that's only one of the intensified relationships arising among the generations. Children have many more years to relate to their parents as adults, as equals, as friends—a

*See page 30, *New York Times Magazine*, March 9, 1997.
**See page 58, *New York Times Magazine*, March 9, 1997.

***See page 70, *New York Times Magazine*, March 9, 1997.

Sure, someone's probably saying: 'Oh, my God! What's this old bag doing in that suit?'
Ann Cole

Age: "Between 59 and Forest Lawn"
Swimsuit Designer

Everyone has certain features that they hate, and that doesn't change much as you get older—it just gets closer to the ground, as Gypsy Rose Lee once said. So you do just grin and bear it, unless you want to sit indoors and grump about it. I get a lot of women who come in and say, "You wouldn't wear that." And I say, "Why, yes I would." I haven't become more comfortable with my body. I've just taken an attitude that it's easier not to care or worry. Just do it. Sure, someone's probably saying: "Oh, my God! What's this old bag doing in that suit?" I've always been a great advocate of people not listening to their children. There used to be a lot of children who weren't happy unless their mother wore a skirted suit down to her knees. They'd say. "Oh, Mom, you can't wear that." I tried to get people over that in the 60's and 70's, because what do they know? You can't be worried about every bump and lump.

fact demonstrated firsthand by the Kotlowitz-to-Kotlowitz letters. ****

SCHOOL: Increasingly, many elders go back to school, to get the education they've always longed for, or to learn new skills—or for the sheer joy of learning. Nearly half a million people over 50 have gone back to school at the college level, giving a senior cast to junior colleges; adults over age 40 now account for about 15 percent of all college students. The 92d Street Y in New York has sponsored activities for seniors since 1874. Suddenly, it finds, many "New Age Seniors" want to do more than play cards or float in the pool. They are signing up by the score for classes on, for instance, Greece and Rome. At a senior center in Westport, Conn., older adults, far from being averse to technology, flock to computer classes and find satisfaction in managing their finances online and traversing the Internet.

****See page 46, *New York Times Magazine,* March 9, 1997.

WORK: American attitudes toward retirement have never been simple. The justifications include a humane belief that retirees have earned their rest; or a bottom-line argument that employers need cheaper workers; or a theoretical contention that a healthy economy needs to make room for younger workers. In any case, scholars find a notable trend toward early retirement, arguably in response to pension and Social Security incentives. Two out of three men on Social Security retire before age 65. One explanation is that they are likely to have spent their lives on a boring assembly line or in debilitating service jobs. Others, typically from more fulfilling professional work, retire gradually, continuing to work part time or to find engagement in serious volunteer effort. In Florida, many schools, hospitals and local governments have come to depend on elders who volunteer their skills and time.

FAMILY, SCHOOL, WORK—AND INSTITUTIONS yet to come: these are the framework for the evolving new stage of later life. But even if happy and healthy, it only precedes and does not replace the last of Shakespeare's age of mankind. One need not be 80 or 90 to understand that there comes a time to be tired, or sick, or caught up by the deeply rooted desire to reflect on the meaning of one's life. For many people, there comes a moment when the proud desire for independence turns into frank, mutual acknowledgment of dependence. As the Boston University sociologist Alan Wolfe wrote in The New Republic in 1995, "We owe [our elders] the courage to acknowledge their dependence on us. Only then will we be able, when we are like them, to ask for help."

That time will come, as it always has, for each of us—as children and then as parents. But it will come later. The new challenge is to explore the broad terrain of longer, fuller life with intelligence and respect. One such explorer, a woman named Florida Scott-Maxwell, reported her findings in "The Measure of My Days," a diary she began in her 80's. "Age puzzles me," she wrote, expressing sentiments that my mother personified. "I thought it was a quiet time. My 70's were interesting and fairly serene, but my 80's are passionate. I grow more intense as I age. To my surprise I burst out with hot conviction. . . . I must calm down."

Studies Suggest Older Minds Are Stronger Than Expected

DANIEL GOLEMAN

The conventional image of the aging brain is that people lose neurons the way balding men lose hair. Brain cells are supposed to start falling away around the age of 20, with everything downhill from there. Some people go bald, or senile, early. Some lucky and unusual ones keep their hair, or their wits, about them into their 90's and beyond.

Science has precious little good news about hair loss, but new findings on the death of brain cells suggest that minoxidil for the mind is unnecessary. Data from men and women who continue to flourish into their 80's and 90's show that in a healthy brain, any loss of brain cells is relatively modest and largely confined to specific areas, leaving others robust. In fact, about 1 of every 10 people continues to increase in mental abilities like vocabulary through those decades.

New imaging techniques, like the PET scan and magnetic resonance imaging, or M.R.I., have shown that the brain does gradually shrink in life's later decades, just not as much as had been thought. Furthermore, the shrinkage of a healthy brain does not seem to result in any great loss of mental ability.

"We used to think that you lost brain cells every day of your life everywhere in the brain," said Dr. Marilyn Albert, a psychologist at Massachusetts General Hospital in Boston. "That's just not so—you do have some loss with healthy aging, but not so dramatic, and in very selective brain areas."

The new imaging techniques have also enabled neuroscientists to discover a flaw in many earlier studies of the aging brain: they included findings from people in the early stages of Alzheimer's disease. Now, both by scanning the brain and by more carefully screening to measure cognitive function, most people with Alzheimer's are excluded from such studies.

Researchers measure brain shrinkage by keeping track of the fjord-like spaces that crease the wrinkled surface layer of the cerebral cortex, the topmost layer that is critical for thought. These tiny crevasses are called ventricles and sulci, and the amount of space in them gradually increases with age, reflecting a loss in the overall mass of the brain.

From age 20 to 70, the average brain loses about 10 percent of its mass, said Dr. Stanley Rapoport, chief of the neuroscience laboratory at the National Institute on Aging in Bethesda, Md.

But that loss "seems related only to subtle differences in cognitive abilities, Dr. Rapoport said. "We think the brain's integrity is maintained because the massive redundancy of interconnection among neurons means that even if you lose some, the brain can often compensate."

Compensation is precisely what studies of the "successful" elderly show. When neuroscientists weed out people with cognitive decline that is a sure sign of illness, the shrinkage is still there, but performance on mental tests is good. And what analyses of healthy old brains show is that old people may use different parts of the brain from young people to accomplish the same task. In some ways a healthy old brain is like a pitcher whose fastball has faded but who can still strike a batter out with other pitches.

Some of the data come from autopsies of 25 men and women from 71 to 95 years old who had volunteered to be part of a control group in a 16-year study of Alzheimer's disease. Dr. John Morris, a neurologist at Washington University in St. Louis who did the study, said the brains of the mentally alert group showed some of the tangles that, more than shrinkage, seem to be the main problem in Alzheimer's disease. But these tangles were in the hippocampus, a structure involved in memory, rather than the centrally important cerebral cortex.

Dr. Morris said his data, which will be published next month in the journal Neurology, suggest "there may be a pool of people who not only have no important cognitive declines, but no brain changes of consequence for mental function, even into their 80's and 90's." Changes in the hippocampus may only slow the rate of retrieval from memory, he said, but not diminish its accuracy.

Similar findings have been made by Dr. Brad Hyman of Massachusetts General Hospital. "We've found no appreciable neuronal loss in people from their 60's to 90's who had retained their mental clarity until they died," said Dr. Hyman, who studied two specific regions of the cortex. "The dire picture we've had of huge cell losses is wrong for a healthy person whose brain remains structurally intact into old age."

Apart from a reduction in the number of brain cells, another aspect of aging in the healthy brain seems to be a drop in the connections between them. Dr. Albert at Massachusetts General said her studies of brain tissue had uncovered specific structures deep in the brain that did show more neuronal loss, even with healthy aging. These include areas important for memory like the basal forebrain.

But, Dr. Albert said, "It's important for mental abilities that most of the neurons in the cortex are retained—they store information once you've learned it."

Some of the most intriguing evidence for the resourcefulness of the aging brain comes from PET scans of the brain at rest and while engaged in mental tasks. In one study using PET scans that compared people in their 20's with those 60 to 75, Dr. Cheryl L. Grady, a neuroscientist at the National Institute on Aging, found that the younger people were indeed quicker and more accurate in recognizing faces, and used more diverse areas of their brains during the task, than did the older people.

But in similar studies at the institute comparing people from 20 to 40 with those 55 and older, the older group was able to recognize the faces with about the same accuracy, though they needed more time to do so than the younger group, Dr. Rapoport said. Images of the brains of the older group showed less activity in visual areas of the brain, but more activity in the prefrontal cortex, suggesting increased mental effort.

Dr. Rapoport said that in older people there seemed to be some loss of circuits involved in visual memory. "So the brain has to recruit other circuits to get the task done," he said.

But recruit it does. The prefrontal cortex, which is the brain's executive area for intellectual activity, appears especially crucial in compensating for areas that no longer function so well in mental tasks.

All is not rosy. The number of people who do end up with Alzheimer's disease and fall into senility is still quite large.

"There are three very different groups among the elderly," said Dr. Guy McKhann, director of the Zanville and Krieger Mind Brain Institute at the Johns Hopkins Medical School. "One does remarkably well, aging very successfully into their 80's and 90's. The second group slides a bit, having some problems with memory and recall, but the problems are typically more aggravating than they are real."

Dr. McKhann said that the third group, which largely consists of people with Alzheimer's disease, suffers inexorable losses in mental function leading to senility. That group accounts for about 15 percent of those in their 70's and 30 percent to 40 percent of those in their 80's.

But for those without disease, the brain can withstand aging remarkably well. "Some people stay very good at intellectual tasks all their lives," said Dr. Judith Saxton, a neuropsychologist at the University of Pittsburgh Medical Center, who is analyzing data from a two-year follow-up of more than 700 men and women from 65 to 92.

"Their overall knowledge and vocabulary continues to grow as they age, even though their speed of retrieval slows a bit," Dr. Saxton added. "I'd guess up to 10 percent of people above 70 fall in this range." The question that interests many people who are headed toward 70, as well as some new and unconventional researchers, is how and why one ends up in the 10 percent. Is a person's neurological fate predetermined? Or is their something that can be done to stay healthy and mentally alert?

Grandparent Development and Influence

Robert Strom and Shirley Strom

Robert Strom is Professor of Lifespan Developmental Psychology, Division of Psychology in Education, Arizona State University, Tempe, Arizona 85287-0611. Shirley Strom is Research Coordinator, Office of Parent Development International Division of Psychology in Education, Arizona State University, Tempe, Arizona 85287-0611.

ABSTRACT

The educational needs of grandparents have been overlooked. They deserve access to a curriculum that can help them adjust to their changing role and illustrates how to build satisfying family relationships. The nation's first educational program developed for grandparents is described in terms of underlying assumptions, measures to assess learning needs, elements of curriculum, and procedures for instruction. Fieldtest evidence regarding the effectiveness of this approach to strengthening families is presented along with implications for the future.

A strong family is one that includes mutually satisfying relationships and the capacity of members to meet each other's needs (Stinnett & DeFrain, 1985). Most efforts to strengthen families involve classes which help parents acquire effective methods of guidance and set reasonable expectations for children. A similar approach could provide greater success for 55 million grandparents in the United States. Observers agree that grandparents have the potential to make a more significant contribution to their families and society should do whatever is necessary to ensure this possibility (Bengston & Robertson, 1985; Elkind, 1990; Kornhaber, 1986). The status of grandparents can be enhanced by (1) better understanding of how family relationships are influenced by technological change, (2) widespread recognition of the need to establish educational expectations for grandparents, and (3) the development of practical curriculum to help them adjust to their emerging role.

FAMILY RELATIONSHIPS AND TECHNOLOGICAL CHANGE

Learning in a past-oriented society. When the older people of today were children, the world was changing less rapidly. Because there was a slower rate of progress, the past dominated the present. Consequently, youngsters learned mostly from adults. In those days a father might reasonably say to his son: "Let me tell you about life and what to expect. I will give you the benefit of my experience. Now, when I was your age..." In this type of society the father's advice would be relevant since he had already confronted most of the situations his son would face. Given the slow pace of change, children could see their future as they observed the day-to-day activities of parents and grandparents.

There are still some past-oriented societies in the world today, places where adults remain the only important source of a child's education. On the island of Bali in Indonesia, parents can be observed passing on their woodcarving and painting skills to sons and daughters who expect to earn a living in much the same way. Similarly, aboriginal tribes in Australia are determined to perpetuate their traditional community. Amish people

This paper was presented to the Japan Society for the Promotion of Science in Tokyo, Japan on July 1, 1991.

in the United States maintain a pattern of living that closely resembles the priorities and routine of their forefathers. For children growing up in each of these static environments, the future seems essentially a repetition of the past. When life is so free of uncertainty, so predictable, it appears justified to teach boys and girls that they should adopt the lifestyle of their elders. Therefore, in every slow-changing culture, grandparents are viewed as experts, as authorities, as models for all age groups. The role expected of children is to be listeners and observers, to be seen but not heard (Strom & Strom, 1987).

Learning in a present-oriented society. When technology is introduced and accelerated in a society, there is a corresponding increase in the pace of social change. Long-standing customs and traditions are permanently modified. Successive generations of grandparents, parents and children come to have less in common. Children today have many experiences that were not part of their parents' upbringing. This means there are some things adults are too old to know simply because we are not growing up at the present time. It is a reversal of the traditional comment to children that "You're too young to understand." Boys and girls now encounter certain conditions which are unique in history to their age group. Access to drugs, life in a single parent family, computer involvement and global awareness are common among children. They are exposed to day care, racially integrated schools, and the fear of life-threatening sexually-transmitted diseases. Adults cannot remember most of these situations because we never experienced them.

The memory of childhood as a basis for offering advice ("When I was your age . . .") becomes less credible as the pace of social change quickens. Because of the gap between experiences of adults and children, there is a tendency to seek advice mostly from peers. An increasing number of people feel that the only persons who can understand them are those at the same stage of life as themselves or who share similar challenges. Unfortunately, when people are limited to their peers for extended conversations, they are less inclined to develop the communication skills needed for successful interaction with other generations.

A peer orientation undermines cultural continuity as it divides the population into special interest groups. Because a rapidly changing society assigns greater importance

to the present than the past, older people cease to be seen as models for everyone. Each generation chooses to identify with famous people of their own or next higher age group. Therefore, respect for the elderly declines. Older adults are no longer regarded as experts about much of anything except aging (Strom, Bernard & Strom, 1989).

Learning in a future-oriented society. The phase of civilization we are entering is referred to as the Information Age. Within this context schooling for children begins earlier, continues longer, and includes a vast amount of knowledge which was unavailable to previous generations of students. Given these conditions, children are bound to view the world from a different vantage and therefore should be seen by adults as an important source of learning. Certainly intergenerational dialogue is necessary to shape the future in a democratic society. Unless such contacts are sustained and mutually beneficial, the future could bring conflict as low birth rates provide fewer working age taxpayers to meet the needs of a growing elderly population. Some social scientists expect relationships between the young and older populations to replace the relationship between races as the dominant domestic conflict in the next half century (Toffler, 1990).

Intergenerational relationships are valuable because they offer a broader orientation than can be gained from any peer group. Until recently, it was supposed that aging is accompanied by a sense of perspective. This assumption still makes sense in slow-changing cultures. But, in technological societies the attainment of perspective requires something more than getting older. Becoming aware of how age groups other than our own see things and feel about the world is necessary for a broad perspective and responding to the needs of others. Unless the viewpoints of younger generations are taken into account, perspective tends to diminish rather than grow as people age (Strom & Strom, 1985, 1991).

ESTABLISHING EDUCATIONAL EXPECTATIONS FOR GRANDPARENTS

Our efforts to help grandparents began by offering a free course for them at senior citizen centers and churches in metropolitan Phoenix. The 400 people who enrolled in these classes were told they would learn something of what it is like for children to be growing up in the contemporary society and how parents view their task of raising children at the present time. In return, the participants agreed to share their experience as grandparents. This format was chosen because the literature on family relations revealed a patronizing attitude toward grandparents instead of educational programs to help them grow. Previous investigators had not made an effort to identify grandparent learning needs so there were no educational solutions. The following assumptions emerged from our preliminary research and guide the continuing project (Strom & Strom, 1989).

Grandparent responsibilities can be more clearly defined. Mothers and fathers have access to parenting courses that help them maintain competence in their changing role but similar opportunities are unavailable to grandparents. Instead, they are left alone to wonder: What are my rights and my responsibilities as a grandparent? How can I continue to be a favorable influence as my grandchild gets older? How well am I doing as a grandparent? These kinds of questions are likely to persist until there are commonly known guidelines for setting goals and self-evaluation. Many grandparents have difficulty defining their role and understanding how they could make a greater contribution. As a result the responsibility for raising youngsters has become disproportionate in many families with grandparents assuming less obligation than is in everyone's best interest.

Grandparents can learn to improve their influence. Mothers and fathers who can count on grandparents to share the load for caregiving and guidance less often seek support outside the family. The success of grandparents requires being aware of the parenting goals of sons and daughters and acting as a partner in reinforcing these goals. However, even though research indicates that people remain capable of adopting new attitudes and skills during middle and later life, grandparent development has not received priority in adult education. This missing element lessens the possibility of a meaningful life for many grandmothers and grandfathers.

The concept of life-long learning should include a concern for curriculum development. This means society has to reconsider its view that continuous learning is essential only for young people. The myth that aging is accompanied by wisdom has misled many older adults to underestimate their need for further education. When grandparents are mentally active, they remain a source of advice. Everyone at every age has a responsibility to keep growing in order to achieve their potential.

A practical grandparent program should be widely available. Older men and women have been led to believe that learning in later life should consist of whatever topics they find interesting without any societal expectations as there are for younger learners. But as people continue to age, they should also continue to grow—and not just in terms of acquiring leisure-oriented skills. Some of education in later life should emphasize obligations and roles, just as curriculum does for younger age groups. Senior citizens are the only population without any defined educational needs or cooperatively planned curricula. Since the size of this group is expected to grow faster than any other age segment, it seems reasonable to provide them educational opportunities which can help strengthen their families.

Society should set higher expectations for grandparents. By themselves grandparents may be unable to generate the motivation necessary to stimulate educational commitment within their peer group. This is a difficult task because so many people think of retirement as a time when they can withdraw from active community responsibility. Peers reinforce the perception that being carefree and without obligation is an acceptable goal in later life. The problem is compounded by age segregation. When older adults are limited to one another for most of their interaction, they establish standards which may not be in accord with what the society as a whole believes is best.

In order to favorably revise existing norms for older adults in terms of greater learning and more significant contributions to the family, younger age groups must raise their expectations and make these known. The talent and potential contribution of seniors could enrich the lives of everyone. Accordingly, we should expect them to demonstrate a commitment to personal growth, concern themselves about others through volunteering, and support the schools to ensure a better future for children. If educational expectations are not established for older adults, they will experience less influence and lower self-esteem.

The benefits of grandparent education can be assessed. Popular support can be expected for programs that help grandparents enlarge the scope of their influence, improve their ability to communicate with loved ones, become more self confident, and experience greater respect in the family. These benefits would be even more credible if the sources confirming them included other persons than just the participating grandparents. By comparing the results from three generational versions of the authors' Grandparent Strengths and Needs Inventory, the merits of various educational approaches to family development can be determined. This inventory also enables educators to adapt curriculum in a way that honors group and individual differences (Strom & Strom, 1990; Strom, Strom & Collinsworth, 1991).

GOALS FOR GRANDPARENT DEVELOPMENT

There are six fundamental aspects of the grandparent experience that we try to influence in our program. Each of them have implications for child and adult development. The goals we pursue are to:

Increase the satisfaction of being a grandparent. It would seem that the longer lifespan today gives grandparents more years to influence their grandchildren. But the actual consequence depends on whether or not a relationship is mutually satisfying. When family members avoid sharing their feelings, or they experience insufficient satisfaction with one another, the relationship is in jeopardy. Grandmothers and grandfathers who enjoy their role are more able to cope with difficulties.

Improve how well grandparents perform their role. The efforts of grandparents to guide grandchildren depend on how self-confident they feel in their family role. Those who seek to support the parenting goals of their sons and daughters will continue to teach grandchildren. These persons realize that it is unreasonable to expect parents to be exclusively responsible for the care and guidance of grandchildren. By being active contributors in the family, they are seen as a valuable and long-term source of influence.

Enlarge the scope of guidance expected of grandparents. There is abundant evidence that, by itself, academic learning is an insufficient preparation for success in life. It follows that grandparents should help grandchildren acquire some of the out of school lessons they need. By defining the aspects of growth that should be obtained at home, it is possible to improve a child's total education and establish a helpful role for grandparents.

Decrease the difficulties of being a grandparent. Grandparents encounter some difficulty in getting along with sons, daughters, in-laws, and grandchildren. The manner in which these problems are handled is a sign of personal effectiveness. Every grandmother and grandfather should have access to education which focuses on their changing role. When grandparents are aware of the childrearing strategies of their sons and daughters and they know the predictable difficulties to expect as grandchildren get older, they can prepare themselves by obtaining the skills necessary for continued success.

Reduce the frustrations experienced by grandparents. Some frustration is to be expected. But grandparents vary in the frequency with which they sense frustration. One way to reduce their discontent is by understanding why certain child behaviors occur and why some of them should be allowed to continue. When the expectations of grandparents are consistent with a child's developmental needs, the tendency is to encourage normative behavior and offer support for a favorable self concept.

Reduce the family information needs of grandparents. Grandparents need accurate perceptions about their grandchild's abilities and their social relationships. Besides the information which teachers and parents provide for them, grandparents should listen to grandchildren themselves to learn about their hopes, fears, goals and concerns. If educational programs for grandparents can regularly include access to the views of people who are the same age as grandchildren, it is easier to understand how family members resemble and differ from their peers.

ELEMENTS OF CURRICULUM AND INSTRUCTION

The learning activities that grandparents consider appealing deserve priority in planning educational programs for them. Just as young students need a variety of teaching methods, older men and women can also benefit from a wide range of instructional techniques. The two courses we have developed on "Becoming A Better Grandparent" and "Achieving Grandparent Potential" follow the same format of focusing on all three generations. Some of the lessons concerning grandparents involve keeping up with the times, giving and seeking advice, communicating from a distance, growing as a couple, and learning in later life. Lessons about the middle generation call for recognizing indicators of parental success, helping single and blended families, developing values and morals, building child self-esteem, and watching television together. The lessons on grandchildren emphasize getting along with others, sharing fears and worries, understanding children's thinking, deciding about sex and drugs, and encouraging the college student. All twenty-four lessons consist of the same instructional elements. In turn, each of these elements deserves a brief explanation.

Discussion and brainstorming. Grandparents meet in small groups to consider agenda from their guidebook that encourages their expression of ideas, concerns, mistakes, goals and solutions (Strom & Strom, 1991a, 1991c). During these discussions the participants inform, challenge, and reassure each other. They quickly discover there is much to gain from sharing feelings and thoughts. Conversations with emotionally supportive peers cause men and women to feel less alone, help them organize their thinking, and increase awareness of the possibilities for becoming a better grandparent. Creative thinking is practiced during each discussion when the group shifts to consideration of a brainstorming task.

Problem solving. The next activity invites grandparents to consider how they might handle a particular problem if they had to cope with it. A family incident is described which offers everyone the same information including several possible solutions. Grandparents like to reflect and then discuss pros and cons they see for each of the given choices. It is stimulating to think of additional options and to identify relevant information that may be missing. Everyone has an opportunity to share their reasoning about the advice they consider to be best. This scenario approach broadens the range of solutions individuals see and discourages premature judgment. Later, in their home, grandparents present the scenarios to relatives and find out their viewpoint.

Grandparent principles. Several written principles accompany each unit. Grandparents rely on these practical guidelines for review, reflection, and personal application. Participants benefit from reading the companion volume of viewpoints which match each lesson in the guidebook (Strom & Strom, 1991b, 1991d). These essays, from which the principles are drawn, offer insights, observations and suggestions for making the grandparent experience more satisfying. In addition, local resource persons can enrich the learning by acquainting grandparents with the way problems are handled in their own community. Be-

cause each individual represents a unique family, grandparents must decide for themselves which principles are most appropriate in their present situation, the ones to apply immediately, and those that can be deferred until a later time.

Self-evaluation and observation. Personal growth requires self-examination. Grandparents are encouraged to practice this important skill as part of their homework. Each homework assignment consists of several multiple-choice questions that give participants a chance to state their feelings about issues such as family relationships, communication problems, and expectations of children. The anonymous homework is submitted at the beginning of each class. After responses are tallied for each item, the previously unknown norms of perception and behavior are announced to the class. This helps individuals know how their experiences as grandparents resemble and differ from peers.

Intergenerational conversations. Grandparents should strive to know each grandchild as an individual. The way to achieve this goal is through interaction with the particular grandchild. However, most grandmothers and grandfathers admit that they sometimes have difficulty keeping a conversation going with youngsters. This is why they appreciate questions focusing on realms of experience that the generations commonly encounter, topics that transcend age. Every lesson includes a set of questions dealing with topics of mutual concern such as music, health, school, money, fears, friends, and careers. These questions facilitate the dialogue that we expect grandparents to initiate face to face or by phone. Most of the inquiries fit all grandchildren while some are more appropriate for teenagers. A portion of each class session is devoted to hearing grandparents comment about the insights they have acquired through intergenerational interviews.

Grandparents also need to know something about the norms of their grandchild's age group. It is unreasonable to suppose that all the information we need about the orientation of relatives will be provided by them alone. In a society where peers have considerable influence it is wise to find out how people in a grandchild's age group think and feel. This improves our understanding of how loved ones resemble and differ from their peers. One approach we use is to videotape interviews with children and parents who express their views on topics like peer pressure, school stress, and family conflict. This method reflects our belief that the broad perspective of life each of us ought to acquire emerges only when the thoughts and feelings of other age groups are taken into account.

EVALUATING GRANDPARENT SUCCESS

The effectiveness of grandparent education has been confirmed by research. In one study 800 people representing three generations evaluated the attitudes and behavior of grandparents before and after their participation in the "Becoming A Better Grandparent" course. At the end of the program grandparents reported that they had made significant improvements. This progress was corroborated by inventory scores of the parents and grandchildren (Strom & Strom, 1990). Specifically, grandparents benefit from the mentally stimulating experience by understanding how their role is changing, acquiring a broader perspective, learning new attitudes, gaining greater confidence and self-esteem, improving communication skills, and strengthening family relationships (Strom & Strom, 1985, 1989; Strom, Strom & Collinsworth, 1990).

These feelings expressed by the grandparents show the importance of the program for them: "I realized that I must keep on growing in order to understand other family members and be seen by them as a positive influence." "Now I understand my privileges as a grandparent as well as the duties I owe my grandchildren." "I found that helping my son and daughter achieve their parenting goals has upgraded my status to that of a valued partner." "I feel so much better about myself as a grandmother and more optimistic about my grandchildren."

Sons and daughters also identified some important benefits of grandparent education: "My parents seem more willing to share their feelings with us and they are more supportive of the way we are bringing up our children." "Taking this class has really helped my mom think about her role in my child's life. She is working hard to get to know my children as individuals." "My Dad has realized that listening and learning from his grandchildren is the key to being respected by them." "My mother has always been kind and loving to all of us but now she is more interesting to be around. It's fun to hear what she is learning."

It would be pleasing to report a balance in the proportion of men and women who seek to improve themselves through grandparent education. However, just as mothers significantly outnumber fathers in parenting classes, grandmothers are over represented in classes for grandparent development. Usually three out of four students in our courses are grandmothers. Does this ratio indicate that grandmothers need more guidance than grandfathers? On the contrary, it suggests grandmothers are more motivated to keep growing in this aspect of life. This conclusion was reached after comparing the influence of 155 grandmothers and 55 grandfathers who had just completed the program. Assessments were made to determine how each gender was perceived by themselves, their sons, daughters and grandchildren. Although the grandmothers reported having less formal education than grandfathers, they were seen as more successful grandparents in the estimate of all three generations (Strom & Strom, 1989).

In this study grandparents, parents and grandchildren portrayed grandmothers as emotionally closer to grandchildren, better informed about family affairs, and more willing to commit themselves to helping others. They were better at seeing the positive side of situations, learning from other family members, and making their feelings known. Grandmothers were credited with knowing more than grandfathers about the fears and concerns of grandchildren and spending more time with them. They were regarded as more effective in teaching grandchildren how to show trust, get along with others, and handle arguments. Grandmothers were viewed as better at passing on family history and cultural traditions, and more willing to accept help from grandchildren.

Strengths of grandfathers were recognized too. They saw themselves as having less difficulty than grandmothers in giving advice to sons and daughters, and were less frustrated by televiewing and listening habits of grandchildren. Parents observed grandfathers as being more satisfied than grandmothers when grandchildren asked for advice. Grandchildren felt their outlook on life was appreciated more by grandfathers.

Perhaps it is unfair to compare grandfathers with grandmothers. Consider the more positive results that emerge when the emphasis is on identifying change in grandfather attitudes and behaviors after instruction. The grandfathers in this study felt they made improvement in terms of satisfaction with their role, success in carrying out their obligations, effectiveness in teaching, overcoming difficulties, coping with frustrations, and becoming more informed. Parents and grandchildren confirmed these gains had occurred. By joining grandmothers as participants in family-oriented education, grandfathers have proven they can learn to build more successful relationships with their spouse, children and grandchildren. Toward this goal grandfathers are urged to grow along with their partner and be actively involved in strengthening the family (Strom & Strom, 1989).

CONCLUSION

As we contemplate the future it is important to bear in mind that the baby-boomers, those persons born between 1946–1964, will become the largest group of older adults in history. This population of 77 million people is going to be better educated, healthier, and live longer than preceding generations. If the preparation they receive for retirement focuses only on financial and leisure readiness, a lifestyle of strictly recreation could become the norm. On the other hand, if getting ready for leisure activities is joined by an emphasis on continued responsibility as family members, then baby-boomers can make an enormous contribution to society. This possibility is supported by the emerging concept of grandparent education (Strom & Strom, 1991e).

REFERENCES

Bengston, V., & Robertson, J. (1985). *Grandparenthood.* Beverly Hills, CA: Sage Publications.

Elkind, D. (1990). *Grandparenting.* Glenview, IL: Scott, Foresman.

Kornhaber, A. (1986). *Between parents and grandparents.* New York: St. Martin's Press.

Stinnet, N., & DeFrain, J. (1985). *Secrets of strong families.* Boston: Little, Brown.

Strom, R., Bernard, H., & Strom, S. (1989). *Human development and learning.* New York: Human Sciences Press.

Strom, R., & Strom, S. (1985). Becoming a better grandparent. In *Growing together: An intergenerational sourcebook,* K. Struntz & S. Reville (eds.). Washington, DC: American Association of Retired Persons and Elvirita Lewis Foundation, pp. 57–60.

Strom, R., & Strom, S. (1987). Preparing grandparents for a new role. *The Journal of Applied Gerontology,* 6(4), 476–486.

Strom, R., & Strom, S. (1989). *Grandparent development.* Washington, DC: American Association of Retired Persons Andrus Foundation.

Strom, R., & Strom, S. (1990). Raising expectations for grandparents: A three-generational study. *International Journal of Aging and Human Development,* 31(3), 161–167.

Strom, R., & Strom, S. (1991a). *Achieving grandparent potential: A guidebook for building intergenerational relationships.* Newbury Park, CA: Sage Publications.

Strom, R., & Strom, S. (1991b). *Achieving grandparent potential: Viewpoints on building intergenerational relationships.* Newbury Park, CA: Sage Publications.

Strom, R., & Strom, S. (1991c). *Becoming a better grandparent: A guidebook for strengthening the family.* Newbury Park, CA: Sage Publications.

Strom, R., & Strom, S. (1991d). *Becoming a better grandparent: Viewpoints on strengthening the family.* Newbury Park, CA: Sage Publications.

Strom, R., & Strom, S. (1991e). *Grandparent education: A guide for leaders.* Newbury Park, CA: Sage Publications.

Strom, R., Strom, S., & Collinsworth, P. (1990). Improving grandparent success. *The Journal of Applied Gerontology,* 9(4), 480–492.

Strom, R., Strom, S., & Collinsworth, P. (1991). The Grandparent Strengths and Needs Inventory: Development and factorial validation. *Educational and Psychological Measurement,* 51(4).

Toffler, A. (1990). *Powershift.* New York: Bantam Books.

The Solace of Patterns

The strange attractors that define life's stages give shape even to grief

ROBERT M. SAPOLSKY

Robert M. Sapolsky is a MacArthur Fellow and a professor of biological sciences and neuroscience at Stanford University. His most recent book, Why Zebras Don't Get Ulcers: A Guide to Stress, Stress-Related Diseases, and Coping, *is published by W. H. Freeman and Company.*

A SHORT TIME AGO MY FATHER died, having spent far too many of his last years in pain and degeneration. Although I had expected his death and tried to prepare myself for it, when the time came it naturally turned out that you really can't prepare. A week afterward I found myself back at work, bludgeoned by emotions that swirled around a numb core of unreality—a feeling of disconnection from the events that had just taken place on the other side of the continent, of disbelief that it was really him frozen in that nightmare of stillness. The members of my laboratory were solicitous. One, a medical student, asked me how I was doing, and I replied, "Well, today it seems as if I must have imagined it all." "That makes sense," she said. "Don't forget about DABDA."

DABDA. In 1969 the psychiatrist Elisabeth Kübler-Ross published a landmark book, *On Death and Dying.* Drawing on her research with terminally ill people and their families, she described the process whereby people mourn the death of others and, when impending, of themselves. Most of us, she observed, go through a fairly well defined sequence of stages. First we deny the death is happening. Then we become angry at the unfairness of it

all. We pass through a stage of irrational bargaining, with the doctors, with God: *Just let this not be fatal and I will change my ways. Please, just wait until Christmas.* There follows a stage of depression and, if one is fortunate, the final chapter, serene acceptance. The sequence is not ironclad; individuals may skip certain stages, experience them out of order or regress to earlier ones. DABDA, moreover, is generally thought to give a better description of one's own preparation for dying than of one's mourning the demise of someone else. Nevertheless, there is a broadly recognized consistency in the overall pattern of mourning: denial, anger, bargaining, depression, acceptance. I was stuck at stage one, right on schedule.

Brevity is the soul of DABDA. A few years ago I saw that point brilliantly dramatized on television—on, of all programs, *The Simpsons.* It was the episode in which Homer, the father, accidentally eats a poisonous fish and is told he has twenty-four hours to live. There ensues a thirty-second sequence in which the cartoon character races through the death and dying stages, something like this: "No way! I'm not dying." He ponders a second, then grabs the doctor by the neck. "Why you little. . . ." He trembles in fear, then pleads, "Doc, get me outta this! I'll make it worth your while." Finally he composes himself and says, "Well, we all gotta go sometime." I thought it was hilarious. Homer substituted fear for depression and got it on the other side of anger. Even so, here was a cartoon suitable to be watched happily by children, and the writers had sneaked in a parody of Kübler-Ross.

But for sheer conciseness, of course, Homer Simpson's vignette has nothing on DABDA. That's why medical students, my laboratory colleague included, memorize the acronym along with hundreds of other mnemonic devices in preparation for their national board examinations. What strikes me now is the power of those letters to encapsulate human experience. My father, by dint of having been human, was unique; thus was my relationship to him, and thus must be my grieving. And yet I come up with something reducible to a medical school acronym. Poems, paintings, symphonies by the most creative artists who ever lived have been born out of mourning; yet, on some level, they all sprang from the pattern invoked by two pedestrian syllables of pseudo-English. We cry, we rage, we demand that the oceans' waves stop, that the planets halt their movements in the sky, all because the earth will no longer be graced by the one who sang lullabies as no one else could; yet that, too, is reducible to DABDA. Why should grief be so stereotypical?

SCIENTISTS WHO STUDY HUMAN thought and behavior have discerned many stereotyped, structured stages through which all of us move at various times. Some of the sequences are obvious, their logic a quick study. It is no surprise that infants learn to crawl before they take their first tentative steps, and only later learn to run. Other sequences are more subtle. Freudians claim that in normal development the child undergoes the invariant transition from a so-called

Reprinted with permission from *The Sciences,* November/December 1994, pp. 14-16. © 1994 by the New York Academy of Sciences. Individual subscriptions are $28 per year. Write to: *The Sciences,* 2 East 63rd Street, New York, NY 10021.

oral stage to an anal stage to a genital stage, and they attribute various aspects of psychological dysfunction in the adult to an earlier failure to move successfully from one stage to the next.

Similarly, the Swiss psychologist Jean Piaget mapped stages of cognitive development. For example, he noted, there is a stage at which children begin to grasp the concept of object permanence: Before that developmental transition, a toy does not exist once it is removed from the child's sight. Afterward, the toy exists—and the child will look for it—even when it is no longer visible. Only at a reliably later stage do children begin to grasp concepts such as the conservation of volume—that two pitchers of different shapes can hold the same quantity of liquid. The same developmental patterns occur across numerous cultures, and so the sequence seems to describe the universal way that human beings learn to comprehend a cognitively complex world.

The American psychologist Lawrence Kohlberg mapped the stereotyped stages people undergo in developing morally. At one early stage of life, moral decisions are based on rules and on the motivation to avoid punishment: actions considered for their effects on oneself. Only at a later stage are decisions made on the basis of a respect for the community: actions considered for their effects on others. Later still, and far more rarely, some people develop a morality driven by a set of their own internalized standards, derived from a sense of what is right and what is wrong for all possible communities. The pattern is progressive: people who now act out of conscience invariably, at some earlier stage of life, believed that you don't do bad things because you might get caught.

The American psychoanalyst Erik Erikson discerned a sequence of psychosocial development, framing it as crises that a person resolves or fails to resolve at each stage. For infants, the issue is whether one attains a basic attitude of trust toward the world; for adolescents, it is identity versus identity confusion; for young adults, intimacy versus isolation; for adults, generativity versus stagnation; and for the aged, peaceful acceptance and integrity versus despair. Erikson's pioneering insight that one's later years represent a series of transitions that must be successfully negotiated is reflected in a quip by the geriatrician Walter M. Bortz II of Stanford University Medical School. Asked whether he was interested in curing aging, Bortz responded, "No, I'm not interested in arrested development."

MOST COMPLEX PATTERNS collapse into extinction. Only a few combinations beat the odds.

Those are some of the patterns we all are reported or theorized to have in common, across many settings and cultures. I think such conceptualizations are often legitimate, not just artificial structures that scientists impose on inchoate reality. Why should we share such patterning? It is certainly not for lack of alternatives. As living beings, we represent complex, organized systems—an eddy in the random entropy of the universe. When all the possibilities are taken into account, it is supremely unlikely for elements to assemble themselves into molecules, for molecules to form cells, for vast assemblages of cells to form us. How much more unlikely, it seems, that such complex organisms conform to such relatively simple patterns of behavior, of development, of thought.

ONE WAY OF COMING TO GRIPS with the properties of complex systems is through a field of mathematics devoted to the study of so-called cellular automata. The best way of explaining its style of analysis is by example. Imagine a long row of boxes—some black, some white—arranged to form some initial pattern, a starting stage. The row of boxes is to give rise to a second row, just below the first. The way that takes place in a cellular automaton is that each box in the first row is subjected to a set of reproduction rules. For example, one rule might stipulate that a black box in the first row gives rise to a black box immediately below it in the next row, only if exactly one of its two nearest neighbors is black. Other rules might apply to a black box flanked by two white boxes or two black boxes. Once the set of rules is applied to each box in the first row, a second row of black and white boxes is generated; then the rules are applied again to each box in the second row to generate a third row and so on.

Metaphorically, each row represents one generation, one tick of a clock. A properly programmed computer could track any possible combination of colored boxes, following any conceivable set of reproduction rules, down through the generations. In the vast majority of cases, somewhere down the line it would end up with a row of boxes all the same color. After that, the single color would repeat itself forever. In other words, the line would go extinct.

Return now to my earlier question: How can it be, in this entropic world, that we human beings share so many stable patterns—one nose; two eyes; a reliable lag time before we learn object permanence; happier adulthoods if we become confident about our identities as adolescents; a tendency to find it hard to believe in tragedy when it strikes? What keeps us from following an almost infinite number of alternative developmental paths? The studies of cellular automata provide a hint.

Not all complex patterns, it turns out, eventually collapse into extinction. A few combinations of starting states and reproduction rules beat the odds and settle down into mature stable patterns that continue down through the generations forever. In general, it is impossible to predict whether a given starting state will survive, let alone which pattern it will generate after, say, n generations. The only way to tell is to crank it through the computer and see. It has been shown, however, that a surprisingly small number of such mature patterns are possible.

A similar tendency in living systems has long been known to evolutionary biologists. They call it convergence. Among the staggering number of species on this planet, there are only a few handfuls of solutions to the problem of how to locomote, how to conserve fluids in a hot environment, how to store and mobilize energy. And among the staggering variety of humans, it may be a convergent feature of our complexity that there are a small number of ways in which we grow through life or mourn its inevitabilities.

IN AN ENTROPIC WORLD, WE CAN TAKE a common comfort from our common patterns, and there is often consolation in attributing such patterns to forces larger than ourselves. As an atheist, I have long taken an almost religious solace from a story by the Argentine minimalist Jorge Luis Borges. In his famous short story, *The Library of Babel,* Borges describes the world as a library filled with an unimaginably vast number of books, each with the same number of pages and the same number of letters on each page. The library contains a single copy of every possible book, every possible permutation of letters. People spend their lives sorting through this ocean of gibberish for the incalculably rare books whose random arrays of letters form something meaningful, searching above all else for the single book (which must exist) that explains everything. And of course, given the completeness of the library, in addition to that perfect book, there must also be one that convincingly disproves the conclusions put forth in it, and yet another book that refutes the malicious solipsisms of the second book, plus hundreds of thousands of books that differ from any of those three by a single letter or a comma.

The narrator writes in his old age, in an isolation brought about by the suicides of people who have been driven to despair by the futility of wandering through the library. In this parable of the search for meaning amid entropy, Borges concludes:

Those who judge [the library to be finite] postulate that in remote places the corridors and stairways and hexagons can conceivably come to an end—which is absurd. Those who imagine it to be without limit forget that the possible number of books does have such a limit. I venture to suggest this solution to the ancient problem: *The library is unlimited and cyclical.* If an eternal traveler were to cross it in any direction, after centuries he would see that the same volumes were repeated in the same disorder (which, thus repeated, would be an order: the Order). My solitude is gladdened by this elegant hope.

I T APPEARS THAT AMID THE ORDER with which we mature and decline, there is an order to our mourning. And my own recent solitude is glad-dened by that elegant hope, in at least two ways. One is inward-looking. This stereotypy, this ordering, brings the promise of solace in the predicted final stage: if one is fortunate, DABDA ends in A.

Another hope looks outward, to a world whose tragedies are inexorably delivered from its remotest corners to our nightly news. Look at the image of a survivor of some carnage and, knowing nothing of her language, culture, beliefs or circumstances, you can still recognize in the fixed action patterns of her facial muscles the unmistakable lineaments of grief. That instant recognition, the universal predictability of certain aspects of human beings, whether in a facial expression or in the stages of mourning, is an emblem of our kinship and an imperative of empathy.

Credits/Acknowledgments

Cover design by Charles Vitelli.

1. Genetic and Prenatal Influences on Development
Facing overview—WHO photo.

2. Development during Infancy and Early Childhood
Facing overview—© 1997 by Cleo Freelance Photography.

3. Development during Childhood: Cognition and Schooling
Facing overview—© 1997 by PhotoDisc, Inc.

4. Development during Childhood: Family and Culture
Facing overview—© 1997 by Cleo Freelance Photography.

5. Development during Adolescence and Young Adulthood
Facing overview—© 1997 by Cleo Freelance Photography.

6. Development during Middle and Late Adulthood
Facing overview—© 1997 by Cleo Freelance Photography.

ANNUAL EDITIONS ARTICLE REVIEW FORM

- NAME: _____ DATE: _____

- TITLE AND NUMBER OF ARTICLE: _____

- BRIEFLY STATE THE MAIN IDEA OF THIS ARTICLE: _____

_____

- LIST THREE IMPORTANT FACTS THAT THE AUTHOR USES TO SUPPORT THE MAIN IDEA:

_____

_____

_____

_____

- WHAT INFORMATION OR IDEAS DISCUSSED IN THIS ARTICLE ARE ALSO DISCUSSED IN YOUR TEXTBOOK OR OTHER READINGS THAT YOU HAVE DONE? LIST THE TEXTBOOK CHAPTERS AND PAGE NUMBERS:

_____

_____

_____

_____

_____

- LIST ANY EXAMPLES OF BIAS OR FAULTY REASONING THAT YOU FOUND IN THE ARTICLE:

_____

_____

_____

_____

- LIST ANY NEW TERMS/CONCEPTS THAT WERE DISCUSSED IN THE ARTICLE, AND WRITE A SHORT DEFINITION:

_____

_____

_____

_____

*Your instructor may require you to use this ANNUAL EDITIONS Article Review Form in any number of ways: for articles that are assigned, for extra credit, as a tool to assist in developing assigned papers, or simply for your own reference. Even if it is not required, we encourage you to photocopy and use this page; you will find that reflecting on the articles will greatly enhance the information from your text.

We Want Your Advice

ANNUAL EDITIONS revisions depend on two major opinion sources: one is our Advisory Board, listed in the front of this volume, which works with us in scanning the thousands of articles published in the public press each year; the other is you—the person actually using the book. Please help us and the users of the next edition by completing the prepaid article rating form on this page and returning it to us. Thank you for your help!

ANNUAL EDITIONS: HUMAN DEVELOPMENT 98/99
Article Rating Form

Here is an opportunity for you to have direct input into the next revision of this volume. We would like you to rate each of the 45 articles listed below, using the following scale:

1. **Excellent: should definitely be retained**
2. **Above average: should probably be retained**
3. **Below average: should probably be deleted**
4. **Poor: should definitely be deleted**

Your ratings will play a vital part in the next revision. So please mail this prepaid form to us just as soon as you complete it.
Thanks for your help!

Rating	Article	Rating	Article
	1. Unraveling the Mystery of Life		24. Children Who Witness Domestic Violence: The Invisible Victims
	2. The World after Cloning		25. The Lasting Effects of Child Maltreatment
	3. Nature's Clones		26. WAAAH!! Why Kids Have a Lot to Cry About
	4. The Role of Lifestyle in Preventing Low Birth Weight		27. TV Violence: Myth and Reality
	5. Prenatal Drug Exposure: Meeting the Challenge		28. The Biology of Soul Murder
	6. Sperm under Siege		29. Children at Risk: Fostering Resilience and Hope
	7. How Breast Milk Protects Newborns		30. Growing Up Goes On and On and On
	8. Fertile Minds		31. Adolescence: Whose Hell Is It?
	9. The Realistic View of Biology and Behavior		32. Working with the Emotionally Sensitive Adolescent
	10. Studies Show Talking with Infants Shapes Basis of Ability to Think		33. What Is a Bad Kid? Answers of Adolescents and Their Mothers in Three Cultures
	11. Your Child's Brain		34. HIV Infected Youth Speaks about Needs for Support and Health Care
	12. Changing Demographics: Past and Future Demands for Early Childhood Programs		35. Psychotrends: Taking Stock of Tomorrow's Family and Sexuality
	13. Parents Speak: Zero to Three's Findings from Research on Parents' Views of Early Childhood Development		36. Who Stole Fertility?
	14. It's Magical! It's Malleable! It's . . . Memory		37. Addicted
	15. Basing Teaching on Piaget's Constructivism		38. Why They Stay: A Saga of Spouse Abuse
	16. A Reconceptualization of the Effects of Undernutrition on Children's Biological, Psychosocial, and Behavioral Development		39. Man's World, Woman's World? Brain Studies Point to Differences
	17. Life in Overdrive		40. Sleep Pays Attention
	18. Bell, Book, and Scandal		41. Getting Over Getting Older
	19. The EQ Factor		42. The Age Boom
	20. Dealing with Misbehavior: Two Approaches		43. Studies Suggest Older Minds Are Stronger than Expected
	21. Fathers' Time		44. Grandparent Development and Influence
	22. Invincible Kids		45. The Solace of Patterns
	23. The Right to a Family Environment for Children with Disabilities		

(Continued on next page)

ABOUT YOU

Name _____ Date _____

Are you a teacher? ❏ Or a student? ❏

Your school name _____

Department _____

Address _____

City _____ State _____ Zip _____

School telephone # _____

YOUR COMMENTS ARE IMPORTANT TO US!

Please fill in the following information:

For which course did you use this book? _____

Did you use a text with this *ANNUAL EDITION*? ❏ yes ❏ no

What was the title of the text? _____

What are your general reactions to the *Annual Editions* concept?

Have you read any particular articles recently that you think should be included in the next edition?

Are there any articles you feel should be replaced in the next edition? Why?

Are there any World Wide Web sites you feel should be included in the next edition? Please annotate.

May we contact you for editorial input?

May we quote your comments?

ANNUAL EDITIONS: HUMAN DEVELOPMENT 98/99